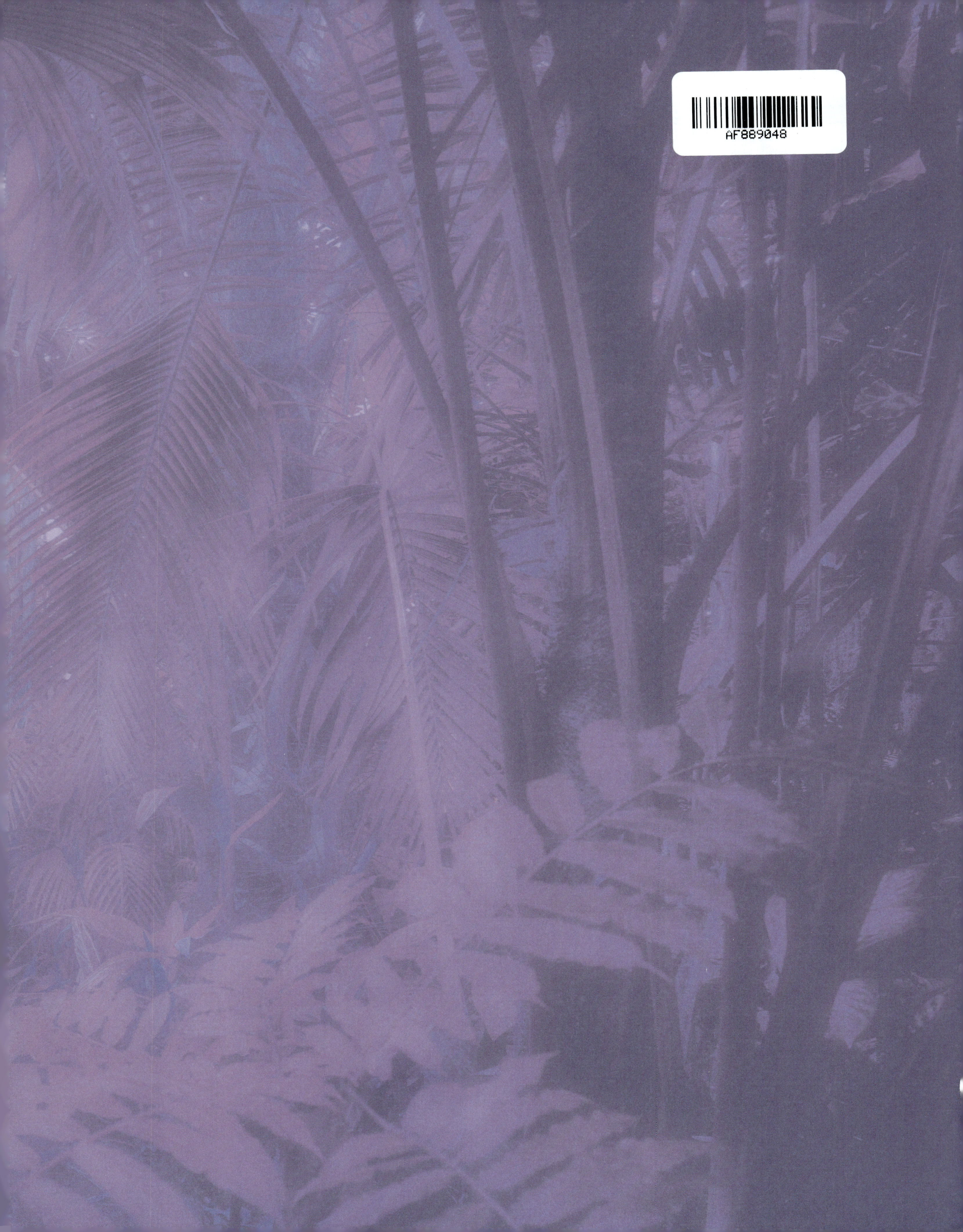

WERNER PAWLOK

GREENHOUSES

CATHEDRALS FOR PLANTS

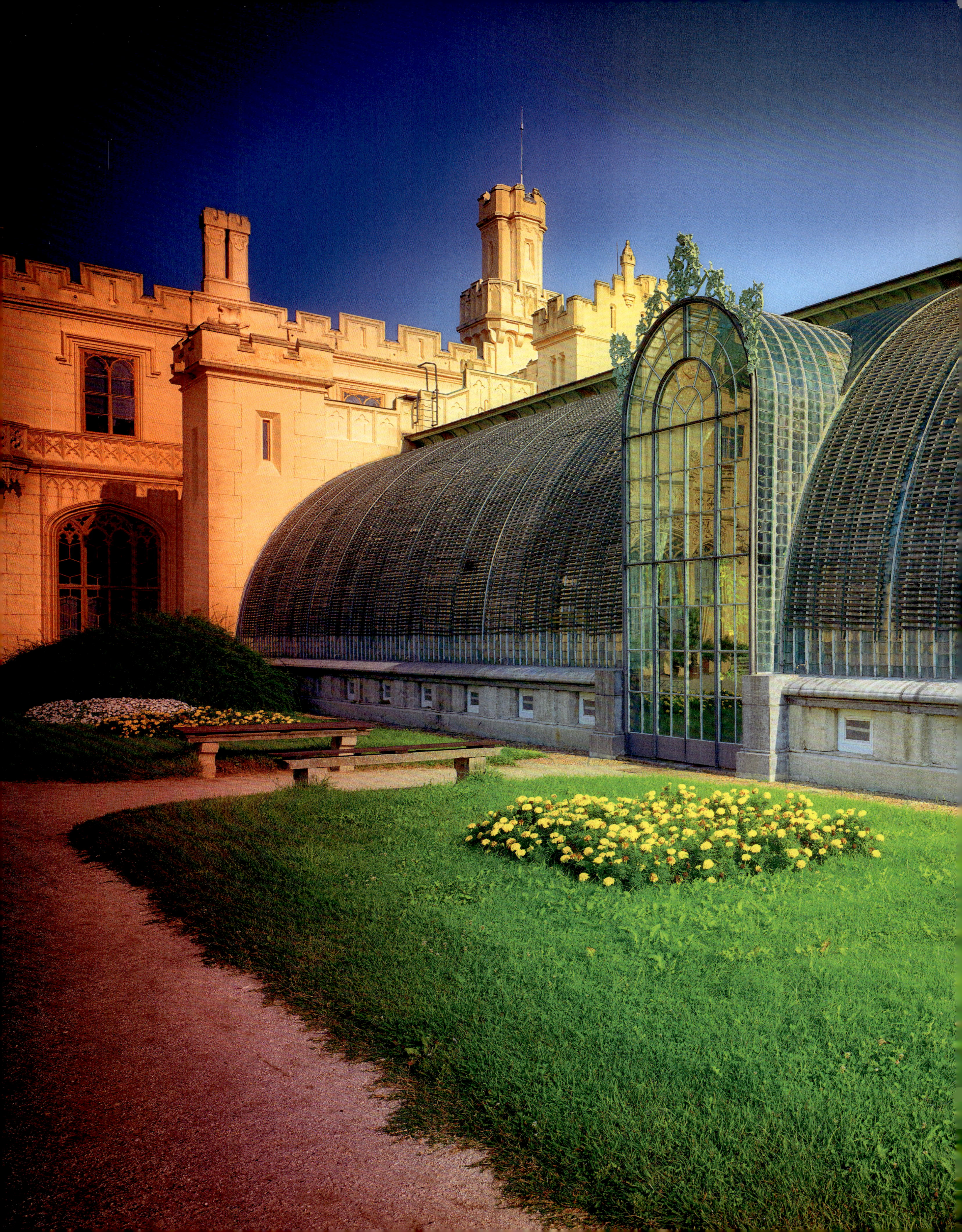

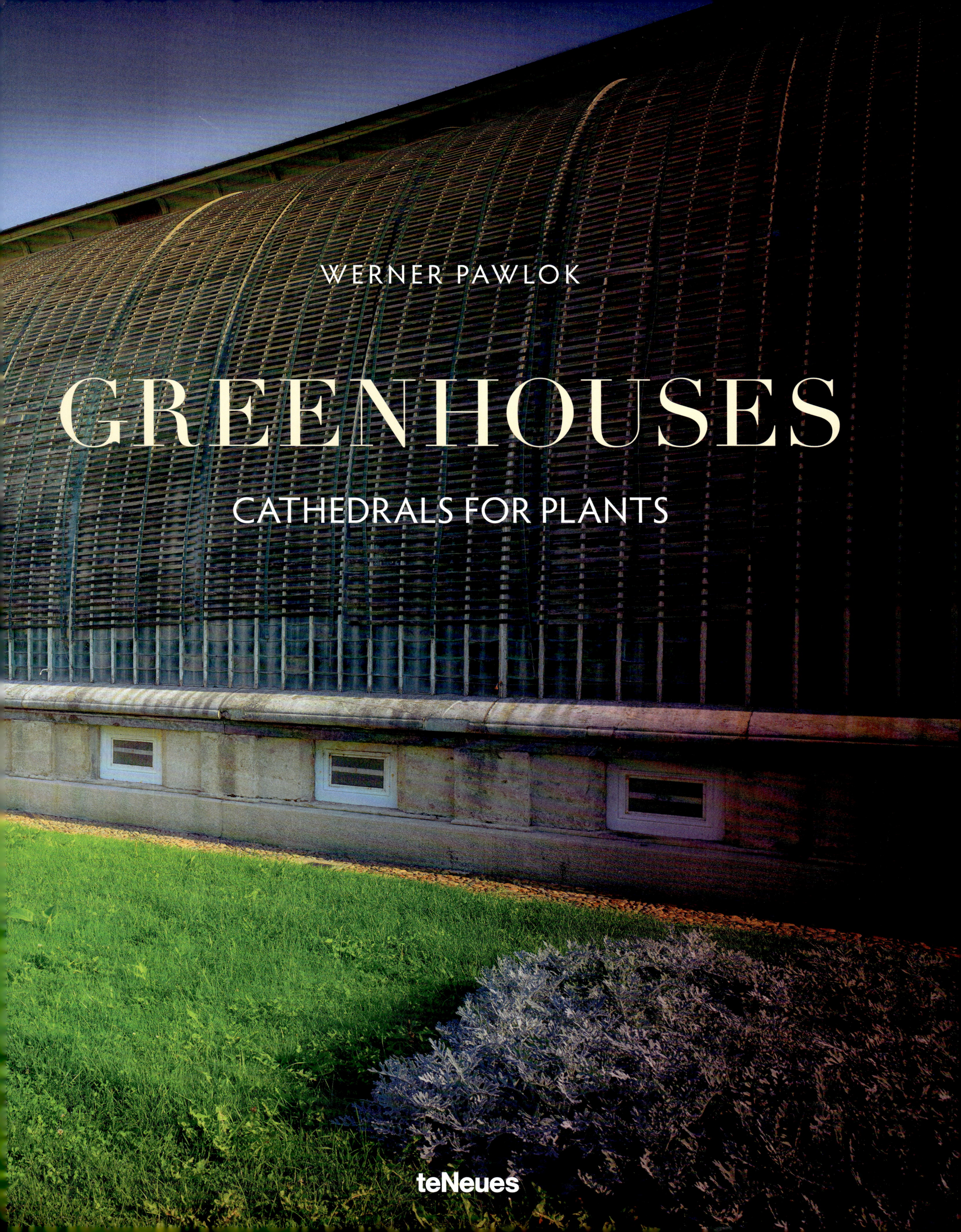

WERNER PAWLOK

GREENHOUSES

CATHEDRALS FOR PLANTS

teNeues

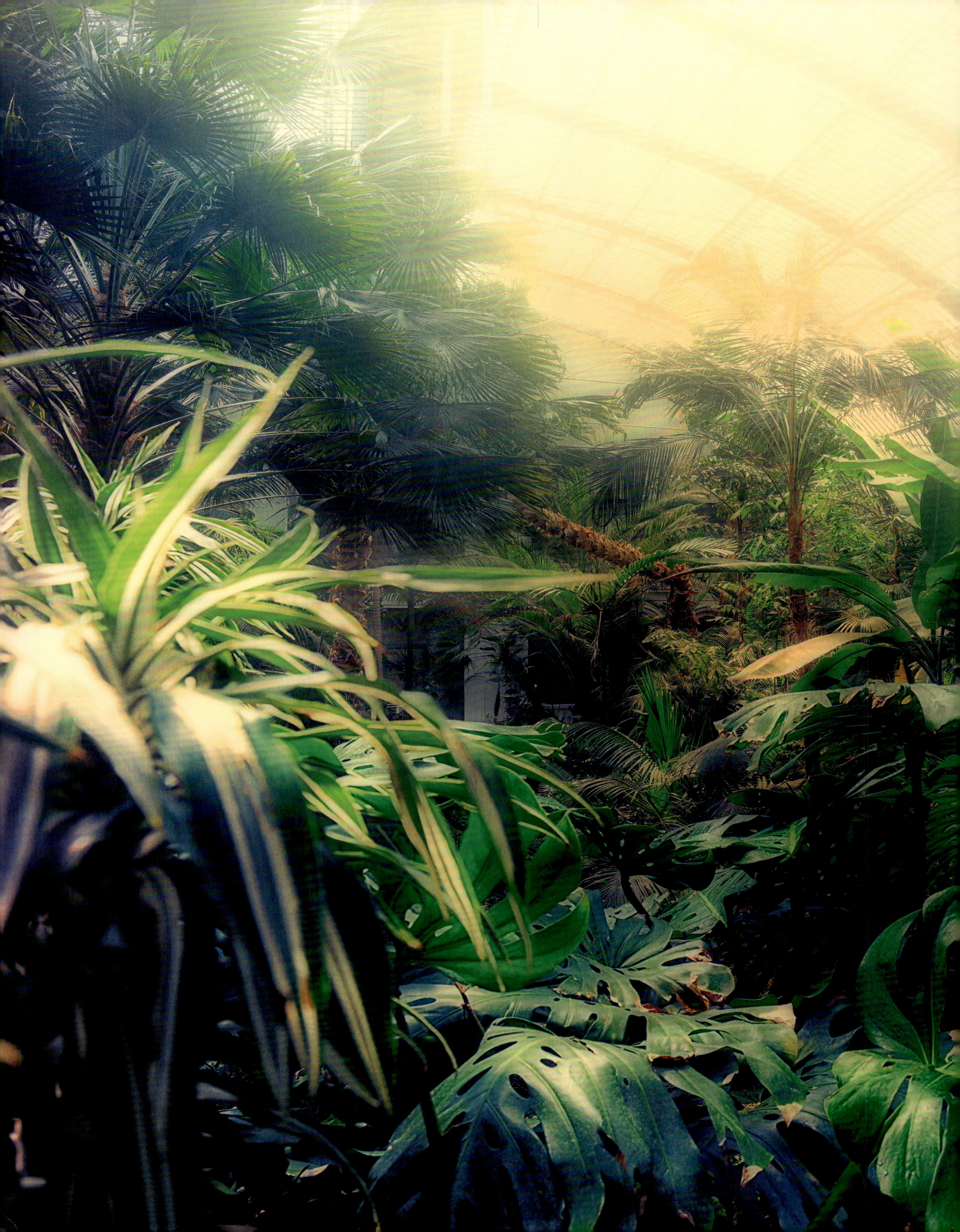

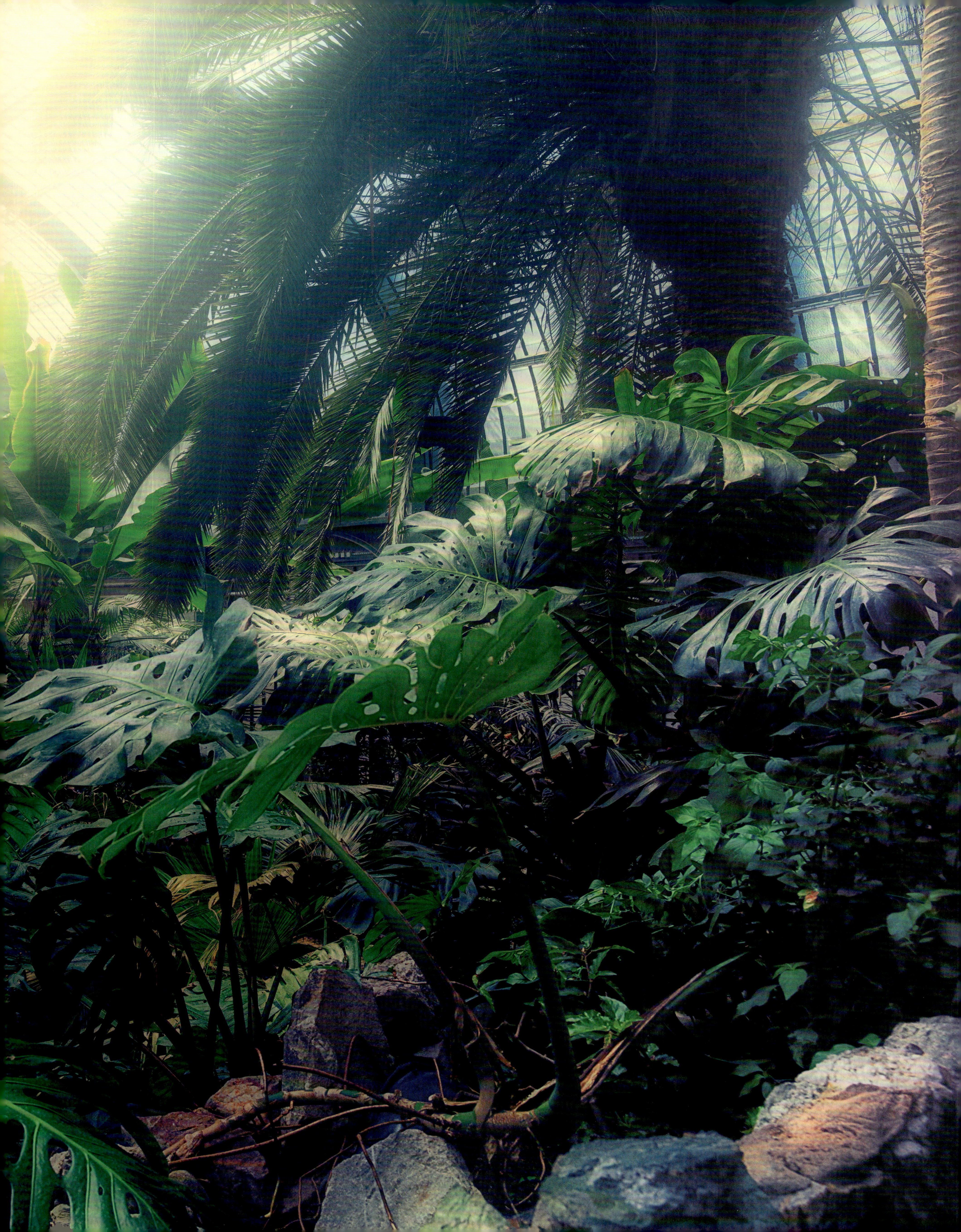

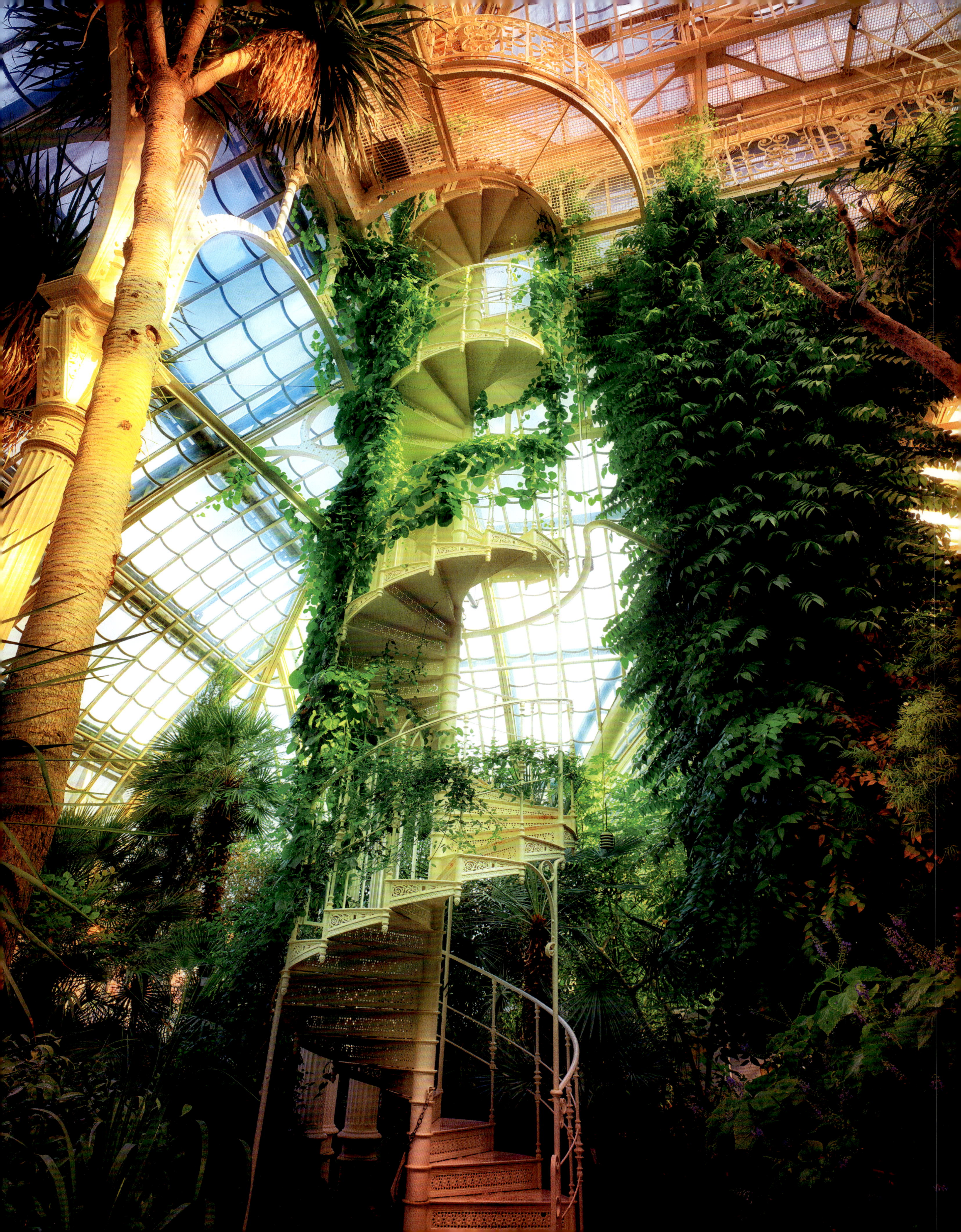

INHALT · CONTENT

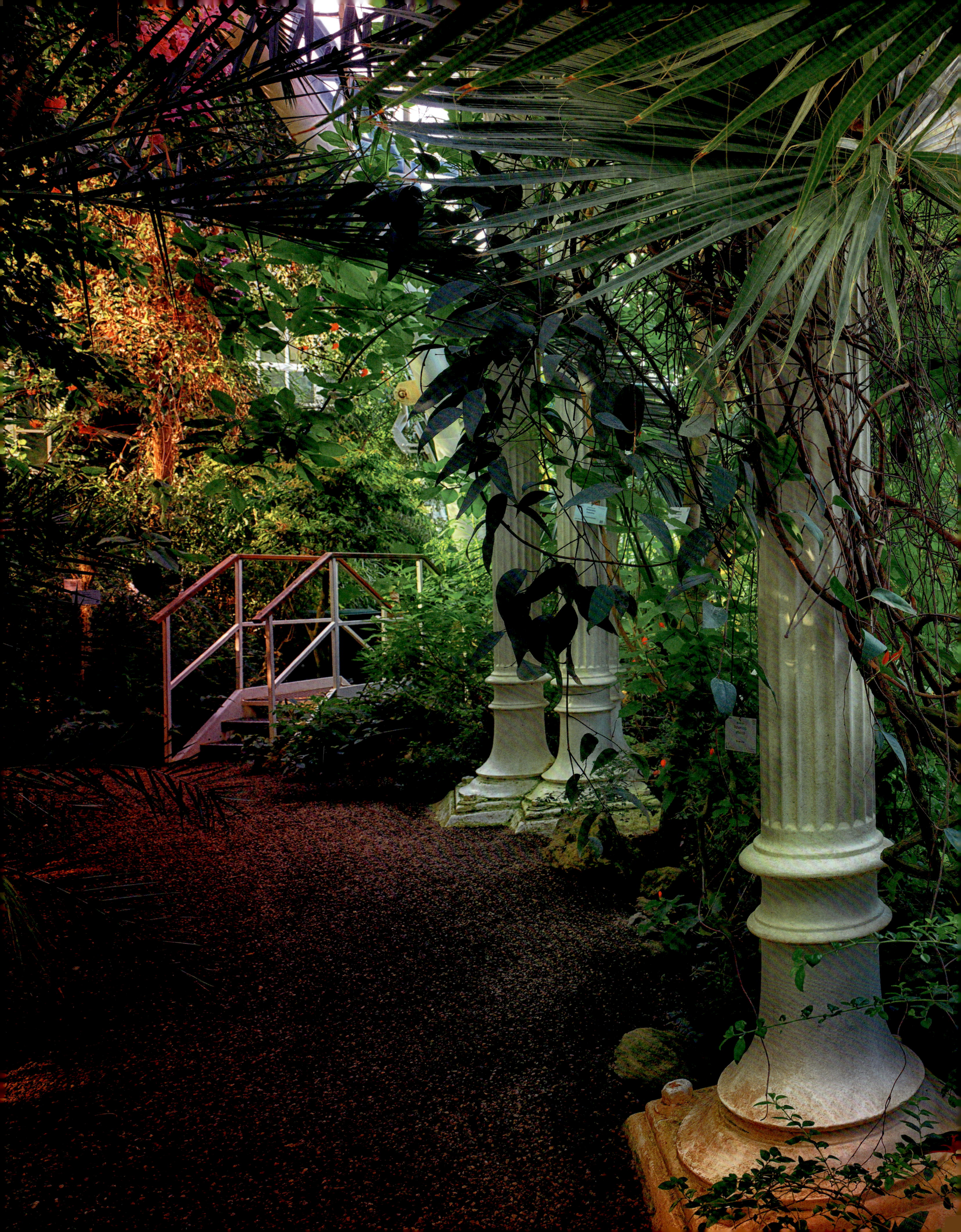

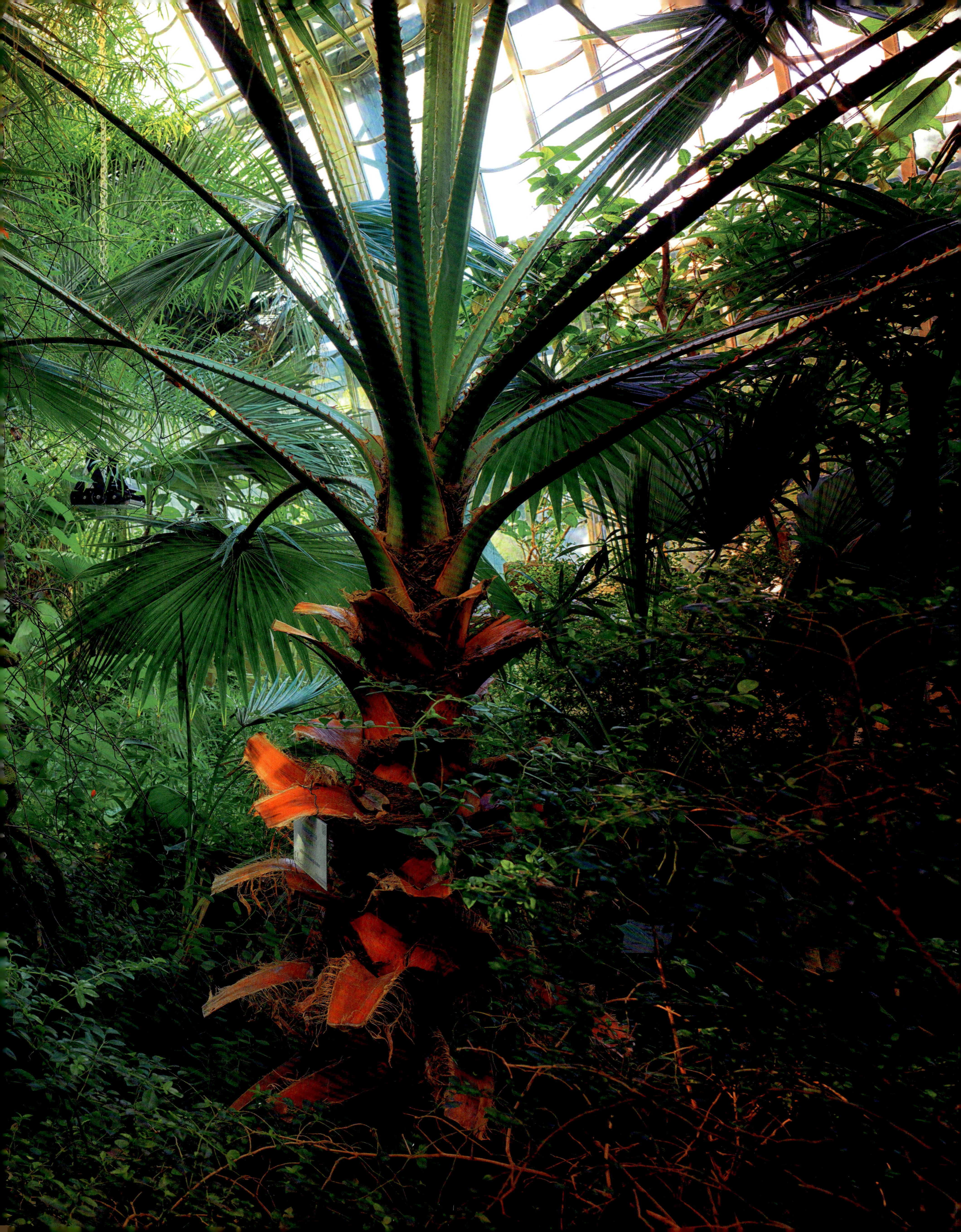

Werner Pawlok

FOTOGRAFIE UND LEIDENSCHAFT

PHOTOGRAPHY AND PASSION

Meine Faszination für Greenhouses ist verbunden mit lebendigen Kindheitserinnerungen: den Zoobesuchen an der Hand meines Vaters. Die Stuttgarter Wilhelma war mehr als ein Tierpark. Neben exotischen Tieren gab es hier märchenhafte Gewächshäuser und Gärten voller seltener Pflanzen. Damals war der beheizte Seerosenteich im maurischen Garten eine der jüngsten Attraktionen der Wilhelma, und mit etwas Glück durfte man als Kind ein schwimmendes Blatt der tropischen Riesenseerose betreten und dessen erstaunliche Tragkraft erproben.

I can trace my fascination with greenhouses back to vivid childhood memories of visiting zoos hand in hand with my father. Stuttgart's Wilhelma was far more than just a zoo. In addition to exotic animals, it was home to fairytale greenhouses and gardens filled with rare plants. Back then, the heated water lily pond in the Moorish Garden was one of Wilhelma's newest attractions, and if you were lucky, as a child you might be allowed to step onto a floating leaf of the giant tropical water lily and test its amazing load-bearing capacity.

Die Wiederbegegnung mit der *Nimphaea victoria* bei dem Greenhouses-Buchprojekt war für mich deshalb eine ganz eigene, sehr berührende Erfahrung. Joseph Paxton, der berühmte Botaniker und Glashausarchitekt, hatte die *Victoria amazonica* in einem eigens für die tropische Seerose entworfenen Gewächshaus mit temperiertem Wasserbecken erstmals in Europa zur Blüte gebracht. Seine gusseisernen Filigran-Konstruktionen waren von den gitterartigen Stützrippen der Victoriapflanze inspiriert. Das englische Vorbild war auch in Stuttgart wirksam: Seit 1851 gab es in der Wilhelma ebenfalls ein gläsernes Gewächshaus für die amazonische Riesenseerose mit dem Namen der Queen.

Die frühen Greenhouses waren technische Meisterleistungen, die den Einsatz neuer, industriell produzierter Baustoffe wie Eisen und Glas virtuos vor Augen führten, und sie waren zugleich Bühne für die ehrgeizigsten Trophäen der Botanik aus der exotischen Pflanzenwelt der Tropen. Ihre Faszinationskraft ist bis heute einzigartig. Diese Traumwelt unter Glas ins Bild zu rücken war eine Herausforderung besonderer Art. Tatsächlich erscheint mir das vorliegende Resultat in manchen Augenblicken wie die visuelle Erinnerung an eine der phantastischen Forschungsreisen des 19. Jahrhunderts.

Es lag bei diesem Projekt auf der Hand, vor allem die Britischen Inseln in den Fokus zu nehmen. Die Erkundungsreisen nach Großbritannien haben meine Partnerin Bettina Herrmann und ich (wie in alten Tagen) vor allem als Backpacker unternommen. Mit der gesamten Ausrüstung im Rucksack hatten wir mit körperlicher Verausgabung gerechnet, nicht aber mit der Intensivierung aller Begegnungen und Eindrücke, die sich am Ende aus dieser Entscheidung ergab. Häufig zu Fuß unterwegs, wurde unsere Wahrnehmung schärfer und die Empfindungen einprägsamer.

For me it was thus a very special and deeply moving experience to once again encounter this water lily, the *Nymphaea victoria*, while working on the *Greenhouses* book project. It was Joseph Paxton, the famed botanist and glass house architect, who was the first to entice the *Victoria amazonica* to flower in Europe thanks to a greenhouse with a temperature-controlled water basin designed specifically for the tropical water lily. His cast iron filigree designs were inspired by the lattice-like support ribs of the Victoria water lily's huge leaves. The English model took root in Stuttgart as well. Since 1851, Wilhelma has also had a glass greenhouse for the Amazonian giant water lily named after the Queen.

The early greenhouses were technical masterpieces that brilliantly showcased the use of new, industrially produced building materials such as iron and glass, while simultaneously providing a stage for the most ambitious botanical trophies from the exotic plant world of the tropics. Their allure remains unique to this day. Capturing this dream world under glass posed a special kind of challenge. In fact, at certain moments the results of my efforts feel like a visual reminder of one of the fantastical voyages of discovery that took place in the 19th century.

For this project, it was an obvious choice to focus primarily on the British Isles. My partner Bettina Herrmann and I made exploratory trips to Great Britain primarily as backpackers, just like in the old days. With all the gear in our backpacks, we had expected physical exhaustion. What we had not expected, however, was that the decision would intensify all of our resulting encounters and impressions. Traveling frequently on foot, our perceptions became sharper and the sensations more memorable.

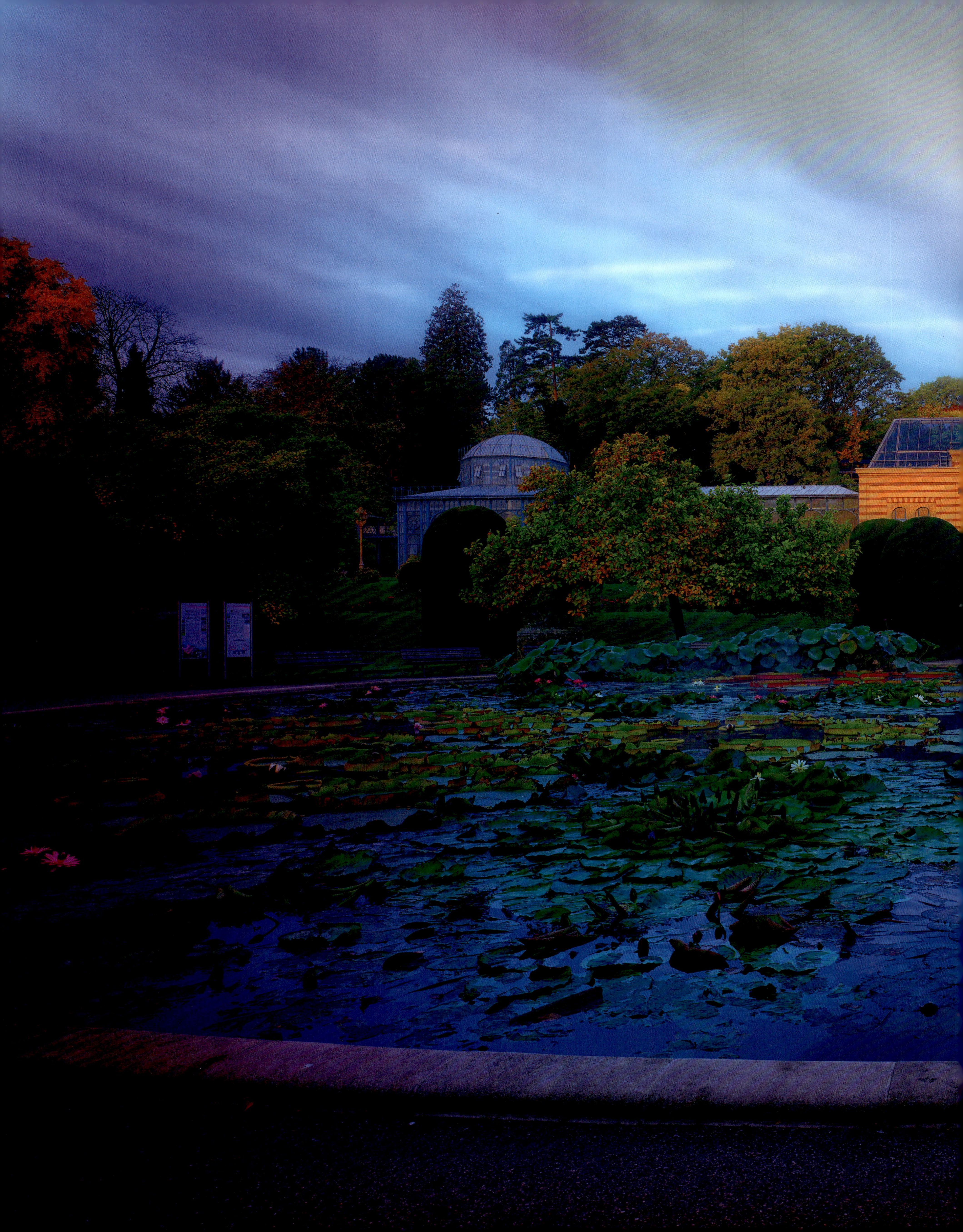

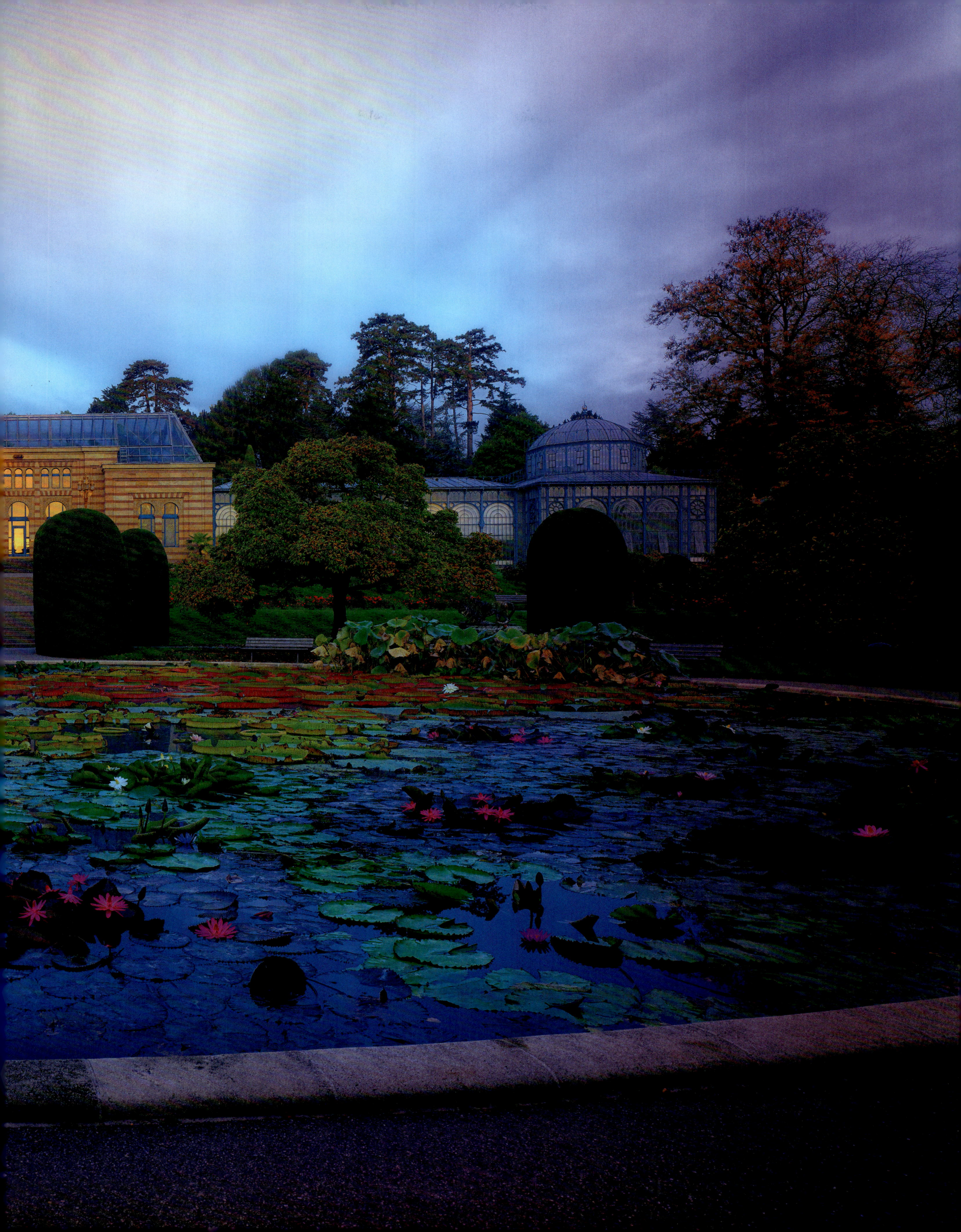

Wie immer, wenn ich mit der Kamera unterwegs bin, verfolge ich keinen vorab exakt festgelegten Plan, sondern versuche, mit der jeweils vorgefundenen Situation intuitiv umzugehen und mit jeder Aufnahme, Bild für Bild, immer tiefer in mein Sujet einzutauchen. Auf diese Art entwickelt sich ein vom fotografischen Instinkt gelenkter Aneignungsprozess, dem ich mich ganz anvertraue. Es geht mir nicht um die fotografische Analyse des Objektes im Sinne einer optimalen Wiedergabe der vorgefundenen Realität. Ich war nie ein Dokumentar.

Mir geht es vielmehr um das Bild als eigenständige Schöpfung. Der Moment der fotografischen Aufnahme ist zwar ein wesentlicher Schritt zum endgültigen Bild, aber es ist in meinem Verfahren eben nur ein erster Schritt. Eine ebenso wichtige Komponente der Bildfindung ist die digitale Nachbearbeitung am Bildschirm. Farbe bringt Kraft und Intensität in meine Motive. Die Greenhouse-Aufnahmen boten dafür einen geradezu idealen Fundus. Von Licht durchflutete Filigran-Konstruktionen in geometrisch strengen Formen kontrastieren mit der unbändigen Vielfalt tropischer Vegetation: Zwischen diesen Eckmotiven liegt ein grünes Farbenmeer verborgen.

Eine Bildserie wie die *Greenhouses* am Ende in einem Bildband der Öffentlichkeit vorstellen zu können, bewirkt einen zusätzlichen Energieschub im kreativen Prozess, denn nur in einem gedruckten Werk kommt nach meiner Meinung die verbindende Seele einer Bildserie wirklich zum Vorschein. Die Bildregie des Autors sucht nach einer gemeinsamen, verbindenden Aura der Bilder – auch dies ein völlig intuitiver Vorgang. Am Ende könnte man sogar für sich selbst den Punkt nicht mehr benennen, an dem diese Verbindungslinien zuerst aufgespürt und in Farbstimmungen oder Kontrastwerte übersetzt wurden.

Whenever I'm out and about with my camera, I don't follow a pre-determined plan. Instead, I simply try to deal intuitively with the situation at hand and to dive deeper and deeper into my subject with every shot, frame by frame. I have learned to trust the photographic instincts I've developed, and I allow those instincts to guide my work. Using photography to analyze an object in the sense of optimally reproducing the reality I find is not something that has ever interested me. I have never been a documentarian.

I prefer to think of the image as a creation in its own right. Although the moment of taking a photograph is an essential step towards the final image, it represents just the first step in my process. When it comes to creating an image, digital post-processing on my computer screen is equally as important. Color infuses my subjects with power and intensity. The images in *Greenhouses* provided an almost ideal pool of material for this. Light-flooded filigree designs in stark geometric shapes form a pleasing contrast with the exuberant diversity of the tropical vegetation: Not only do these motifs form the cornerstones of this project, they also frame a sea of green.

In the end, being able to publicly present a series of images such as *Greenhouses* in the form of a coffee-table book infuses the creative process with an additional boost of energy, because in my opinion only a printed work can truly reveal the unifying soul of a series of images. In his compositions, the author is searching for a shared, unifying aura – this, too, is a completely intuitive process. In the end, it would be impossible to name – even in your own mind – the point at which these connecting lines were first discovered and then translated into chromatic moods or contrast values.

Der Moment der fotografischen Aufnahme ist zwar ein wesentlicher Schritt zum endgültigen Bild, aber es ist in meinem Verfahren eben nur ein erster Schritt.

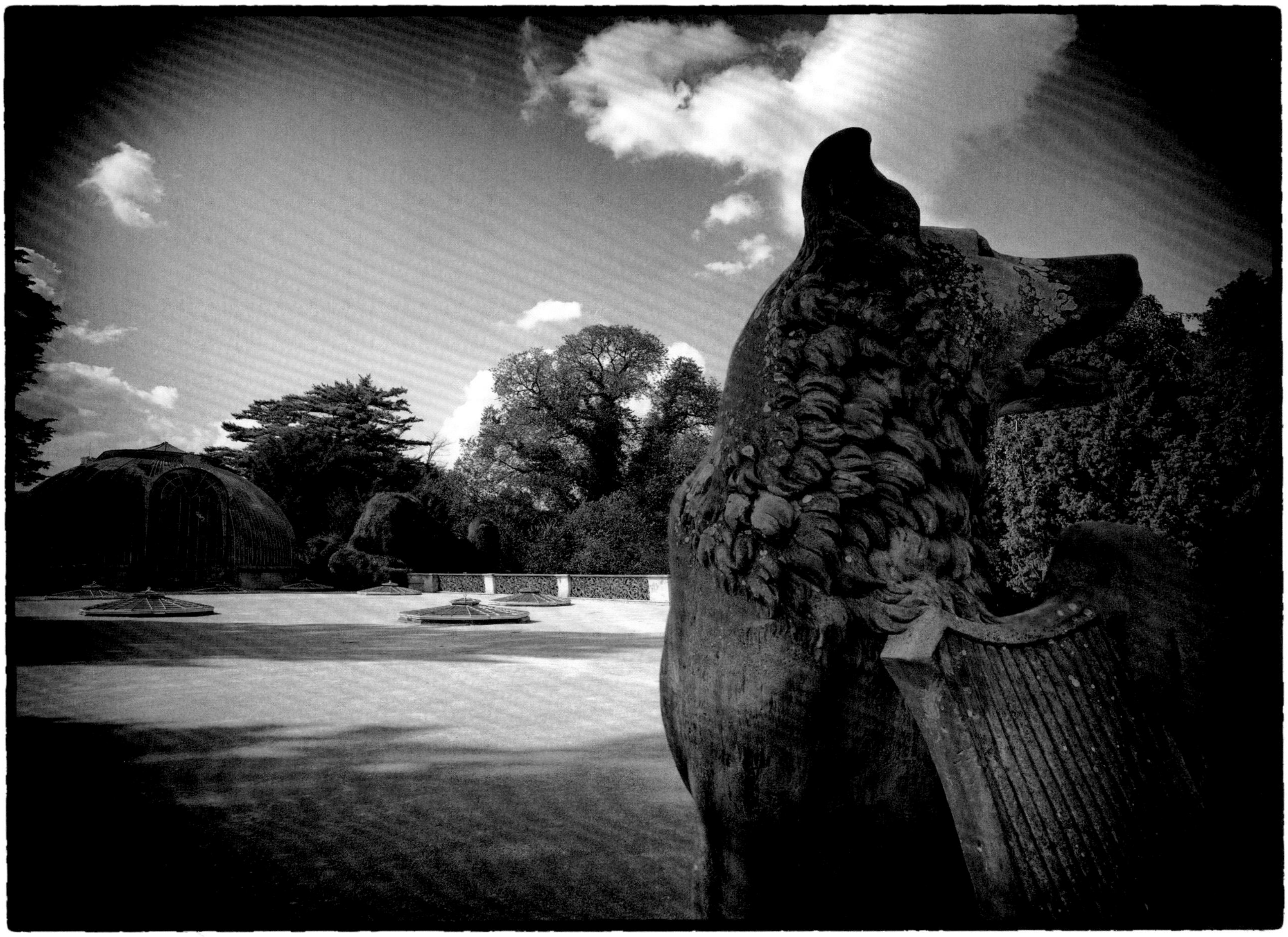

Although the moment of taking a photograph is an essential step towards the final image, it represents just the first step in my process.

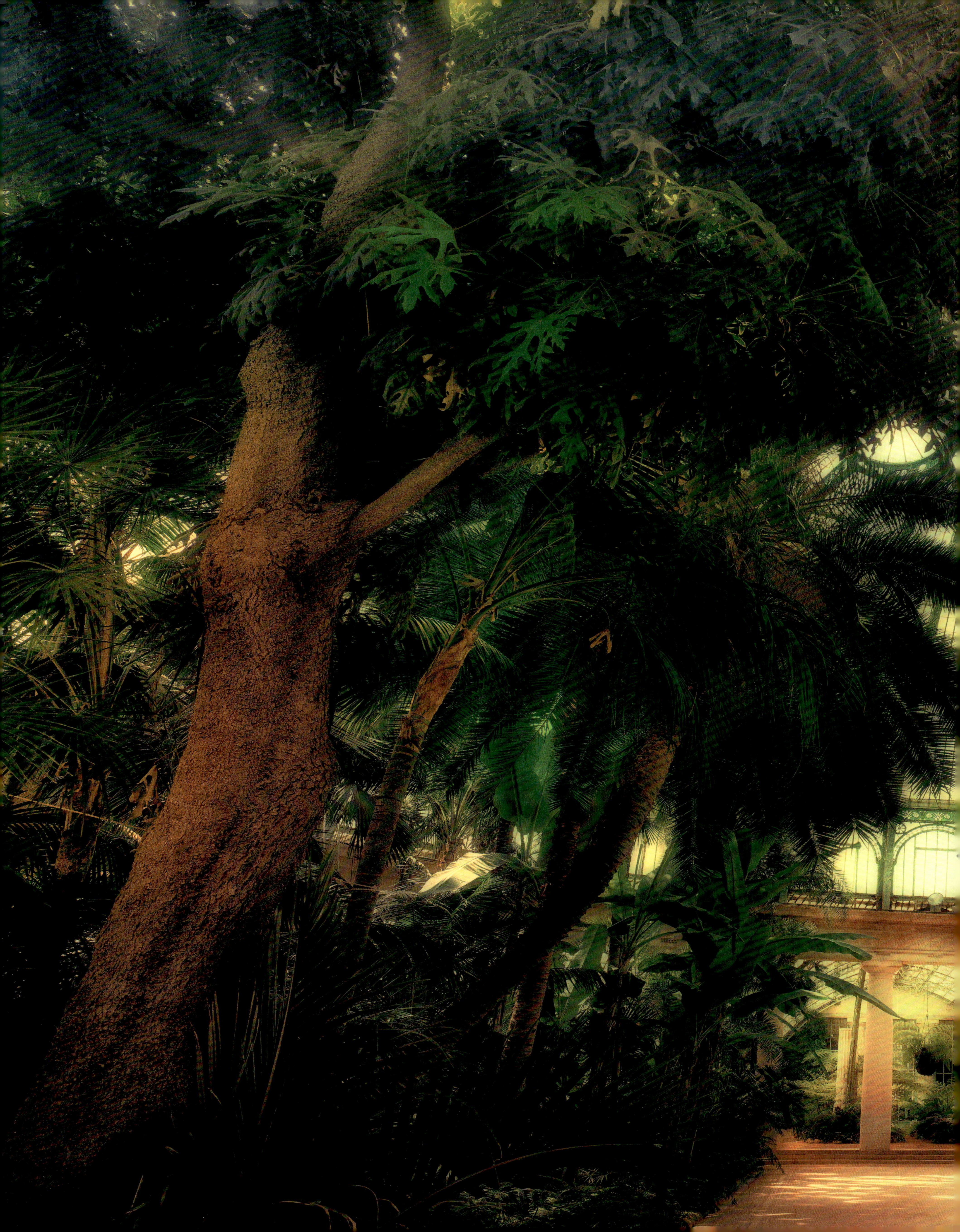

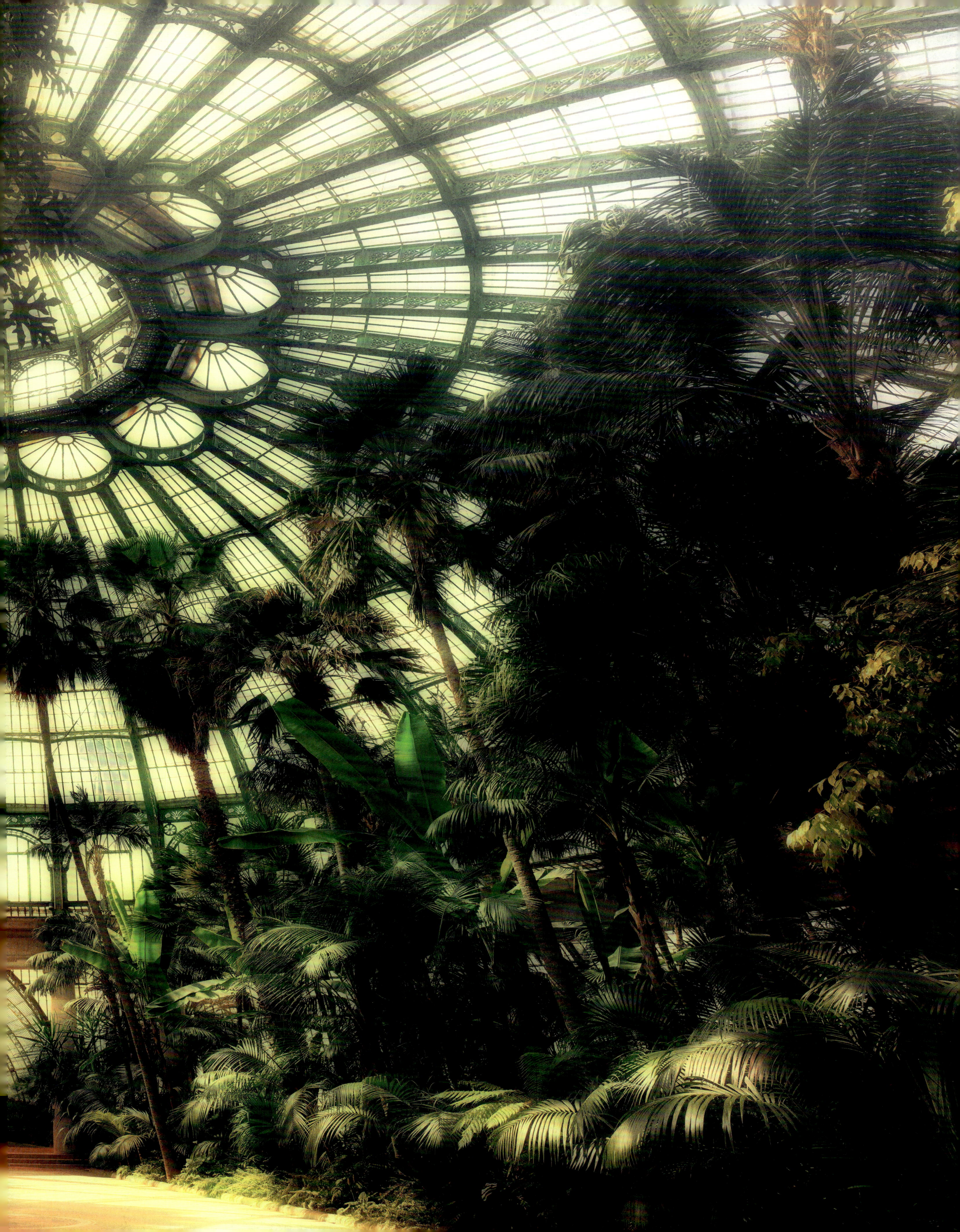

Stephan Reisner

TRAUMWELT UNTER GLAS

DREAM WORLD IN GLASS

Botanische Glashäuser sind filigrane, Licht durchflutete Paläste der europäischen Kultur und Architektur. Im Zentrum der formschönen Treibhäuser stehen überseeische Pflanzenwelten und seltene vegetative Arten. Für einen intuitiven Fotografen wie Werner Pawlok sind diese Orte die reinsten Wunderkammern: Form trifft auf Farbe, Licht auf hohe Räume, architektonische Konstruktion auf unbändige natürliche Vielfalt. Bereits in seinem umfangreichen *Cuba*-Projekt zeigte sich die kraftvolle Präsenz von exotischen Pflanzen im Kontrast zu architektonischen Formen. Nun rücken die Pflanzen

Botanical greenhouses are latticework palaces filled with light that showcase European culture and architecture. The elegant conservatories center around plant habitats from distant lands and rare species of flora. An intuitive photographer like Werner Pawlok finds these enclosures to be place of utmost wonder. They are where form meets color, light meets vast space, architectural design meets the boundless diversity of nature. As early as his extensive *Cuba* project, he contrasted the powerful presence of exotic plants with architectural shapes. His latest work focuses more

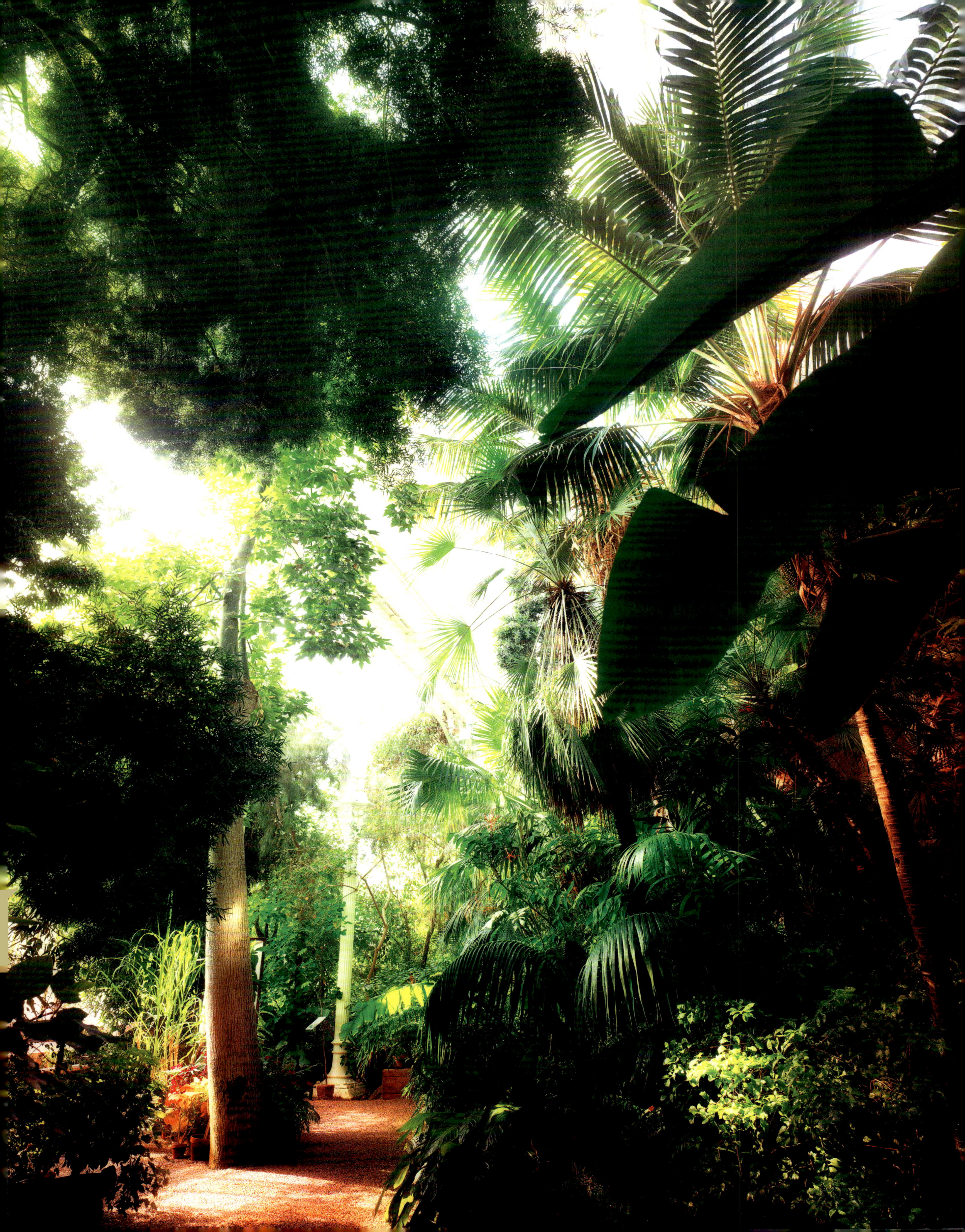

noch deutlicher in den Fokus seiner Arbeiten, kunstvoll umrahmt von den raumgreifenden Architekturen viktorianischer Ingenieure und Baumeister.

Insgesamt fünfzehn europäische Gewächshäuser besuchte der Stuttgarter Fotograf auf einer Rundreise, die er in modernen Siebenmeilenstiefeln und mit ausgesuchtem Fotoequipment zurücklegte. Ausgestattet mit Großbildkamera, Stativ und einem schmalen ausgehandelten Zeitfenster betrat er die beeindruckenden und sehr individuellen Orte einer Jahrhunderte alten Nischenkultur, bei der Architektur und Pflanzenwelten erlebnisreiche Ensembles bilden.

Es sind vielerlei Kräfte und visuelle Momente in den versammelten Fotografien am Wirken.

Die schwüle Hitze und exotische Exzentrik der künstlichen Biotope ist nicht leicht ins Bild zu setzen. Durch die hohe Luftfeuchtigkeit beschlagen die Kamera-Objektive schnell. Ein Motiv will also gut ausgewählt sein, bevor es sich ins Bild verwandelt. Normalerweise lässt sich Werner Pawlok bei der Motivwahl viel Zeit und fühlt sich intensiv ins lokale Sujet ein. Das Verständnis des kulturellen Kontextes und des sozialen Umfeldes ist für ihn immens wichtig, um in einen kreativen Dialog mit den Motiven zu kommen.

Bei dieser ungewöhnlichen Reise galt es, schnell und präzise zu handeln, das Auge umgehend an die komplexen Verhältnisse im Innern der flirrenden Glashäuser zu gewöhnen und die eigene sensitive Erfahrung mit der fotografischen Intuition kurzzuschließen.

clearly on the plants themselves, artistically framed by the spacious architecture of Victorian engineers and builders.

The Stuttgart-based photographer toured a total of fifteen European greenhouses, covering the distance in modern Seven League Boots and carrying selected photo equipment. Outfitted with a large-format camera, a tripod, and with a narrow, negotiated time window, he visited the impressive and highly individual sites of a centuries-old niche culture, one where architecture and the world of plants form an eventful ensemble.

It is not easy to capture the muggy heat and exotic eccentricity of the manmade biotopes on film. The camera lens can quickly fog up in such high humidity. It is important to select a subject carefully before turning it into a photograph. Werner Pawlok usually takes his time making this choice, and he likes to get a strong sense of the local setting. He believes that it is essential to gain an understanding of the cultural context and social environment in order to enter into creative dialog with his subjects.

When undertaking this extraordinary journey, he needed to work quickly and precisely, accustom his eye rapidly to the complex environment within the shimmering hothouses, and to bring his sensitive experience into direct contact with his photographic intuition.

A great many forces and visual moments are at work in the collection of photographs, which compiles the individual images into an exclusive and impressive series of greenhouse photographs. The most captivating and astounding aspect is the brilliant, expressive color scheme, which attaches an additional aura to the natural appearance of the plants and places the historical connections between humans and nature, architecture and botany, in a new light in the truest sense of the word. The pictures show that 19th century architecture and

Es sind vielerlei Kräfte und visuelle Momente in den versammelten Fotografien am Wirken, die die Bilder zu einer herausgehobenen und beeindruckenden Serie der Gewächshaus-Fotografie kompilieren. Allem voran besticht und erstaunt die fulminante expressive Farbgebung, die die natürliche Erscheinungsweise der Pflanzen mit einer zusätzlichen Aura ausstattet und die zeitgeschichtlichen Zusammenhänge zwischen Mensch und Natur, Architektur und Botanik im wahrsten Sinne des Wortes in ein neues Licht taucht. Die Bilder zeigen auf, dass die seinerzeit äußerst innovative Architektur und botanische Wissenschaft im 19. Jahrhundert zu einer überaus sinnlichen Formensprache avancierte, deren Gestaltungen bis heute zu Reflexionen anregen, wenn nicht sogar zu ganz neuen Betrachtungen und Einsichten über das Verhältnis von Mensch und Natur führen können.

Wir begegnen in den Bildern kühnen Effekten der Farbexplosion und gewagten kompositorischen Bildüberspannungen. Wie ein emblematisches Pfauenrad überwölbt die Kuppel des majestätisch anmutenden Königlichen Botanischen Gartens in Brüssel das fotografische Stationendrama. Dieses Haus öffnet nur einmal jährlich dem Publikum die Türen, was die Exklusivität der Fotografien noch einmal steigert. Aber auch die kleineren und weniger bekannten, dafür umso überraschenderen und in ihrer Eigentümlichkeit sehr inspirierenden Gewächshäuser wie im schottischen Benmore oder im tschechischen Lednice unterstreichen eine Form der Kultur, deren sinnliche Impulse und reichhaltig ausschwärmende Assoziationssporen bis in die Gegenwart reichen und von der zeitgenössischen Fotografie noch gar nicht recht entdeckt zu sein scheinen. Weniger die nüchterne dokumentarische Abbildung des Zeitgeschichtlichen und Pflanzlichen steht dabei im Vordergrund der Bilderreise, als vielmehr eine bewusste Verwandlung des Bestehenden in Sphären der sinnli-

botanical science, which were extremely innovative in their day, evolved into an entirely sensual form language, whose compositions inspire people to reflect, even to see them in entirely new ways, and to gain insight into the relationship between humans and nature.

A great many forces and visual moments are at work in the collection of photographs.

In the photos, we see what bold effect the explosion of colors has on us, and we encounter the daring tensions of visual compositions. The vaulted dome of the majestic Royal Botanical Garden in Brussels fans out over the photographic station drama like an peacock's emblematic display of plumage. This garden opens its doors to the public only once a year, which lends even greater exclusivity to the photographs. But the smaller and less well known greenhouses, such as those in Benmore, Scotland, or Lednice, Czech Republic, are all the more surprising and inspiring in their uniqueness. They underscore a kind of culture that sends sensual stimuli and abundantly spreading tendrils of association all the way to the present without seeming to ever have been properly discovered by contemporary photographers. The visual journey is less a sober, documentary depiction of history and the plant world and more an intentional transformation of what is already present into spheres of sensual exposition and thematic transfer. The photos attempt to evoke an emotional rather than a visual response. They try to bring countless worlds and ideas together and make them blossom. The colors intentionally clear a path to the expressive and, in doing so, open up new spaces for reflection.

chen Exposition und motivischen Übertragung. Die Bilder wollen wirken, nicht abbilden. Sie versuchen, etliche Welten und Vorstellungen zusammenzuführen und zum Blühen zu bringen. Dabei schlägt die Farbgebung bewusst Schneisen ins Expressive und eröffnet darüber neue Räume der Reflexion.

Je nach Darstellungsmittel lässt das Medium der Fotografie Wahrnehmungen zu, die über die rein dokumentarische Abbildungsfunktion des Sichtbaren hinausreichen und neue Perspektiven der Rezeption eröffnen. Die ausgesuchte und sehr bedachtsam angewendete farbliche Anreicherung der Bilder erzeugt hier Träume und Sehnsüchte, die wie ein Rauschmittel für die Vorstellung wirken. Bei der Betrachtung der Bilderserie gewinnt man den Eindruck, ein jedes Bild würde dem anderen zusätzliche kompositorische Kraft und fotografische Farbfeuchtigkeit verleihen. Das Innere der Glashäuser erscheint über alle geografischen Grenzen hinweg in einen umfassenderen Zusammenhang gestellt. Licht und Luftfeuchtigkeit gehen farblich wechselnde und nahezu haptische Symbiosen ein. Einzelne Farbströme und Konturlinien von Pflanzen und Architekturen treffen sich im archimedischen Punkt der Detailgenauigkeit und verästeln sich daraufhin zu ästhetischen Drehmomenten einer über das rein Äußerliche weit hinausreichenden Darstellung.

Das Farbschema, die Filter und die Vignetten überwölben, umhüllen und umschließen die Pflanzen und Architekturen. Sie sind selbst wie ein künstliches Treibhaus, in dem etwas herangezogen wird. Der fotografische Referent im Sinne des Naturgetreuen, des Realen, Pflanzlichen und des architektonischen Details wird durch die Kolorierung in einen neuen Kontext gestellt. Dieser besitzt durchaus Anschlüsse an die Malerei. Sehnsucht, Traum und Wirklichkeit verschmelzen zu einem somnambulen Rausch. Es ist ein

Depending on the presentation medium, photography allows us to perceive things in a way that goes well beyond the simple function of documenting what we see and offers us new reception modalities. The images have a carefully selected and deliberately applied richness of color that evokes dreams and a sense of longing that have an intoxicating effect on the mind. While viewing the series, we are left with the impression that each photo has lent the next one additional compositional power and a photographic color humidity. The hothouse interiors appear to be set against a more comprehensive context that transcends all geographic boundaries. Light and humidity enter into a nearly haptic symbiosis of alternating colors. Individual color streams and contour lines of plants and architectures meet at the Archimedean point where detail comes into focus and then branch out to aesthetic twists and turns of a representation that goes far beyond the purely external.

The color scheme, filters, and vignettes envelope, embrace, and arch over the plants and architectures. They form a sort of artificial hothouse of their own, where things are grown. The use of color places the photographic reportage in a new context in terms of faithfulness to nature, real life, the plant world, and architectural detail. This storytelling has much in common with painting. Yearnings, dreams, and reality blend into a somnambulant exhilaration. It is like looking through a phantasmagoric lens, where unexpected discoveries are made in the thicket of nature, bringing new images to life that exist beyond real and literal experience. The greenhouse thus transforms into a kind of oversized camera obscura, a botanical circular cinema, and a nearly tactile venue for sensory immersion. The inner world contrasts with the external one, time with the instantaneous moment, history with the present. The macrocosm is reflected in the microcosm and vice versa.

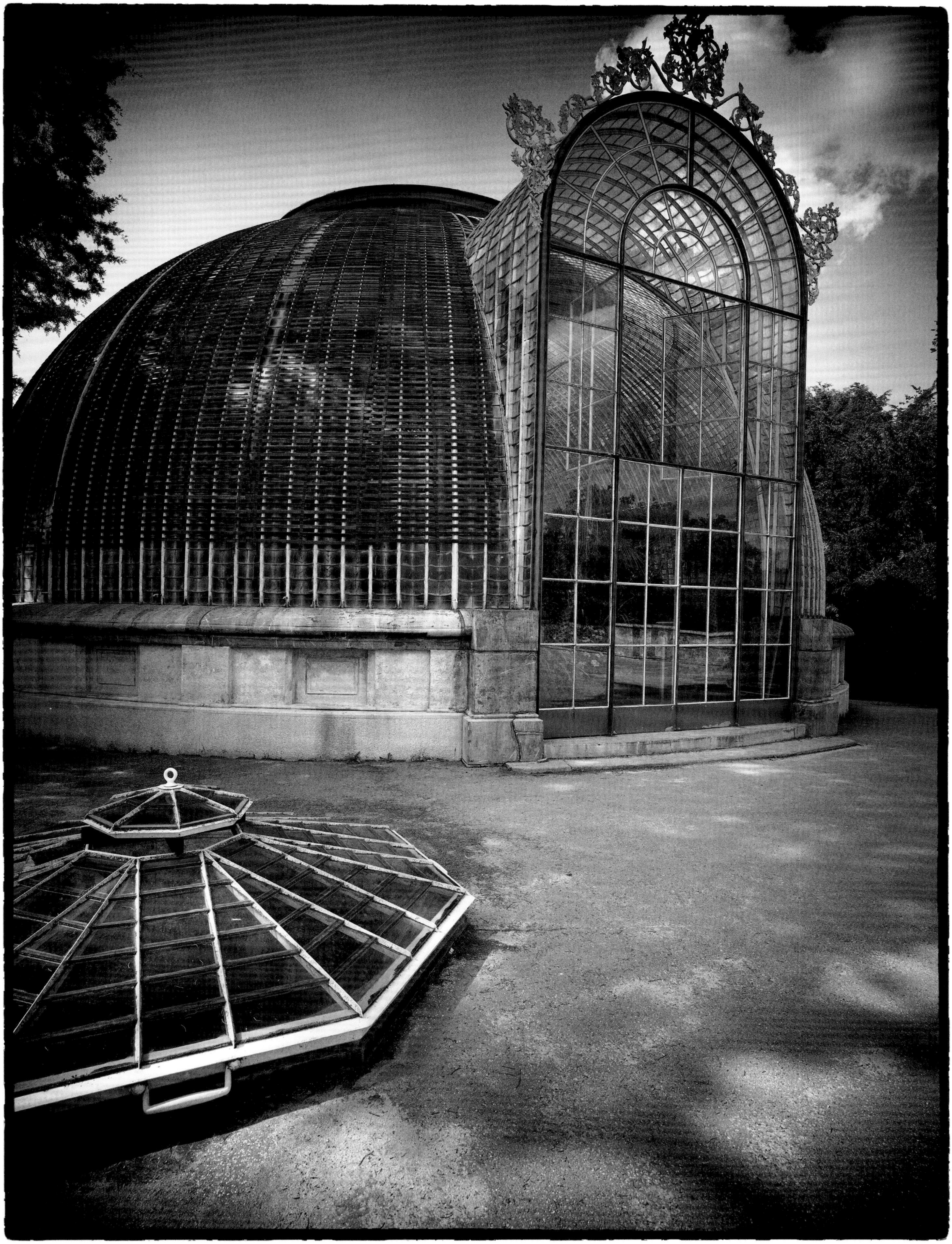

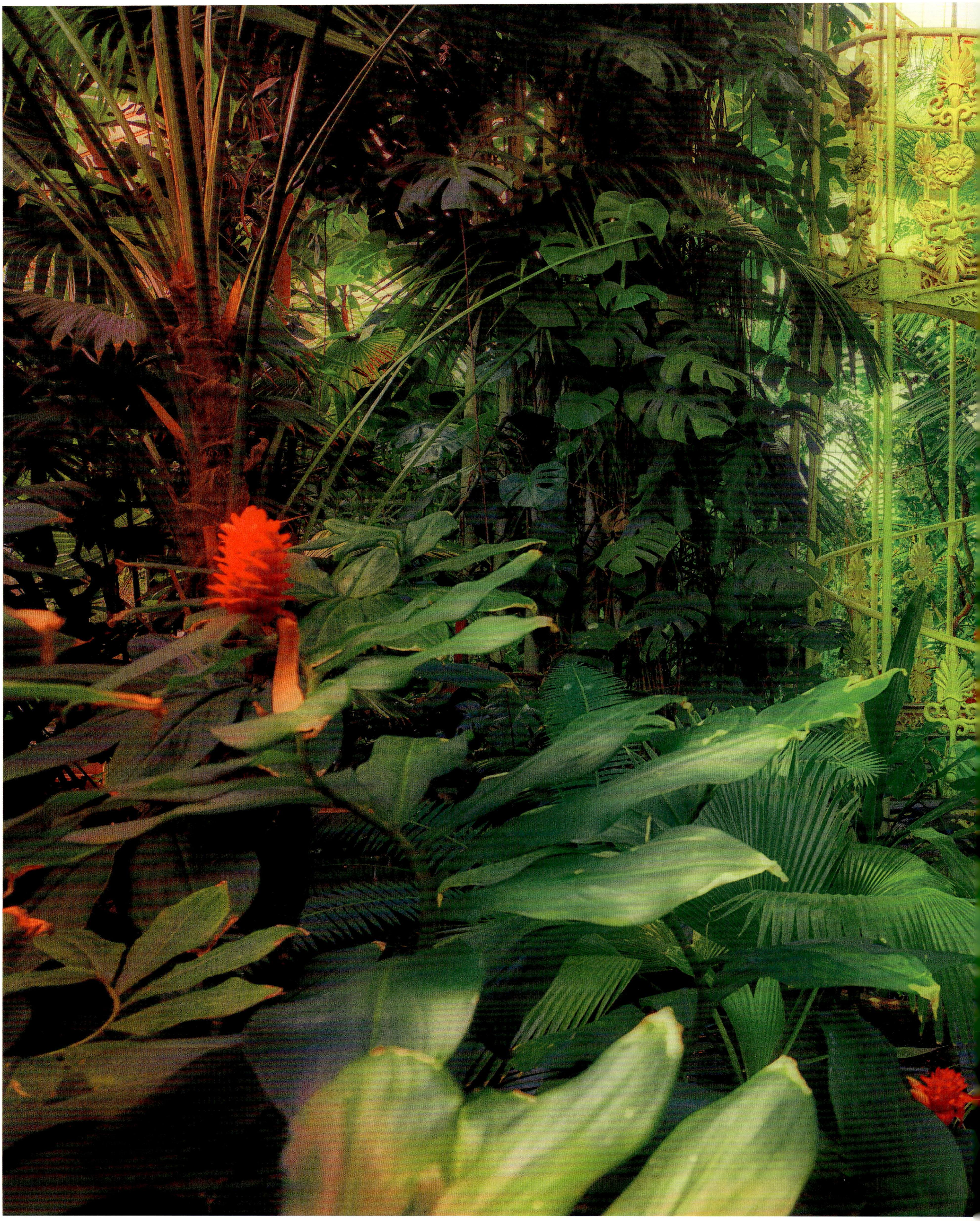

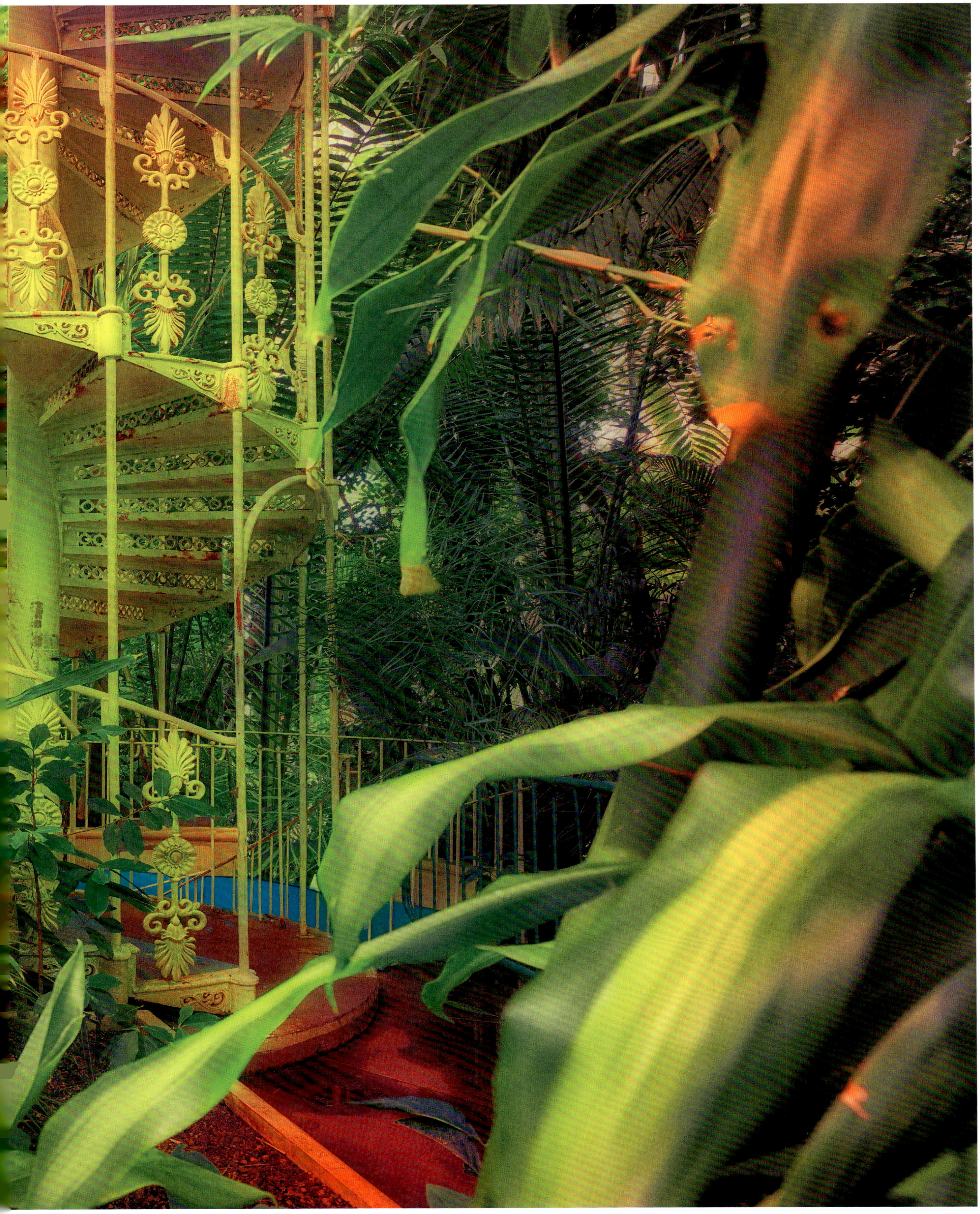

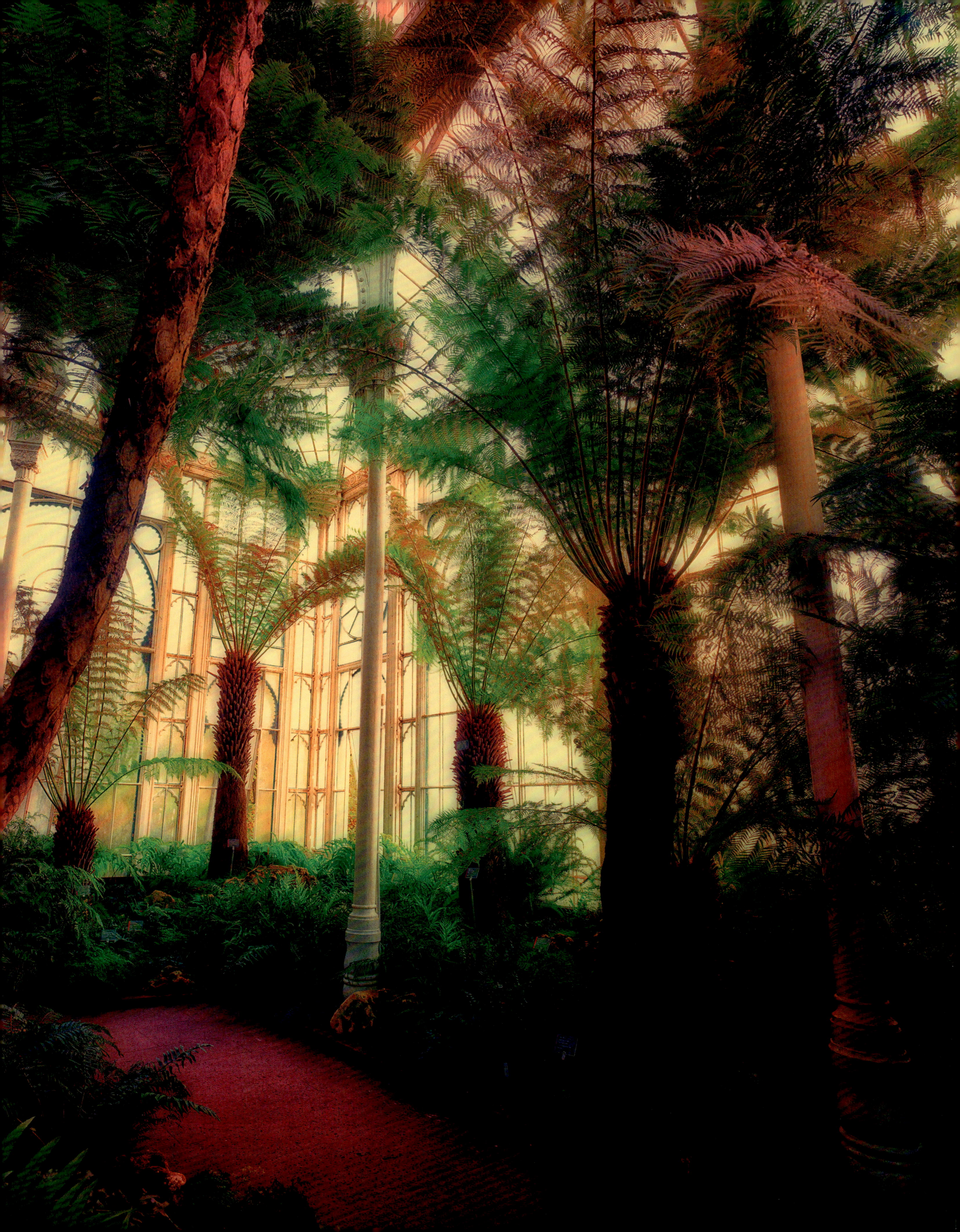

phantasmagorisches Sehen, das im Dickicht des Natürlichen unerwartete Entdeckungen macht und neuartige Bilder aktiviert, die jenseits des Wirklichen und Tatsächlichen liegen. So verwandelt sich das Gewächshaus in eine Art überdimensional große Camera obscura, in ein botanisches Rundkino und in einen immersiven, nahezu taktilen Erlebnisraum. Innenwelt und Außenwelt, Zeit und Augenblick, Geschichte und Gegenwart setzen sich ins Verhältnis, der Makrokosmos spiegelt sich im Mikrokosmos wider und umgekehrt.

Die exzeptionelle Architektur als solche kommt dabei in keinem der Werke zu kurz. Auch sie wird gefeiert und fotografisch exponiert wie eine seltene und abenteuerlich blühende Pflanzenart. Zu ihrer Entstehungszeit waren diese Bauwerke Wunderwerke der Filigran-Architektur, die ein Maximum an Licht bereitstellten, dafür jedoch nur ein Minimum an tragender Konstruktion verlangten. Welche architektonische Noblesse in ihnen steckt und wie sehr dabei die exotische Pflanzenwelt und das künstliche Gehäuse motivisch ineinander greifen, auch dies setzen die Bilder außergewöhnlich in Szene. Teilweise geht das Bildkonzept des Fotografen so weit, dass die Bilder ins Anachronistische kippen. Es wirkt, als ahme er jene Malerei nach, die im 19. Jahrhundert als erstes in diese neuen beeindruckenden Glaspaläste trat, um sich die exotischen Innenwelten und das künstliche Raumklima motivisch zu erschließen.

Der Fotograf Karl Blossfeldt hat den motivischen Zusammenhang von Natur und Architektur, von Rittersporn und Jugendstil, in den 1920er-Jahren fotografisch detailreich herausgearbeitet. Er nannte sein taxonomisches Bilderwerk *Urformen der Kunst*. Hier nun windet sich eine schmiedeeiserne Wendeltreppe wie eine metaphorische DNA-Spindel durch den Raum, verziert von mäandernden Schlingpflanzen. Die Linien und Kurven von Pflanzen ahmen die Bögen und Rostränder der architektonischen

Exceptional architecture as such does not come up short in any of the pieces. It is celebrated and exposed through the lens like a rare and quixotically blooming species of plant. At the time they were built, these structures were marvels of latticework architecture, which maximized light while requiring only minimal structural support. The images also form an extraordinary backdrop for showcasing their architectural noblesse and the thematic interweaving of flora and its artificial home. To a certain extent, the photographer's vision even goes so far as to push the pictures to the brink of anachronism. It is as though he were imitating the 19th century school of painting that was first seen in these new striking glass palaces as a way to thematicize the exotic interiors and their artificial climates.

In the 1920s, the photographer Karl Blossfeldt developed a richly detailed photographic style that depicted the thematic connection between nature and architecture, between larkspur and Art Nouveau. He titled his taxonomic book of photography *Urformen der Kunst* (Architypes of Art). Here now wrought-iron spiral staircase winds through space like a metaphorical coil of DNA, adorned with meandering vines. The lines and curves of plants mimic the arches and edges of grates in architectural structures. Columns and pillars, in turn, resemble the trunks of palms and trees. A South American mask placed on a rock turns into the head of a stone primate. Elsewhere, a graceful white Art Nouveau bench invites the viewer to sit down and rest for a while. Next to it, the leaves of an exotic palm fan out with an openness that is similarly inviting. Who is the real imitator here? Does art imitate nature or does nature imitate art?

Photographs cannot reproduce scents. We cannot hear any voices, no buzzing of bees, no chirping of birds. Nor can we see dewdrops fall to the ground

Konstruktionen nach. Säulen und Stützen wiederum gleichen Stämmen von Palmen und Bäumen. Eine auf einem Felsen abgelegte südamerikanische Maske verwandelt sich in den Kopf eines steinernen Primaten. An anderer Stelle lädt eine filigrane weiße Jugendstil-Bank zum Verweilen ein. Gleich daneben fächern sich die Blätter einer exotischen Palme in ähnlicher einladender Offenheit auf. Wer ahmt dabei wen nach? Die Kunst die Natur oder die Natur die Kunst?

Eine Fotografie reproduziert keine Gerüche, wir hören keine Stimmen, kein Summen, kein Zwitschern, wir sehen auch keinen Tautropfen vom wiegenden Palmblatt zu Boden platschen. Zwar werden Schwüle und Luftfeuchtigkeit anhand von Kondenswasser an Fensterscheiben und auf Palmblättern ablesbar, aber werden sie auch spürbar?

Spürbar wird in den Bildern etwas anderes und Besonderes: Eine Art Traum oder Rausch von eigenwillig verschobenen Dimensionen, in dem sich das Menschliche und Künstliche mit dem Natürlichen und Geschichtlichen neuartig verbindet. Im fotogenen Zusammenspiel von Architektur und Pflanzen, Kunst und Natur eröffnen die Bilder einen Assoziationsraum, dessen Elemente uns selbst zu einer mannigfaltigen Reaktion verleiten. Wir vollführen eine Art mentale Fotosynthese, denn unsere Vorstellungskräfte und Sehnsüchte werden durch die Werke aktiviert und schütten dabei einen energiereichen Assoziationszucker aus. Die Bilder belichten die fantastischen Anteile und schwärmerischen Samen in uns und lassen uns weit in den Raum des Vorstellbaren wachsen. Mit etwas Glück überwinden wir den gewohnten Erdkreis unserer Anschauung und gelangen bis ins Kosmische hinein. So wölben sich die mächtigen Waben des südenglischen Eden-Projekts, die an Buckminster Fullers ingeniöse Formensprache anknüpfen, wie extraterrestrische Tropfen über unseren kühnsten Vorstellungen.

from swaying palm fronds. We can get a sense of mugginess and humidity from condensation on window panes and palm leaves, but can we actually feel them physically?

What we can do is feel something different and special in the photos. A kind of dream or intoxication evoked by deliberately shifted dimensions, in which the human and the artistic combine with natural and historical phenomena in entirely new ways. In the photogenic interplay between architecture and plants, art and nature, the pictures open up room for association, whose elements produce a manifold response in us. We complete a kind of mental photosynthesis, for our imagination and yearnings are stimulated by the works and energize us with the sweetness of association. The photos expose the fantastical within us and plant the seeds of enthusiasm, allowing us to grow far into the space of the imaginable. With a bit of luck, we break out of the earthly realm of our world view and soar to the cosmos. Like extraterrestrial pods, the magnificent honeycombs of the Eden Project in southern England, reminiscent of Buckminster Fuller's ingenious form language, vault over our most audacious perceptions.

But don't we also lose something in this dream world encased in glass? Where is the actual nature, the reality of growth and decay? Are the photos too pretty to be real?

Through the pictures, we sense the connection between finality and continuity, repetition and revolution. They allow us to glimpse the cycle of growth and decay. We turn into a monad who passes through a plethora of perceptions and discovers the world reflected in itself. Assisted by the images, we rush through the geological

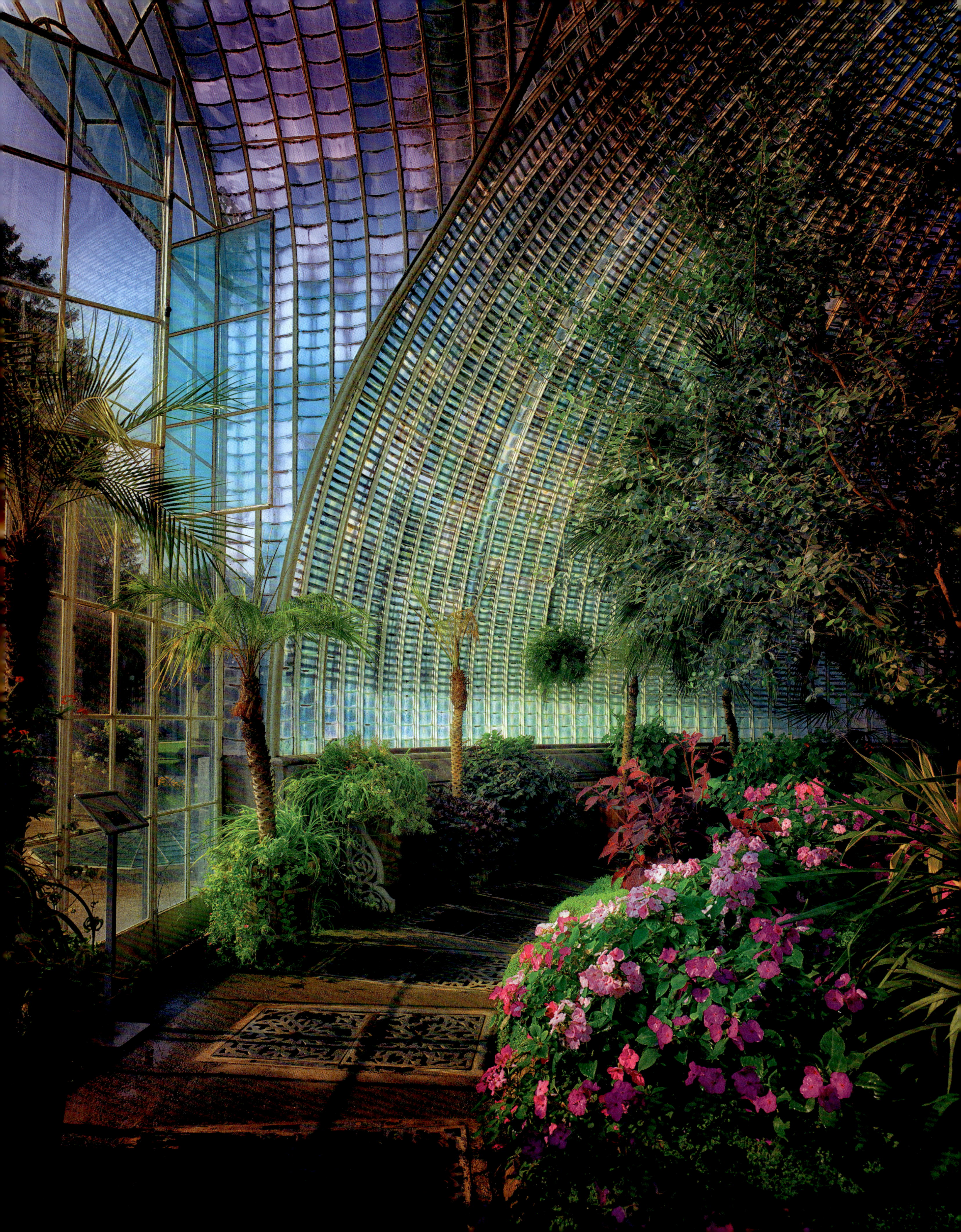

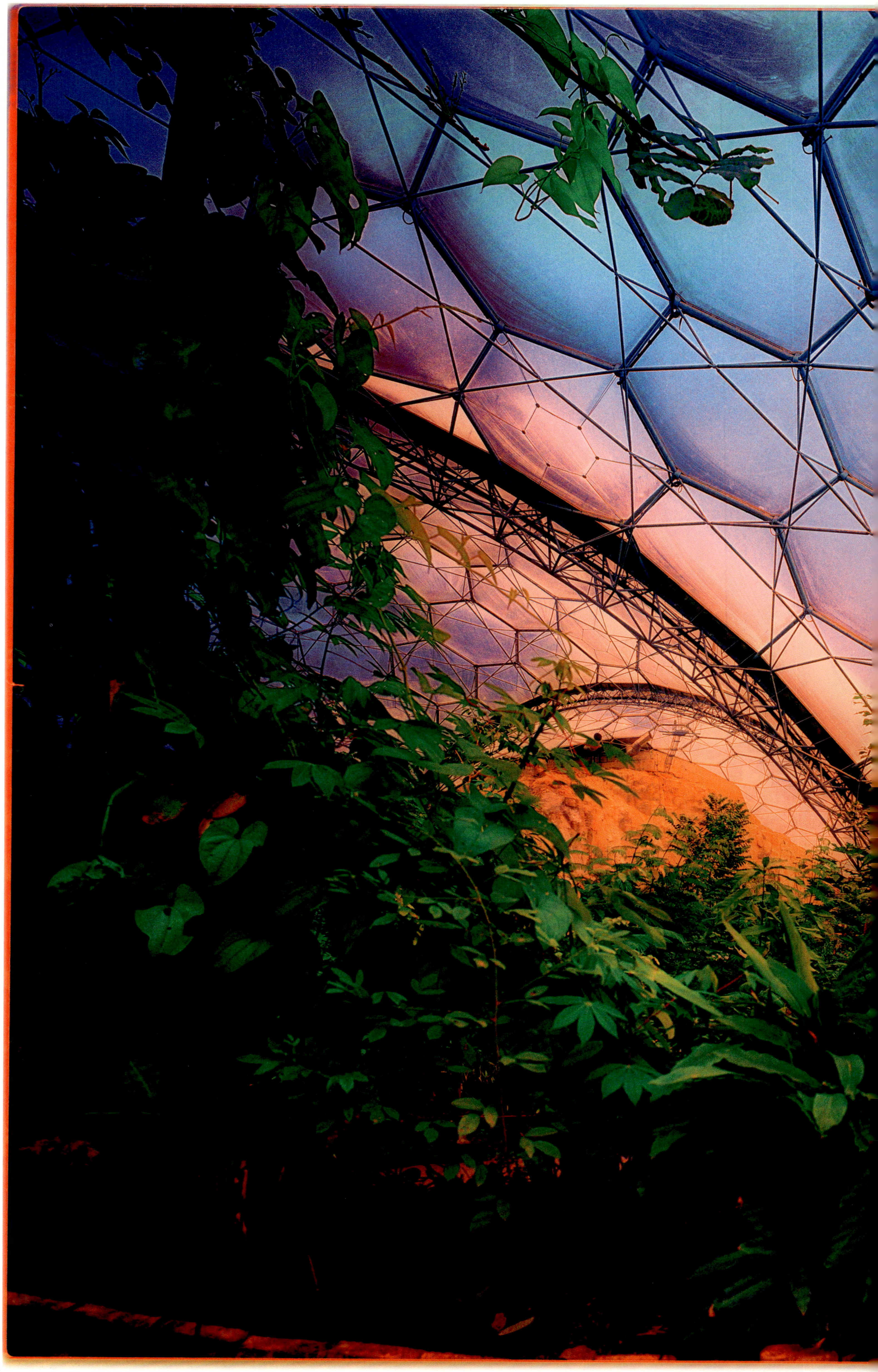

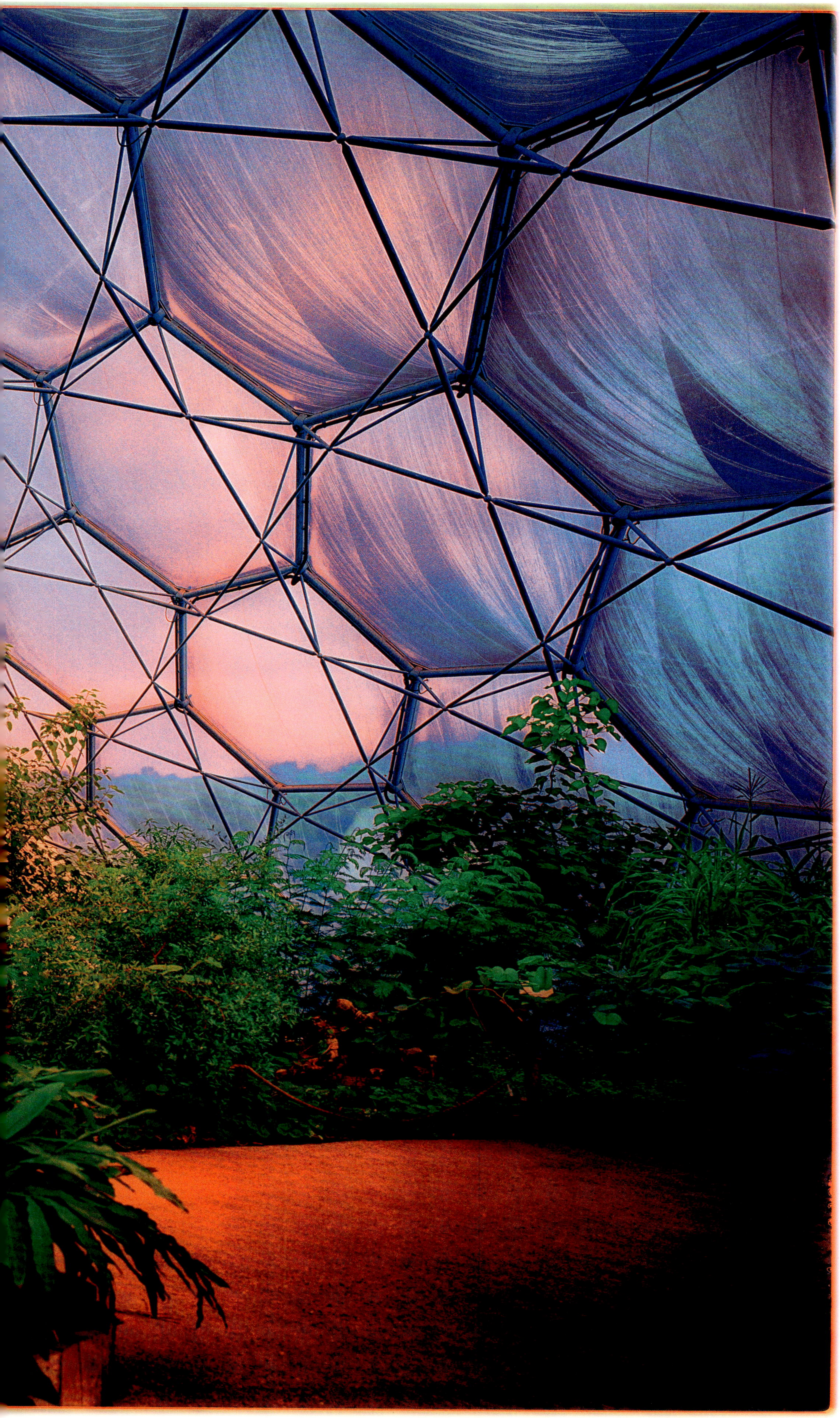

Aber verlieren wir uns nicht auch etwas in dieser Traumwelt unter Glas? Wo ist die tatsächliche Natur, die Wirklichkeit des Werdens und Vergehens? Sind die Bilder zu schön, um wahr zu sein?

Über die Bilder erahnen wir den Zusammenhang von Endlichkeit und Dauer, von Zyklus und Revolution, wir blicken mit ihnen in den Kreislauf des Werdens und Vergehens. Wir werden zu einer Monade, die eine Fülle an Perzeptionen durchläuft und im Spiegel ihrer selbst die Welt entdeckt. So durcheilen wir mit Hilfe der Bilder die erdgeschichtlichen Zeitalter, die Jahrhunderte, die Jahrtausende und blicken für einen kurzen Moment auf unsere menschliche Kultur im Verhältnis zur Natur. Für einen flüchtigen, aber sinnlich eindringlichen Moment begreifen wir den Zusammenhang von Leben und Evolution, menschlicher Kultur und Wissenschaft. Die Bilder werden zu einem Spiegel unseres Staunens und unseres menschlichen Wirkens in der Zeit. Vielleicht erreichen sie niemals den tatsächlichen Breitengrad der Wirklichkeit, der jenseits der Glaswände existiert und unsere Spezies überragt. Aber zumindest ist jede dieser Fotografien, jedes Bild und jede Vorstellung von ihr etwas, das wie eine unbekannte Lebensform in uns austreibt und sich der Wahrnehmung zuwendet.

Dem Fotografen Werner Pawlok kommt dabei das besondere Verdienst zu, sich an all diese außergewöhnlichen und wunderbaren Orte begeben zu haben, um sie atmosphärisch für uns im Bild zu erfassen und in neue Zukunftsträume zu übersetzen. Seine Bilder sind eine Einladung zur Reise. Im Grunde ist er ein moderner fotografischer Forschungsreisender, der im Sinne der Botanik und Kunst die Botanisiertrommel und das taxonomische Skizzenbuch gegen Kamera, Stativ und einen Rucksack voller Objektive eingetauscht hat.

ages, the centuries, the millennia, and for just a moment glimpse our own humanity in relation to nature. For a fleeting yet sensually penetrating instant, we comprehend the connection between life and evolution, human culture and science. The photos begin to mirror our amazement and our human impact through time. We may never reach the actual latitude of reality that exists beyond the glass walls and towers over our species. However, at least each of these photographs, each image, and each perception of it is something that sprouts within us like an unknown life form and applies itself to our awareness.

It is to the photographer Werner Pawlok's great credit that he visited all these extraordinary and wonderful places in order to capture their atmosphere in pictures for us and translate them into new dreams of the future. His photos are an invitation to travel. He is in essence today's version of a traveling photographic researcher, who, in the interest of botany and art, has exchanged his specimen glass and taxonomic sketchbook for a camera, tripod, and backpack filled with lenses.

Kew Garden XI • Peoples Palace Glasgow ▼

Die Bilder werden zu einem Spiegel unseres Staunens und unseres menschlichen Wirkens in der Zeit.

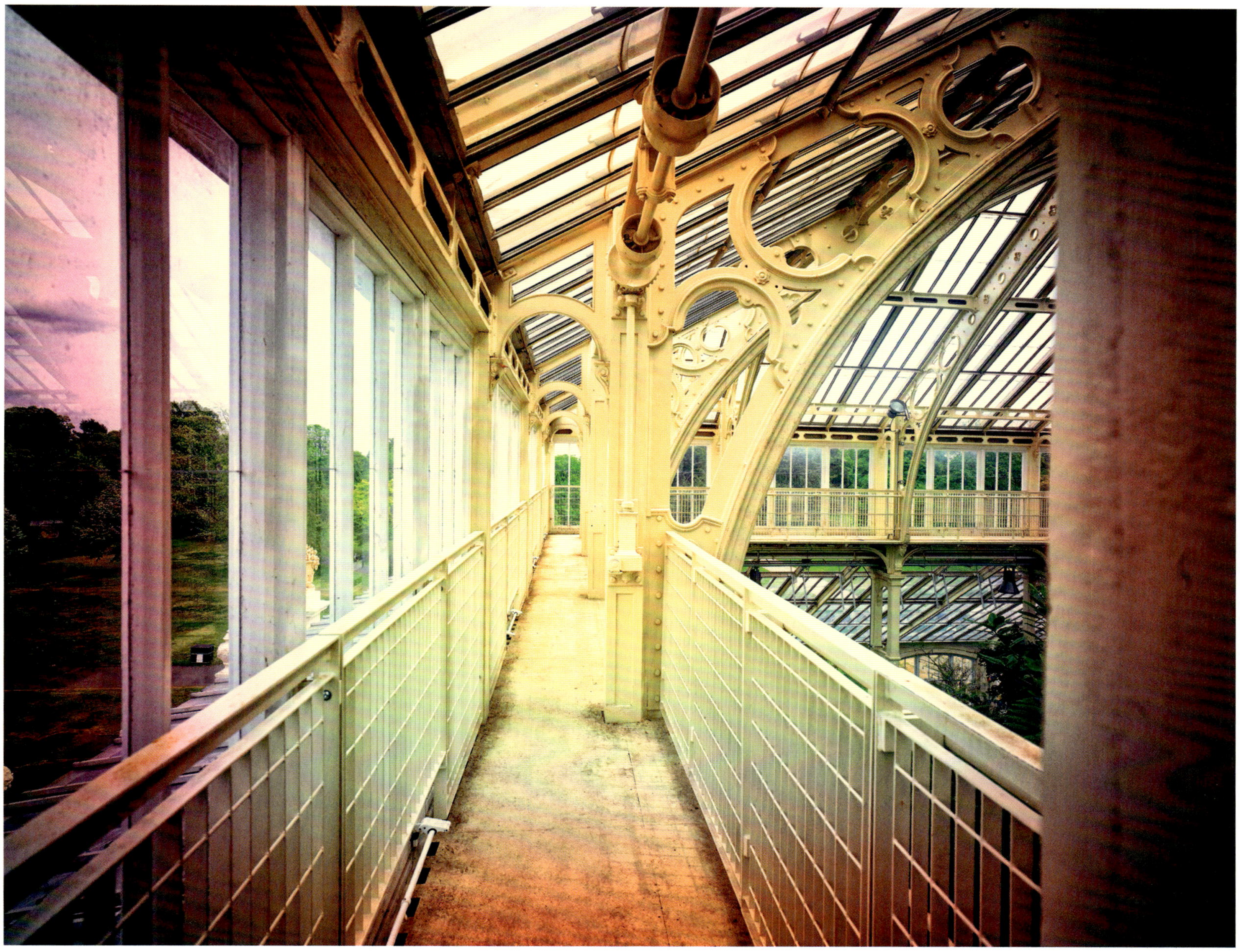

The photos begin to mirror our amazement and our human impact through time.

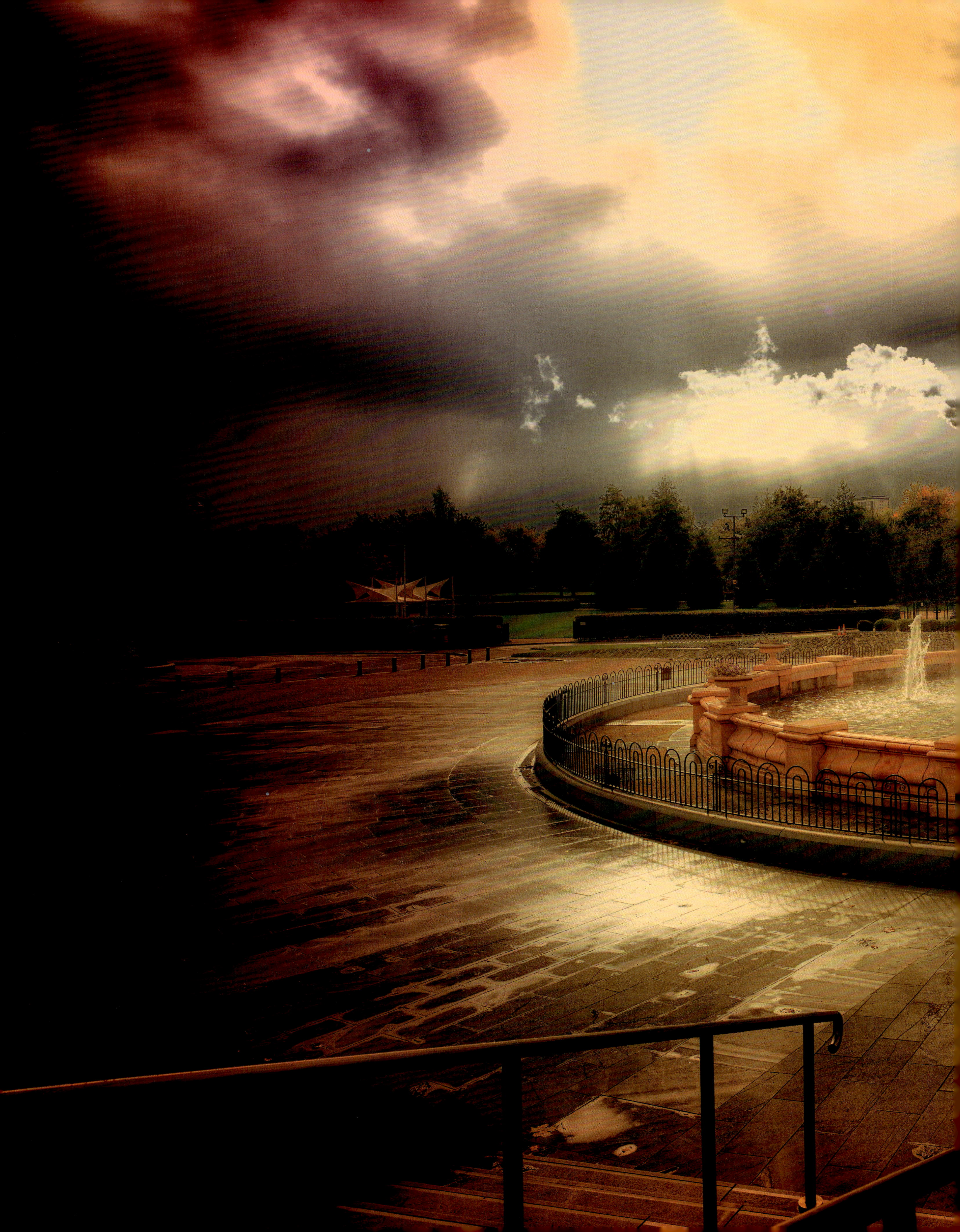

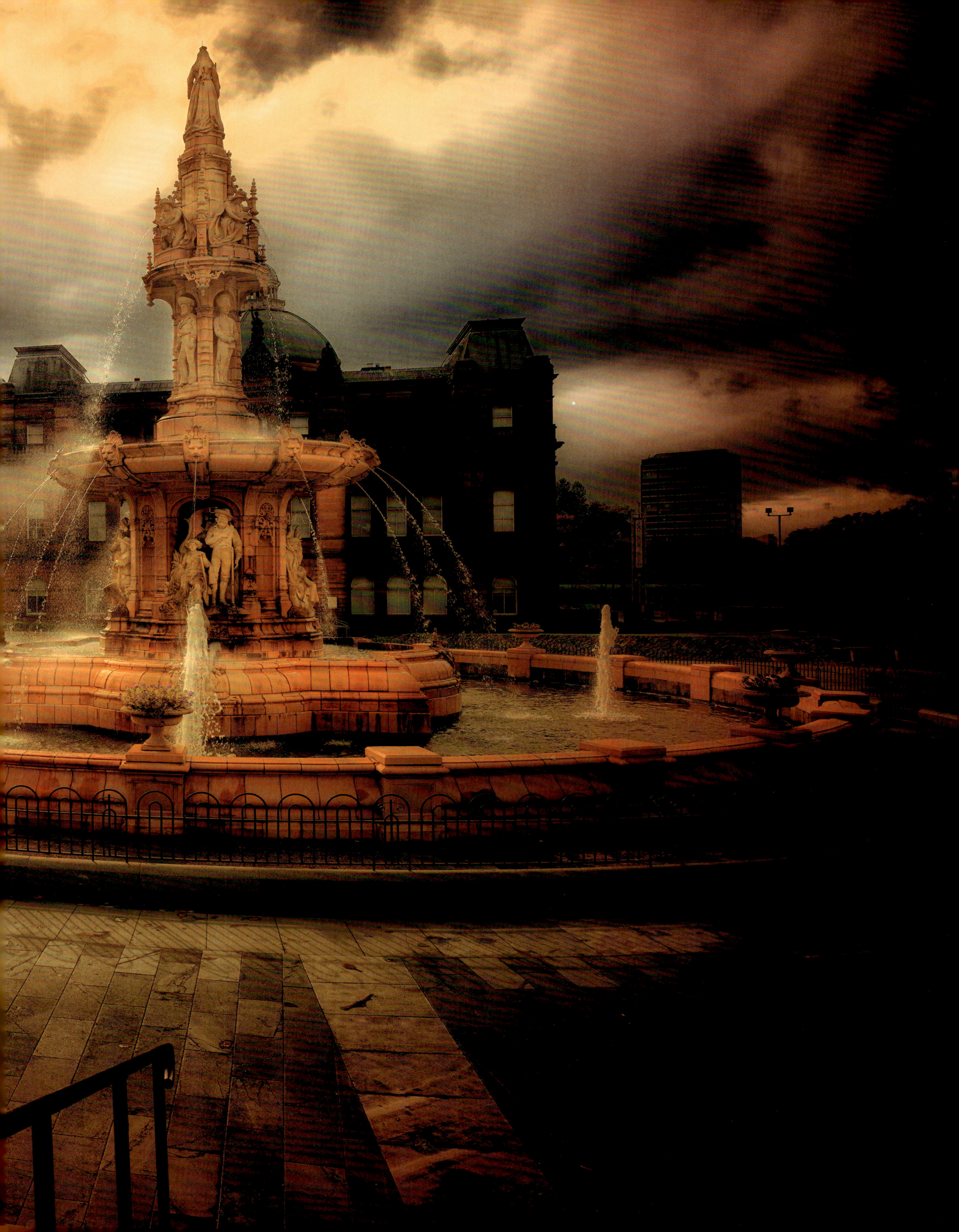

Alexandra Schmöger

PARADIESE VON MENSCHENHAND

MANMADE GARDENS OF EDEN

Grüne Palmen, die sich majestätisch in der warmen Südseebrise wiegen – nicht nur in der heutigen Zeit eine Sehnsucht, in der sich der Wunsch nach dem Paradies auf Erden manifestiert. Schon das 19. Jahrhundert kennt dieses Wunschbild. Geografisch ist die Erde durch die großen Entdeckerfahrten seit dem 15. Jahrhundert vermessen, jedoch gab es weiterhin unermessliche Pflanzenschätze zu heben. Die Palme mit ihrem hohen Wuchs galt schnell als über alle anderen Pflanzen herrschende Fürstin, die „Bewohnerin der glücklichen Länder der Tropen, wo die Strahlen der Sonne immer

Green palms sway majestically in the warm South Sea breeze. This image evokes a sense of longing, manifested in a desire for paradise on earth – and not only in our modern times. This idyll was just as prevalent in the 19th century. Adventurers may have been mapping the Earth's geography since the 15th century on their great voyages of discovery, but there were still vast number of botanical treasures to be uncovered. Palm trees, with their towering growth, were soon viewed as the sovereigns of the plant world, "the natives of those happy countries within the tropics, where the rays of

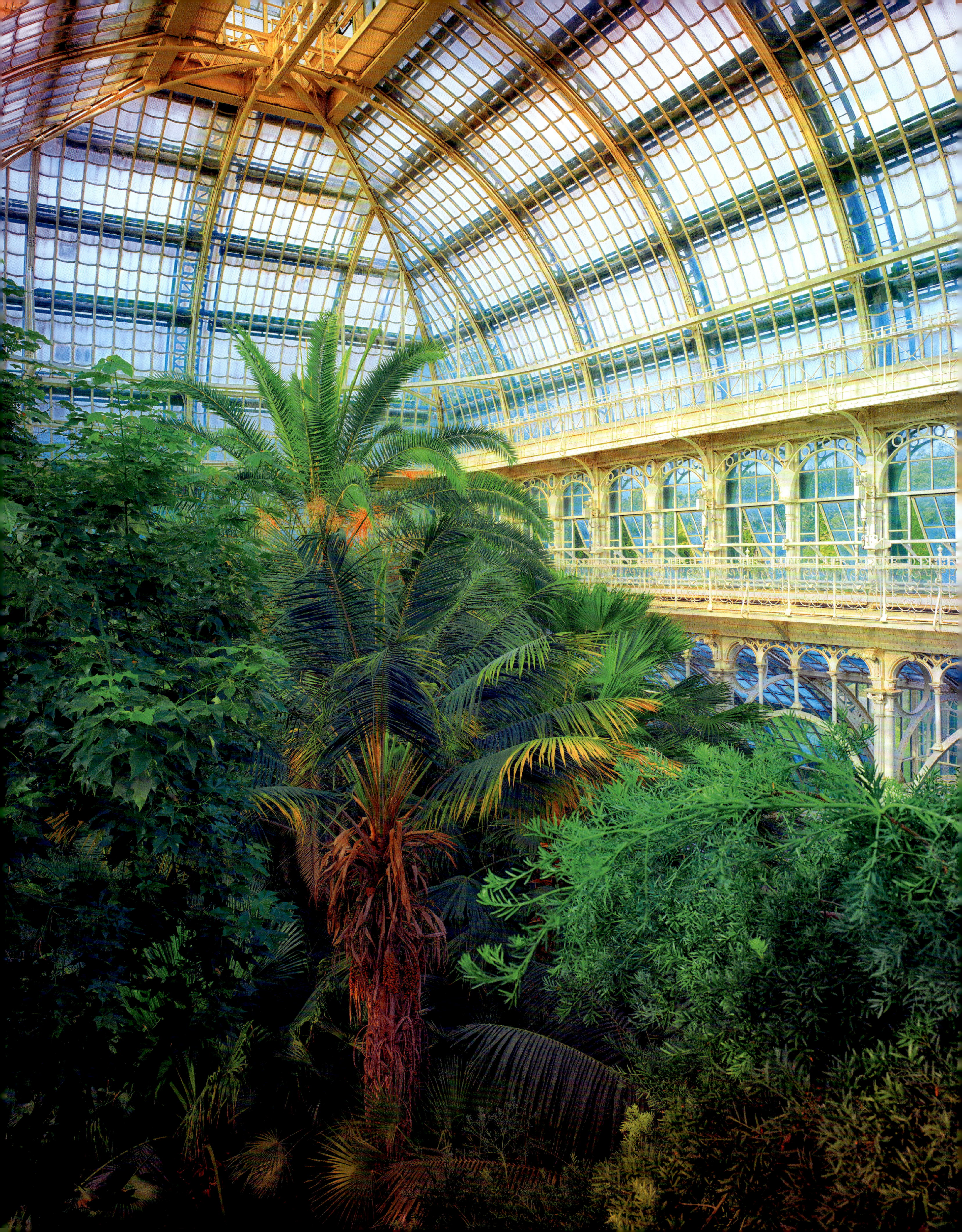

scheinen" (Karl Friedrich von Martius, Direktor Botanischer Garten München). Die Südsee entwickelte sich zur Idealvorstellung eines unverfälschten Paradieses, in dem die Flucht aus der Alltagswelt möglich war. Allerdings brachen nur wenige wie der Maler Paul Gauguin auf, um in der nach monatelanger Seereise erreichten Südsee ein vermeintliches Paradiesleben zu führen. Die Sehnsucht bestand darin, sich dieses Paradies zumindest in Form der Palmen, Farne und anderer exotischer Pflanzen nach Europa zu holen. Das Überleben dieser Pflanzen in den kalten europäischen Breitengraden sicherten beheizbare Gewächshäuser. Neben spektakulären Palästen aus Glas gab es immer mehr private Wintergärten. Deren Besitzer orientierten sich im Kleinen an den im Glaspalast entstandenen exotischen Welten aus tropischer Flora, Brunnen und Dekorationen und eiferten diesen nach.

VON DER ORANGERIE ZUM GLASHAUS

Die Orange, in ihrer leuchtenden Farbe, duftend in Blüte und Frucht, rückte an den Fürstenhöfen in Nordeuropa ab der Renaissance in den Fokus. Sie war nicht nur ein prestigeträchtiges, aus dem Süden stammendes Gewächs, sondern wurde für das Selbstverständnis der Herrschenden elementar. Die Frucht wurde mit den Äpfeln der Hesperiden gleichgesetzt. Eine der Aufgaben des Herkules war es, diese zu gewinnen. Als Sohn des Göttervaters Zeus / Jupiter ist der Held an Kraft, Intelligenz sowie moralischer Integrität den Menschen überlegen. Diese Eigenschaften übertrugen die Fürsten mit dem Erwerb der Pflanzen auf sich. Die Orange ist jedoch ein Gewächs des Südens und musste im Winter vor Kälte, Wind und Schnee geschützt werden. Zunächst wurden die in der Erde stehenden Orangenbäume im Winter durch Holzbauten geschützt, die zum Sommer abgebaut wurden. Durch das Anpflanzen in Kübeln war es schließlich möglich, sie in der kalten Jahreszeit in

the latter are ever beaming" (Karl Friedrich von Martius, Director of the Munich Botanical Garden). However, few were able to emulate the artist Paul Gauguin and lead this presumably idyllic life on a tropical island, which could be reached only after many months at sea. The South Seas became the epitome of an untouched paradise, where one could escape from the humdrum of everyday life. People expressed this aspiration by attempting to bring this piece of heaven back to Europe, at least in the form of palms, ferns, and other exotic plants. Heated greenhouses ensured that the plants could survive in the chilly European latitudes. Along with spectacular palaces made of glass, private winter gardens also became increasingly popular. Their owners emulated the exotic biospheres they encountered in the glass palaces on a smaller scale by filling the space with tropical flora, fountains, and decorative elements.

FROM THE ORANGERY TO THE GLASSHOUSE

The orange tree, with its brilliant color, fragrant blossoms, and delicious fruit, earned its place as the centerpiece of the northern European royal courts in the years following the Renaissance. Not only did these plants of southern origin lend prestige to their owners, they were elementary to the rulers' very self-image. The fruit was set on a par with the golden apples of the Hesperides, which Hercules was supposed to gather as one of his labors. As the son of the god Zeus/Jupiter, the hero possessed strength, intelligence, and moral integrity superior to that of humans. The nobility adopted these qualities as their own by acquiring the trees. However, oranges grow in southern climates and had to be protected against cold, wind, and snow during the winter months. At first, the orange trees were planted in the ground, with wooden shelters built around them

Das Überleben exotischer Pflanzen in den kalten europäischen Breitengraden sicherten beheizbare Gewächshäuser.

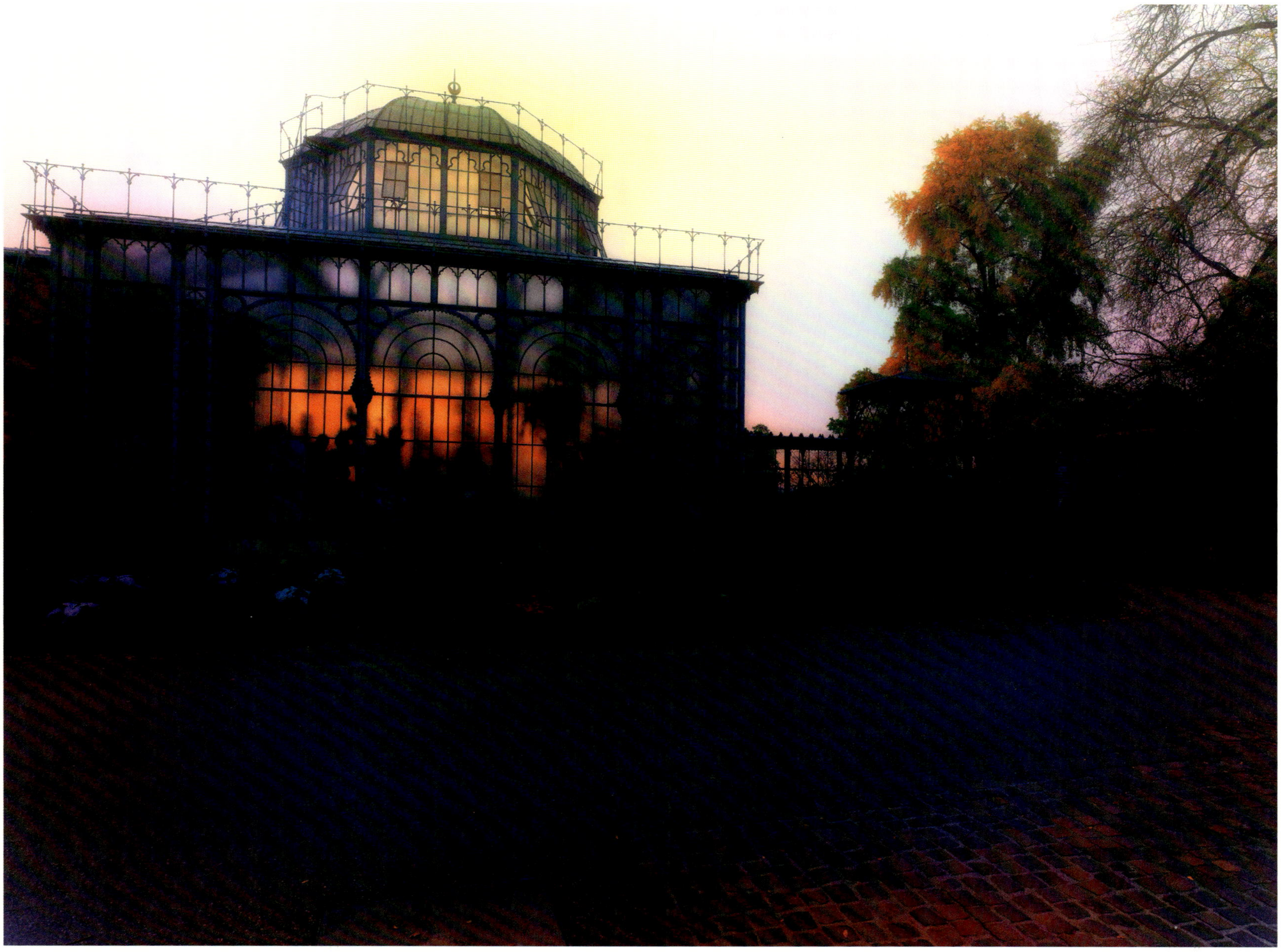

Heated greenhouses ensured that the plants could survive in the chilly European latitudes.

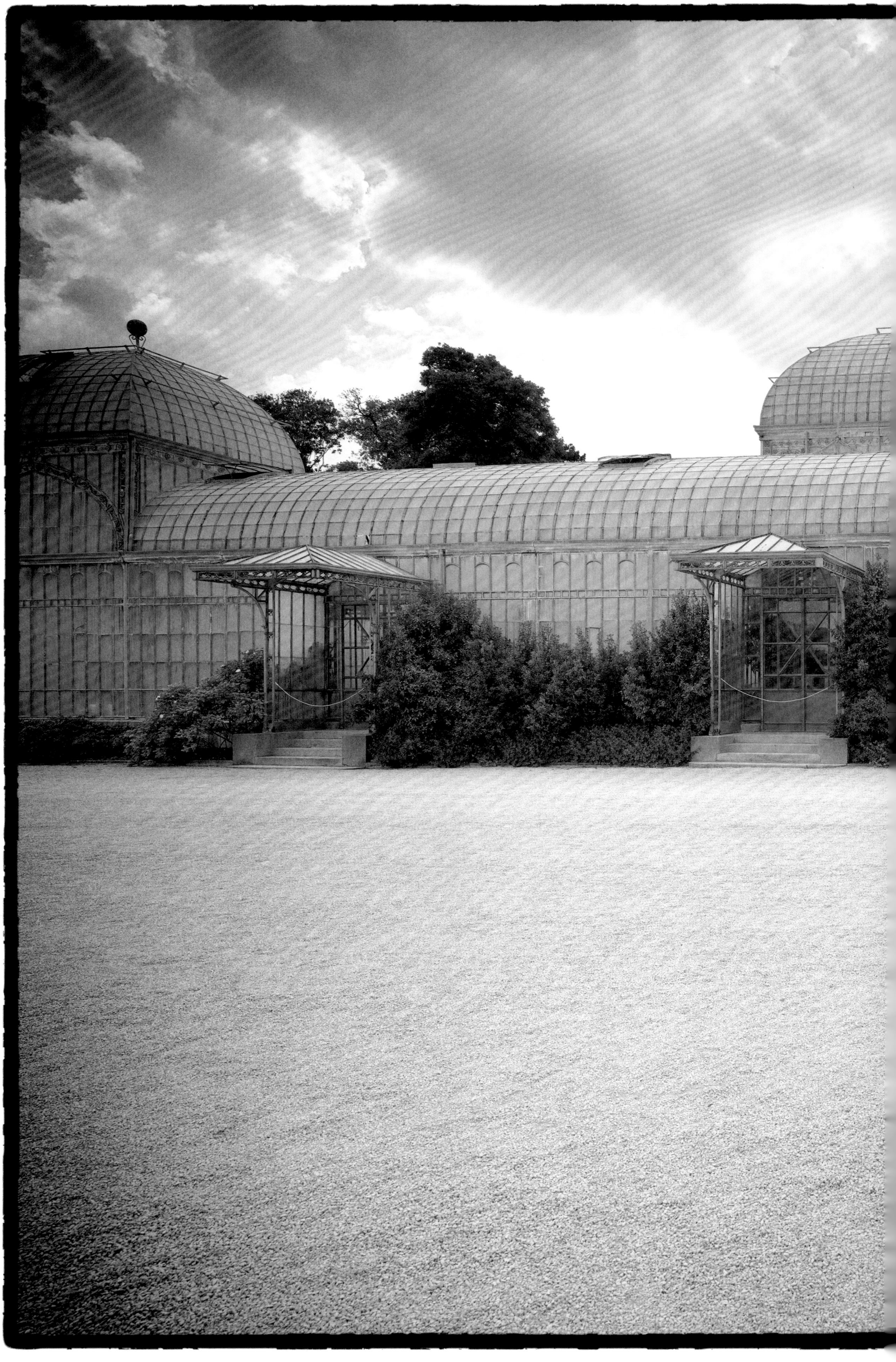

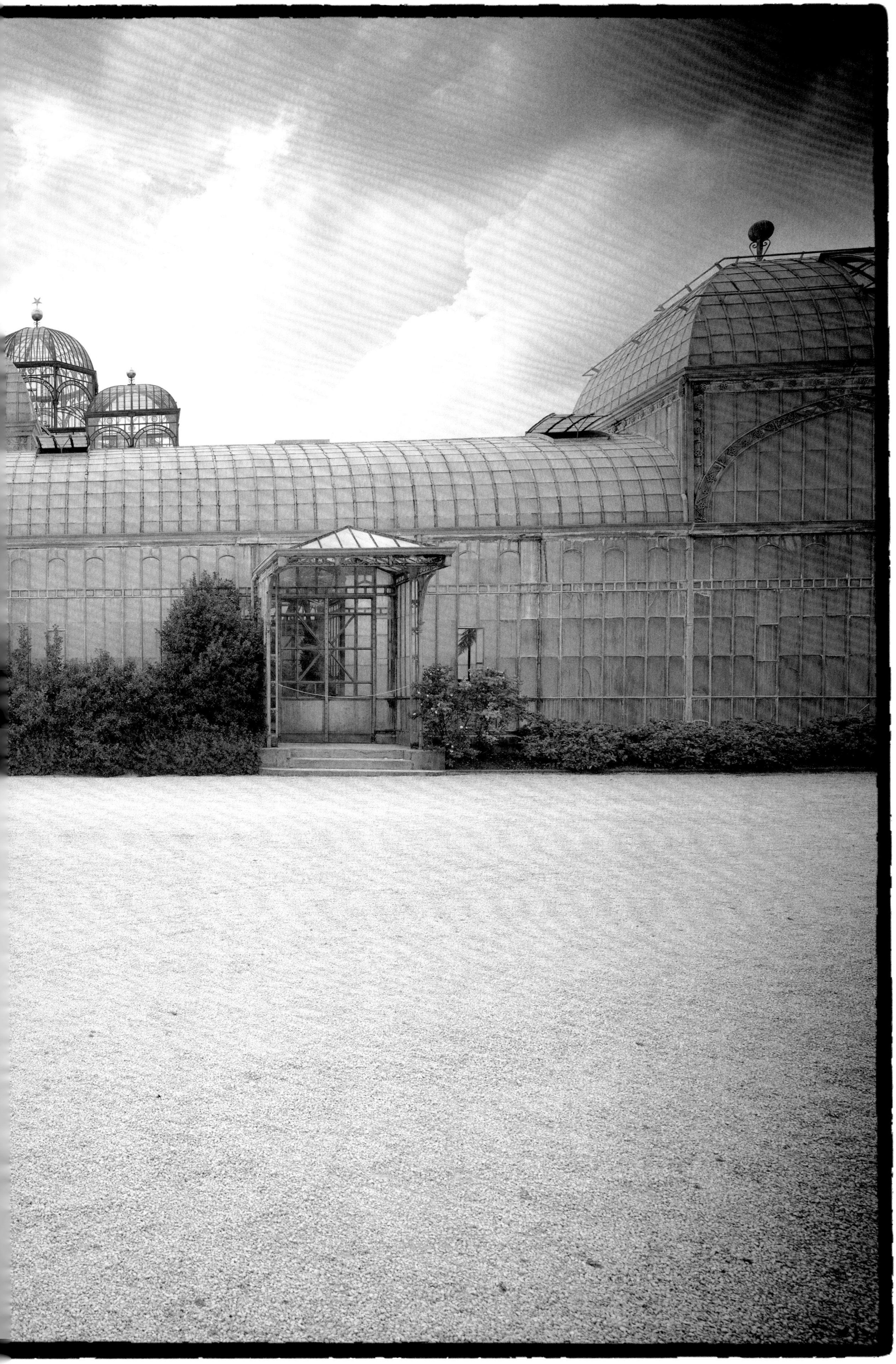

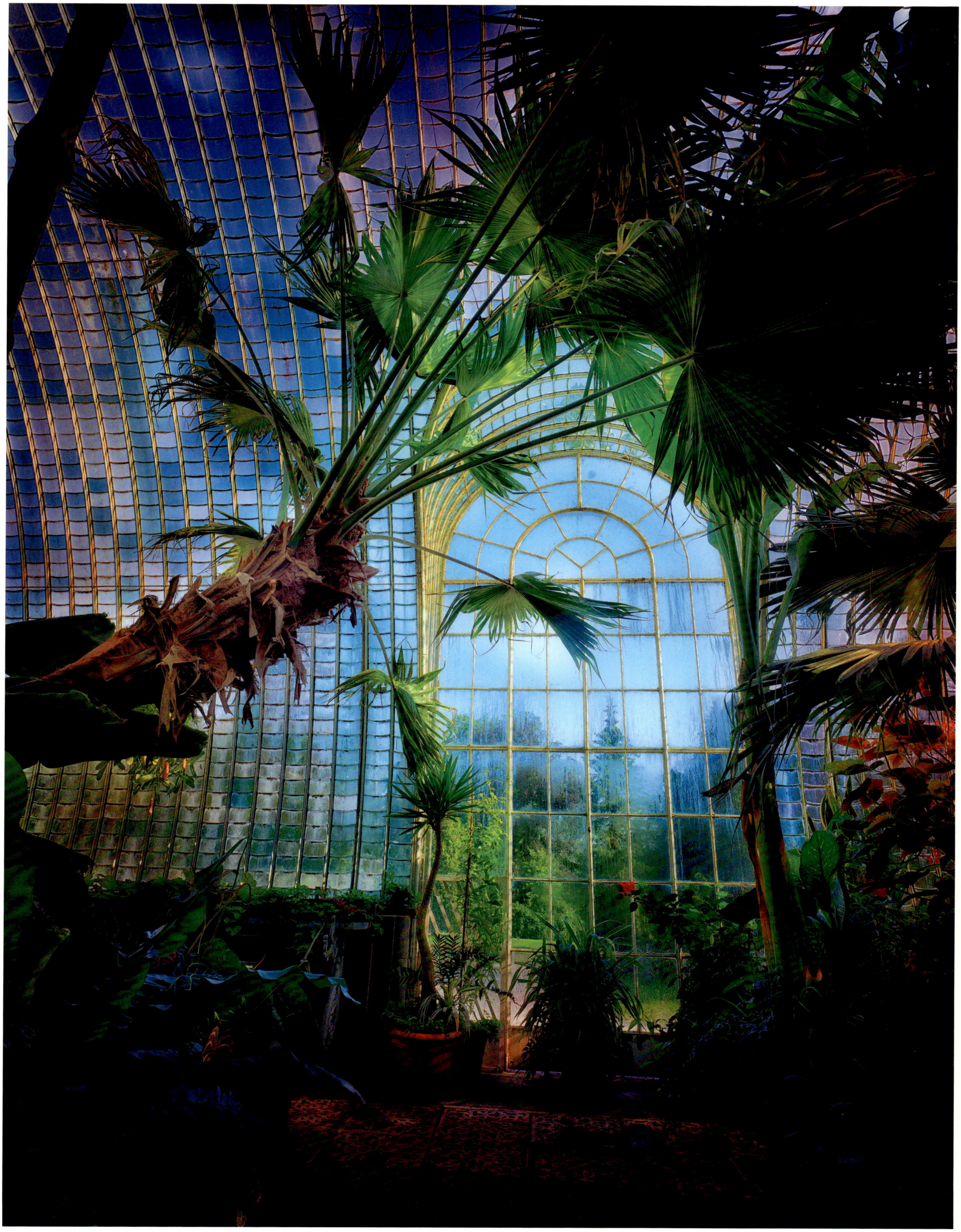

beheizbare, fest errichtete Steingebäude zu verbringen. So entstand der im 17. und 18. Jahrhundert wichtige Bautyp der Orangerie.
Ein zweiter Vorläufer des modernen Glashauses ist das Gewächshaus. Obst und Gemüse – unabhängig von natürlichen Erntezeiten – ganzjährig zur Verfügung zu haben, war wie bei den Orangen, nicht nur ein kulinarisches Bedürfnis, sondern entwickelte sich ebenfalls zum Ausdrucksmittel der absoluten Gewalt der Herrschenden. Beide Gebäudetypen waren in der Regel nach Süden ausgerichtet und hier verglast. Aus ihnen entwickelten sich die Glashäuser des 19. Jahrhunderts, indem sukzessive die bisher aus Stein ausgeführten Bauteile in Glas und Eisen überführt wurden.

DAS ZEITALTER DER GLASHÄUSER

Ende des 15. Jahrhunderts wurden die Seewege nach Amerika, Westafrika und schließlich Indien erkundet und zum Import nach Europa genutzt. Ganze Pflanzen sowie Samen und Zwiebeln exotischer Gewächse gelangten nach Europa. Bis zur Erfindung der Wardschen Kästen im Jahr 1829 überlebte jedoch nur eine von 100 Pflanzen den langen Transport nach Europa. Nathaniel Ward erfand einen verglasten Kasten, in dem die Pflanze in Erde gesetzt wurde. Dieser wurde fest geschlossen und an Deck der Schiffe verschraubt. Sie erhielten so genug Licht während der langen Seereise, waren gegen das Salzwasser geschützt und bekamen genug Wasser, da die tagsüber erwärmte Luft nachts kondensierte und die Feuchtigkeit an die Pflanzen abgab.
Aus finanziellen Gründen waren die ersten Empfänger Adelshöfe. Der Kauf erfolgte aus verschiedenen Interessen: dekorative, repräsentative, kulinarische oder wissenschaftliche. Es entstanden aber auch Pflanzensammlungen reicher Bürger und Universitäten.
1533 wurde in Padua der erste öffentliche Botanische Garten gegründet. Im gleichen Jahrhundert folgten die

in winter and subsequently removed in summer. Later they were grown in tubs, which allowed them to be brought into permanent stone buildings that could be heated during the cold season. This led to the orangery as an important architectural form of the 17th and 18th centuries.
The second stage in the evolution of the modern glasshouse was the greenhouse. The ability to have fruit and vegetables on hand year round, regardless of their natural harvest times, was not only a culinary necessity but, like the oranges, also developed into a expression of the rulers' hegemony. Both types of buildings were usually oriented to face south and encased in glass. The 19th century glasshouses emerged from these earlier greenhouses by successively replacing the components made of stone with glass and iron.

THE AGE OF THE GLASSHOUSE

In the late 15th century, explorers discovered maritime routes to the Americas, West Africa, and finally India and used them to import goods to Europe. Not only seeds and bulbs of exotic plants but entire plants reached the continent this way. Yet until the Wardian case was invented in 1829, only one in 100 of the plants survived the long journey. Nathaniel Ward came up with a glass case that was placed over plants set in soil. It was hermetically sealed and screwed to the decks of ships. The vegetation received enough light during the long voyage, had adequate protection against salt water, and received sufficient fresh water. This was because the air, which heated up during the day, formed condensation at night and released its moisture to the plants.
For financial reasons the first recipients were members of the nobility. They did so for different reasons: as decorative objects, for their own prestige, for cooking, or for scientific research. However, wealthy townsfolk and universities also collected plants. In 1533, the first

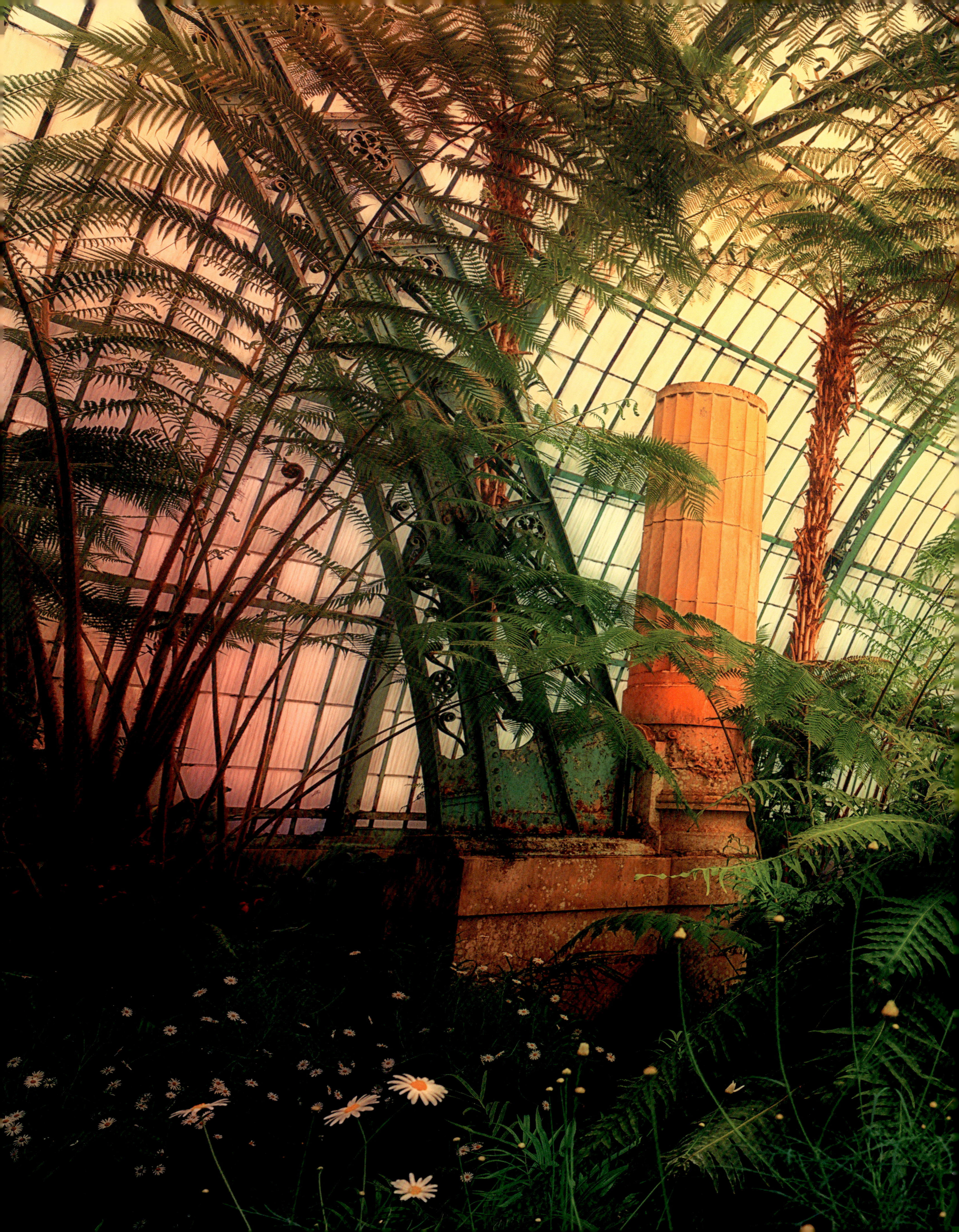

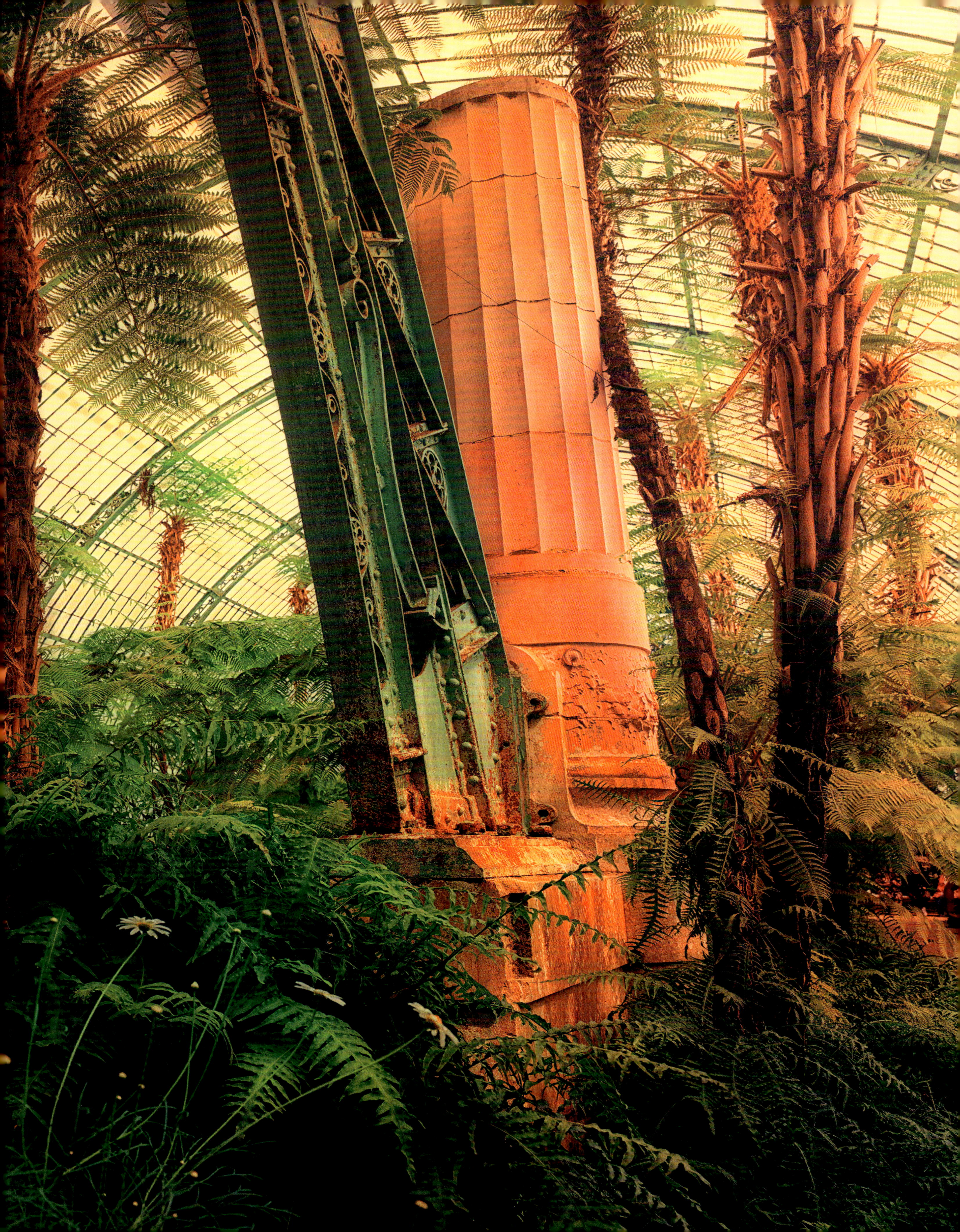

Sammlungen in Pisa, Leiden, Leipzig und Oxford. Alle Sammler und Institutionen tauschten untereinander Samen und Pflanzen.

Die privaten botanischen Gesellschaften mit ihren Gärten und Gewächshäusern erhielten im 19. Jahrhundert Konkurrenz durch von Privatleuten gegründete Aktiengesellschaften zum Bau von Wintergärten. Diese waren ebenfalls mit exotischen Pflanzen gefüllt und oftmals durch Cafés, Billardsäle, Raucherzimmer oder Ballsäle ergänzt. Diese wurden zu gesellschaftlichen Treffpunkten. Tagsüber wandelte man zur Bildung unter dem Glasdach, staunte über die weitgereisten Farne, Palmen oder nie gesehenen Blumenschmuck. Dazu trank man einen Kaffee, der auch aus der Ferne importiert war und genoss die Atmosphäre. Abends zog sich die gute Gesellschaft ins Glashaus zurück, um nach dem Tanz im dazugehörigen Ballsaal Atem zu schöpfen. Das Frankfurter Palmenhaus ist ein Beispiel hierfür.

Mit den Bauten in Birmingham, Liverpool, Lancaster, Glasgow oder Kopenhagen finden wir Beispiele für privates Mäzenatentum. Öffentliche Institutionen und Parkanlagen erhielten aufwendige Glashäuser. Im Falle der kaiserlichen und königlichen Anlagen von Wien, London, Stuttgart und Brüssel führten gesellschaftlicher Wandel oder politischer Druck zur Öffnung der ursprünglich privaten Gewächshäuser mit ihren fremdländischen Pflanzensammlungen.

Die industrielle Revolution in Großbritannien schuf die Grundlagen für den modernen Typus des Gewächshauses. Dazu gehörten Erfindung und Weiterentwicklung des Gusseisens, neue Heizungstechniken sowie die Produktion großformatiger Glasscheiben. Letztere wurde befördert durch die Senkung der Glassteuer, die bis 1845 die Produktion großer Glasscheiben unrentabel gemacht hatte.

Zwei britische Spezialisten für Gartenbau, Landwirtschaft sowie Eisen- und Glaskonstruktion, John Claudius Loudon (1783 – 1843) und Joseph Paxton (1803 – 1865), waren

public botanical garden was established in Padua. Before the century was out, other collections followed in Pisa, Leiden, Leipzig, and Oxford. All collectors and institutions exchanged seeds and plants with each other.

In the 19th century, private botanical societies, with their gardens and greenhouses, began to face competition from corporations founded by private citizens to build winter gardens. These were also filled with exotic plants and many of them housed cafes, billiard halls, smoking rooms, and ballrooms as places for social gatherings. During the day, visitors could take an educational stroll beneath the glass roof, admire the well-traveled ferns, palms, or never-before-seen flower arrangements. They would soak in the pleasant atmosphere while drinking coffee, which had also been imported from distant lands. In the evening, high society would withdraw to the glasshouse to catch their breath after dancing in the adjoining ballroom. The Palm House in Frankfurt is one example of this.

The greenhouses in Birmingham, Liverpool, Lancaster, Glasgow, and Copenhagen were the recipients of private patronage. Elegant glasshouses were built on the grounds of public institutions and in parks. Social change and political pressure forced imperial and royal families in Vienna, London, Stuttgart, and Brussels to open what had originally been private greenhouses with foreign plant collections to the public.

The industrial revolution in Great Britain laid the foundation for modern greenhouse design. Among the innovations were the invention and further development of wrought iron, new heating technologies, as well as the ability to manufacture large-format glass panels. Manufacturers began to produce more of these windows after the tax on glass was reduced in 1845, which had previously made the production of large glass windows unprofitable.

John Claudius Loudon (1783 – 1843) and Joseph Paxton (1803 – 1865) were two British innovators who were responsible for modern greenhouse design, specializing in

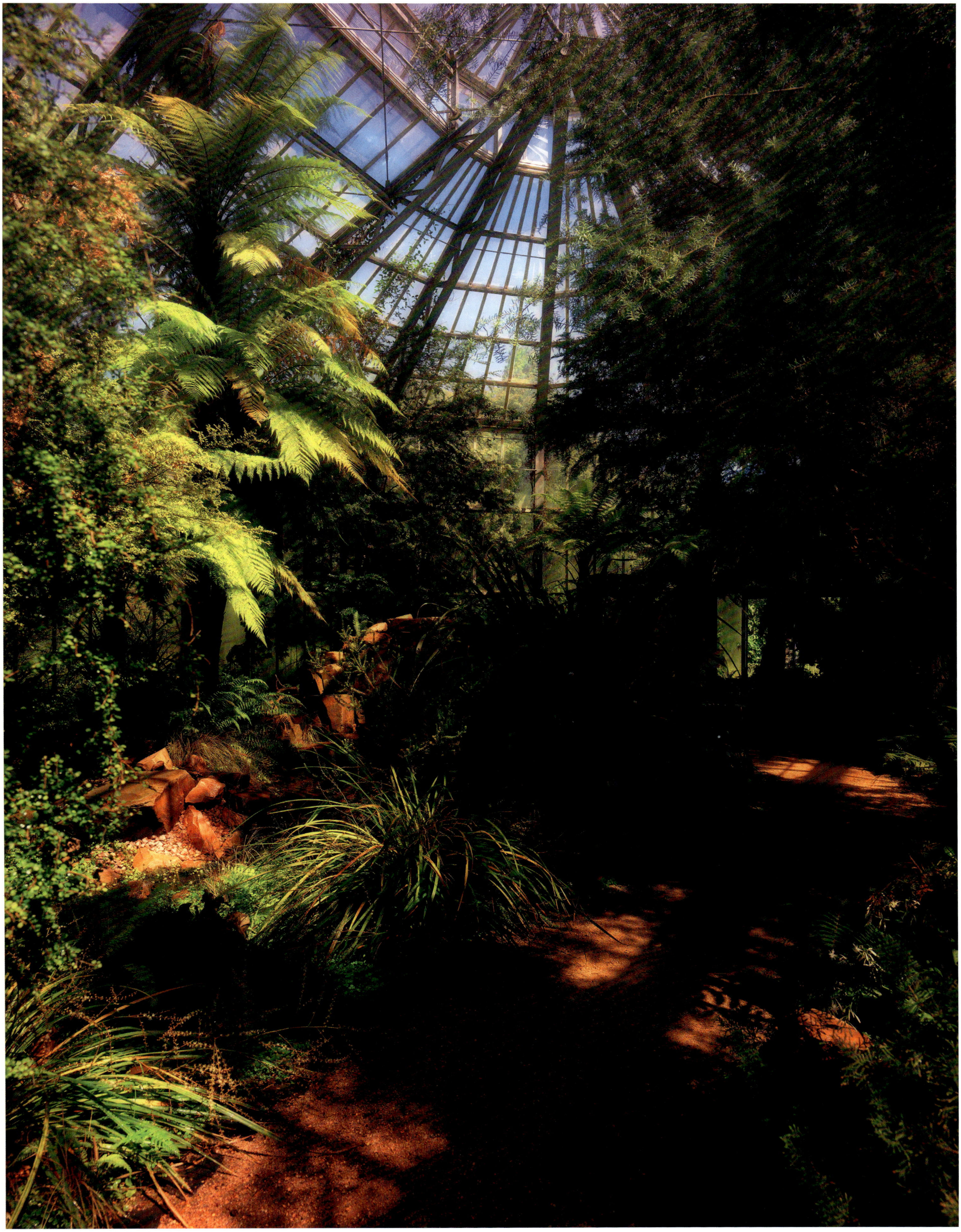

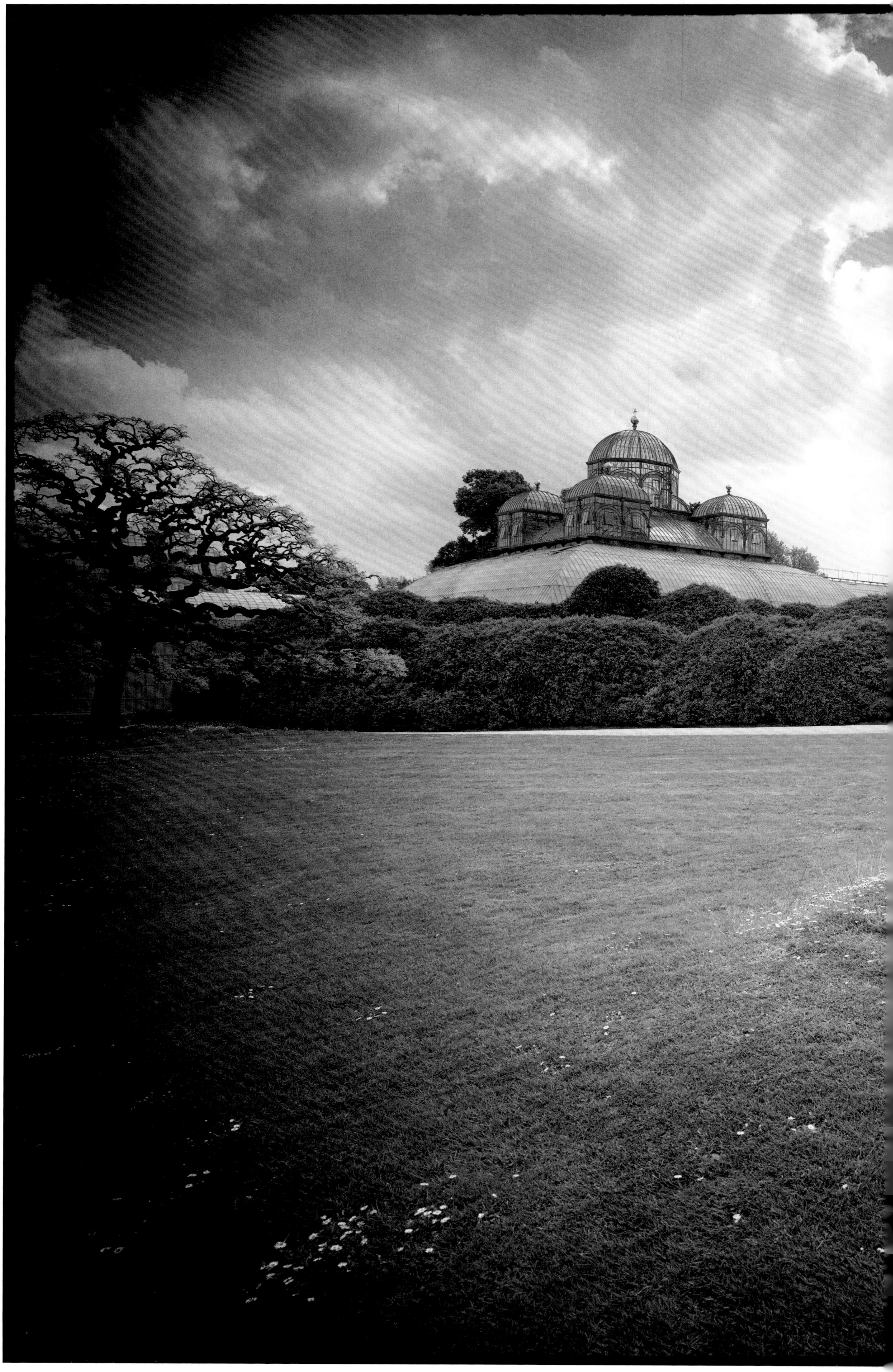

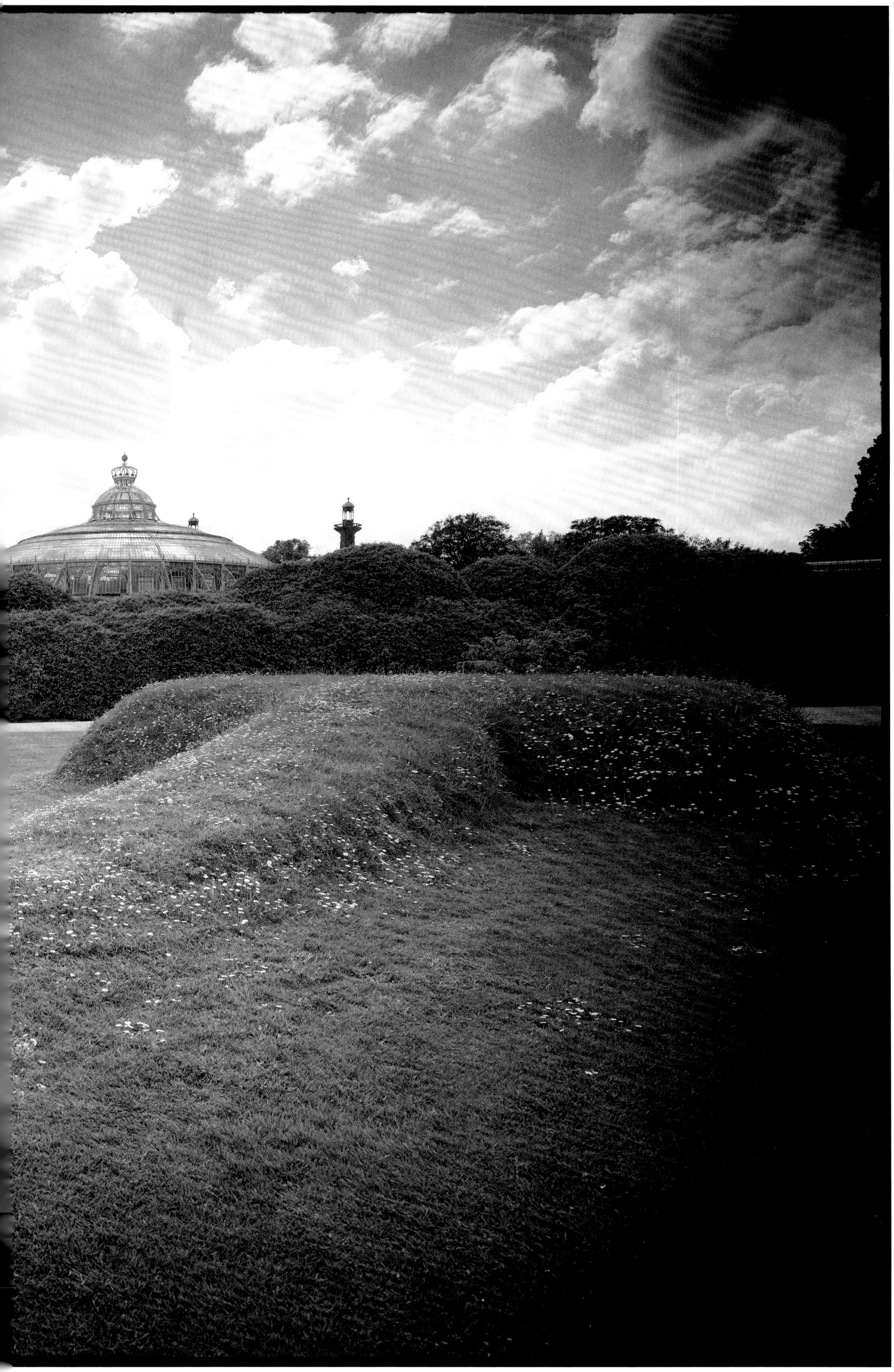

die Innovatoren, welche die moderne Gestalt der Gewächshäuser entwickelten. Loudon setzte sich mit den nötigen Neigungswinkeln der Glasflächen zur optimalen Ausnutzung der Sonneneinstrahlungen für den Glashausbau auseinander, die zu sphärischen oder kurvenlinearen Konstruktionsformen führten. Der einzige erhaltene Bau dieser Art auf kontinentaleuropäischem Boden ist der Wintergarten von Lednice in Tschechien. Der Architekt Georg Wingelmüller orientierte sich offensichtlich an Loudon. Die Faszination des Innenraums entsteht durch den fast durchgehend licht erscheinenden Raum. Dicht an dicht sind schmale, gebogene Eisenrippen nebeneinander gesetzt, die sich auf einem Natursteinsockel bis zur Laterne erheben. Gleich Fischschuppen sind zwischen die Rippen 62, nur 20 x 16 Zentimeter schmale, einander leicht überlappende Glasscheiben gesetzt. Der Rippenkrümmung folgend ergibt sich im durchscheinenden Licht auch ein unterschiedlich schimmerndes Glasbild. Mit dem dazugehörigen Kontrast der satten grünen Pflanzen und der Farbtupfer einzelner Blüten entsteht die Impression einer mittelalterlichen Kathedrale. Unterstützt wird der Eindruck durch die Verwendung von Säulen, auf denen die Laterne aufliegt. Passend zur Funktion des Wintergartens als exotische Pflanzenhalle sind sie in Form von Bambus ausgeführt.
Bis heute nimmt uns die Atmosphäre der Gewächshäuser sofort gefangen. Umhüllt von warmer Luft intensivieren sich die Pflanzenfarben. Gleichzeitig scheinen die gläsernen Hüllen die Grenze zwischen Innenraum und Himmel aufzulösen und nicht nur der Besucher der Vergangenheit erhielt den Eindruck eines fernen, ursprünglichen Paradieses. Werner Pawloks Fotografien lassen uns dieser Sehnsucht und Faszination nachspüren und nehmen uns mit auf eine Reise unter Palmen zum Ursprung unserer Kultur: dem Garten Eden.

horticulture, agriculture, and iron and glass construction. Loudon grappled with ways to adjust the angle of greenhouse windows to make the best possible use of incident sunlight, designs that led to spherical and curvilinear forms of construction. The only structure of this type still standing in Continental Europe is the Winter Garden in Lednice, Czech Republic, whose architect, Georg Wingelmüller, clearly drew inspiration from Loudon. The interior draws the eye with a space that appears luminous almost throughout. Slender, curved iron ribs are set close together and rise to the lantern from a base of natural stone. 62 narrow, slightly overlapping glass panes, measuring only 20 by 16 centimeters in size, are set between the ribs like fish scales. As the light shines through the windows and follows the curvature of the ribs, it produces a variably shimmering glass pattern. Contrasted with the lush green plants and splashes of color from individual blossoms, the scene creates the impression of a Medieval cathedral. The use of columns on which the lantern rests only reinforces this impression. In keeping with the winter garden's function as a hall of plants, the columns are shaped to look like bamboo.
Greenhouses continue to captivate us even today with their lush atmosphere. Enveloped in warm air, the plants intensify their colors. At the same time, the glass enclosures seem to dissolve the boundary between interior space and the sky, so that visitors of ages past aren't the only ones to imagine themselves in a distant, primordial paradise. Werner Pawlok's photographs allow us to experience this yearning and fascination, and they take us on a journey among palm trees to the source of our culture: the Garden of Eden.

Bis heute nimmt uns die Atmosphäre der Gewächshäuser sofort gefangen. Umhüllt von warmer Luft intensivieren sich die Pflanzenfarben.

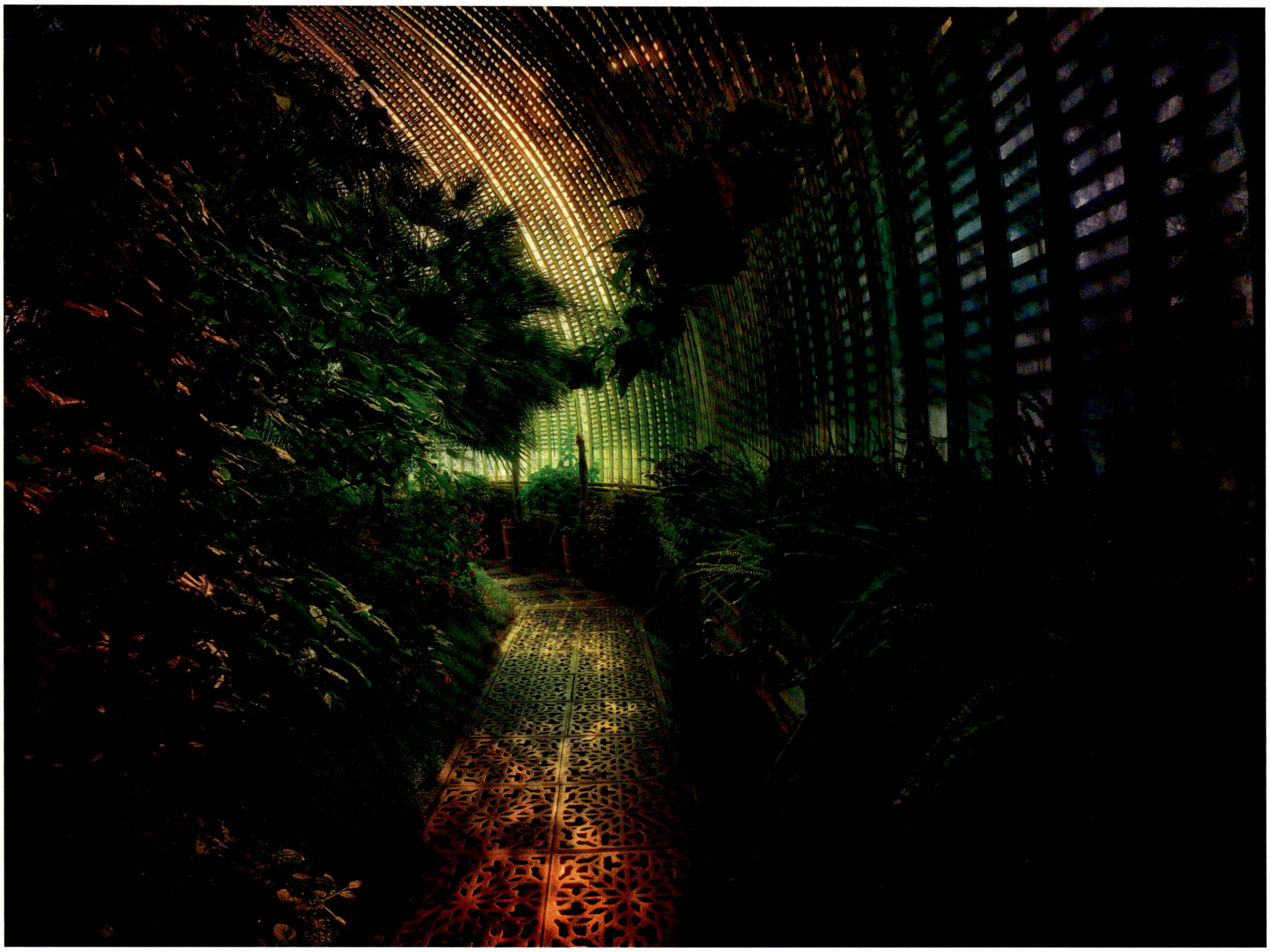

Greenhouses continue to captivate us even today with their lush atmosphere. Enveloped in warm air, the plants intensify their colors.

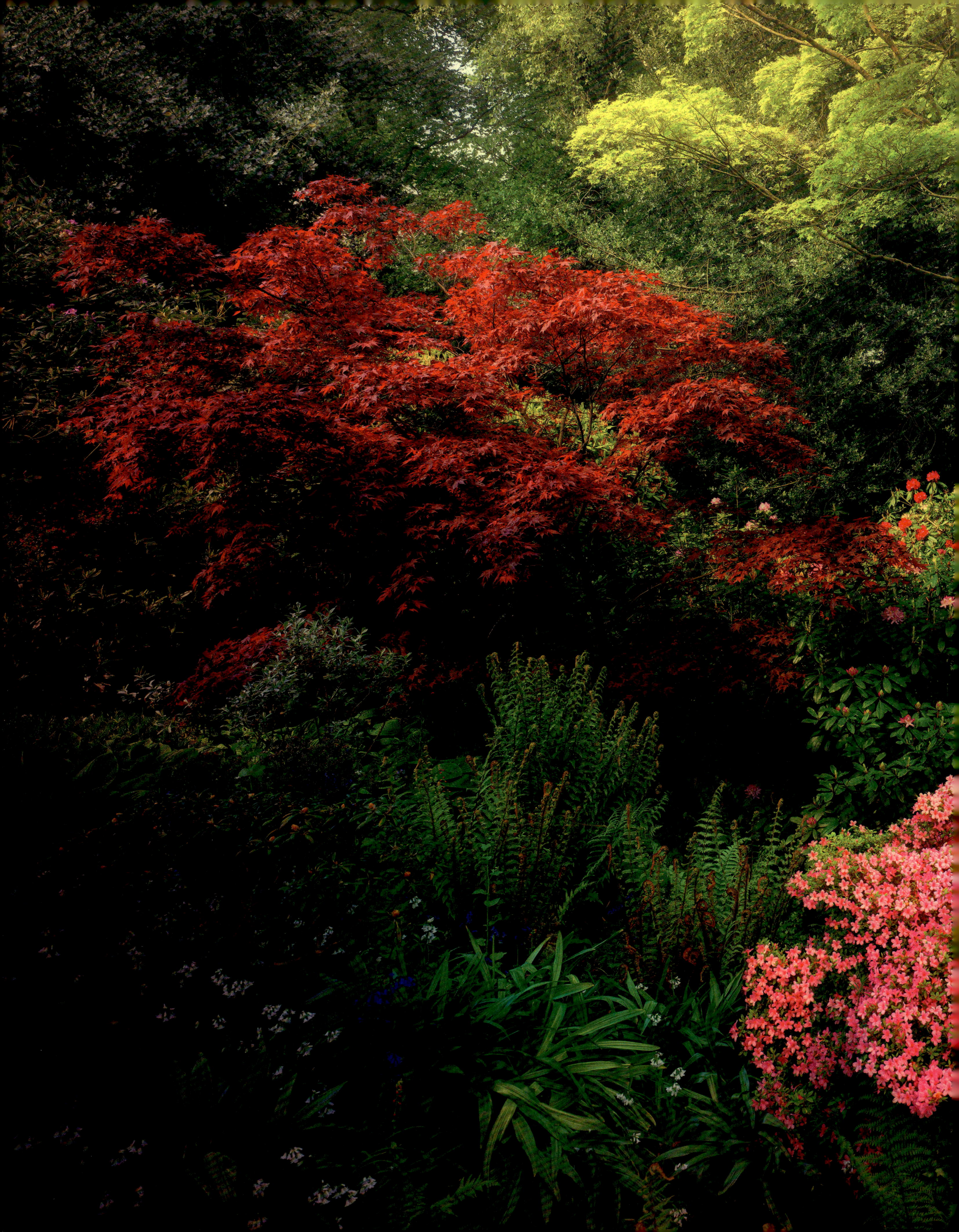

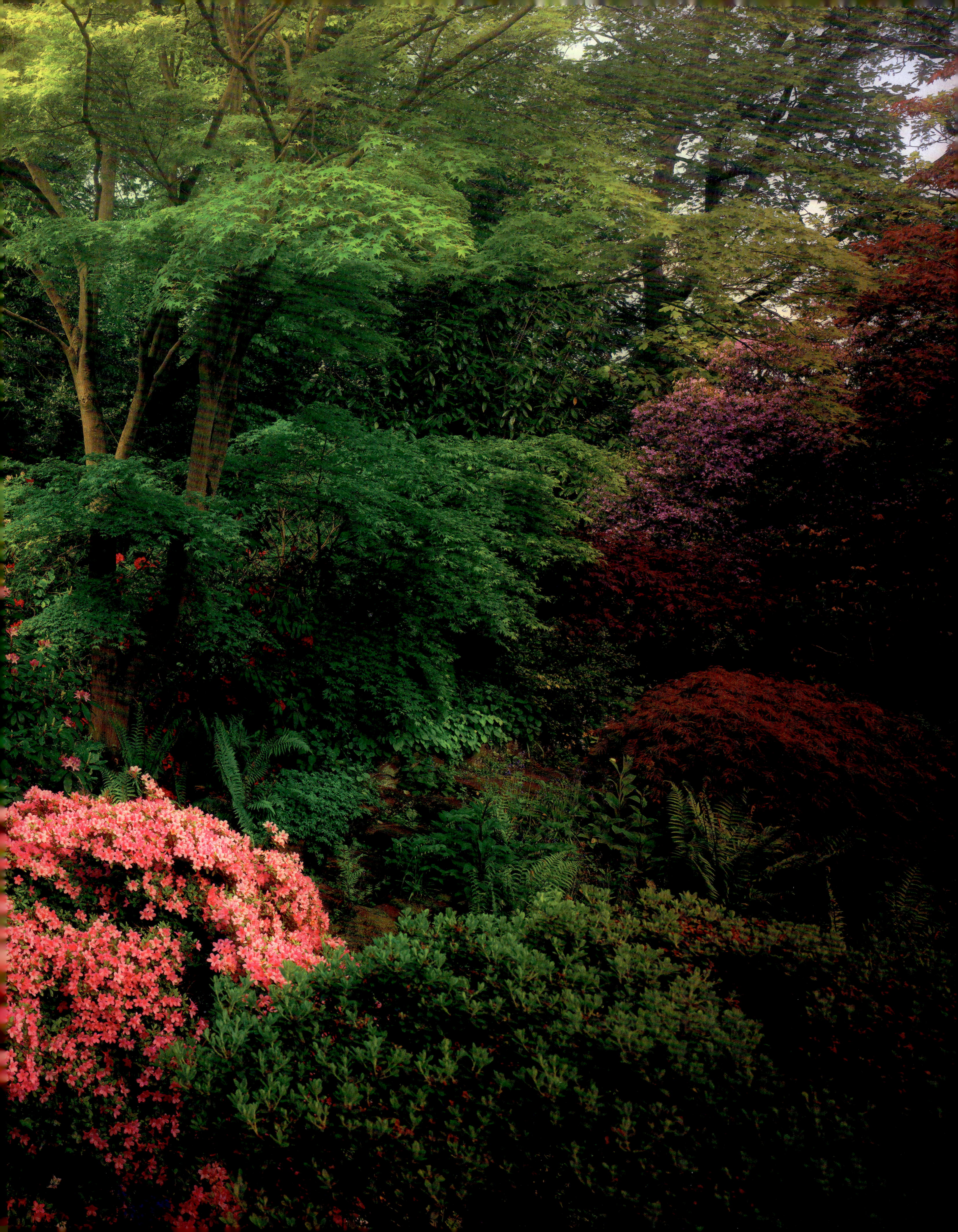

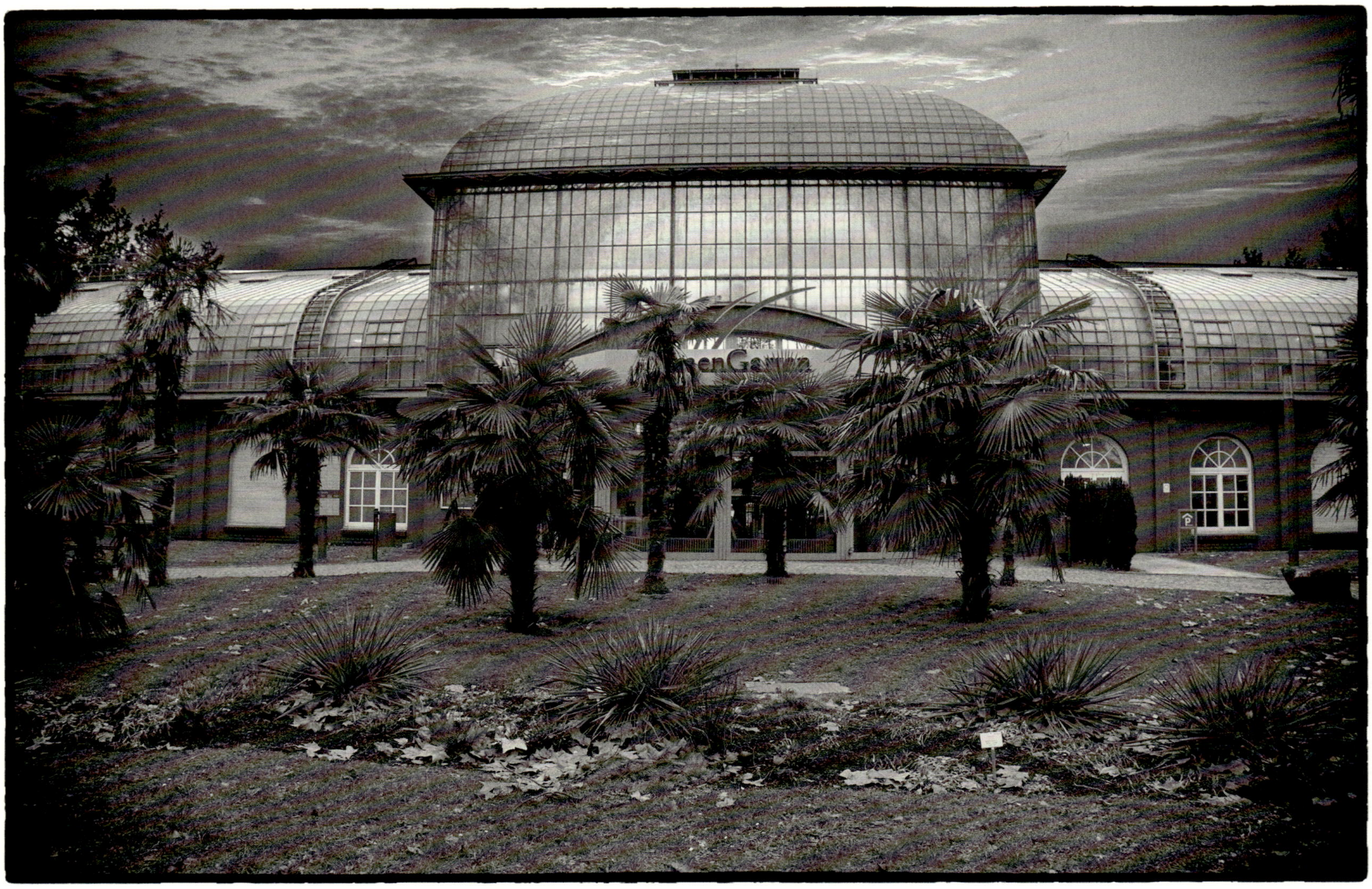

PALMENGARTEN

FRANKFURT

PALMENGARTEN

ORT
Frankfurt am Main, Deutschland

GRÖSSE
52,6 m lang; 30,5 m breit;
an der Scheitelhöhe 18,5 m hoch

ENTSTEHUNG
1868–1869
Entwurf: Friedrich Kayser

ARCHITEKTUR
Stützenfreie Glashalle über rechteckigem Grundriss. Das Palmenhaus lebt durch den Kontrast zwischen der lichten Glashalle und dem vorgelagerten steinernen Gesellschaftshaus. Die Eisen-Glas-Konstruktion nach Patent der Pariser Weltausstellung 1867 schafft einen weiten Raum, unter dessen Dach sich eine grüne Oase ausbreitet.

PFLANZEN
Im Palmenhaus finden sich vor allem Palmen: Petticoat-, Fischschwanz-, Betelnuss- und Bergpalmen. Dazu kommen Araukarien, Palm- und Baumfarne.

BESONDERHEITEN
1868 Bürgerschaftliche Gründung einer Aktiengesellschaft, um die 200 exotische Pflanzen umfassende Sammlung Herzogs Adolph von Nassau aus den Wiesbaden-Biebricher Schlosswintergärten zu kaufen. Der Palmengarten mit seiner Kombination aus vorgelagertem Gesellschaftshaus und Glashalle sollte zugleich Treffpunkt der Gesellschaft und Botanischer Schauraum sein.

LOCATION
Frankfurt am Main, Germany

SIZE
52.6 m long; 30.5 m wide;
18.5 m high (at apex)

ESTABLISHED
1868–1869
design: Friedrich Kayser

ARCHITECTURE
Hall of glass without supporting pillars on a rectangular footprint. The contrast between the bright hall of glass and an anterior stone building, the Society House, is what brings the Palm House to life. The iron and glass design modeled on a patent from the 1867 World's Fair in Paris creates a vast expanse which encompasses a sprawling oasis of green under its roof.

PLANTS
The Palm House is primarily home to palms, including petticoat, fishtail, betel nut, and mountain palms. It also features monkey puzzle trees, fern palms, and tree ferns.

ADDITIONAL NOTES
Citizen's initiative to establish a joint-stock company in 1868 to purchase Duke Adolph of Nassau's collection of 200 exotic plants from his castle gardens in Wiesbaden-Biebrich. The Palmengarten, with its combination of a Society House situated in front of an adjoining glass hall, was intended to serve as both a social center and a botanical exhibition hall.

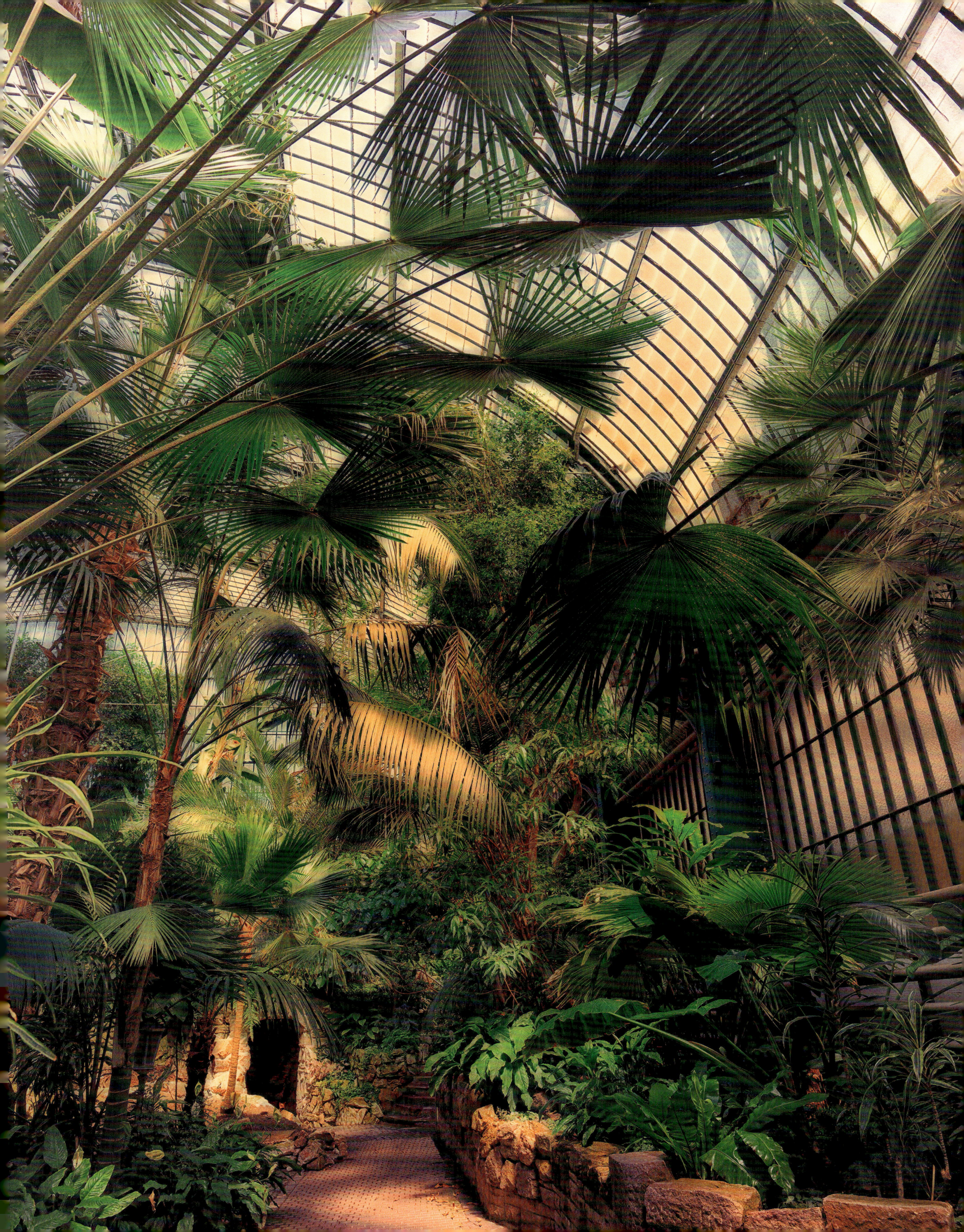

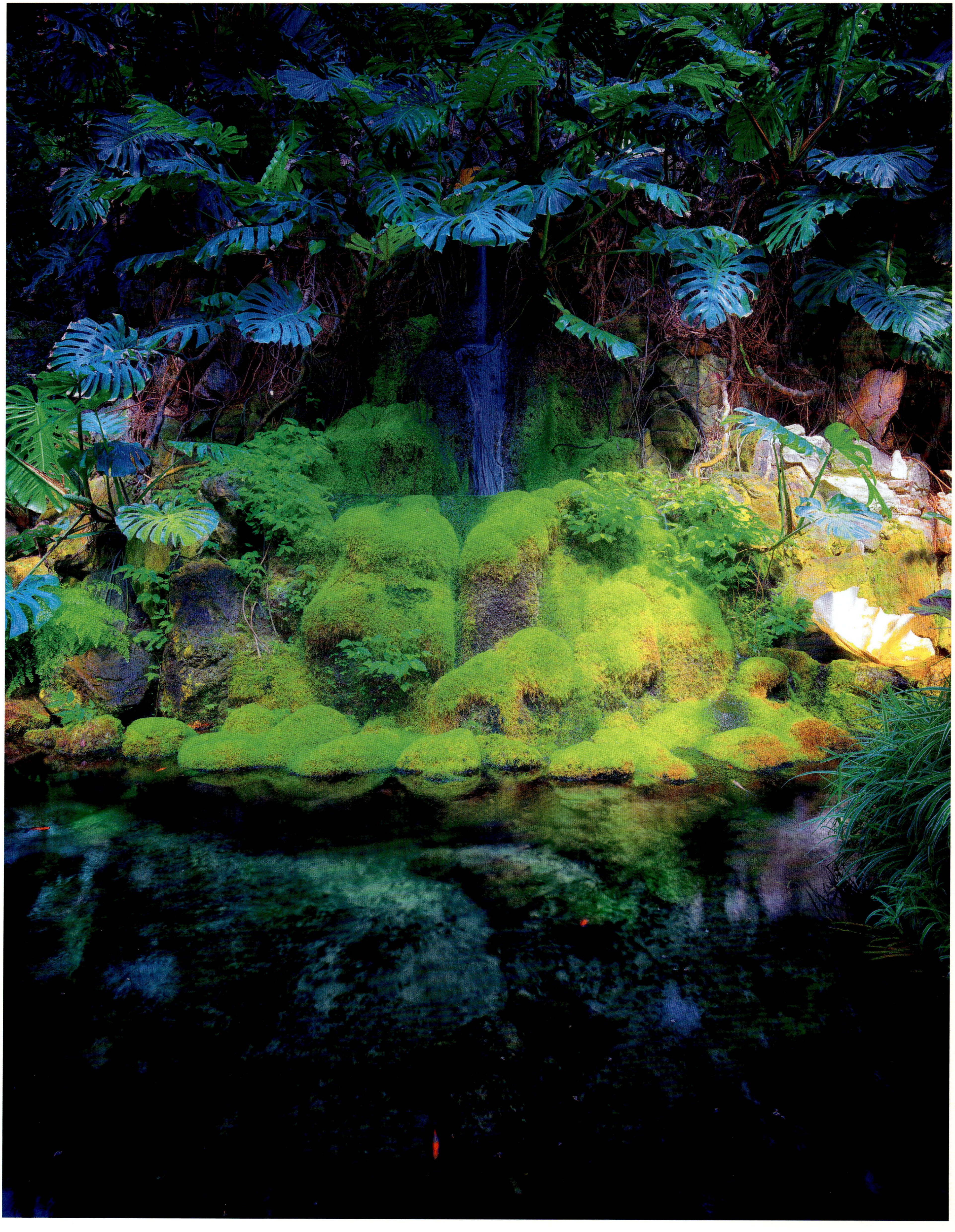

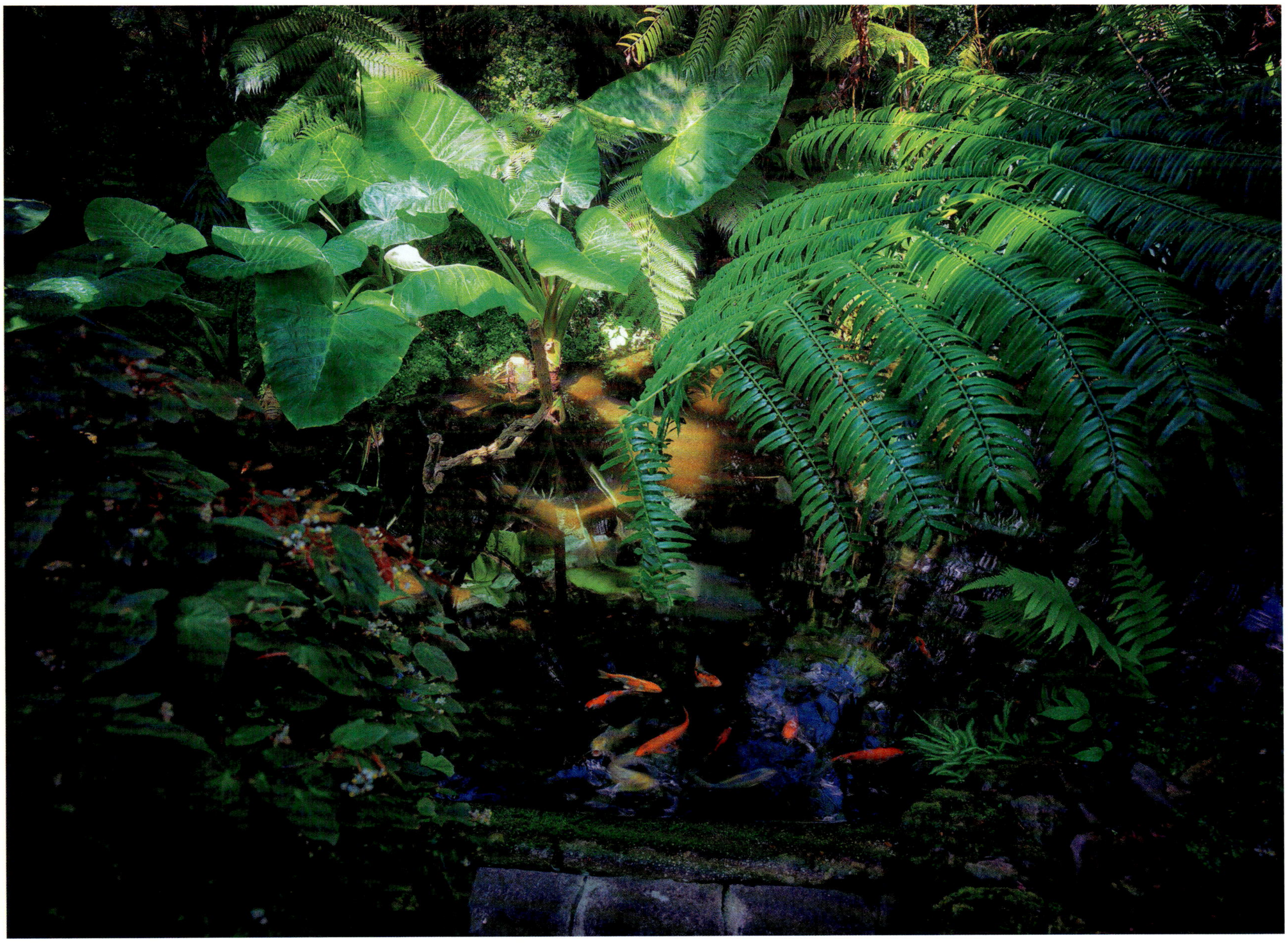

Palmengarten Frankfurt IX · Palmengarten Frankfurt XVI

Palmengarten Frankfurt XII

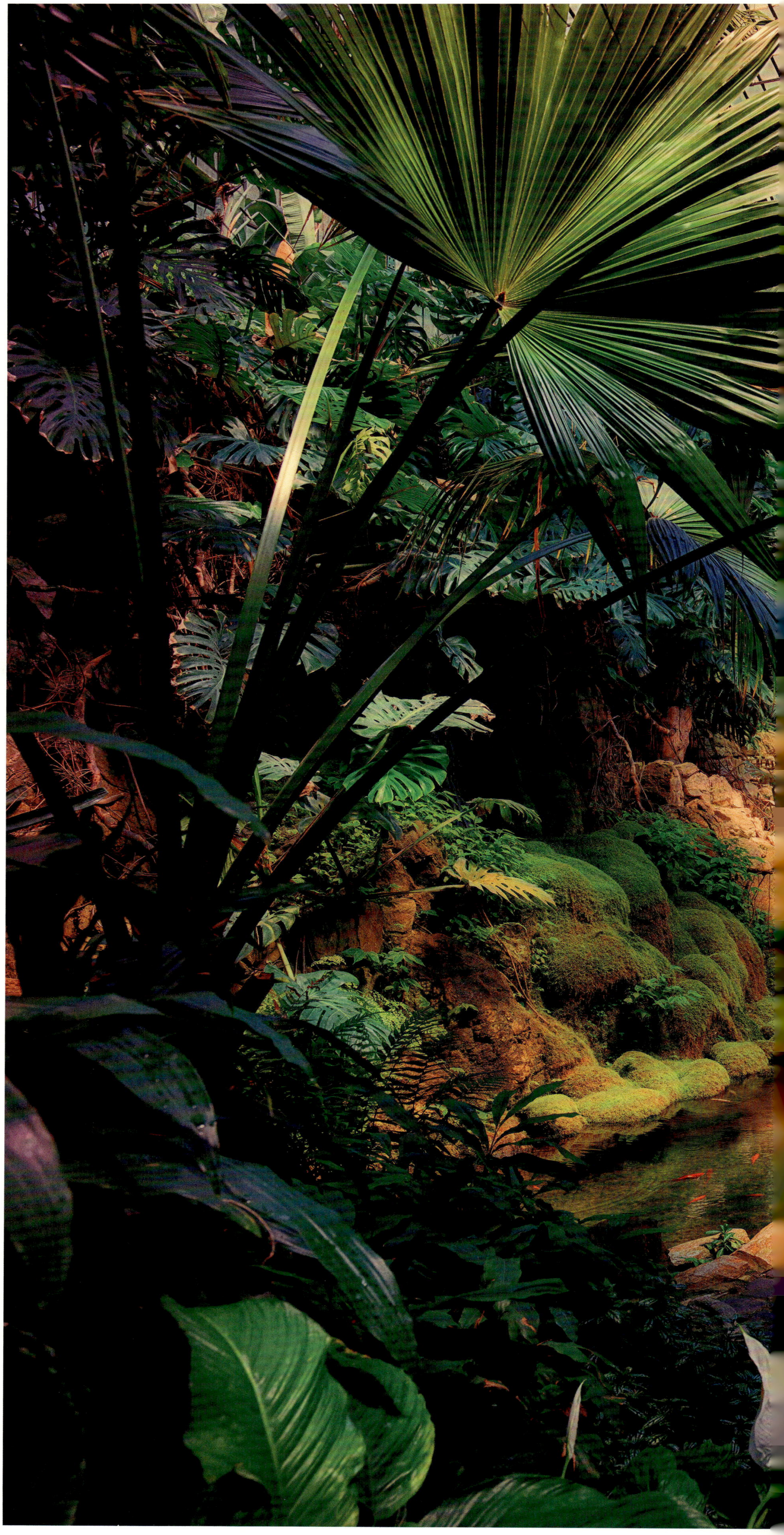

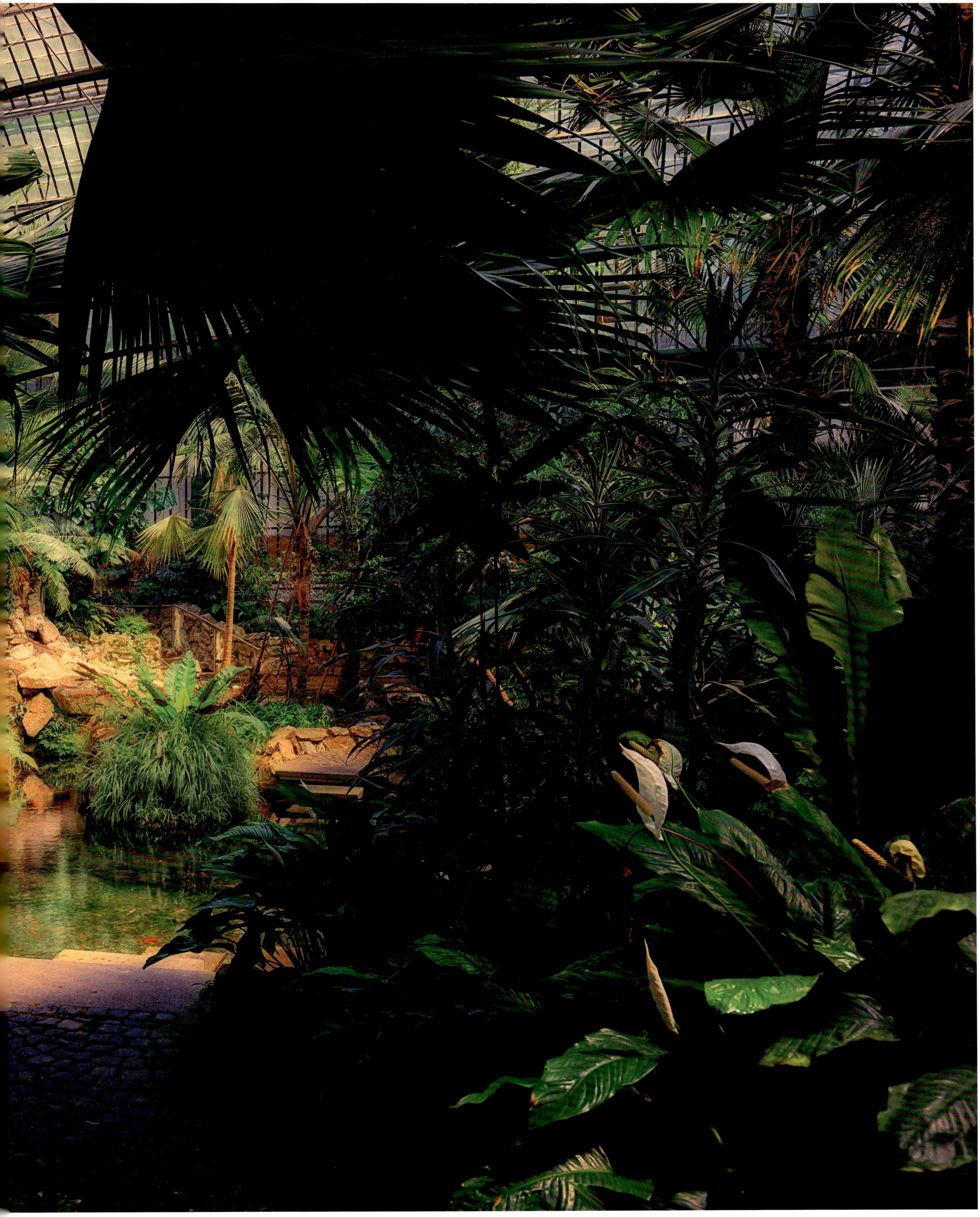

Diese wunderbaren Glaspaläste betreten und ihr grün duftendes, tropisches Innenleben mit der Kamera erkunden zu dürfen, kam mir wie eine Expedition ins Herz des 19. Jahrhunderts vor.

WERNER PAWLOK

Stepping into these wonderful glass palaces and being allowed to explore their fragrant, verdant tropical interiors with my camera made me feel like I was embarking on an expedition into the heart of the 19th century.

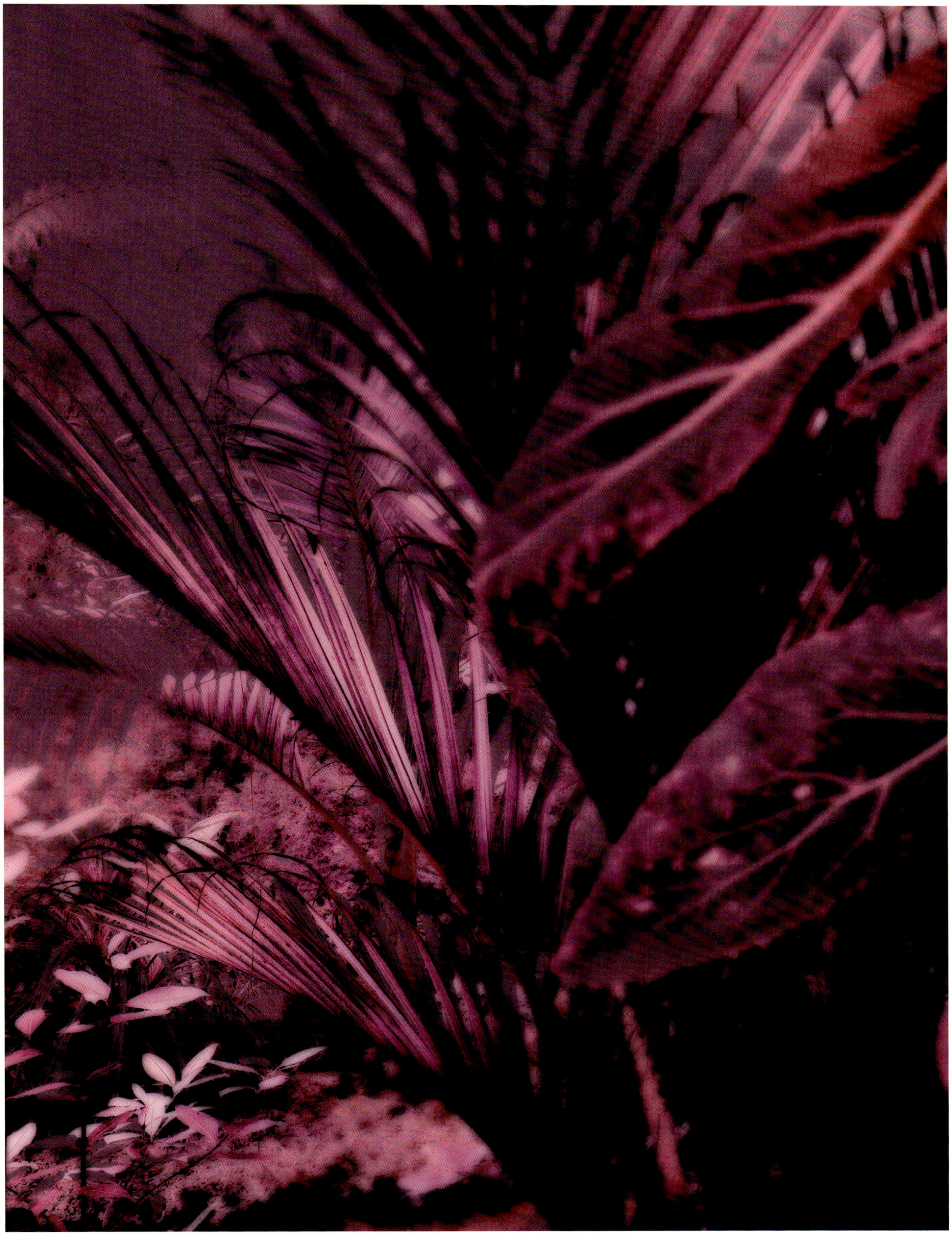

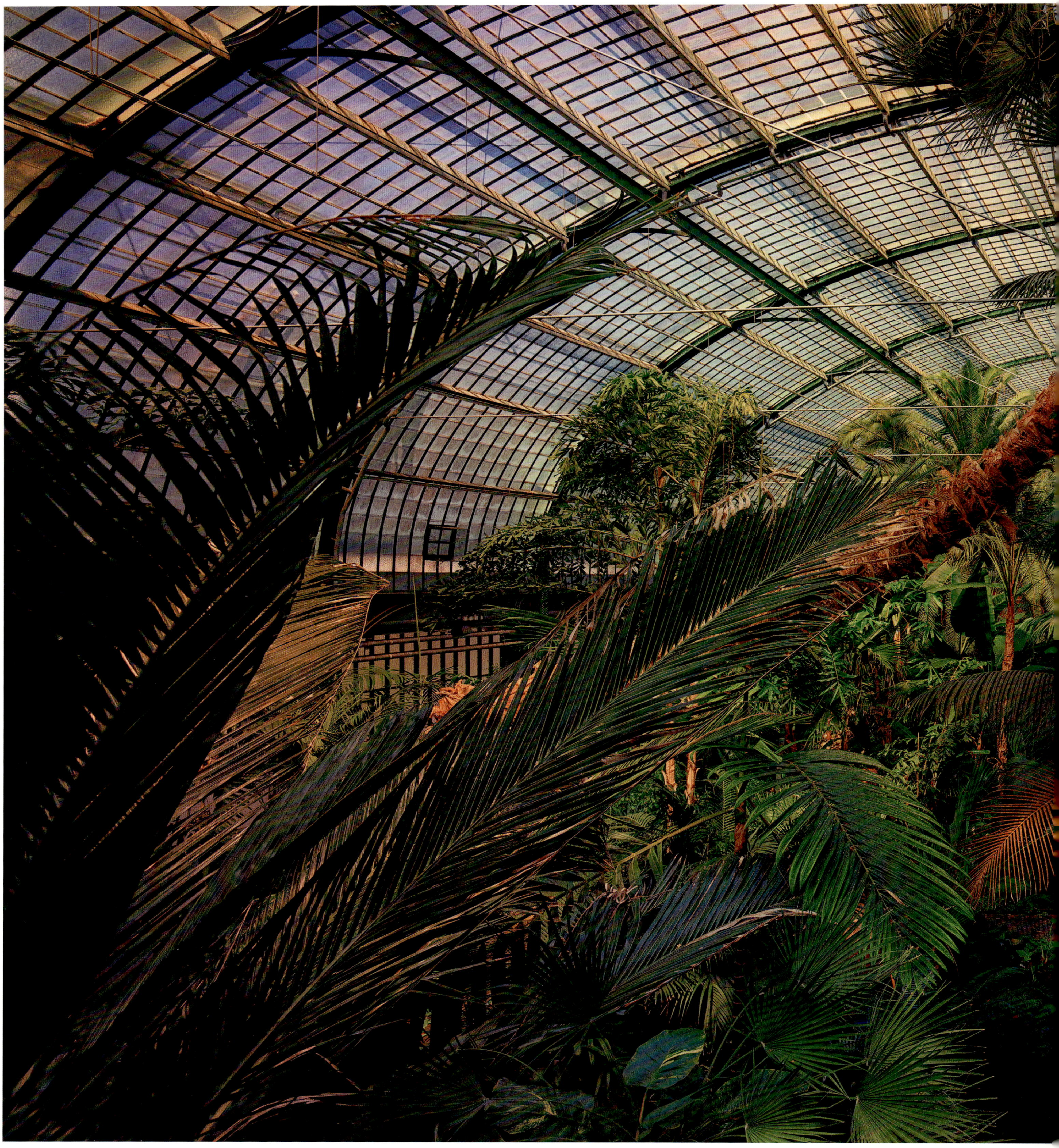

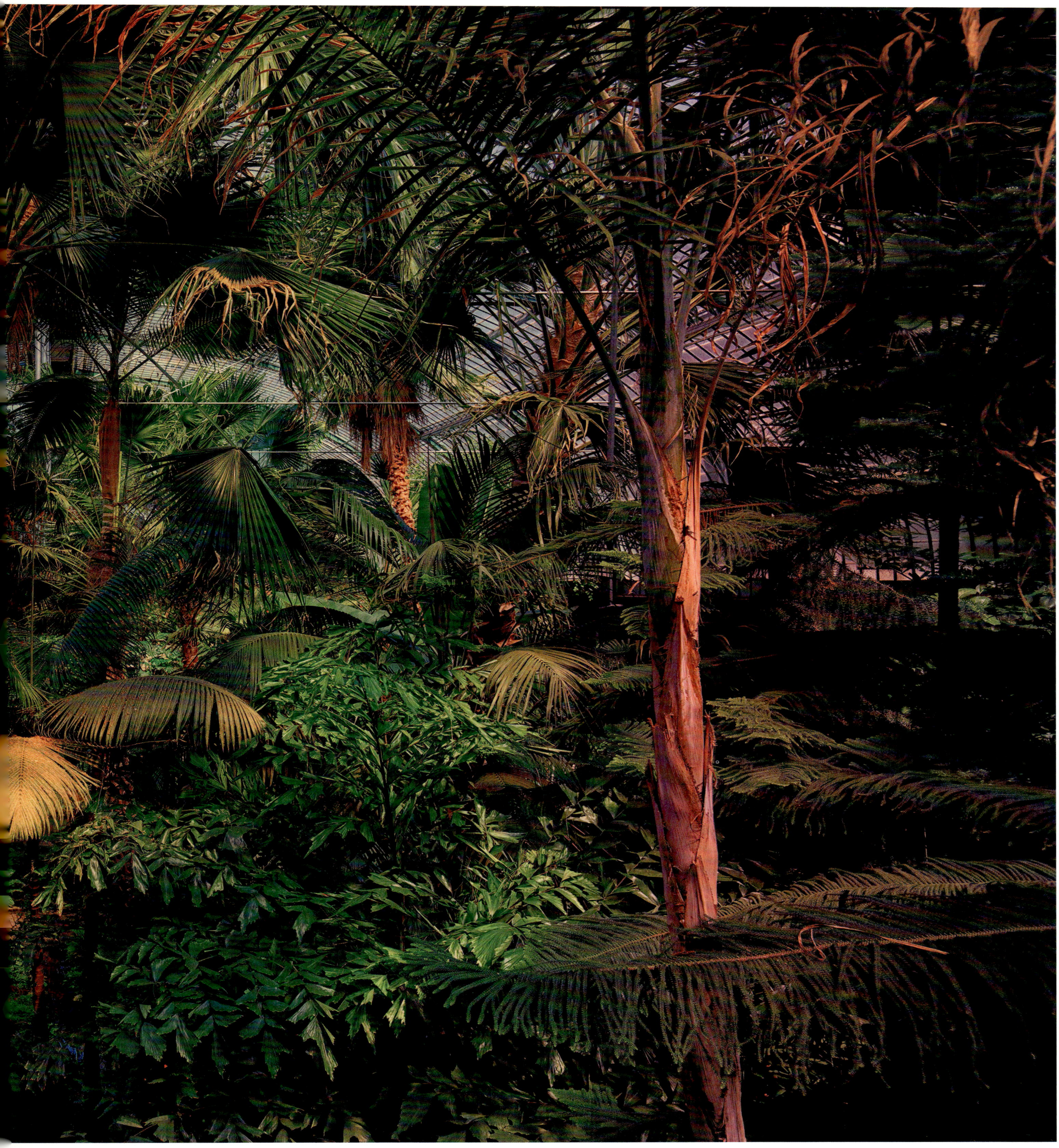

Palmengarten Frankfurt XVIII

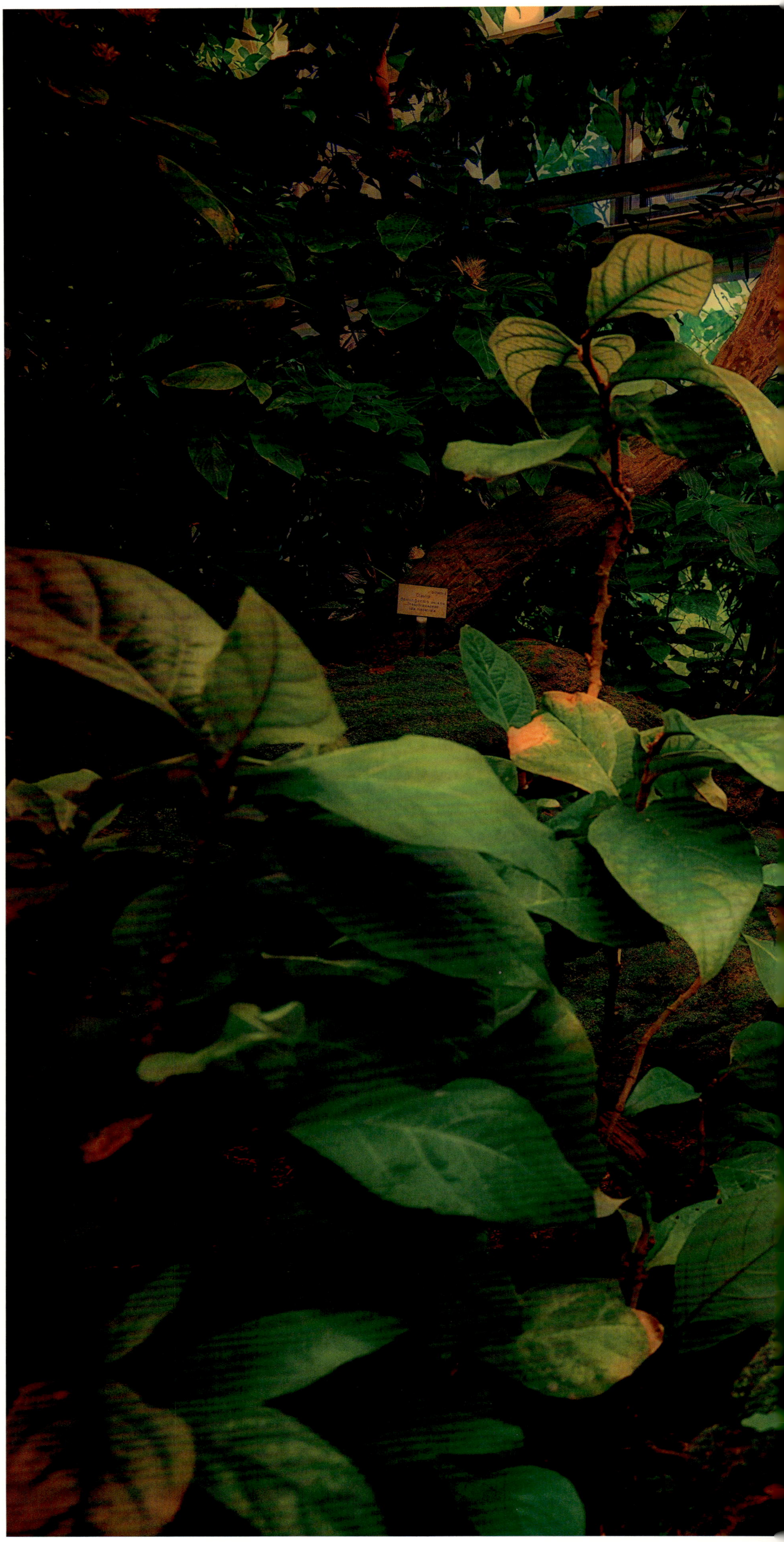

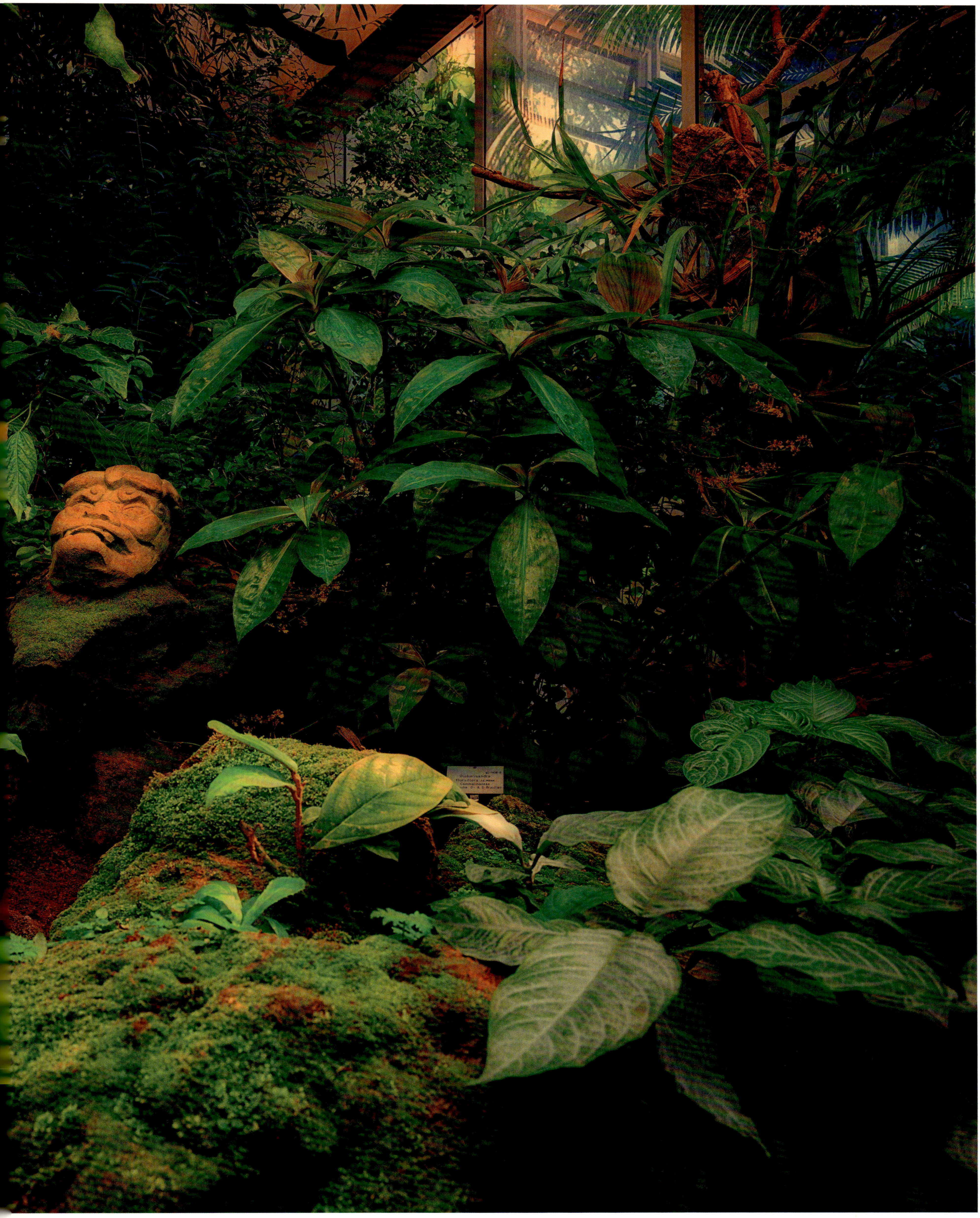
Dichorisandra
thyrsiflora J.C.Mikan
Commelinaceae

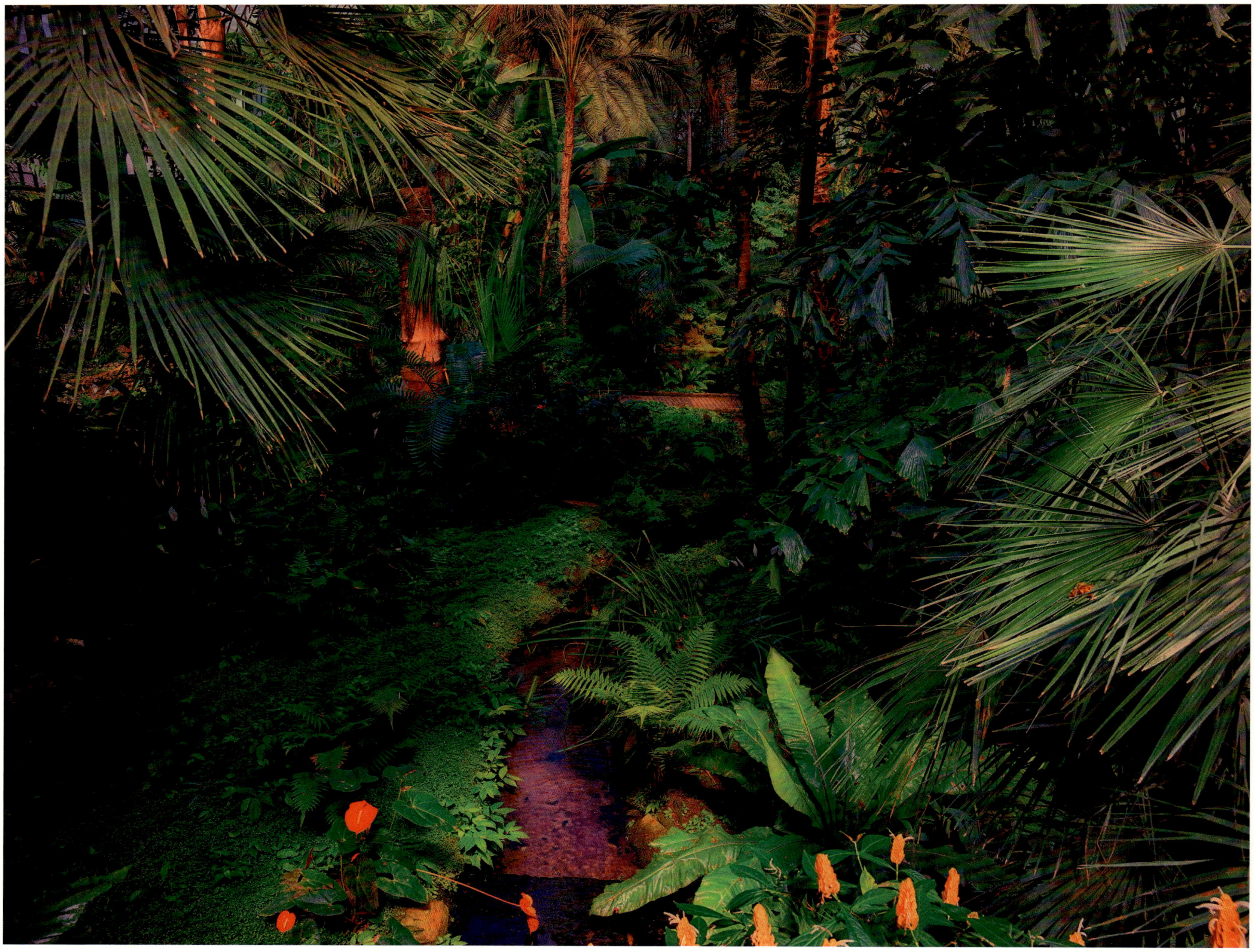

Palmengarten Frankfurt IV

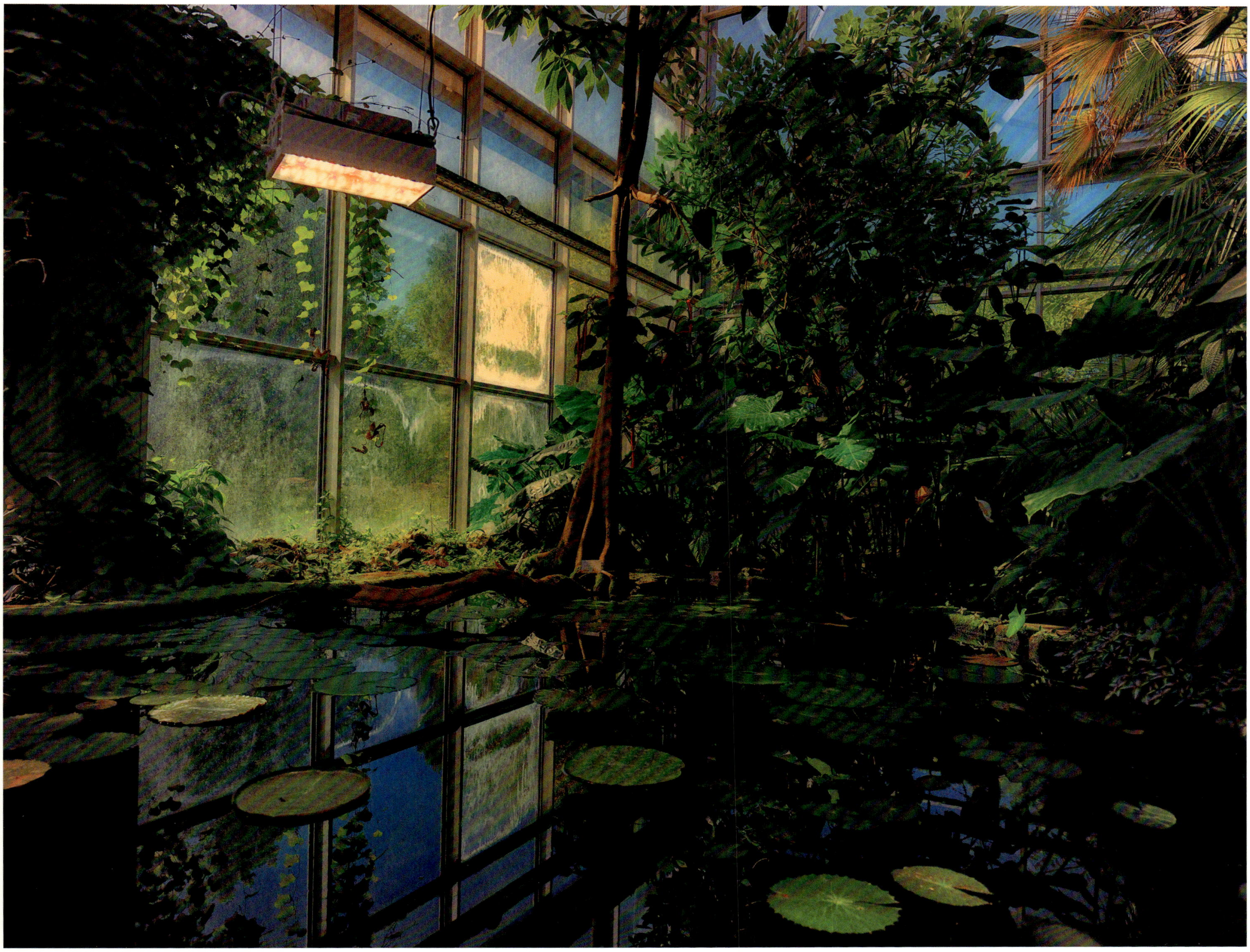

Palmengarten Frankfurt XVII · Palmengarten Frankfurt XV

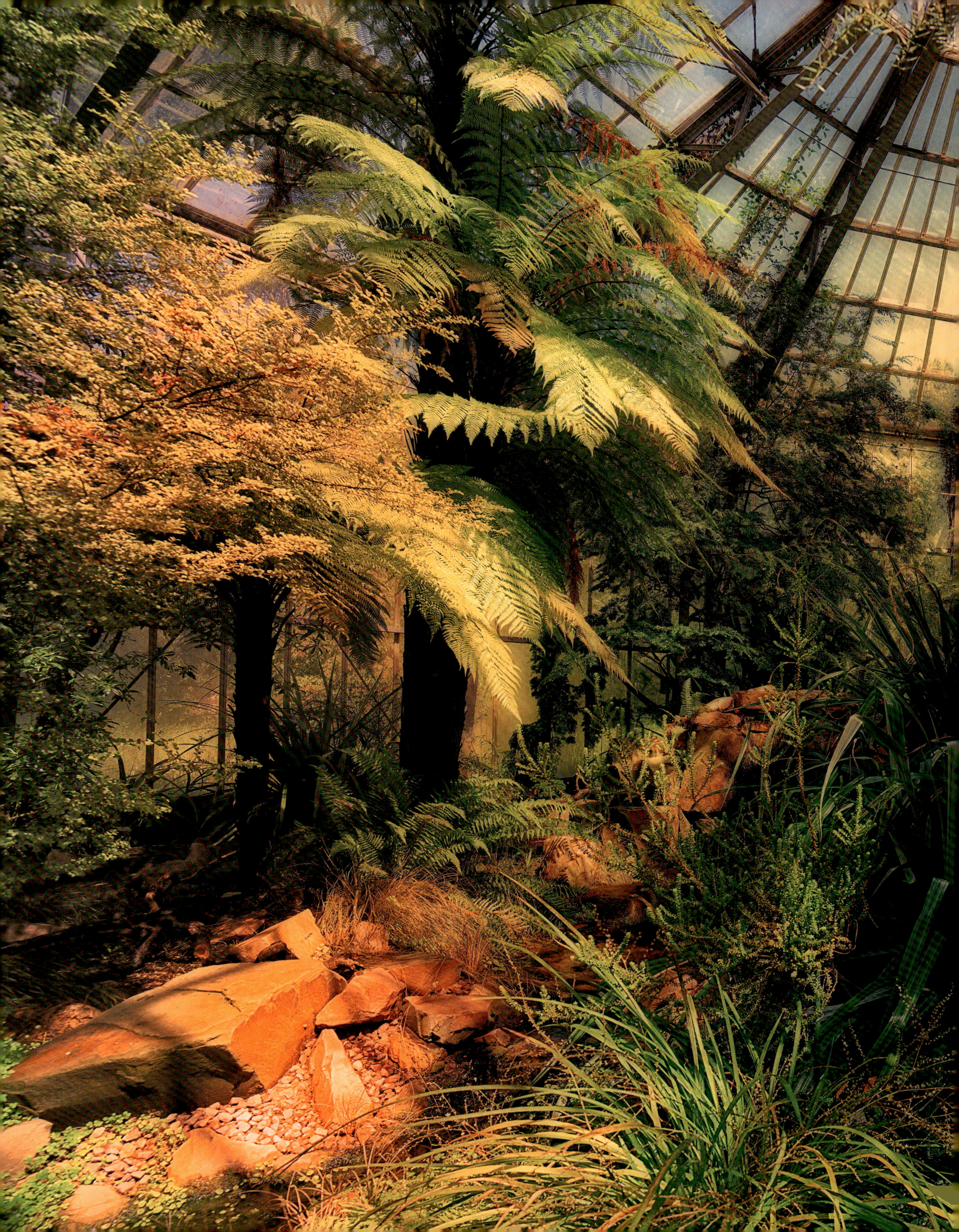

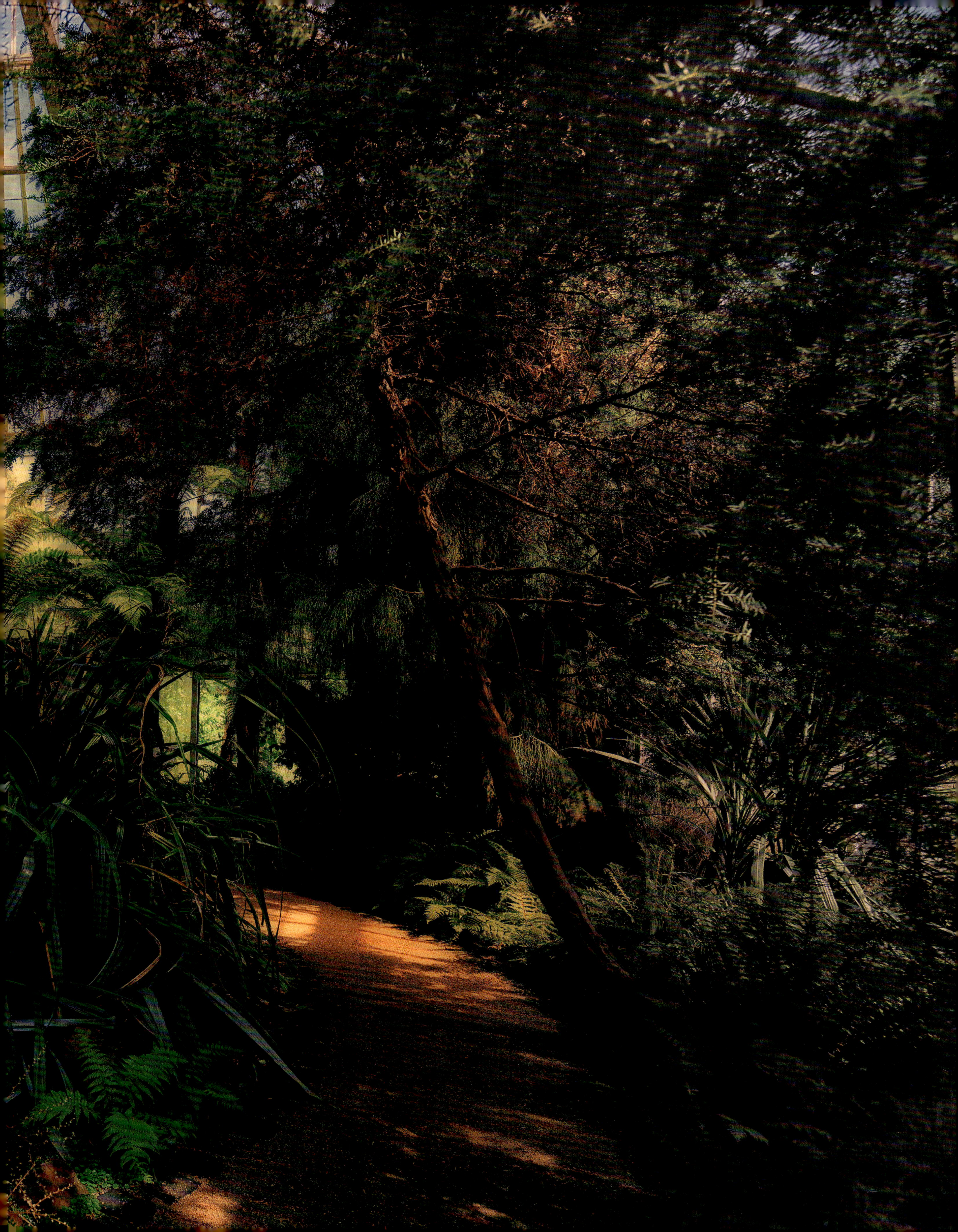

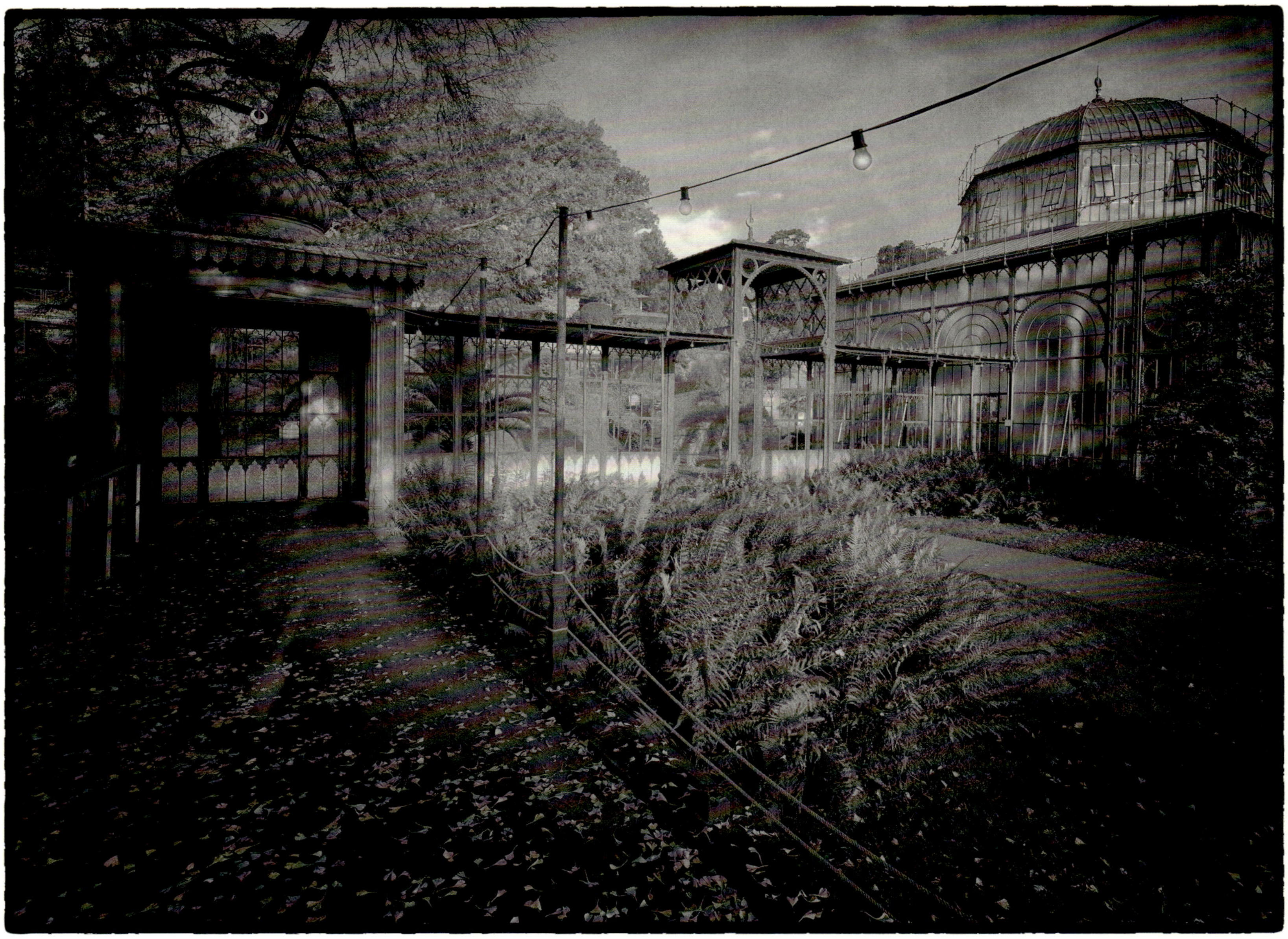

WILHELMA

STUTTGART

WILHELMA

ORT
Stuttgart, Deutschland

GRÖSSE
Gesamtgebäude: 93 m lang;
23 m breit; 11,50 m hoch (Eckpavillon)

ENTSTEHUNG
1842–1846
Entwurf: Ludwig von Zanth

ARCHITEKTUR
Das fürstliche Wohngebäude aus Stein nach maurischen Vorbildern mit Hufeisenbögen liegt im Zentrum der Anlage. Die zwei anschließenden gusseisernen Gewächshäuser enden in Eckpavillons. Sie sind mit vorgefertigten Teilen im Modularsystem montiert. Das Hufeisenbögen Motiv wird hier ebenfalls verwandt und schafft eine stilistische Einheit mit dem ehemaligen Wohngebäude.

PFLANZEN
Kakteen, tropische Nutzpflanzen, tropische Farne und Baumfarne

BESONDERHEITEN
Benannt nach seinem königlichen Bauherrn Wilhelm I. von Baden-Württemberg ist im Bau der Wille zu königlicher Repräsentation in historischer Bautradition mit dem Stolz auf die Leistungsfähigkeit der modernen, heimischen Eisenindustrie des Hüttenwerks Wasseralfingen vereint. 1852–1853 wurden weitere Gewächshäuser durch von Zanth errichtet. Erst ab 1880 gab es für Jedermann Eintrittskarten zur Wilhelma, die heute den Stuttgarter Zoo beherbergt.

LOCATION
Stuttgart, Germany

SIZE
Entire building: 93 m long;
23 m wide; 11.50 m high (corner pavilion)

ESTABLISHED
1842–1846
design: Ludwig von Zanth

ARCHITECTURE
Featuring a Moorish style with horseshoe arches, the royal residence is made of stone and situated in the center of the complex. The two adjoining cast-iron greenhouses end in corner pavilions. They have a modular design with prefabricated parts. The horseshoe arch motif, which is used here as well, blends harmoniously with the style of the former residential building.

PLANTS
Cacti, tropical crops, tropical ferns, and tree ferns

ADDITIONAL NOTES
Named after its royal owner, Wilhelm I of Baden-Württemberg, the building combines the desire for royal representation in historical building tradition with a pride in the efficiency of the modern, domestic iron industry of the Wasseralfingen ironworks. In 1852–1853, von Zanth built additional greenhouses. It was not until 1880 that the general public could buy tickets to Wilhelma, which is now also home to the Stuttgart Zoo.

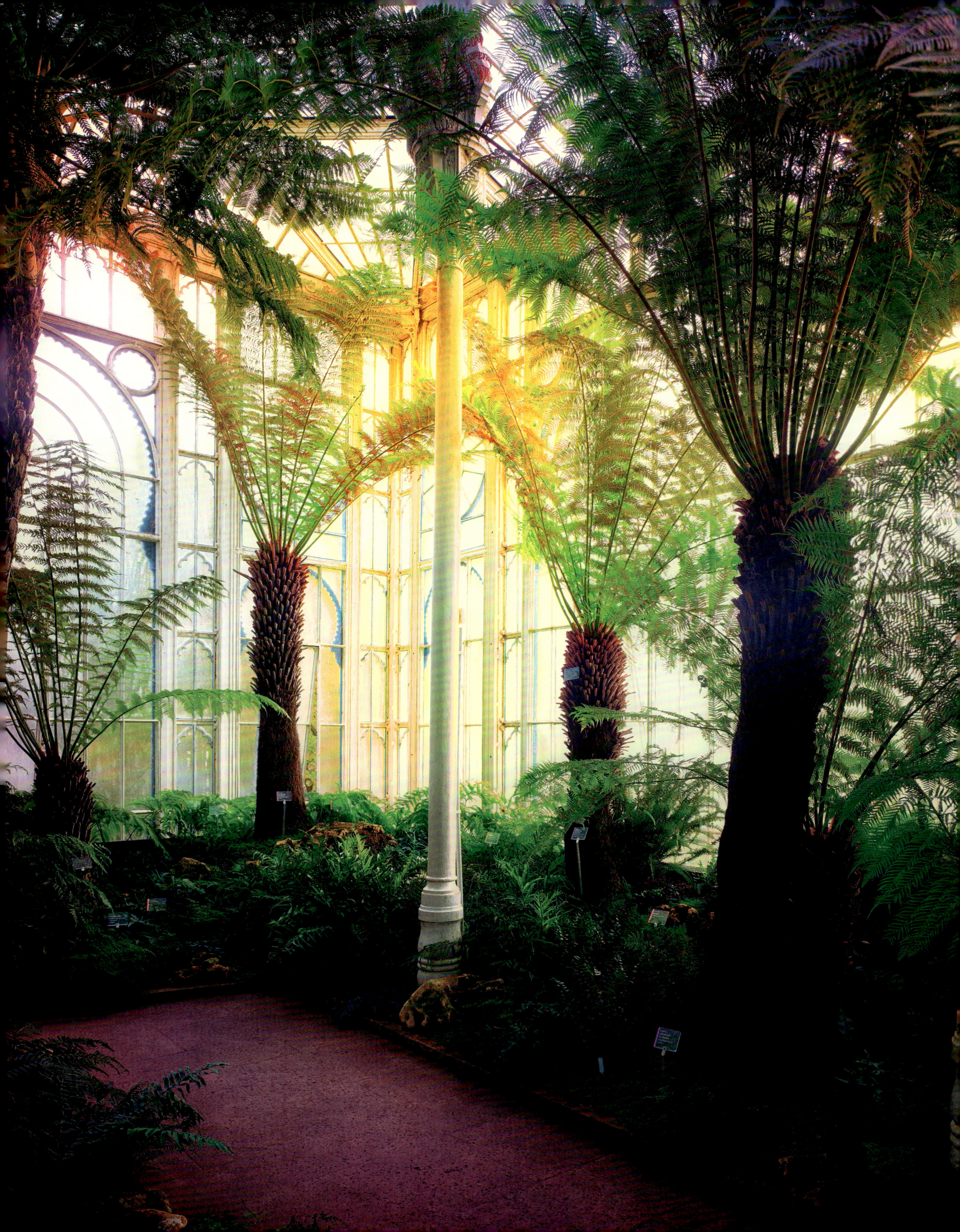

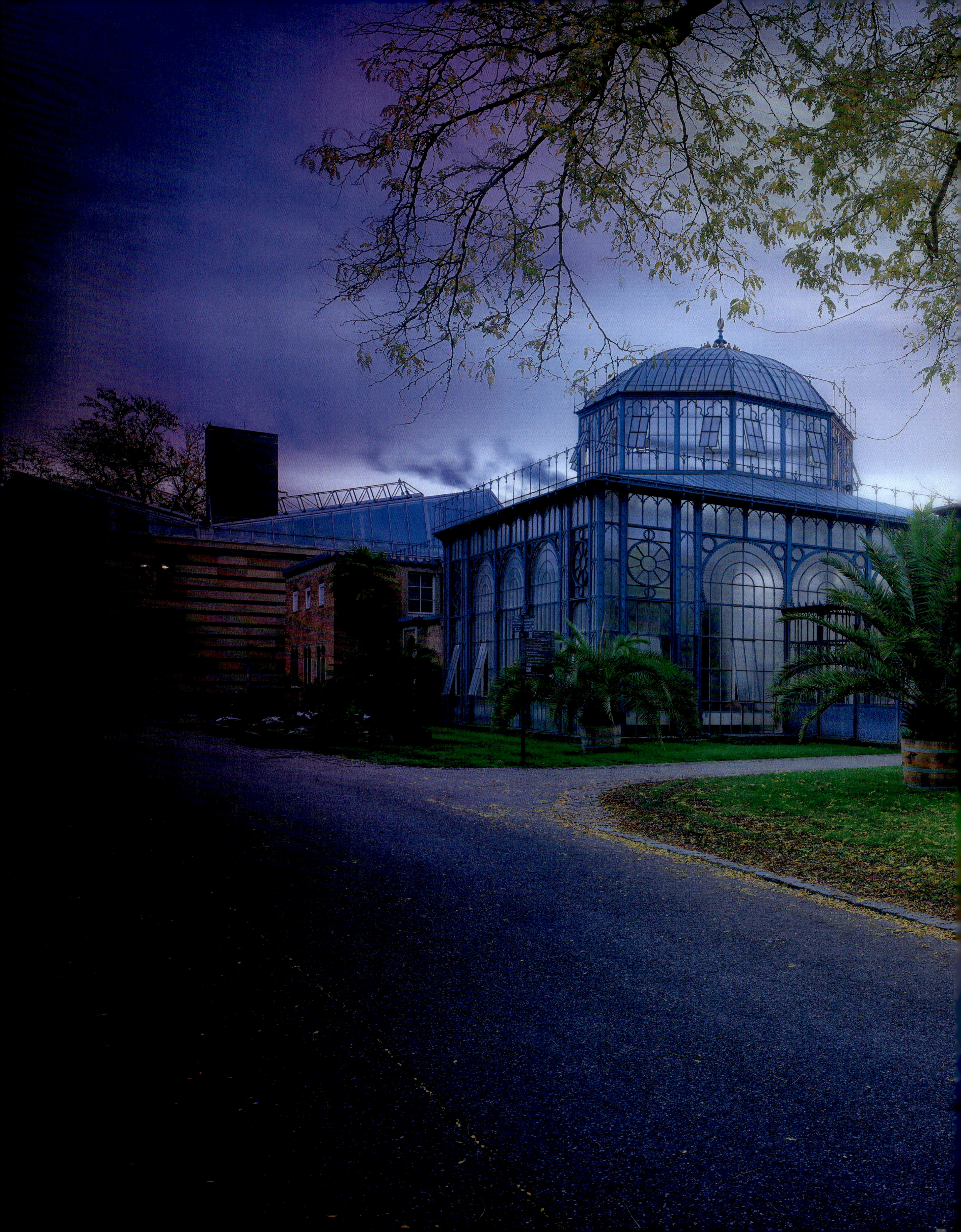

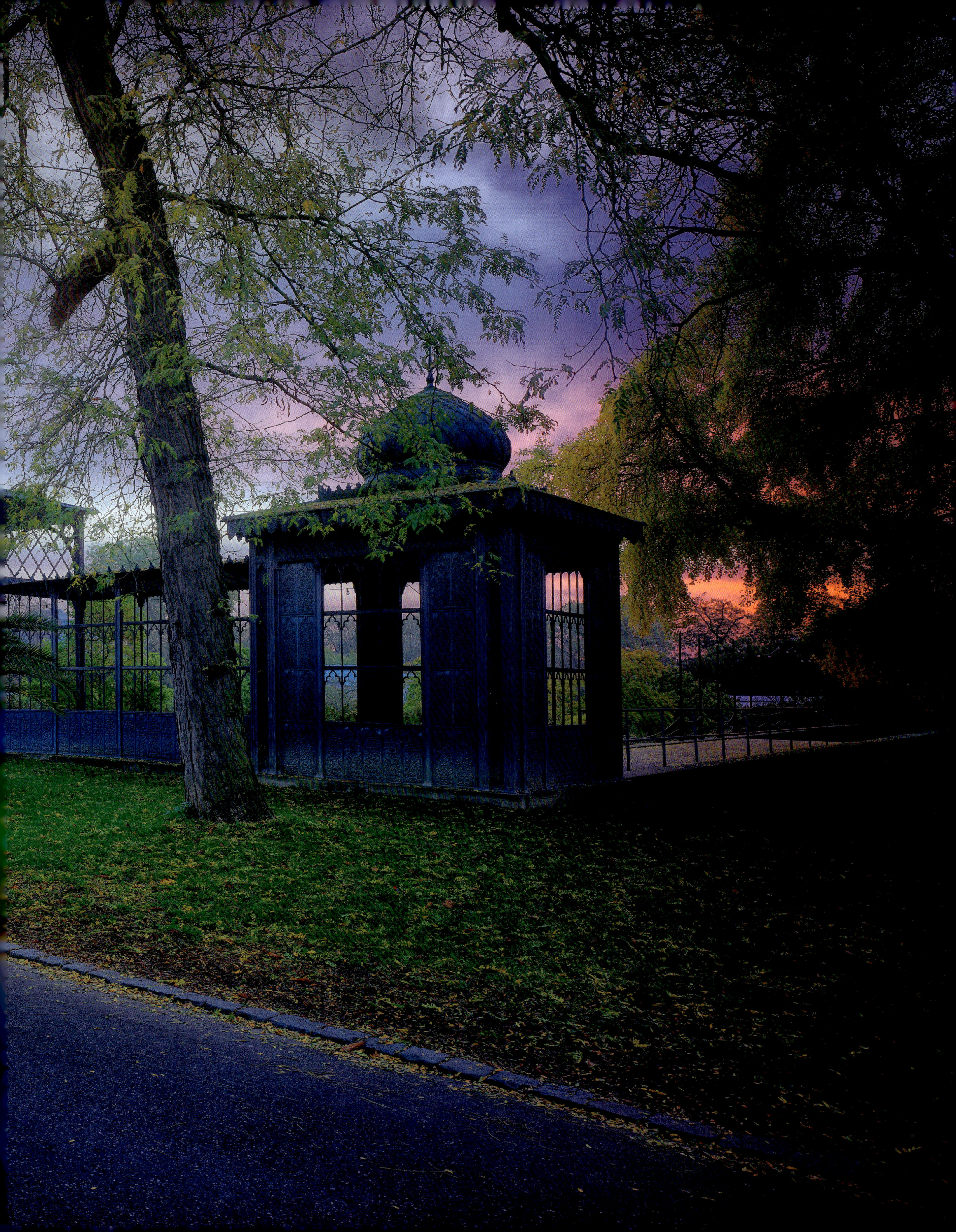

Wie immer, wenn ich mit der Kamera unterwegs bin, verfolge ich keinen vorab exakt festgelegten Plan, sondern versuche, mit der jeweils vorgefundenen Situation intuitiv umzugehen und mit jeder Aufnahme, Bild für Bild, immer tiefer in mein Sujet einzutauchen.

WERNER PAWLOK

Whenever I'm out and about with my camera, I don't follow a pre-determined plan. Instead, I simply try to deal intuitively with the situation at hand and to dive deeper and deeper into my subject with every shot, frame by frame.

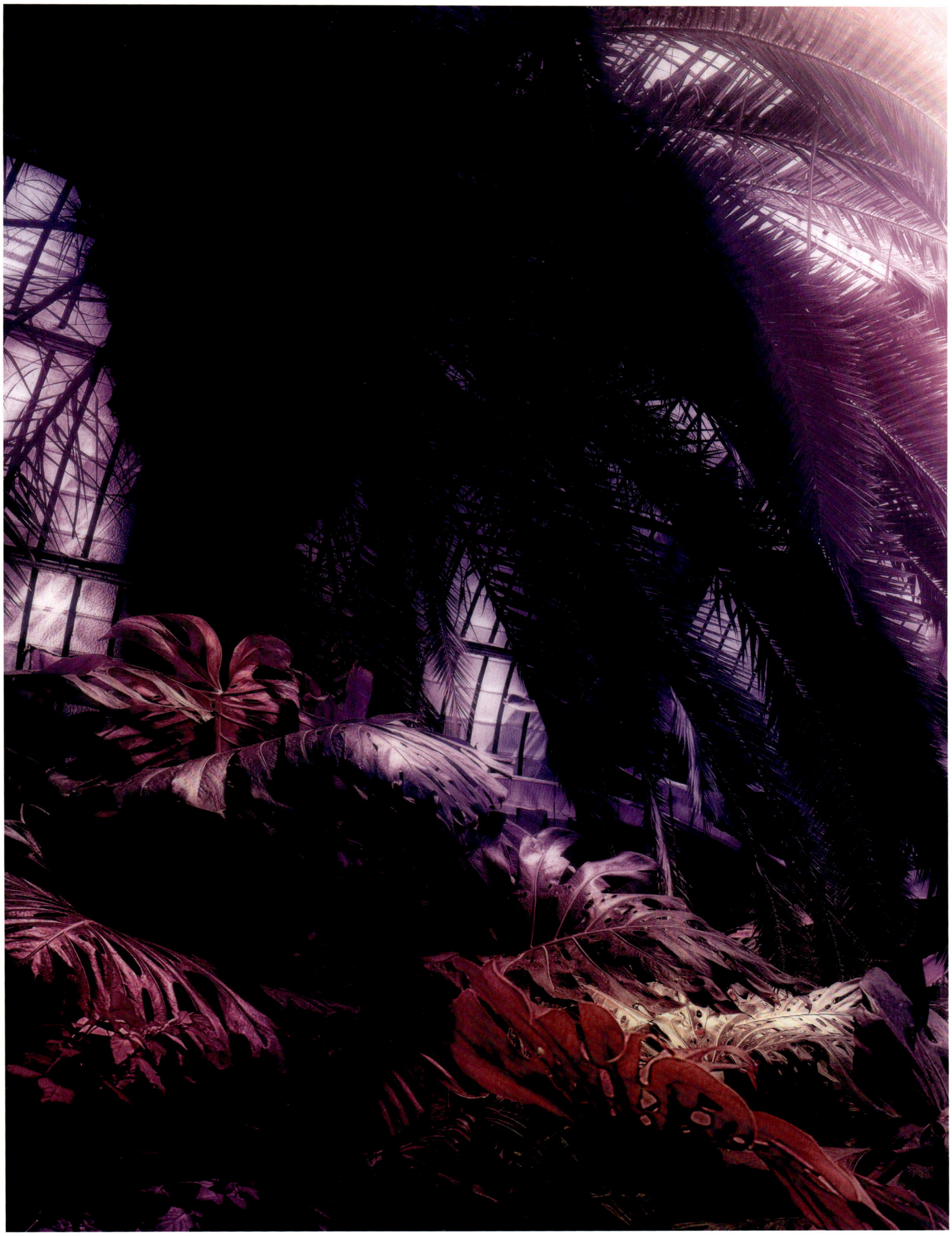

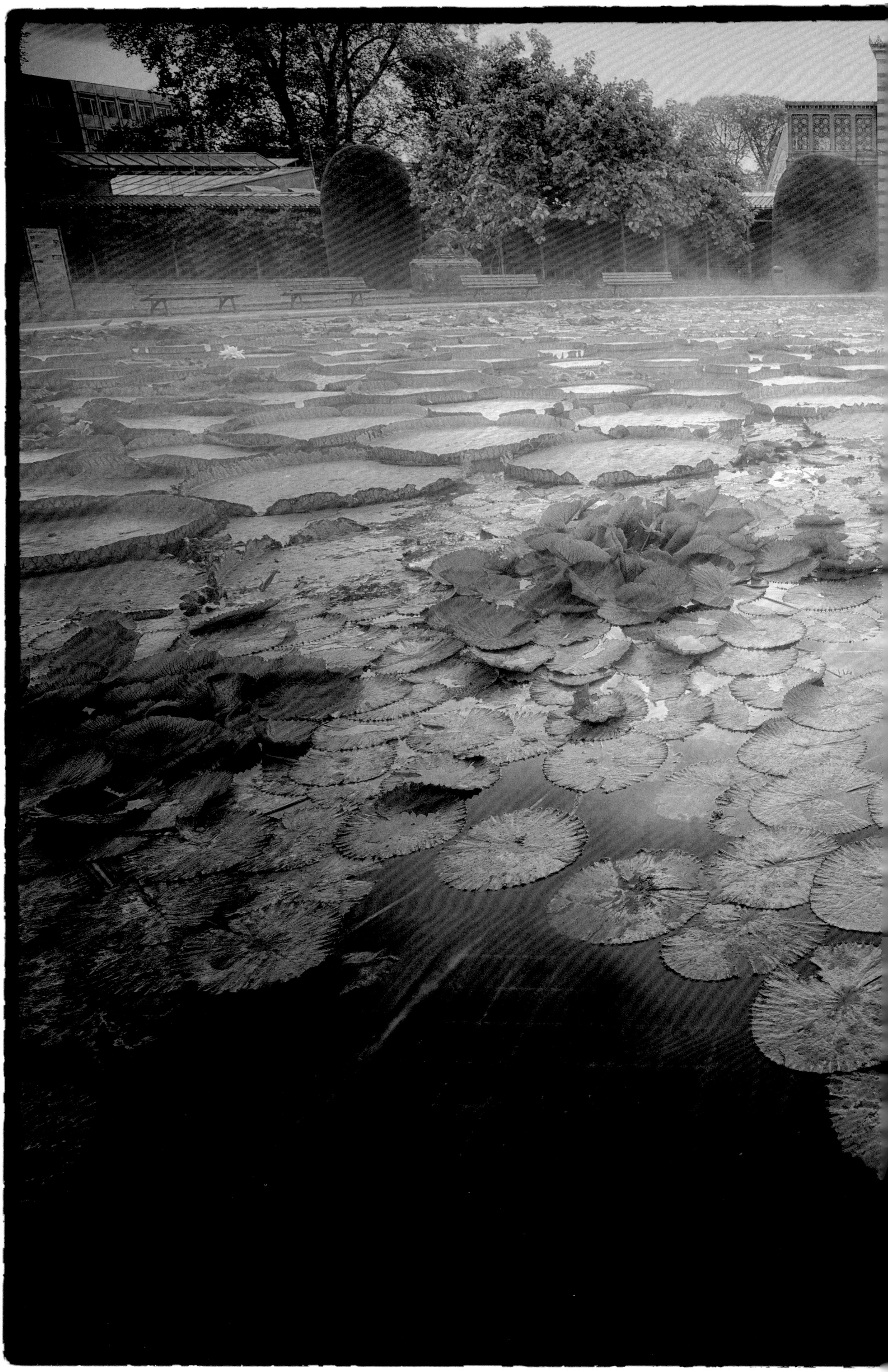

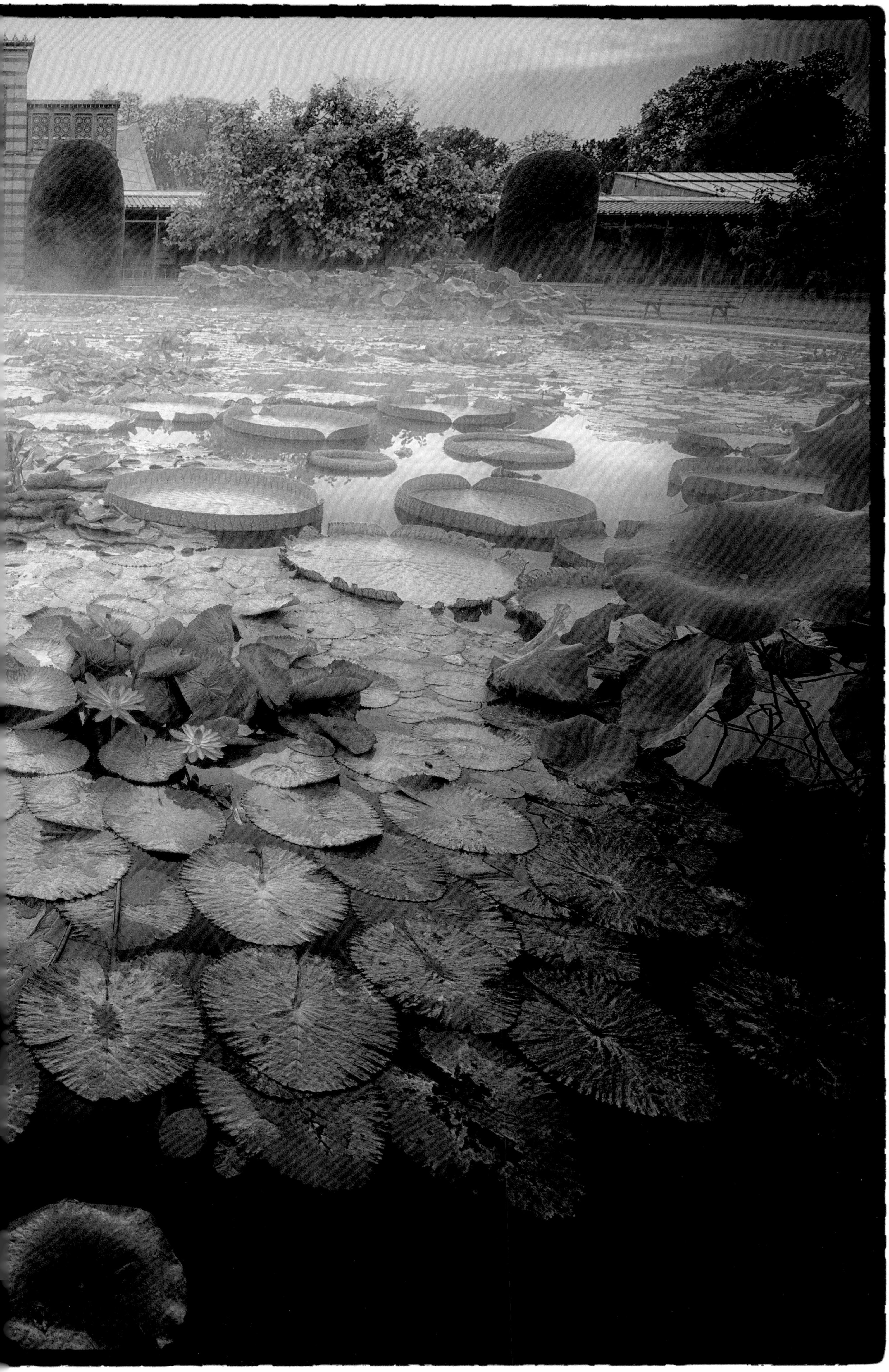

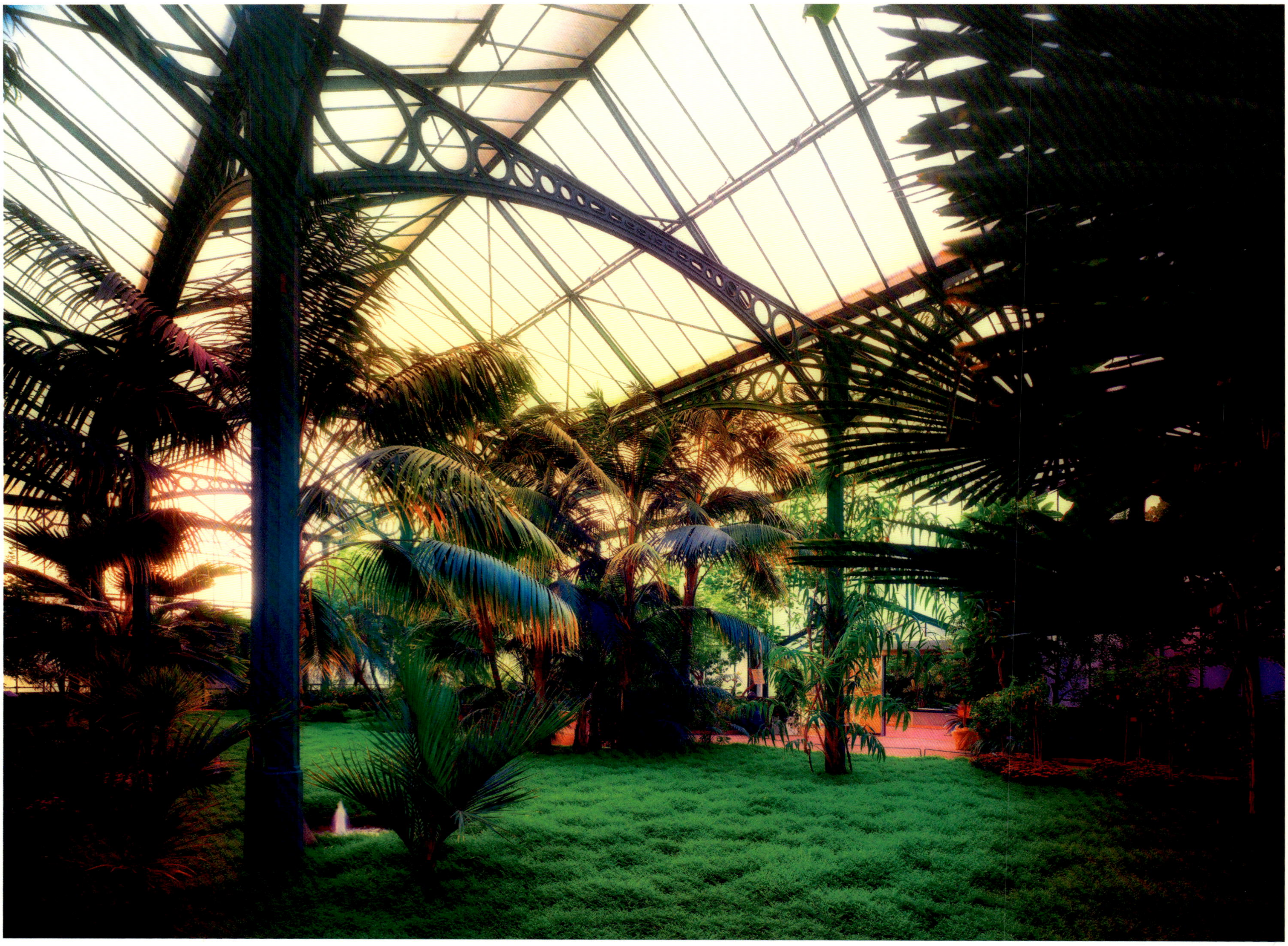

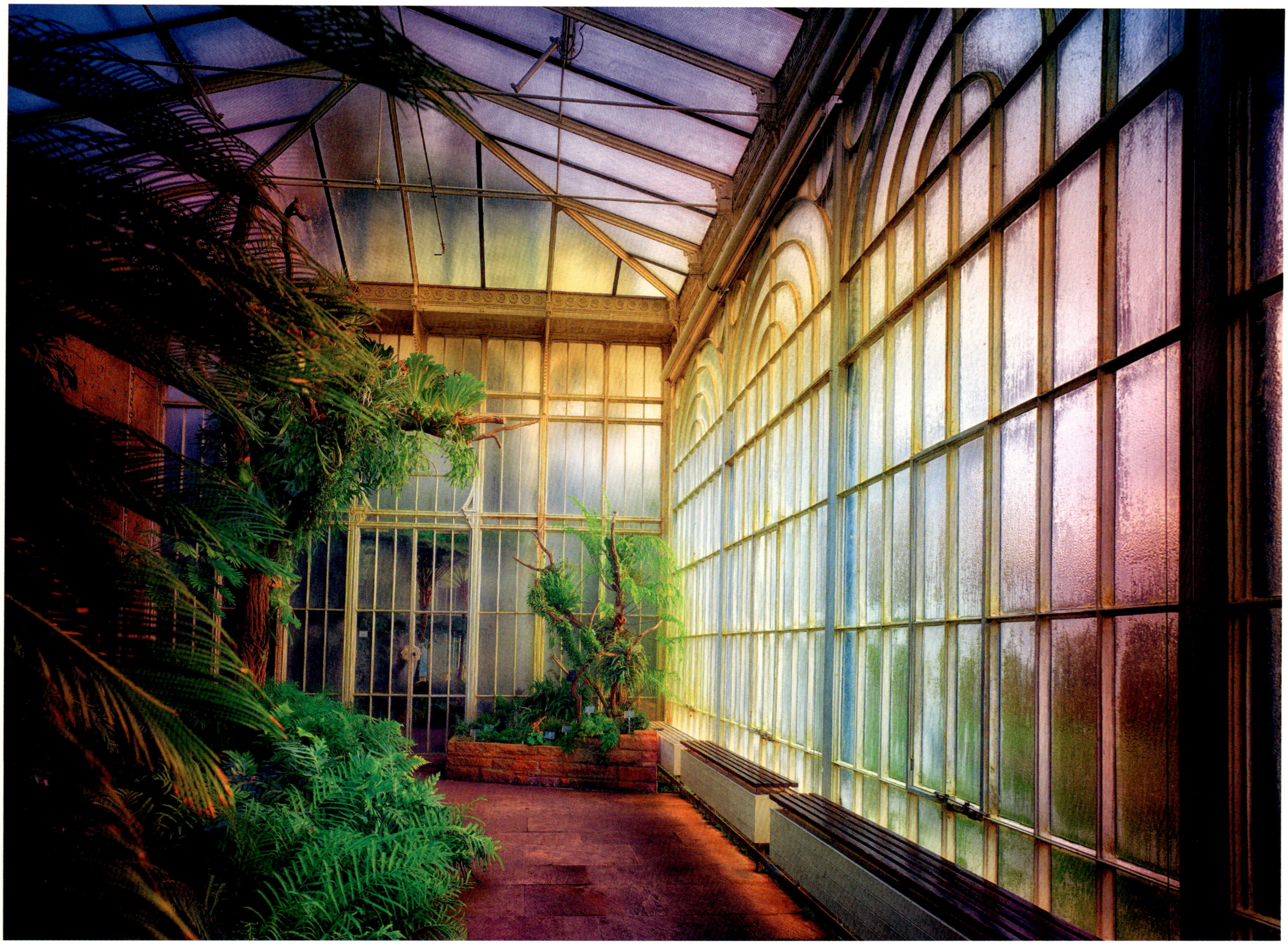

Wilhelma Stuttgart XVI

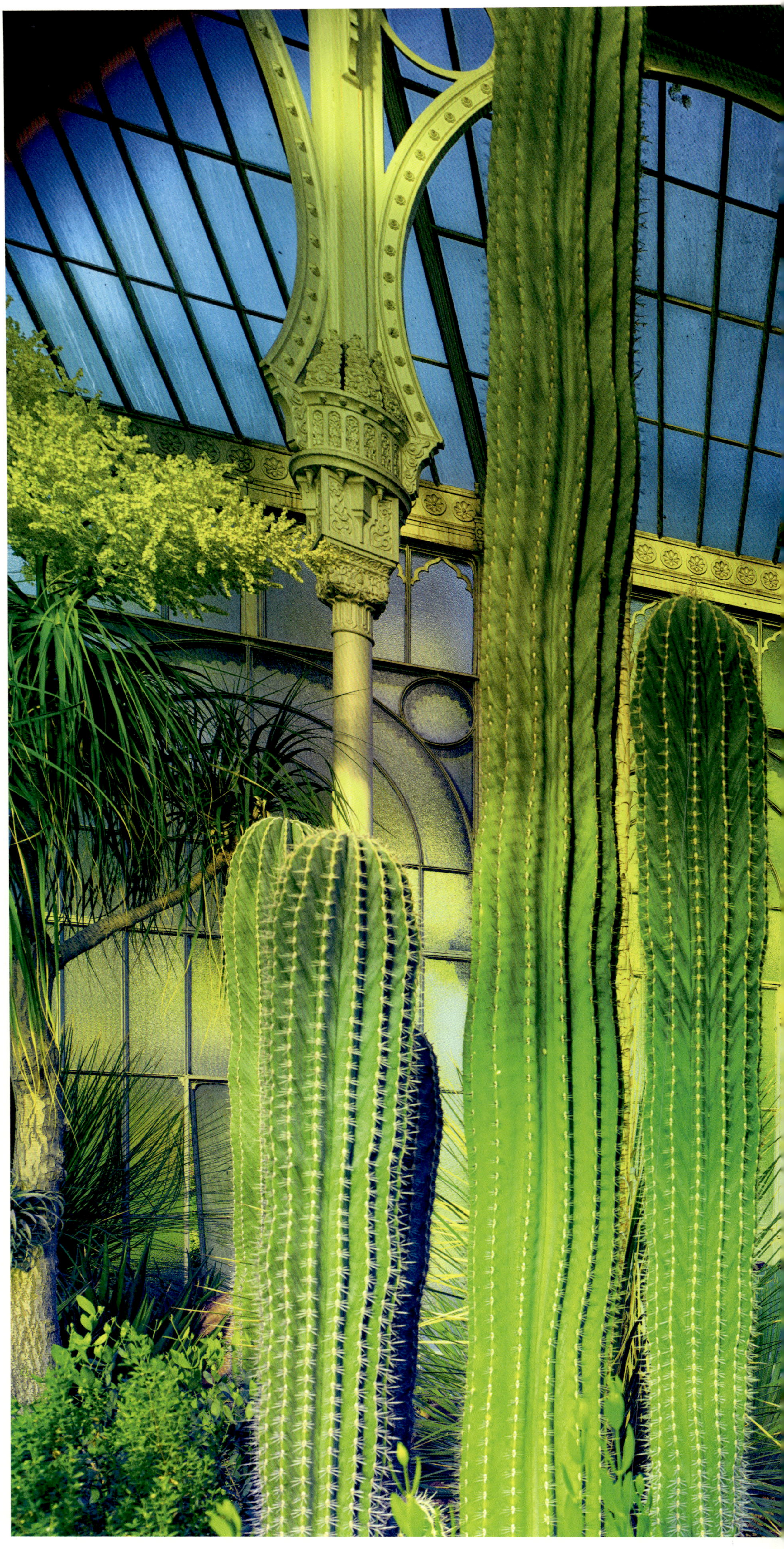

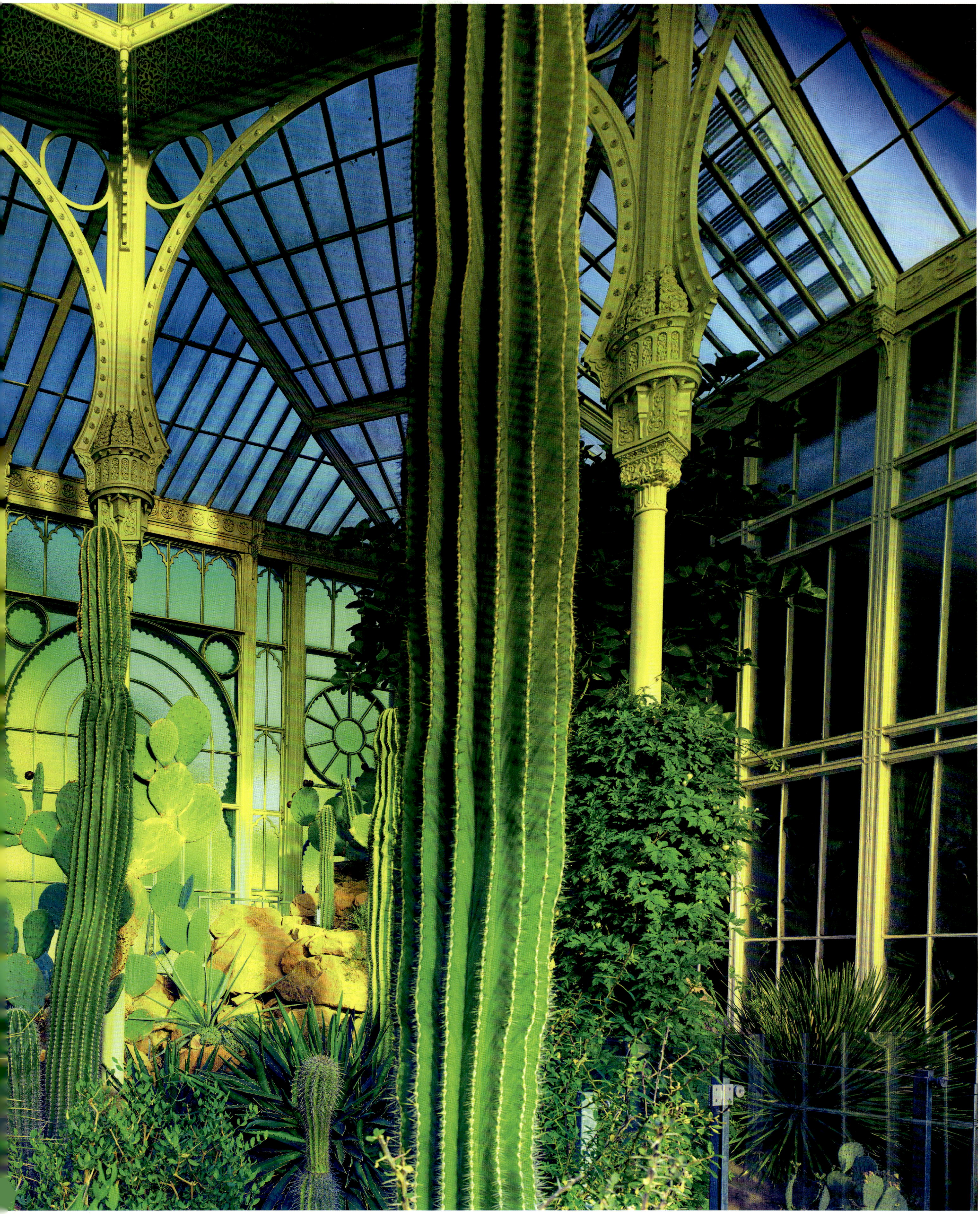

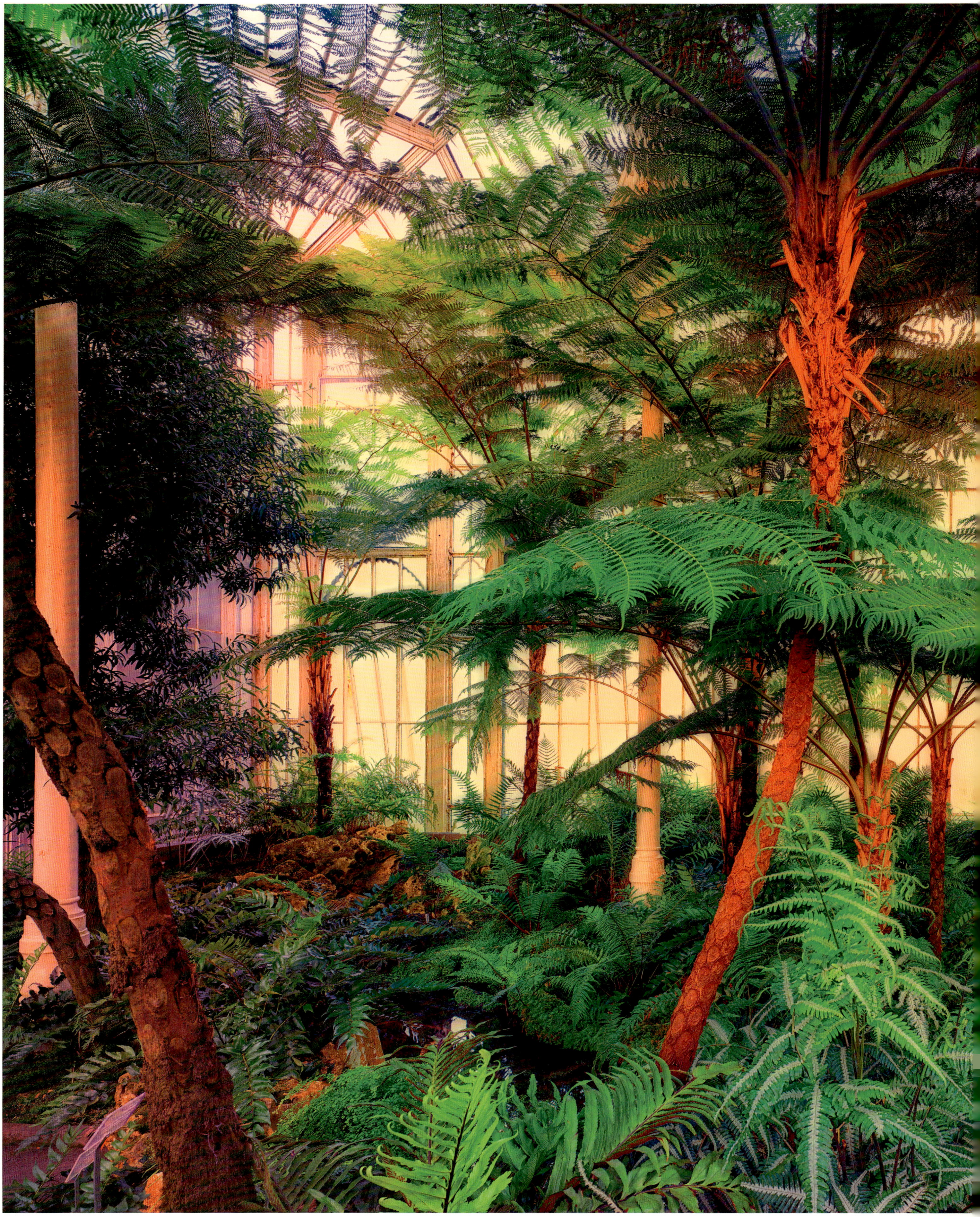

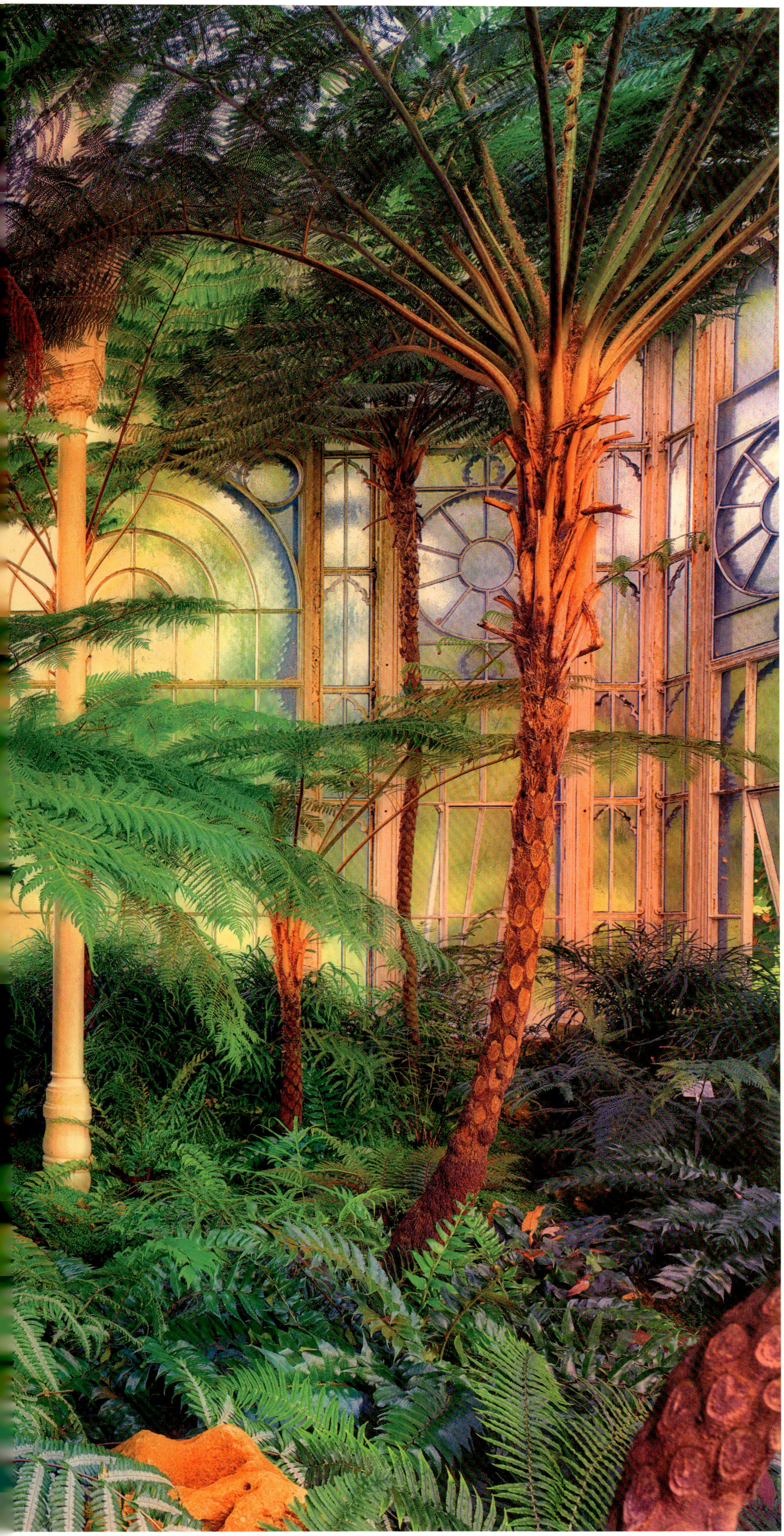

Wilhelma Stuttgart IX
Wilhelma Stuttgart VIII ▼
Wilhelma Stuttgart XV ▼▼

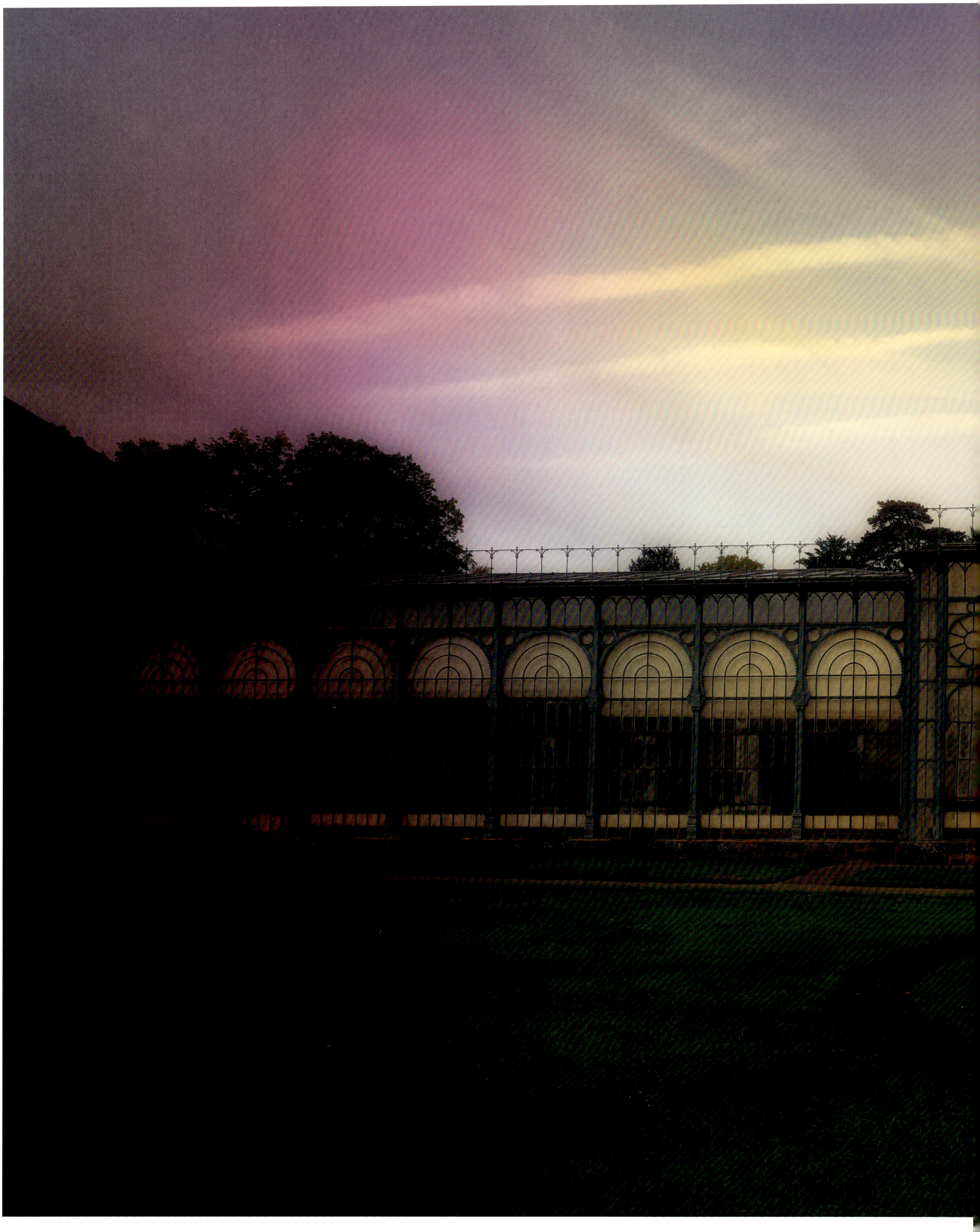

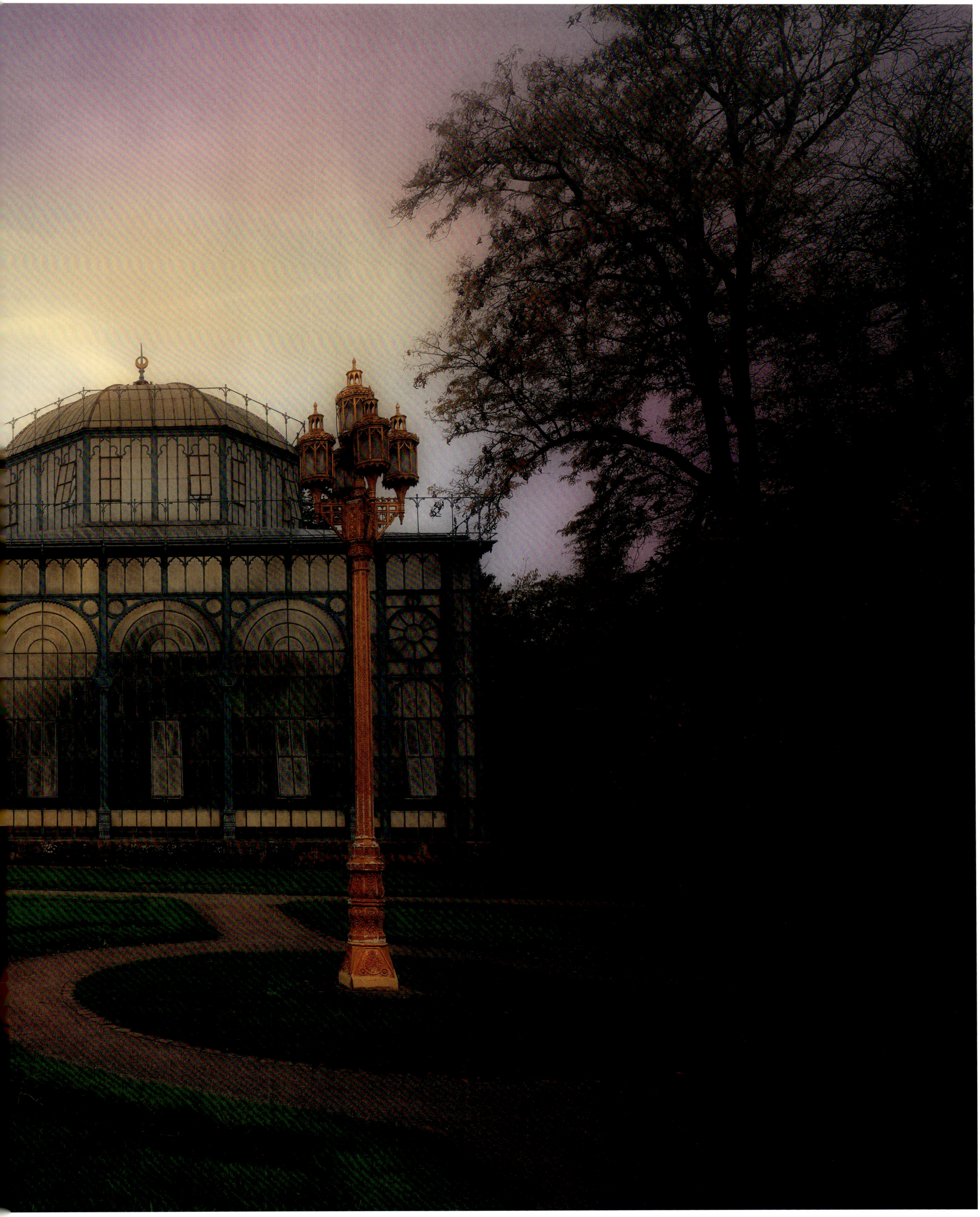

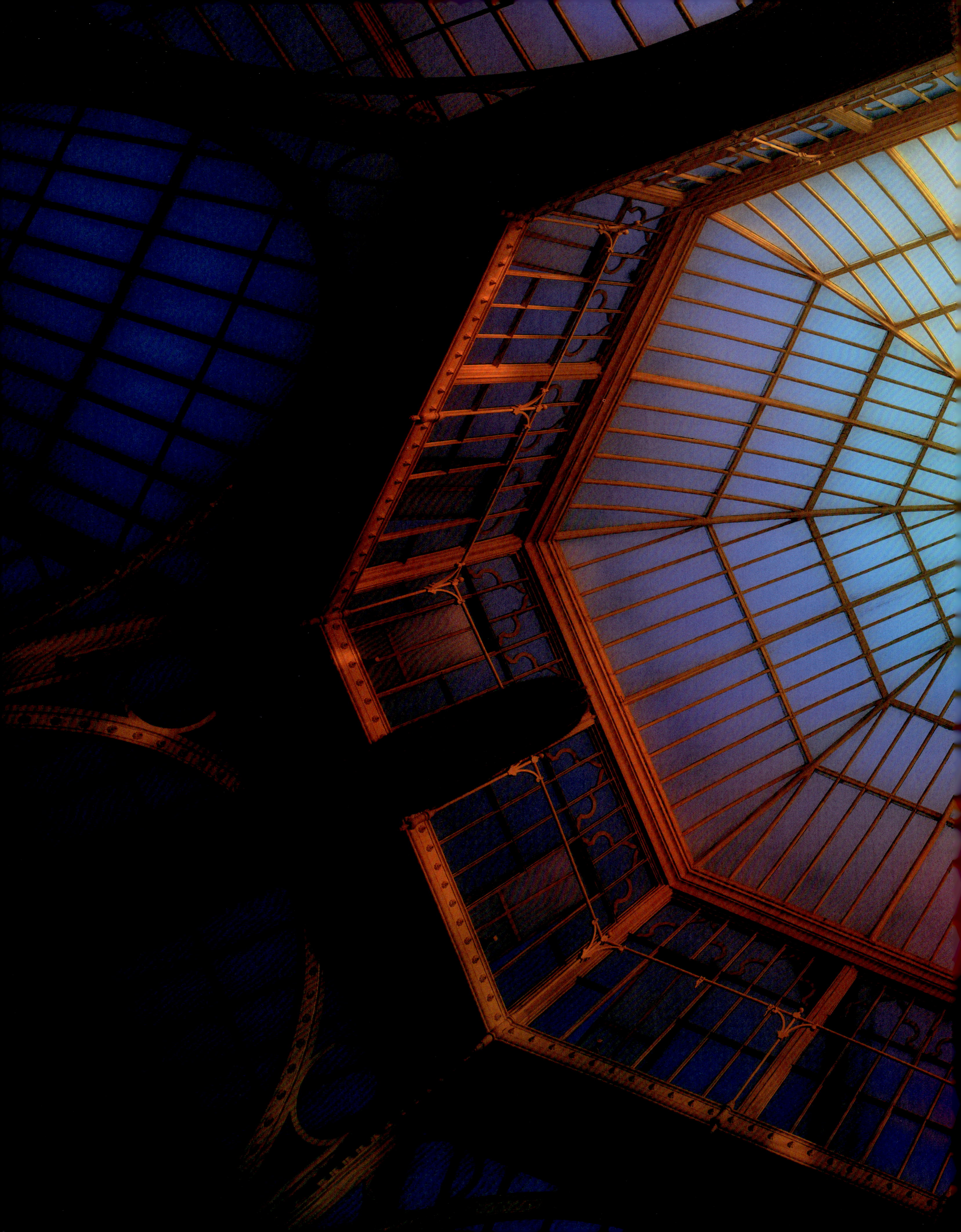

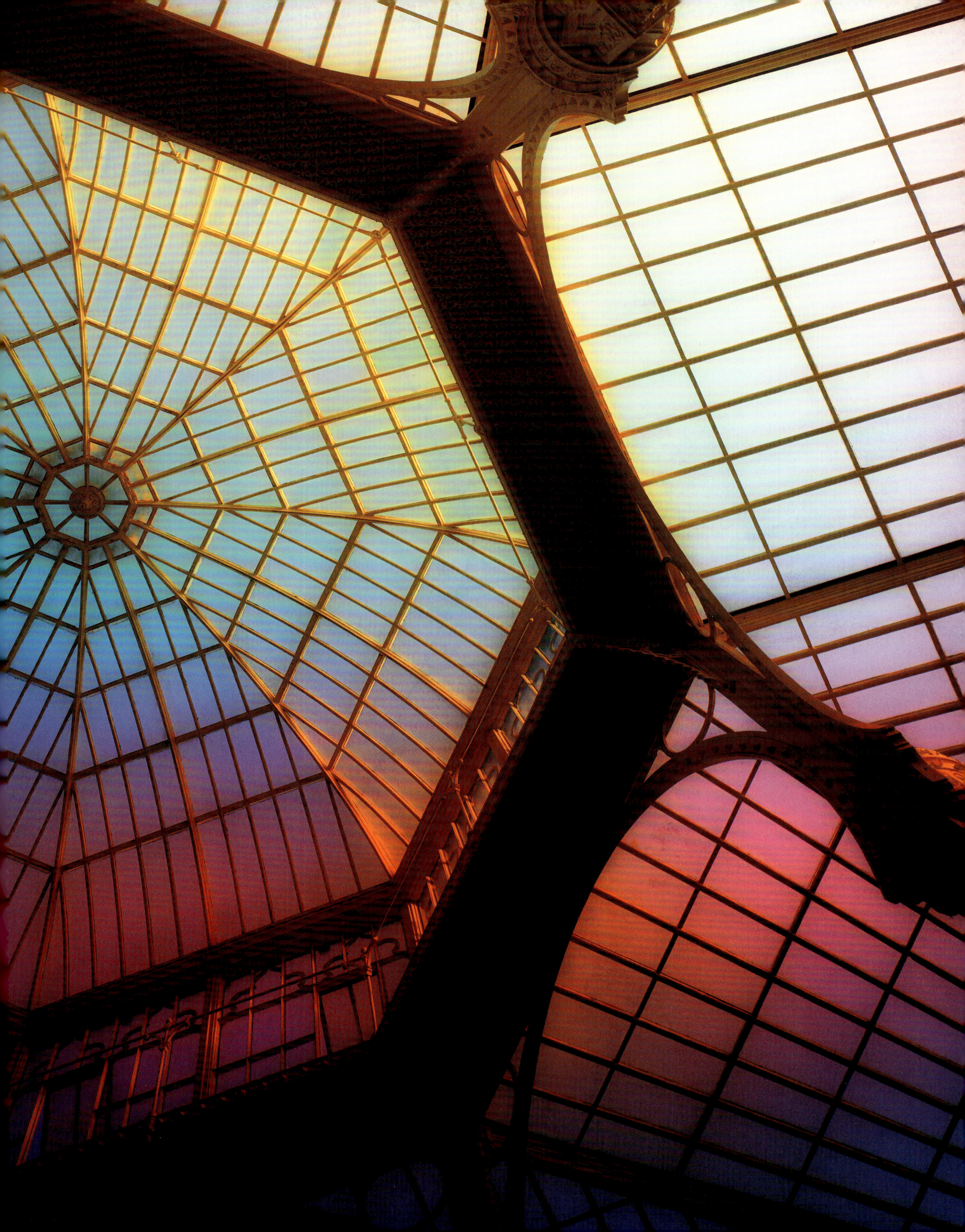

Wilhelma Stuttgart XII
Wilhelma Stuttgart XIII

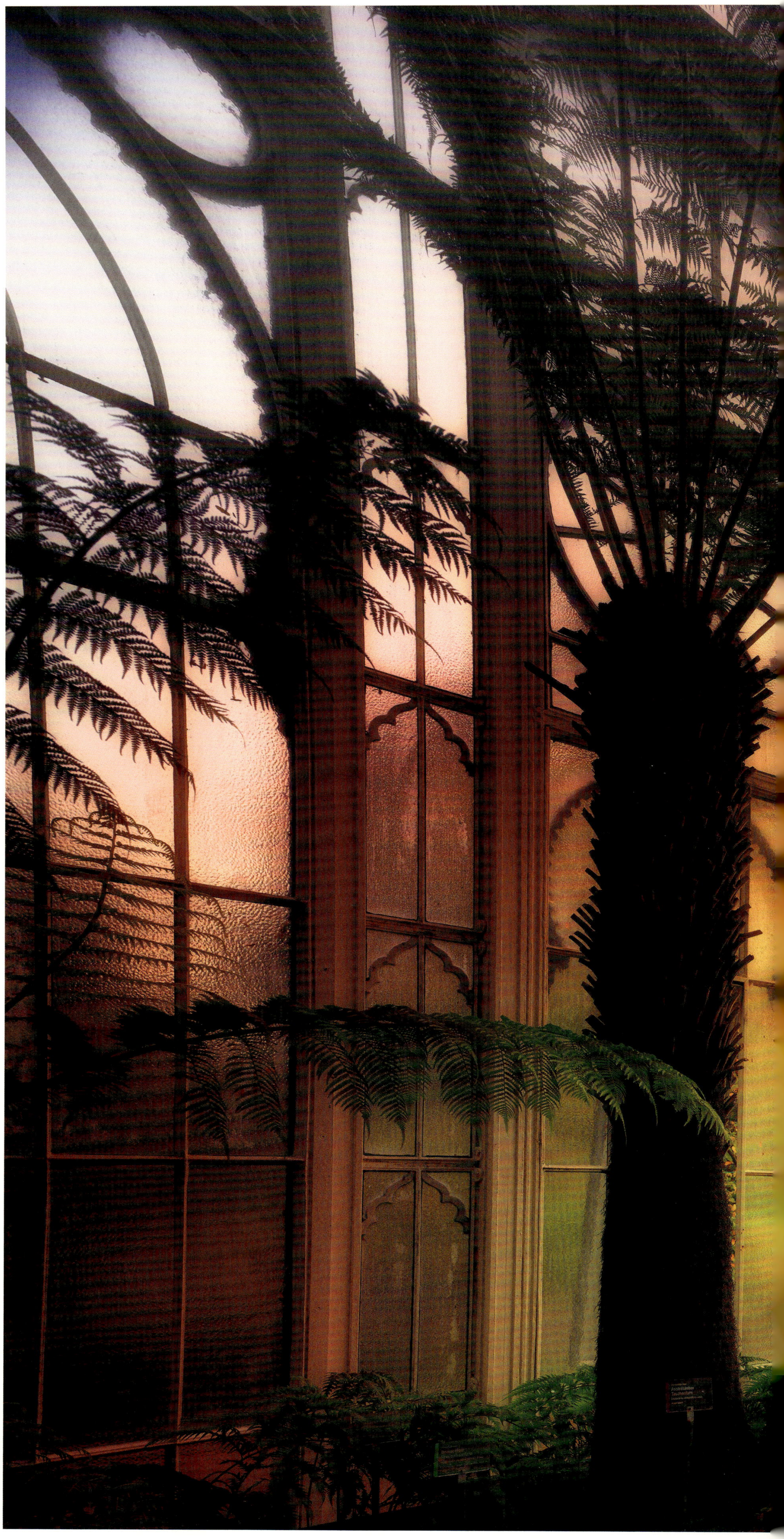

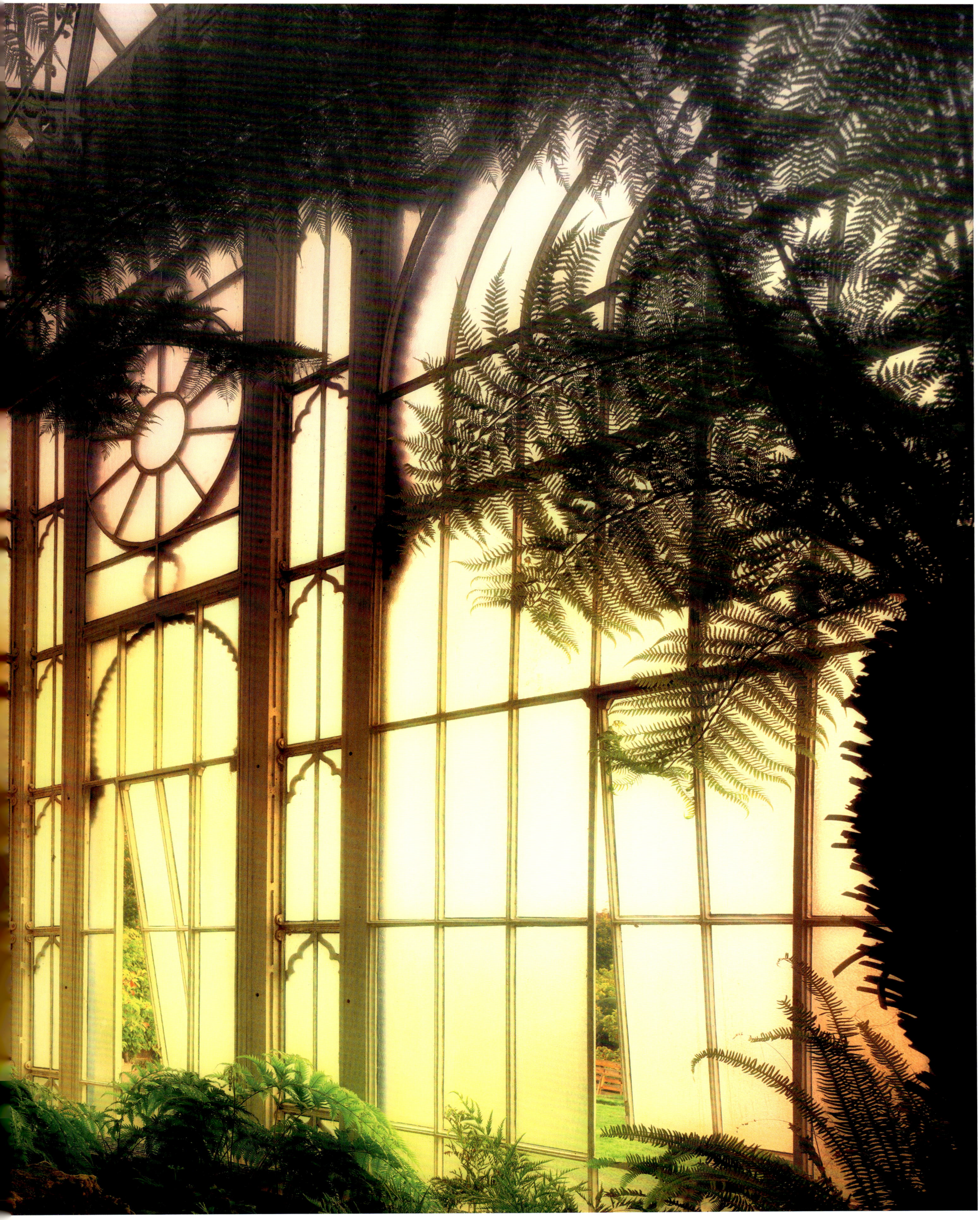

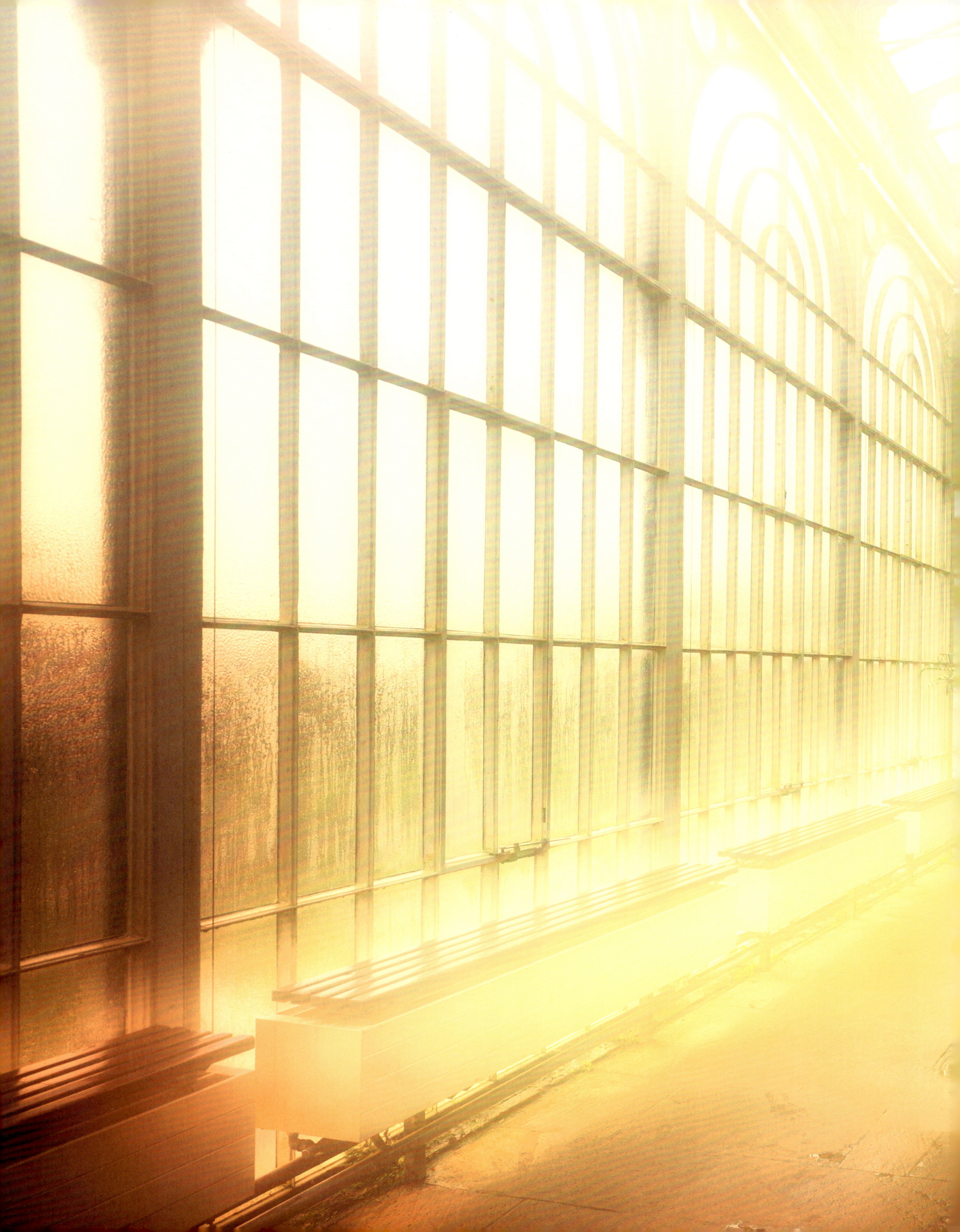

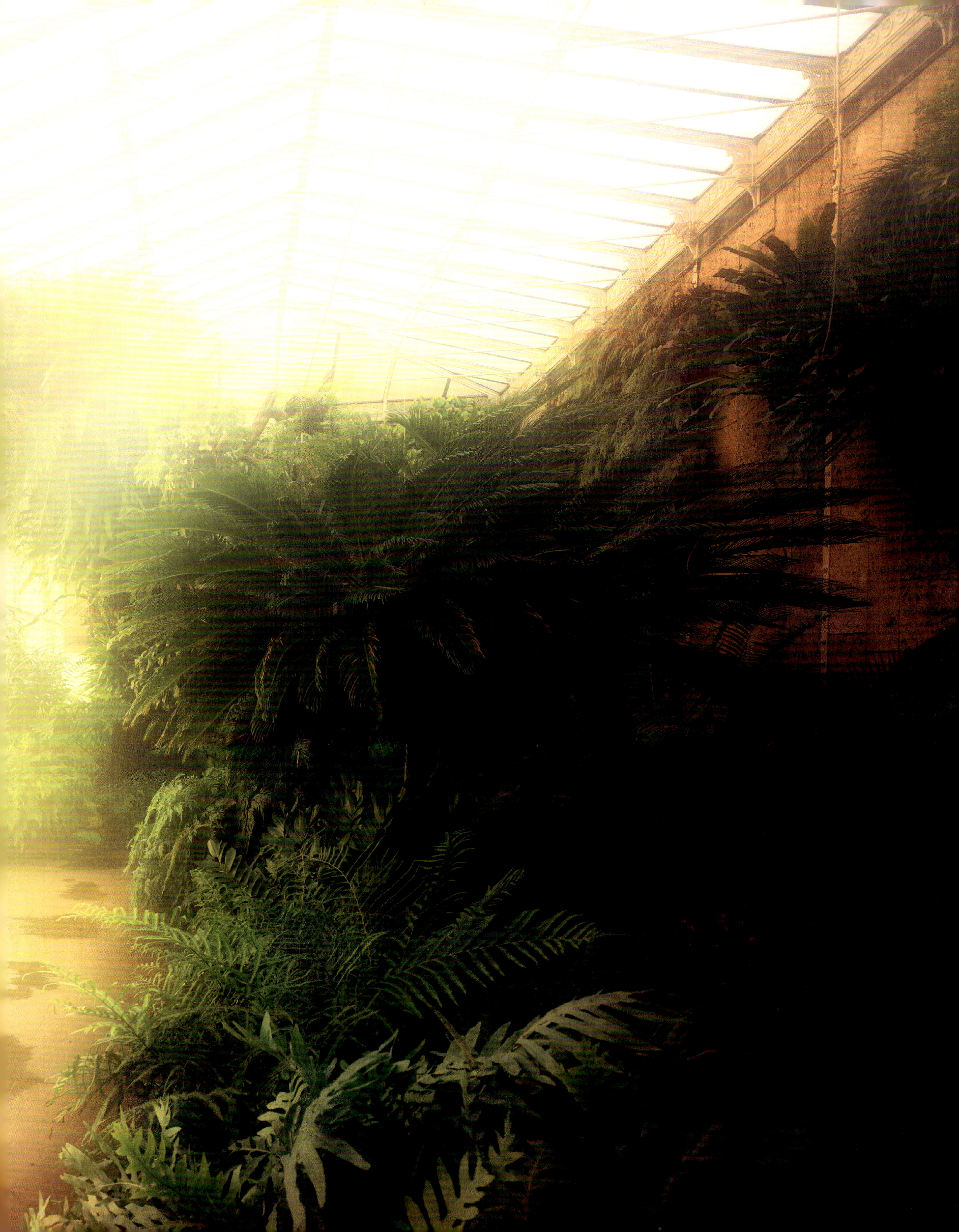

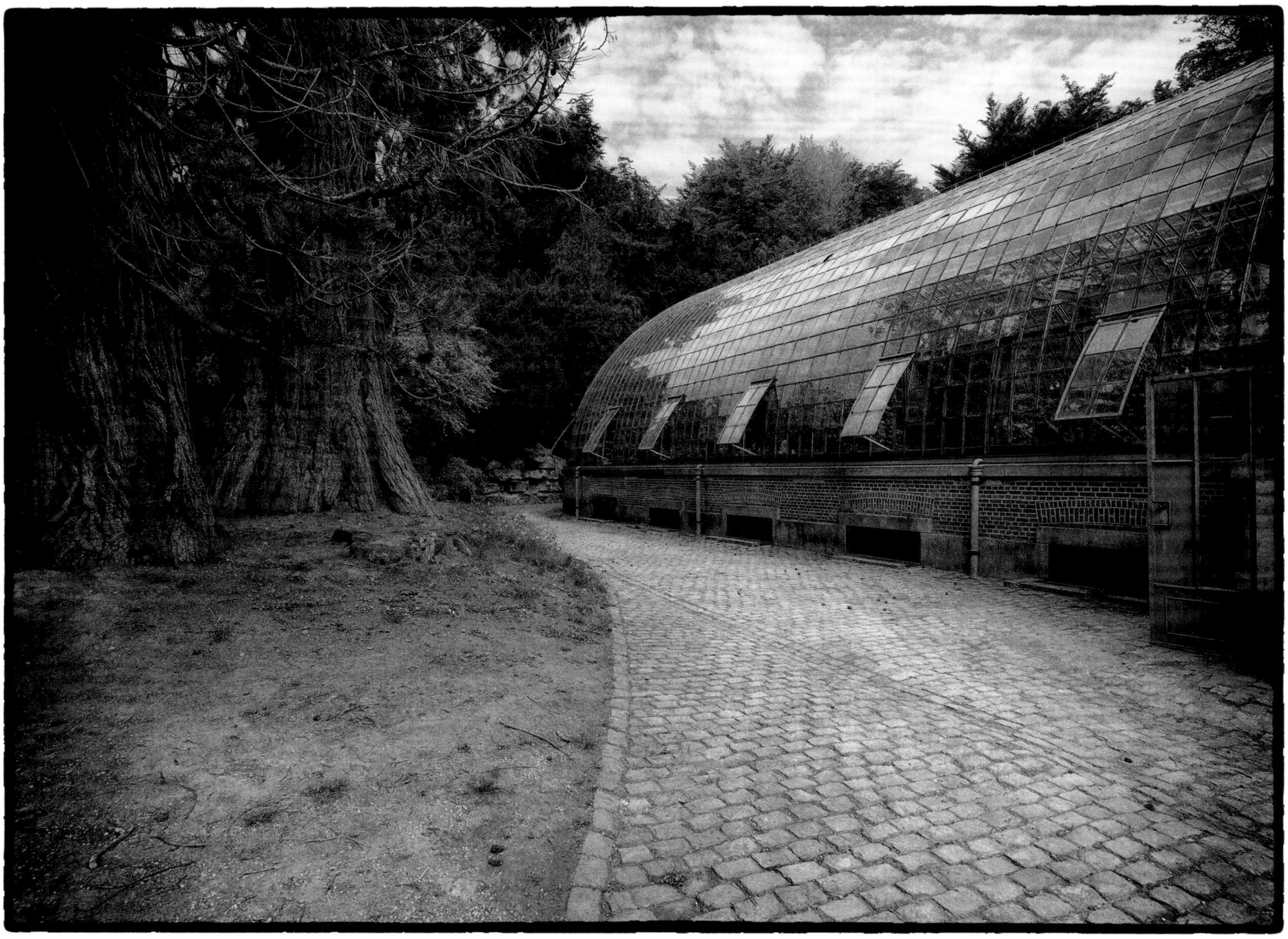

ROYAL GREENHOUSES OF LAEKEN

BRUSSELS

ROYAL GREENHOUSES OF LAEKEN

ORT
Brüssel, Belgien

GRÖSSE
Größter Gewächshauskomplex Europas. Die 36 Gebäude bilden einen zusammenhängenden Innenraum von 1,6 km Länge. Höhepunkt der Anlage ist der kreisrunde Wintergarten mit einem Durchmesser von 56 m und einer Kuppelhöhe von ca. 30 m.

ENTSTEHUNG
1865–1890
Entwurf: Alphonse Balat

ARCHITEKTUR
In der axialen Abfolge von Orangerie, Wintergarten, Kongohaus und Embarcadère bildet der Wintergarten den großartigsten Glaszentralbau Europas. Gleich einer Glocke erheben sich die Eisenrippen dreistufig zur sich im Zentrum am höchsten Punkt befindlichen Königskrone.

PFLANZEN
Wintergarten: Palmen wie die kanarische Dattelpalme, Fächerpalme oder Kentiapalme. Zimtbäume, verschiedene Farnsorten und Blumen wie die Datura oder Paradiesvogelblume.

BESONDERHEITEN
Viele der exotischen Pflanzen stammten aus dem als „Freistaat" berüchtigtem Kongo, der im Privatbesitz Leopolds II. war. Die enormen Ausgaben für den Bau führten zum Konflikt mit dem Parlament. So war der König gezwungen den Komplex einmal im Jahr für zwei Wochen der Öffentlichkeit zugänglich zu machen, was bis heute der Fall ist.

LOCATION
Brussels, Belgium

SIZE
Largest greenhouse complex in Europe. The 36 buildings form a continuous interior space of 1.6 km in length. The highlight of the complex is the circular Winter Garden with a diameter of 56 m and a dome height of approx. 30 m.

ESTABLISHED
1865–1890
design: Alphonse Balat

ARCHITECTURE
The Orangery, Winter Garden, Congo Greenhouse, and the Pier Greenhouse are arranged in sequence along an axis; of the four, the Winter Garden forms the most magnificent central glass building in all of Europe. Like a bell, the iron ribs rise in three tiers to the royal crown at the highest point in the center.

PLANTS
Winter Garden: Palm trees, such as the Canary Island date palm, fan palm, and Kentia palm. Cinnamon trees, different varieties of ferns, and flowers like the datura and bird of paradise.

ADDITIONAL NOTES
Many of the exotic plants came from the Congo "Free State", which became infamous during the time that it was privately owned by Leopold II. The enormous expenses for the construction led to conflict with the parliament. As a result, the king was forced to open the complex to the public once a year for two weeks, a custom which continues to this day.

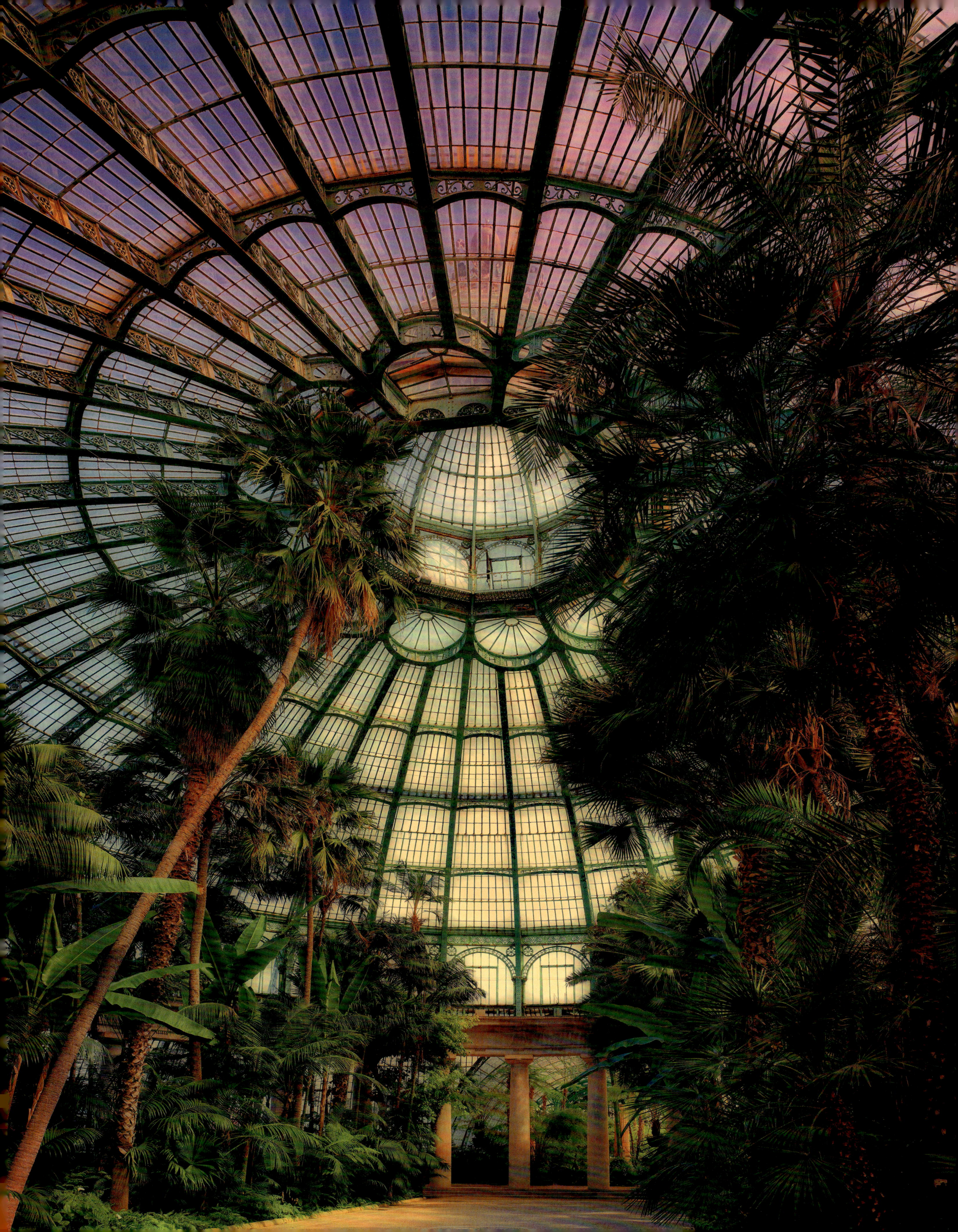

Royal Garden Brussels X
Royal Garden Brussels VIII ▼
Royal Garden Brussels III ▼▼

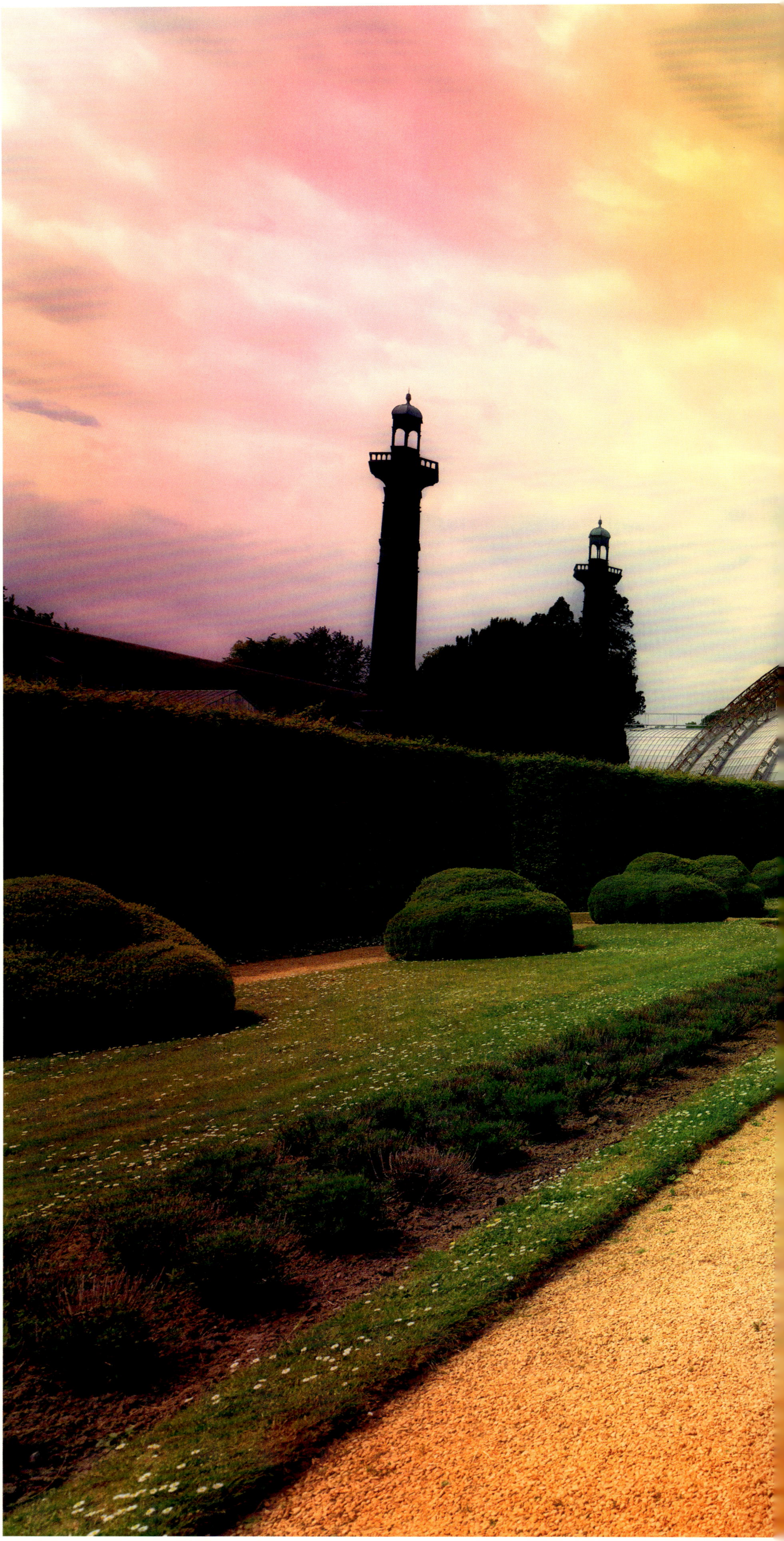

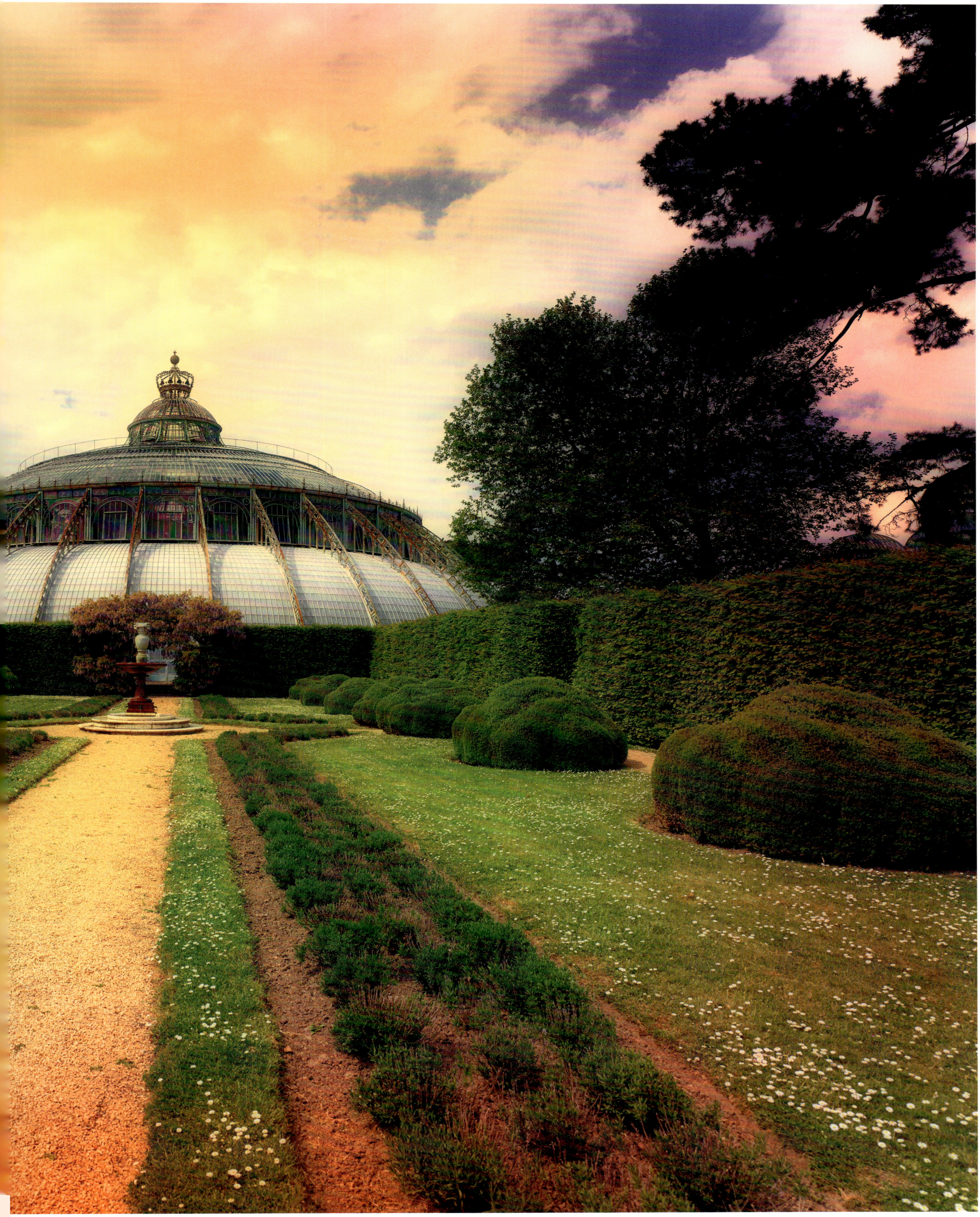

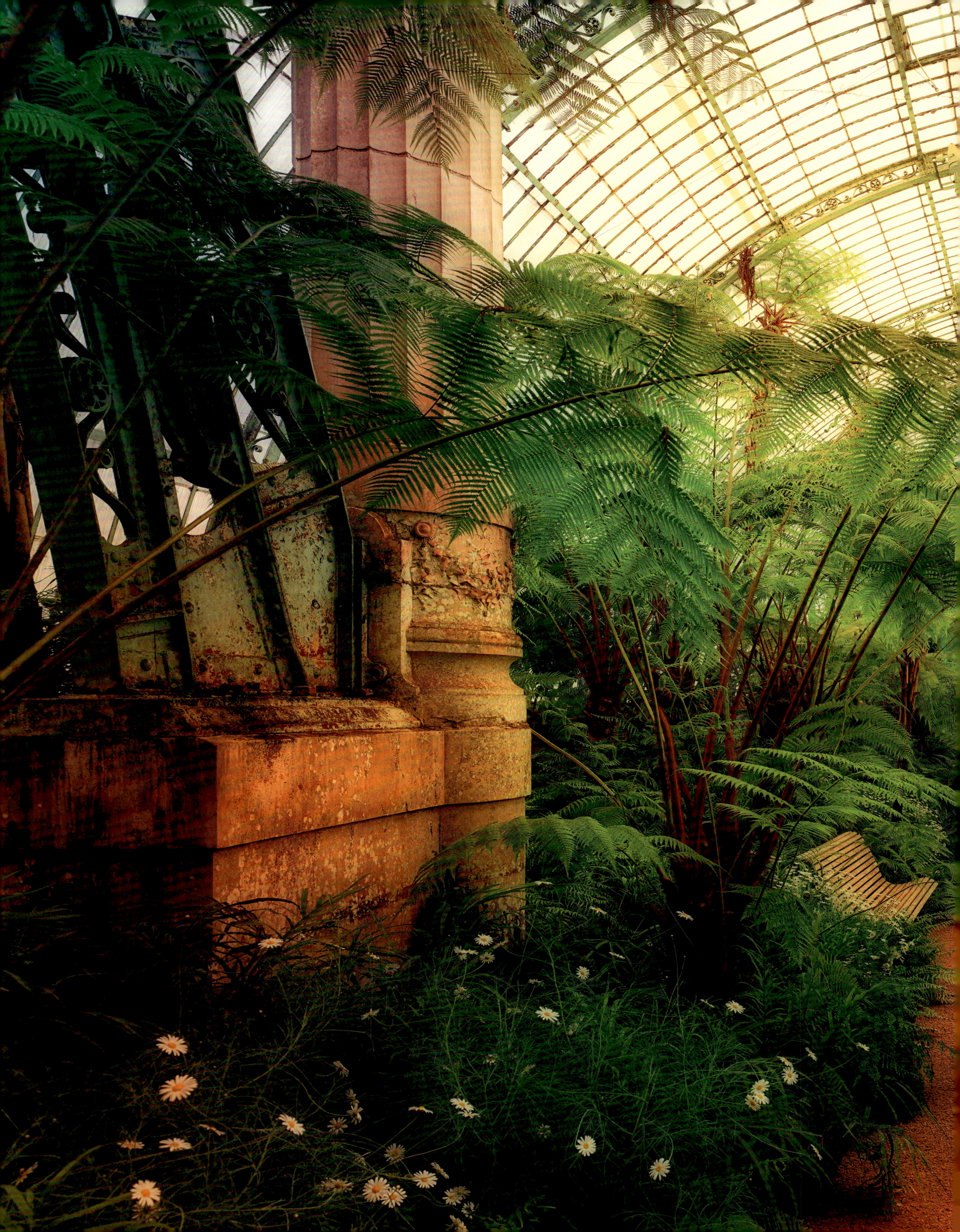

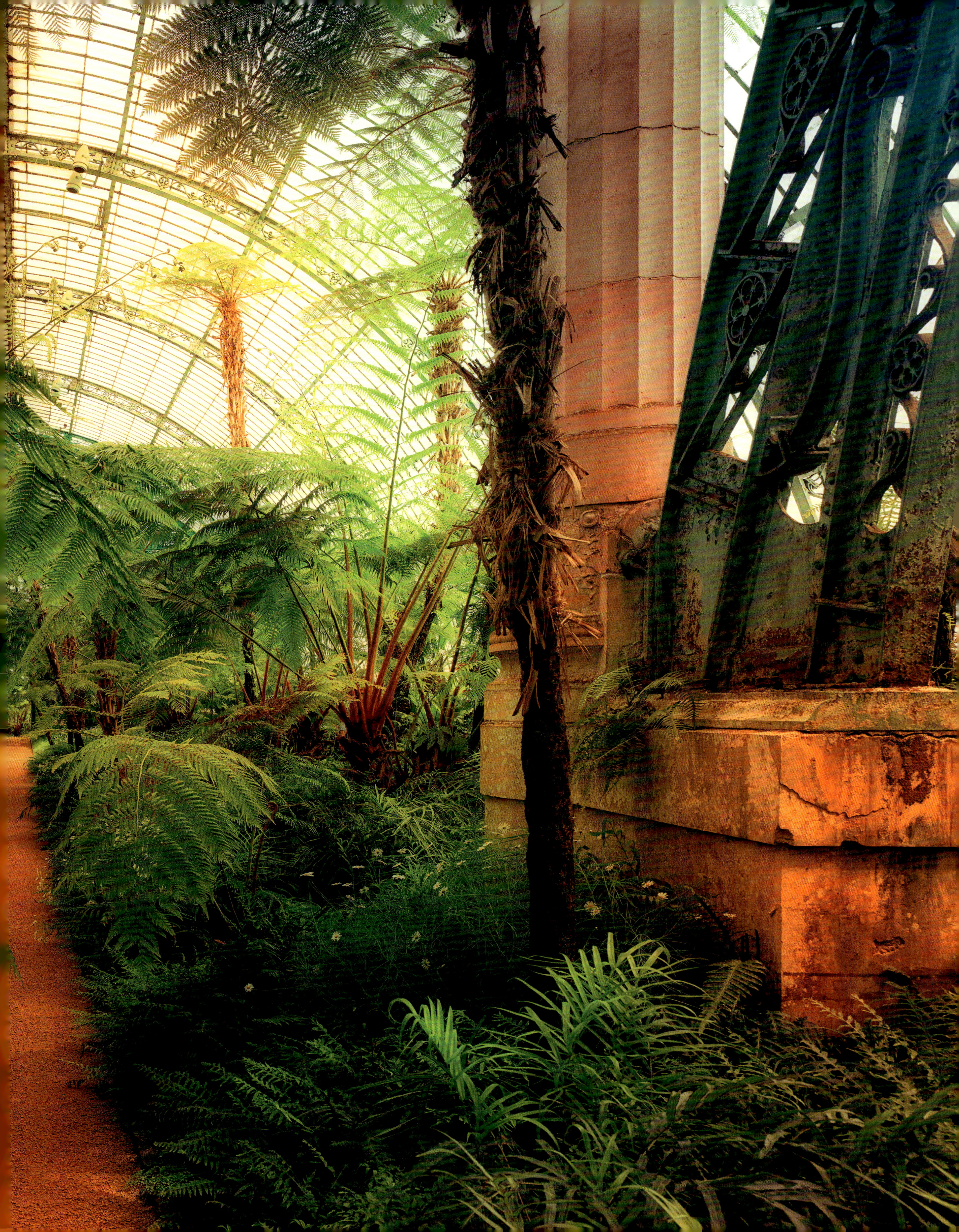

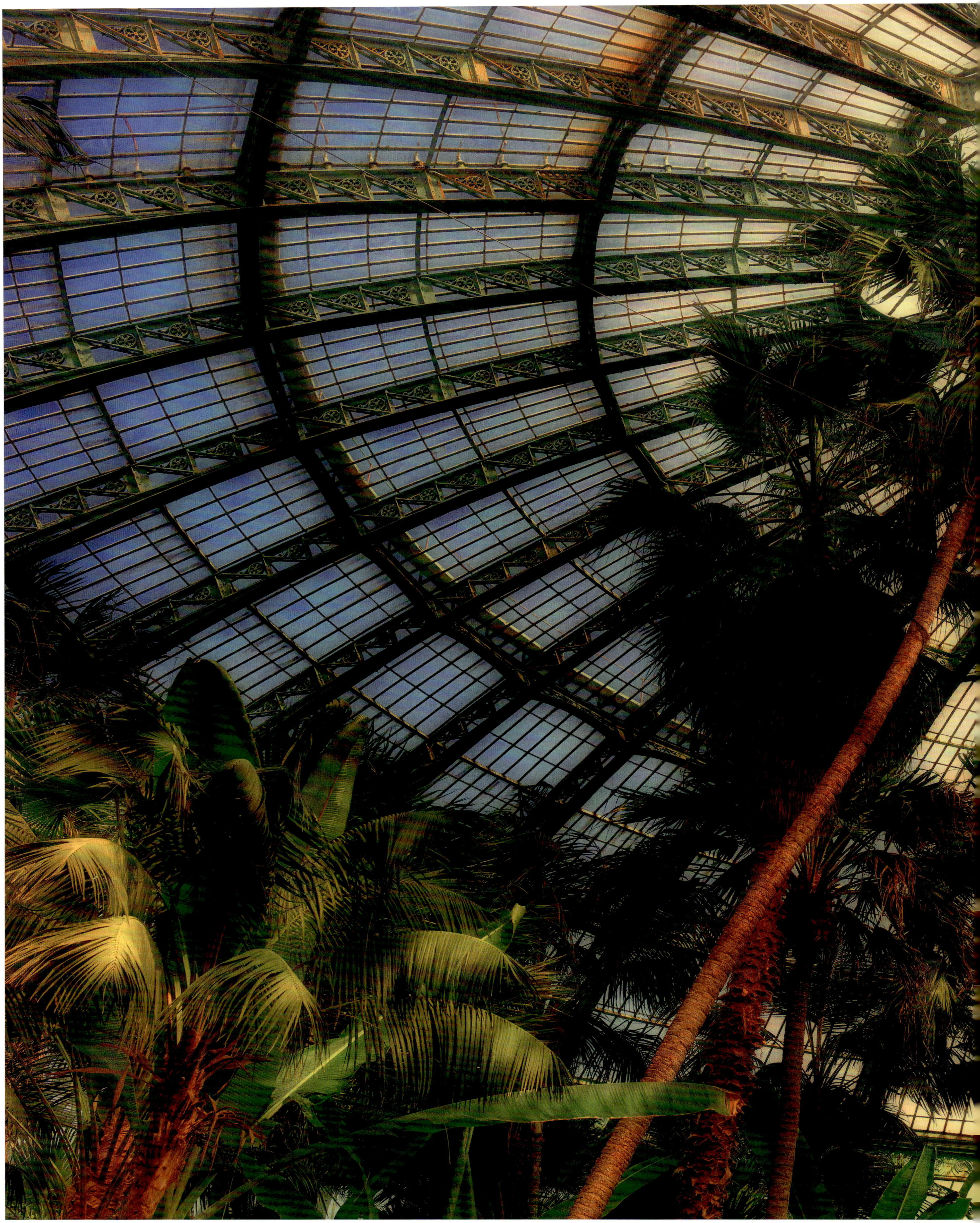

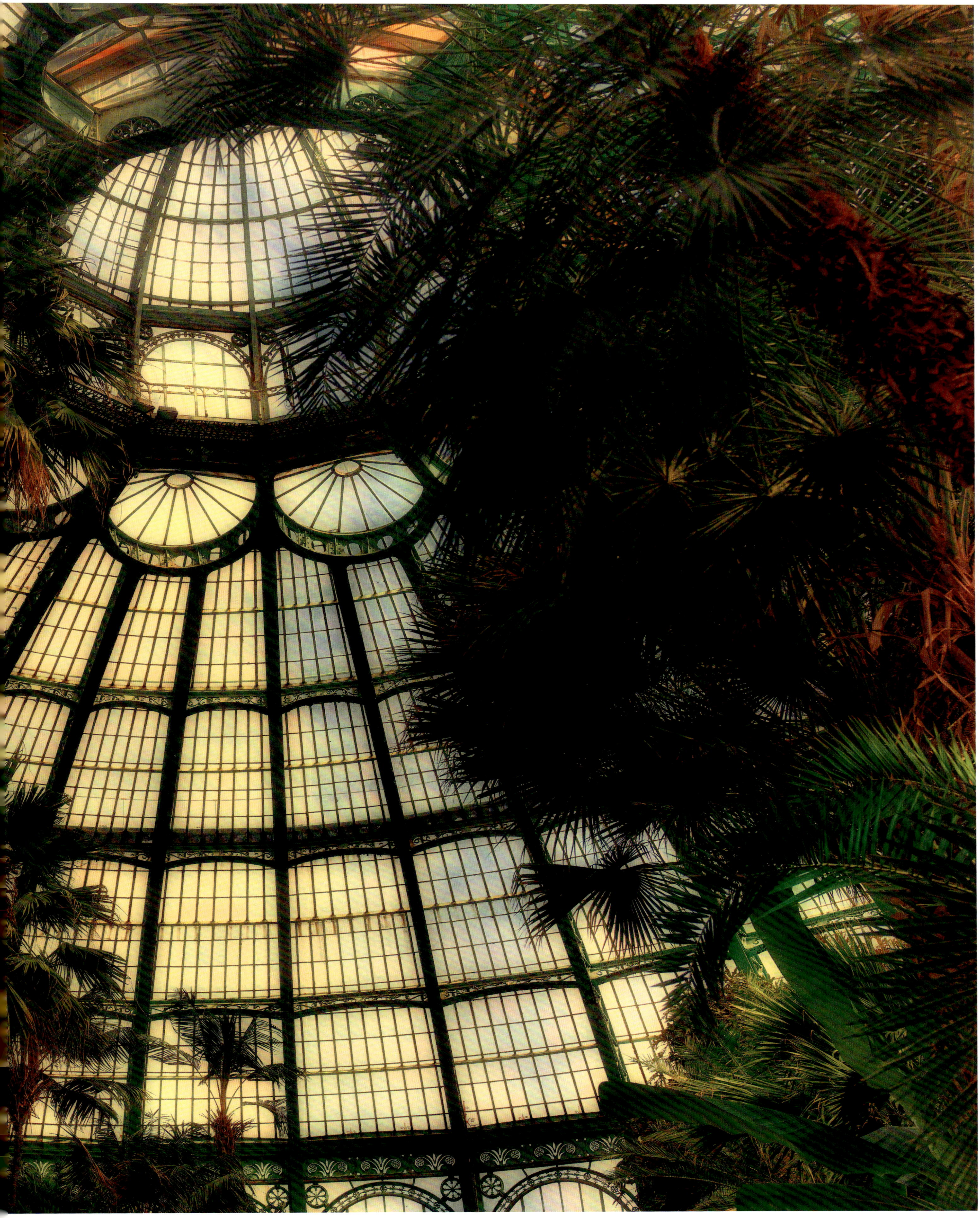

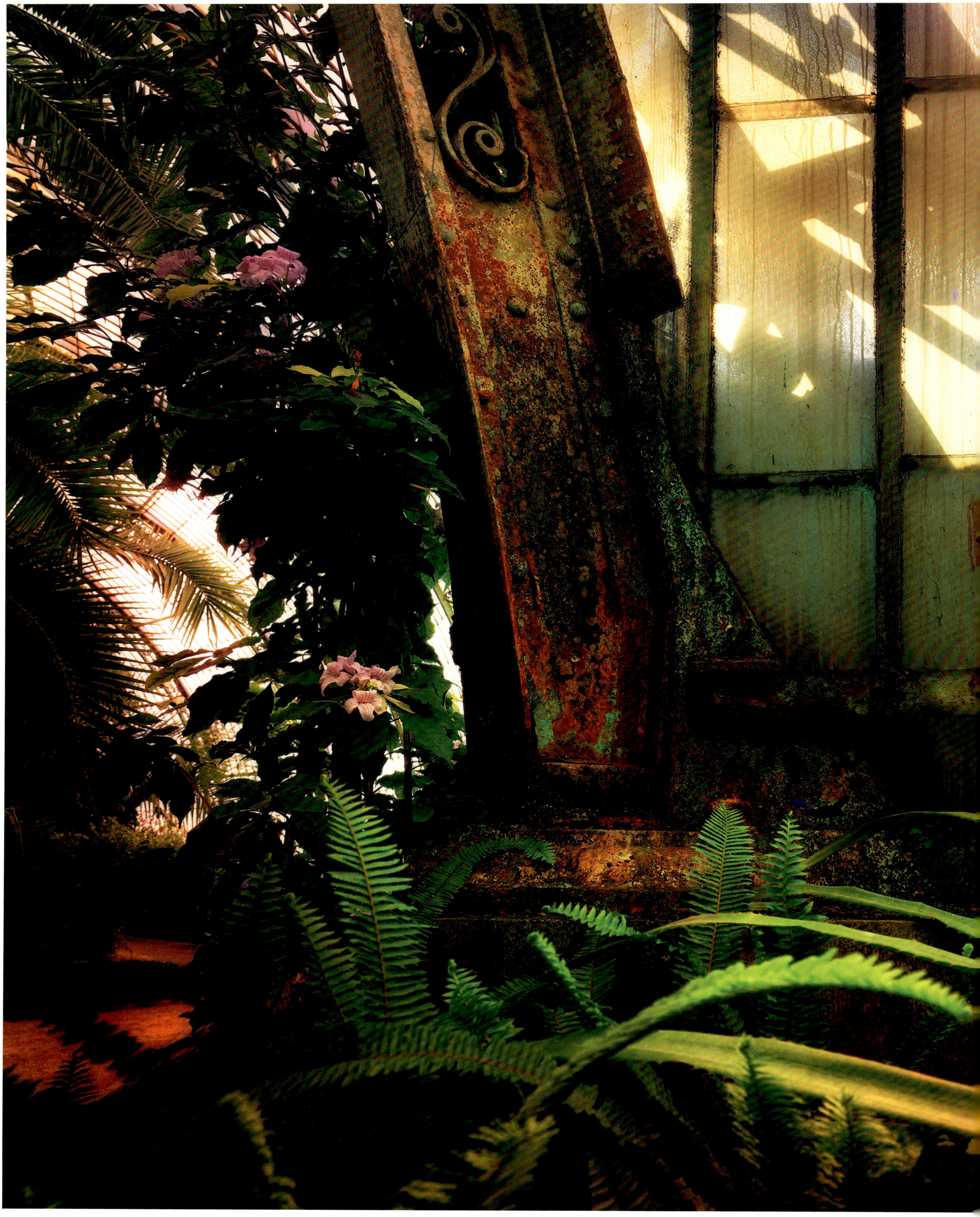

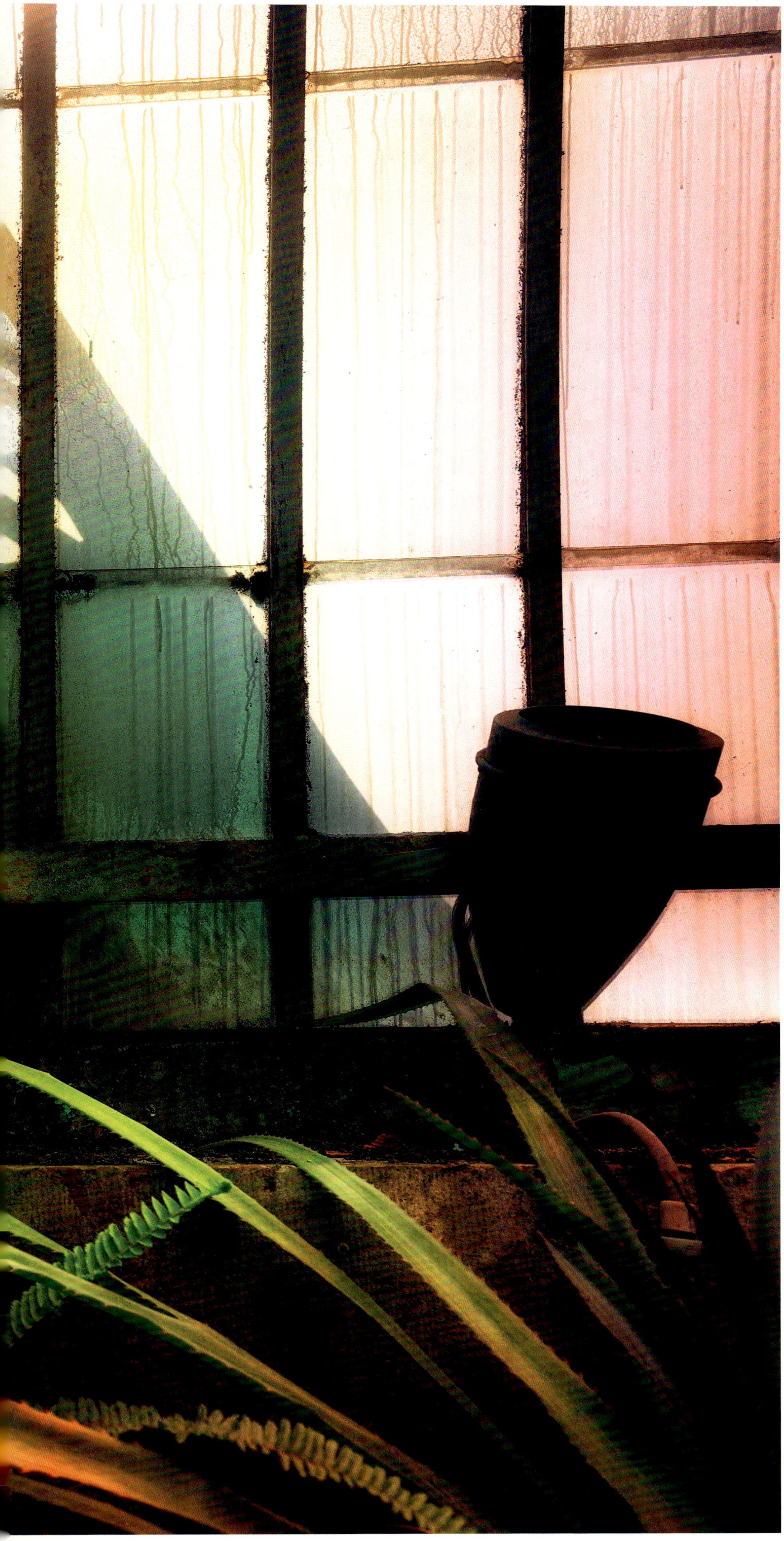

Royal Garden Brussels IV
Royal Garden Brussels VII ▼

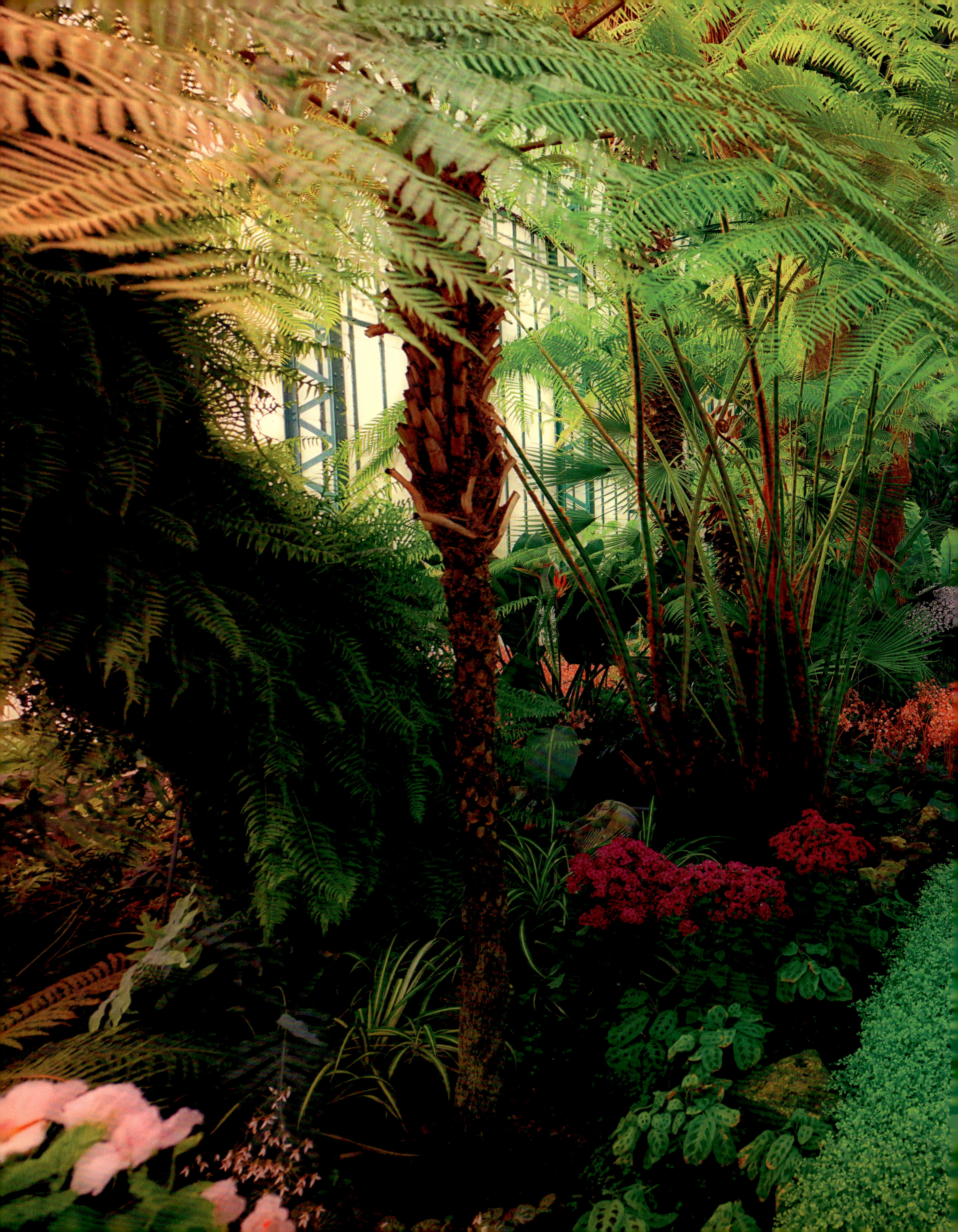

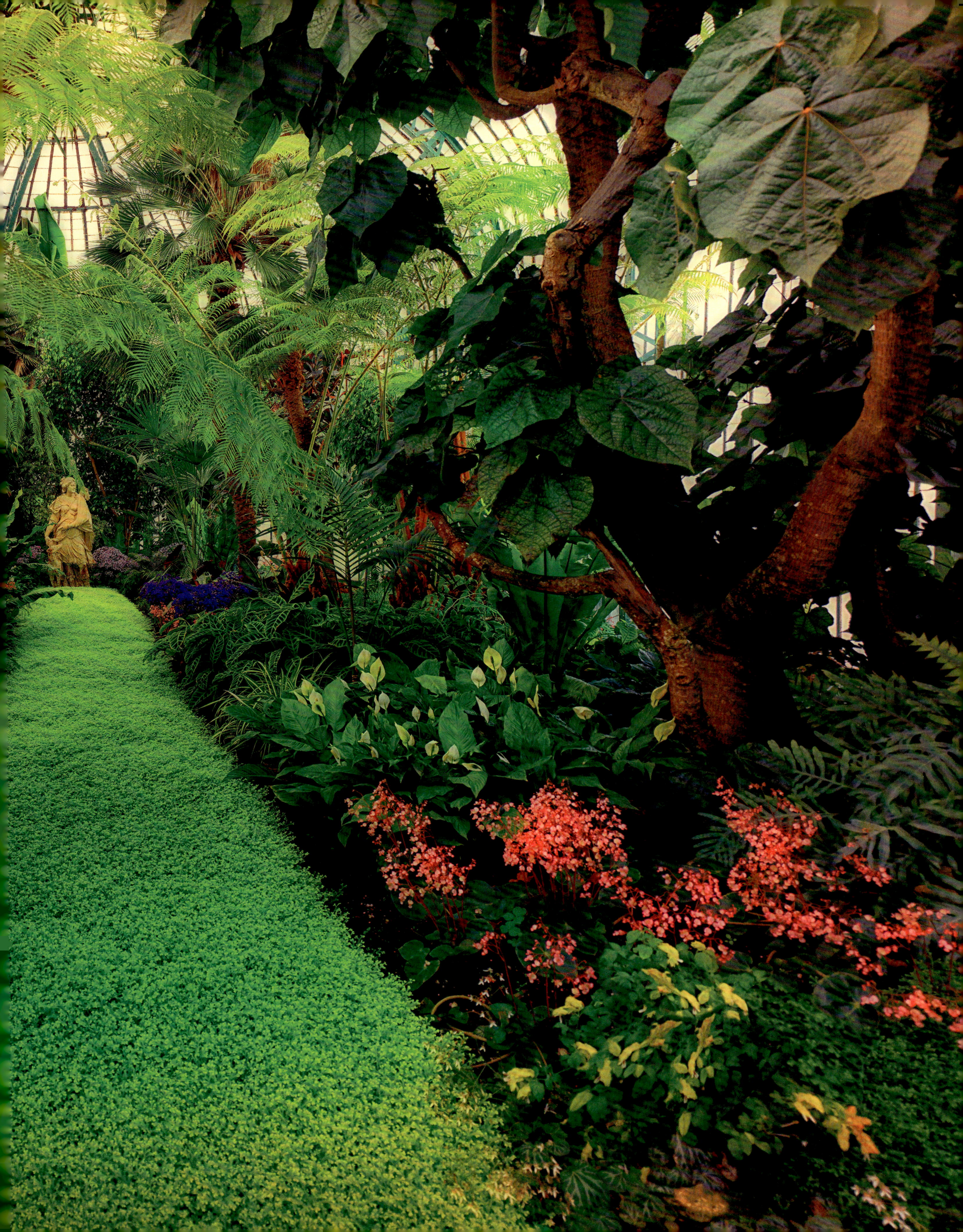

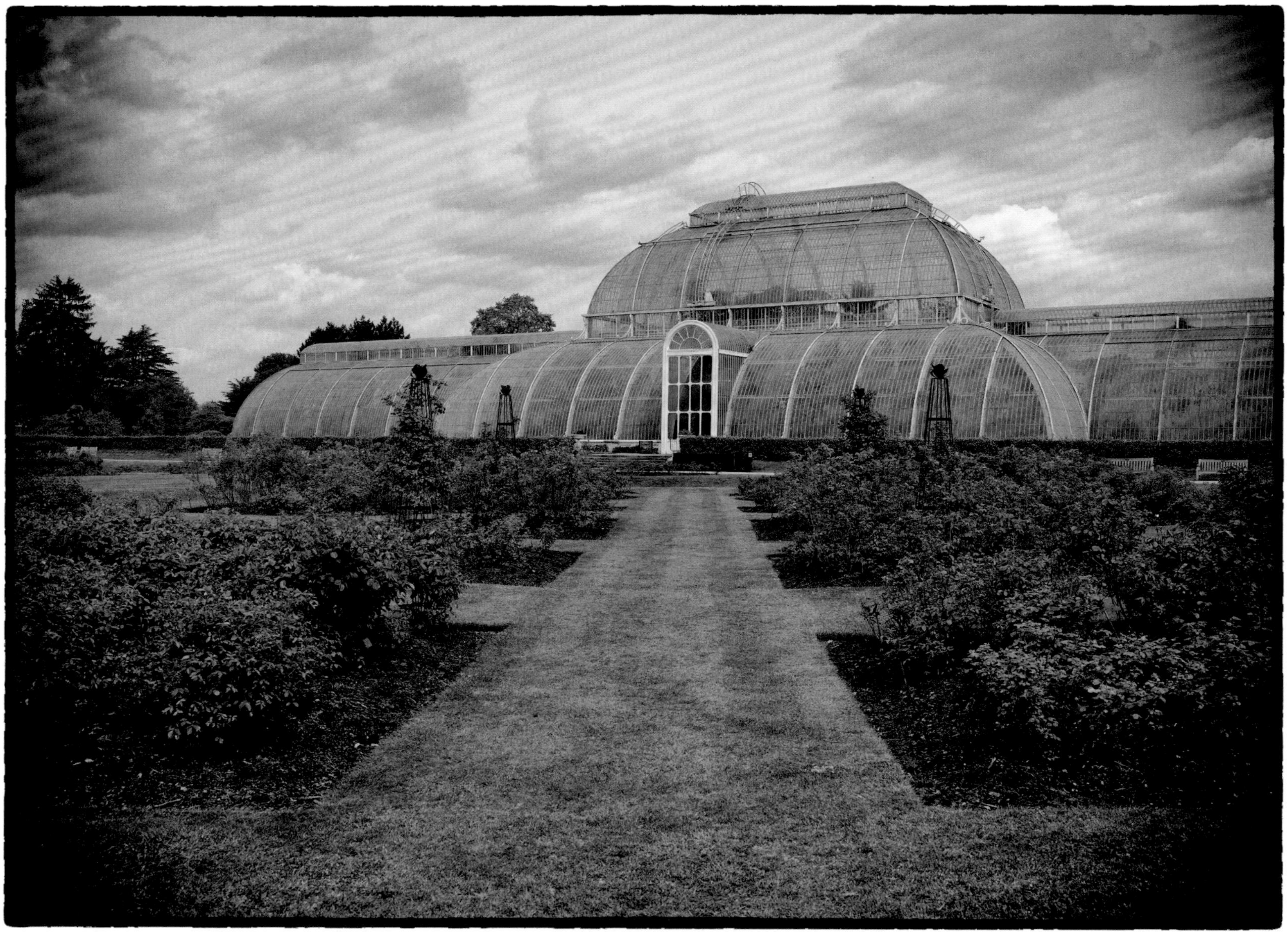

ROYAL BOTANIC GARDENS KEW

LONDON

ROYAL BOTANIC GARDENS KEW

ORT
Kew, London, England,
Vereinigtes Königreich Großbritannien

LOCATION
Kew, London, England,
United Kingdom, Great Britain

GRÖSSE
Mehrere Gewächshäuser von verschiedener Größe.
Palmenhaus:
110,5 m lang; 30,05 m breit; 19,20 m hoch
Temperiertes Gewächshaus:
5 Gebäude, Gesamtlänge 177 m
Mittleres Haus:
64 m lang; 42 m breit; 18 m hoch

SIZE
A number of greenhouses of various sizes.
Palm House:
110.5 m long; 30.05 m wide; 19.20 m high
Temperate House:
5 buildings, total length 177 m
Central house:
64 m long; 42 m wide; 18 m high

ENTSTEHUNG
Palmenhaus: 1844–1848
Entwurf: Richard Turner und Decimus Burton
Temperiertes Gewächshaus: 1859–1863
Entwurf: Decimus Burton

ESTABLISHED
Palm House: 1844–1848
design: Richard Turner and Decimus Burton
Temperate House: 1859–1863
design: Decimus Burton

ARCHITEKTUR
Die verschiedenen Glashäuser unterscheiden sich in ihrer äußeren Gestalt. So stellt das Palmenhaus mit seinen gebogenen, verglasten Streben ein perfektes Beispiel für ein kurvenlineares Gewächshaus dar. Im Gegensatz zu diesem gibt es beim temperierten Gewächshaus eine architektonische Unterscheidung von Wand und Dach. Die flach geneigten Glasdachflächen liegen auf einer gemauerten, durchfensterten und dekorierten Steinwand auf.

ARCHITECTURE
The various glass houses differ in terms of their external appearance. With its curved, glazed struts, for example, the Palm House is a perfect example of a curvilinear greenhouse. In contrast to this, the temperate greenhouse creates an architectural distinction between the wall and the roof. The sloped glass roofs rest on a stonework wall featuring windows and decorative elements.

PFLANZEN
Unter anderem Afrikanische Ölpalmen, Kautschukbäume oder Palmfarne sowie Raketenblumen oder Nadelkissen

PLANTS
A wide variety of plants, including African oil palms, rubber trees, palm ferns, as well as rocket flowers, and pincushions

BESONDERHEITEN
Der ursprünglich Königliche Botanische Garten wurde 1841 in staatlichen Besitz überführt. Seit dem 18. Jahrhundert wurden Expeditionen in die ganze Welt geschickt, um botanische Besonderheiten zu sammeln.

ADDITIONAL NOTES
The original Royal Botanical Garden was transferred to state ownership in 1841. Starting in the 18th century, expeditions were sent all over the world to collect botanical curiosities.

Kew Garden I · Kew Garden VII ▼

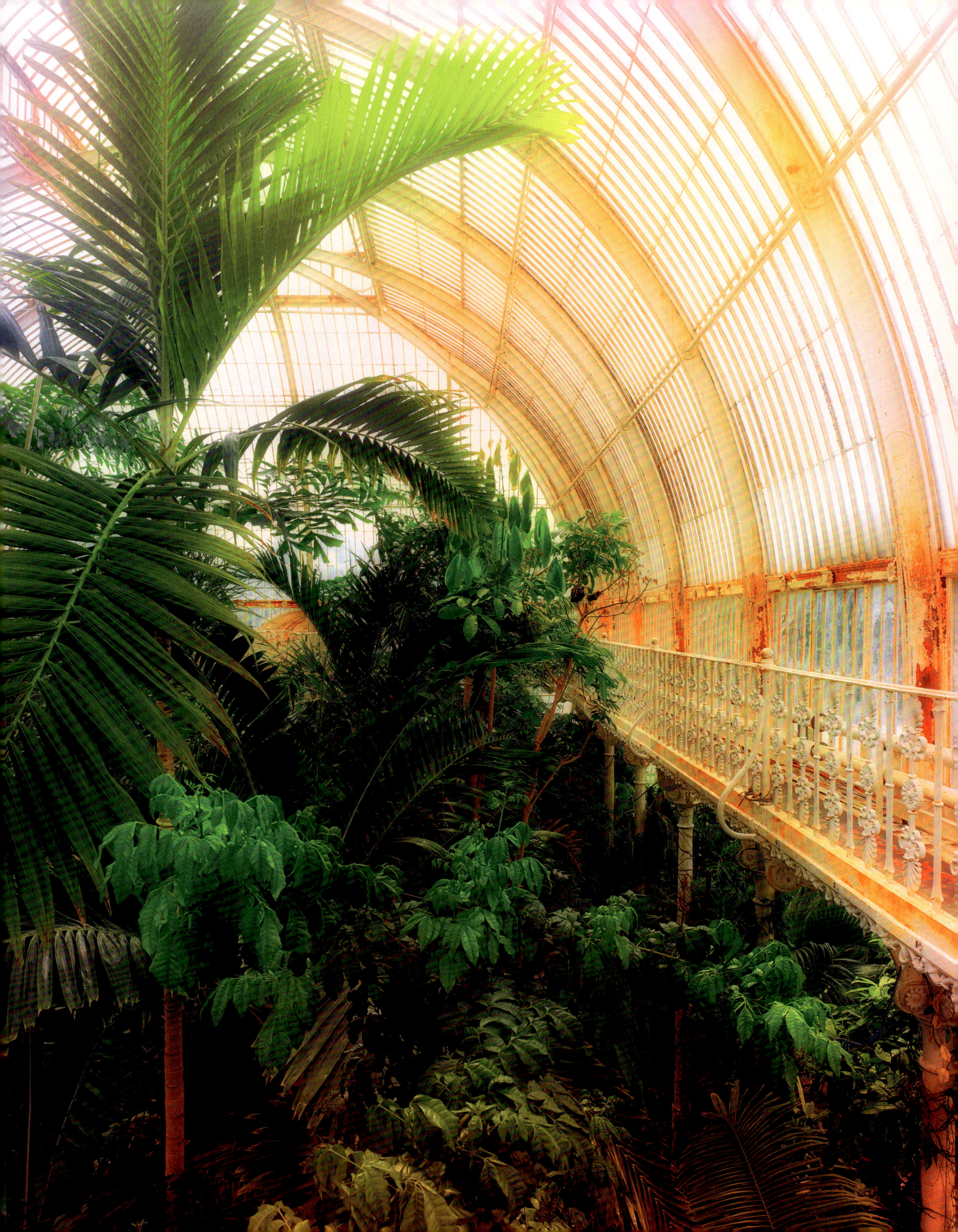

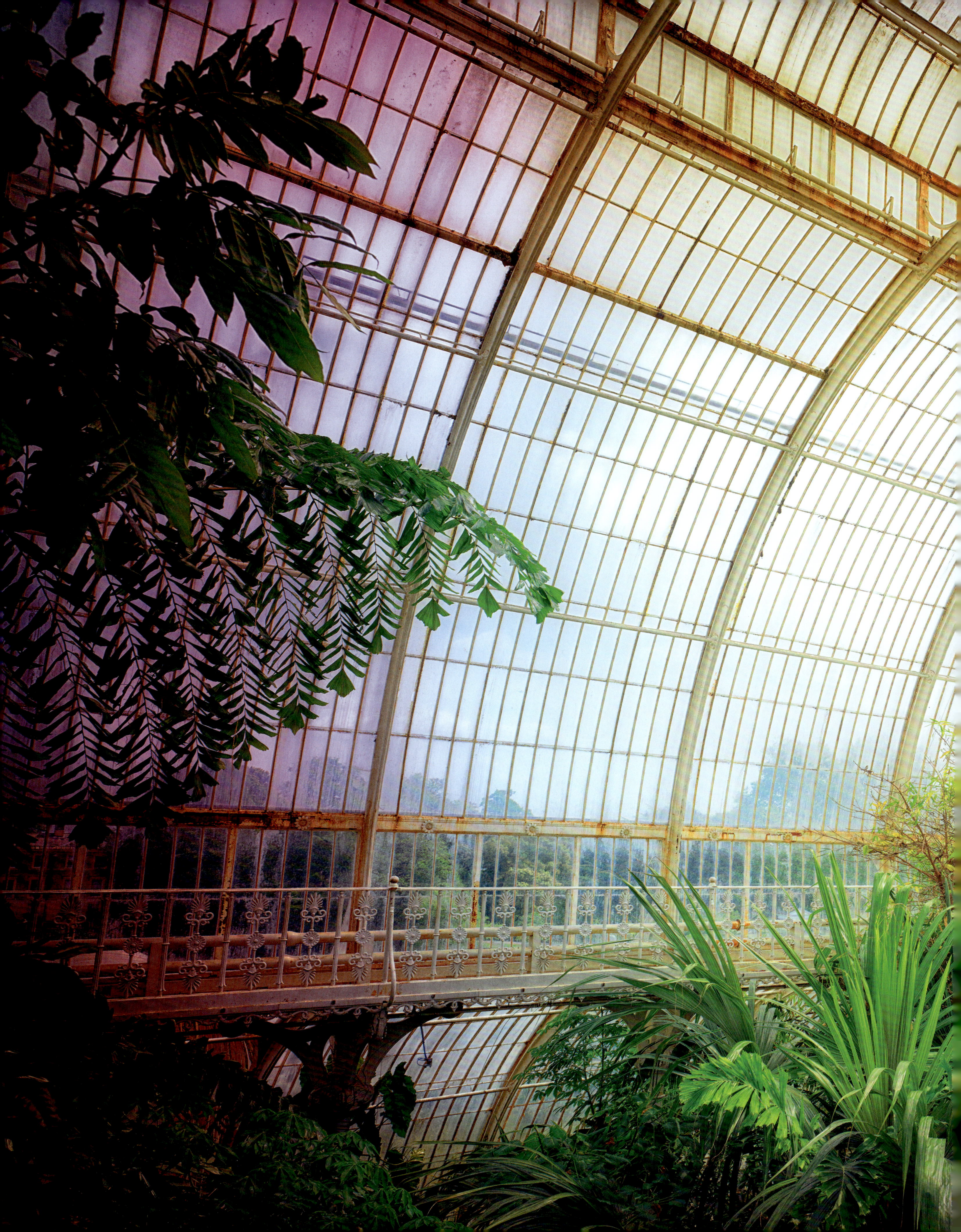

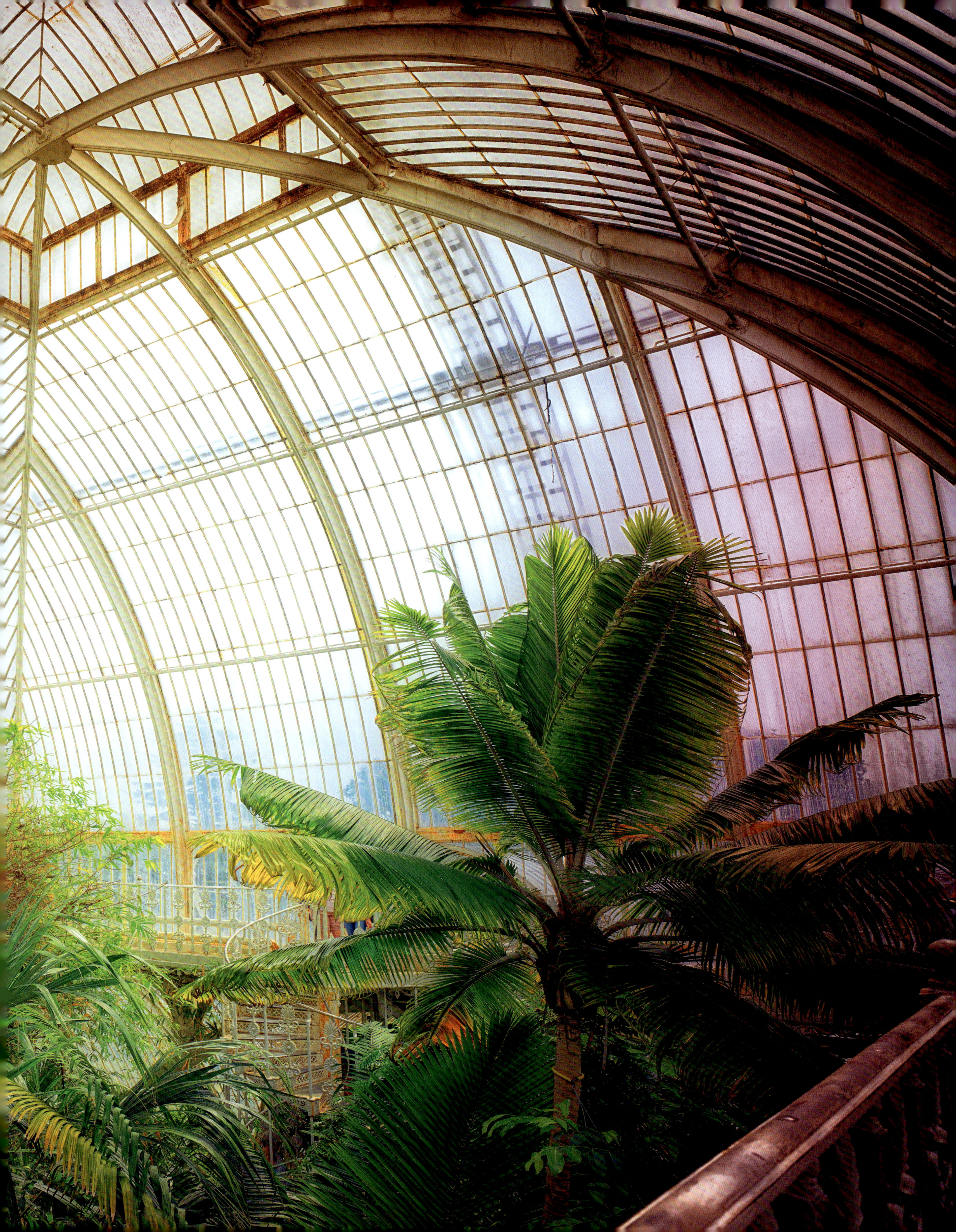

Kew Garden VI

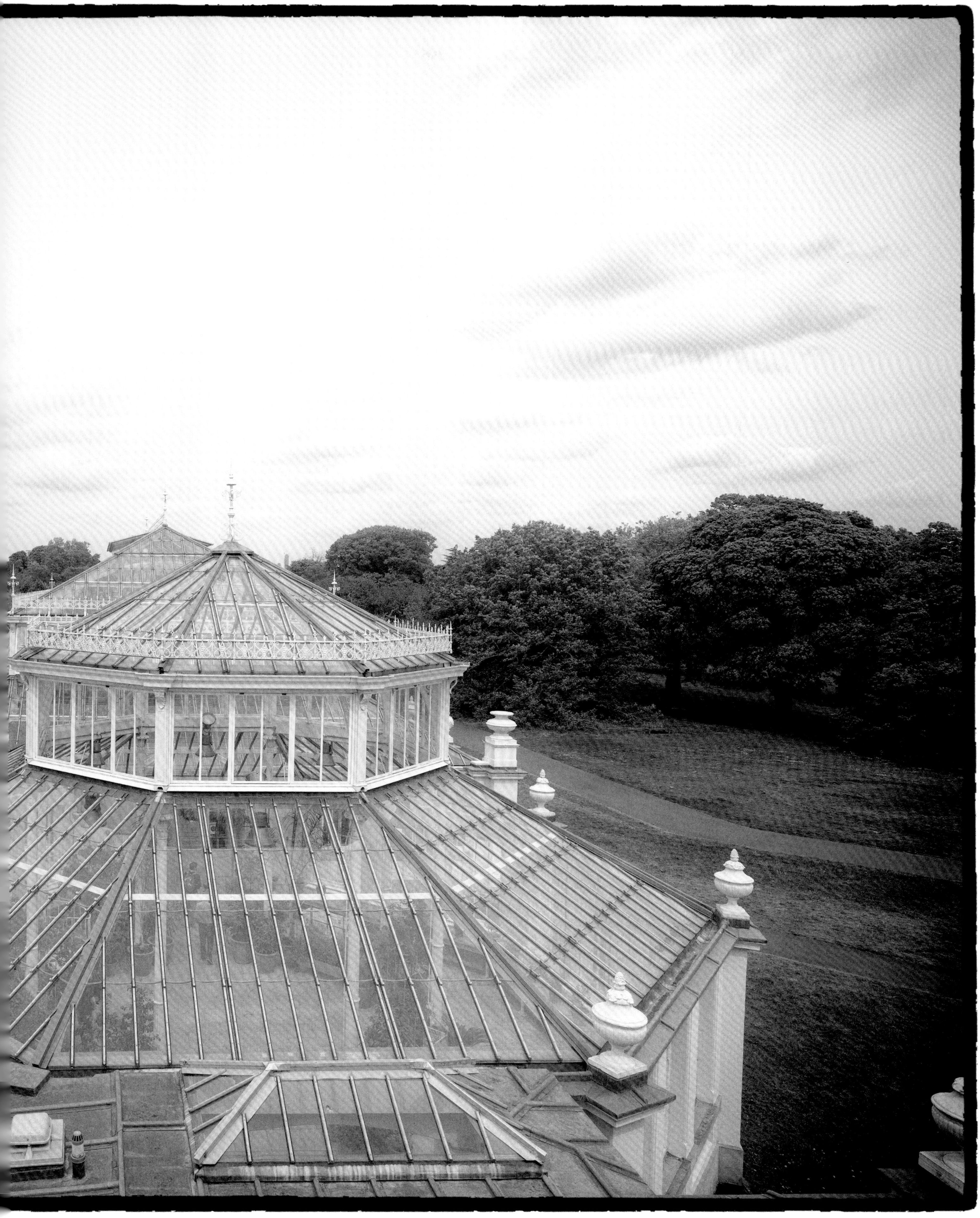

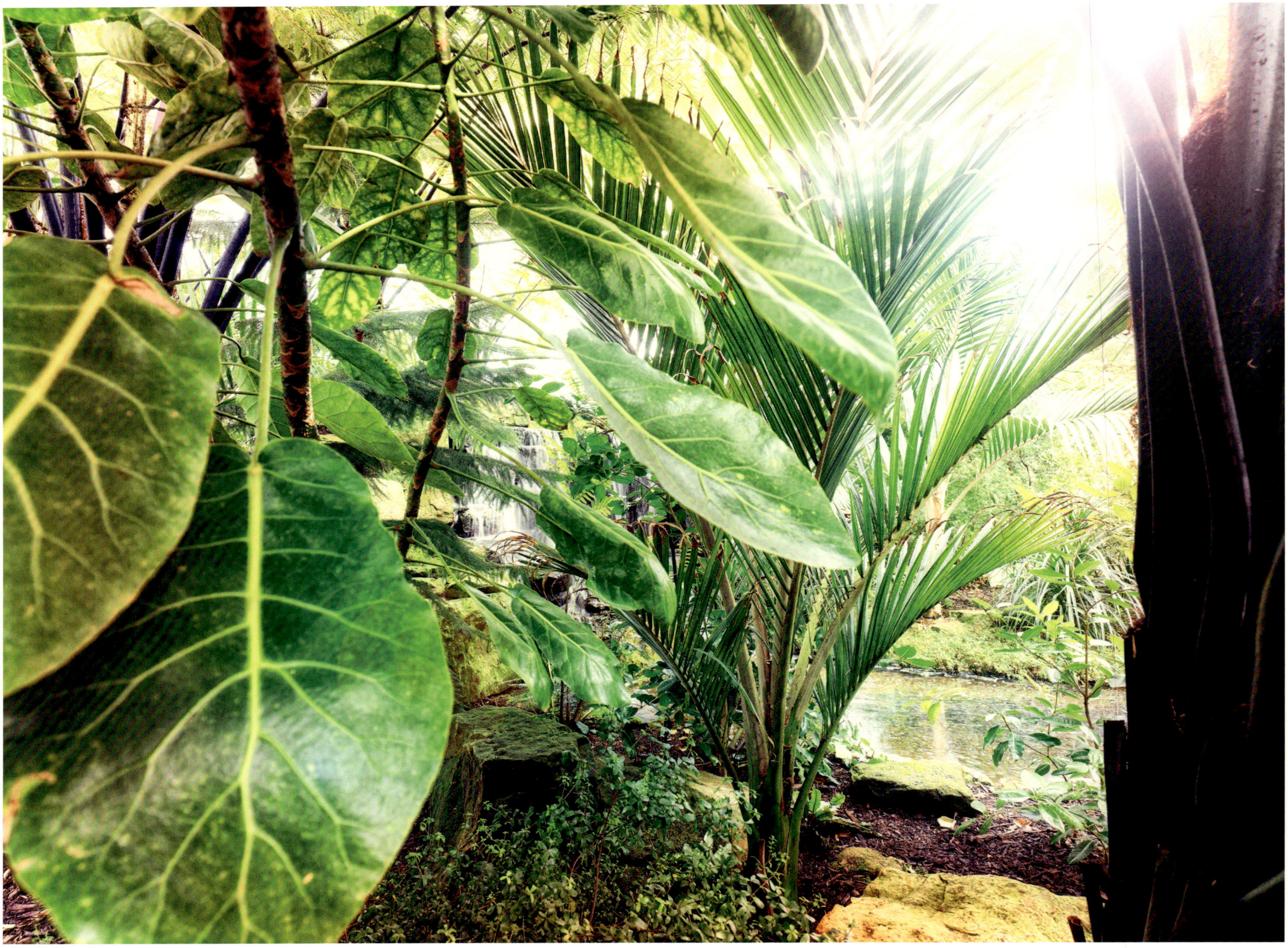

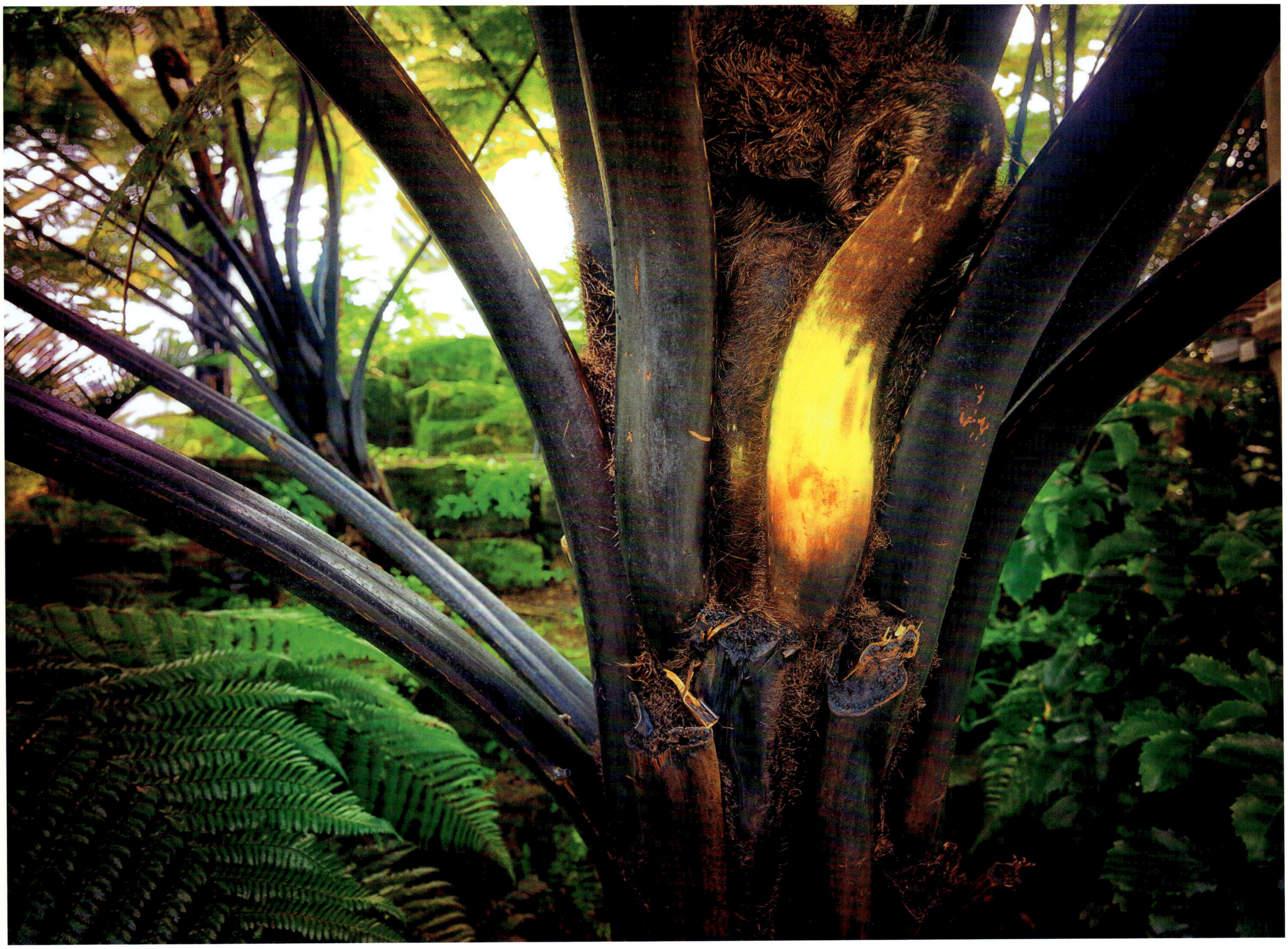

Kew Garden XVII

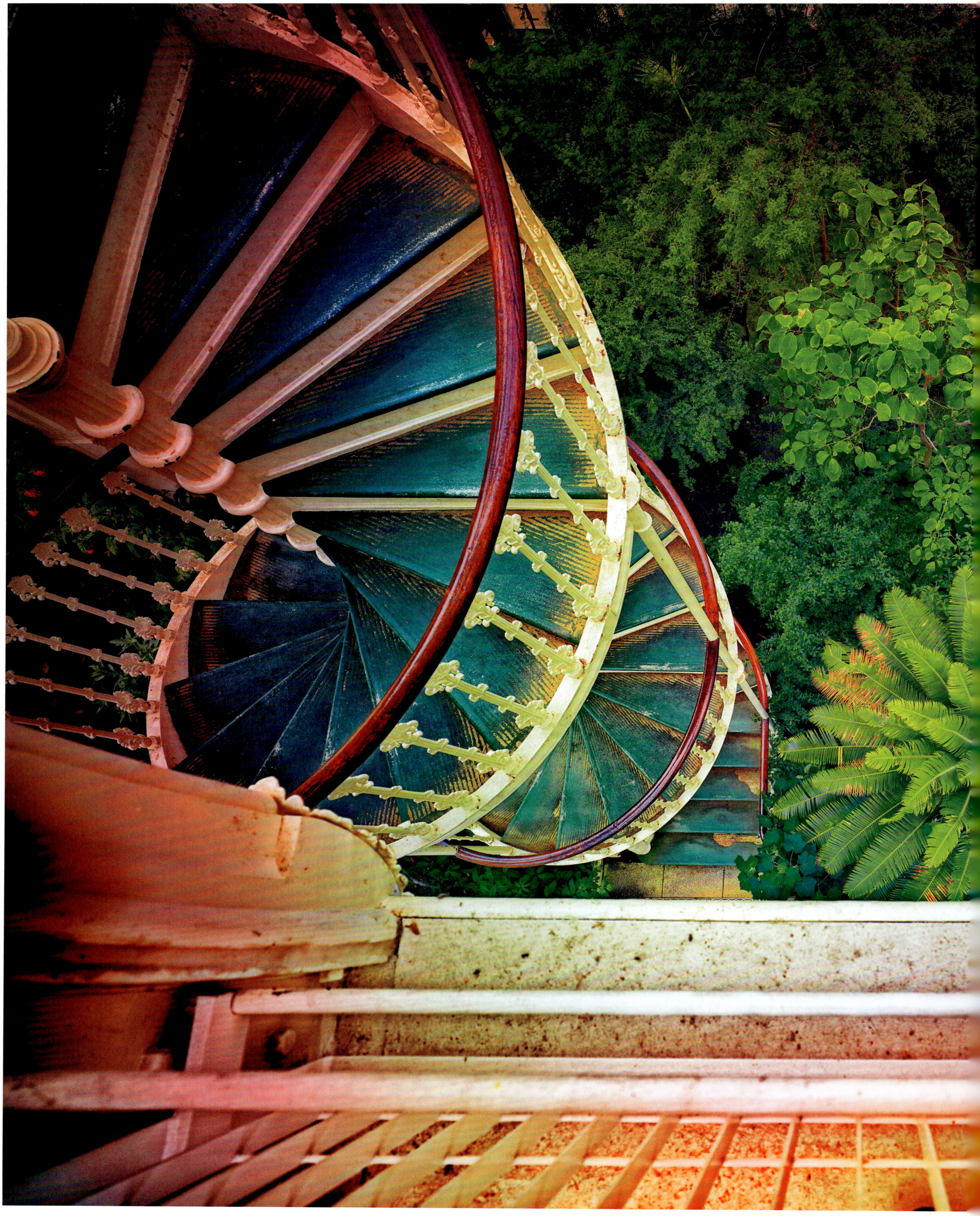

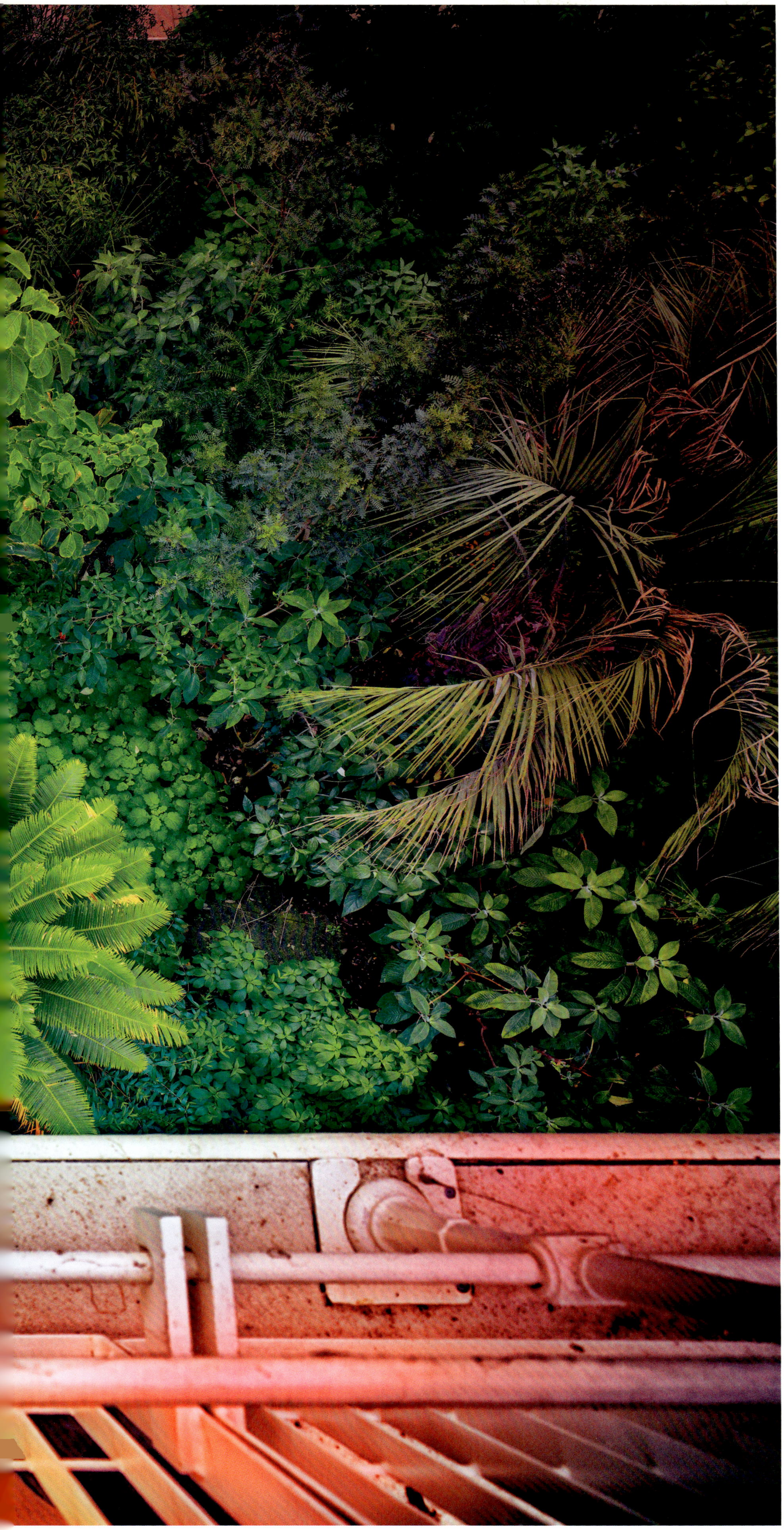

Kew Garden XII
Kew Garden X ▼

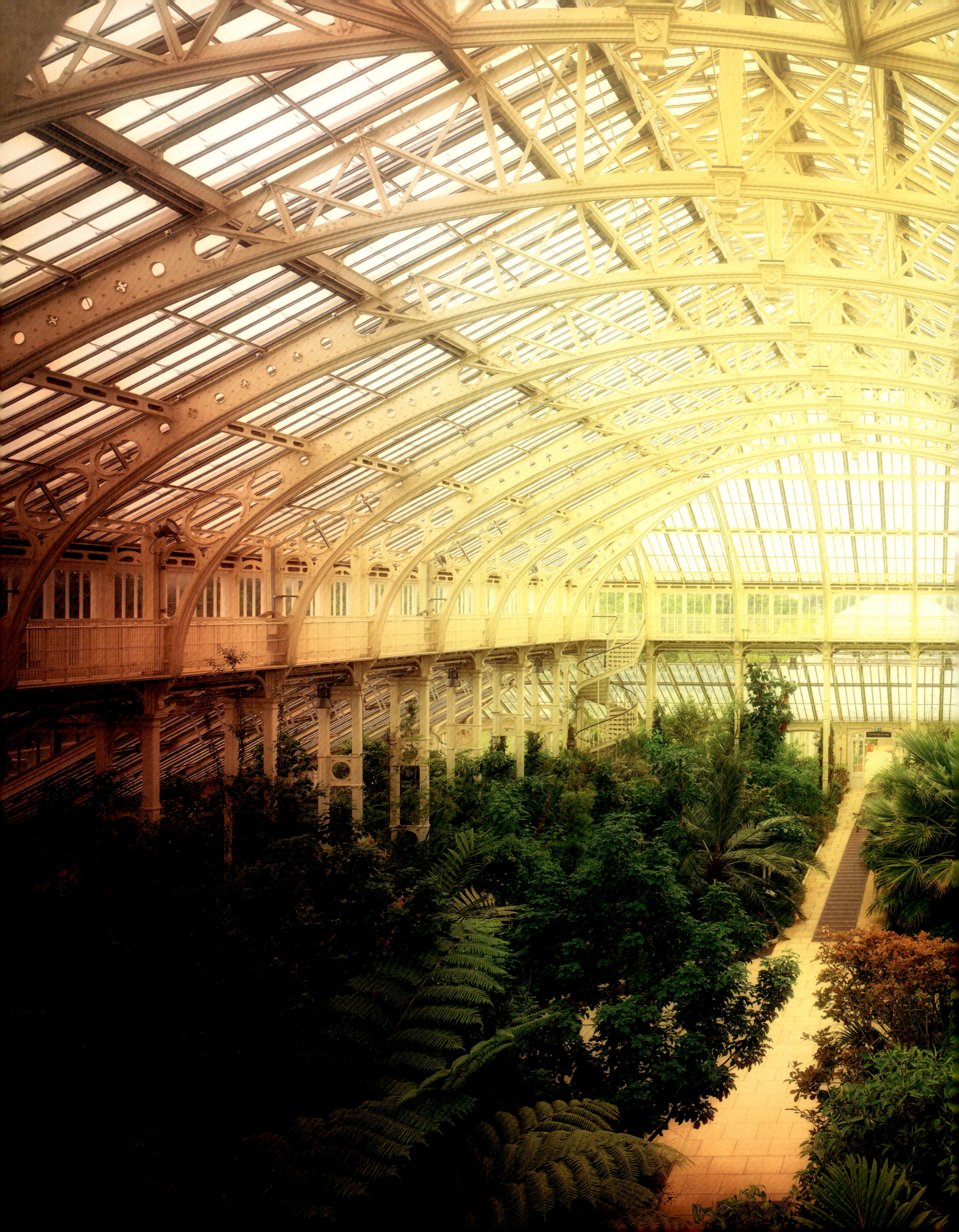

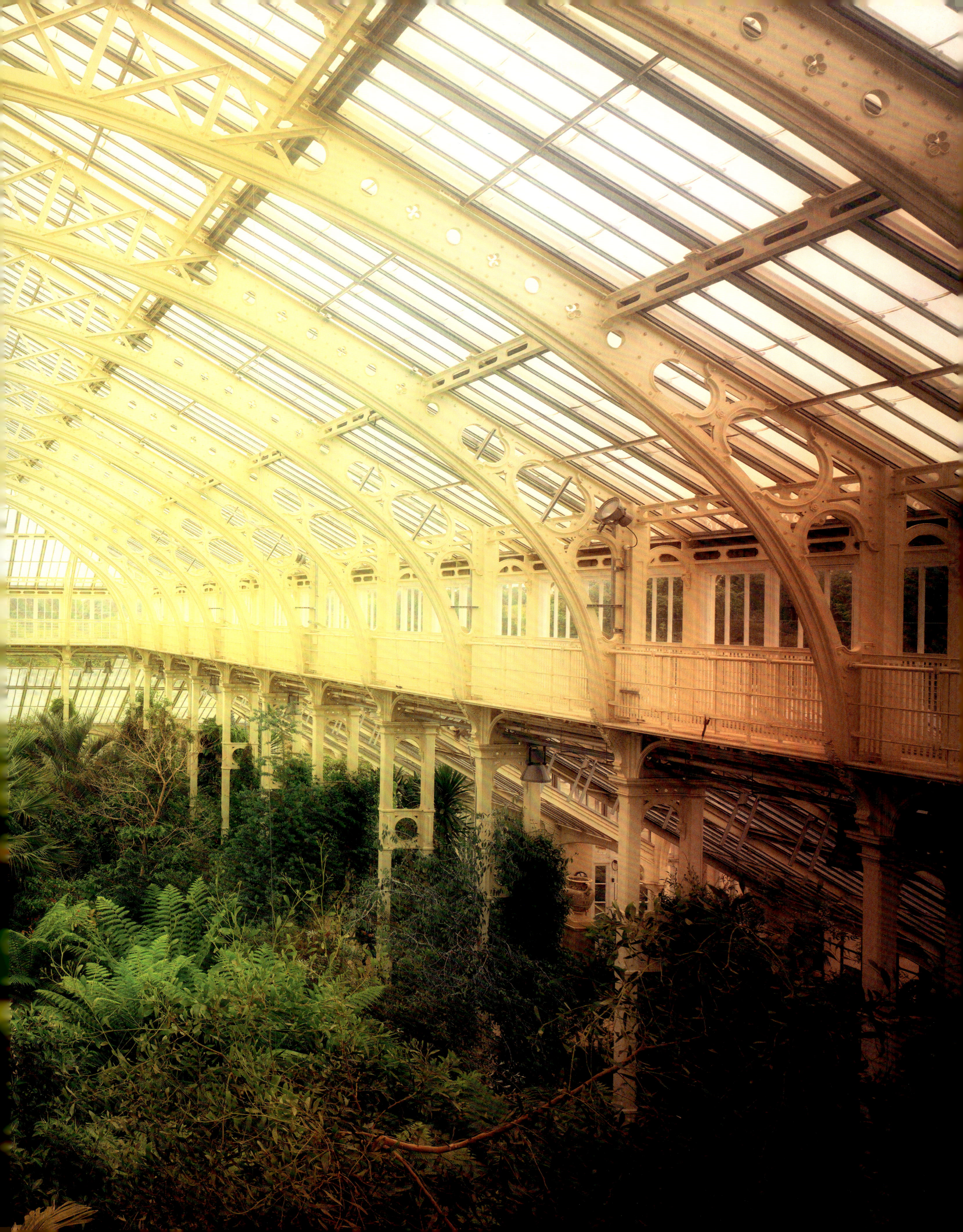

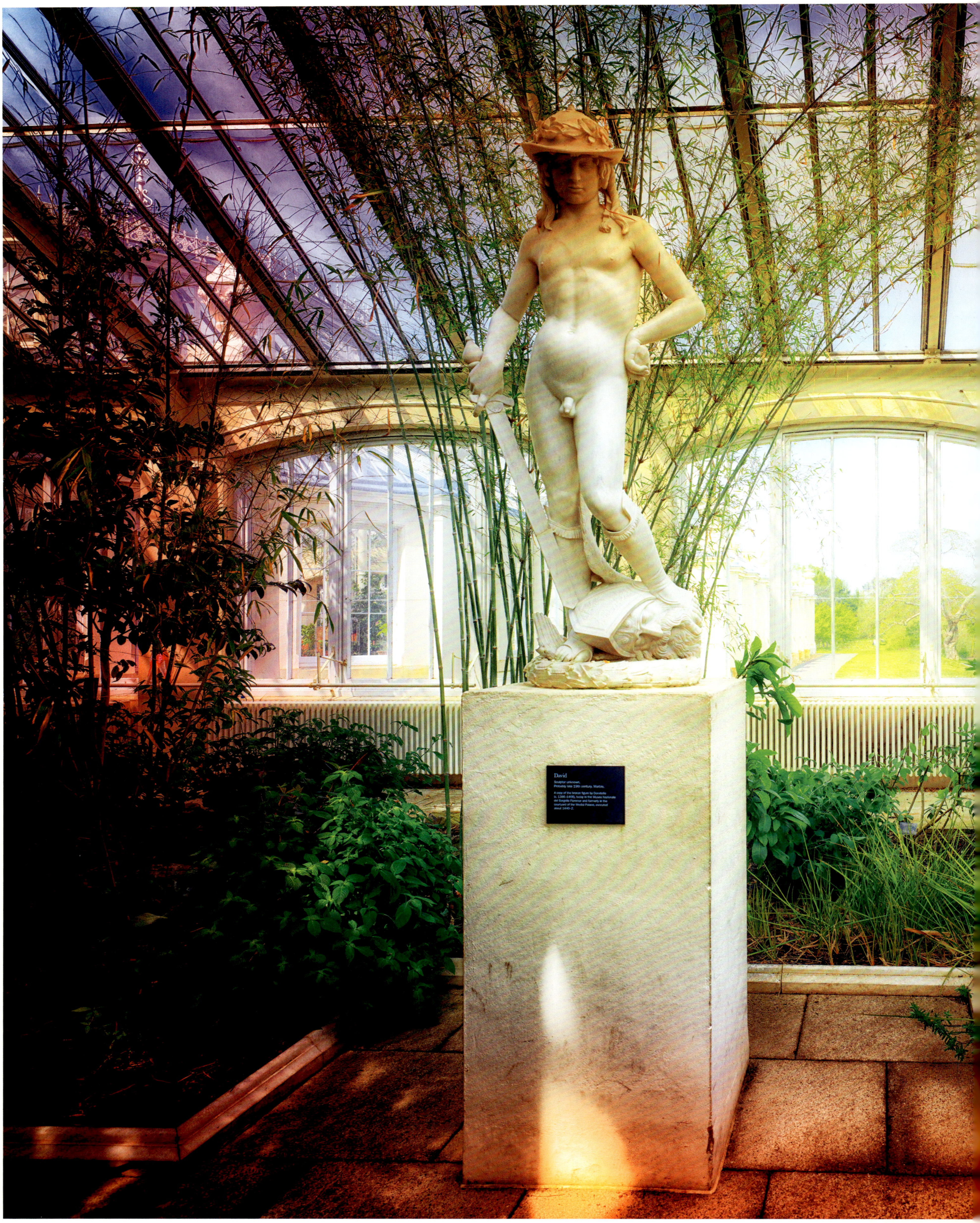
David
Sculptor unknown.

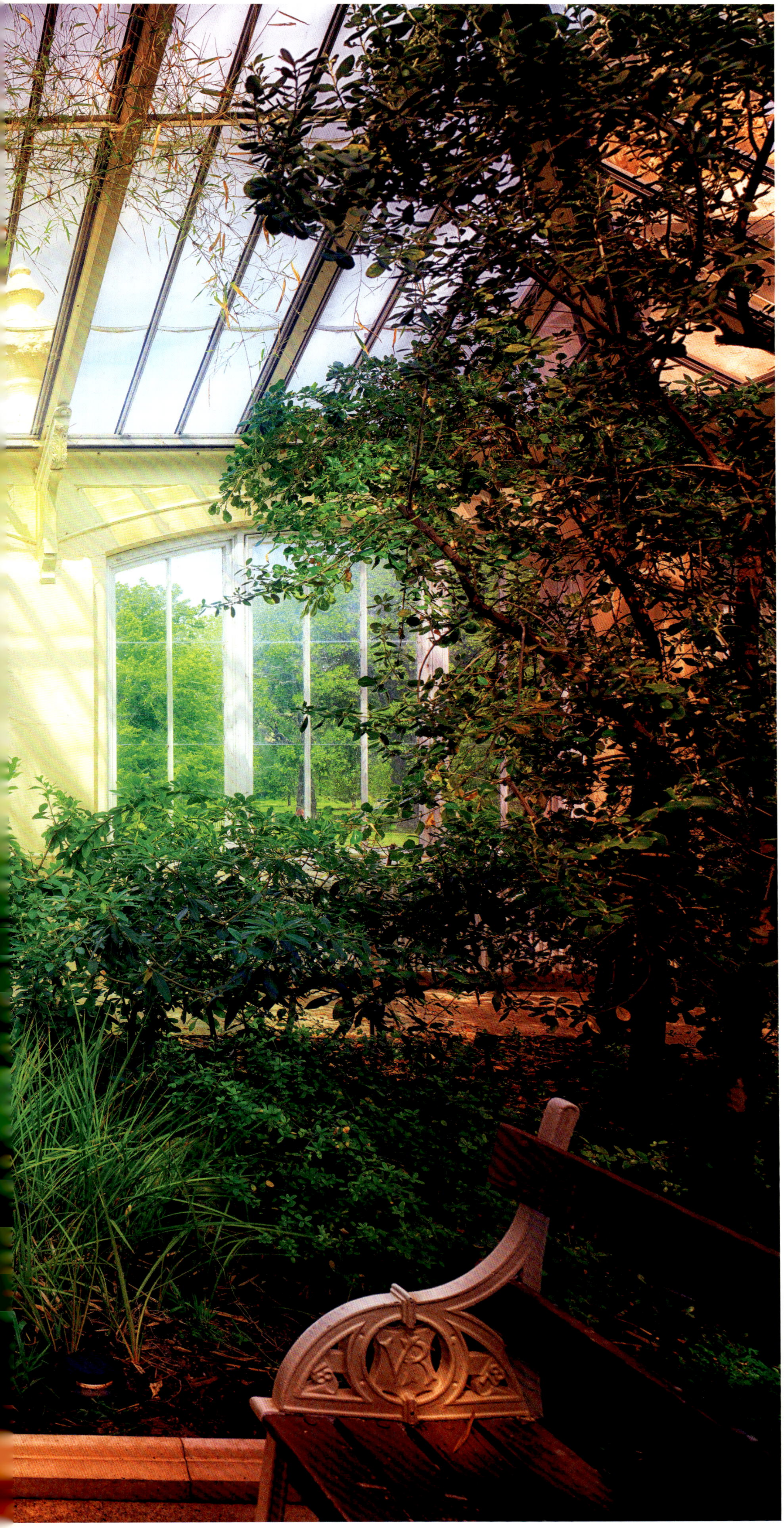

Kew Garden XVI

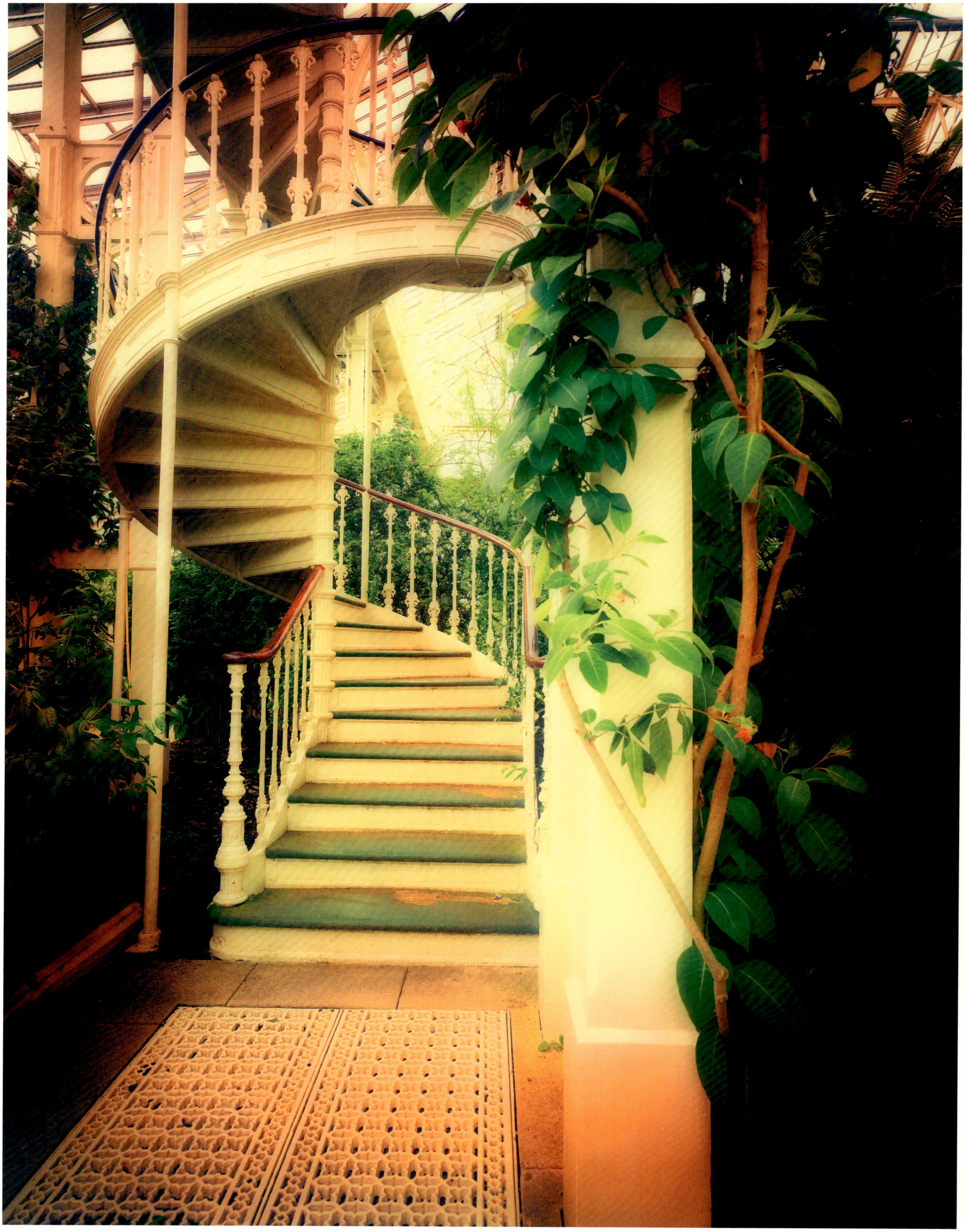

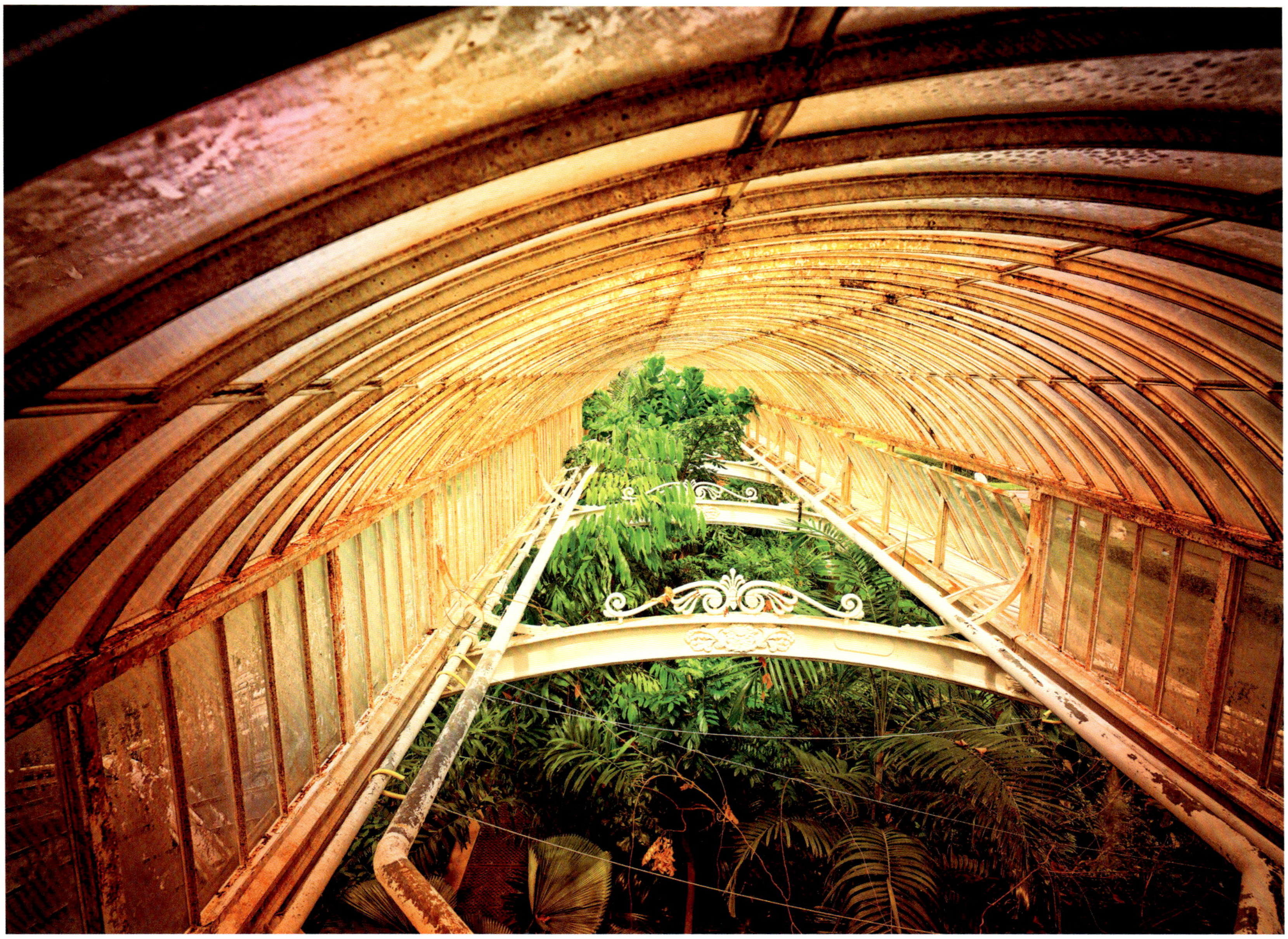

Kew Garden XIII • Kew Garden VIII

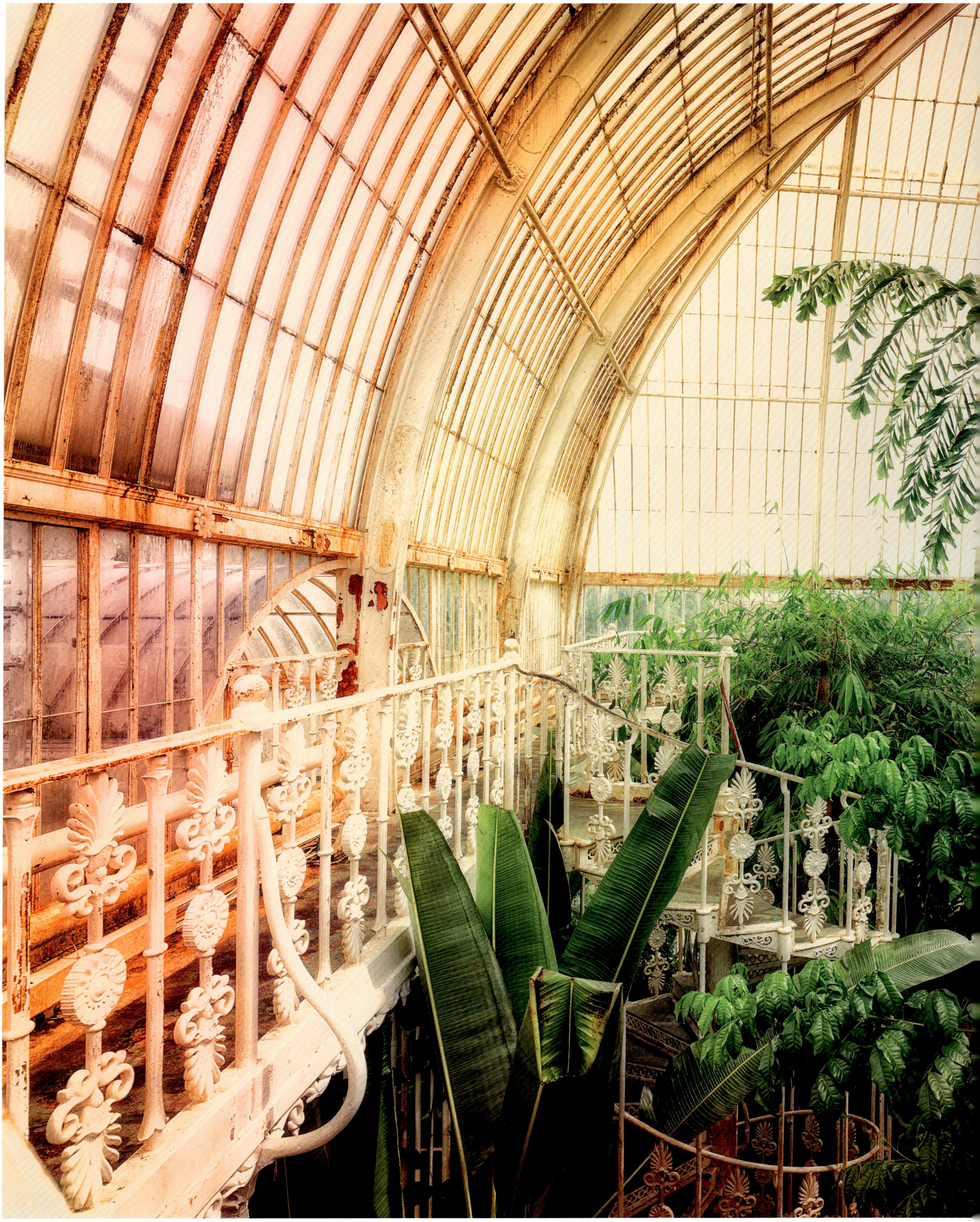

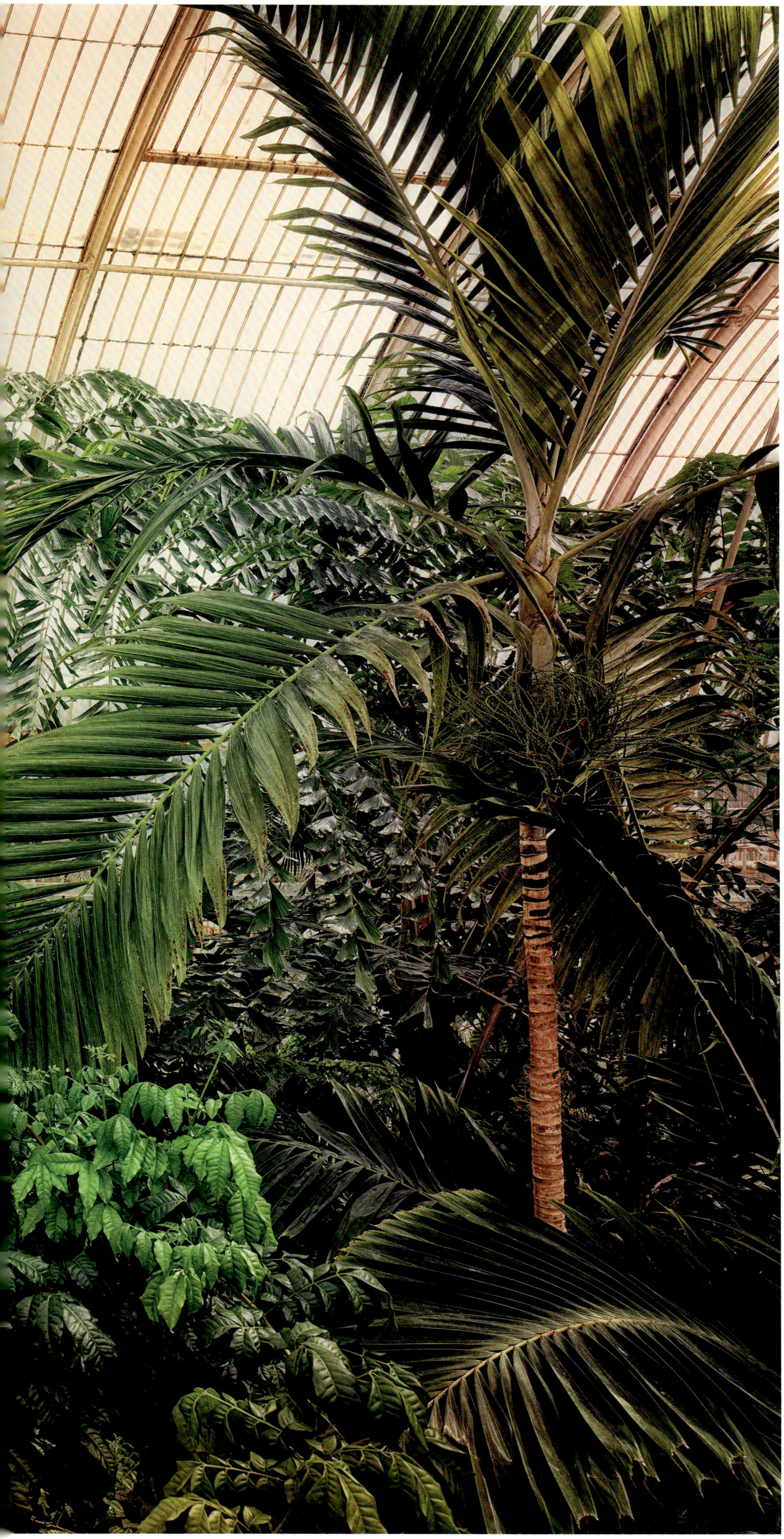

Kew Garden II

Kew Garden V
Kew Garden IV ▼

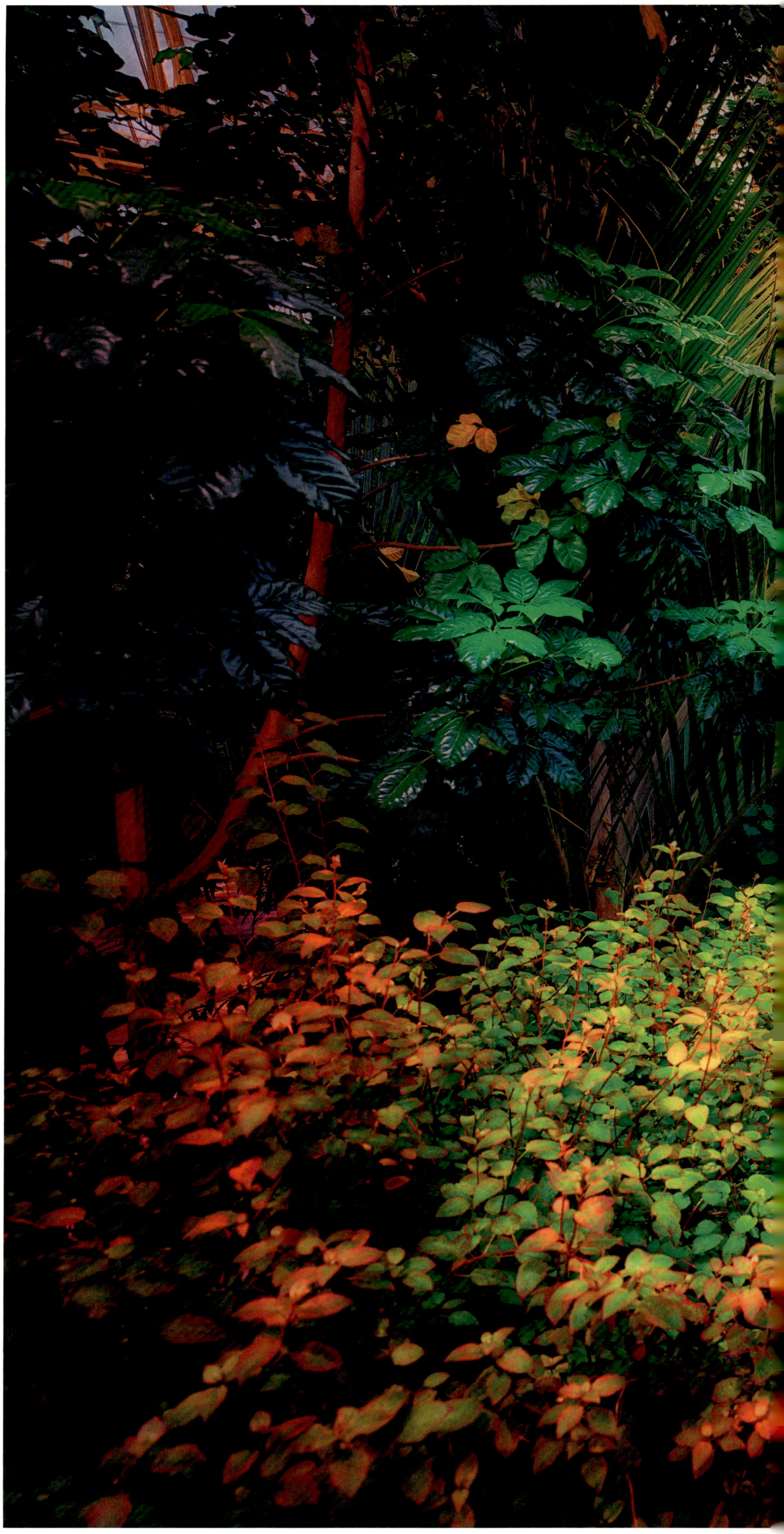

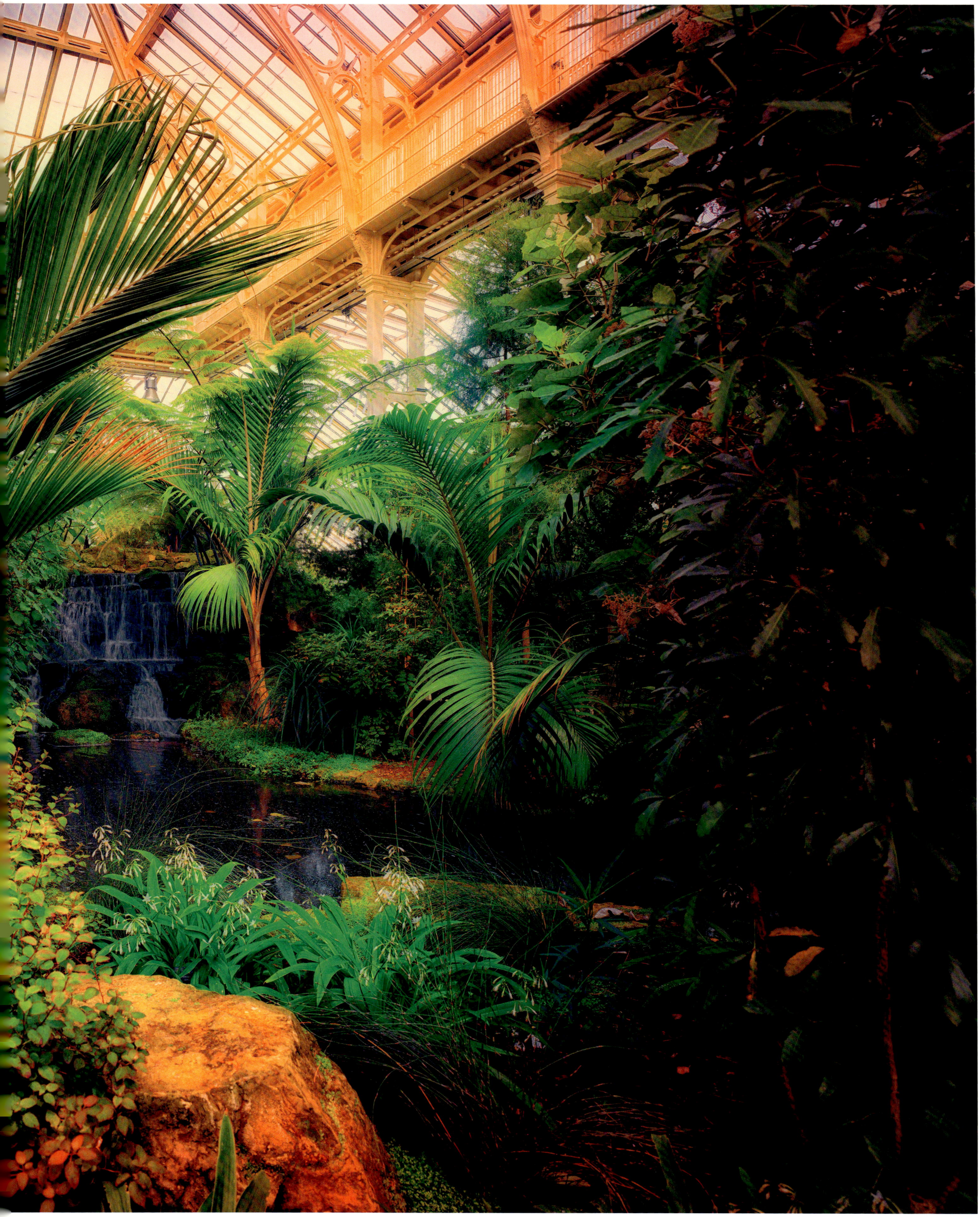

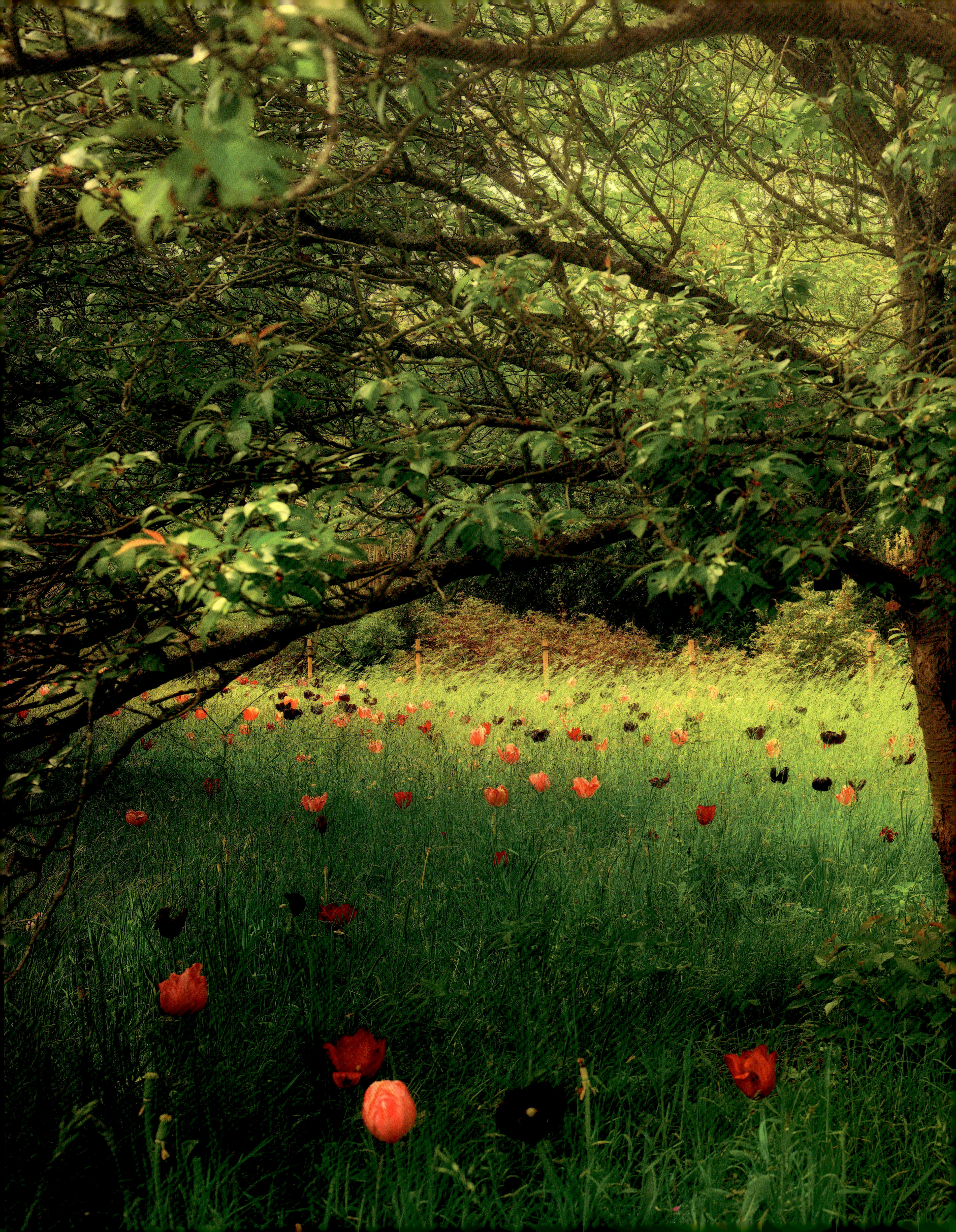

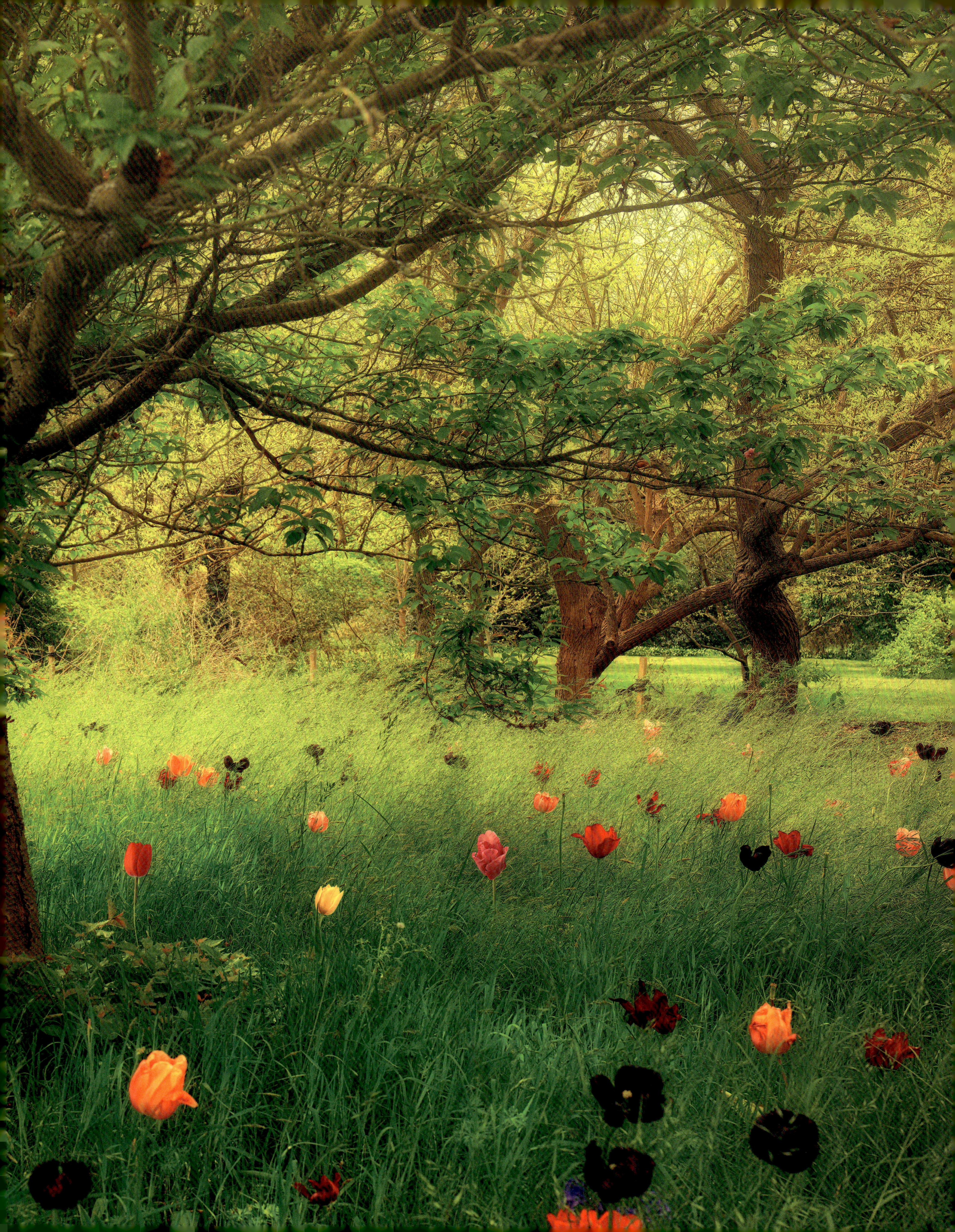

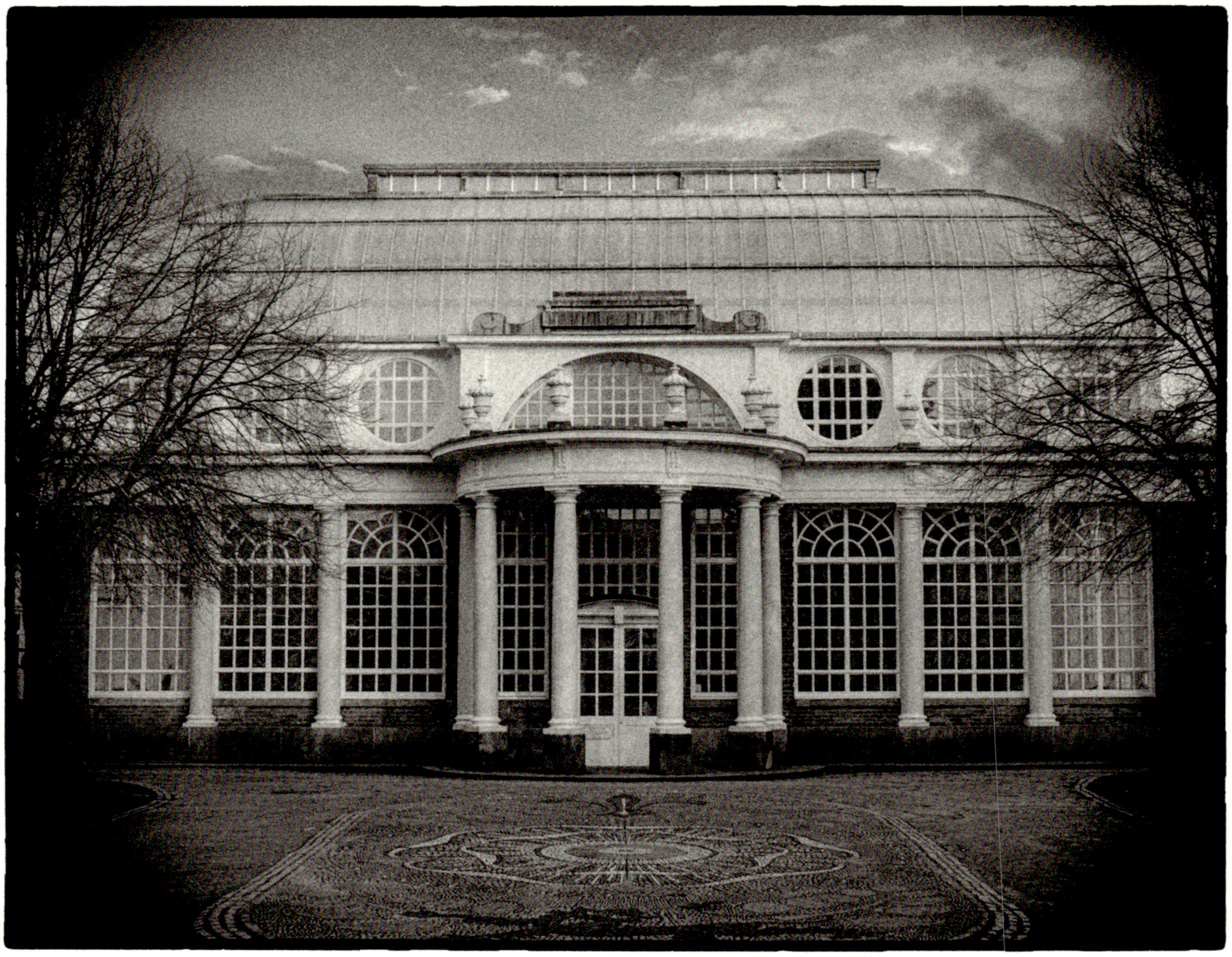

BUTTERFLY HOUSE

WILLIAMSON PARK
LANCASTER

BUTTERFLY HOUSE WILLIAMSON PARK

ORT
Lancaster, England,
Vereinigtes Königreich Großbritannien

ENTSTEHUNG
1909
Entwurf: John Belcher und John Joass

ARCHITEKTUR
Neobarockes Gebäude auf rechteckigem Grundriss. Das unterste Geschoss ist gemauert und auf drei Seiten mit durch Säulen getrennten Fenstern versehen. Im anschließenden Halbgeschoss finden sich Rundfenster. Den Abschluss bildet ein gläsernes Walmdach.

PFLANZEN
Tropische Pflanzen

BESONDERHEITEN
Williamson Park ist die Stiftung des Fabrikanten James Williamson (nach seiner Erhebung in den Adelsstand Baron Ashton) und seines Vaters, der zeitweise Bürgermeister Lancasters war. Heute beherbergt das ehemalige Palmenhaus viele Schmetterlingsarten sowie Kois, Schildkröten und andere Tiere.

LOCATION
Lancaster, England,
United Kingdom, Great Britain

ESTABLISHED
1909
design: John Belcher and John Joass

ARCHITECTURE
Neo-Baroque structure on a square footprint. The ground floor is made of brick and has windows separated by columns on three sides. The adjoining mezzanine features round windows. The building is topped by a glass hipped roof.

PLANTS
Tropical plants

ADDITIONAL NOTES
Williamson Park was founded by James Williamson (Baron Ashton after his elevation to the peerage), a manufacturer, and his father, who was mayor of Lancaster for a time. Today, the former palm house is home to many species of butterflies as well as koi, turtles, and other animals.

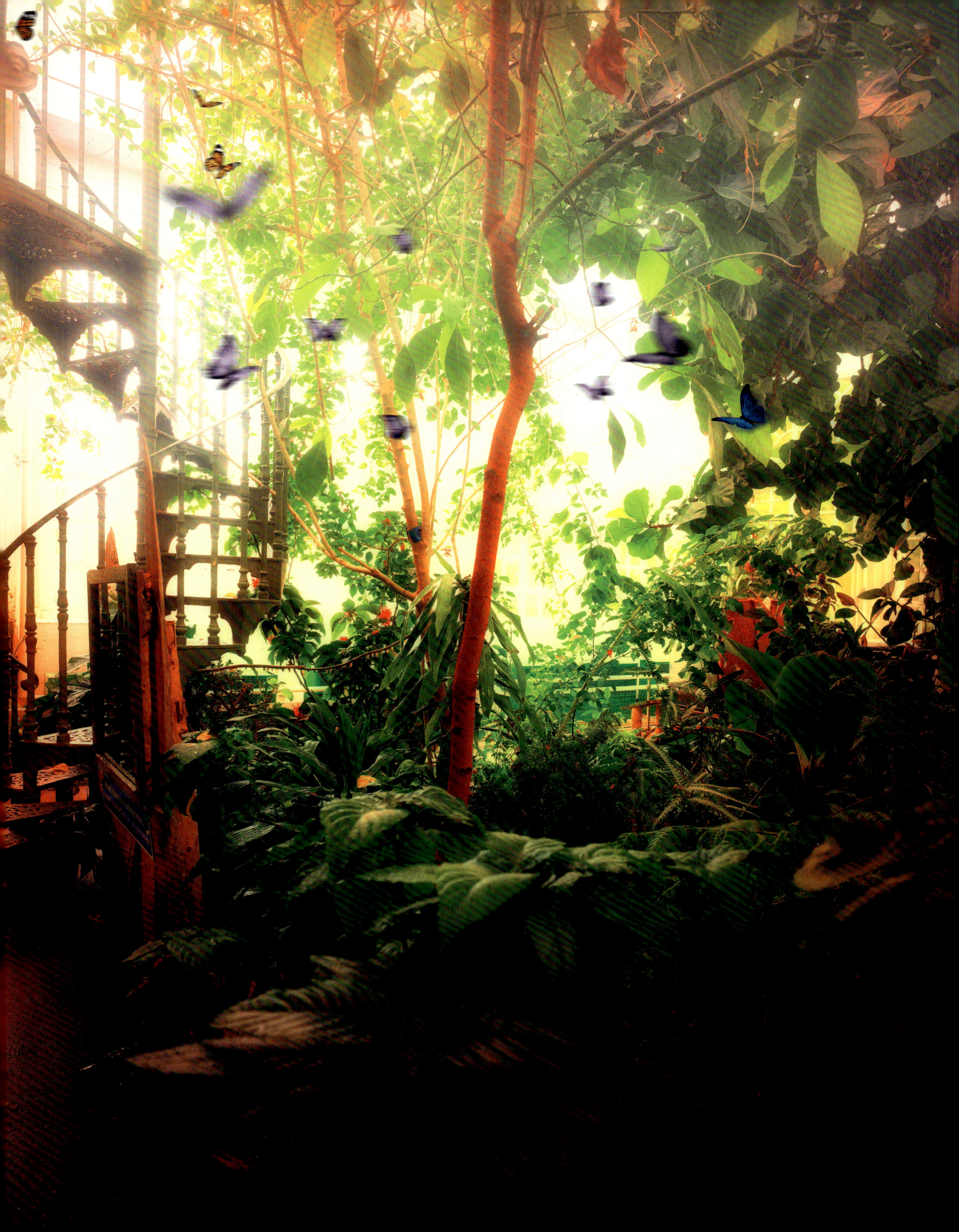

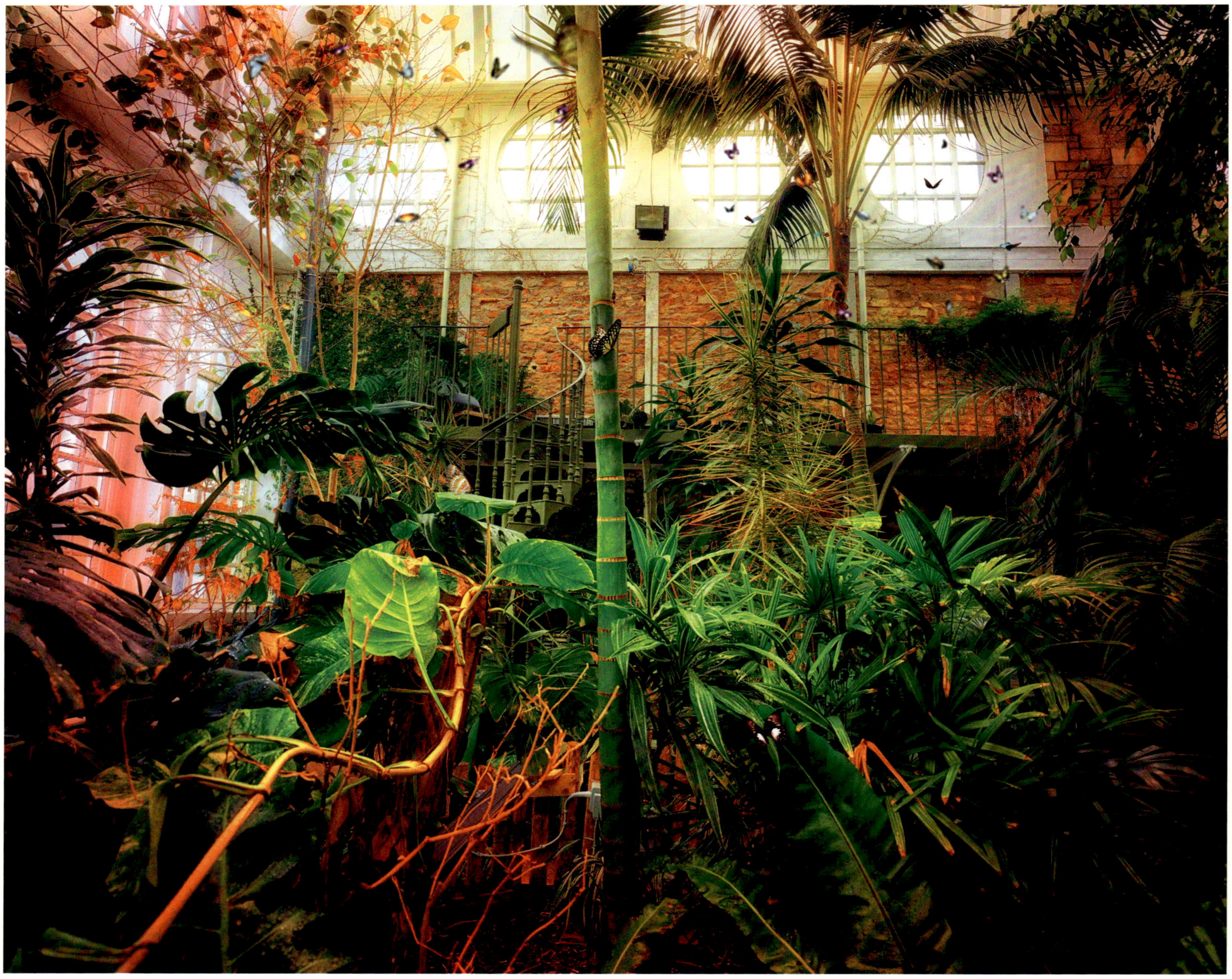

Butterfly House Lancaster III • Butterfly House Lancaster I

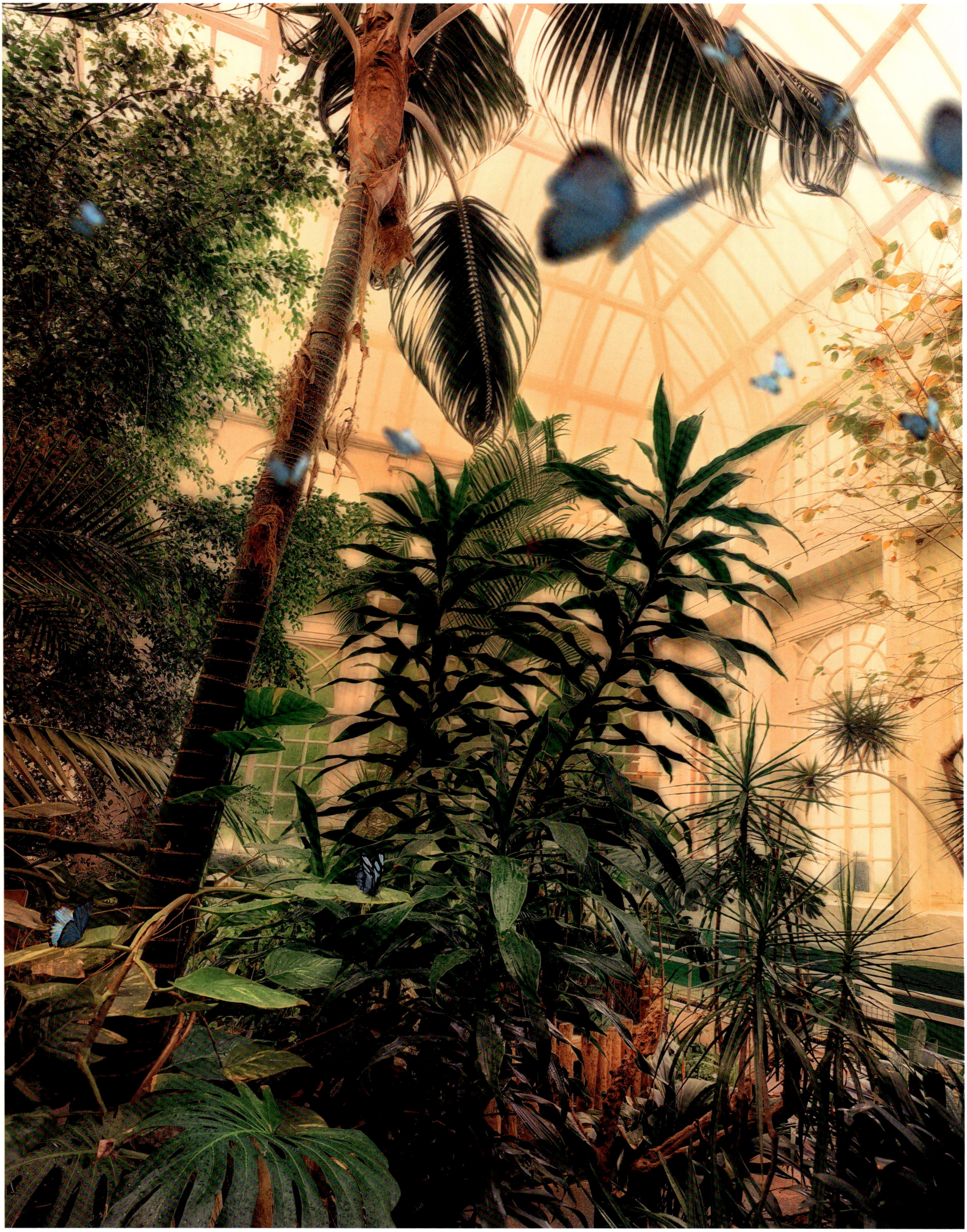

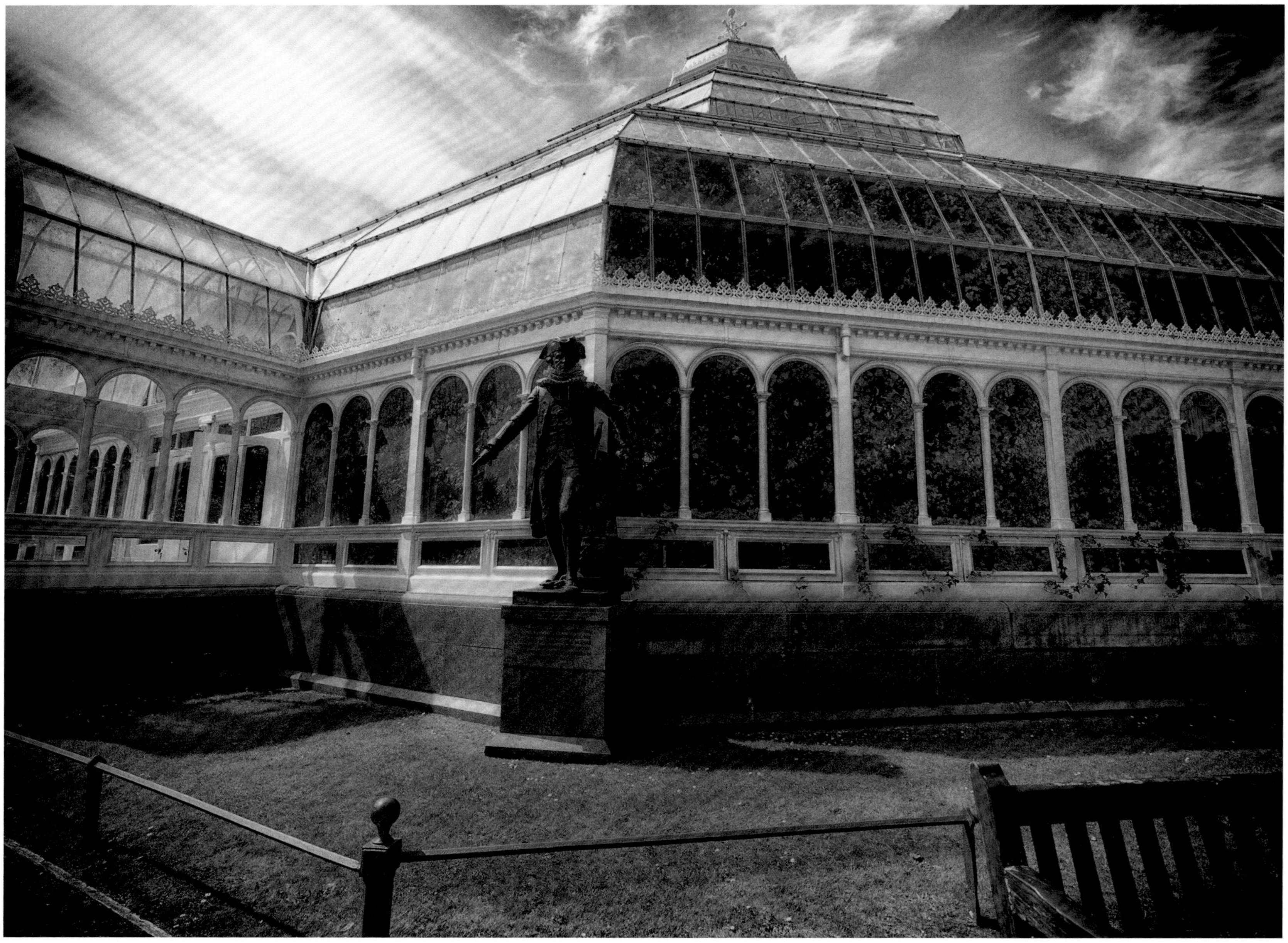

PALM HOUSE

SEFTON PARK
LIVERPOOL

PALM HOUSE SEFTON PARK

ORT
Liverpool, England,
Vereinigtes Königreich Großbritannien

GRÖSSE
Durchmesser 32 m; Kuppelhöhe 22,5 m

ENTSTEHUNG
1896
Entwurf: Gewächshausfirma Mackenzie & Moncur

ARCHITEKTUR
Zentralbau auf achteckigem Grundriss. Darüber erhebt sich eine dreistufige Glasglocke aus Gusseisenrippen, die Modular aneinandergefügt wurden.

PFLANZEN
20 Palmsorten wie die Kanarische Dattelpalme oder die Palmettopalme sowie 23 Orchideenarten. Dazu Blumen wie gelber Oleander und Bougainville.

BESONDERHEITEN
Das Palmenhaus ist eine private Stiftung von Henry Yates Thompson. Das umgebende Gelände wurde dem Graf Sefton durch ein bürgerliches Komitee zwecks Einrichtung des öffentlichen Parks abgekauft. Yates Thompson stiftete neben den Pflanzen auch Statuen berühmter Gärtner, Botaniker und Entdecker, die bis heute den Außenbau schmücken. Die Entwerfer des Palmenhauses Mackenzie und Moncur waren Inhaber der im 19. Jahrhundert führenden Firma der Gewächshausherstellung. Sie waren auch mit der Errichtung der äußeren Rechteckbauten des temperierten Gewächshauses in Kew beauftragt.

LOCATION
Liverpool, England,
United Kingdom, Great Britain

SIZE
32 m in diameter; dome height of 22.5 m

ESTABLISHED
1896
design: conservatory company Mackenzie & Moncur

ARCHITECTURE
Central structure on an octagonal footprint. Rising above the central structure is a three-tiered glass dome made of cast iron ribs joined together in a modular design.

PLANTS
20 palm varieties, including Canary Island date palms and palmetto palms, as well as 23 species of orchids in addition to flowers such as yellow oleander and bougainvillea.

ADDITIONAL NOTES
Henry Yates Thompson gifted funds to the city for the construction of the Palm House. The city council purchased the surrounding land from the Earl of Sefton for the development of a public park. In addition to the plants, Yates Thompson also donated statues of famous gardeners, botanists, and explorers, which still adorn the exterior of the structure. The designers of the Palm House, Mackenzie and Moncur, were owners of the 19th century's leading conservatory construction company. They were also commissioned to build the exterior rectangular structures of the temperature-controlled greenhouse at Kew Gardens.

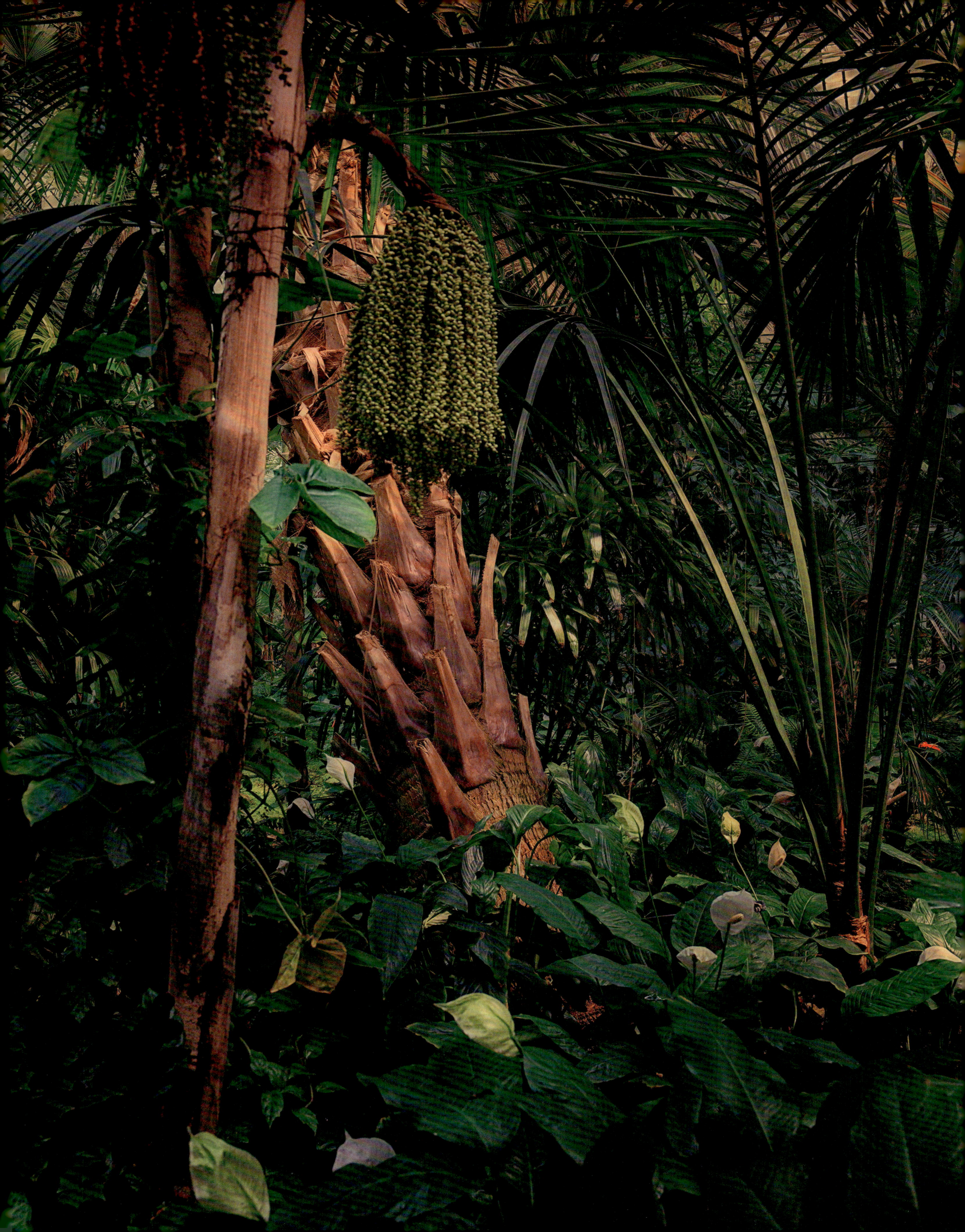

Es geht mir nicht um die fotografische Analyse des Objektes im Sinne einer optimalen Wiedergabe der vorgefundenen Realität. Ich war nie ein Dokumentar. Mir geht es vielmehr um das Bild als eigenständige Schöpfung.

WERNER PAWLOK

Using photography to analyze an object in the sense of optimally reproducing the reality I find is not something that has ever interested me. I have never been a documentarian. I prefer to think of the image as a creation in its own right.

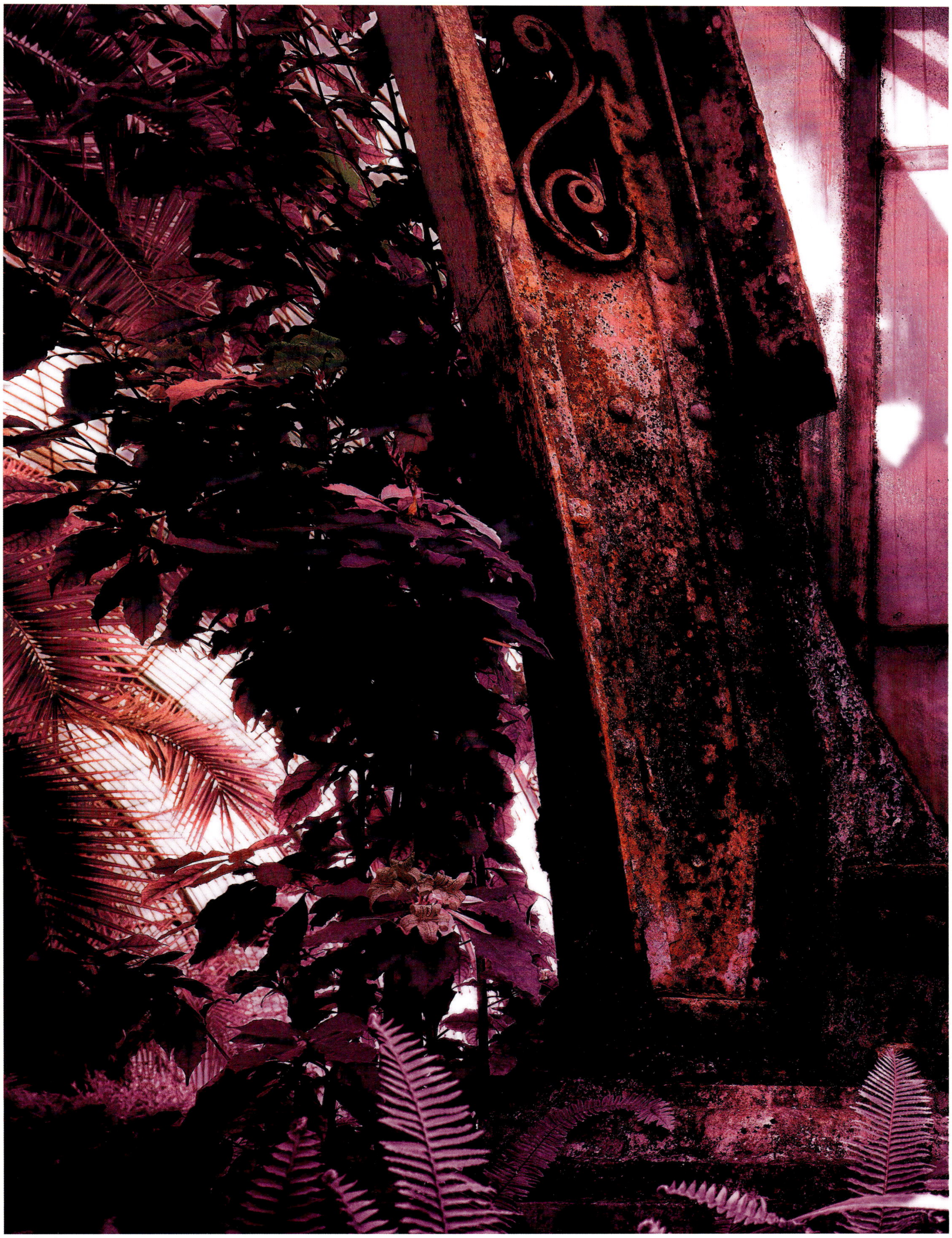

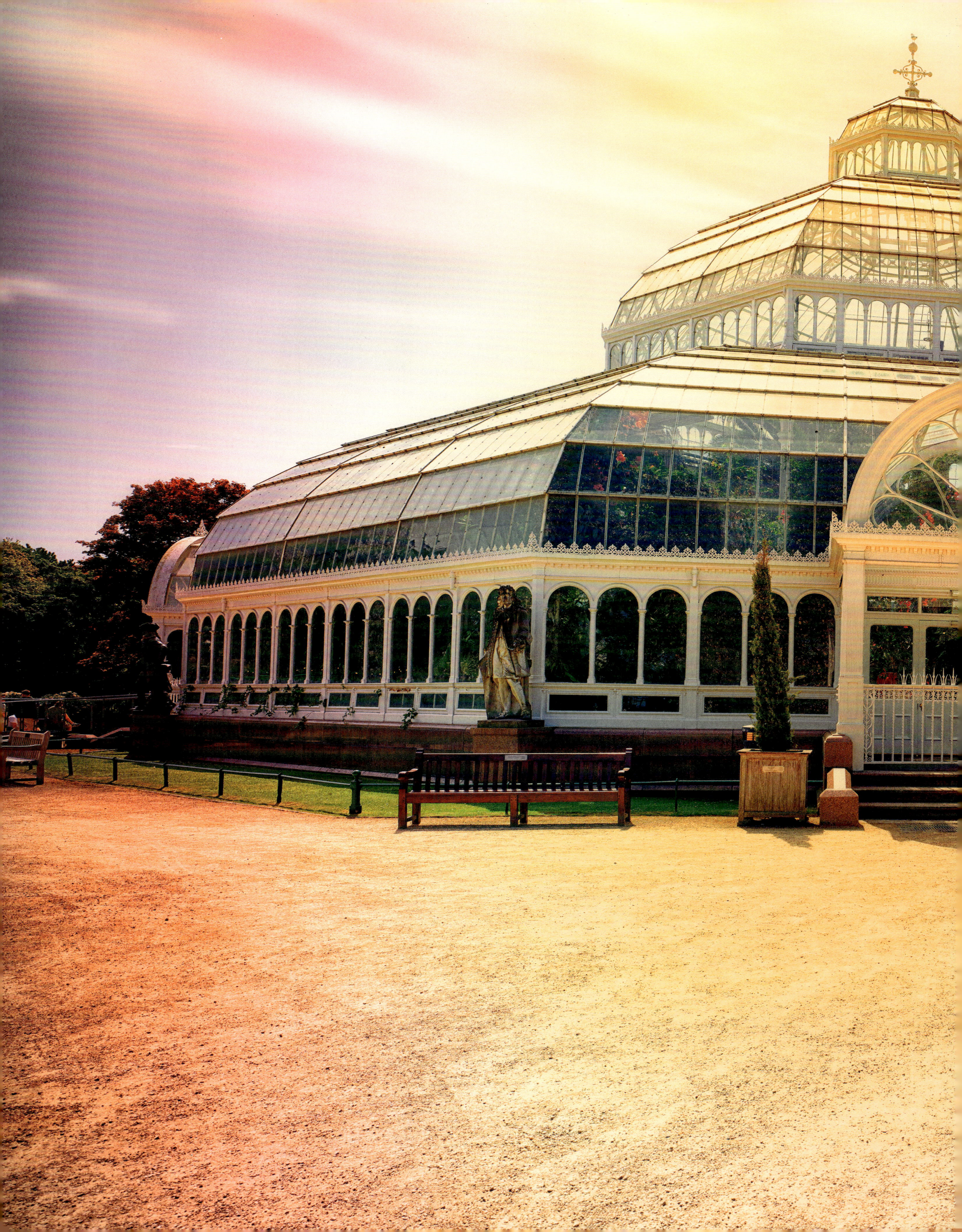

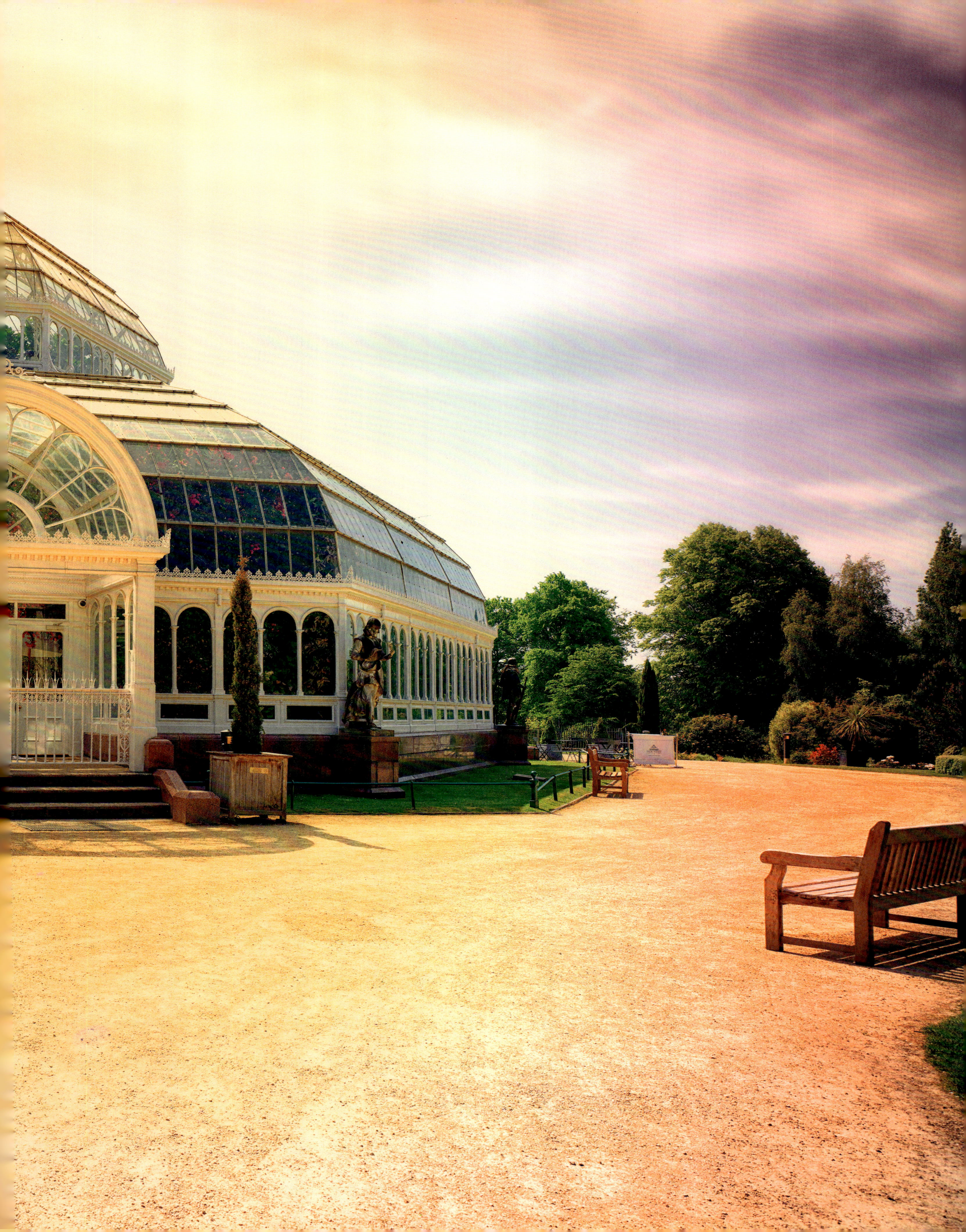

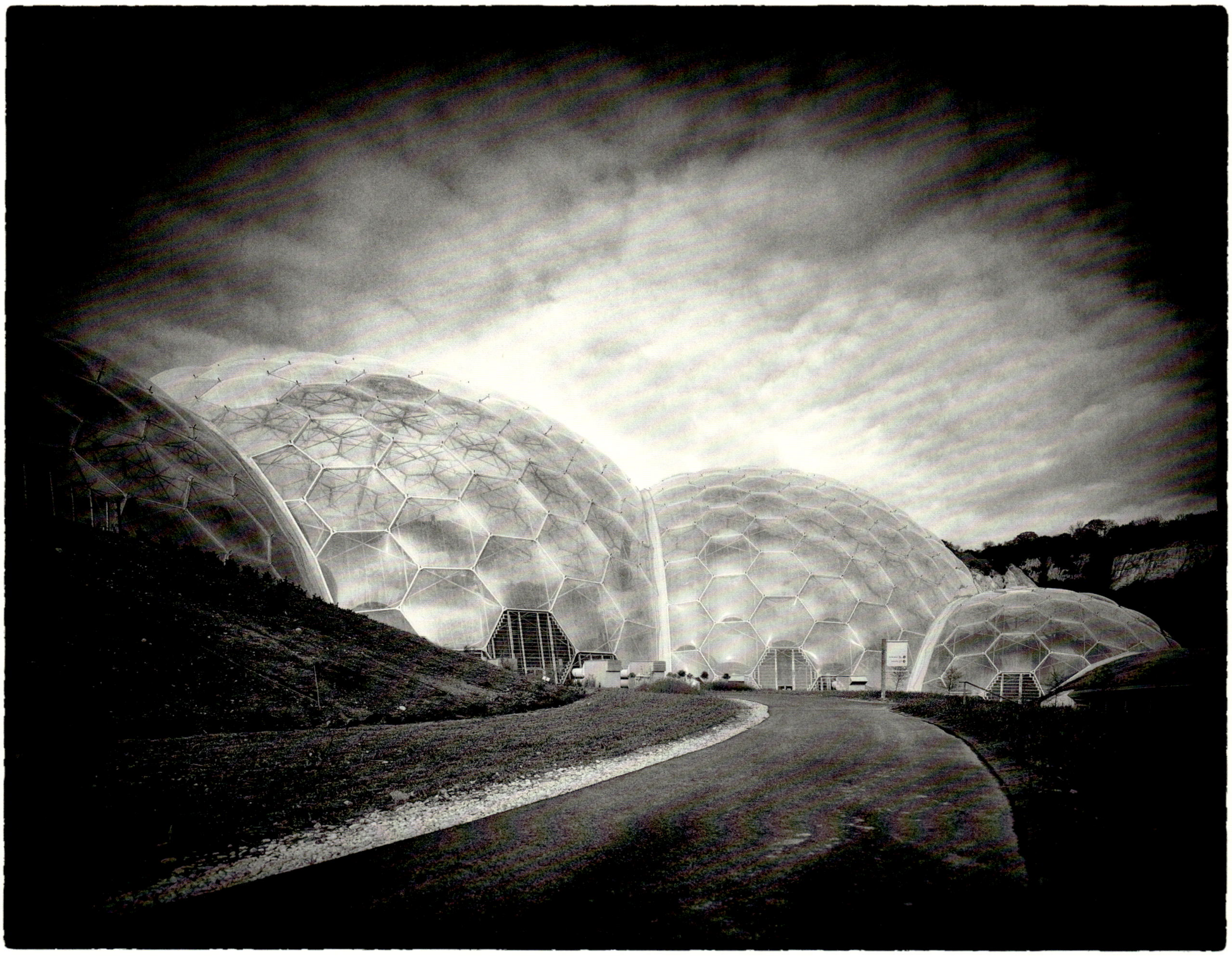

EDEN PROJECT

CORNWALL

EDEN PROJECT

ORT
Bodelva, England,
Vereinigtes Königreich Großbritannien

GRÖSSE
Zwei Gewächshäuser, hier Biome genannt:
Regenwald Biom: 240 m lang; 110 m breit; 50 m hoch
Mediterranes Biom: 135 m lang; 65 m breit; 35 m hoch

ENTSTEHUNG
1998–2001
Entwurf: Sir Nicholas Grimshaw

ARCHITEKTUR
Zwei verbundene Komplexe aus jeweils vier ineinander geschobenen Halbkugeln. Standort ist eine ehemalige Tongrube. Die Kuppeln bestehen aus einer Stahlkonstruktion und insgesamt 625 sechseckigen, 16 fünfeckigen und 190 dreieckigen Texlon® ETFE Folienkissen. Aufgrund der gewaltigen Dimensionen der Anlage konnte wegen des hohen Gewichts kein Glas als Material verwendet werden.

PFLANZEN
Regenwald Biom:
über 1000 Arten wie Zuckerrohr,
Kautschukbäume, Titanwurz
Mediterranes Biom:
über 1000 Arten wie Duftpflanzen im Parfümgarten,
Oliven und Zitruspflanzen

BESONDERHEITEN
Der Name ist abgeleitet vom Garten Eden, dem biblischen Paradies. Der Botanische Garten umfasst nach dem Willen der Gründer über 5000 Arten. Diese sollen einen Genpool bilden, um deren Aussterben zu verhindern.

LOCATION
Bodelva, England,
United Kingdom, Great Britain

SIZE
Two greenhouses, referred to as biomes.
Rainforest Biome: 240 m long; 110 m wide; 50 m high
Mediterranean Biome: 135 m long; 65 m wide; 35 m high

ESTABLISHED
1998–2001
design: Sir Nicholas Grimshaw

ARCHITECTURE
Two connected complexes, each consisting of four adjoining domes. The location is a former clay mine. The domes consist of a steel structure and 625 hexagons, 16 pentagons, and 190 triangles featuring Texlon® ETFE panels. Due to the enormous dimensions of the complex, glass could not be used as a material because of its considerable weight.

PLANTS
Rainforest Biome:
more than 1,000 varieties of plants, such as sugar cane,
rubber trees, and titan arum
Mediterranean Biome:
more than 1,000 varieties of plants, such as scented plants
in the Perfume Garden, olives, and citrus plants

ADDITIONAL NOTES
The project was named after the Garden of Eden, the biblical paradise. The founders' intention was for the botanical garden to include more than 5,000 varieties of plants in an effort to create a gene pool that would prevent their extinction.

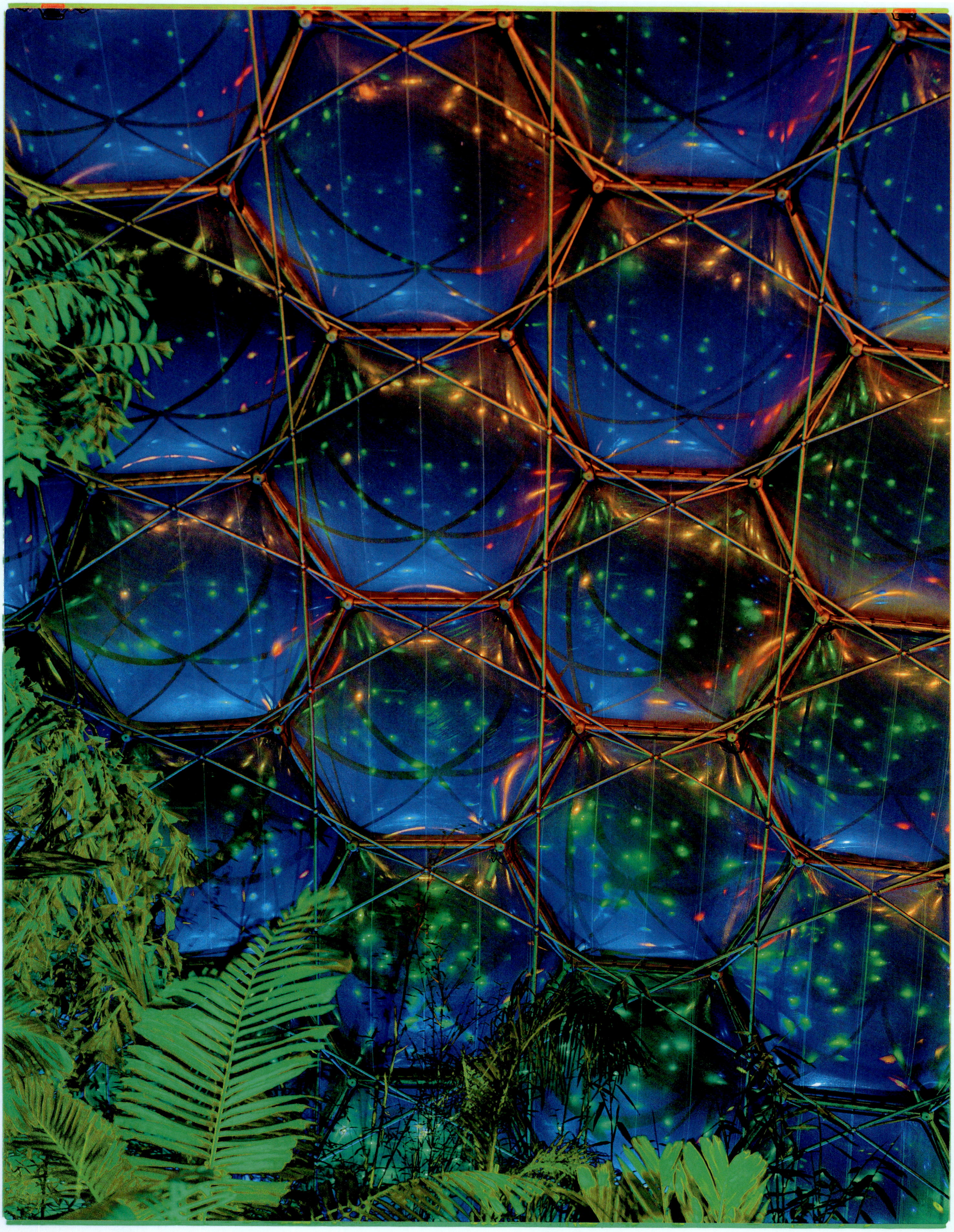

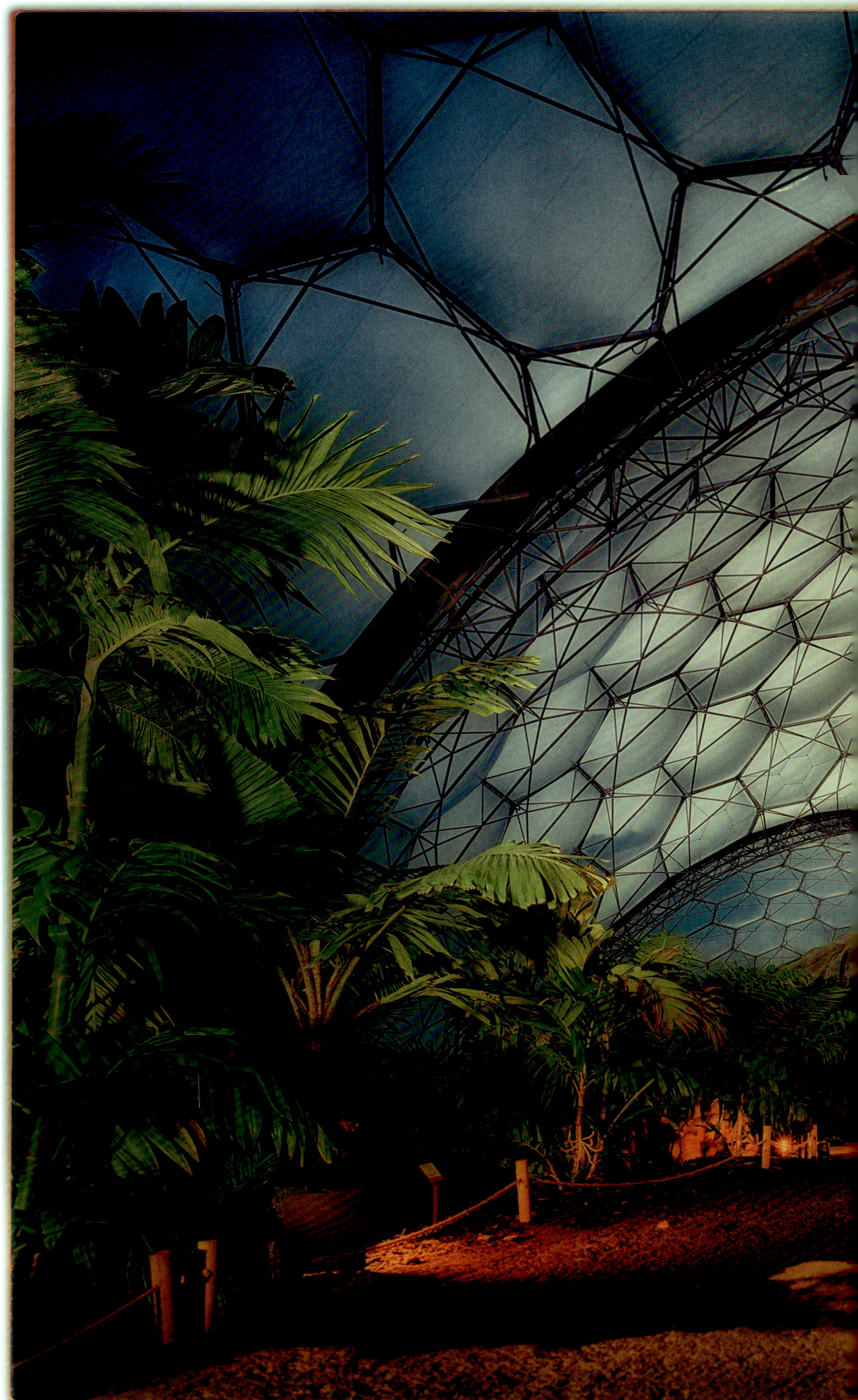

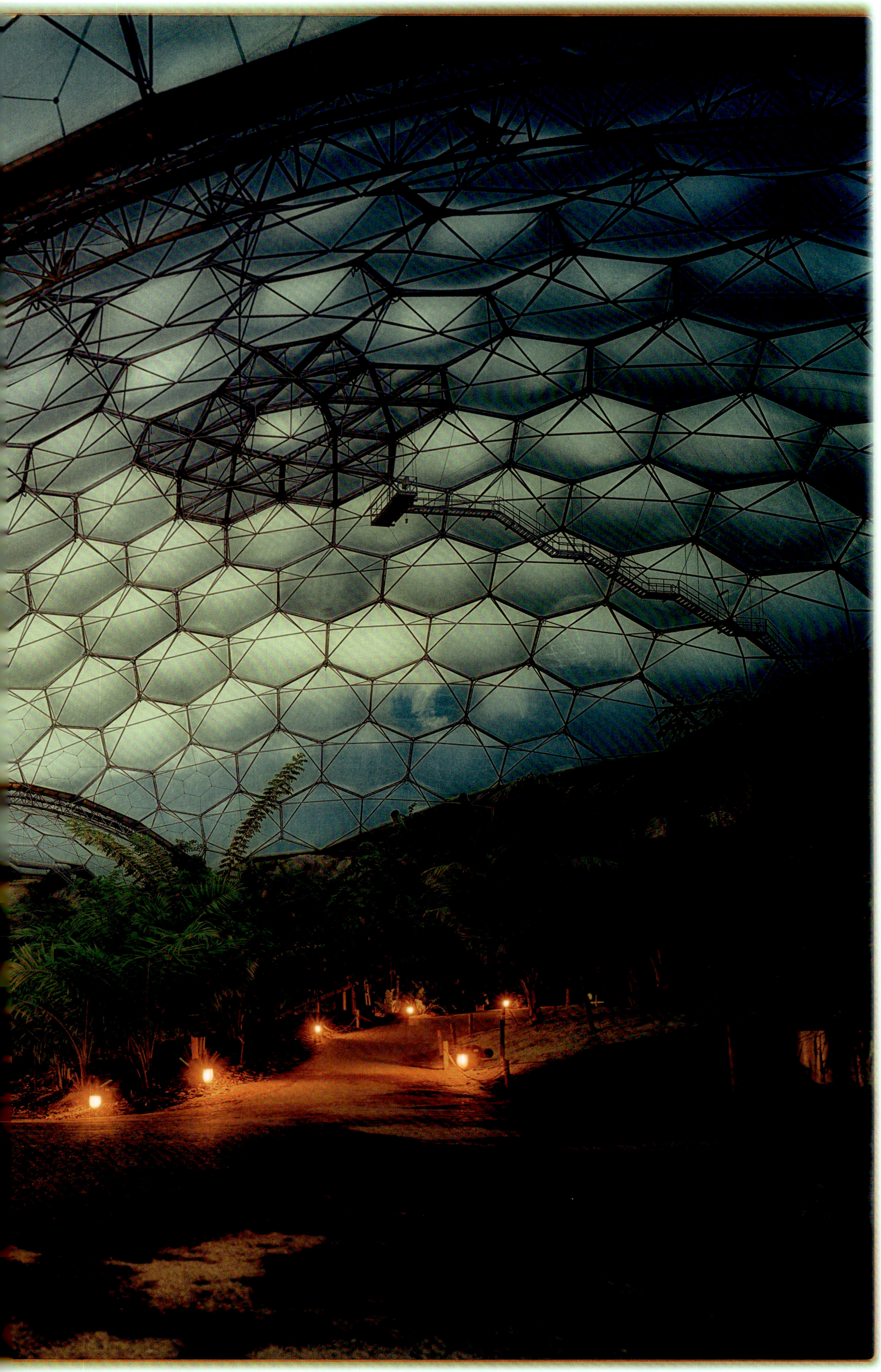

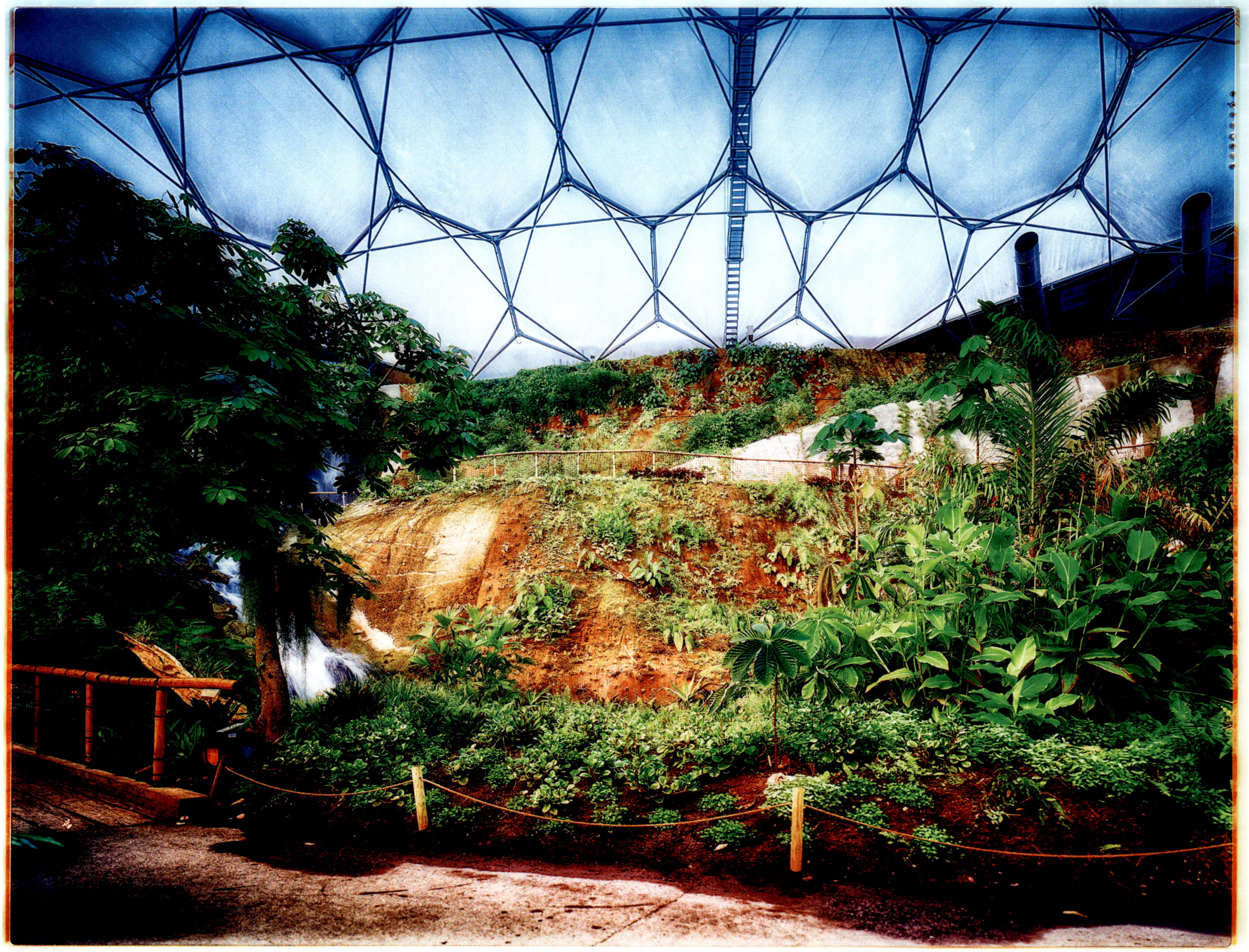

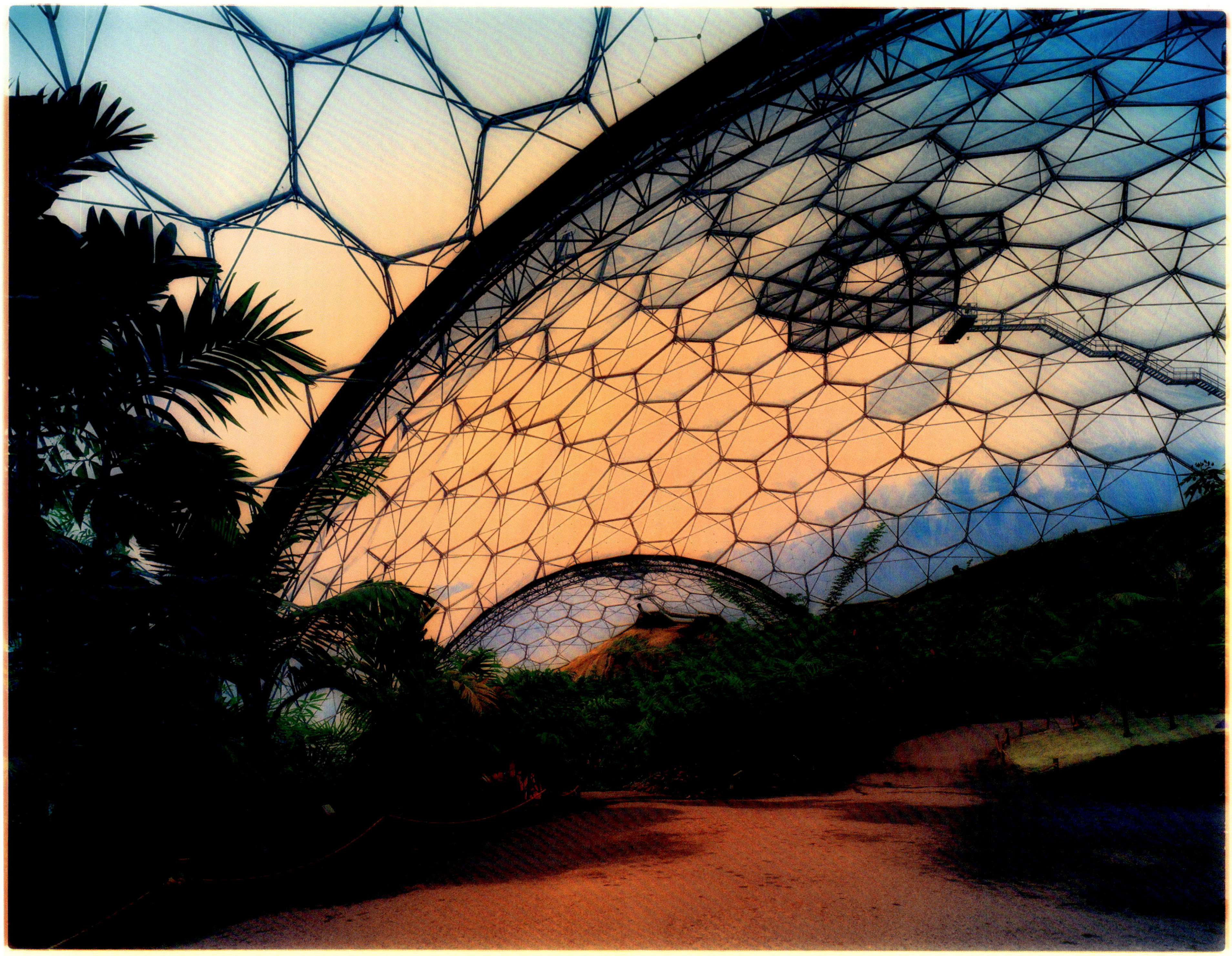

Eden Project III • Eden Project VIII

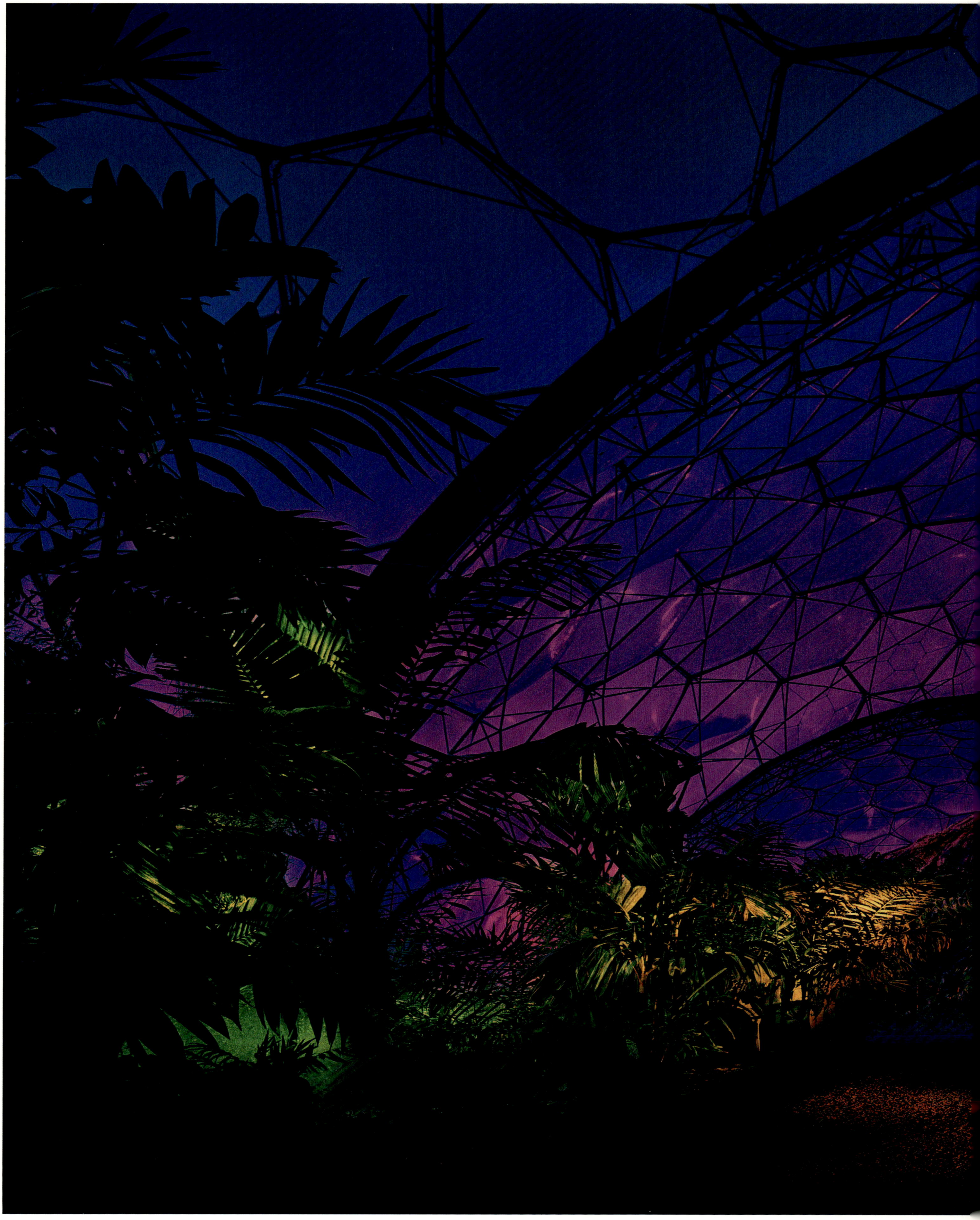

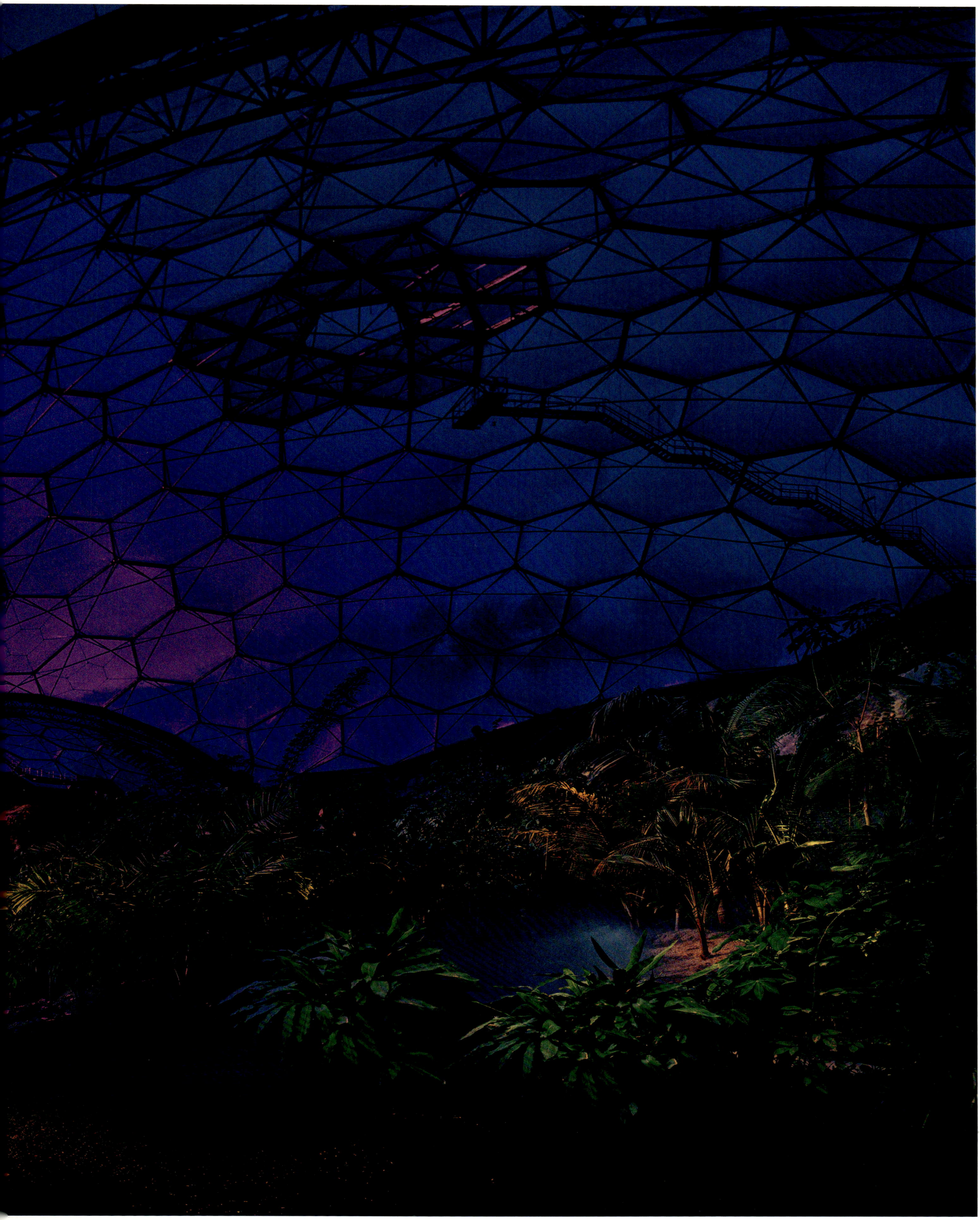

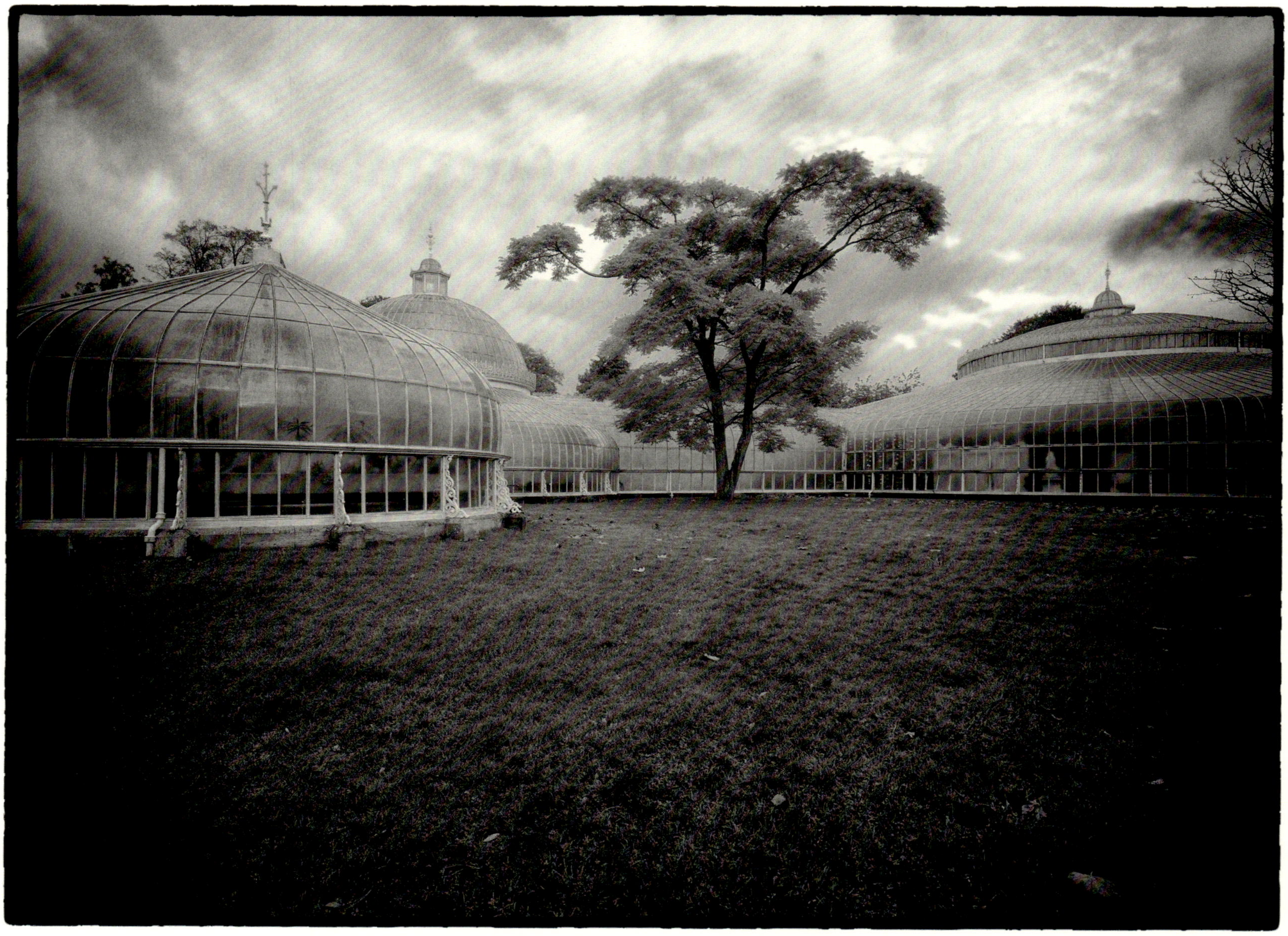

KIBBLE PALACE

GLASGOW

KIBBLE PALACE

ORT
Glasgow, Schottland,
Vereinigtes Königreich Großbritannien

LOCATION
Glasgow, Scotland,
United Kingdom, Great Britain

GRÖSSE
Zentralkuppel: 44,5 m Durchmesser
Kuppelhöhe mit Laterne: 13 m

SIZE
Central cupola: 44.5 m in diameter
cupola with lantern: 13 m high

ENTSTEHUNG
1872–1873
Entwurf: John Kibble

ESTABLISHED
1872–1873
design: John Kibble

ARCHITEKTUR
Der große Kuppelbau ist über einen Glaskorridor mit einem länglichen Glashaus mit halbrunden Abschlüssen verbunden. Durch das Glasgewölbe oberhalb des Verbindungsbereiches zum länglichen Baukörper entsteht der beherrschende Eindruck einer Doppelkuppel.

ARCHITECTURE
A glass corridor connects the large domed structure to an elongated greenhouse terminating in a semicircular design. The glass vault above the connecting area to the elongated structure creates the overarching impression of a double dome.

PFLANZEN
Vorrangig verschiedene Farne und Baumfarne wie Australische Baumfarne

PLANTS
Primarily a variety of ferns and tree ferns, such as Australian tree ferns

ANERE BESONDERHEITEN
1865 als privates Gewächshaus auf dem Grundstück John Kibbles erbaut. Versetzung als von Kibble gestifteten Kristallpalast in den Botanischen Garten Glasgows. Hierbei Vergrößerung und Nutzung als öffentlicher Ausstellungsraum für Kunst und Blumen sowie Veranstaltungen. Nach 1881 erwarb es die Königliche Botanische Vereinigung von Kibble und baute es mit einer Heizung zum Wintergarten für tropische Pflanzen, vorrangig Farne, um.

ADDITIONAL NOTES
Built in 1865 as a private greenhouse on John Kibble's property. Relocated to Glasgow Botanic Gardens as a crystal palace funded by Kibble. It was enlarged as part of that process and used as a public exhibition space for art and flowers, as well as events. After 1881, the Royal Botanic Institution of Glasgow acquired it from Kibble and converted it, with heating, into a conservatory for tropical plants, primarily ferns.

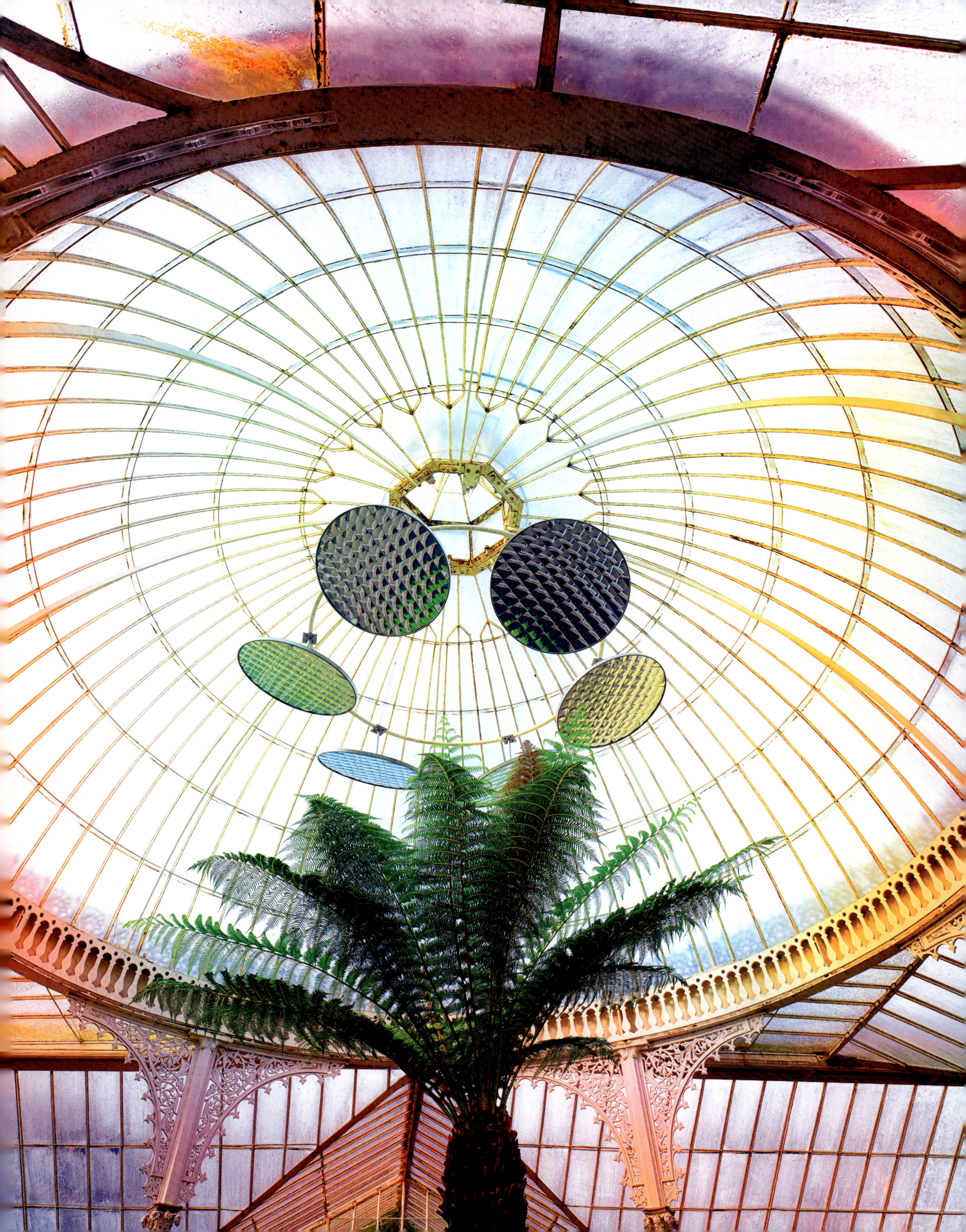

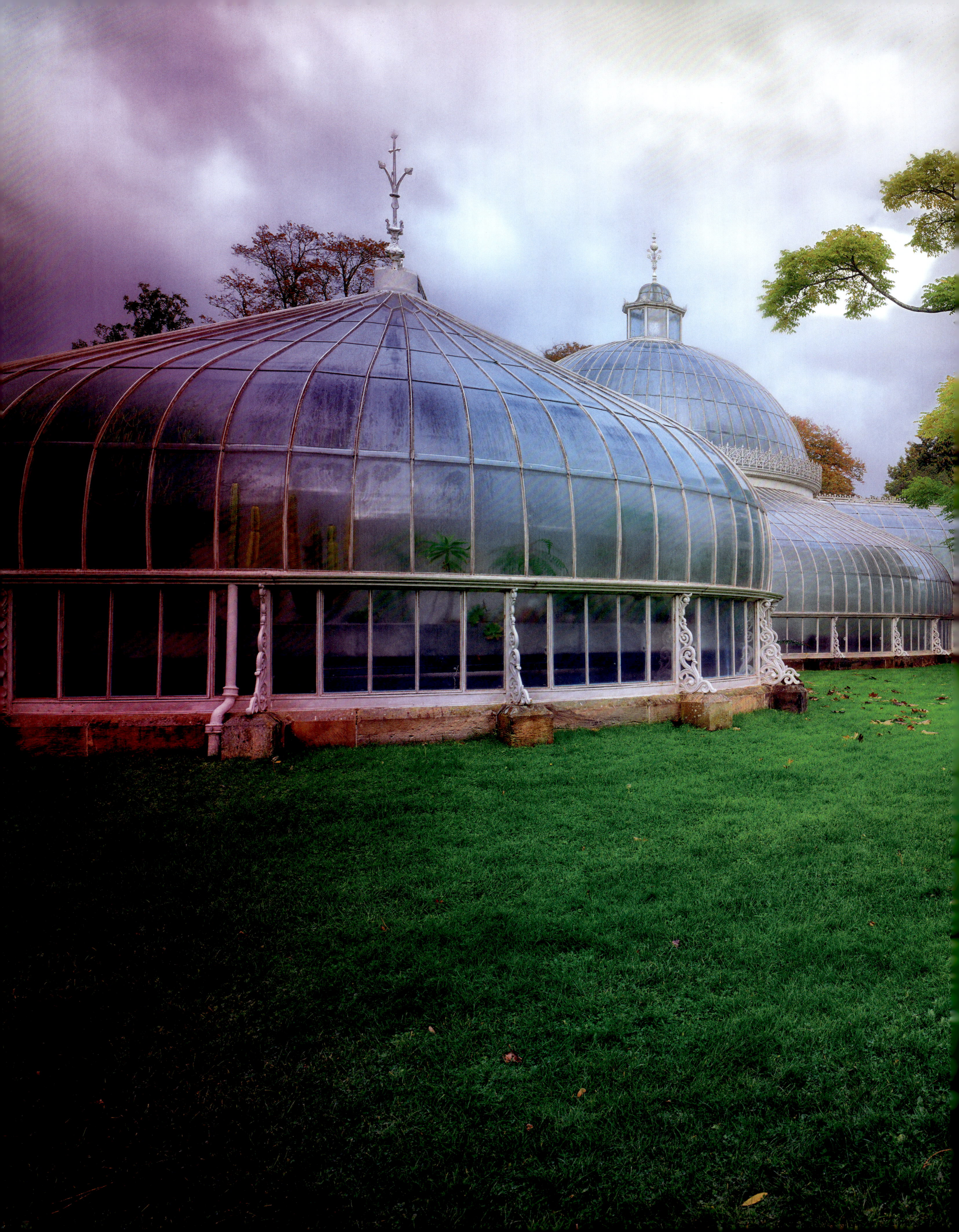

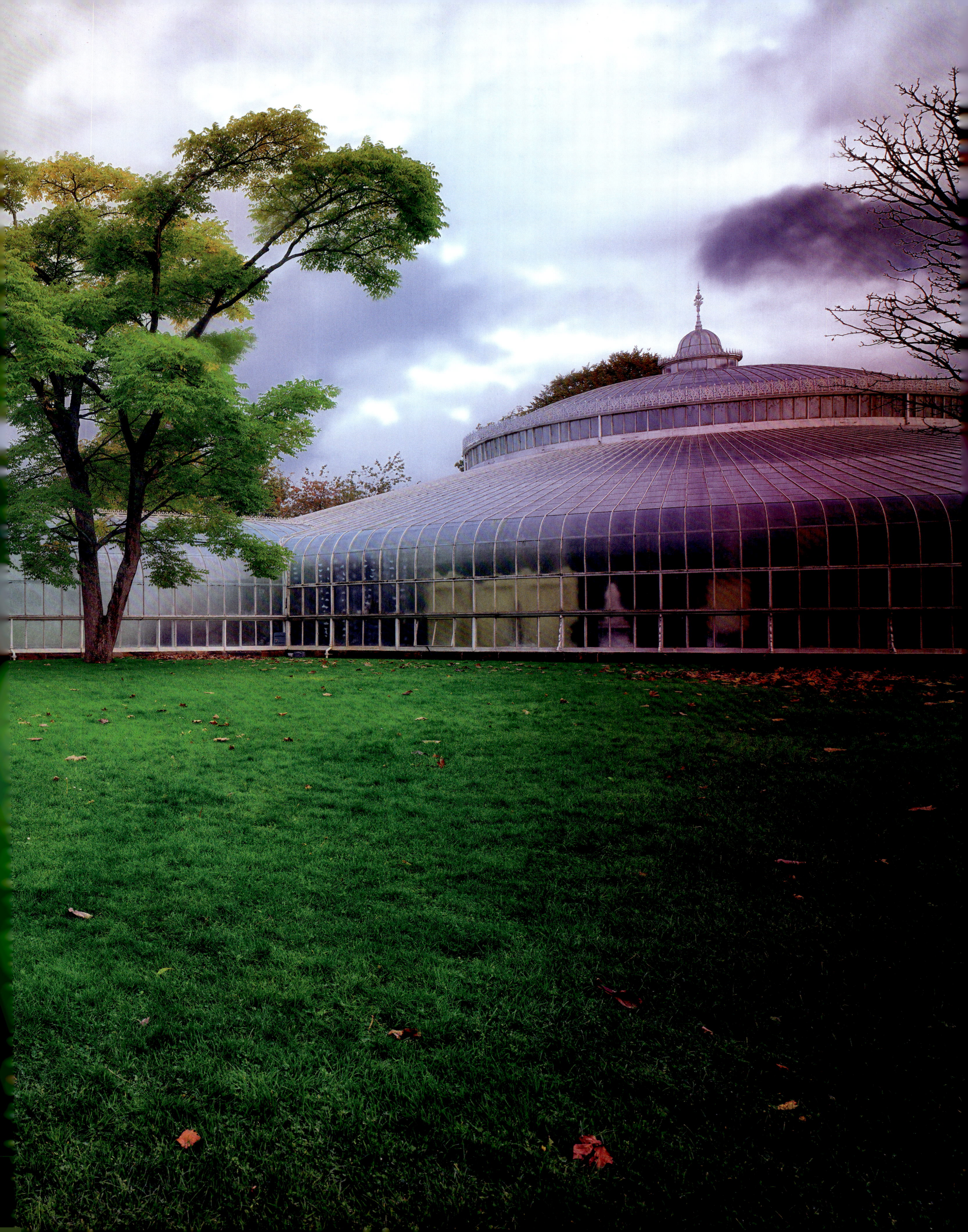

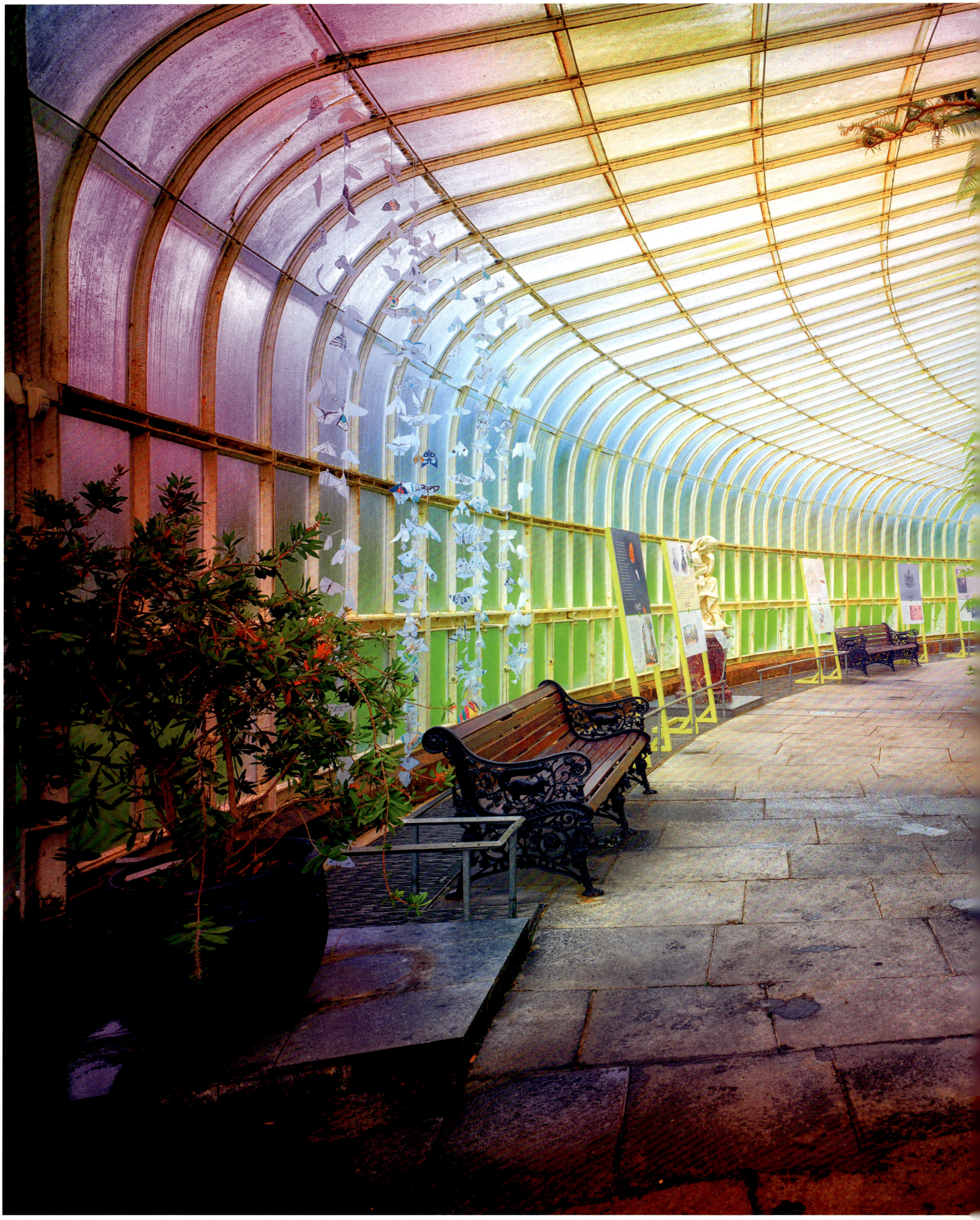

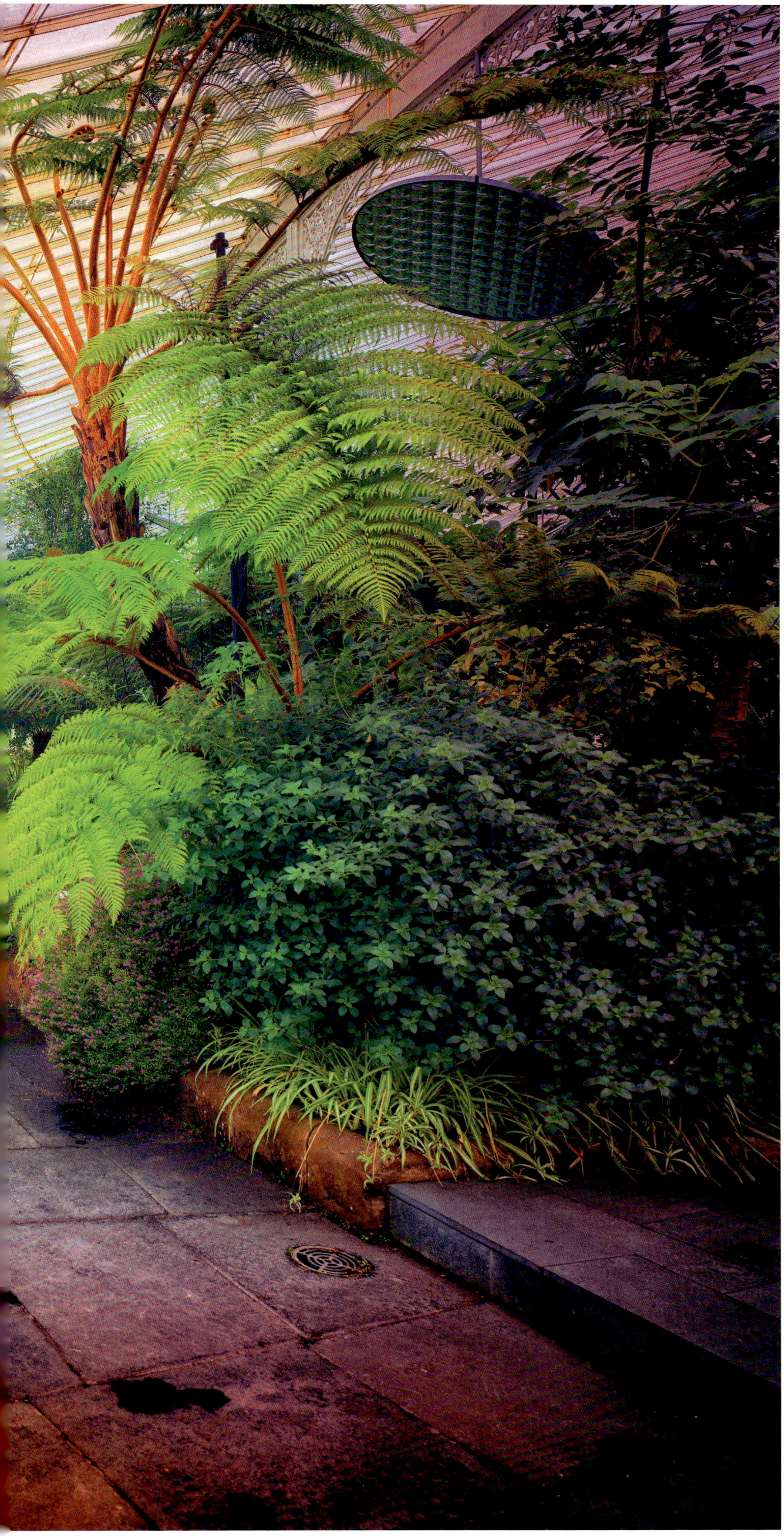

Kibble Palace Glasgow II

Eine Fotografie reproduziert keine Gerüche, wir hören keine Stimmen, kein Summen, kein Zwitschern. Spürbar wird in den Bildern etwas anderes und Besonderes: Eine Art Traum oder Rausch von eigenwillig verschobenen Dimensionen.

STEPHAN REISNER

Photographs cannot reproduce scents. We cannot hear any voices, no buzzing of bees, no chirping of birds. What we can do is feel something different and special in the photos. A kind of dream or intoxication evoked by deliberately shifted dimensions.

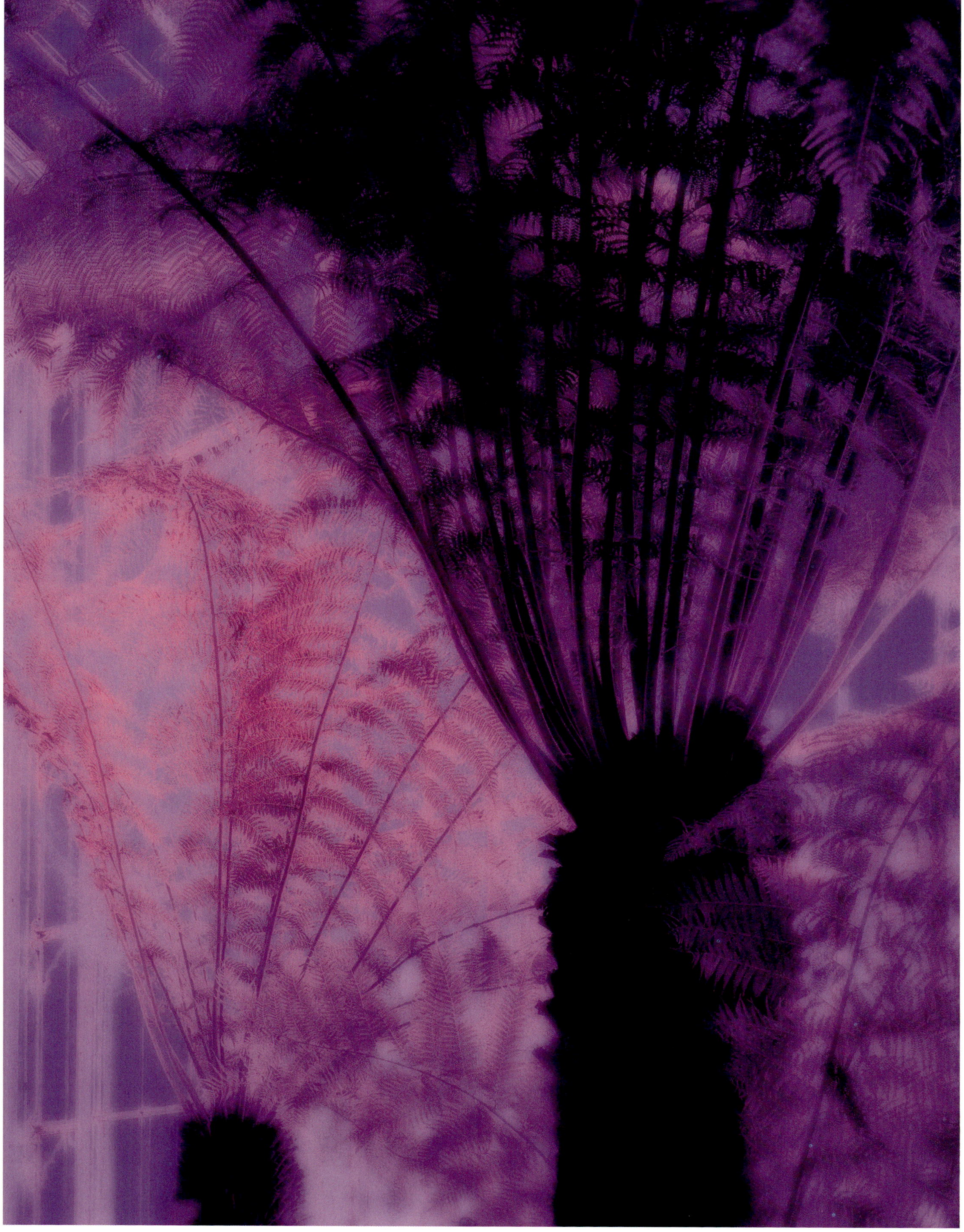

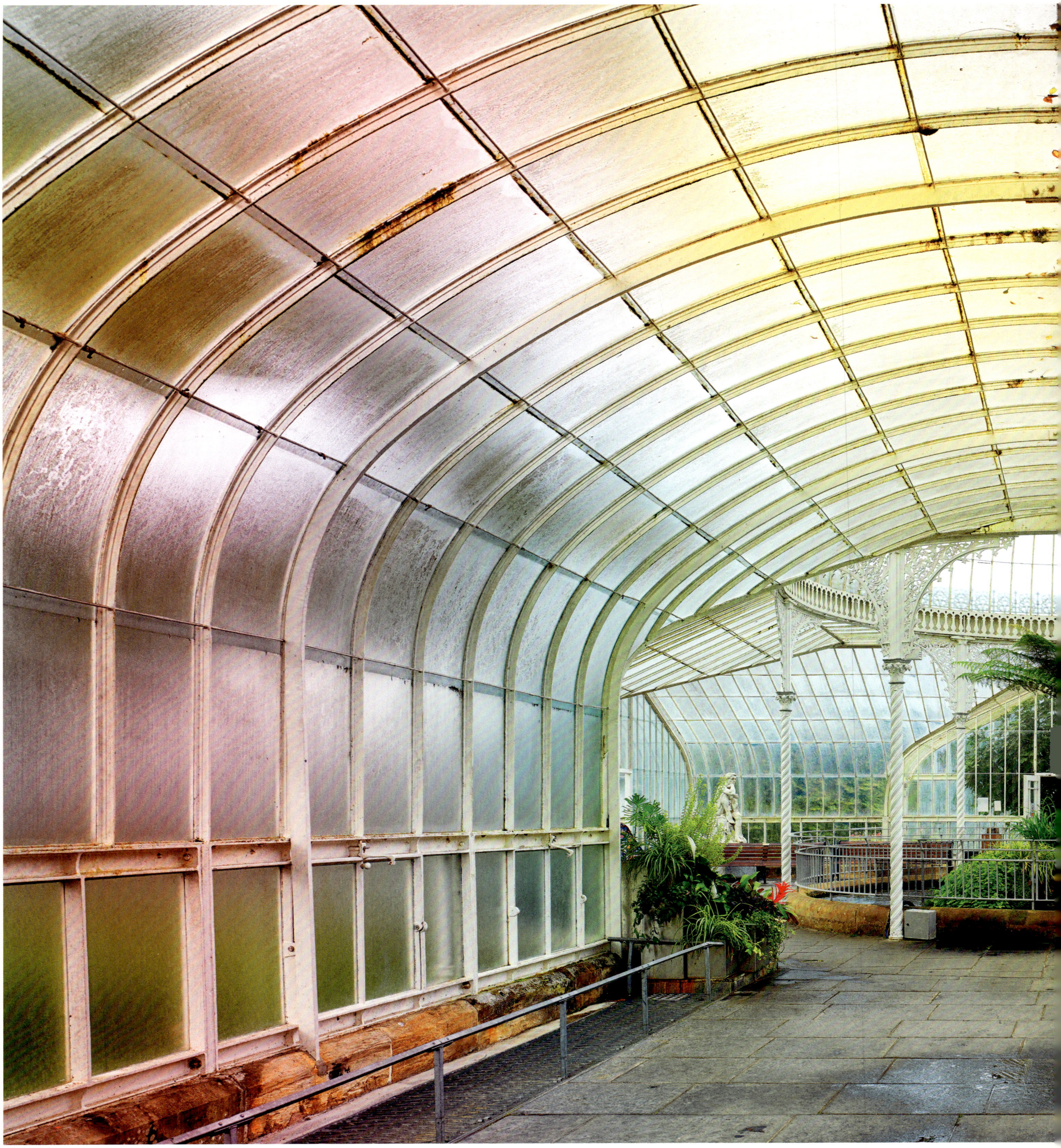

Kibble Palace Glasgow III

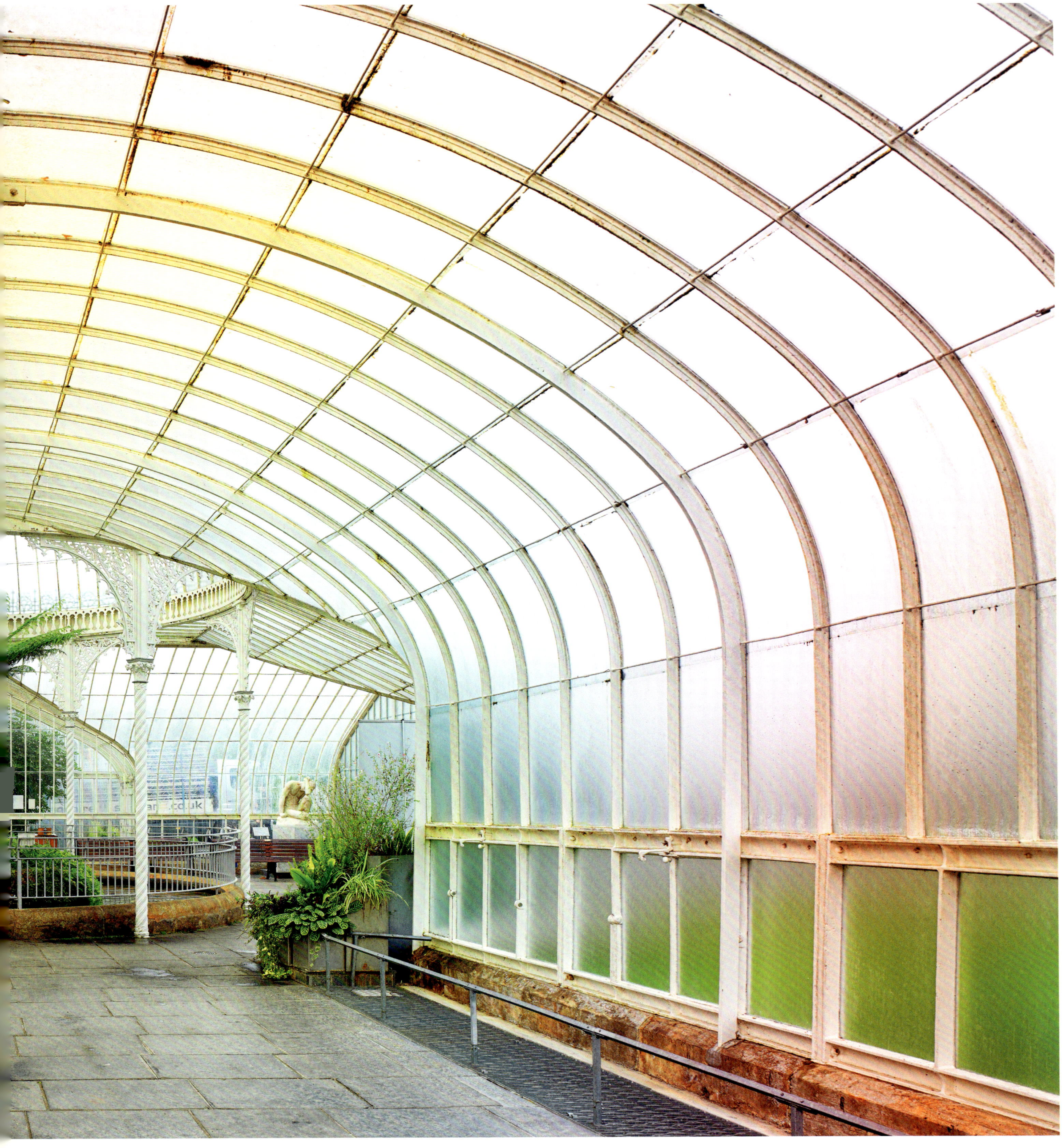

Kibble Palace Glasgow VII
Kibble Palace Glasgow V ▼

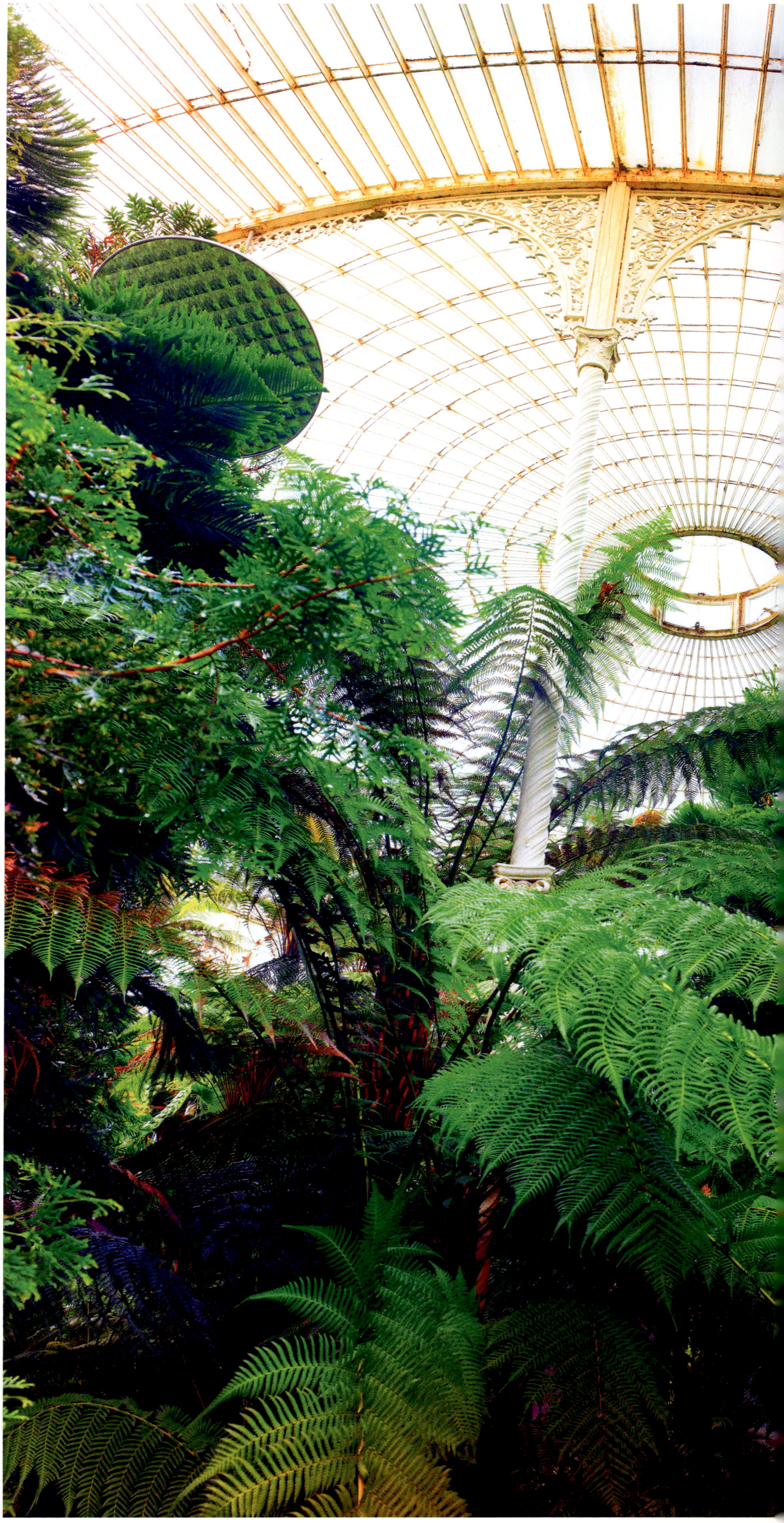

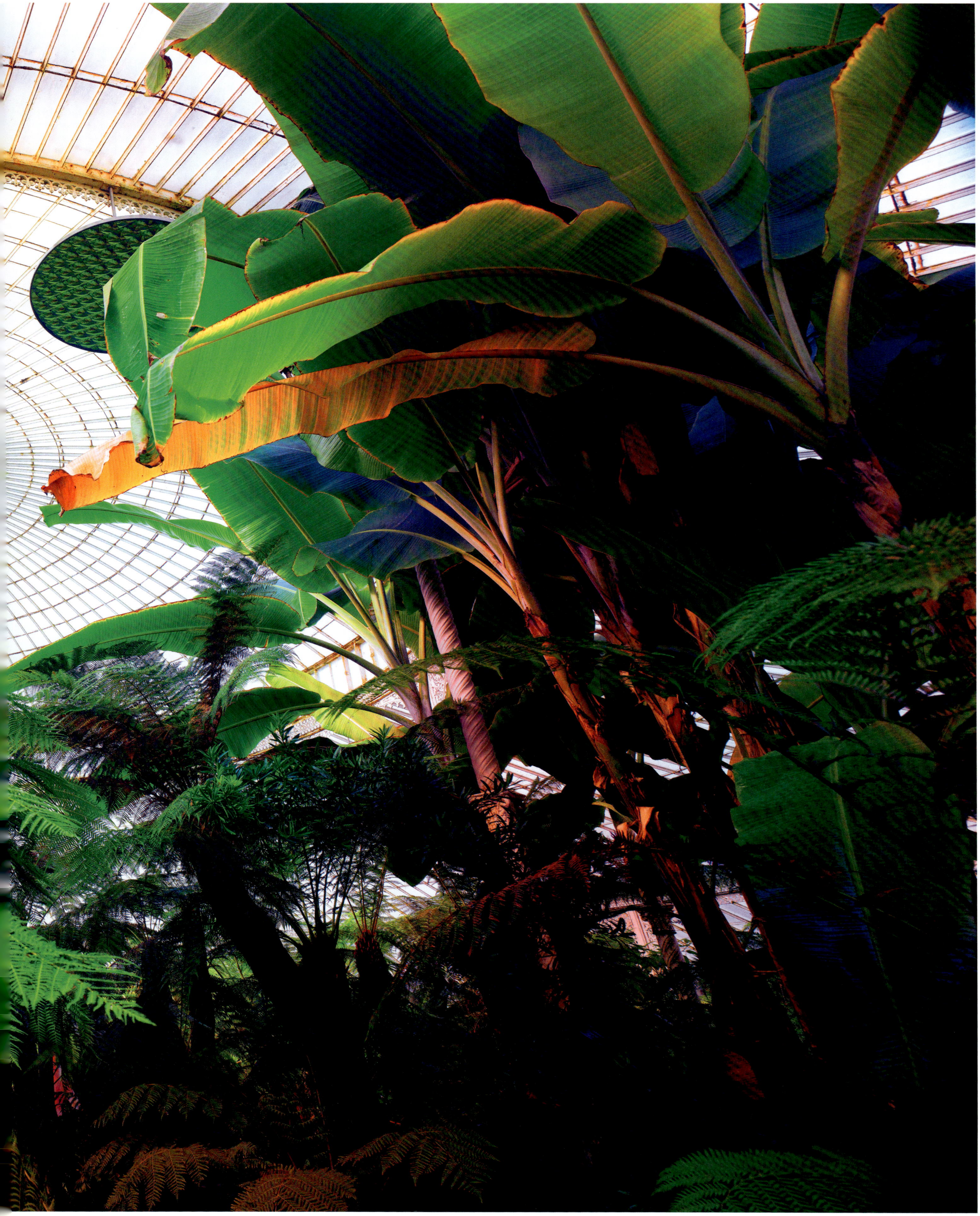

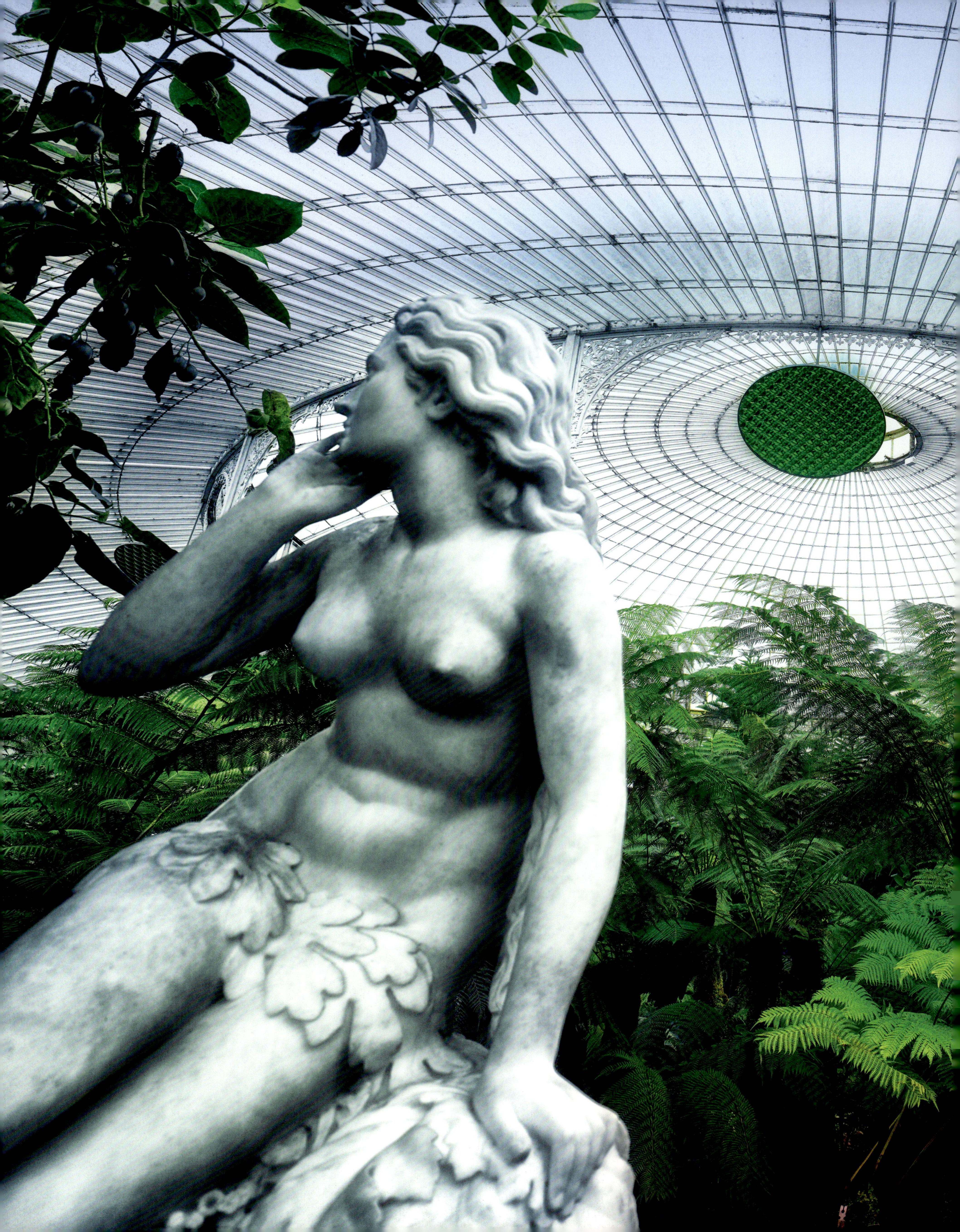

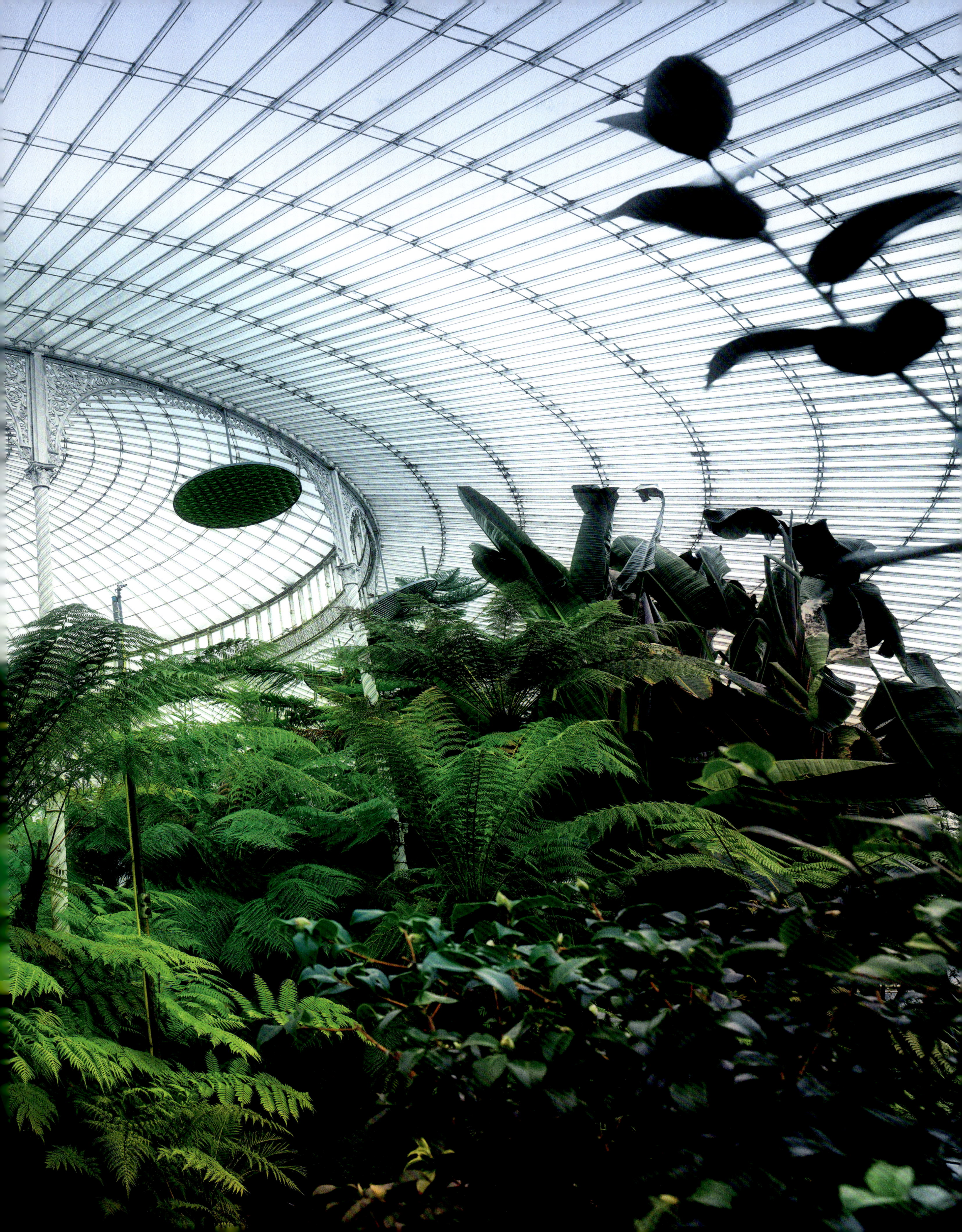

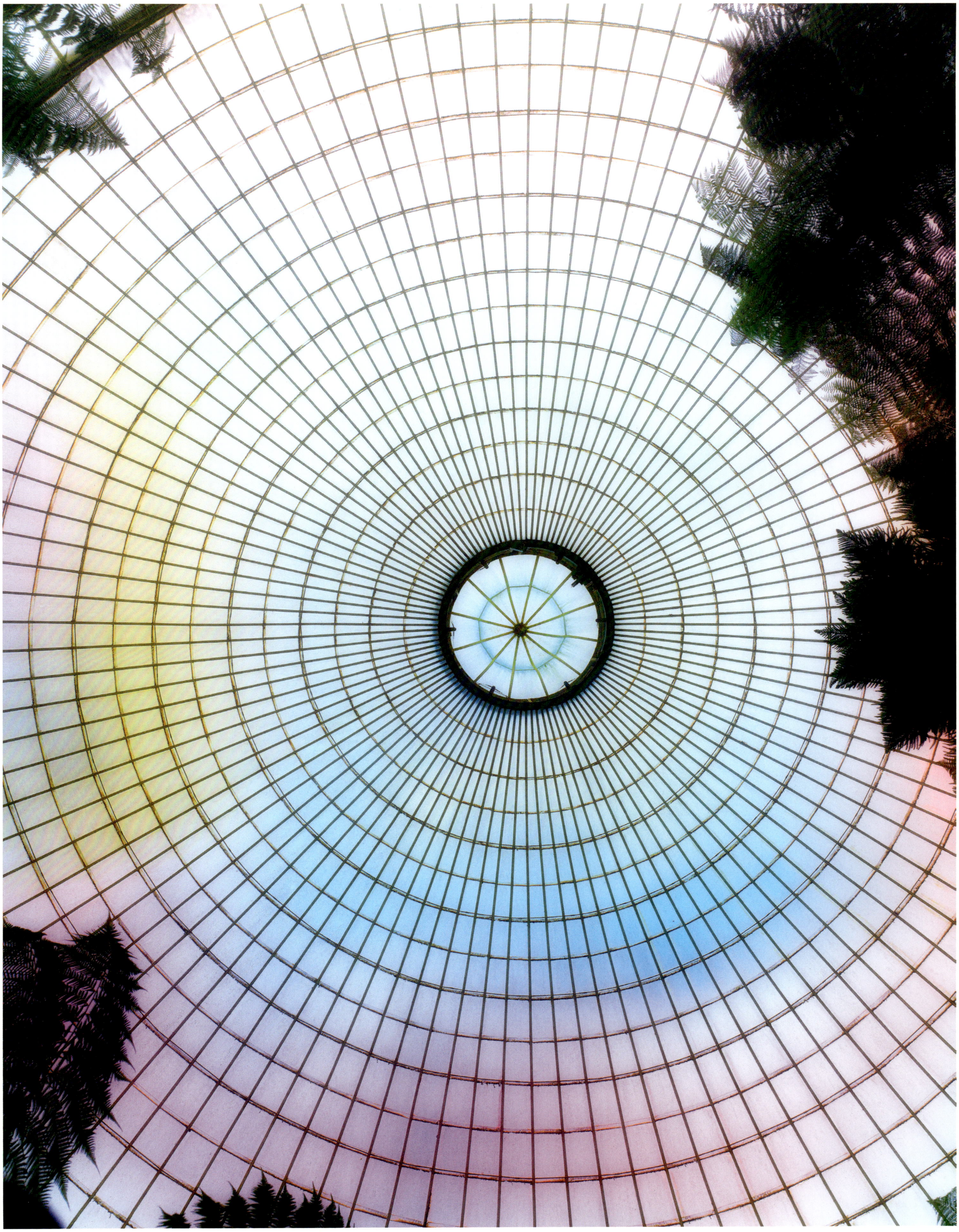

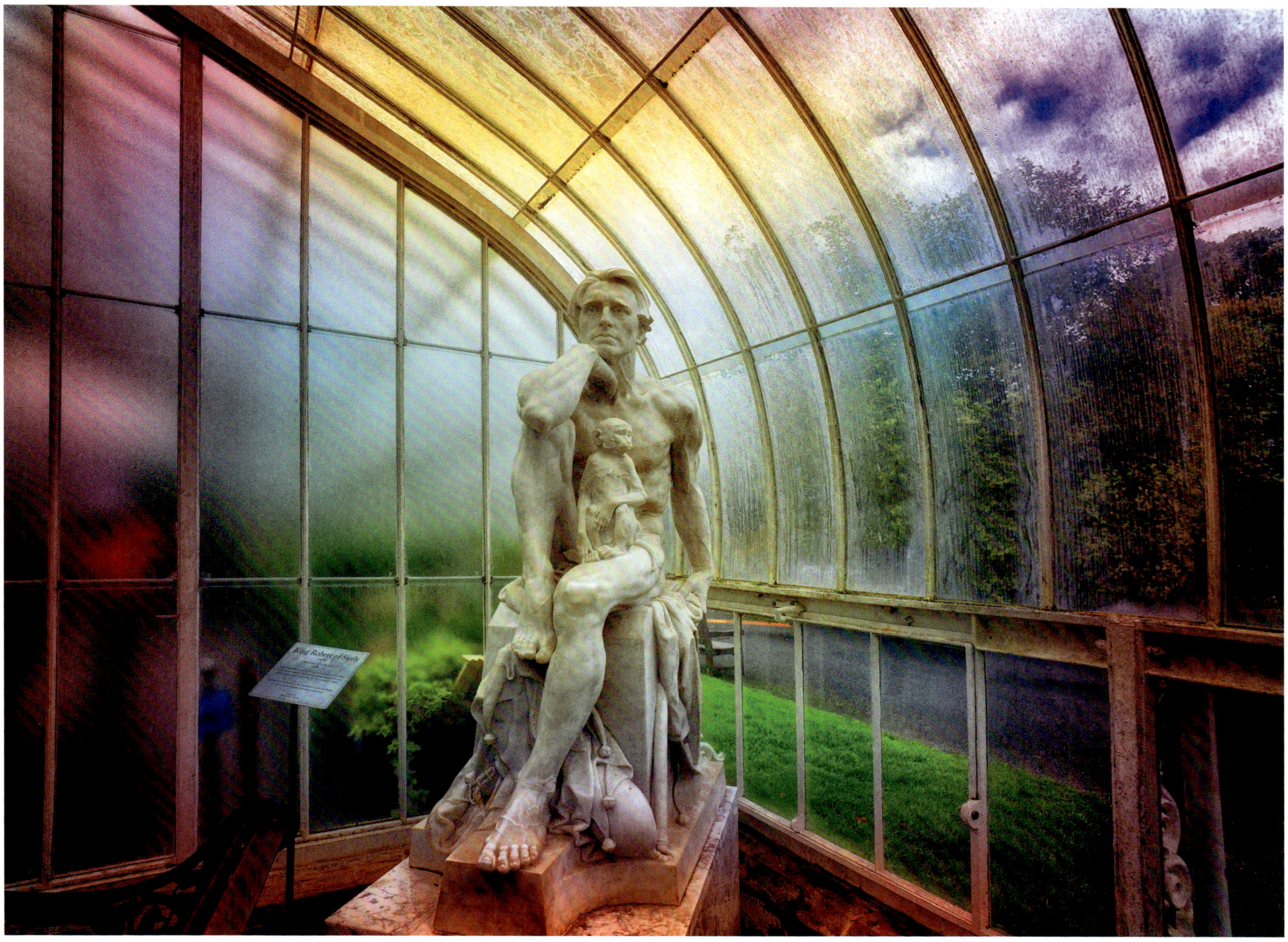

Kibble Palace Glasgow VI • Kibble Palace Glasgow IX
Kibble Palace Glasgow VIII ▼

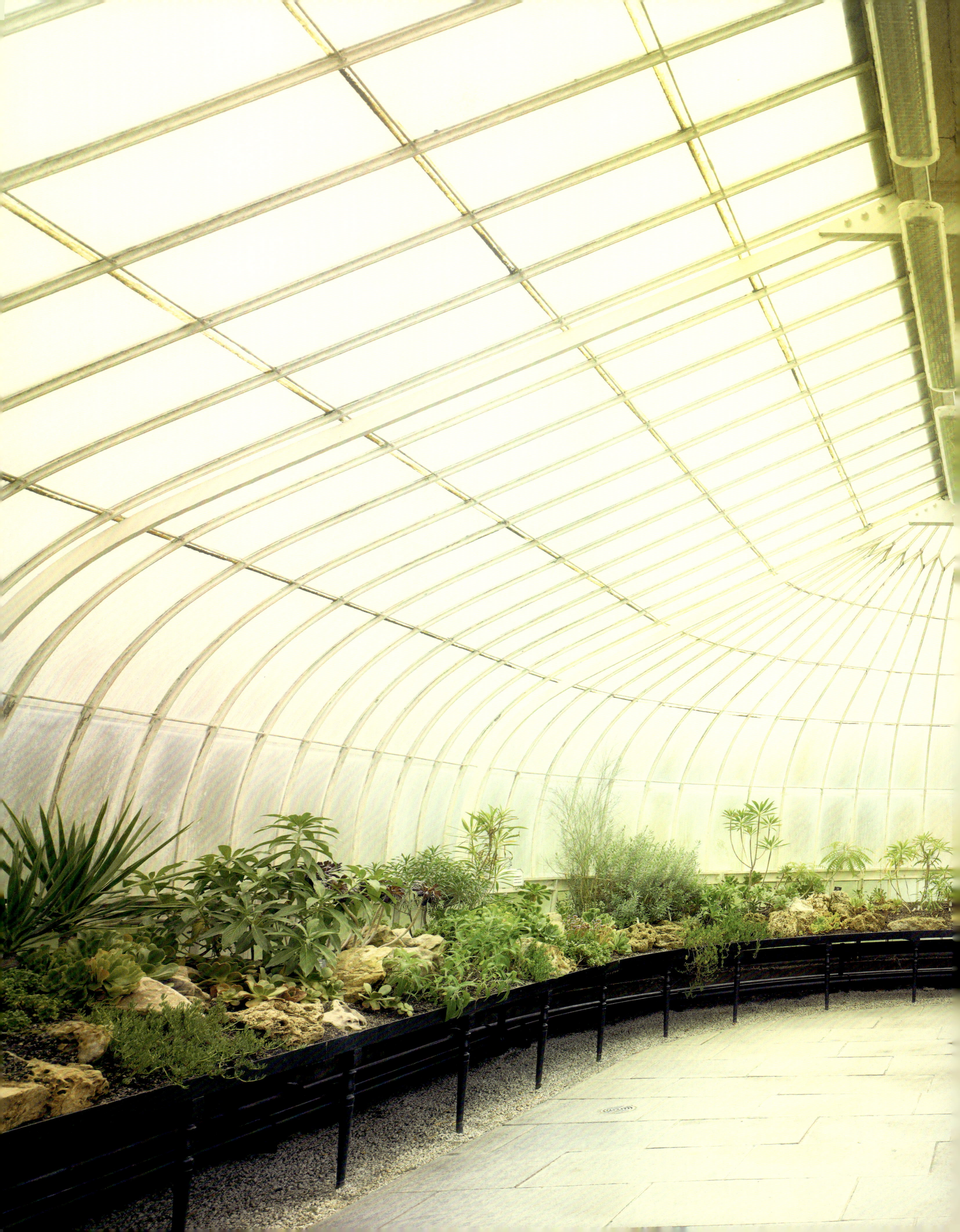

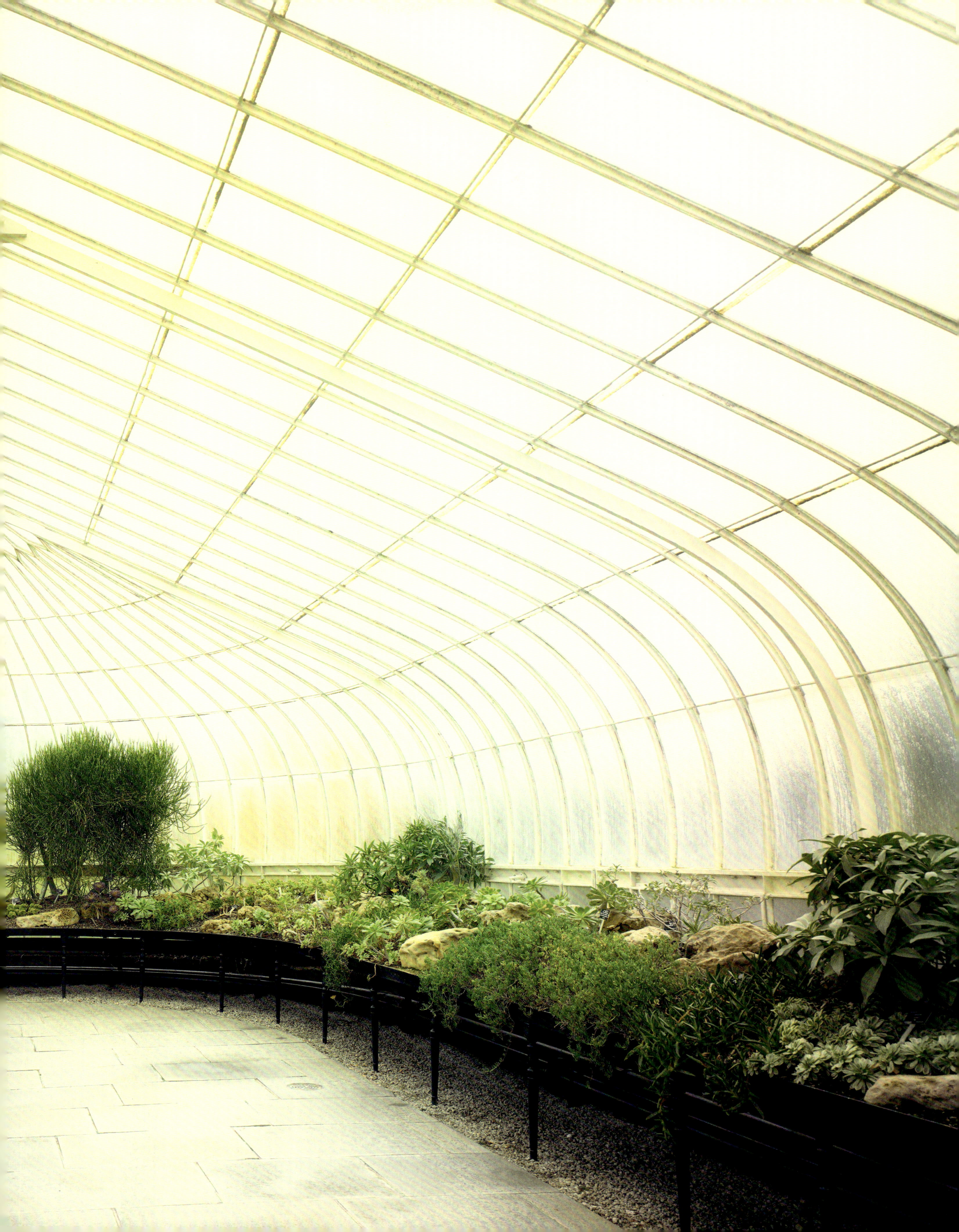

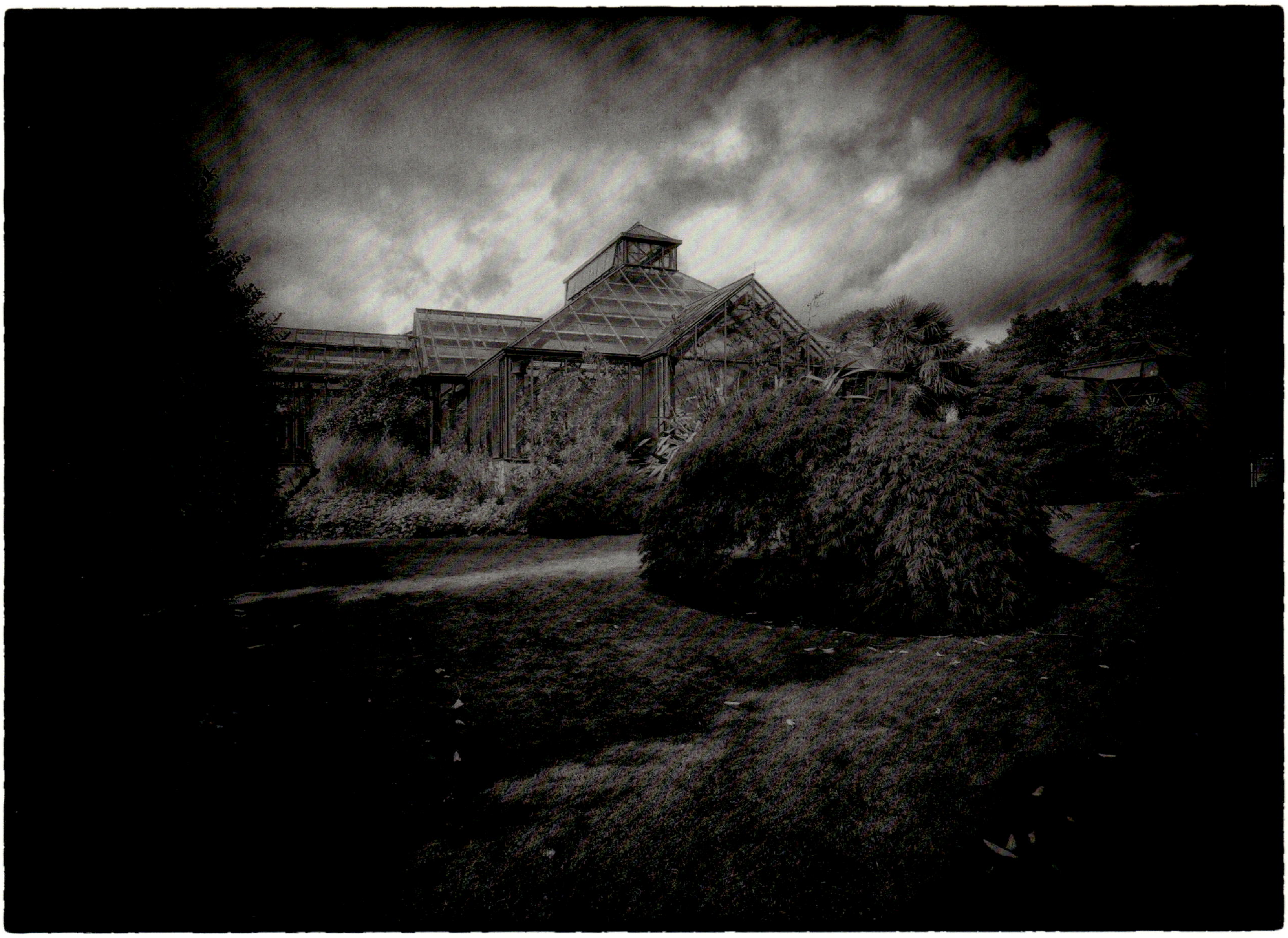

CONSERVATORY PALM HOUSE

GLASGOW

CONSERVATORY AND PALM HOUSE

ORT
Glasgow, England,
Vereinigtes Königreich Großbritannien

ENTSTEHUNG
1878,
Restaurierungen 1988 und 2004 (Westflügel)

ARCHITEKTUR
Einer dreistufigen Pyramide gleich verjüngt sich der Bau auf quadratischem Grundriss zum Walmdach. Seitlich schließen hieran mehrere Glasflügel auf rechteckigem Grundriss mit Satteldach.

PFLANZEN
Verschiedene Temperatur- und Feuchtigkeitsbereiche mit unterschiedlicher Bepflanzung von tropischem Regenwald- bis zum Wüstenklima

BESONDERHEITEN
Die Materialwahl 1878 von Teakholz knüpfte bewusst an das historische Baumaterial eines Gewächshauses aus Holz an. Das beständige Tropenholz verkörperte Exotik und verdeutlichte zugleich die Unterschiede zum kurz zuvor errichteten Kibble Palace aus Glas und Eisen. Bei den Restaurierungen ersetzte man das Teakholz durch Stahl.

LOCATION
Glasgow, Scotland,
United Kingdom, Great Britain

ESTABLISHED
1878,
restorations in 1988 and 2004 (west wing)

ARCHITECTURE
Like a three-tiered pyramid, the building with its square footprint tapers to a hipped roof. Several glass wings featuring a rectangular footprint and a pitched roof connect to the sides of the building.

PLANTS
Different temperature and humidity zones with a variety of plantings ranging from tropical rain forest to desert climates

ADDITIONAL NOTES
In 1878, the decision to use teakwood as a material was a deliberate reference to the historic building material of a wooden greenhouse. The durable tropical wood embodied the exotic while at the same time underscoring its differences to Kibble Palace, which had been built of glass and iron only a short time before. During the restorations, the teak was replaced by steel.

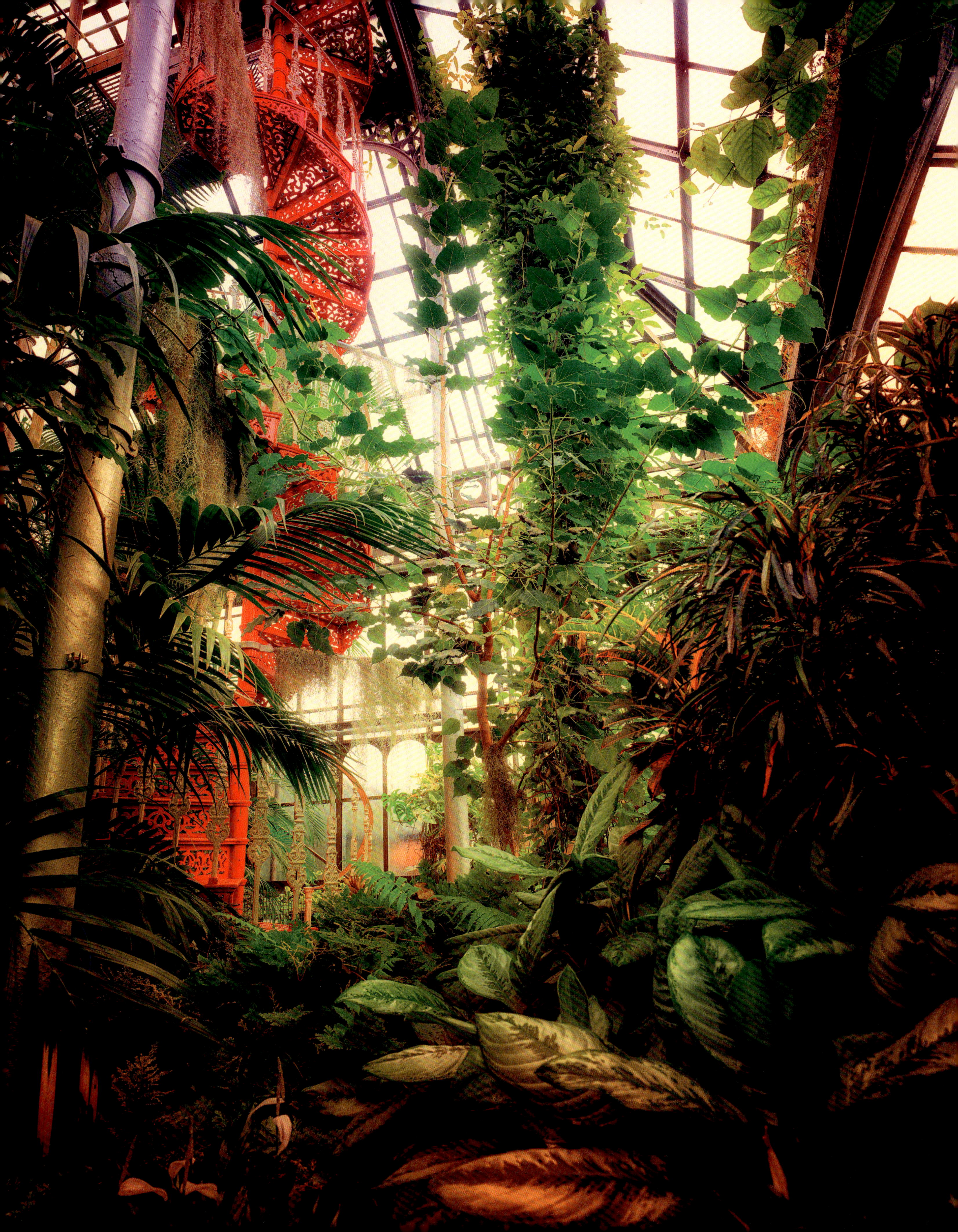

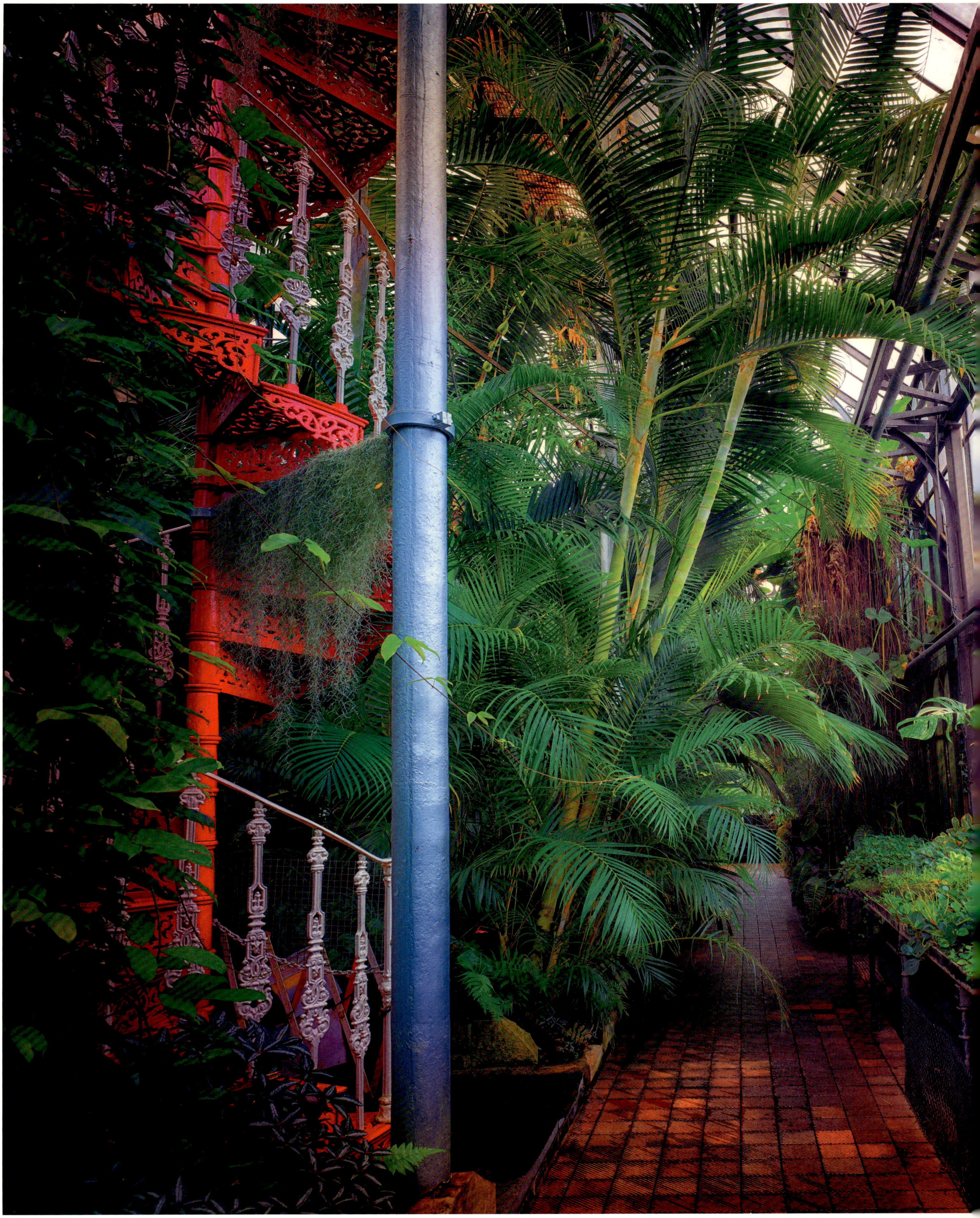

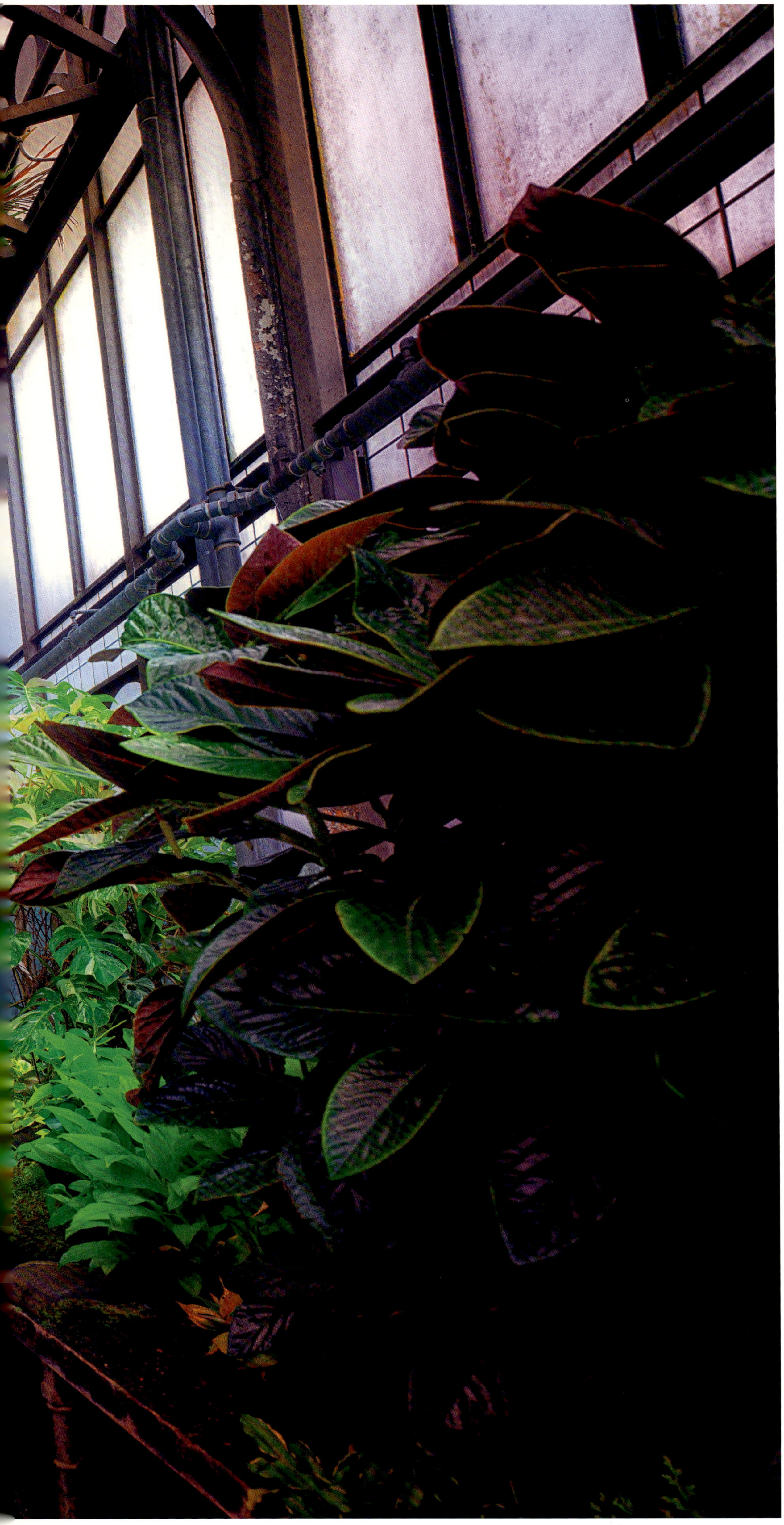

Glasgow Palmhouse III
Glasgow Palmhouse IV ▼

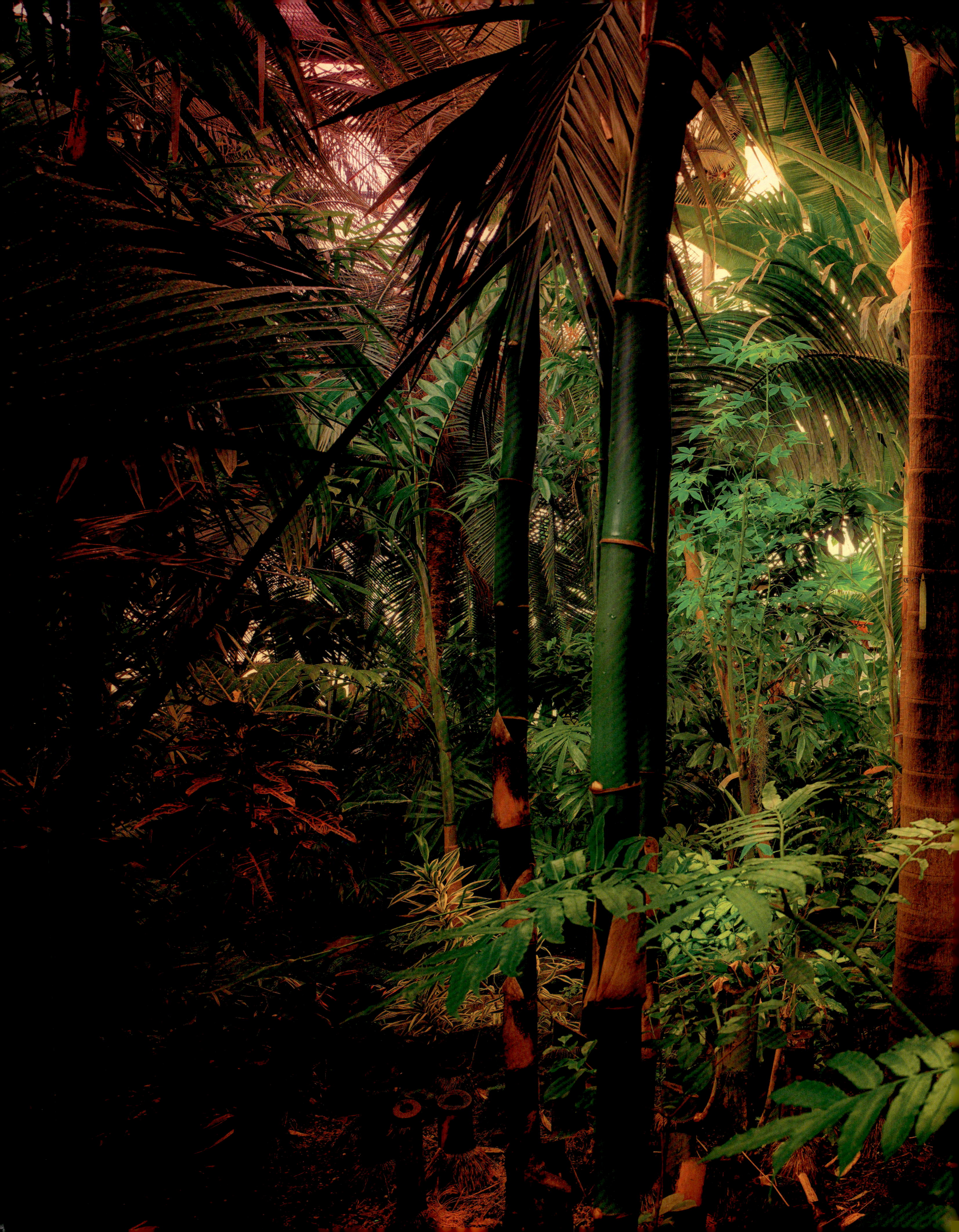

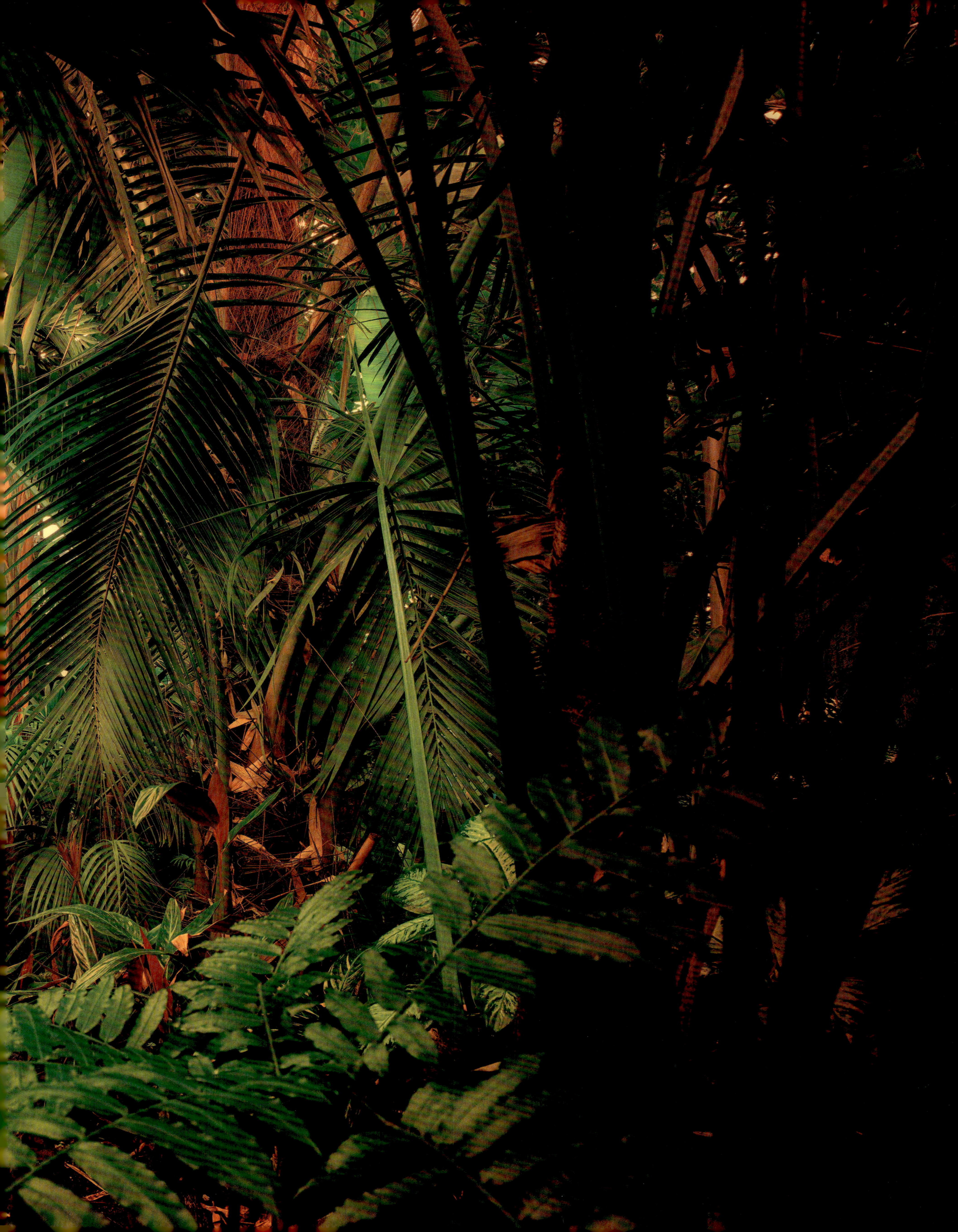

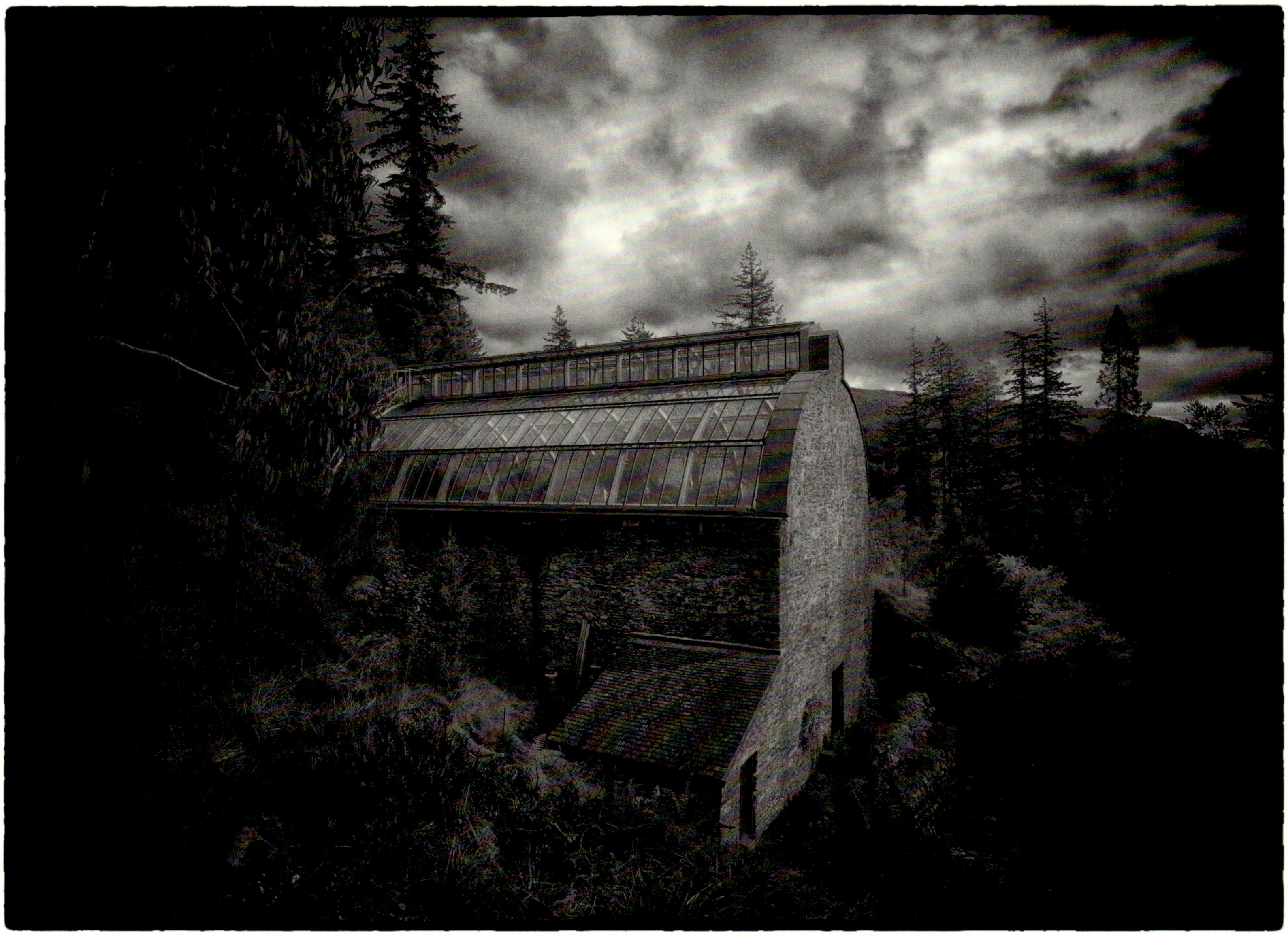

BOTANIC GARDEN

BENMORE

BOTANIC GARDEN FERNERY

ORT
Benmore, Schottland,
Vereinigtes Königreich Großbritannien

ENTSTEHUNG
Zu Beginn der 1870er-Jahre,
rekonstruiert 2008–2009

ARCHITEKTUR
Eingepasst in eine enge Schlucht mit steilen Seiten, erhebt sich das Farnhaus auf rechteckigem Grundriss. Drei Wände sind aus Schieferbruchstein gemauert, während die vierte Wand durch das Felsgestein der Schlucht gebildet wird. Das Tonnengewölbe aus Glas liegt auf Stahlrippen. Landschaftlich eingefügt, erwächst das Farnhaus aus der Naturumgebung. Durch die Anpassung an die natürliche Lage ergibt sich im Raum ein dreistufiges Bodenniveau.

PFLANZEN
Farne und Baumfarne mit weltweiter und regionaler Herkunft

BESONDERHEITEN
Anfang der 1870er-Jahre als privates Gewächshaus für James Duncan, einen Zuckerfabrikanten, errichtet. Das Gewächshaus war Ausdruck der Farnmode („fern craze") des viktorianischen Zeitalters. Nach seinem Bankrott verkaufte Duncan Benmore 1879 und das Farnhaus verfiel. Heute ist es Teil des Königlichen Botanischen Gartens Edinburgh.

LOCATION
Benmore, Scotland,
United Kingdom, Great Britain

ESTABLISHED
In the early 1870s,
reconstructed 2008–2009

ARCHITECTURE
Nestled in a narrow, steep-sided cleft, the Fernery rises on a rectangular footprint. Three walls are constructed of schist rubble, while the fourth wall is formed by the rock of the cleft itself. The barrel vault made of glass rests on steel ribs. Incorporated into the landscape, the Fernery grows out of the natural environment. Thanks to how the design adapted to the natural setting, the space features three different floor levels.

PLANTS
Ferns and tree ferns with global and regional origins

ADDITIONAL NOTES
Built in the early 1870s as a private greenhouse for James Duncan, a sugar refiner. The greenhouse was an expression of the fern craze that had become common during the Victorian era. After his bankruptcy, Duncan sold Benmore in 1879 and the Fernery fell into disrepair. Today it is part of the Royal Botanic Garden Edinburgh.

Benmore IV • Benmore IX ▼

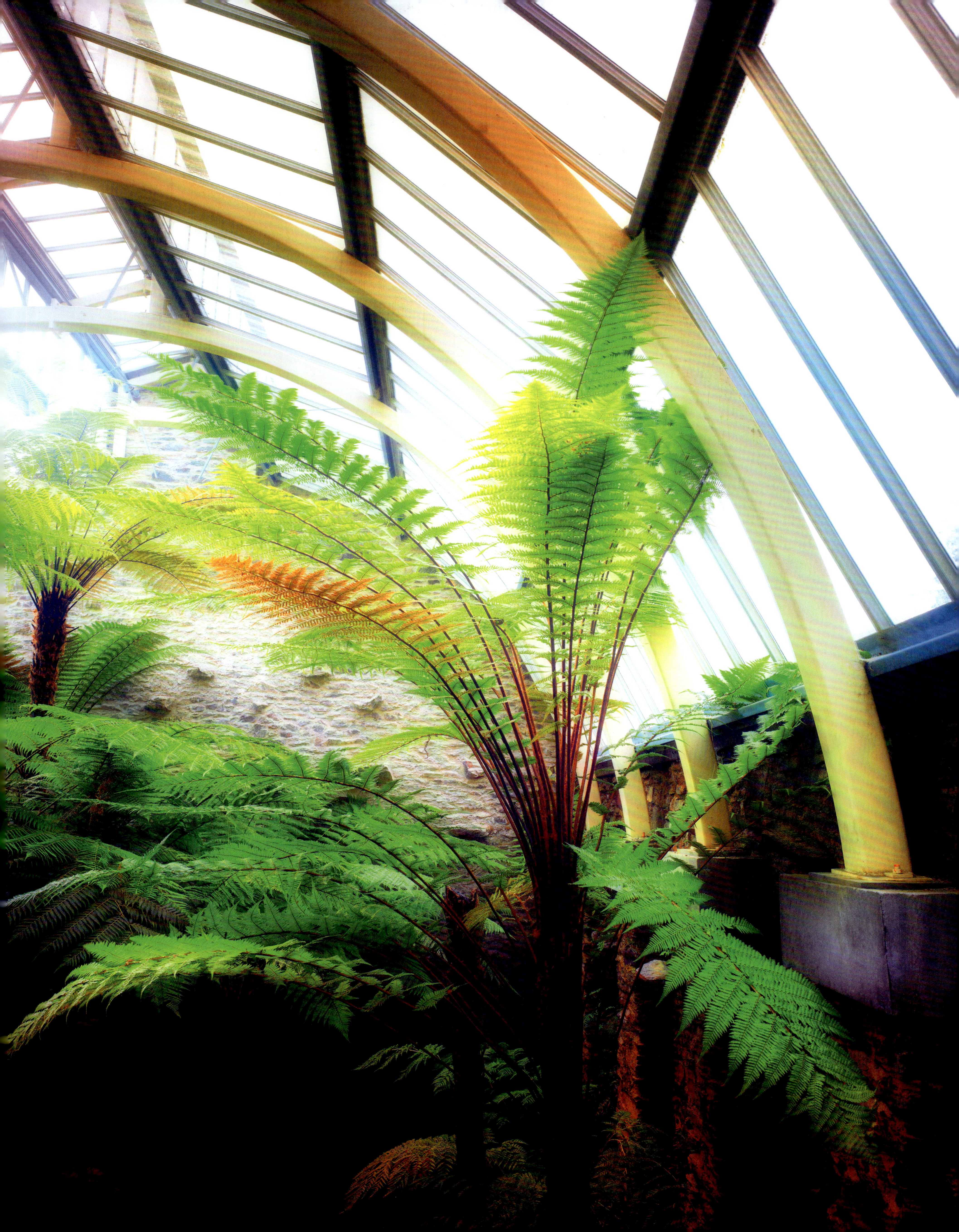

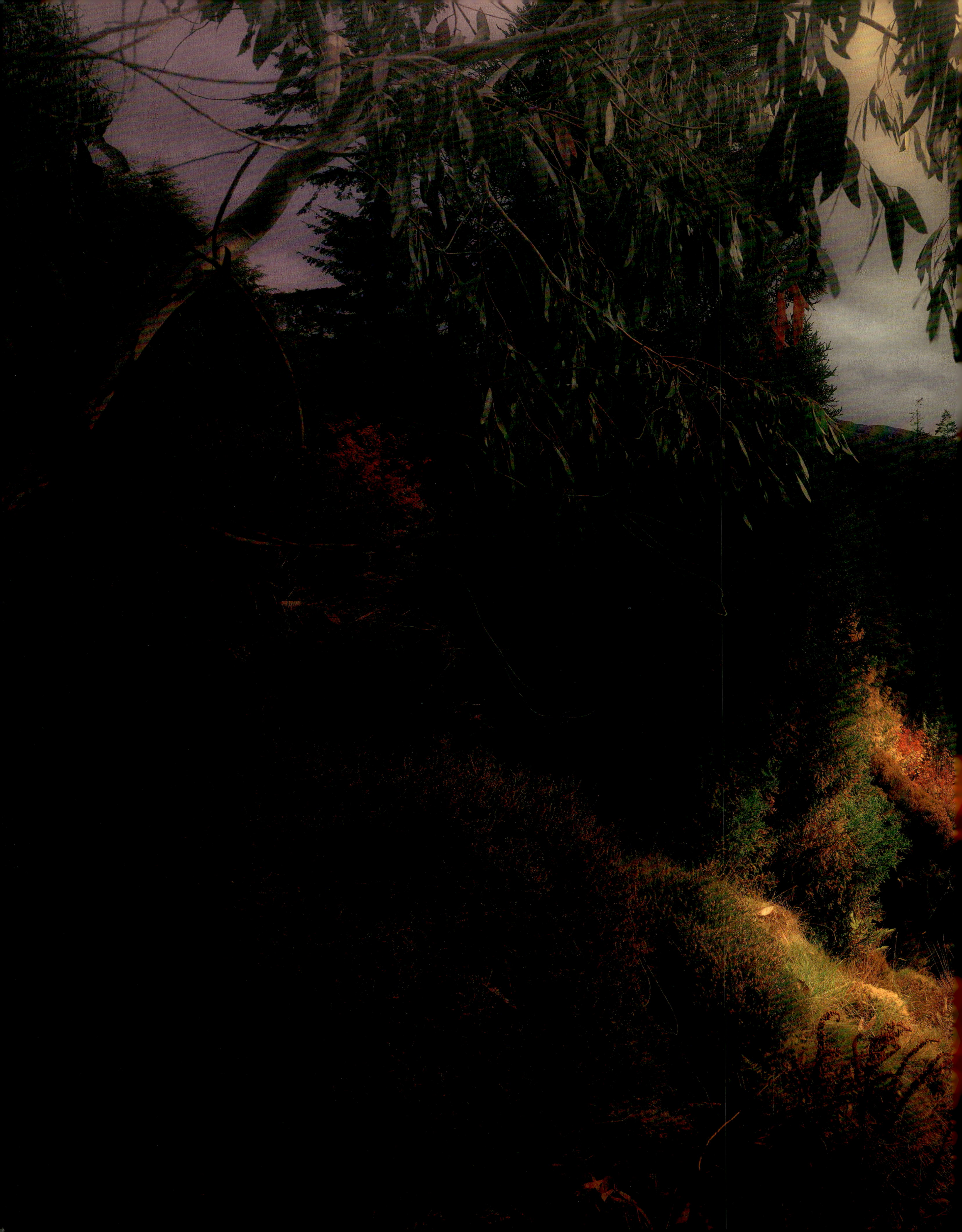

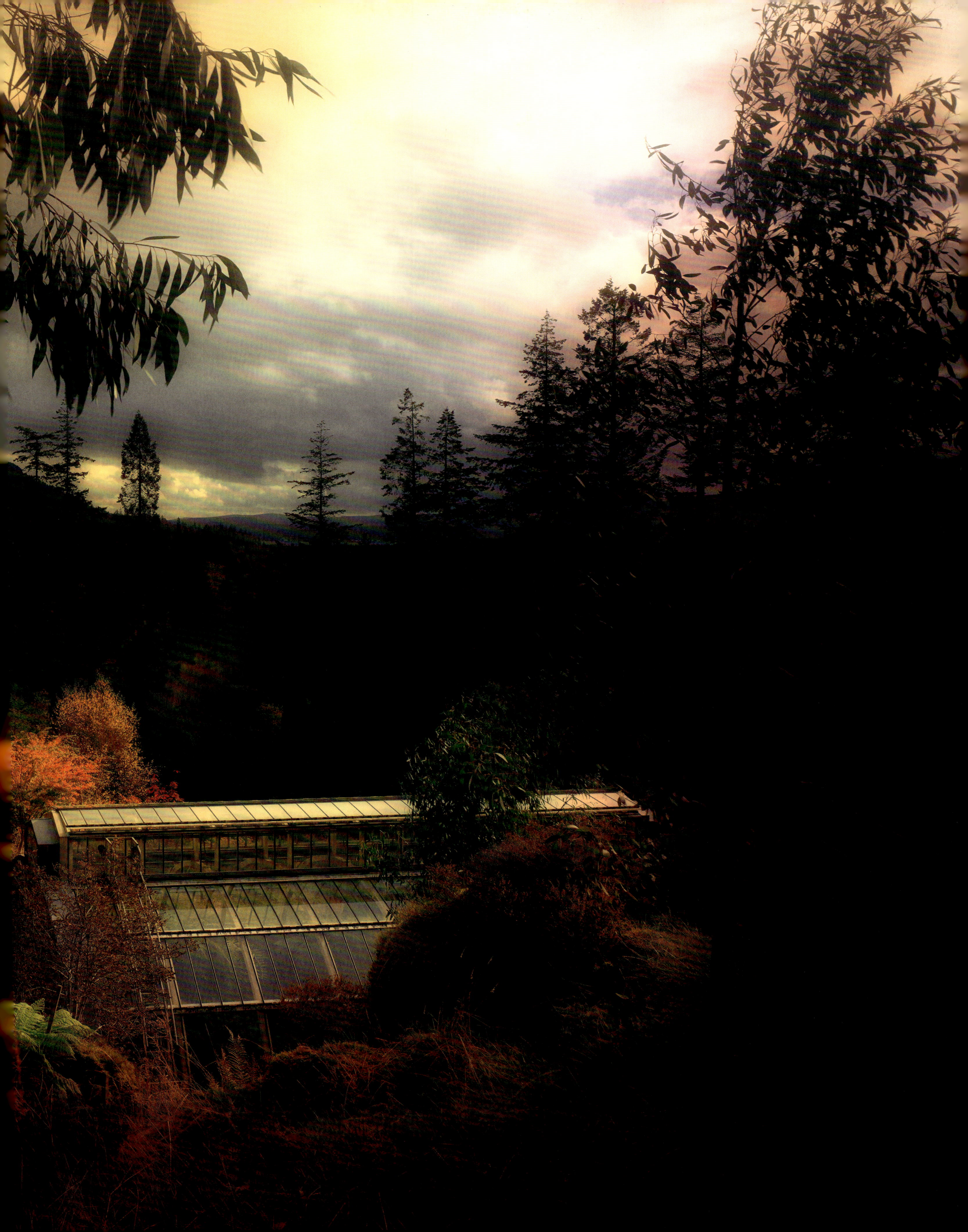

Benmore I

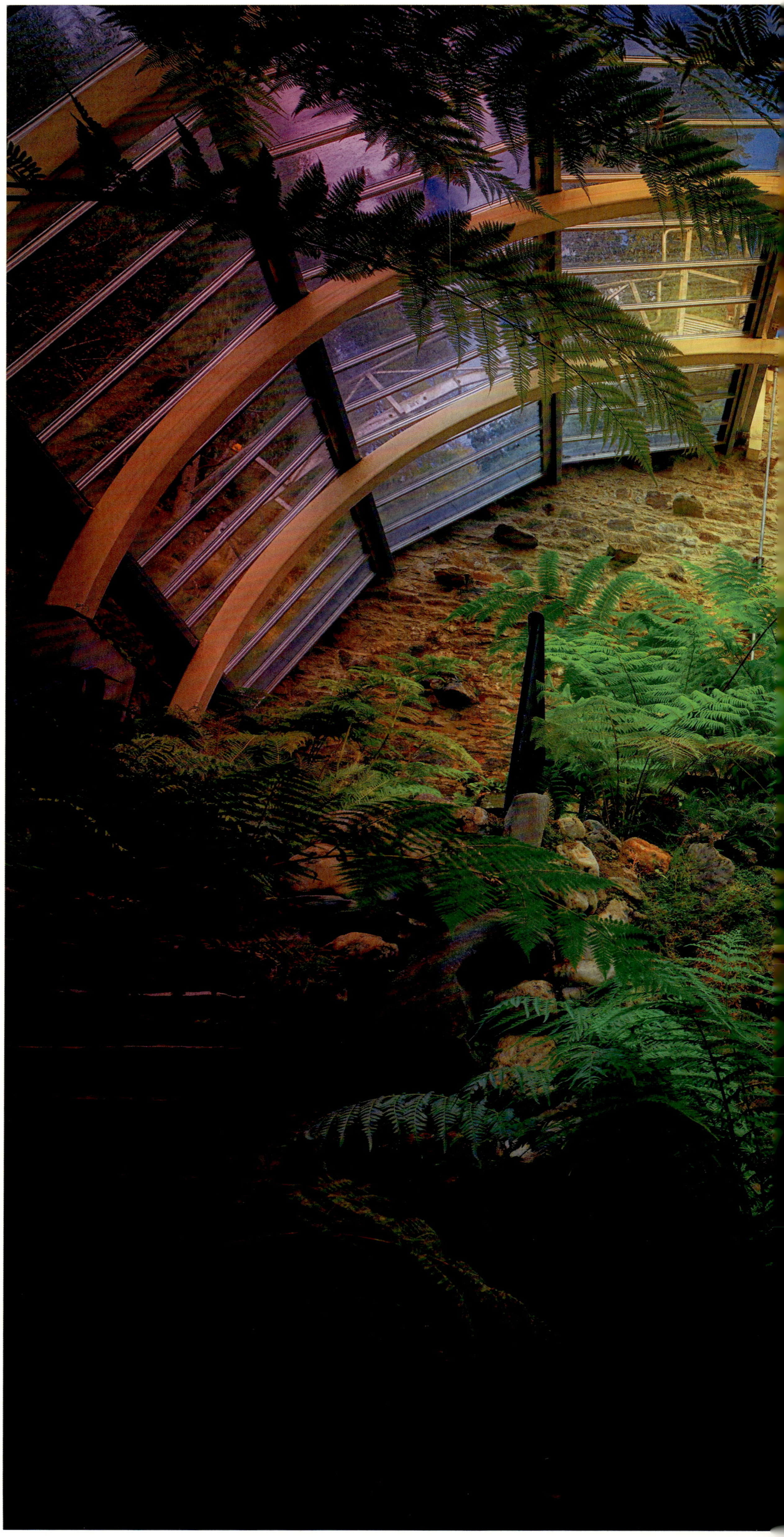

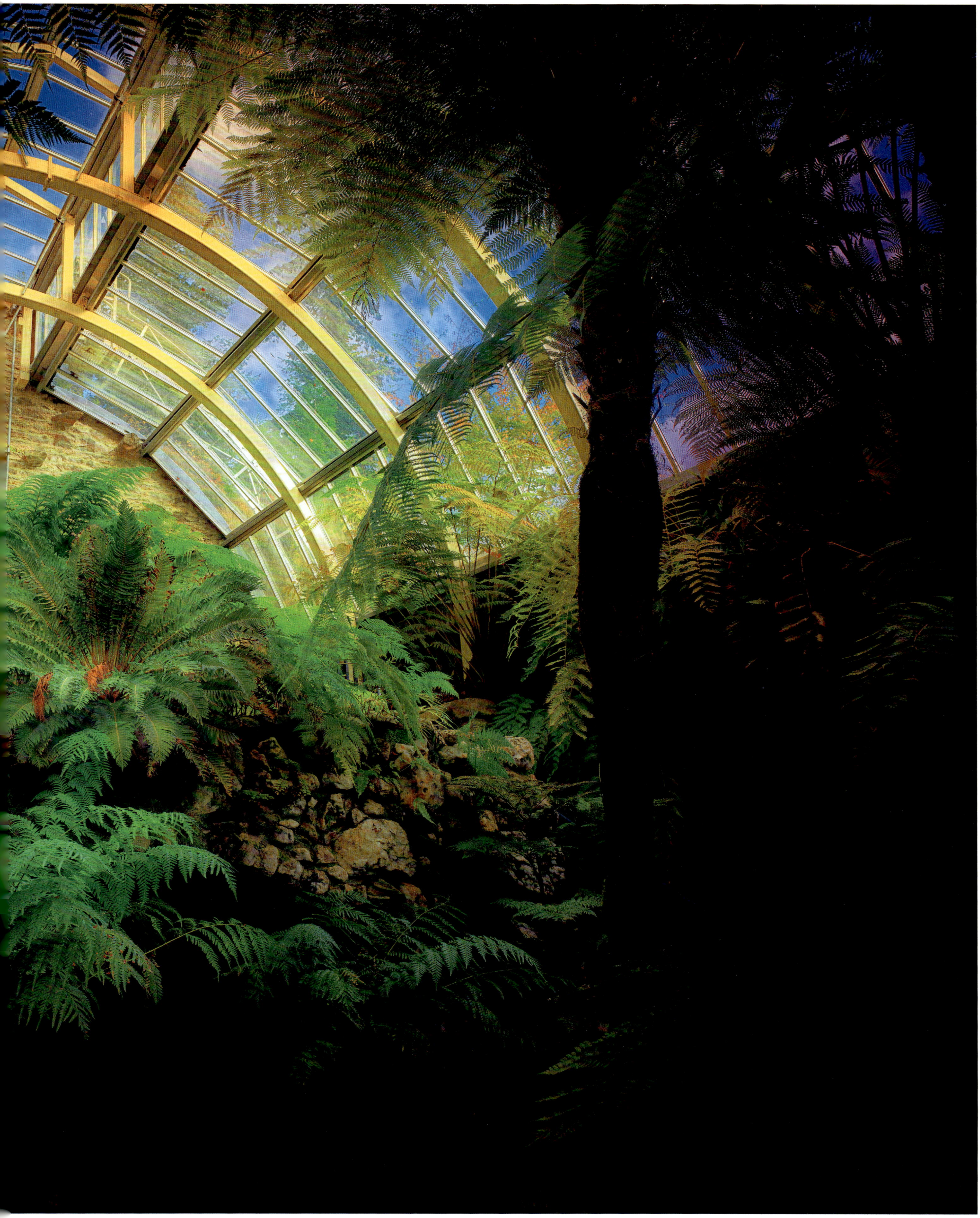

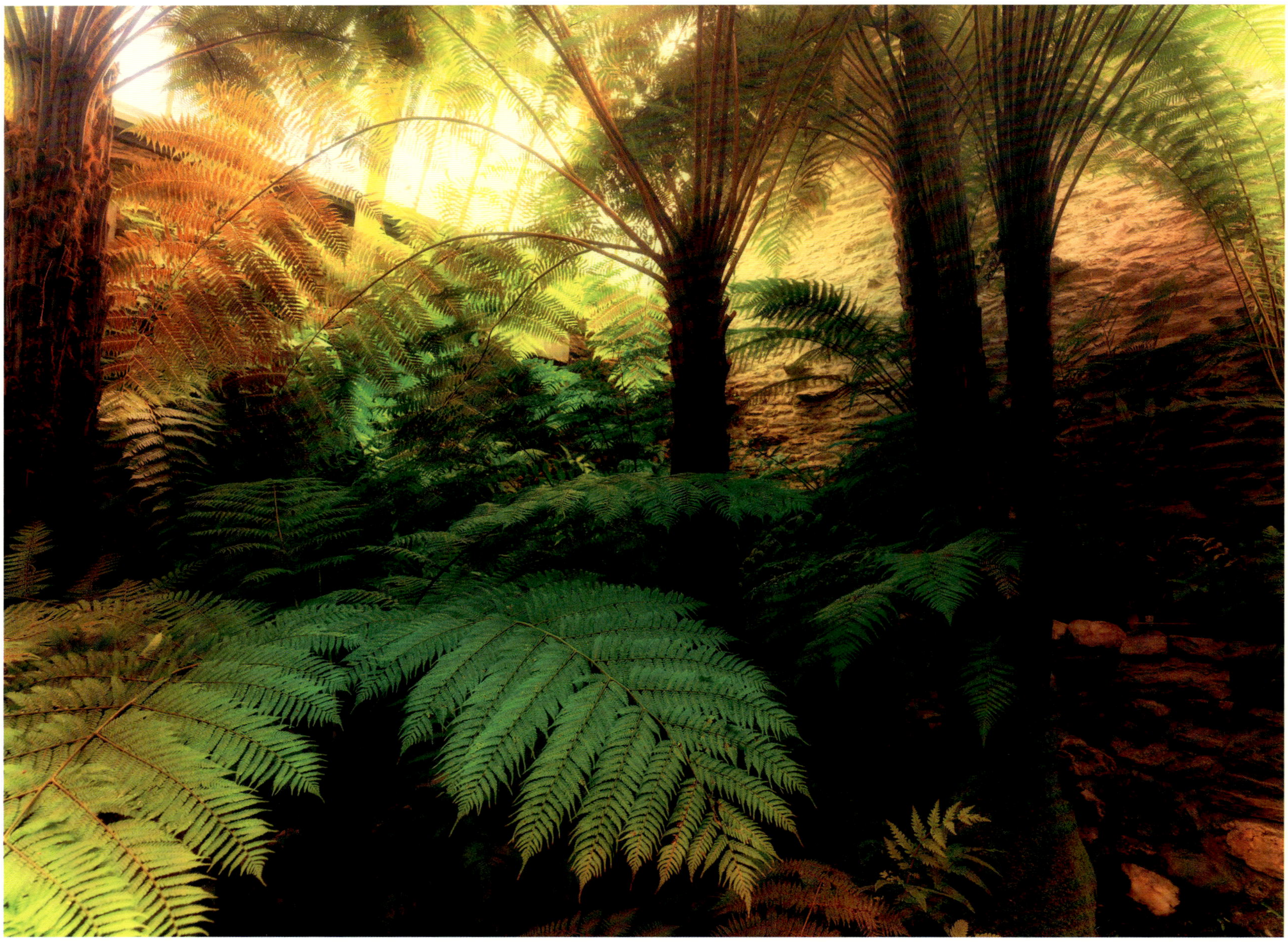

Benmore III · Benmore II

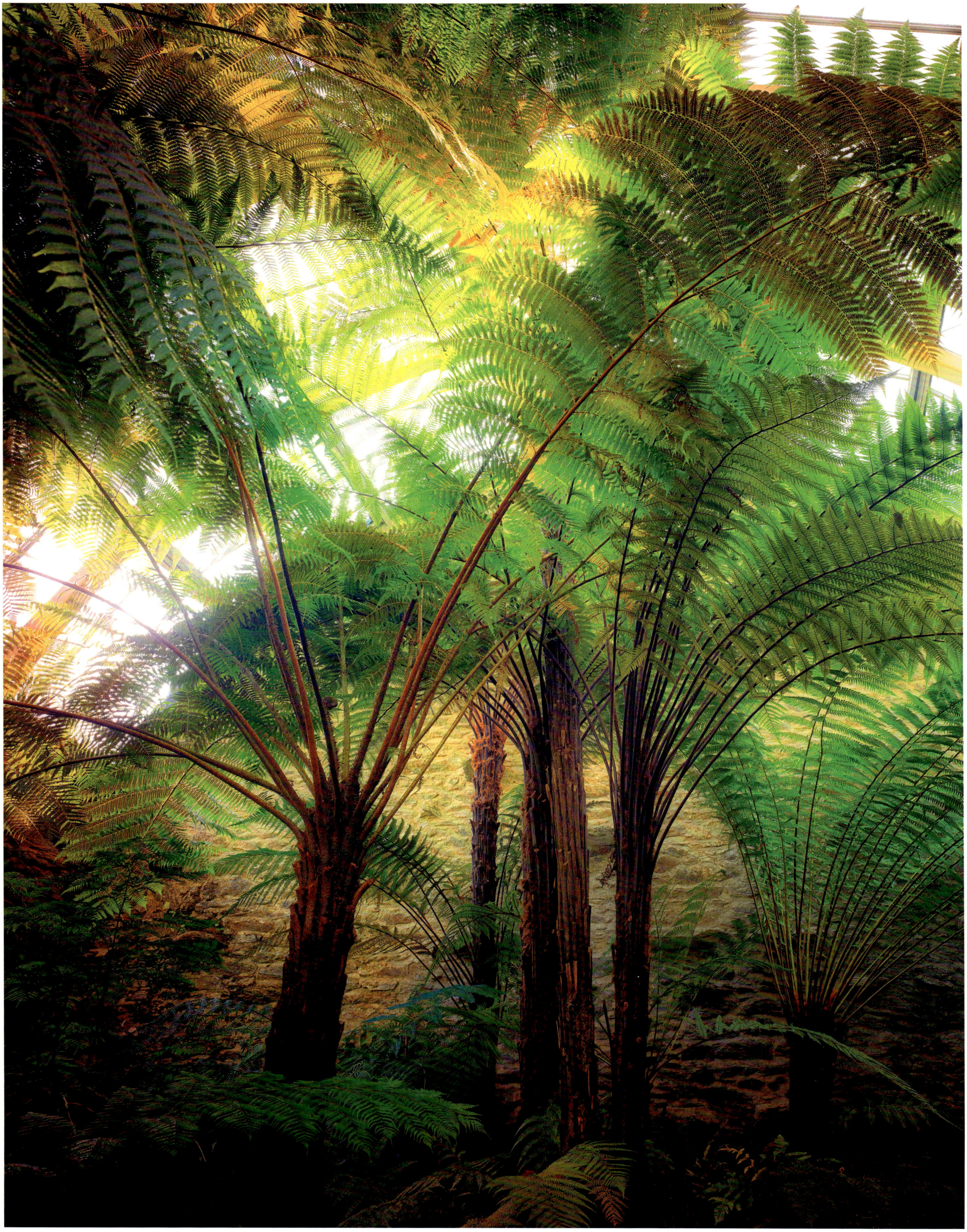

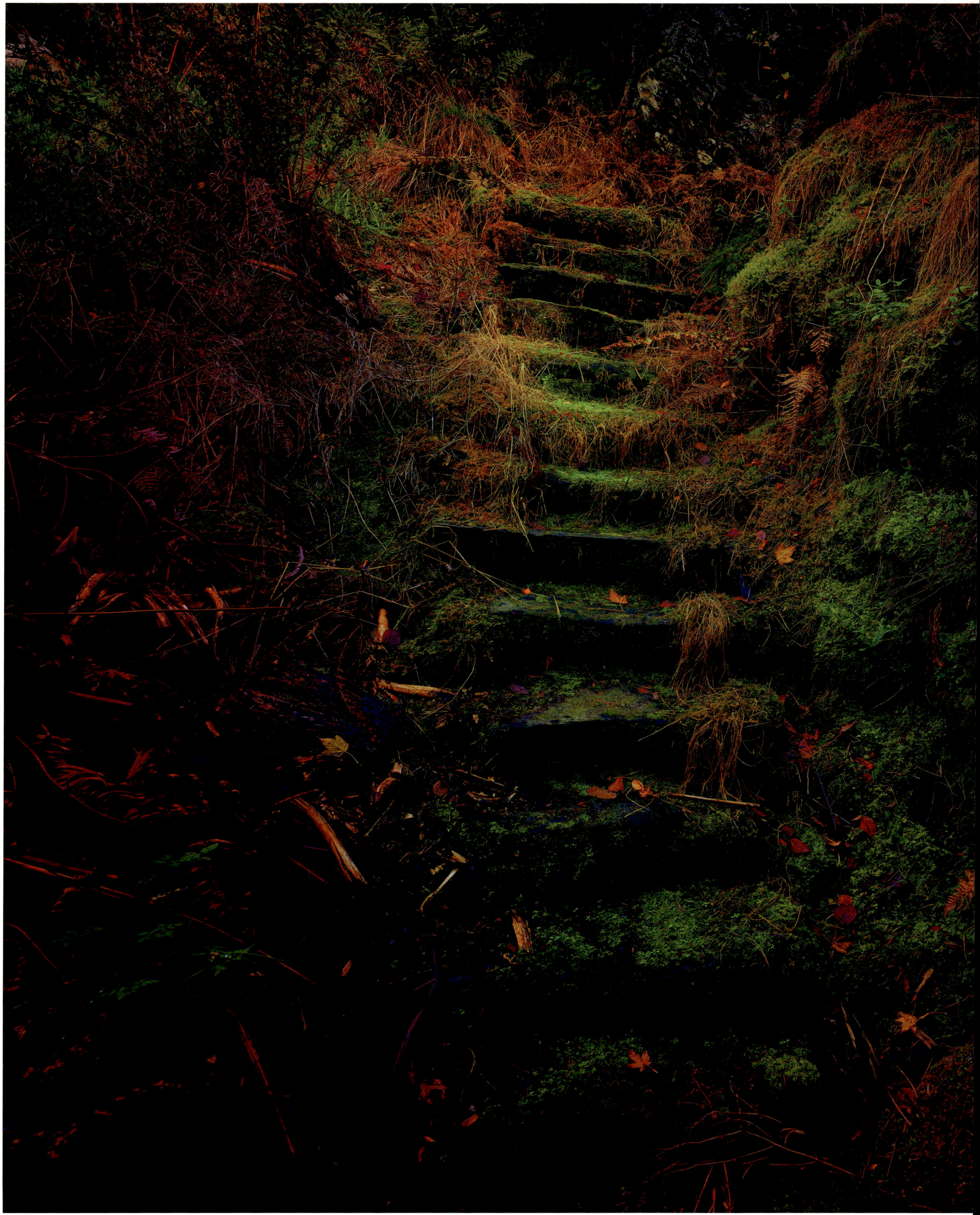

Benmore VI
Benmore X ▼

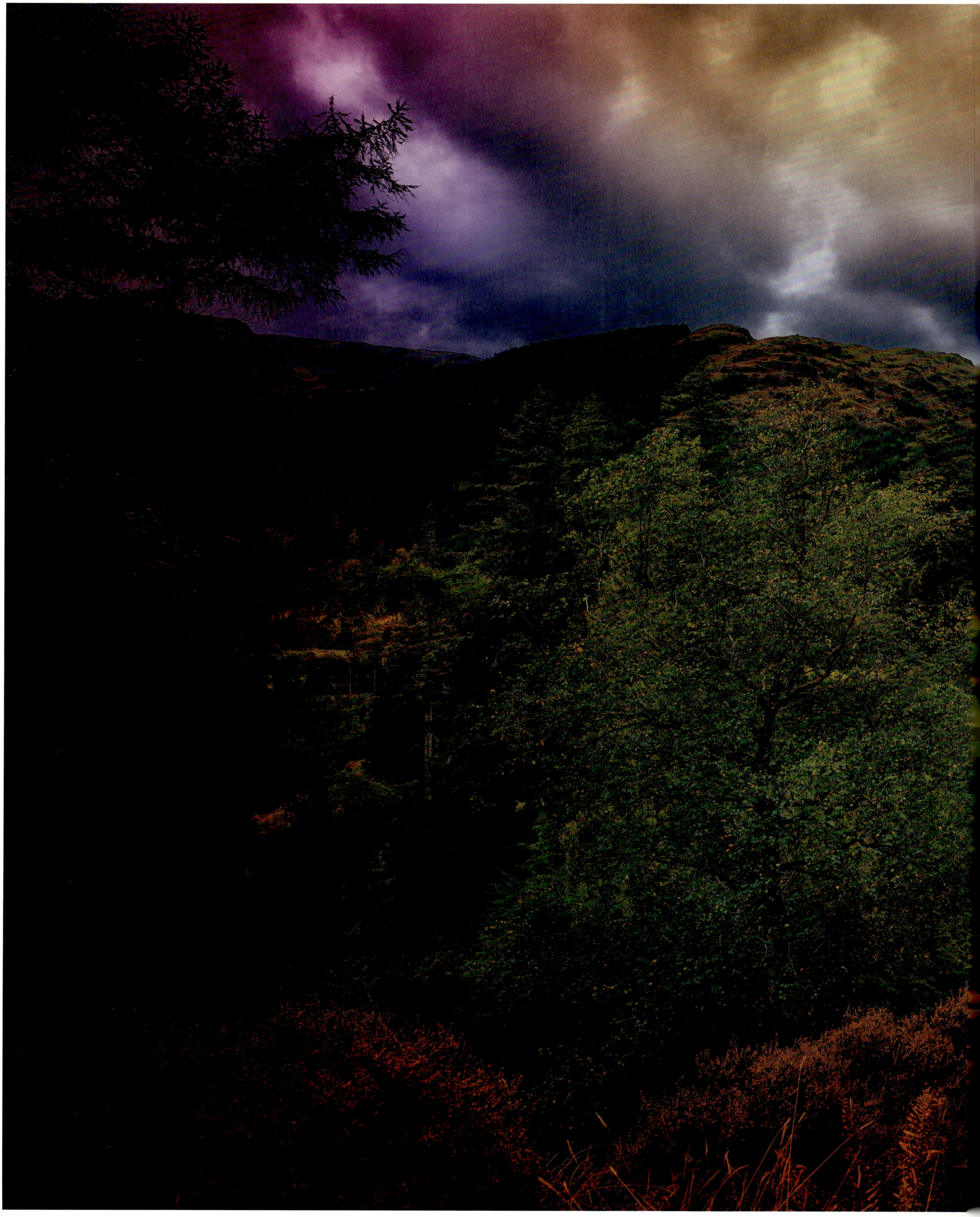

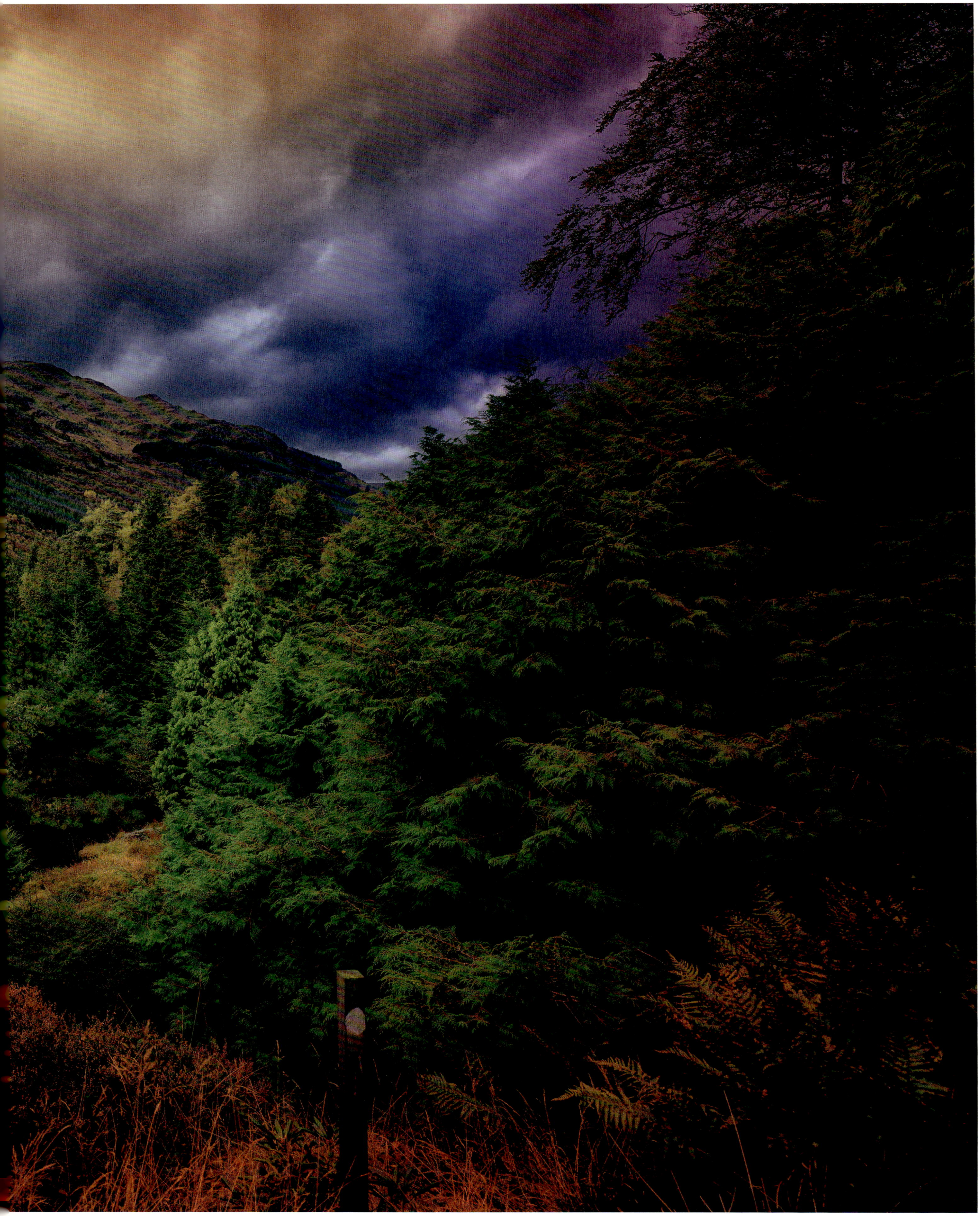

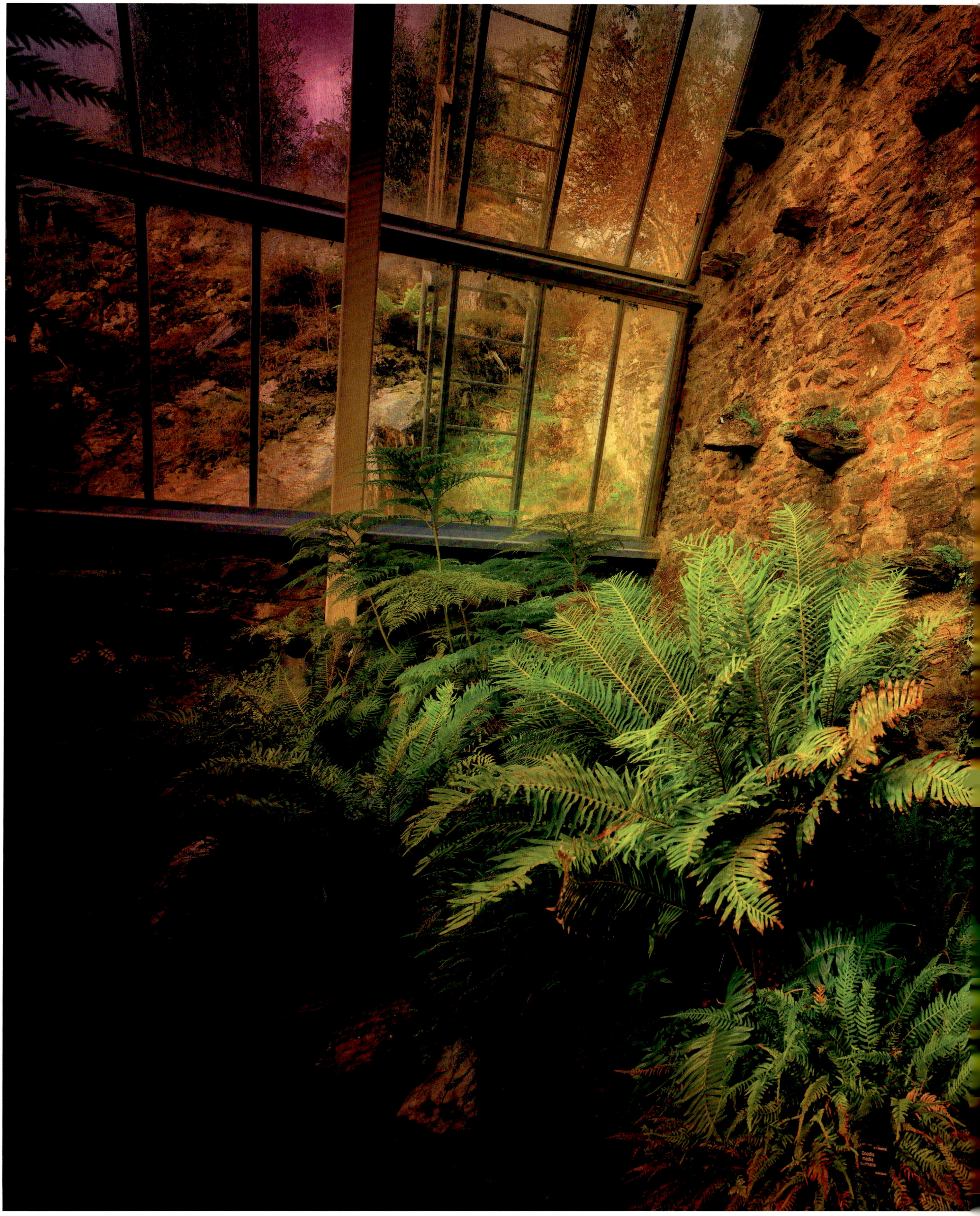
Doodia
media
australis

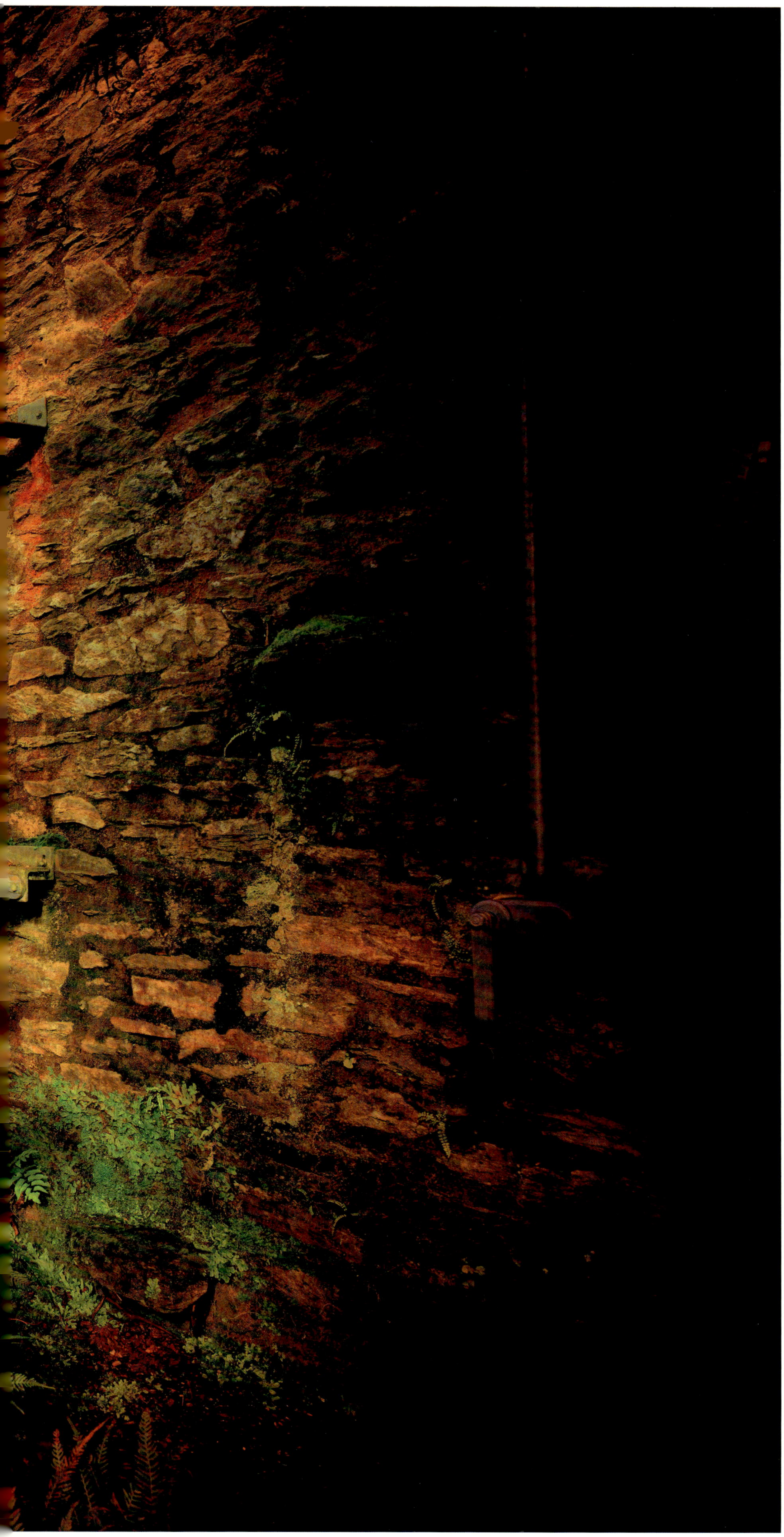

Benmore VII
Benmore XI ▼

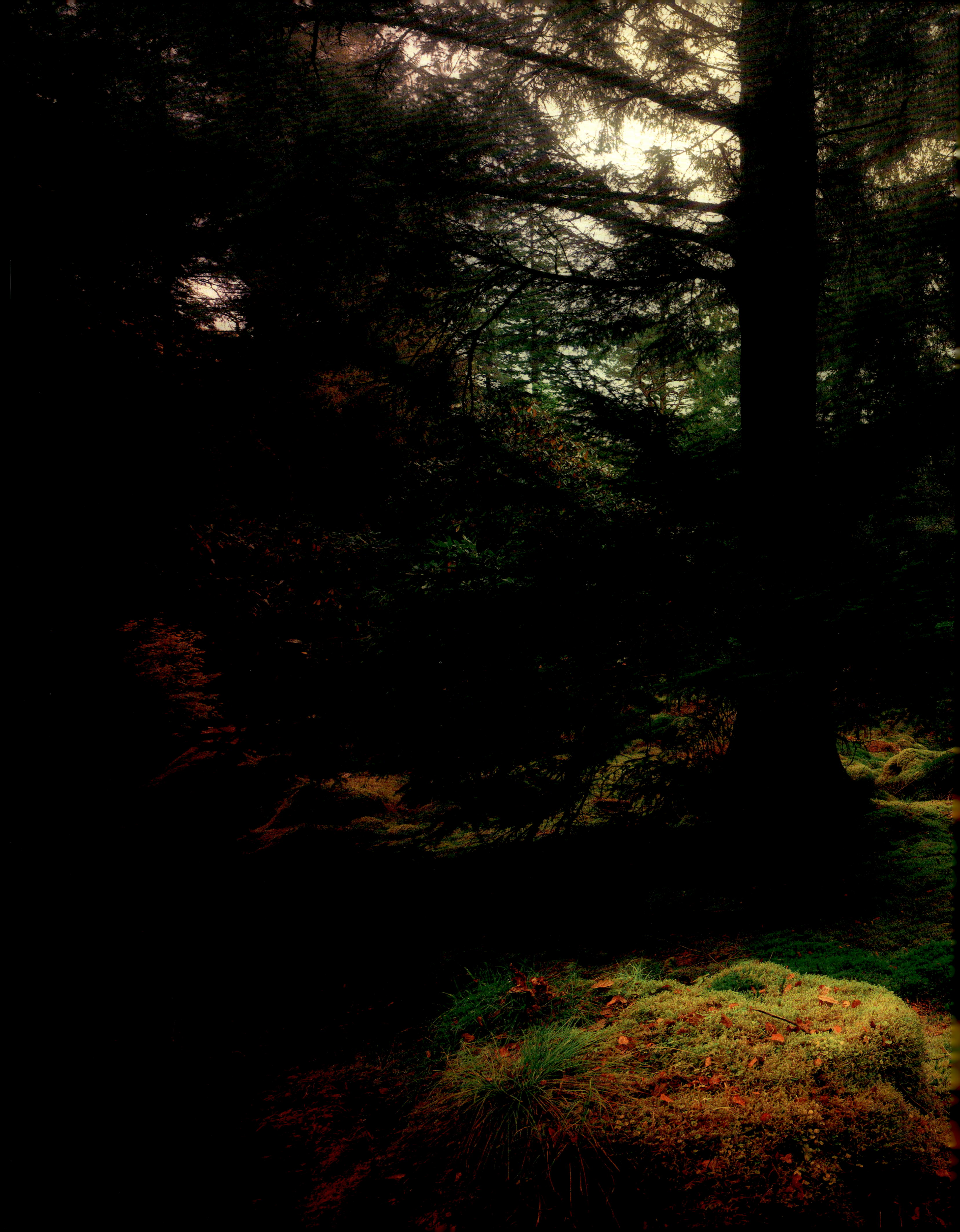

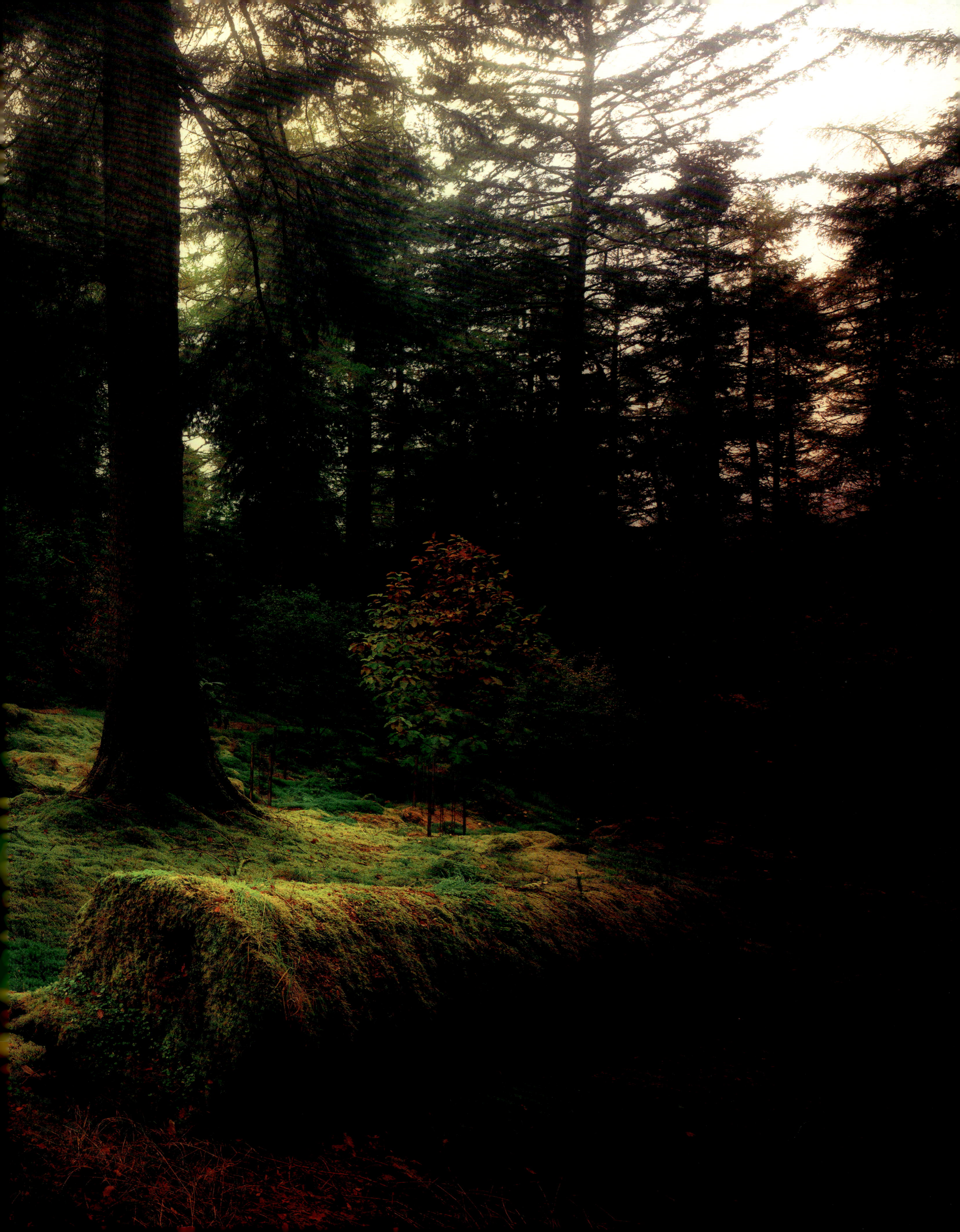

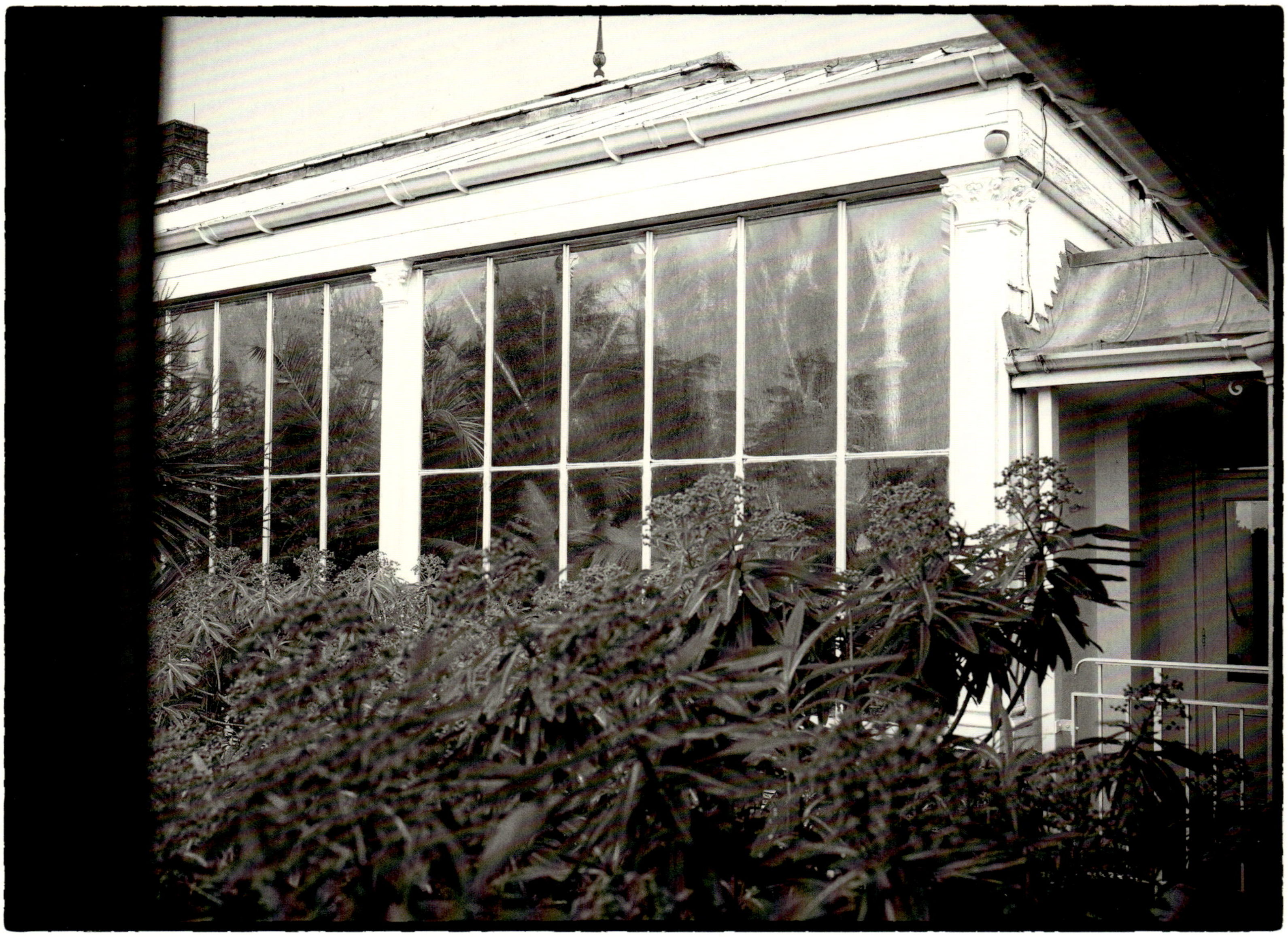

BOTANICAL GARDENS

BIRMINGHAM

BOTANICAL GARDENS AND GLASSHOUSES

ORT
Birmingham, England,
Vereinigtes Königreich Großbritannien

LOCATION
Birmingham, England,
United Kingdom, Great Britain

GRÖSSE
L-förmige Anlage aus vier miteinander verbundenen Gewächshäusern.

SIZE
L-shaped complex consisting of four interconnected greenhouses.

ENTSTEHUNG
Botanischer Garten ab 1829, Gewächshäuser 1852–1884
Entwurf: John Claudius Loudon,
Ausführung der Gewächshäuser später aus Kostengründen durch verschiedene Architekten.

ESTABLISHED
The botanical gardens in 1829, greenhouses 1852–1884
design: John Claudius Loudon;
due to cost constraints, various architects later handled the construction of the greenhouses.

ARCHITEKTUR
An das zentrale Palmenhaus auf quadratischem Grundriss schließen sich die Gewächshäuser auf rechteckigem Grundriss an. Die ursprünglich mehrgeschossigen Eisengusskonstruktionen wurden im 20. Jahrhundert verändert. Im gleichen Jahrhundert wurden auch die Volieren aus Eisenguss in den Botanischen Garten eingefügt, welche die einzigen Überbleibsel der ab den 1910er-Jahren bestehenden zoologischen Abteilung darstellen.

ARCHITECTURE
Featuring a square footprint, the central Subtropical House is adjoined by greenhouses with a rectangular layout. The original multistory cast iron structures were modified in the 20th century. In the same century, the cast iron aviaries were added to the botanical garden; they are the only remnants of the zoological department that existed from the 1910s.

PFLANZEN
Palmen, Baumfarne sowie andere subtropische Pflanzen

PLANTS
Palms, tree ferns, as well as other subtropical plants

BESONDERHEITEN
Die Botanische Vereinigung Birmingham, 1829 als Aktiengesellschaft zur Anlage des Gartens gegründet, plante neben den Botanischen Schaubereichen Verkaufsflächen. Wegen Unrentabilität der Anlage wurde der dritte Erweiterungsbereich Anfang der 1840er-Jahre der Edgbaston Archery & Lawn Tennis Society überlassen, die hier anschließend die heute noch bestehenden, weltweit ersten Rasentennisplätze anlegen ließ.

ADDITIONAL NOTES
When the Birmingham Botanical and Horticultural Society was founded as a joint-stock company in 1829 for the development of the garden, the aim was to create retail areas in addition to the botanical display areas. Because the site was deemed unprofitable, the third expansion area was given to the Edgbaston Archery & Lawn Tennis Society in the early 1840s. The club subsequently had the world's first lawn tennis courts built there, which still exist today.

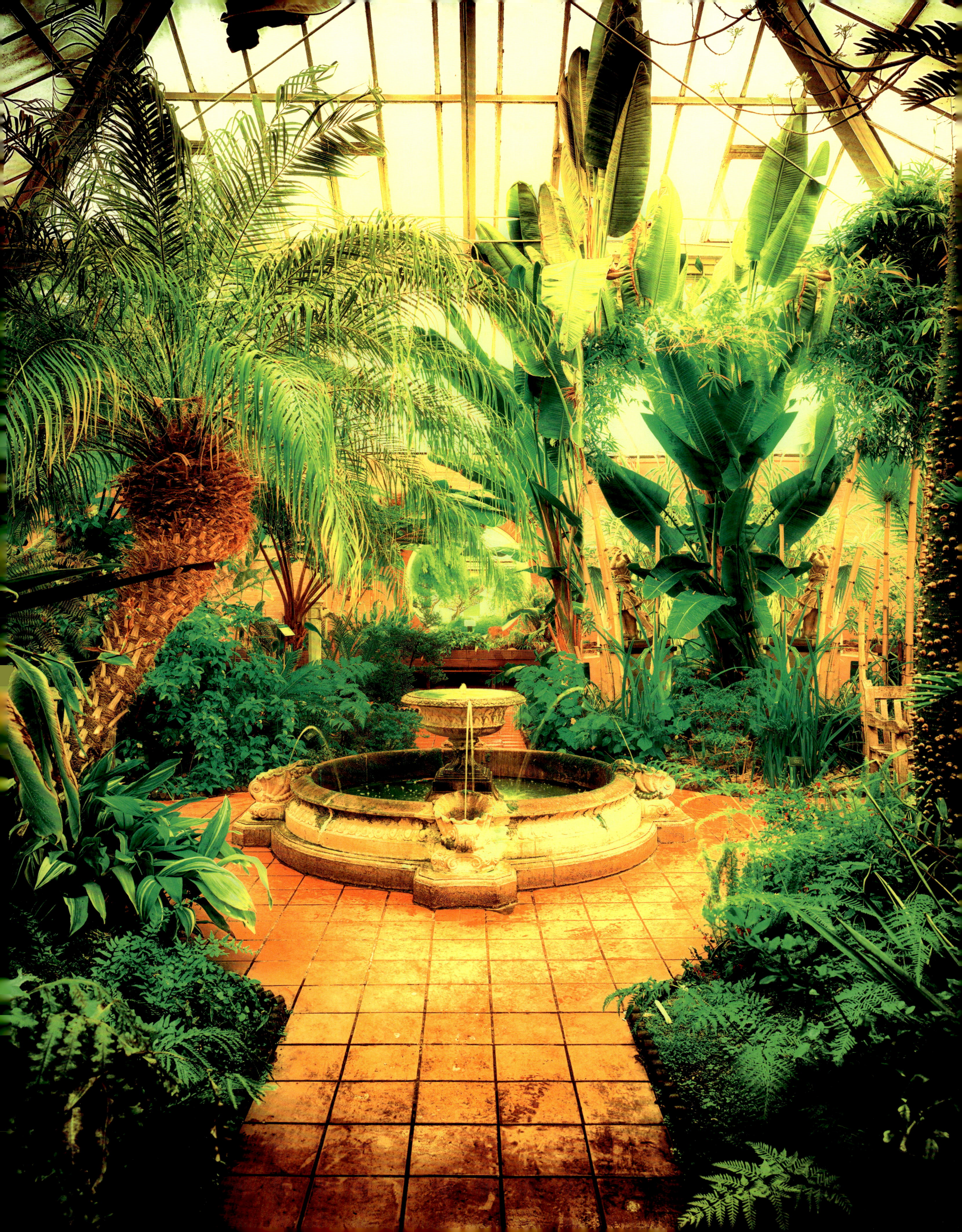

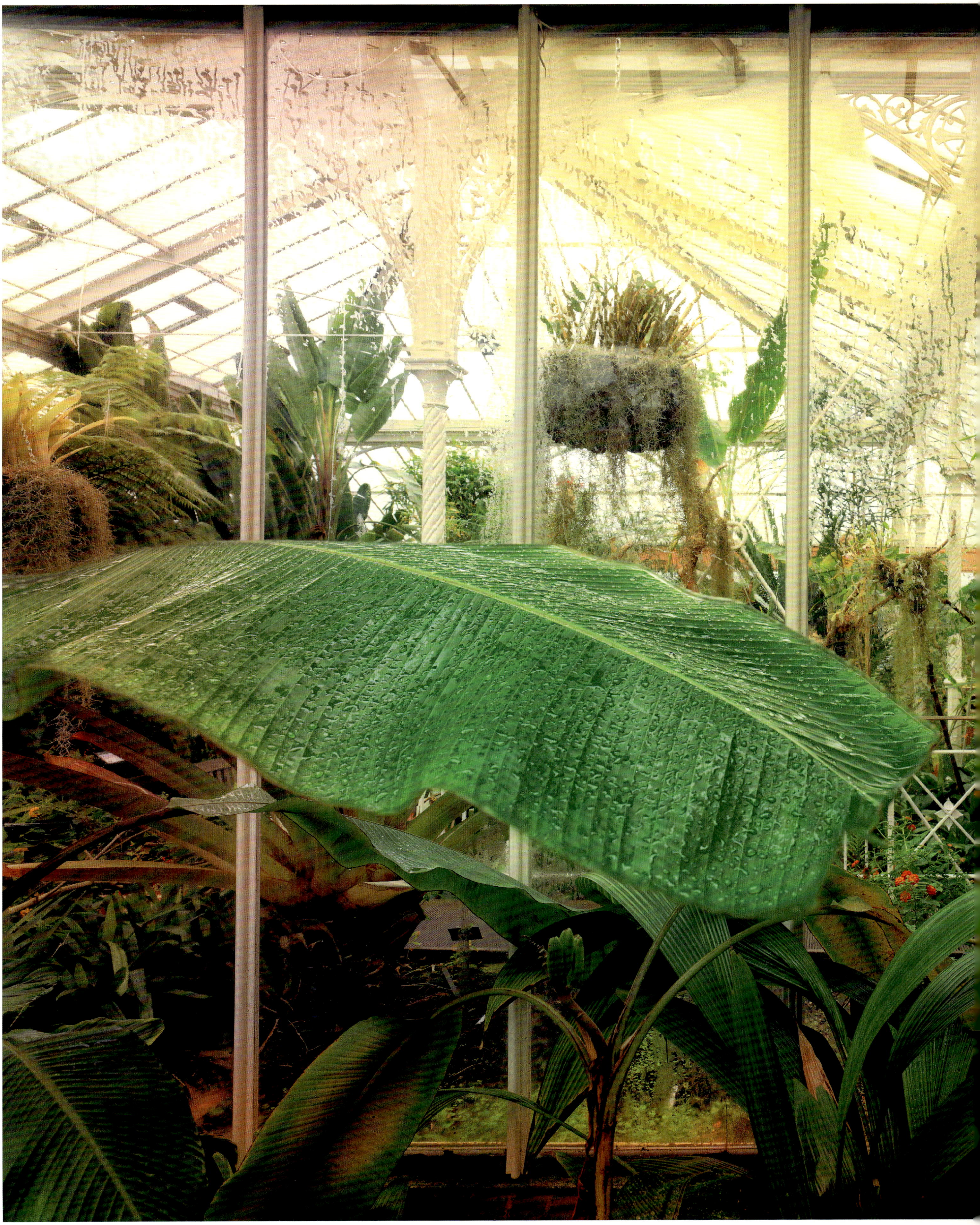

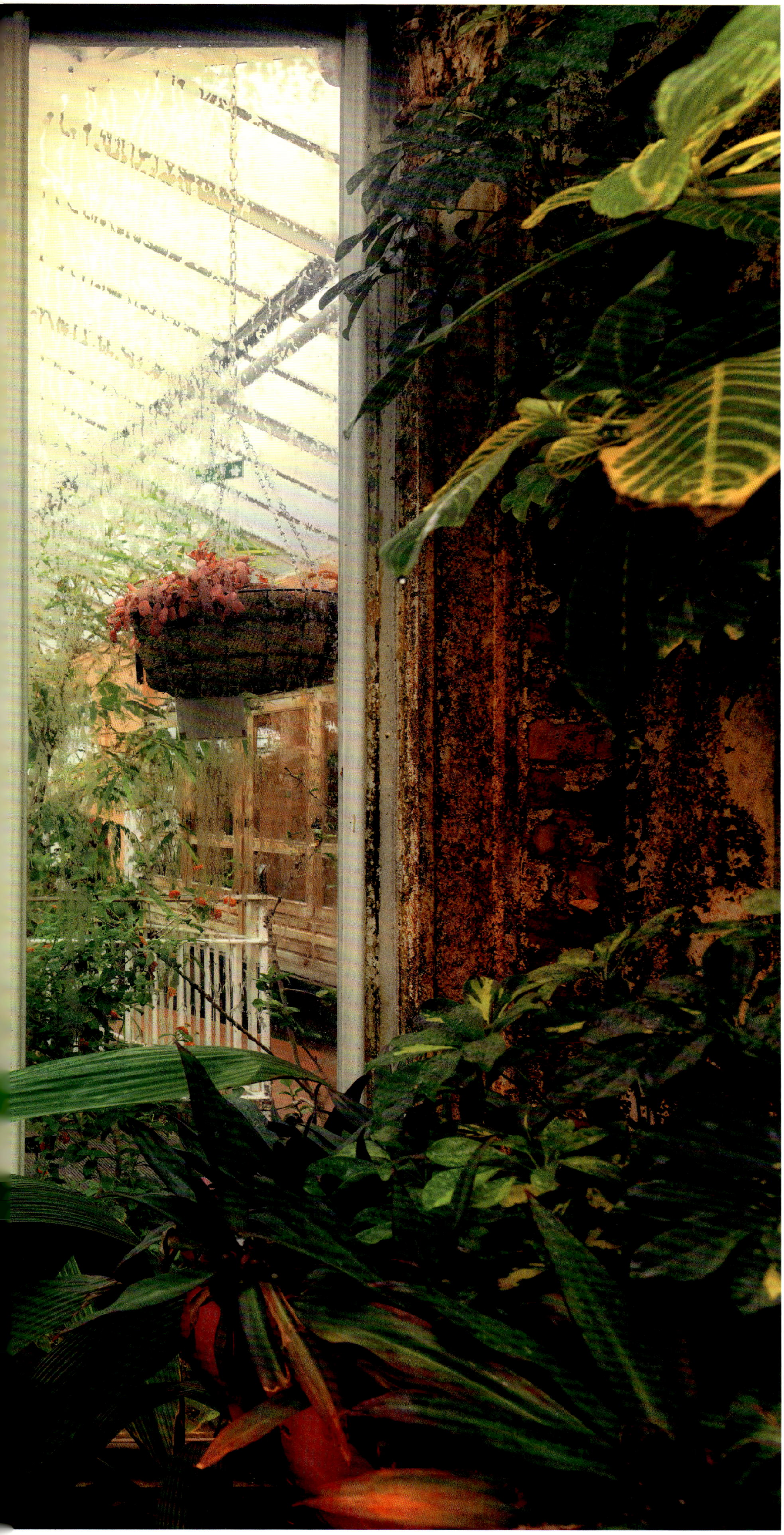

Birmingham Botanical Garden IV
Birmingham Botanical Garden V ▼

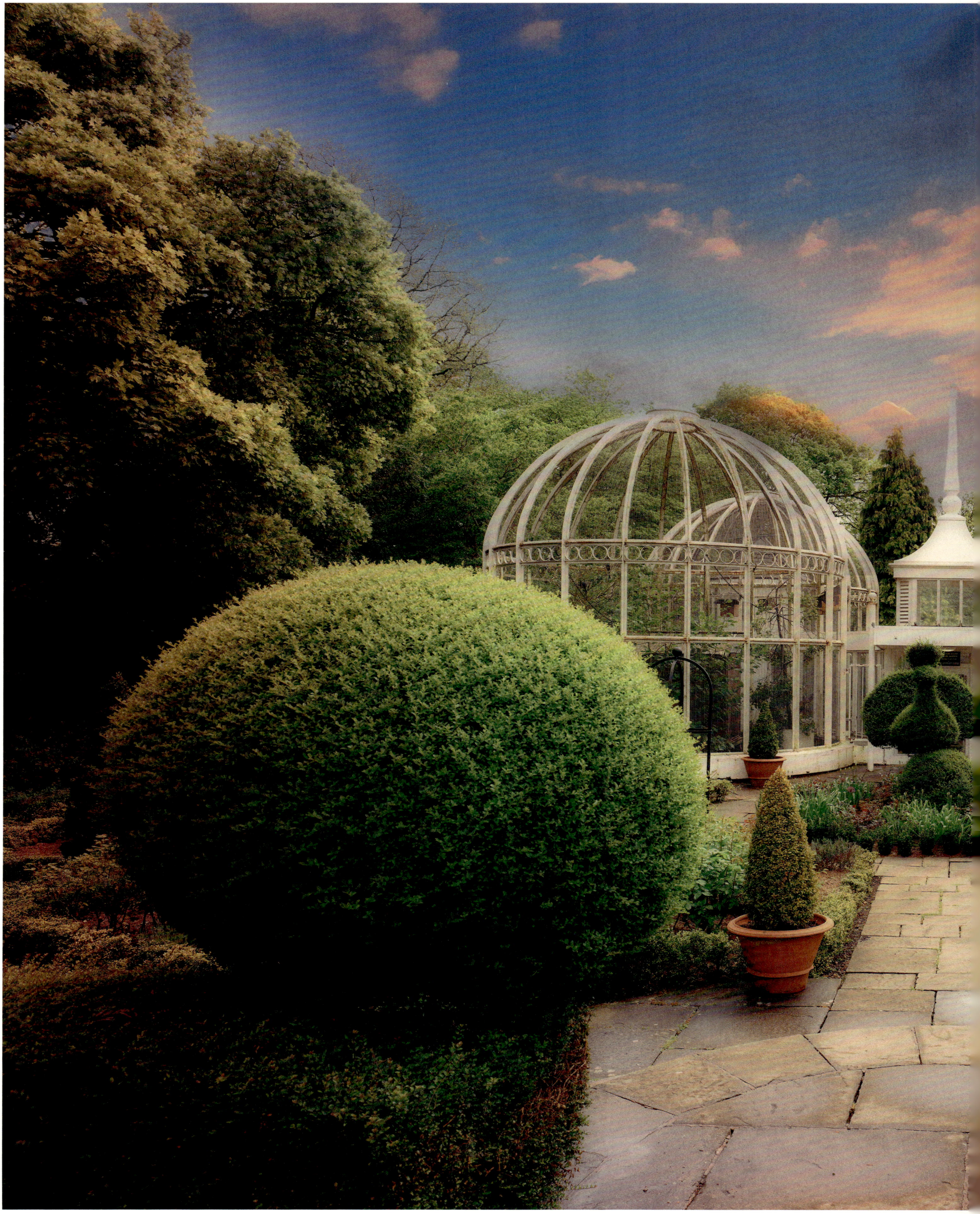

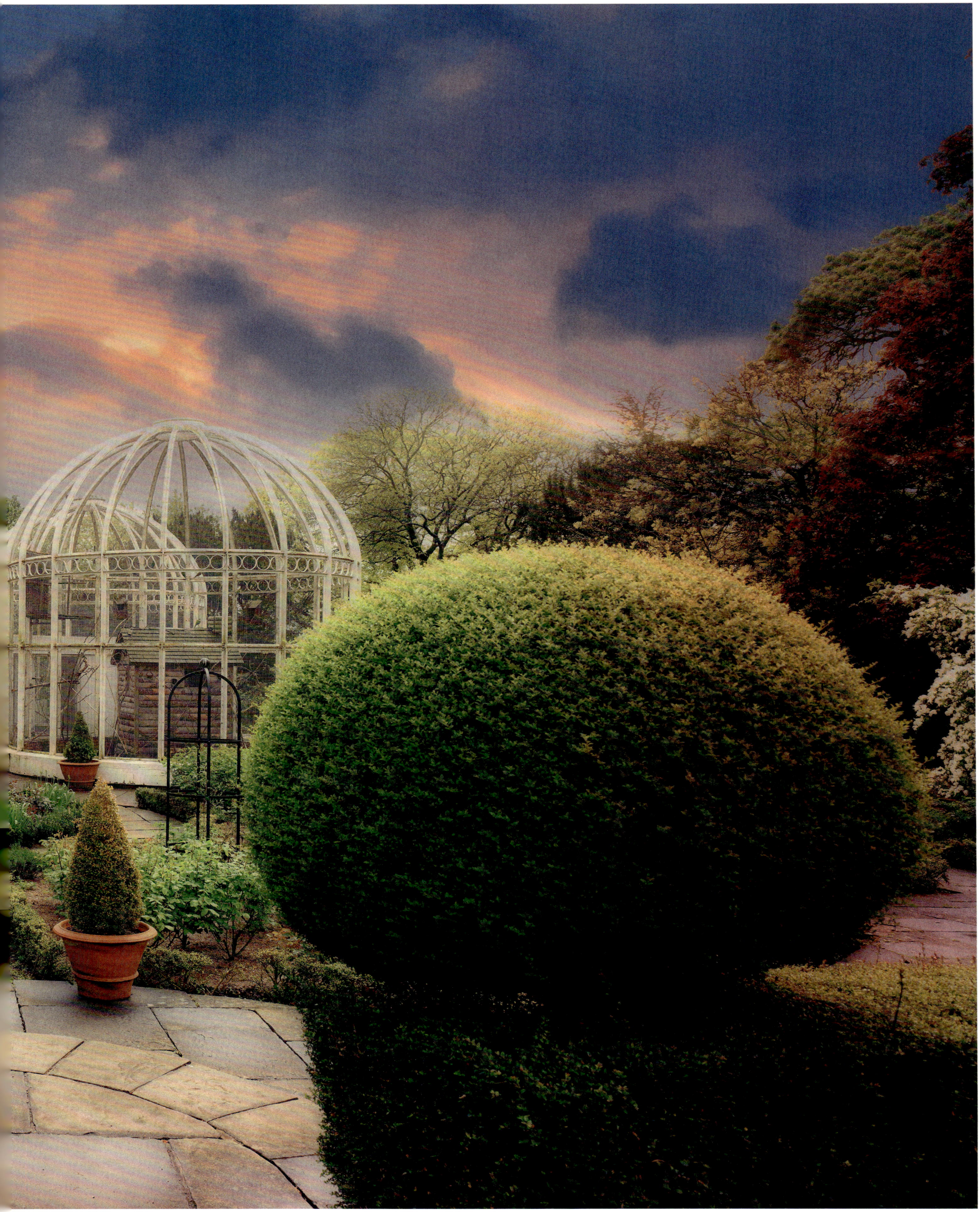

Die Bilder wollen wirken, nicht abbilden. Sie versuchen, etliche Welten und Vorstellungen zusammenzuführen und zum Blühen zu bringen.

STEPHAN REISNER

The photos attempt to evoke an emotional rather than a visual response. They try to bring countless worlds and ideas together and make them blossom.

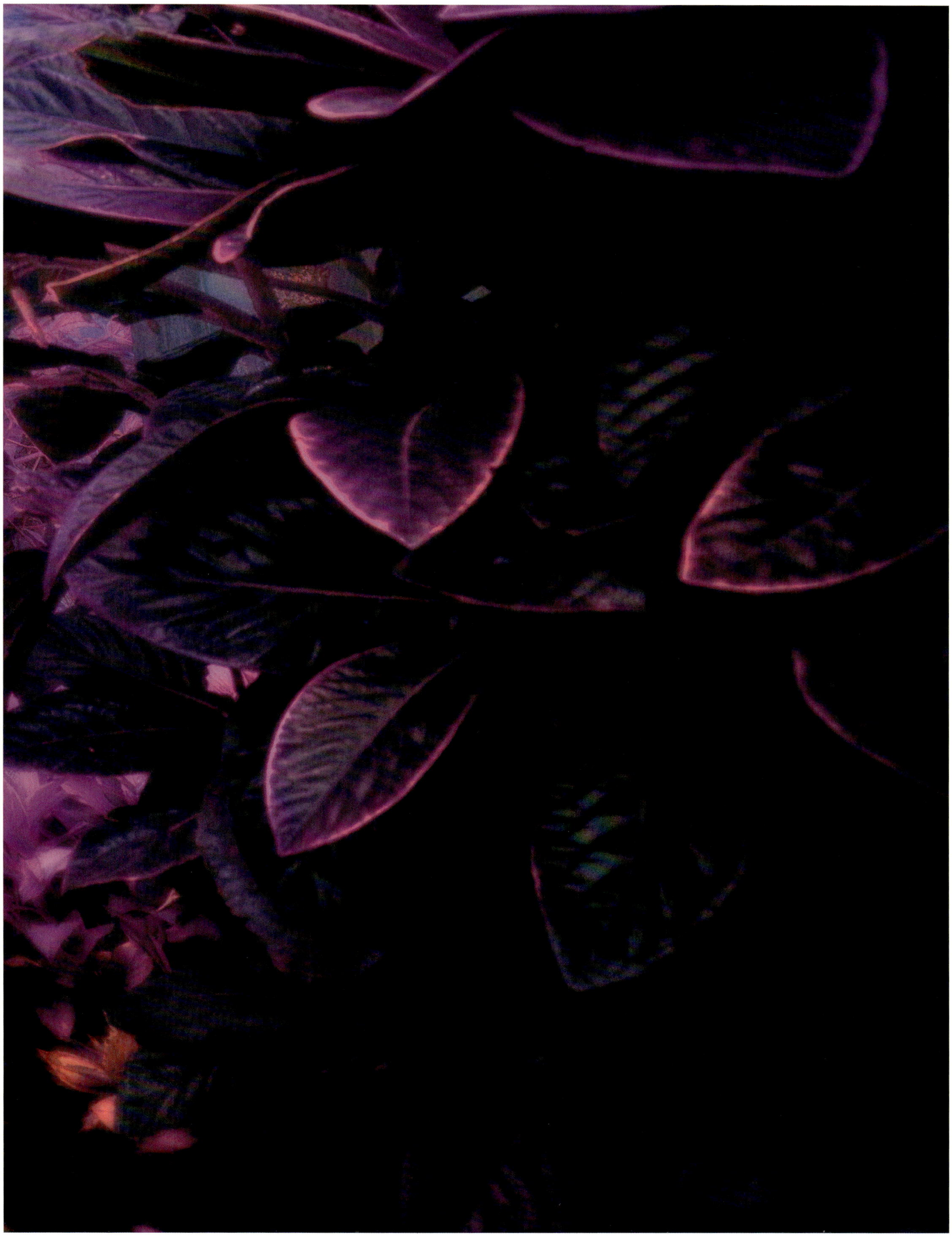

Birmingham Botanical Garden VII

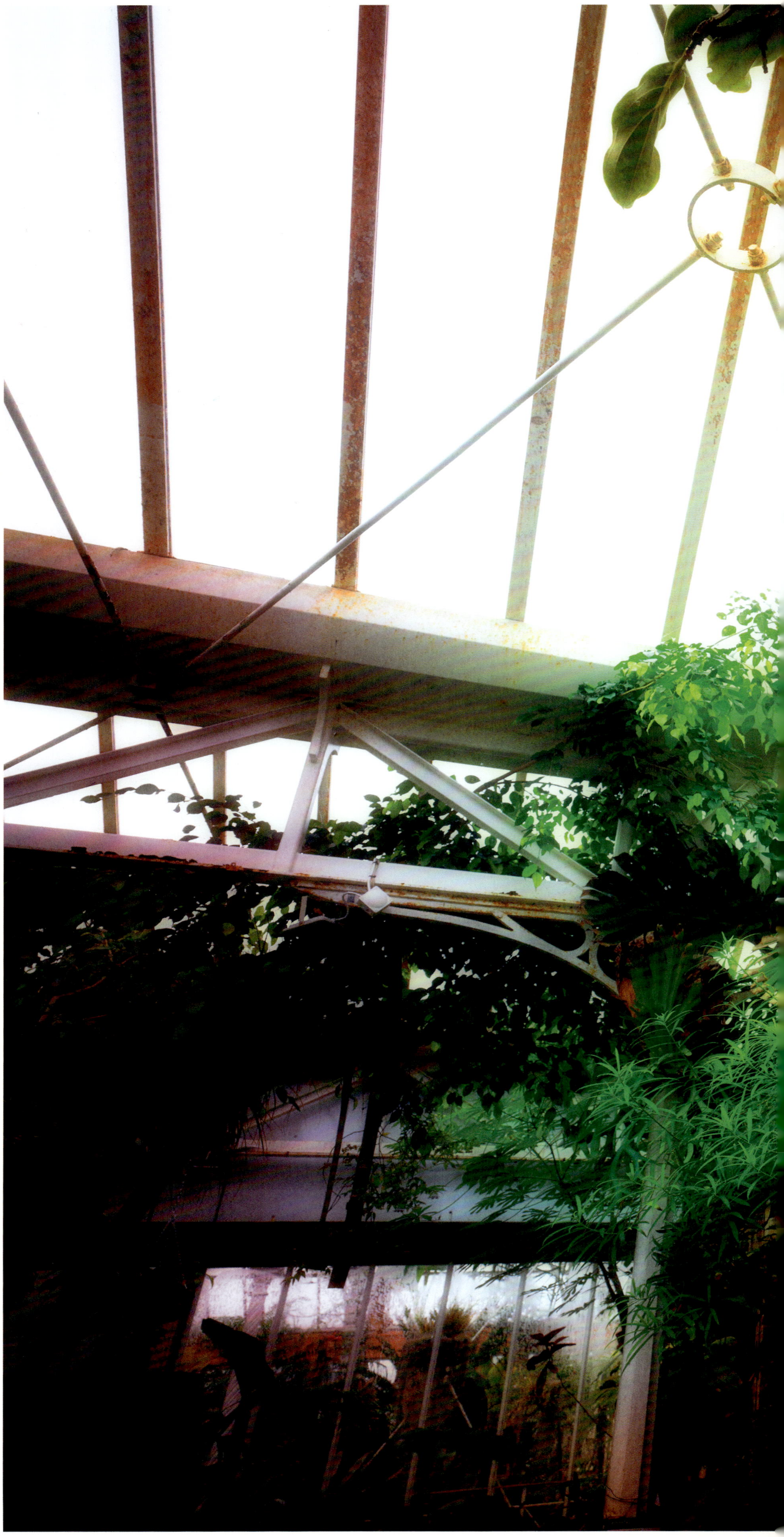

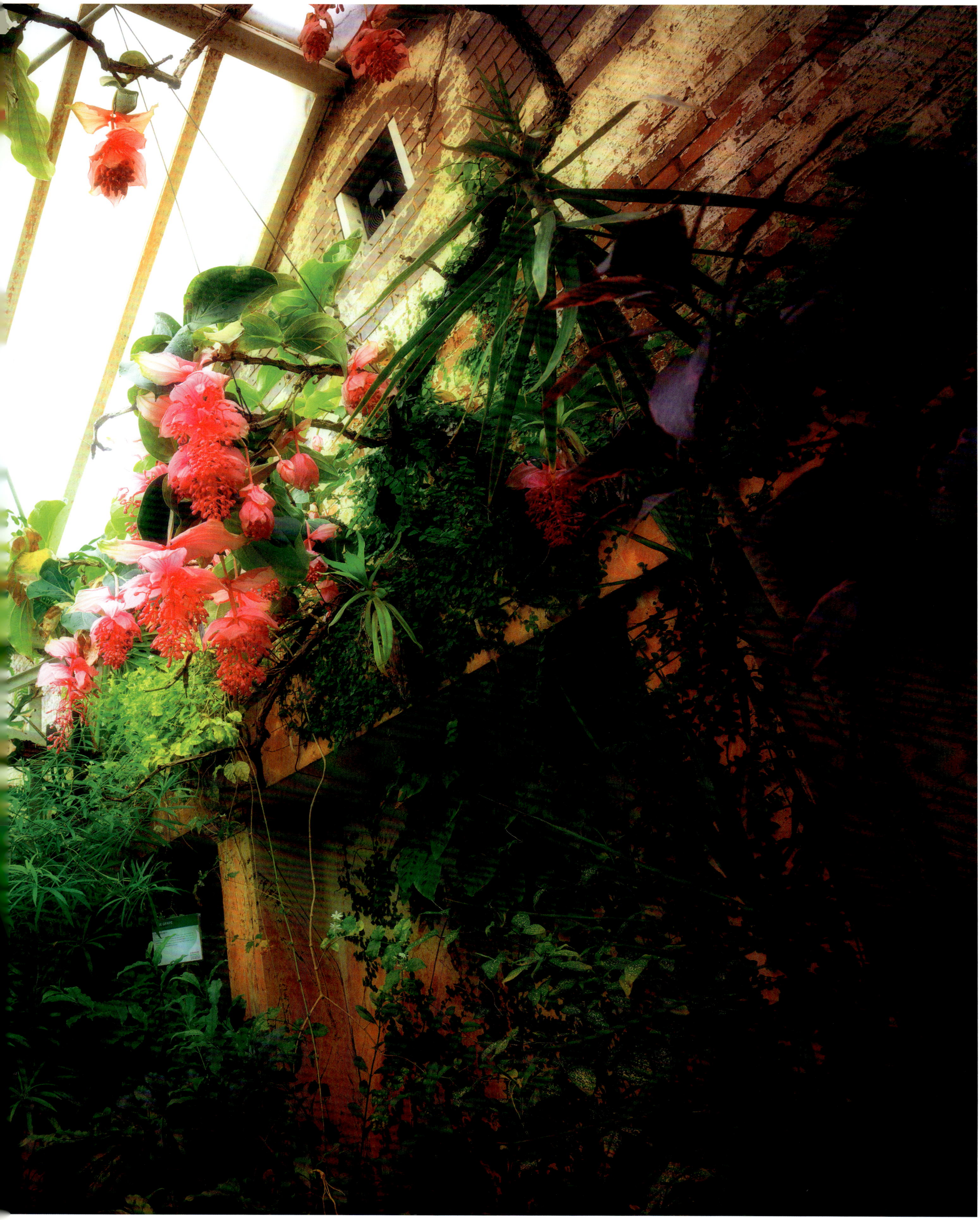

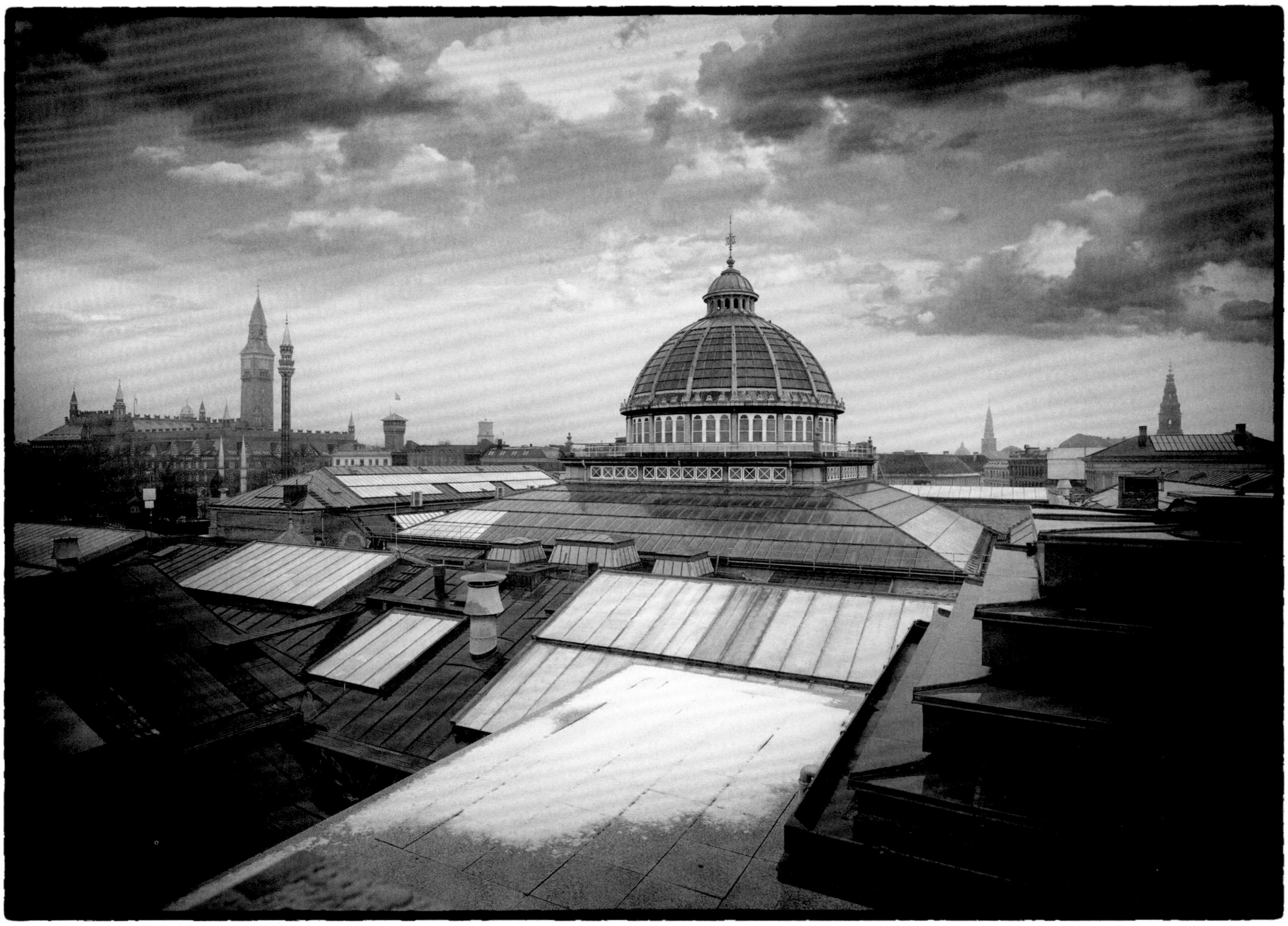

NY CARLSBERG GLYPTOTEK

COPENHAGEN

NY CARLSBERG GLYPTOTEK

ORT
Kopenhagen, Dänemark

GRÖSSE
43 m lang; ca. 40 m hoch

ENTSTEHUNG
1904–1906
Entwurf: Vilhelm Dahlerup

ARCHITEKTUR
Das Museum besteht aus drei Flügeln um einen Hof, der durch eine Wand abgeschlossen wird. Dieser wird durch eine gläserne Kuppelkonstruktion zu einem Wintergarten geschlossen.

PFLANZEN
Verschiedene Palmen (Kanarische Dattelpalme)

BESONDERHEITEN
Der Besitzer der Carlsberg Brauerei, Johann Carl Jacobsen, war ein großer Befürworter von Glas-Eisen-Konstruktionen. Er besaß privat einen Wintergarten und stiftete das Palmenhaus des Kopenhagener Botanischen Gartens. Auf ihn ging die Anregung zurück, die Glyptotek, die seine der Öffentlichkeit gestiftete Kunstsammlung aufnahm, mit einem großartigen Entree in Form eines Wintergartens zu schmücken. Hier sollten die Bürger Kopenhagens „vom Grün zur Kunst gezogen werden". Der erst sieben Jahre nach der Eröffnung des Museums hinzugefügte Wintergarten sollte auf die mediterrane Herkunft vieler der Exponate einstimmen.

LOCATION
Copenhagen, Denmark

SIZE
43 m long; approx. 40 m high

ESTABLISHED
1904–1906
design: Vilhelm Dahlerup

ARCHITECTURE
The museum consists of three wings around a courtyard, which is closed off by a wall. The courtyard was later transformed into a winter garden through the addition of a glass dome.

PLANTS
Various palms (Canary Island date palms)

ADDITIONAL NOTES
The owner of Carlsberg Brewery, Johann Carl Jacobsen, was a huge proponent of glass and iron structures. He privately owned a conservatory and was a major donor to the Palm House in the Copenhagen Botanical Garden. He was the one who suggested adding a grand entrance in the form of a winter garden to the Glyptotek, which housed the art collection he had donated to the public. It was his hope that the citizens of Copenhagen would be "drawn in by the greenery and then to the art."
The winter garden, added only seven years after the museum's opening, was intended to evoke the Mediterranean origins of many of the exhibits.

Copenhagen Glyptotek VII · Copenhagen Glyptotek VI ▼
Copenhagen Glyptotek XII ▼▼

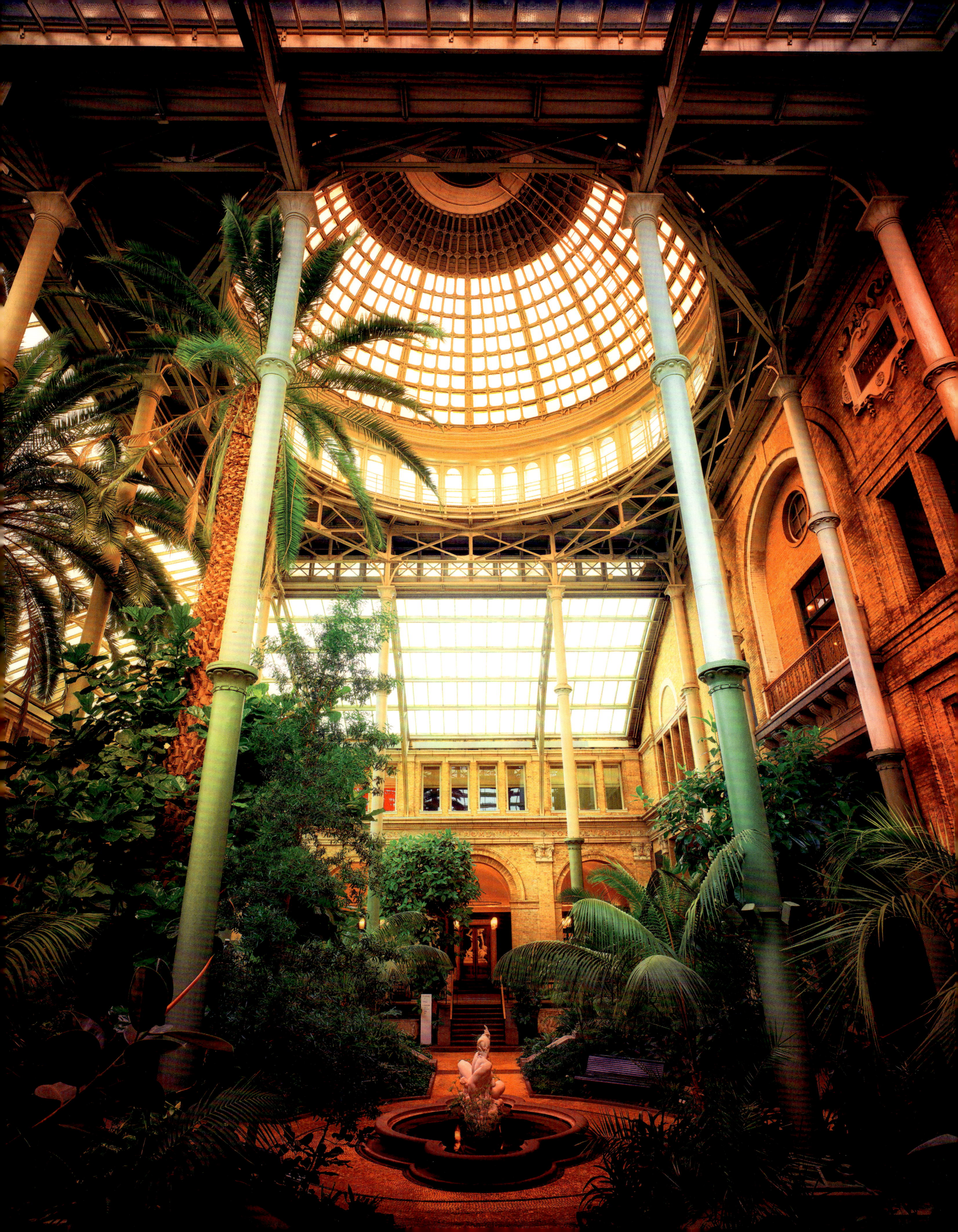

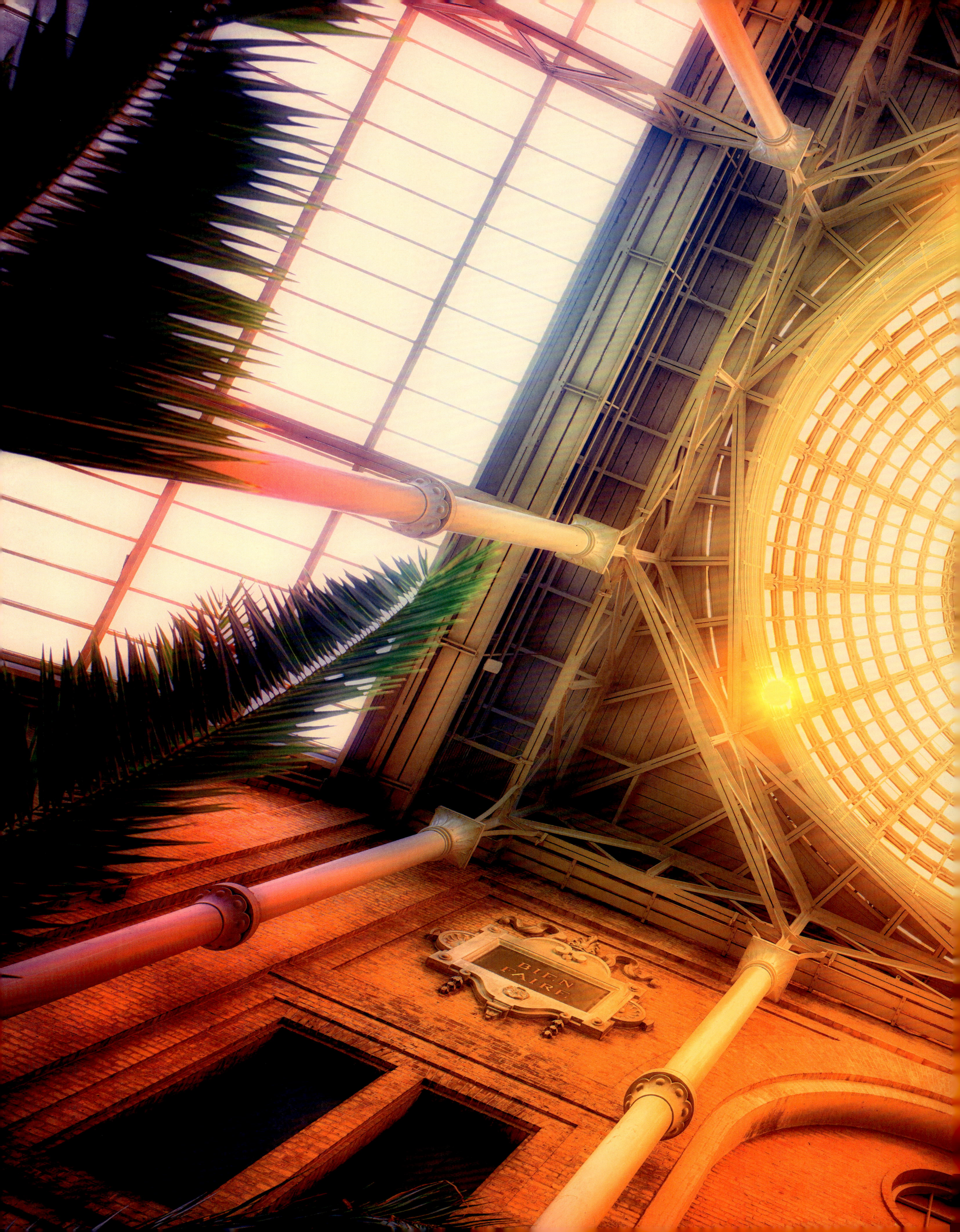
BIEN FAIRE

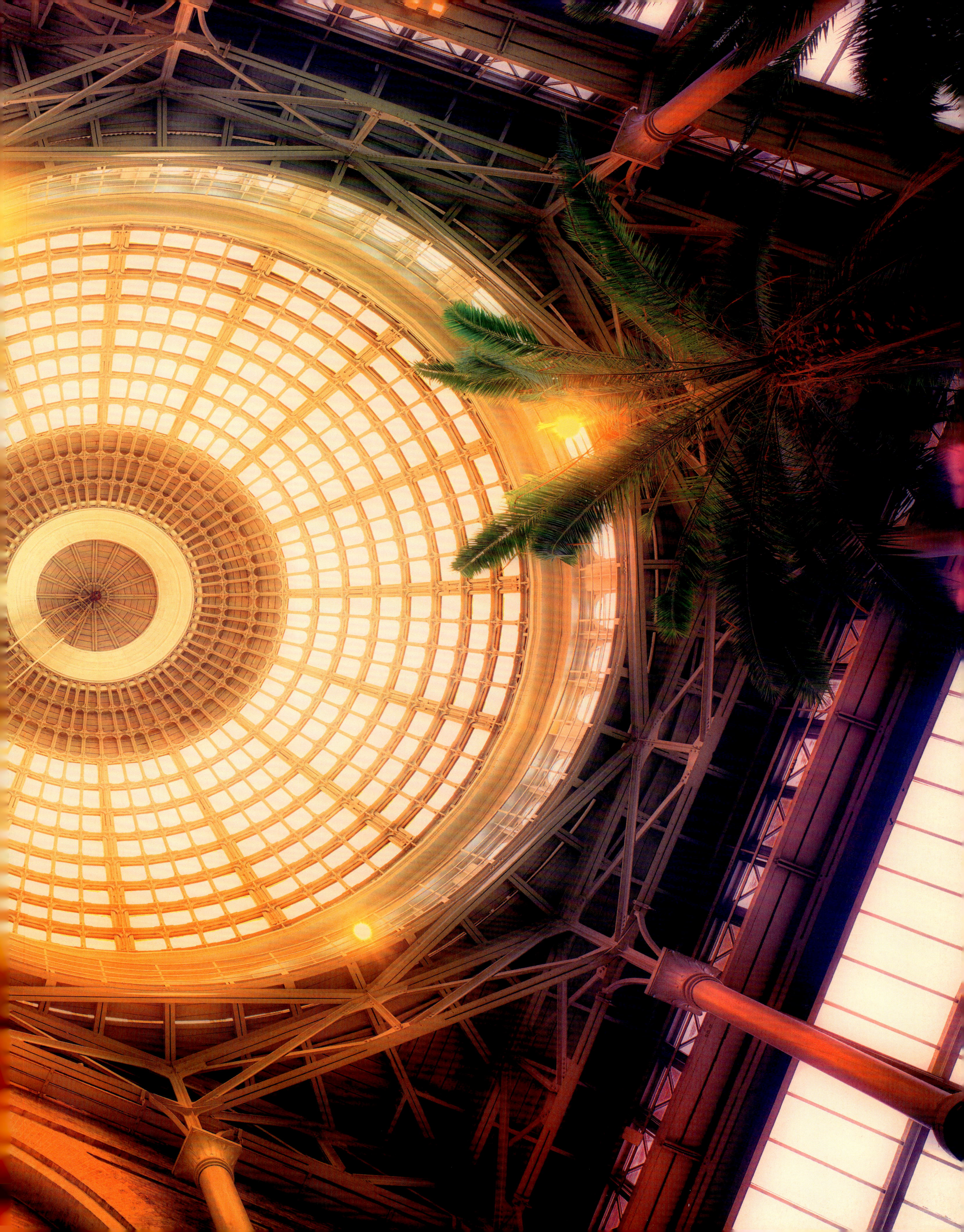

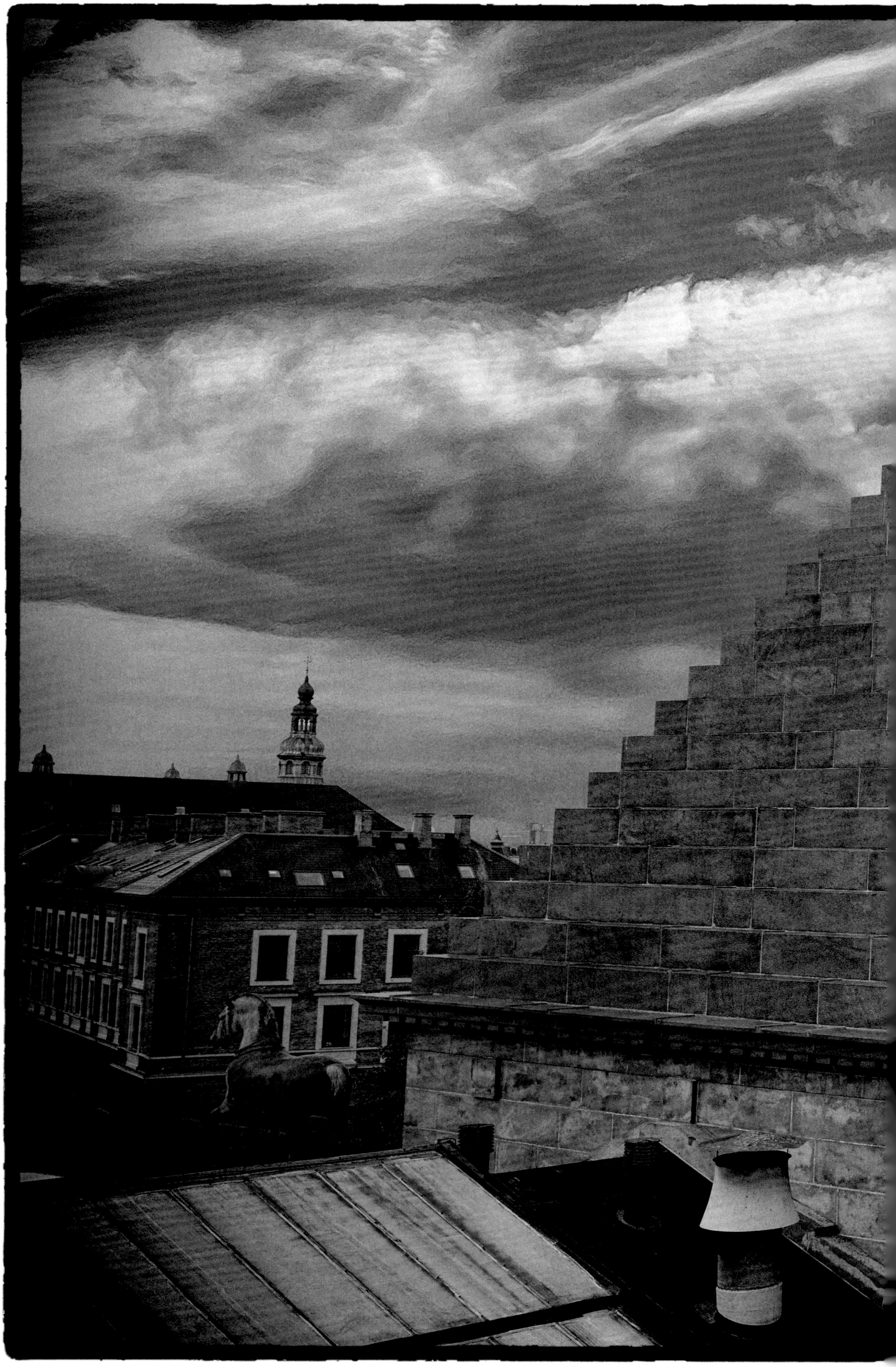

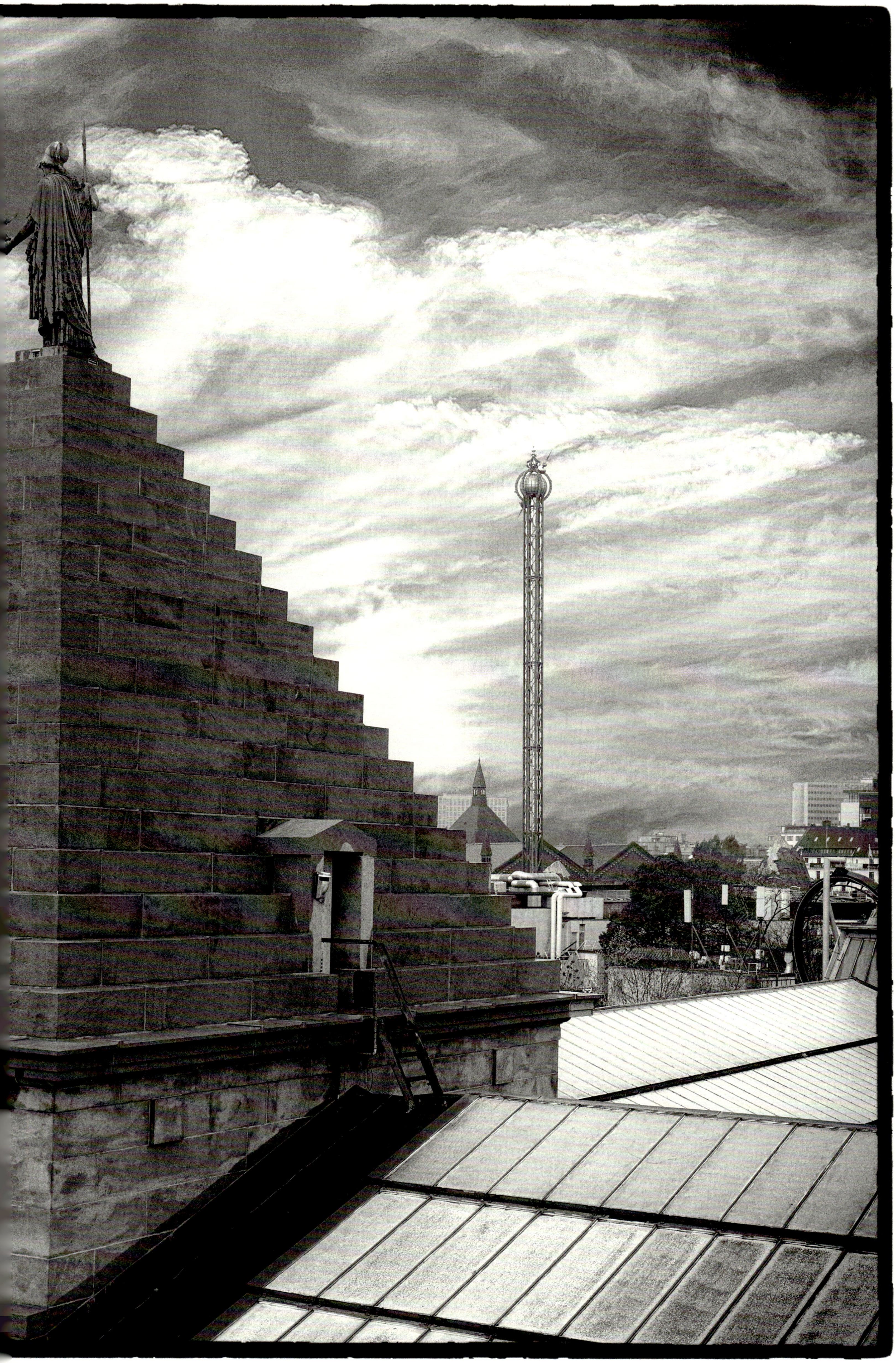

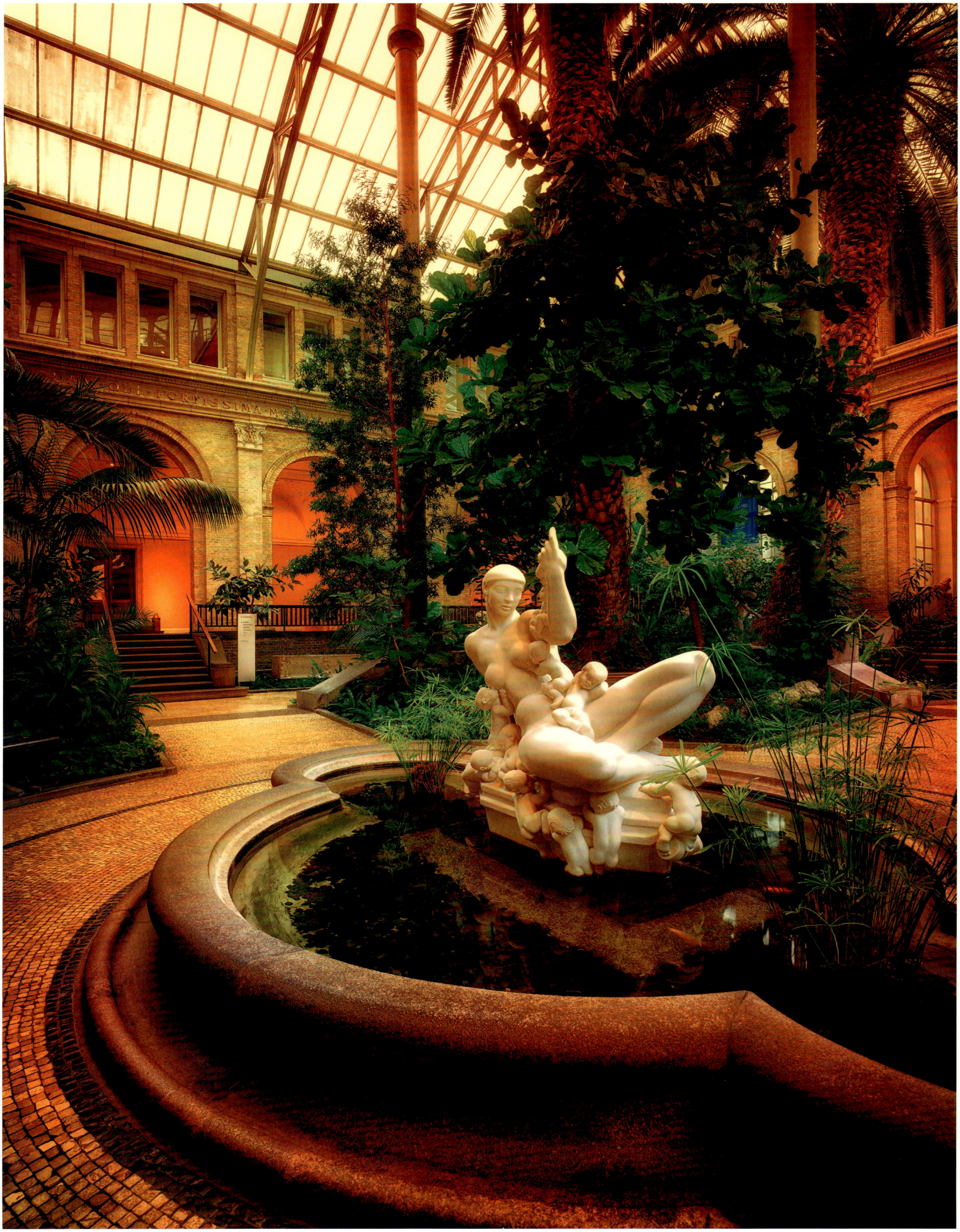

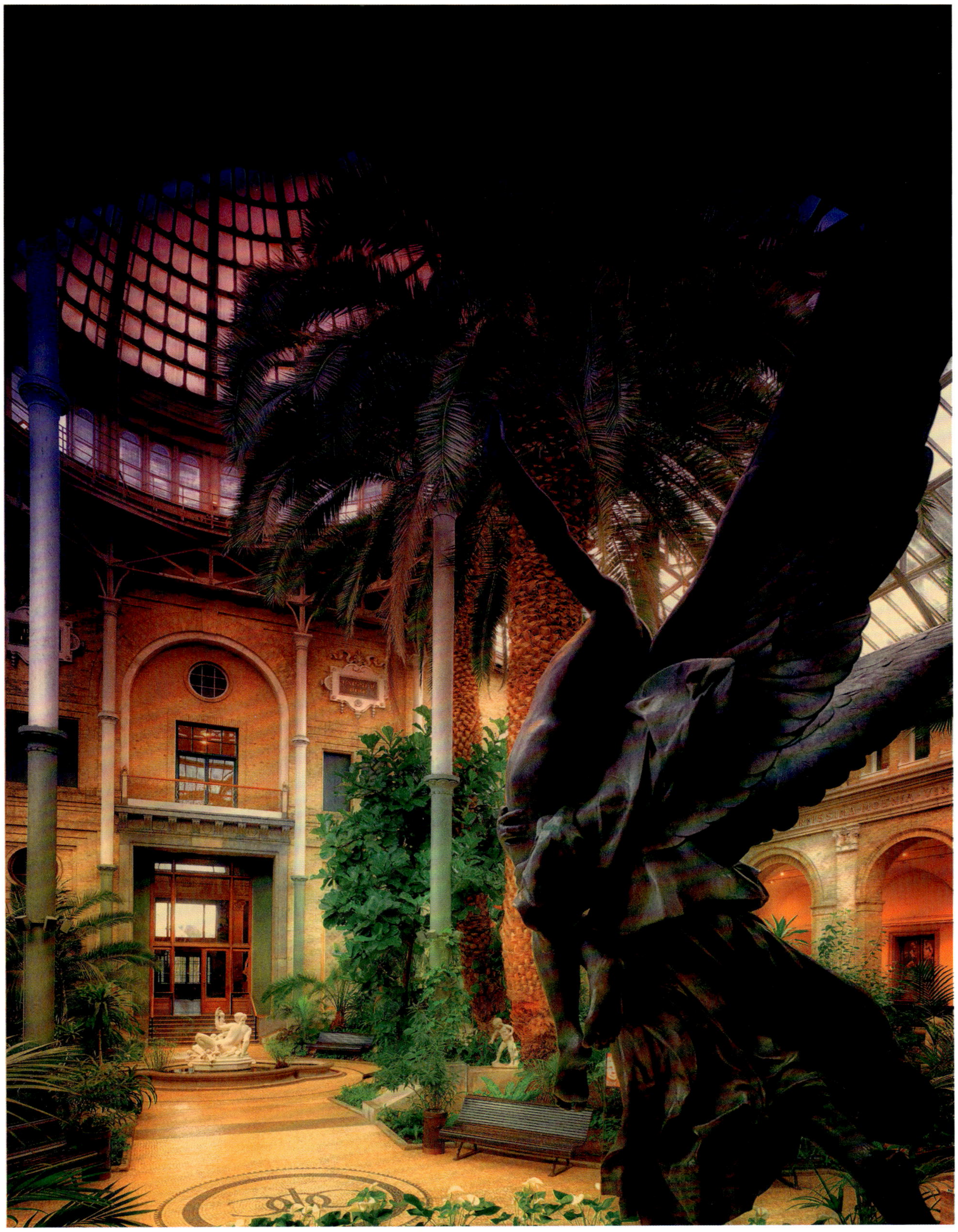

Copenhagen Glyptotek X

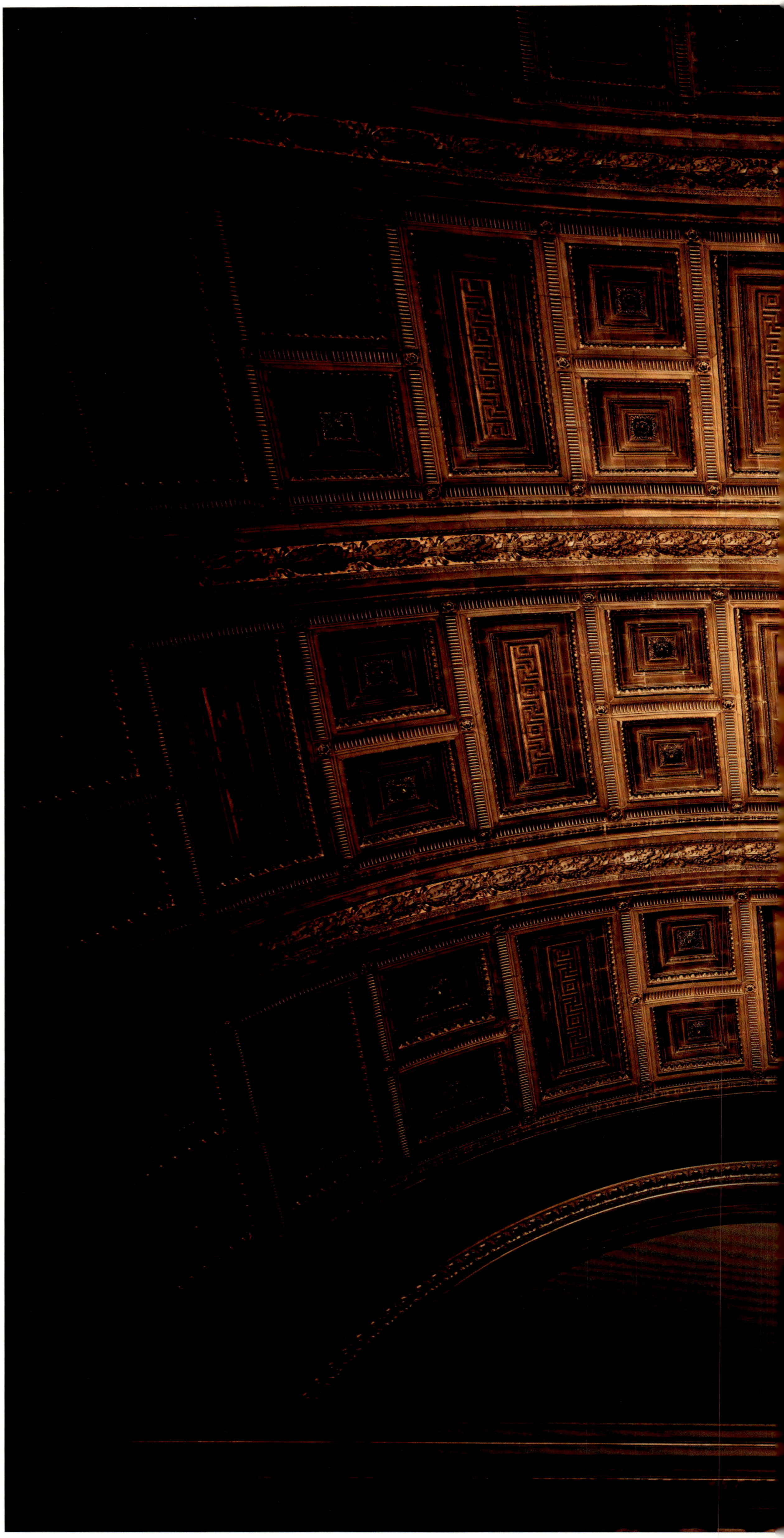

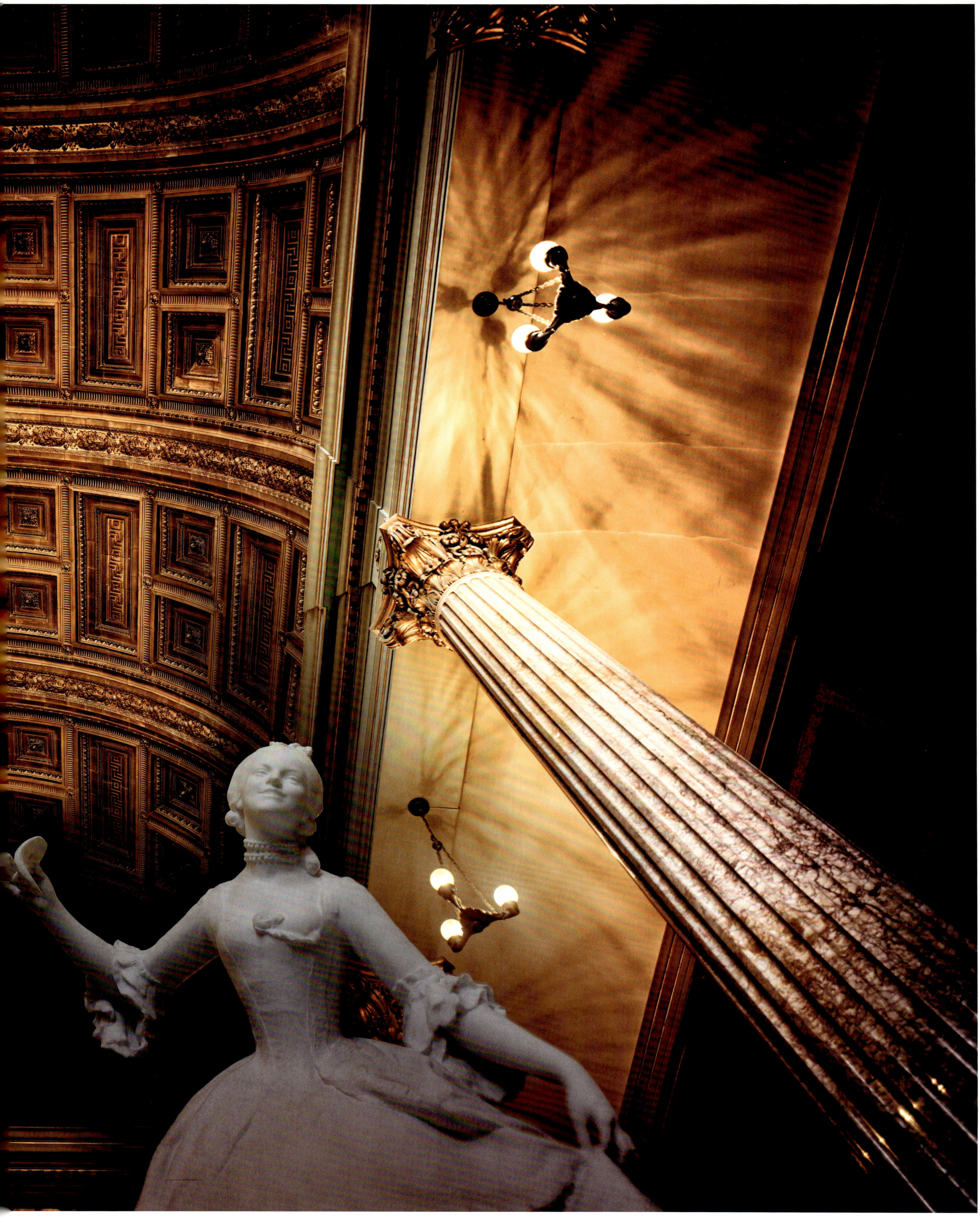

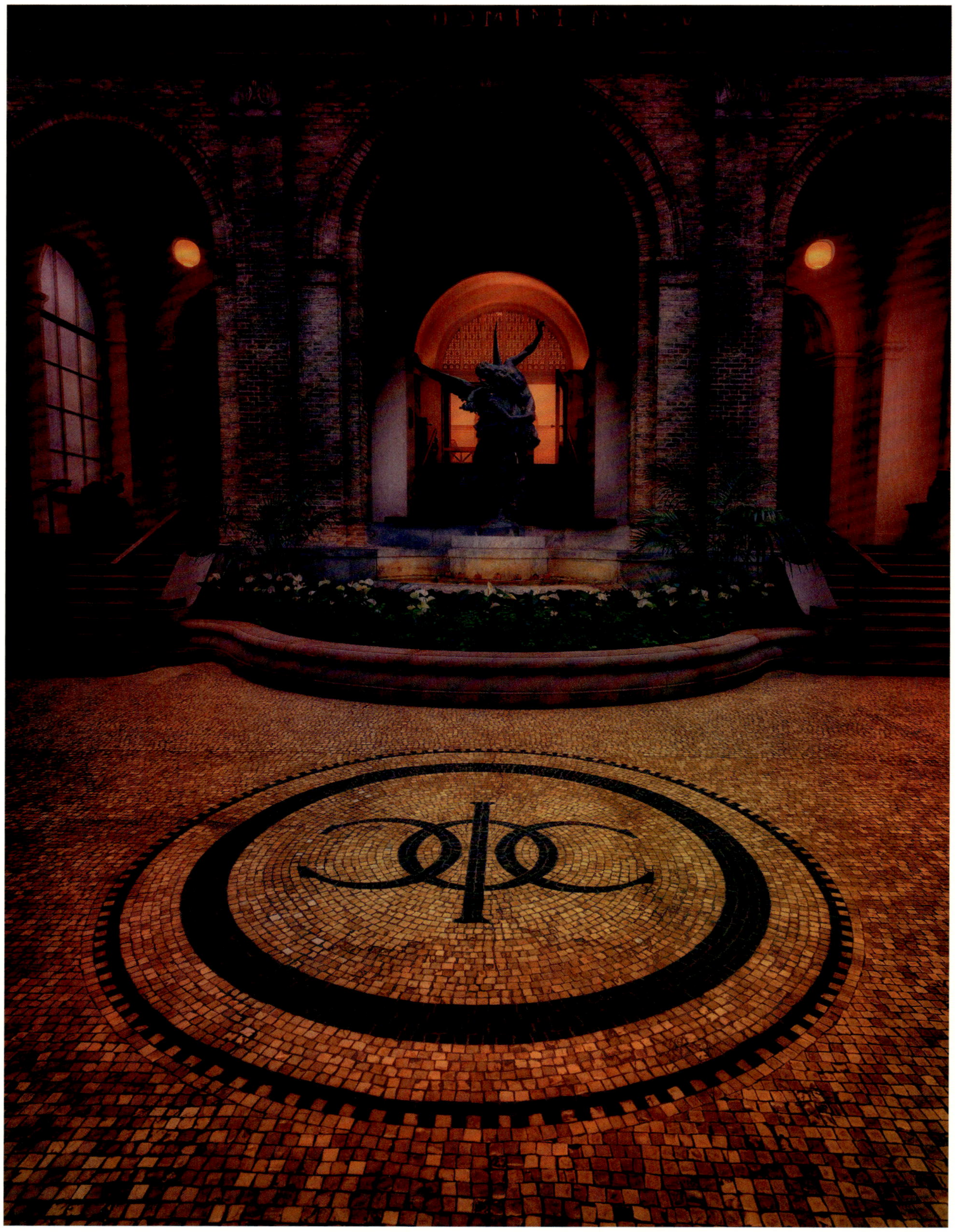

Copenhagen Glyptotek I · Copenhagen Glyptotek III
Copenhagen Glyptotek IX

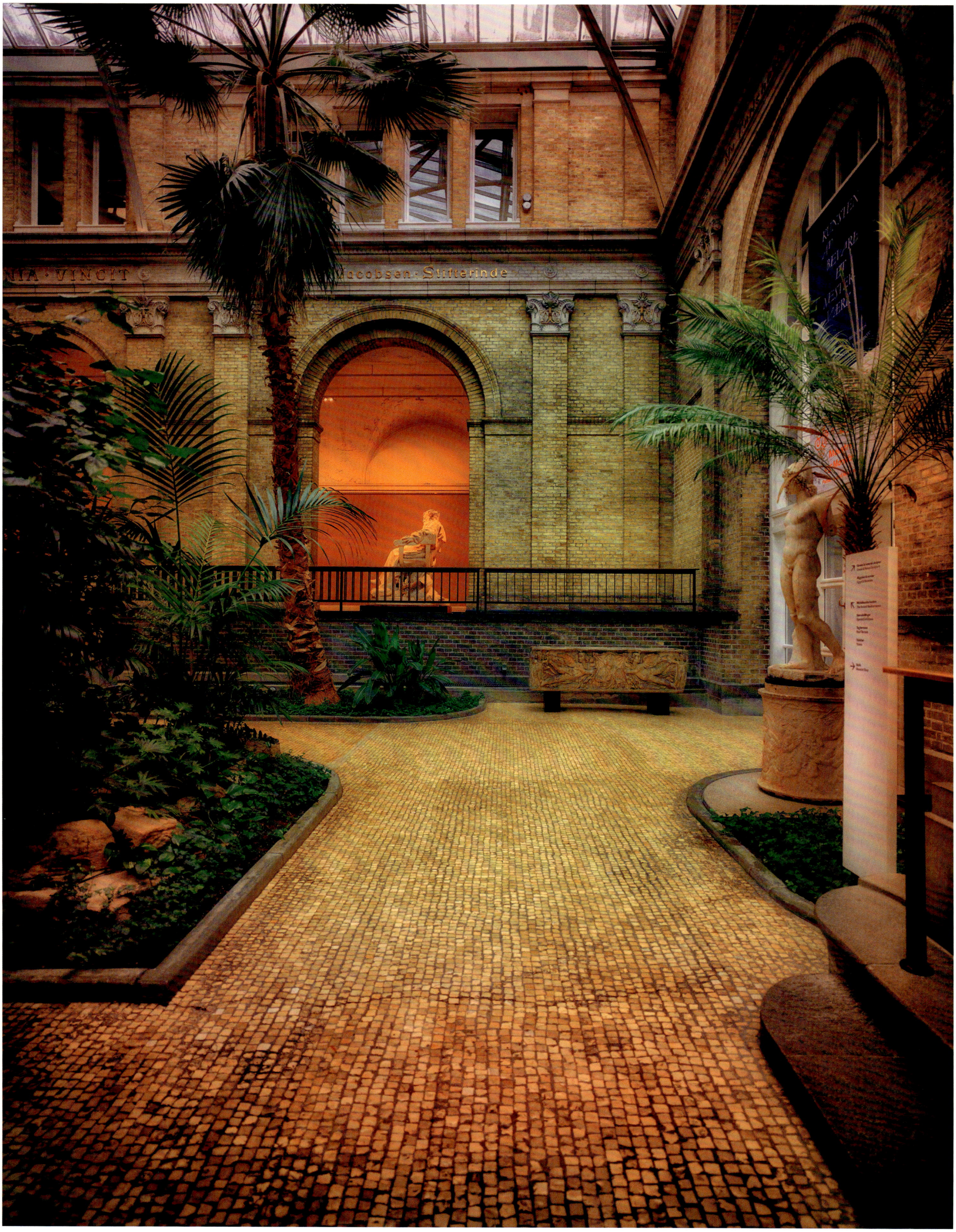
VINCIT
Stifterinde

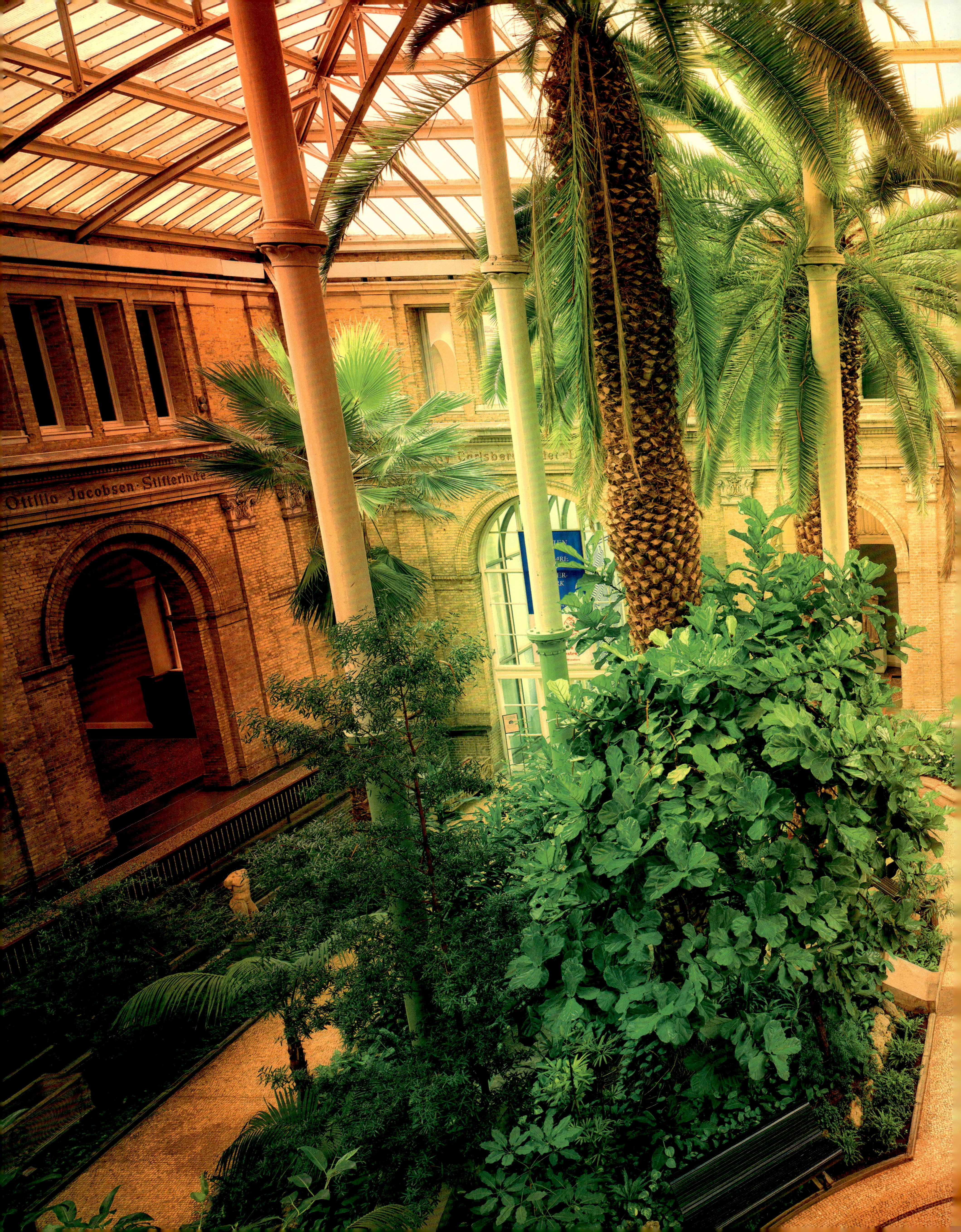
Ottilia Jacobsen · Stifterinde

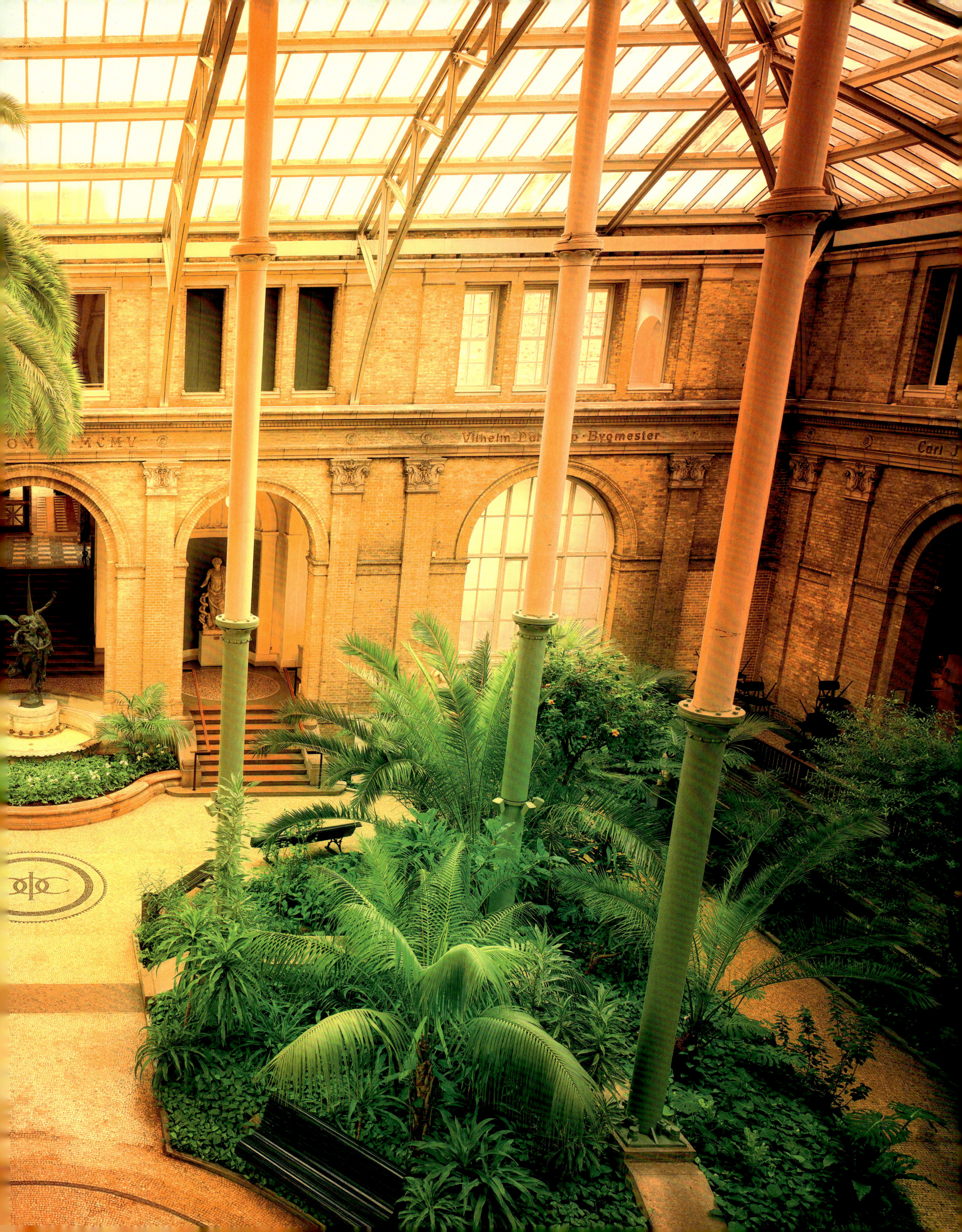
MCMV
Bygmester

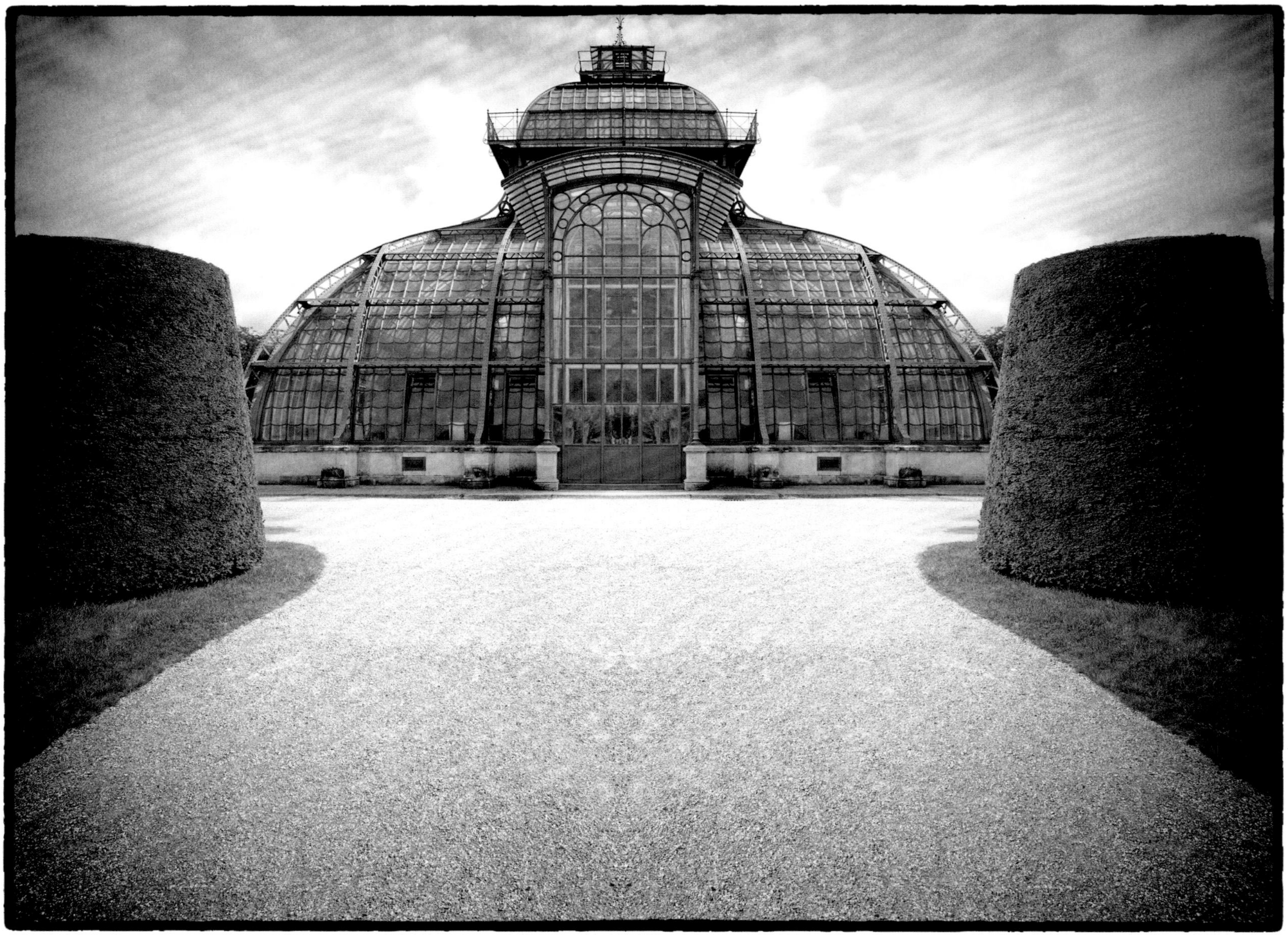

GROSSES PALMENHAUS SCHÖNBRUNN

VIENNA

GROSSES PALMENHAUS SCHÖNBRUNN

ORT
Wien, Österreich

GRÖSSE
Gesamtgebäude: 111 m lang; 28 m breit; 25 m hoch

ENTSTEHUNG
1880–1882
Entwurf: Franz Xaver Segenschmid

ARCHITEKTUR
Längsrechteckiges Gebäude mit drei in der Breite hervorspringenden Pavillons an den Enden und in der Mitte. Die Glaskuppel des Mittelpavillons ist fast doppelt so groß wie die der Eckpavillons. Der optische Eindruck wird dominiert durch die Eisenrippenkonstruktion. Üblicherweise bildet die Verglasung die äußere Hülle eines Gewächshauses, hier sieht der Betrachter zunächst die Eisenträger, welche die Außengestalt des Gebäudes bestimmen.

PFLANZEN
Das Palmenhaus im Zentrum zeigt verschiedene Palmen wie die chinesische Schirmpalme. Im Tropenhaus finden sich Blattpflanzen, während das Kalthaus Farne und Azaleen zeigt.

BESONDERHEITEN
Das Palmenhaus erinnert in Grundriss und Form an das Palmenhaus in Kew. Jedoch legte Segenschmid Wert auf die gestalterische Darstellung der Tragekonstruktion. Turner hatte diese in Kew zugunsten des Raumeindrucks als gläserne Hülle nahezu aufgelöst. Zu seiner Entstehung war das Palmenhaus das größte Glashaus Europas.

LOCATION
Vienna, Austria

SIZE
Entire building: 111 m long; 28 m wide; 25 m high

ESTABLISHED
1880–1882
design: Franz Xaver Segenschmid

ARCHITECTURE
Long rectangular building with three pavilions that protrude widthwise at the ends and in the center. The glass cupola of the central pavilion is almost twice as large as that of the corner pavilions. The iron ribbed design makes a strong visual impact. Whereas the glazing normally forms the outer shell of a greenhouse, here viewers first see the iron girders that define the exterior shape of the building.

PLANTS
Situated in the center of the structure, the Palm House displays various palms, such as the Chinese umbrella palm. The tropical zone features foliage plants, while the cold house showcases ferns and azaleas.

ADDITIONAL NOTES
In terms of its footprint and shape, the Palm House is reminiscent of the Palm House at Kew Gardens. In this case, however, Segenschmid attached great importance to the design of the supporting structure. Turner had almost completely done away with this at Kew Gardens in favor of creating a spatial impression as a glass shell. At the time of its construction, the Palm House at Schönbrunn was the largest glasshouse in Europe.

Großes Palmenhaus Schönbrunn XVII
Großes Palmenhaus Schönbrunn XXVII ▼

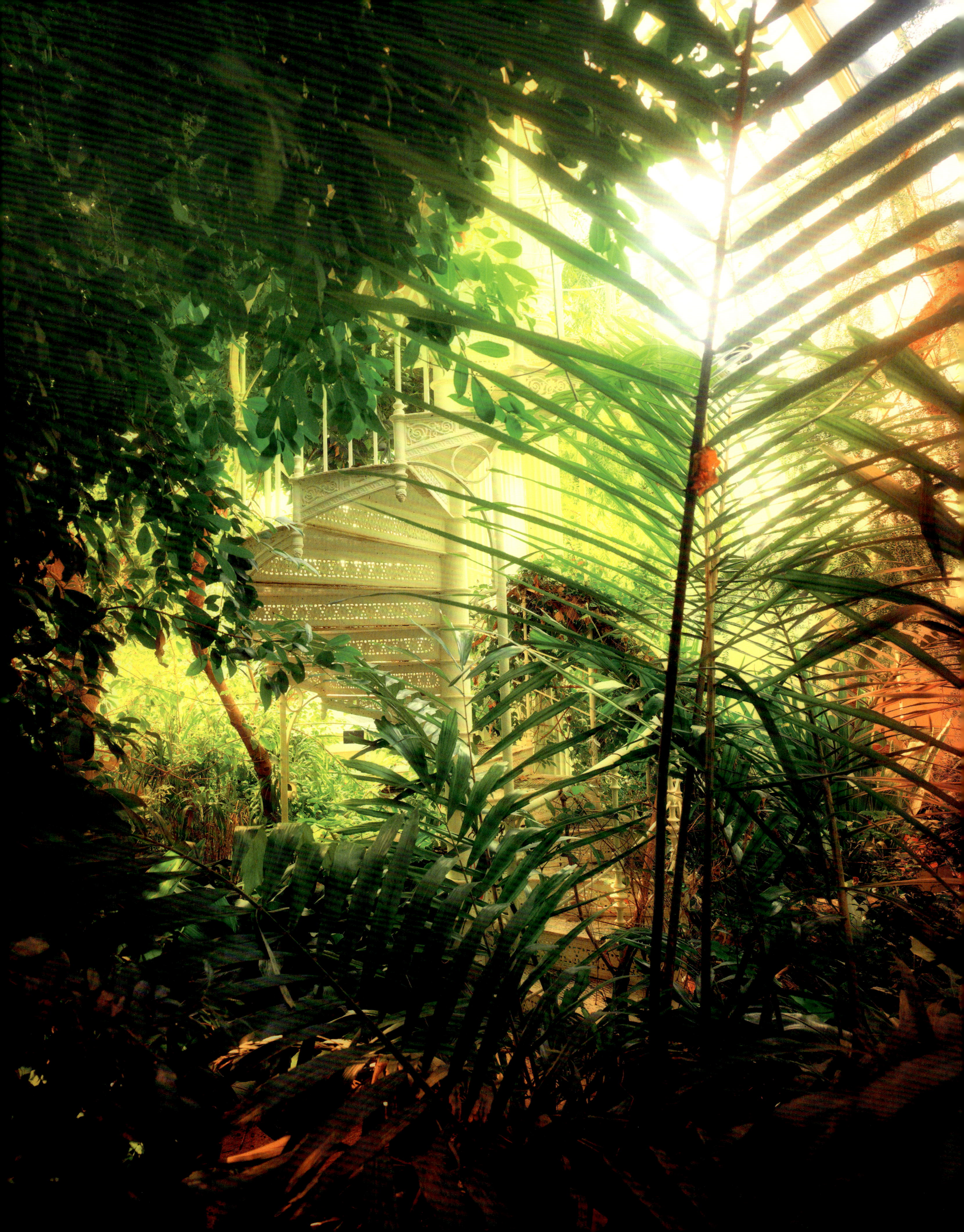

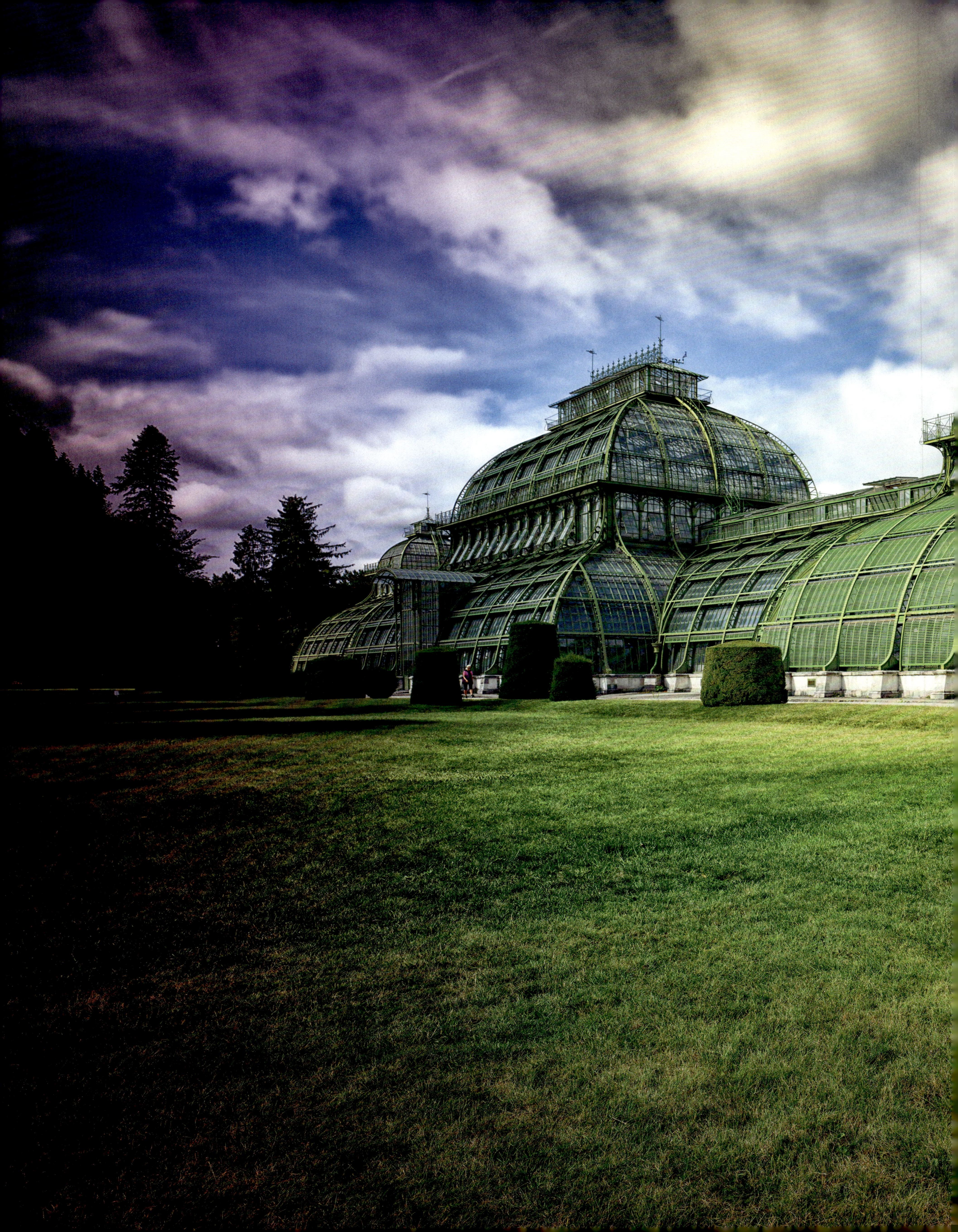

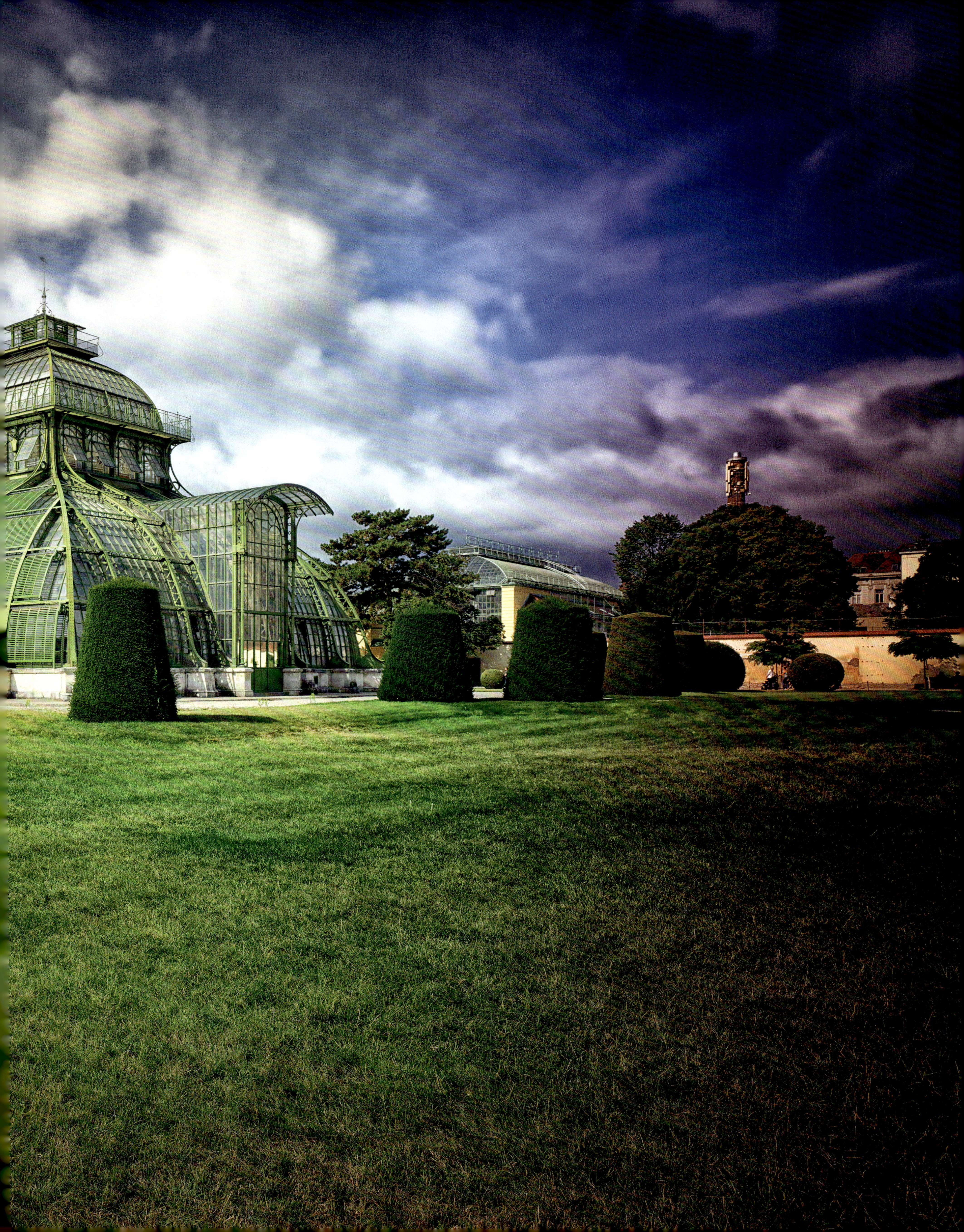

Großes Palmenhaus Schönbrunn XXIII

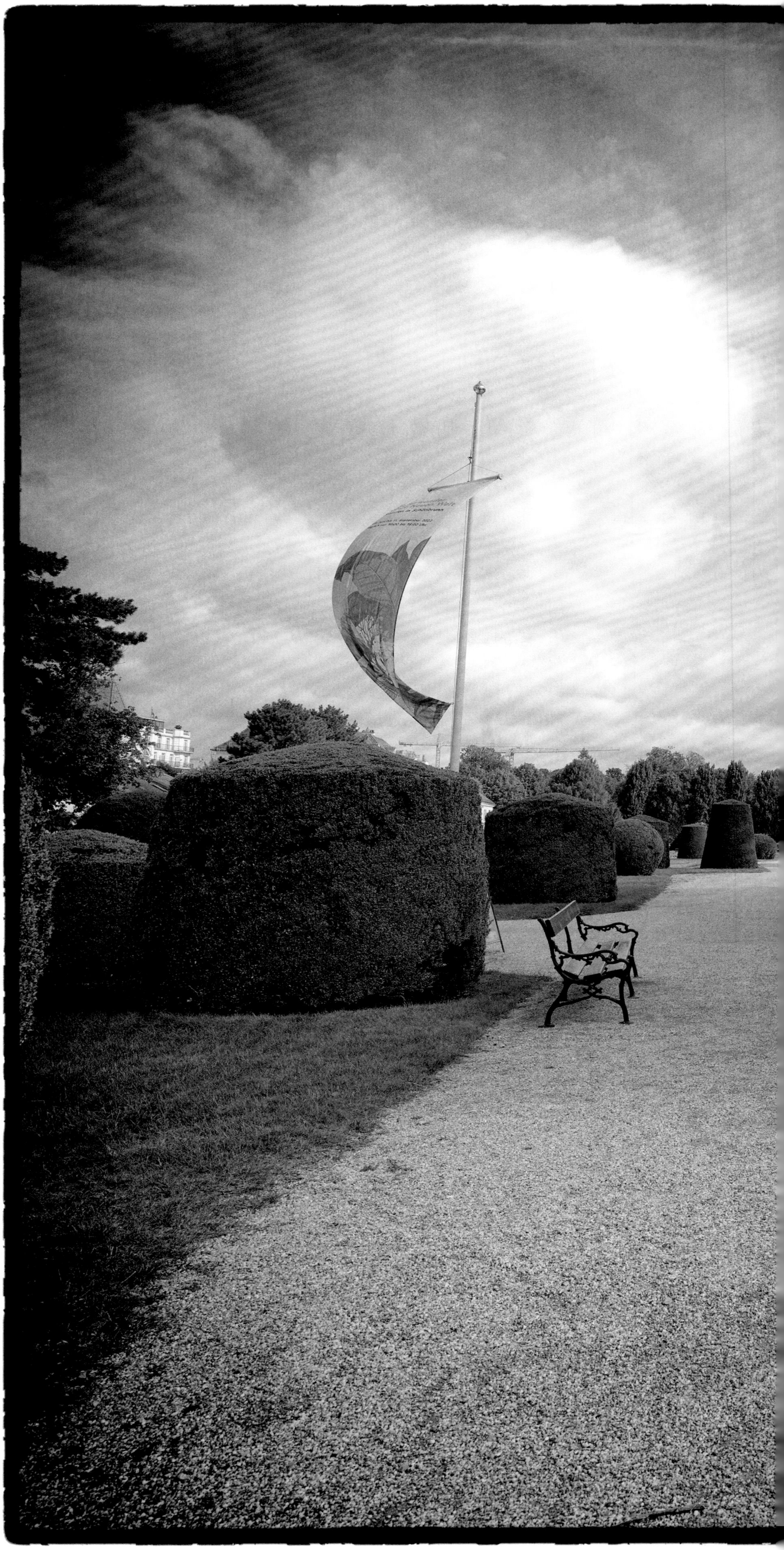

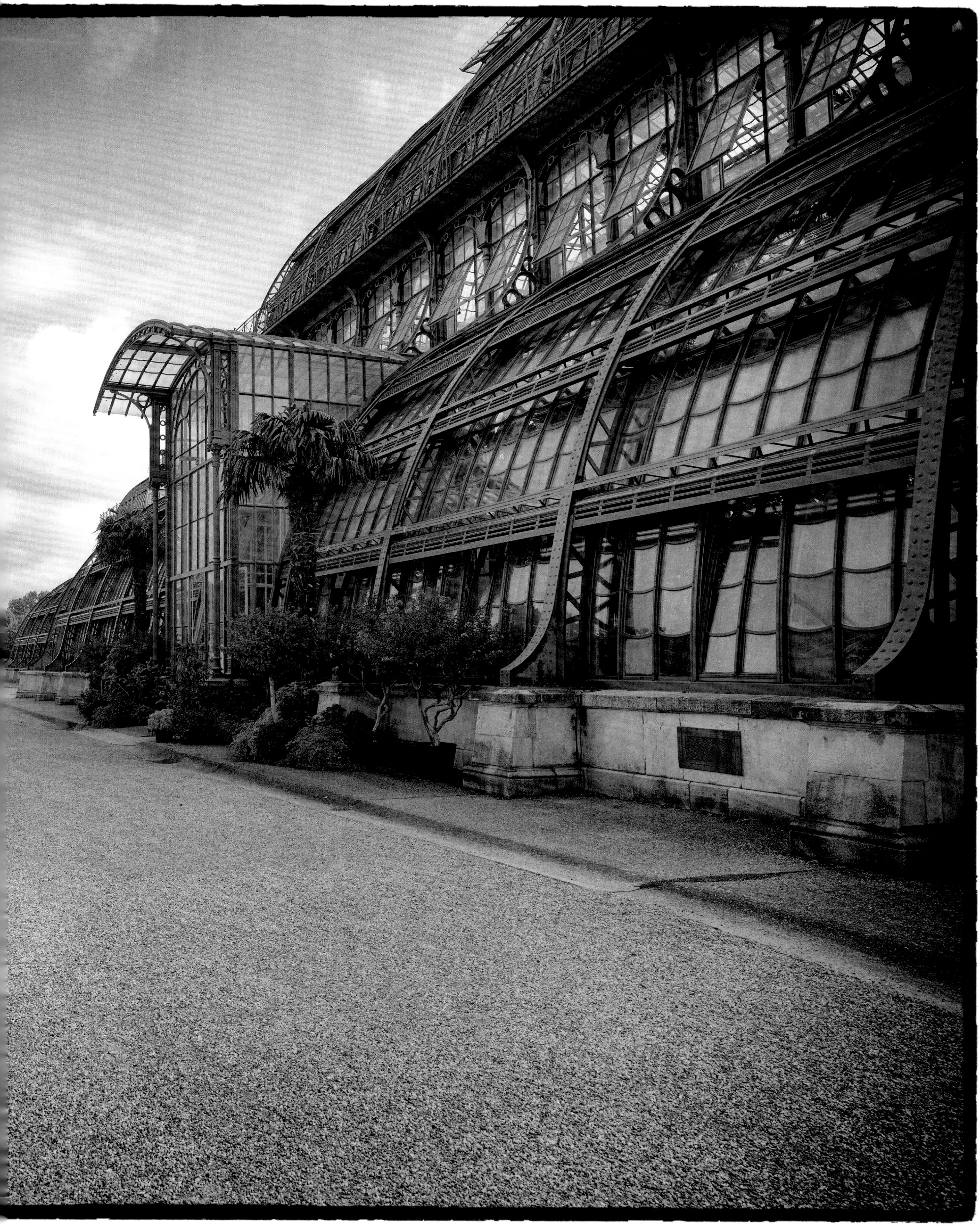

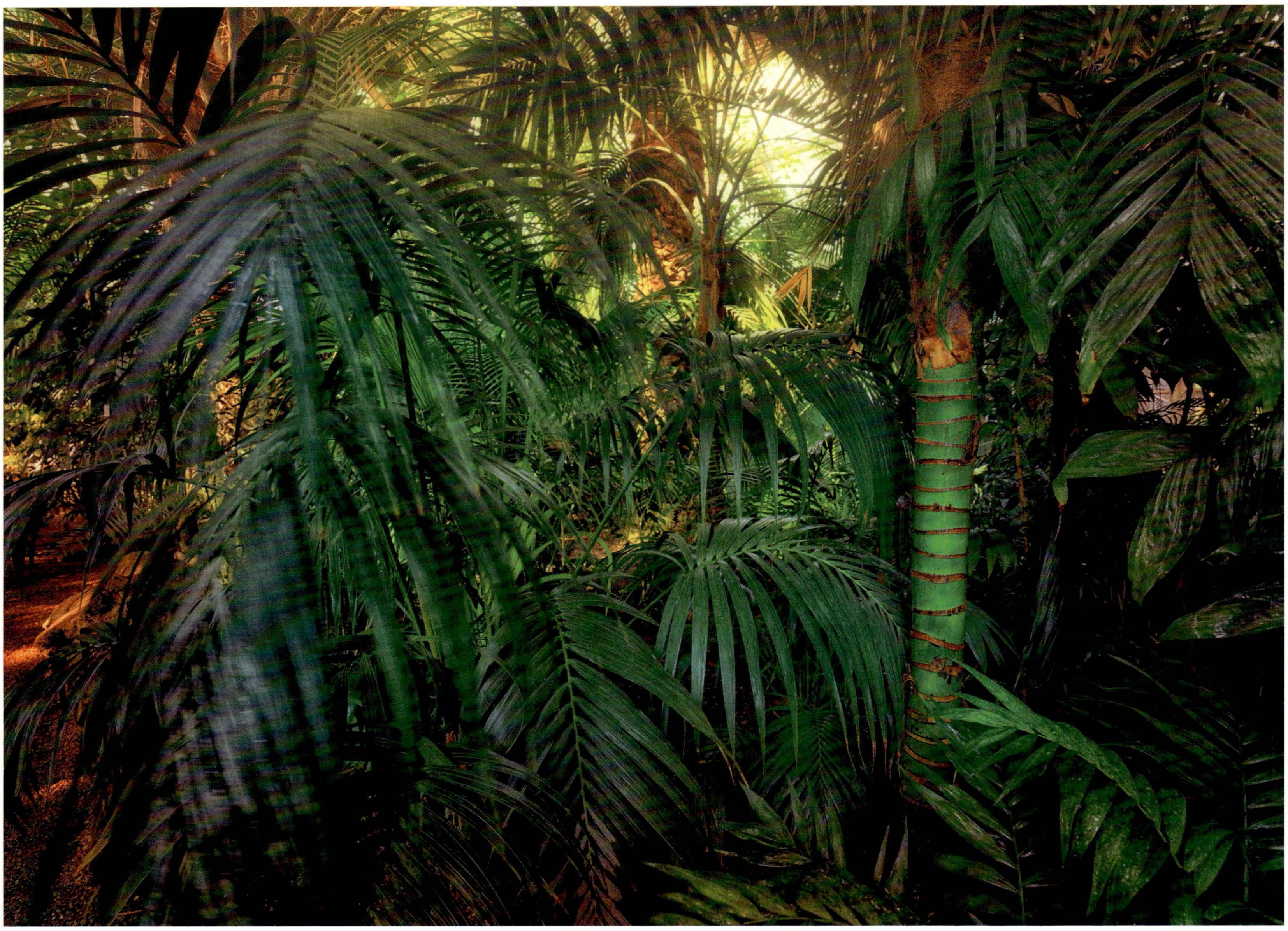

Großes Palmenhaus Schönbrunn XIX • Schönbrunn Wüstenhaus XXVIII
Großes Palmenhaus Schönbrunn IV ▼

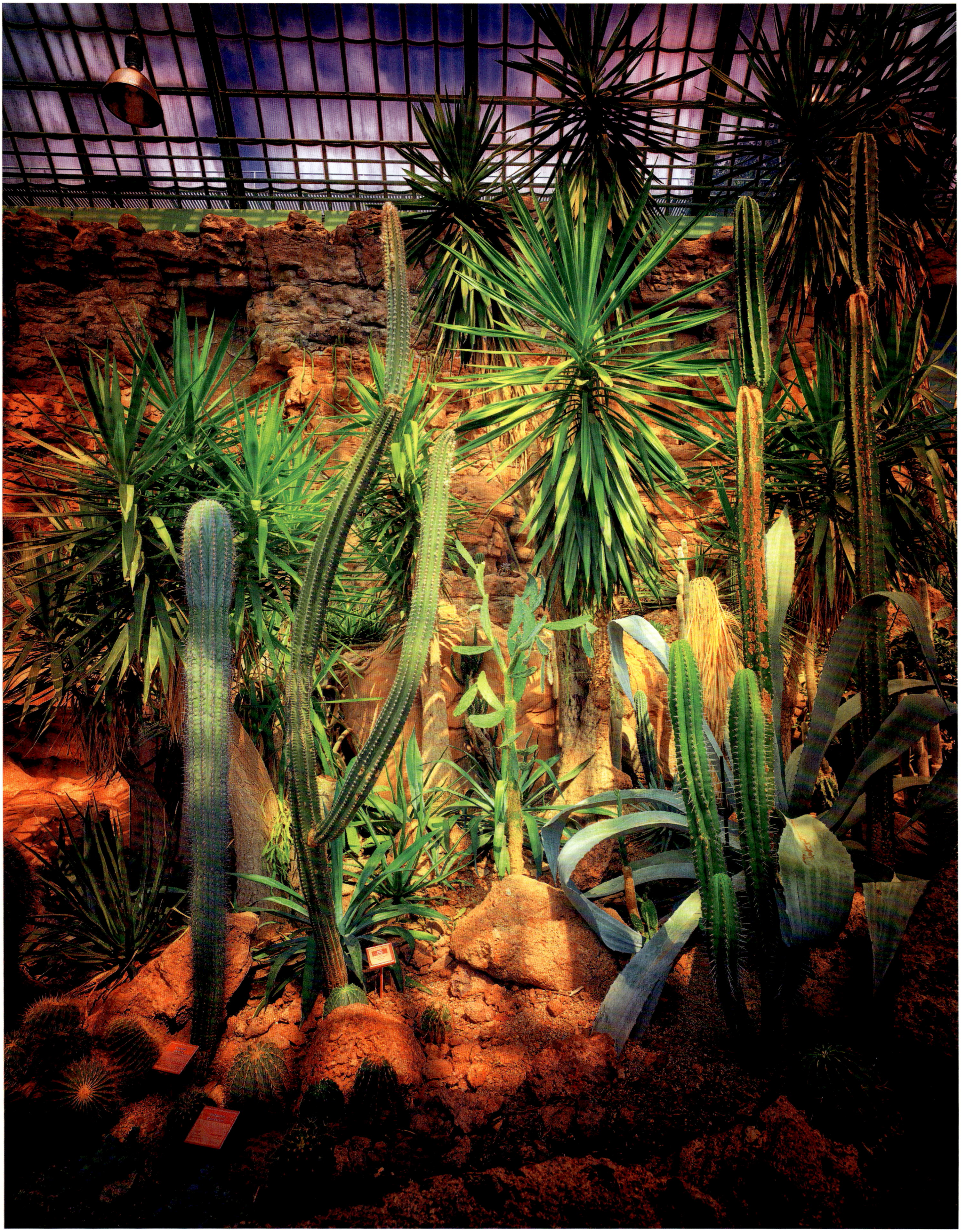

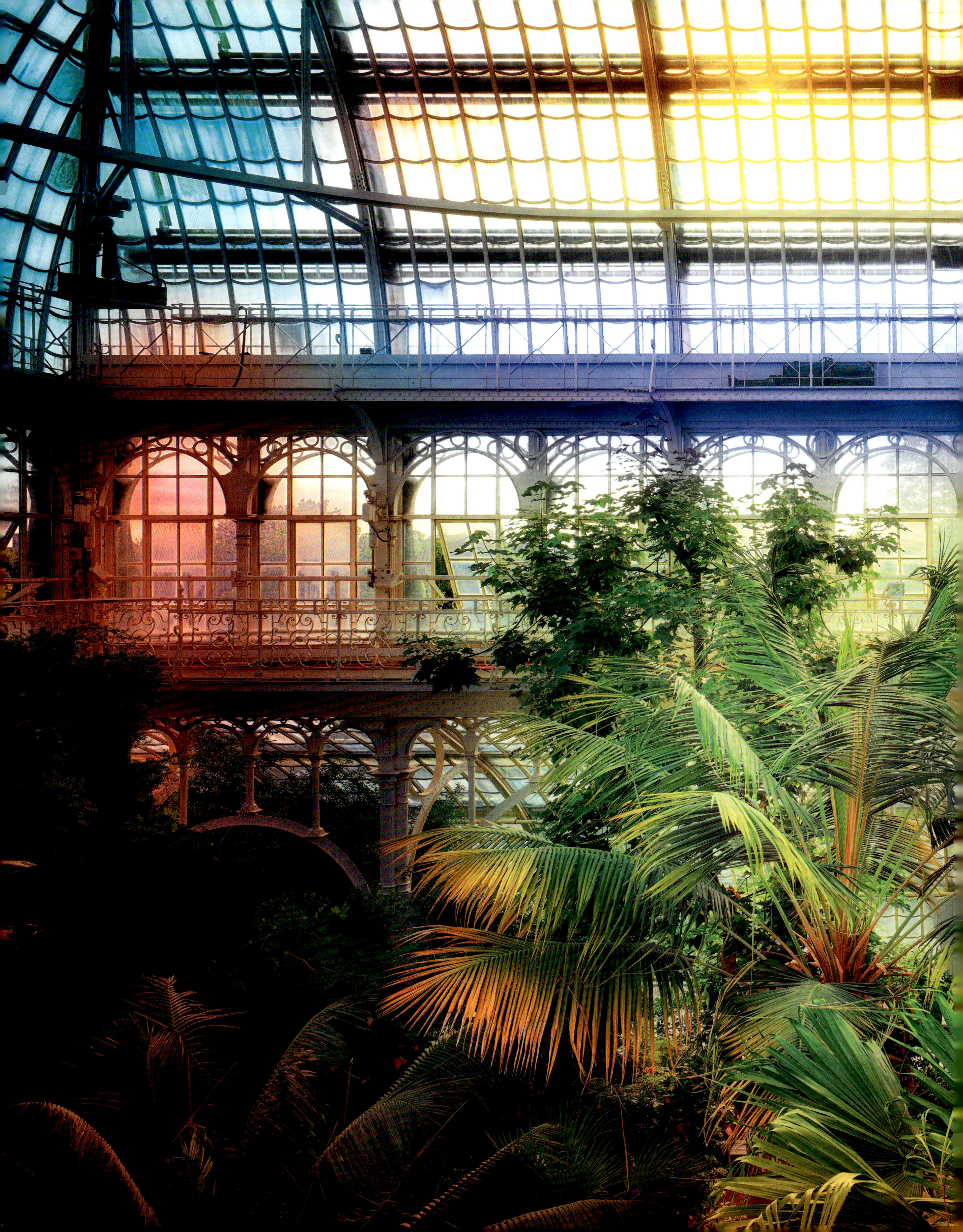

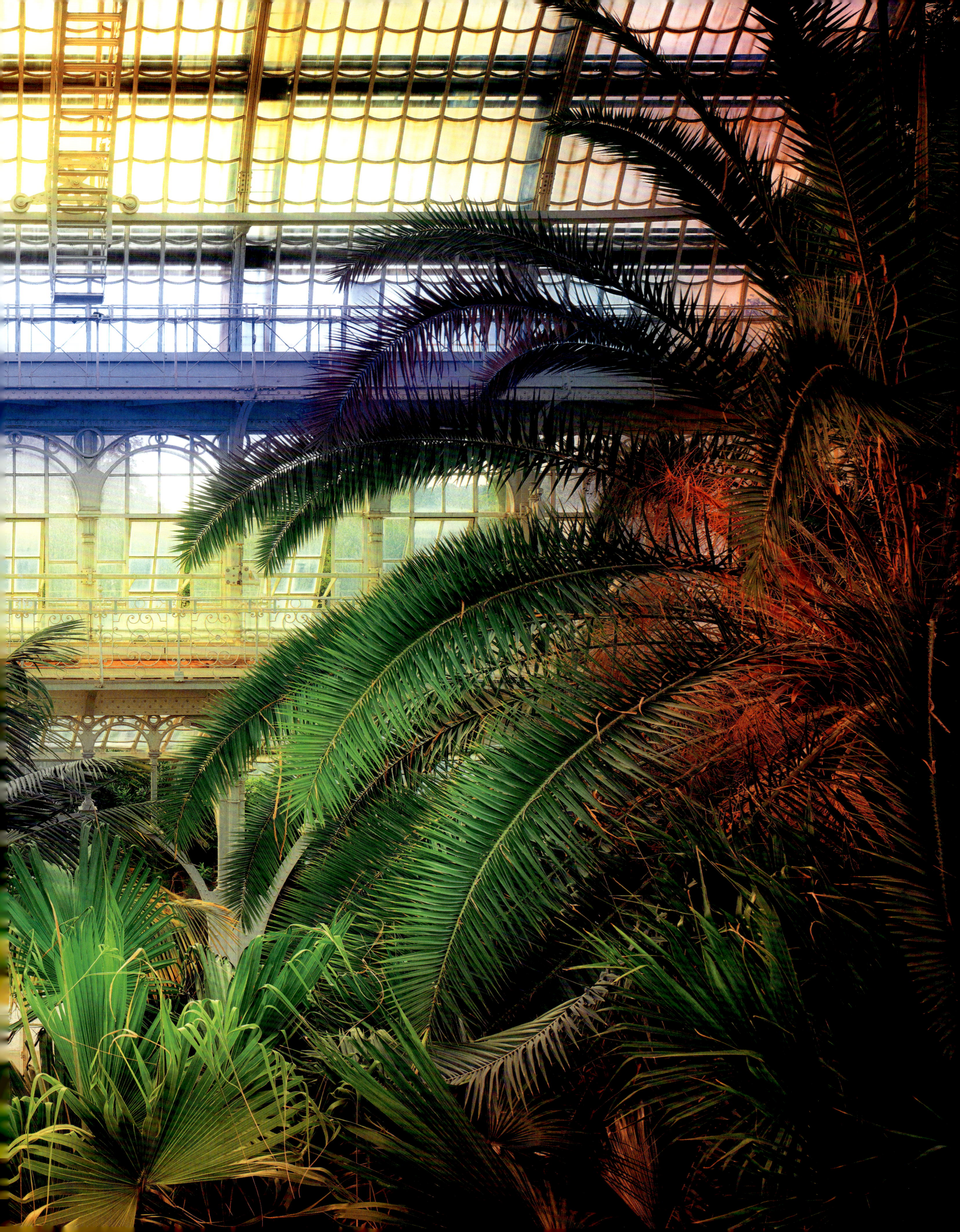

Großes Palmenhaus Schönbrunn XVIII

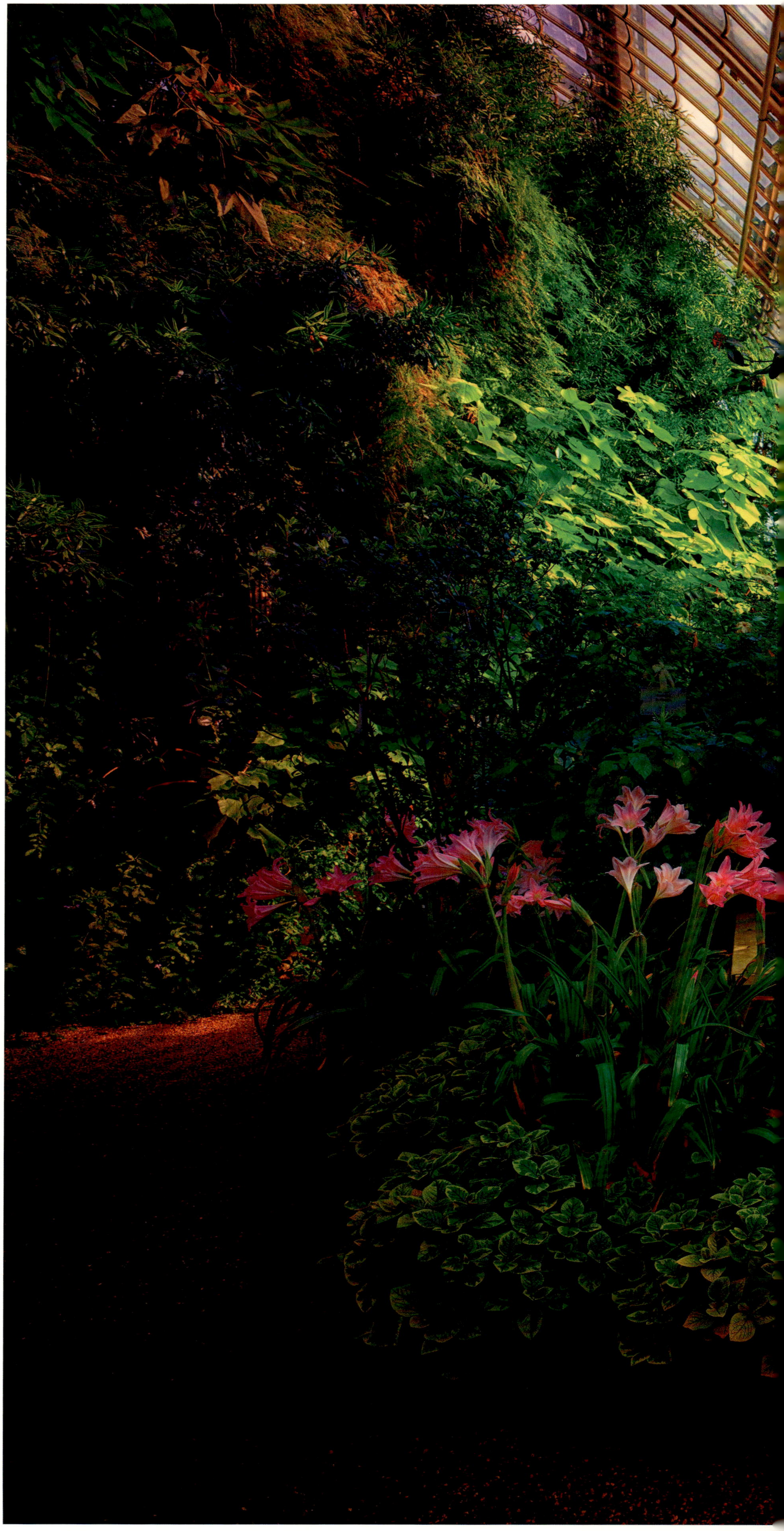

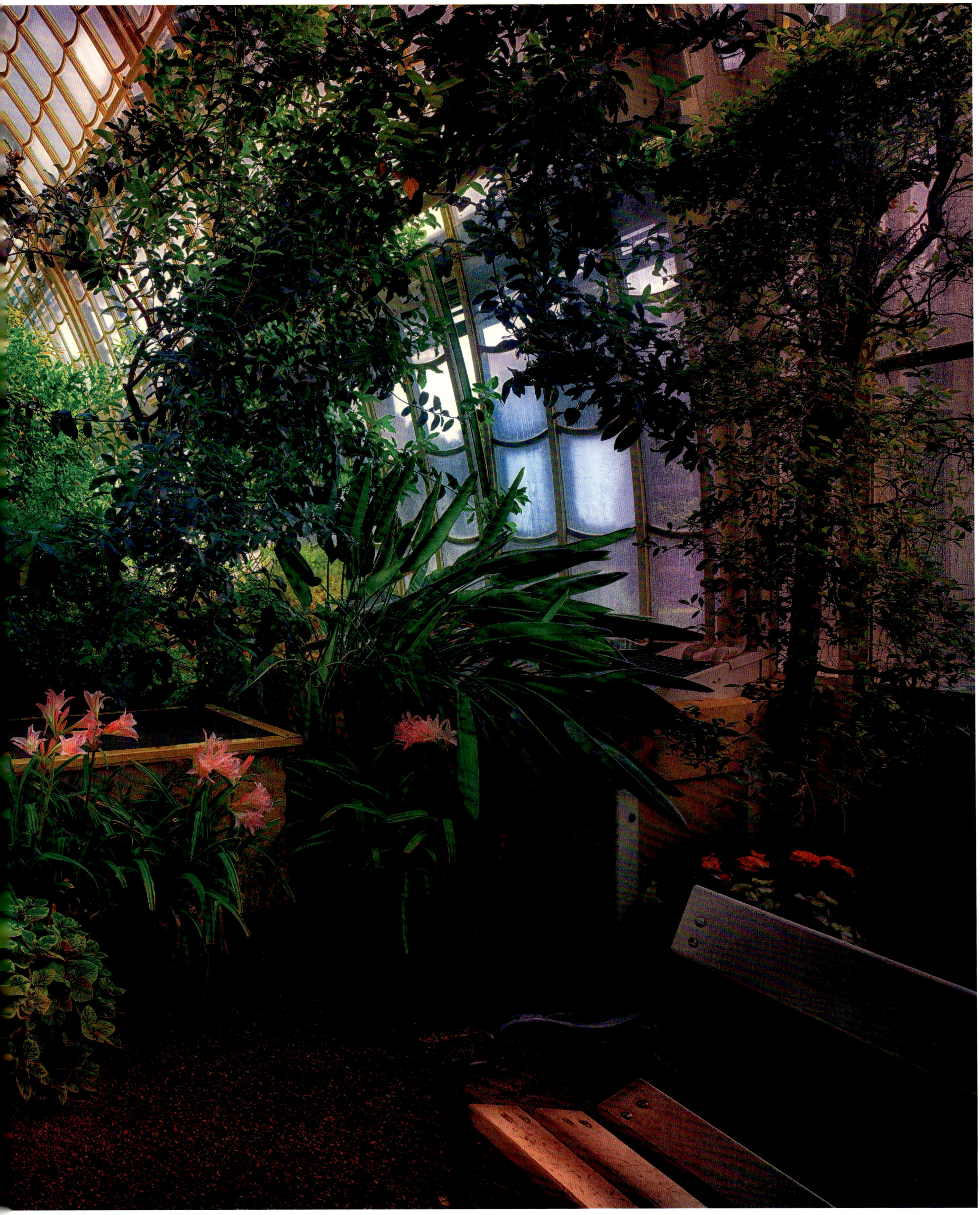

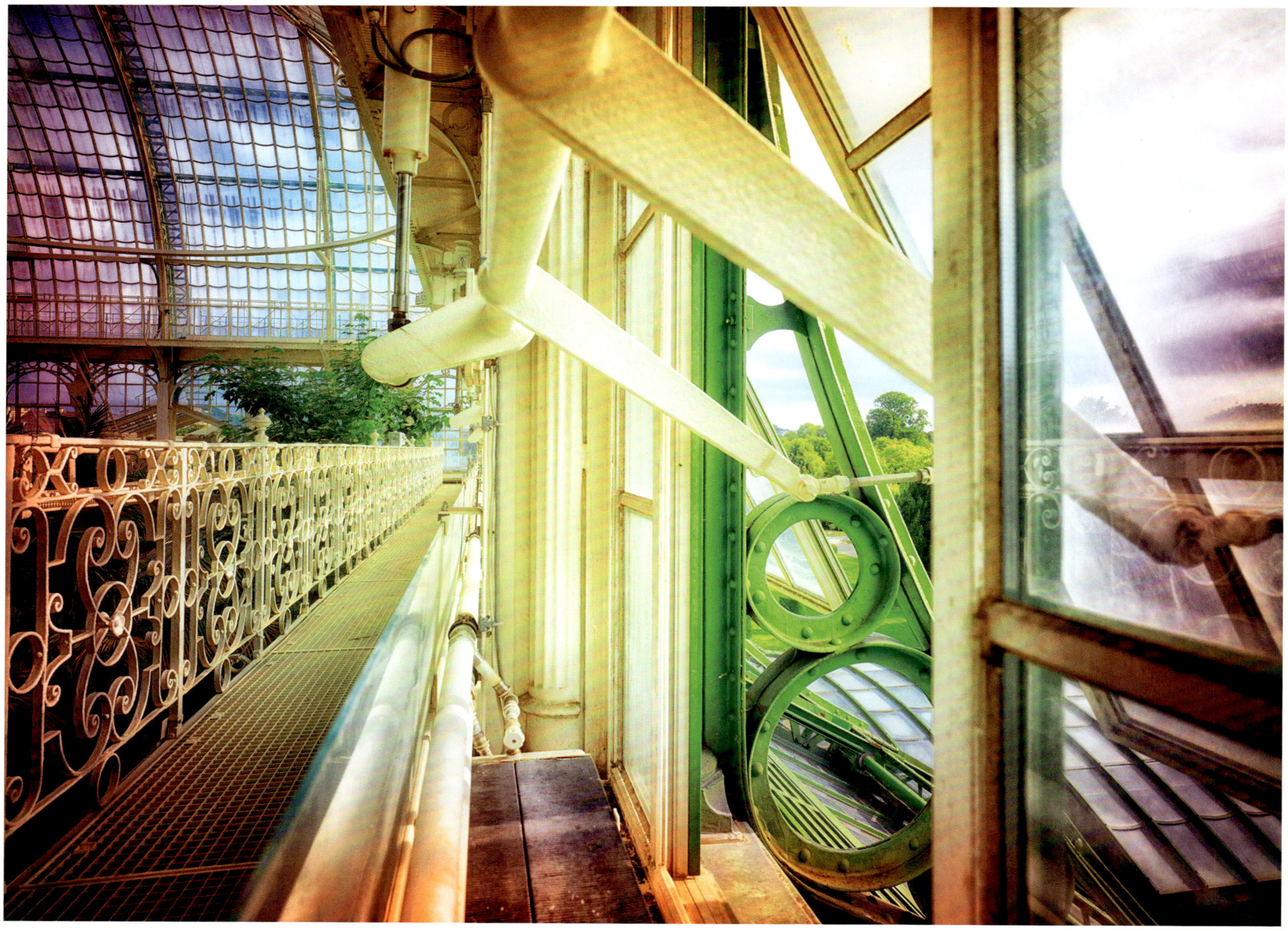

Großes Palmenhaus Schönbrunn XII • Großes Palmenhaus Schönbrunn XVI
Großes Palmenhaus Schönbrunn XV

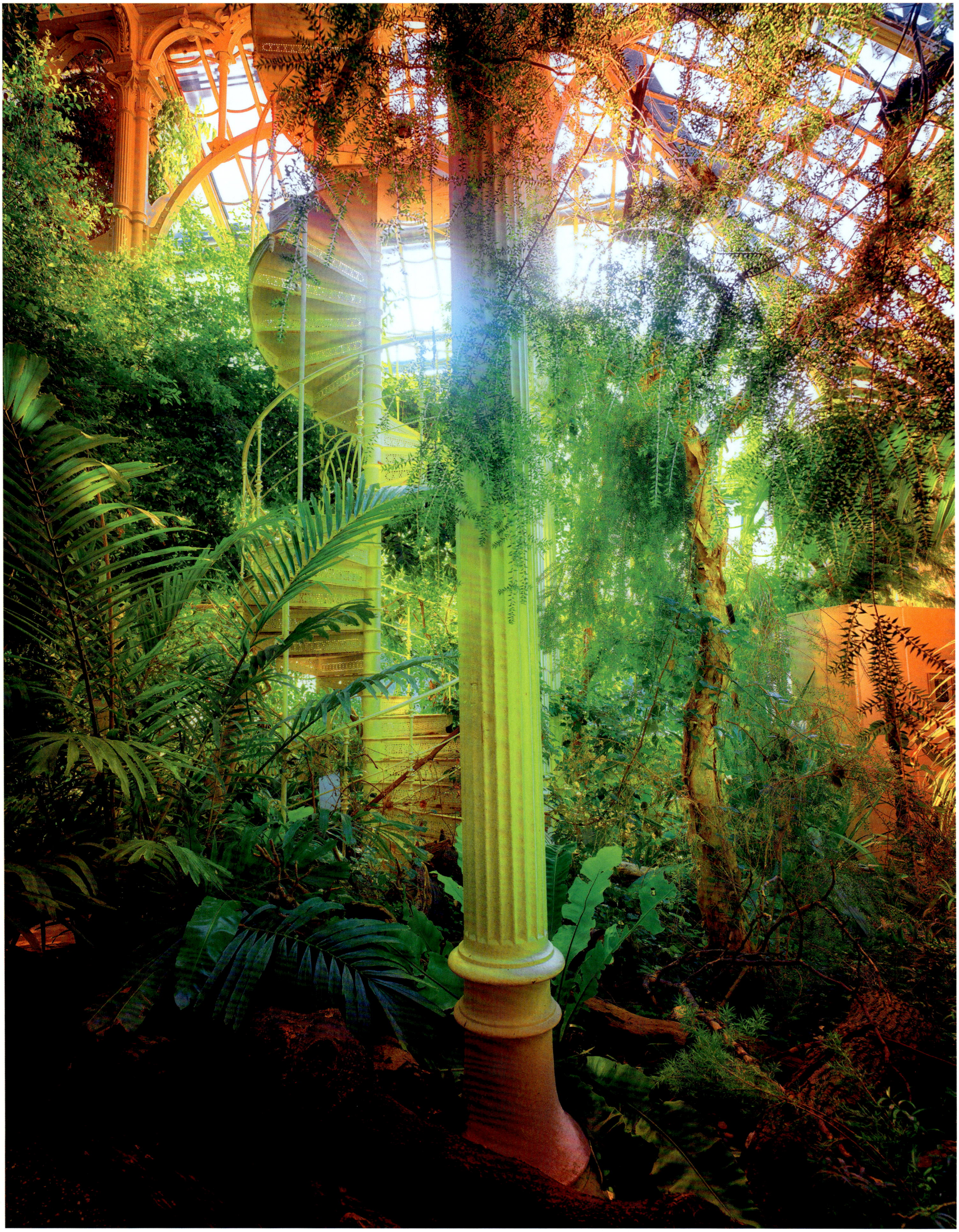

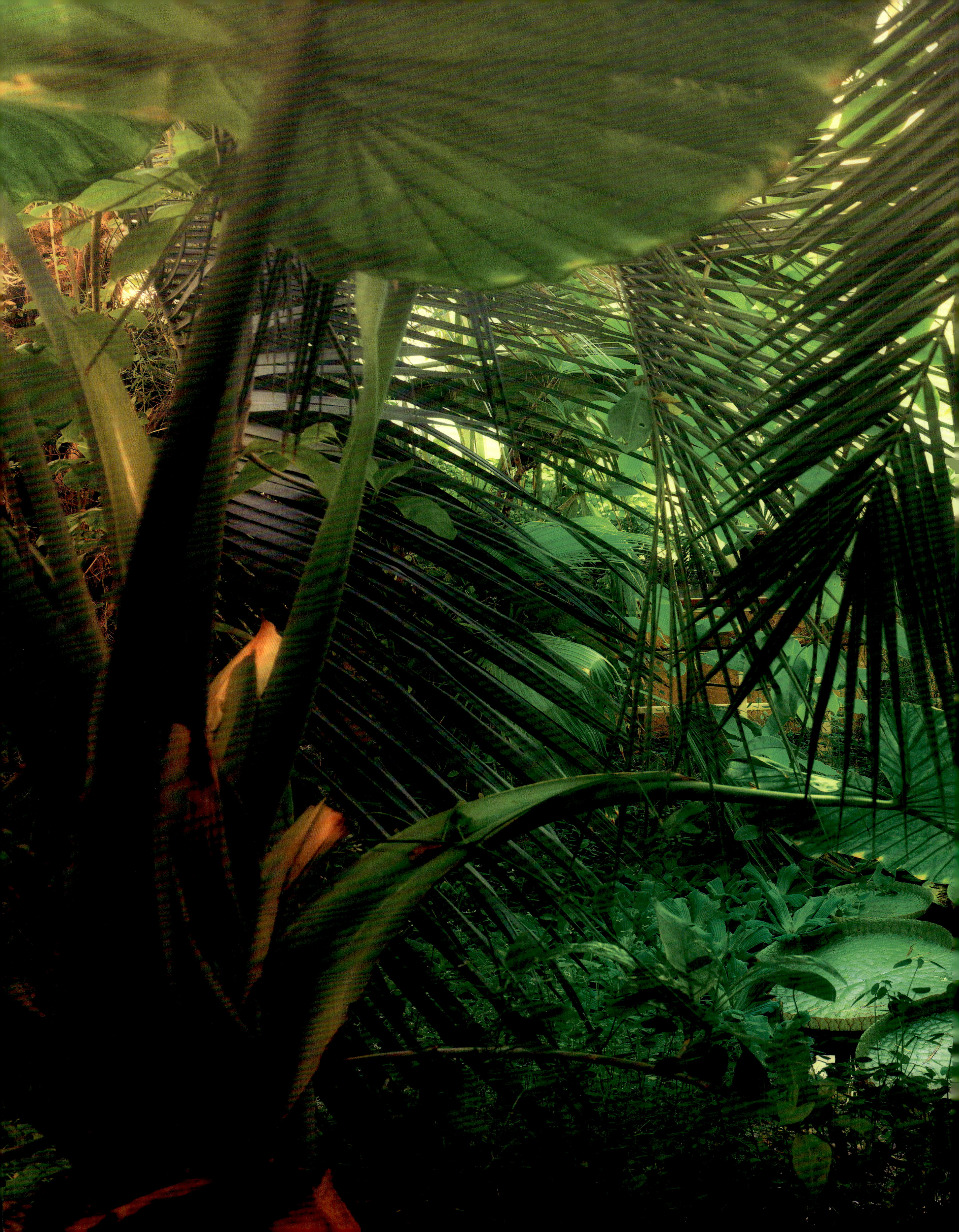

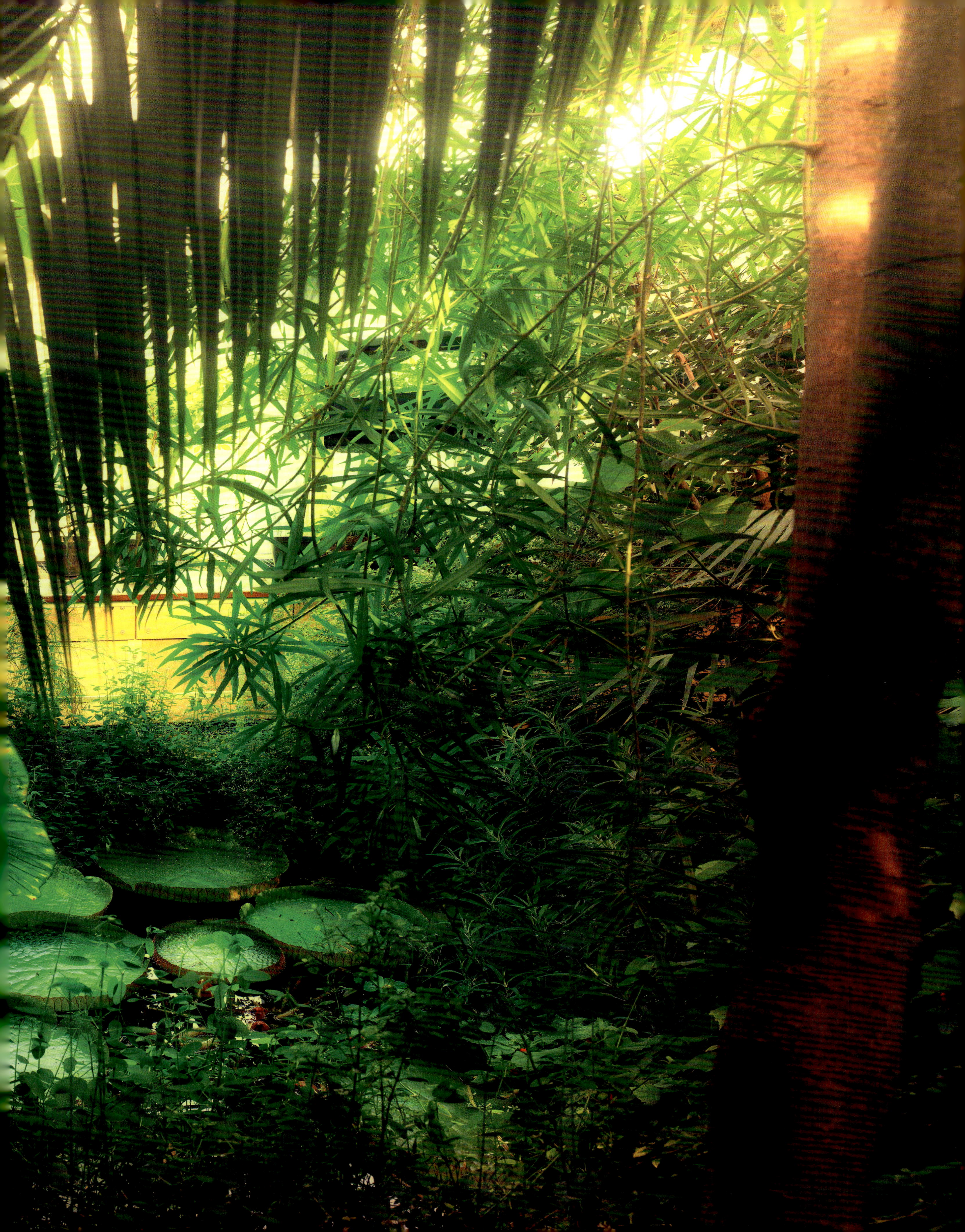

Großes Palmenhaus Schönbrunn II
Großes Palmenhaus Schönbrunn I ▼

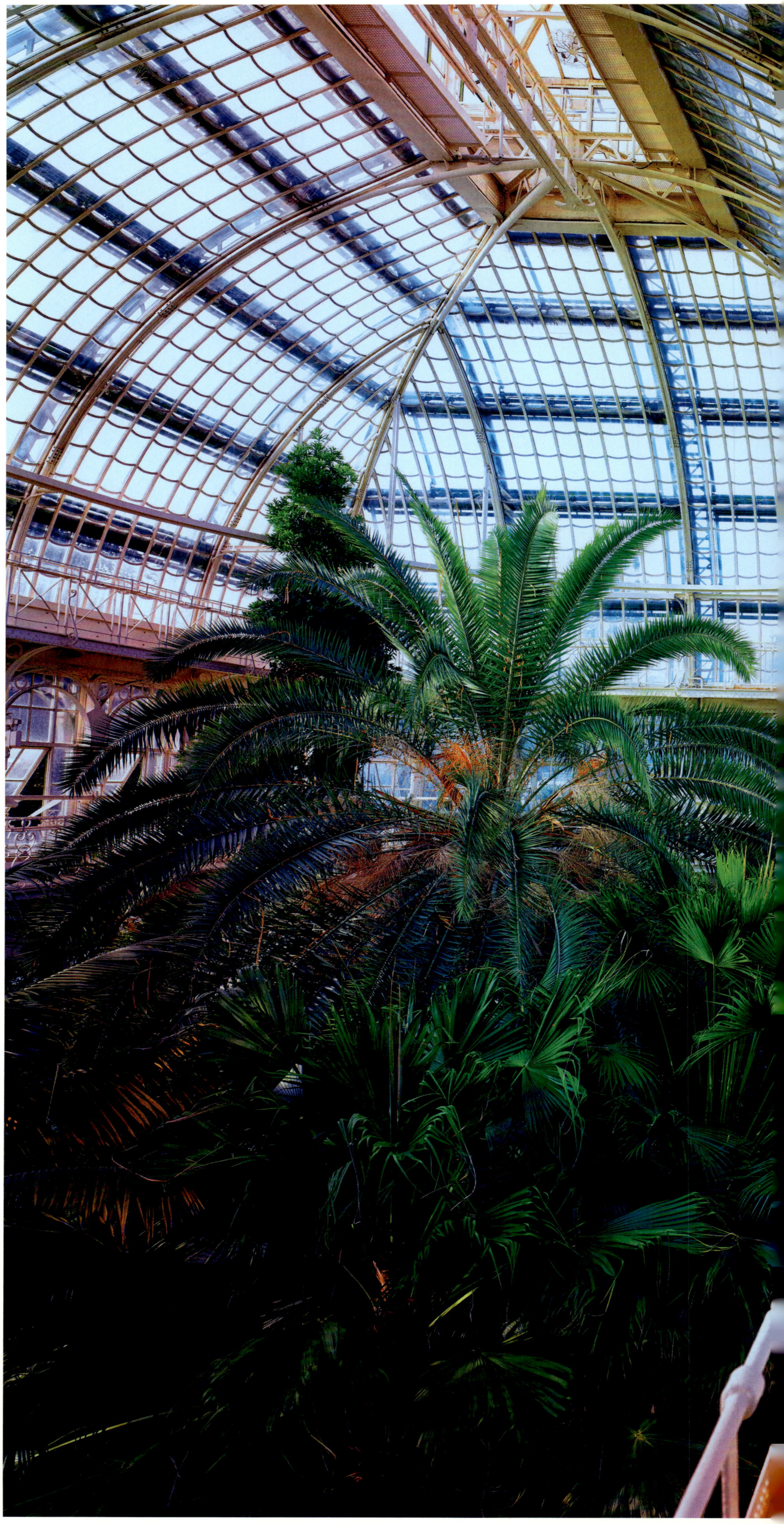

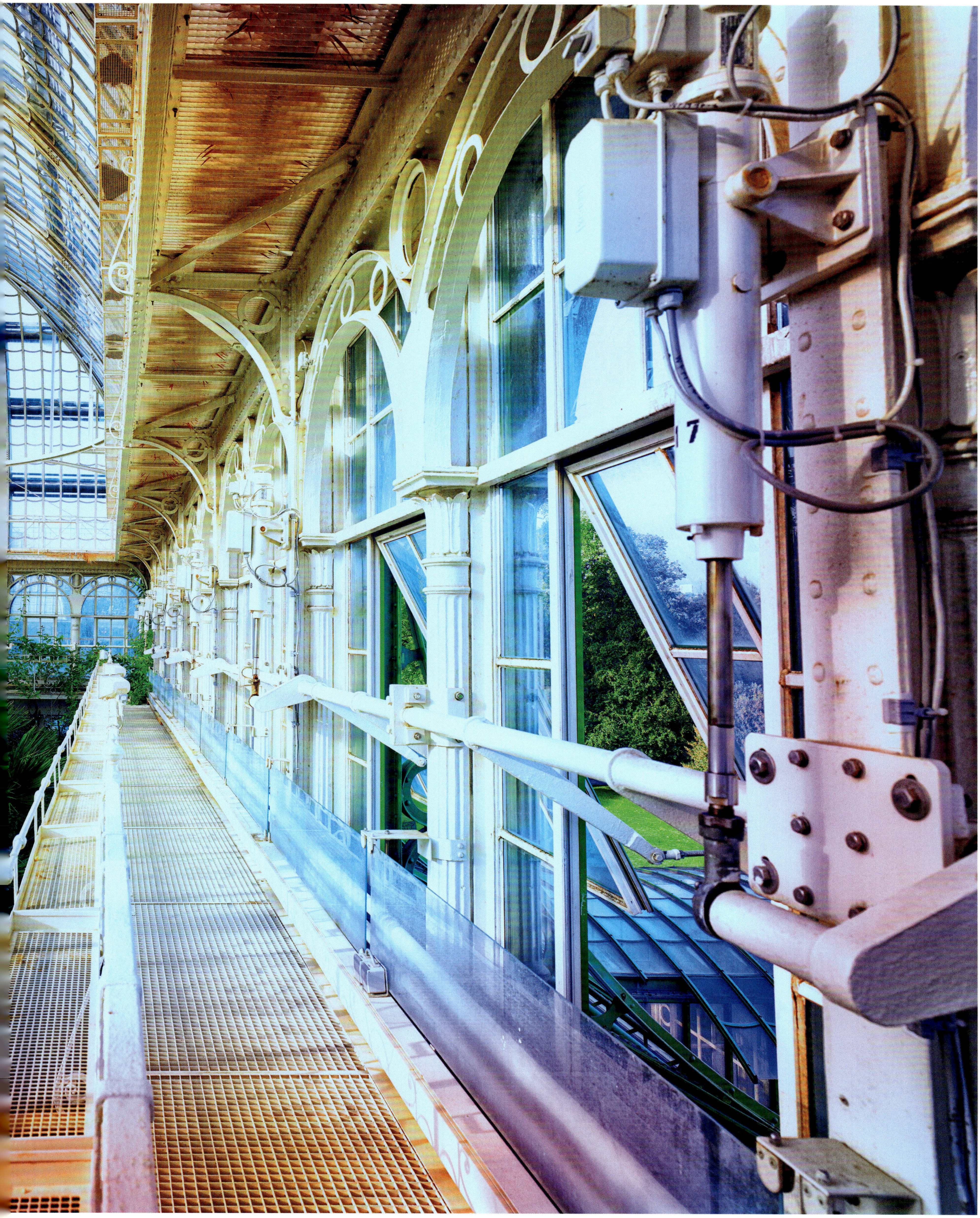

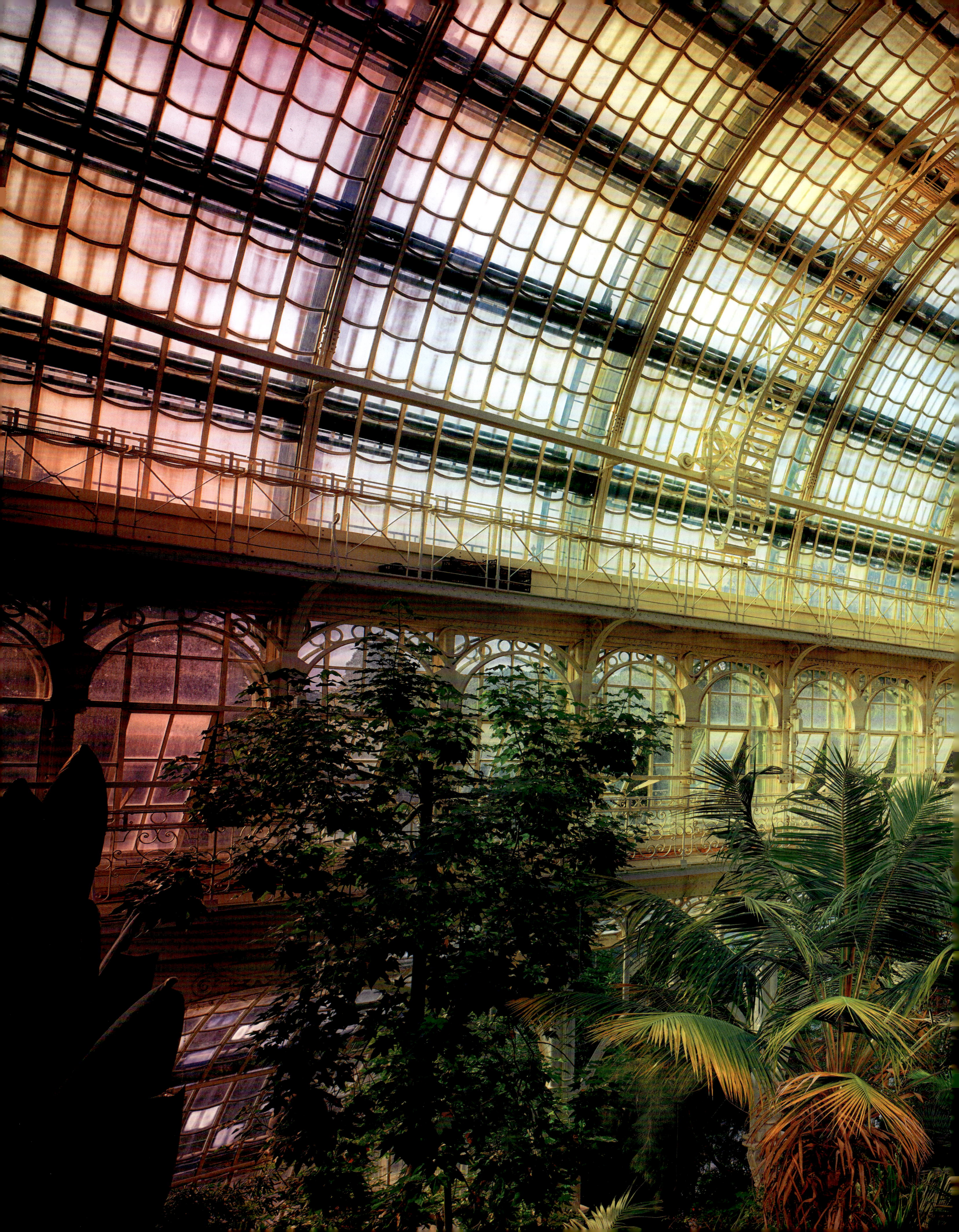

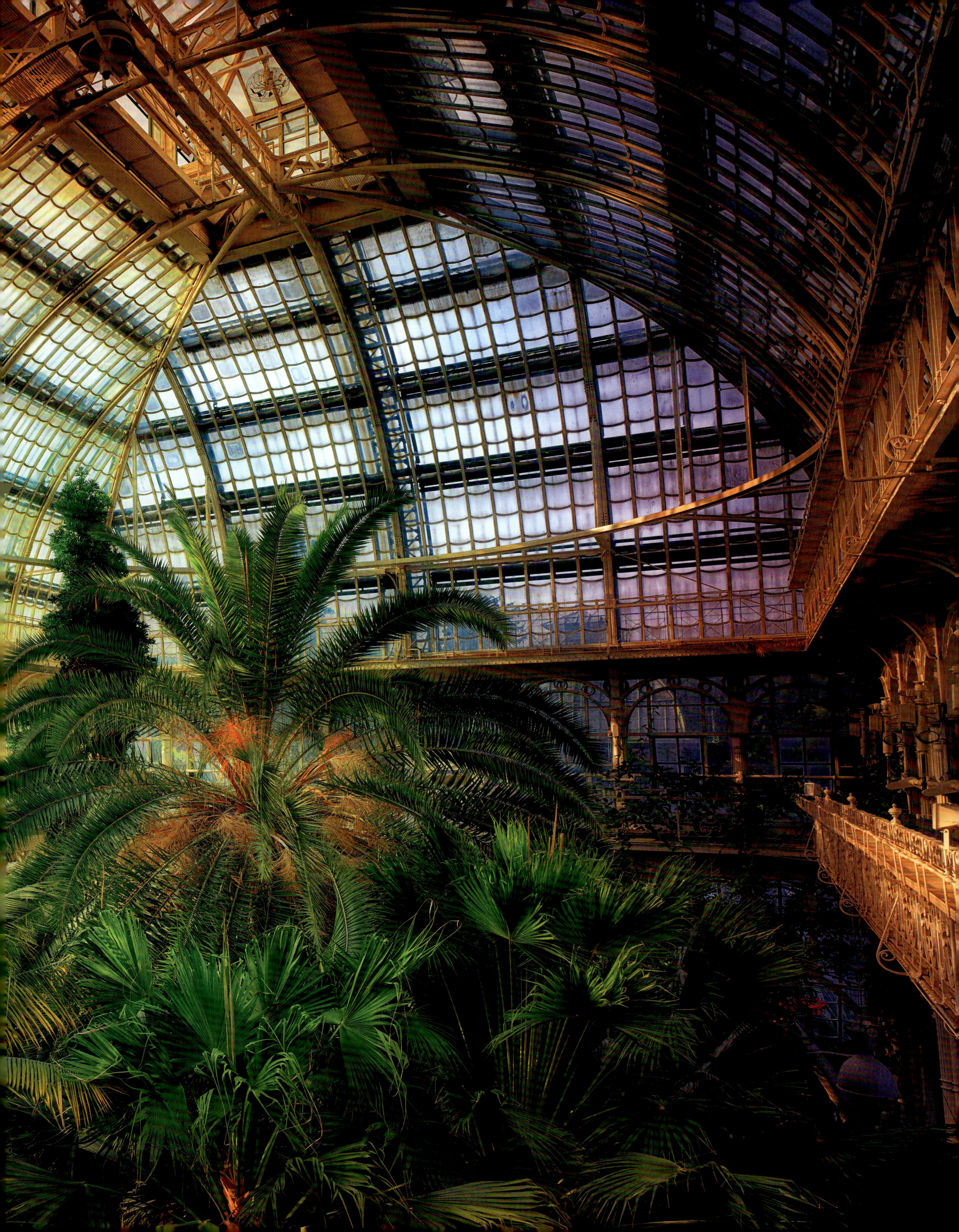

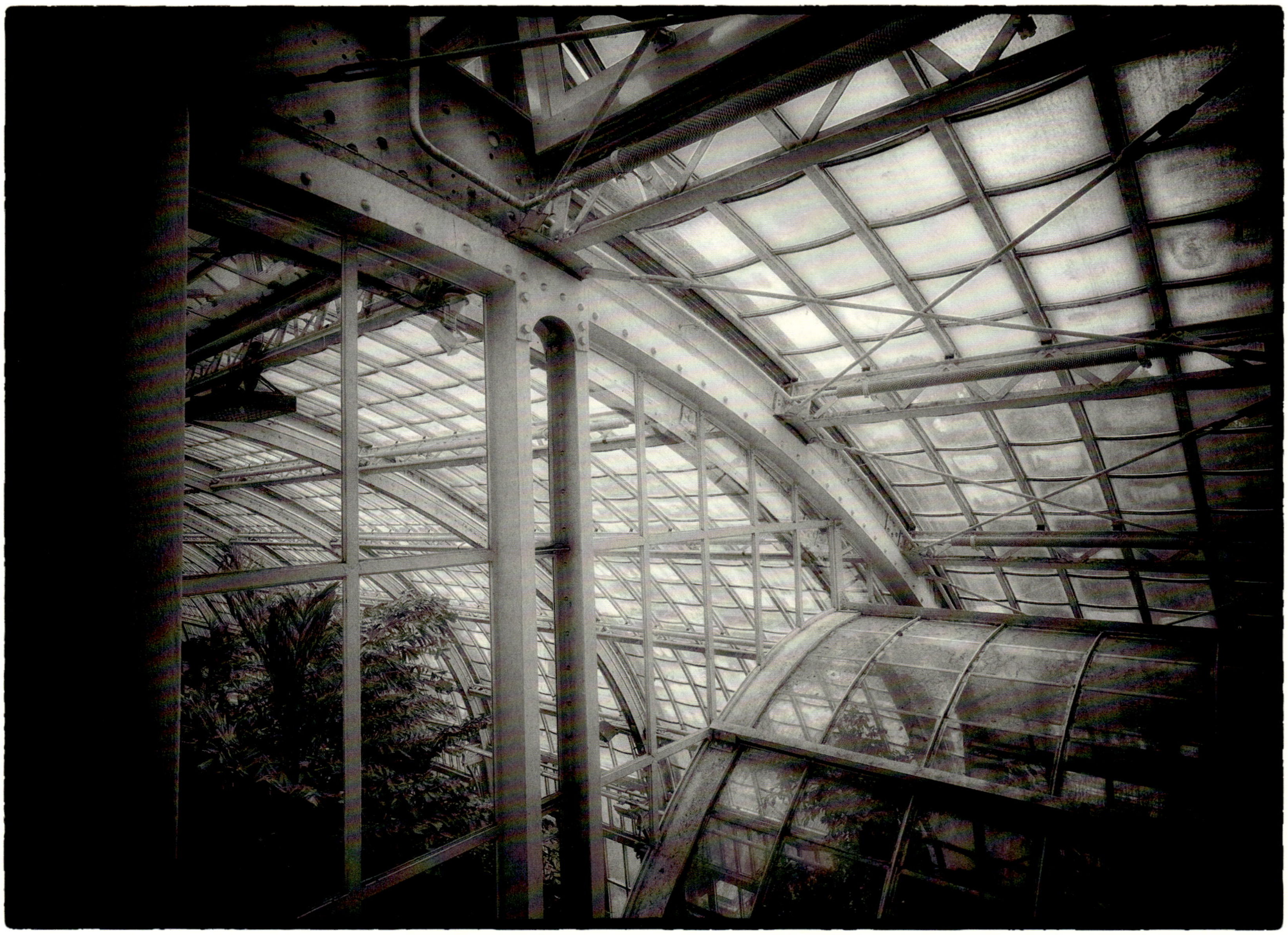

SCHMETTERLINGS-
HAUS

BURGGARTEN HOFBURG

VIENNA

SCHMETTERLINGSHAUS BURGGARTEN HOFBURG

ORT
Wien, Österreich

GRÖSSE
120 m lang; 16 m breit; 17 m hoch

ENTSTEHUNG
1901–1903
Entwurf: Friedrich Ohmann

ARCHITEKTUR
Längsrechteckiges Gebäude mit einem Richtung Burggarten in der Breite nach vorn springendem Mittelpavillon mit erhöhtem Glasgewölbe. Die fünfachsige Fassade des Mittelpavillons wird durch ionische Säulen geschmückt. An den Enden steinerne Pavillons mit pyramidenförmigen Dächern, welche durch den Jugendstil beeinflusst sind.

PFLANZEN
Tropische Pflanzen des Lebensraums der über 50 Schmetterlingsarten

BESONDERHEITEN
Bis zum Ende der Donau Monarchie 1918 waren weder der Burggarten noch das Palmenhaus der Öffentlichkeit zugängig. Heute ist der Mittelteil ein Café, der linke Flügel das Schmetterlingshaus, währenddessen der rechte Flügel als Überwinterungshaus für die Botanische Sammlung der Österreichischen Bundesgärten genutzt wird. Der leergeräumte rechte Flügel dient im Sommer als Ort für Veranstaltungen.

LOCATION
Vienna, Austria

SIZE
120 m long; 16 m wide; 17 m high

ESTABLISHED
1901–1903
design: Friedrich Ohmann

ARCHITECTURE
The building is rectangular in length and has a central pavilion with a raised glass vault that juts out widthwise in the direction of the castle garden. The five-axis façade of the central pavilion is decorated with Ionic columns. Stone pavilions with pyramid-shaped roofs inspired by the Art Nouveau style are situated at the ends.

PLANTS
Tropical plants from the habitat of more than 50 species of butterflies

ADDITIONAL NOTES
Until the end of the Habsburg monarchy in 1918, neither the Castle Garden nor the Palm House were open to the public. Today, the central part is a café, the left wing is the Butterfly House, while the right wing is used as an overwintering house for the botanical collection of the Austrian Federal Gardens. That same right wing, which is cleared out in the summer, then serves as an event venue.

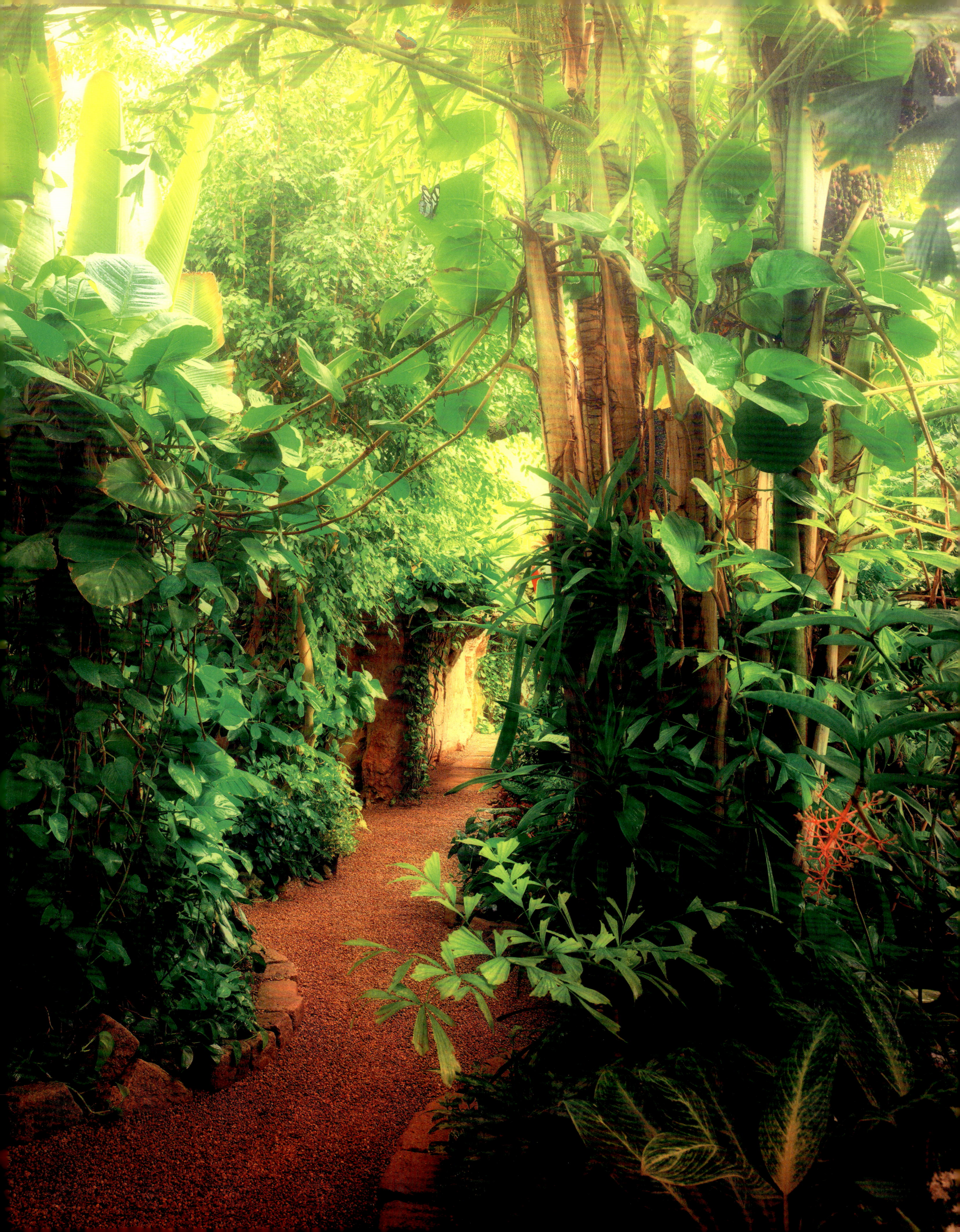

Hofgarten Wien Schmetterlinghaus III

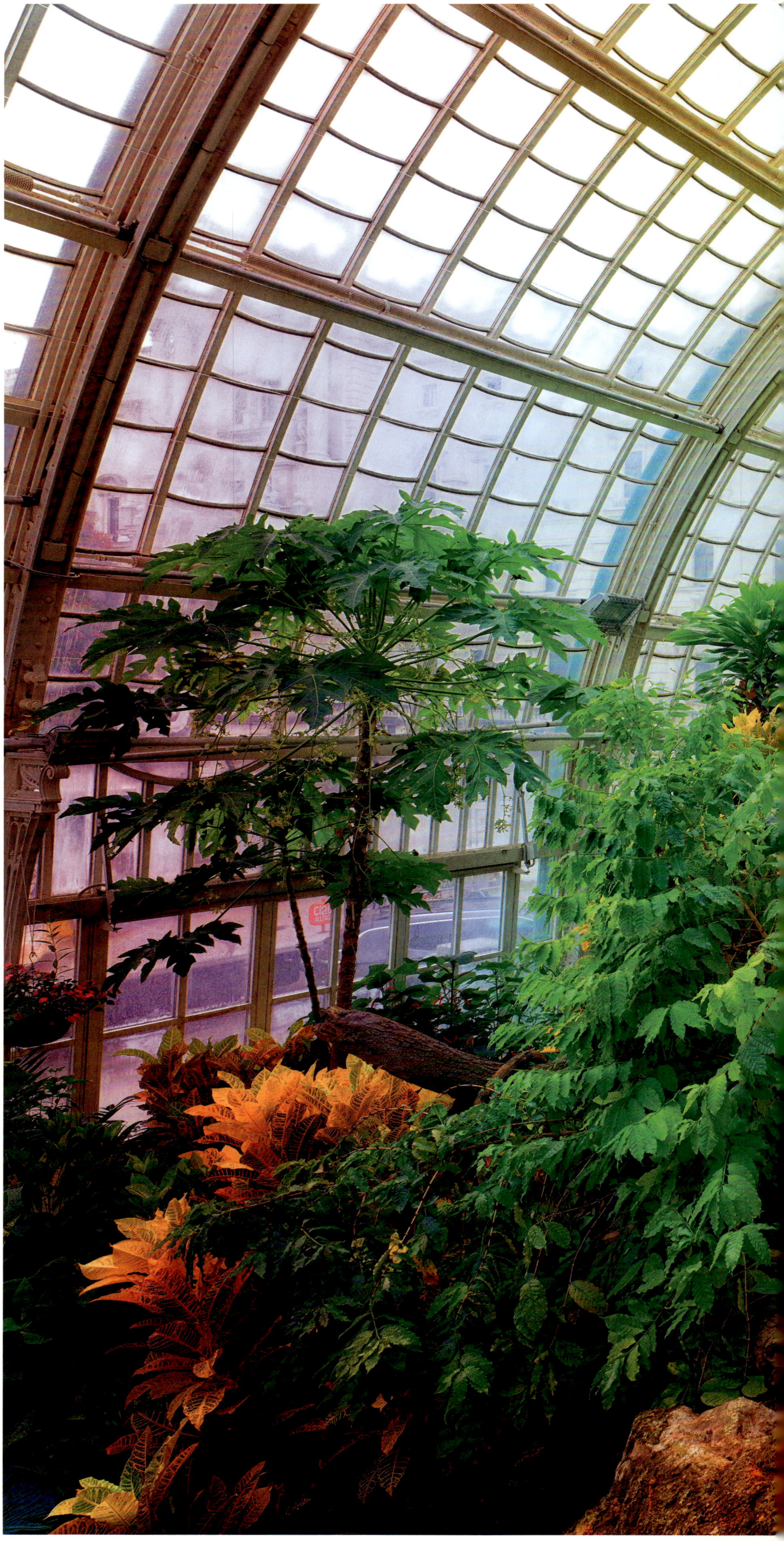

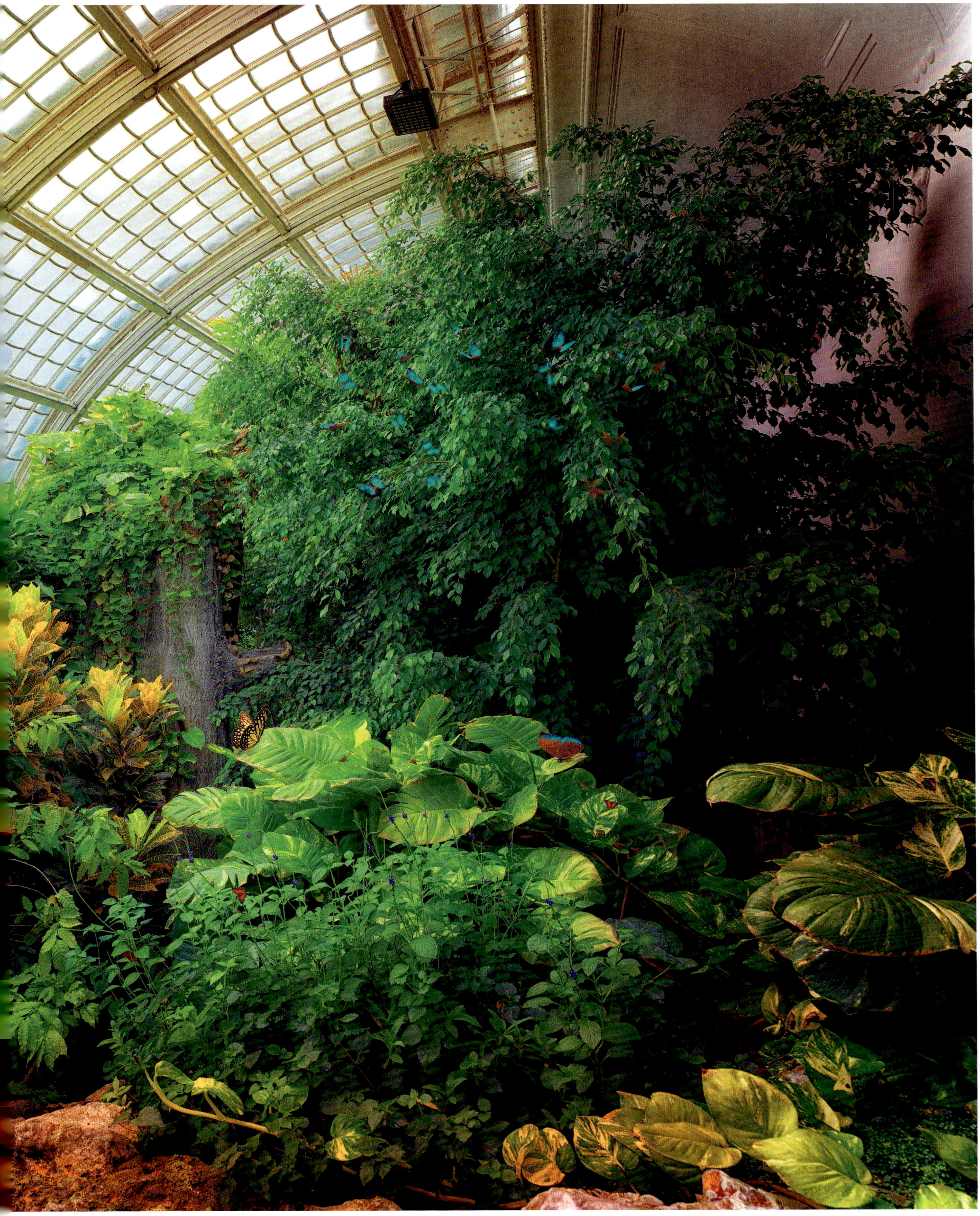

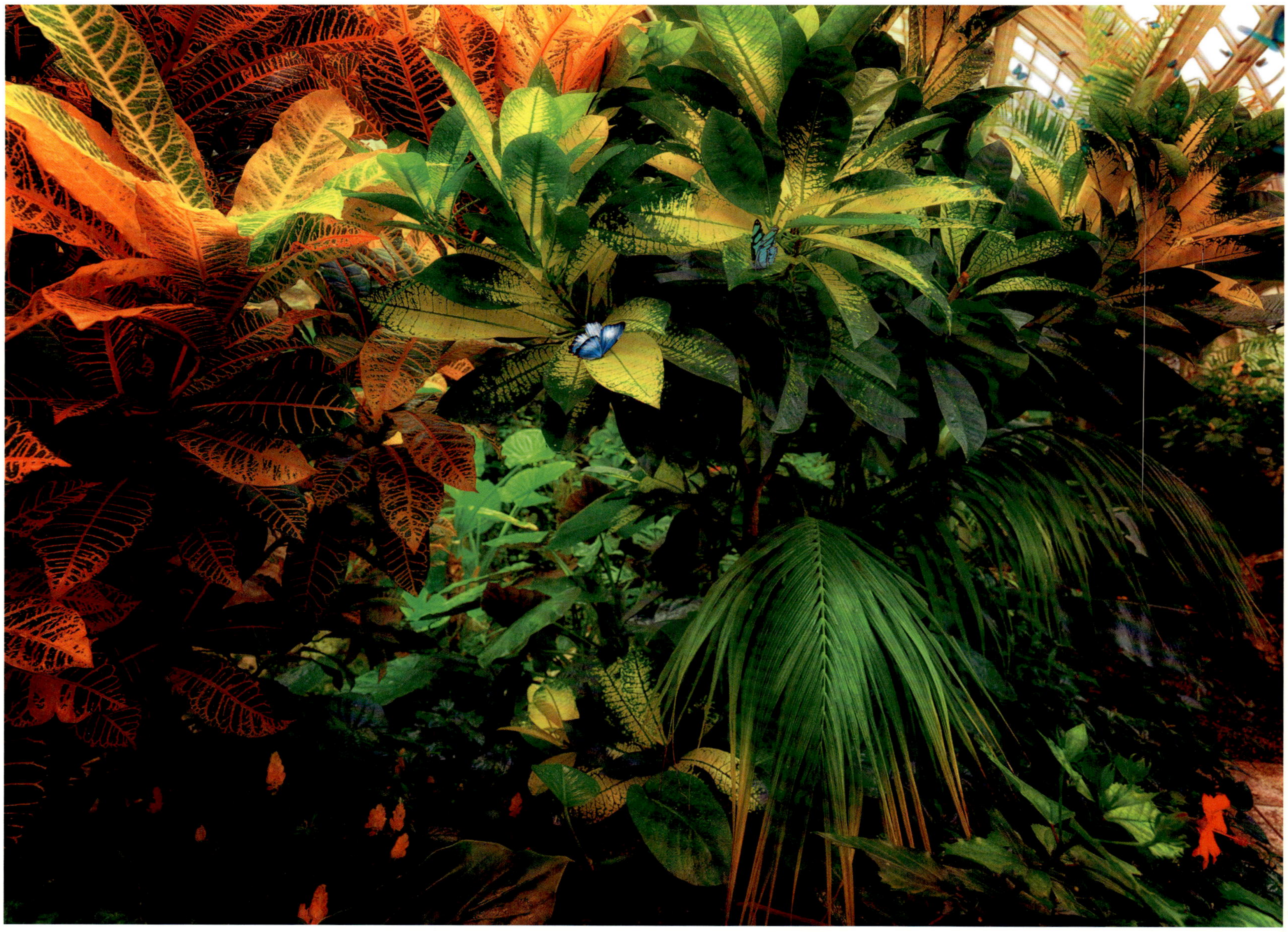

Hofgarten Wien Schmetterlinghaus V · Hofgarten Wien Schmetterlinghaus IV

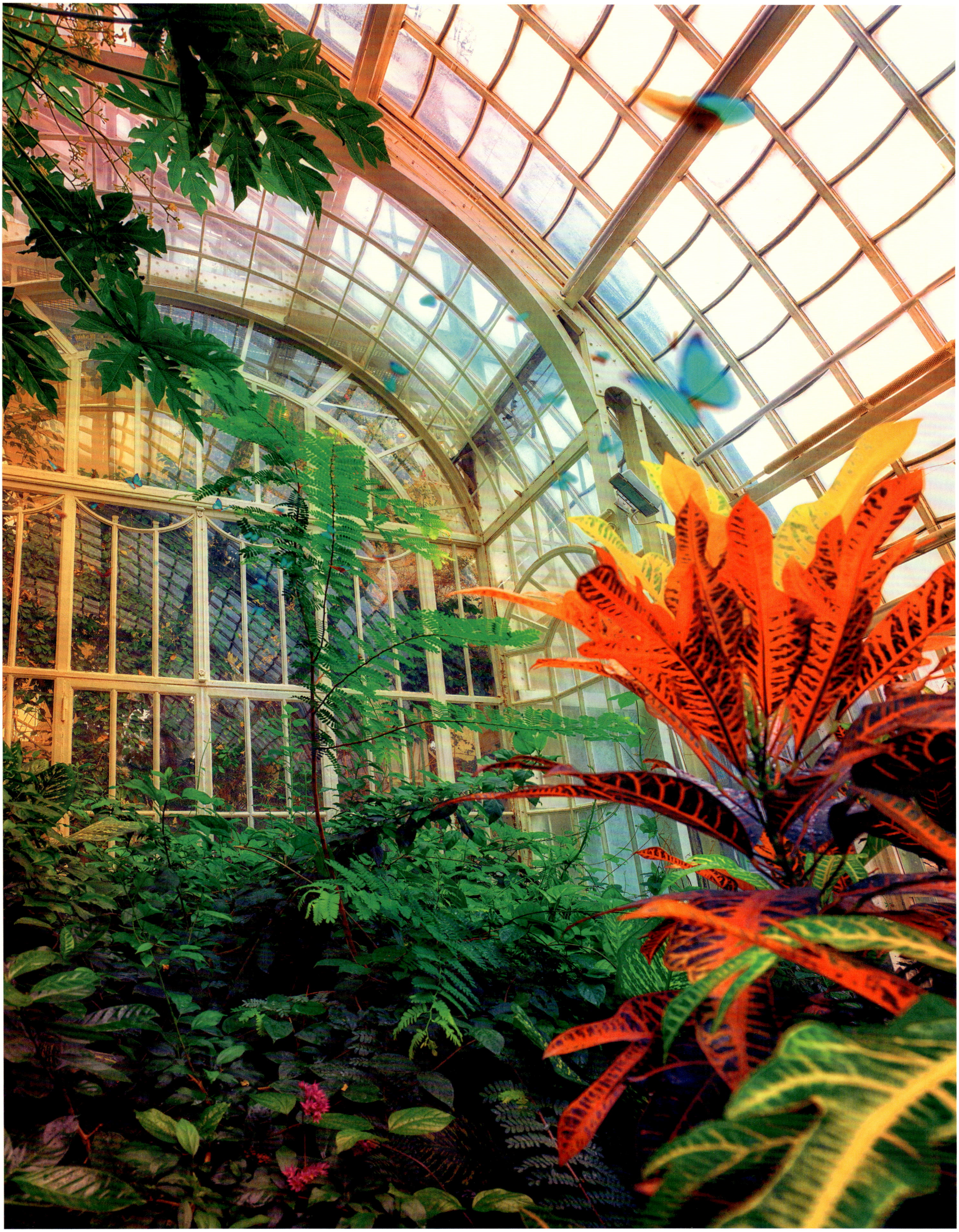

Hofgarten Wien Schmetterlinghaus VI

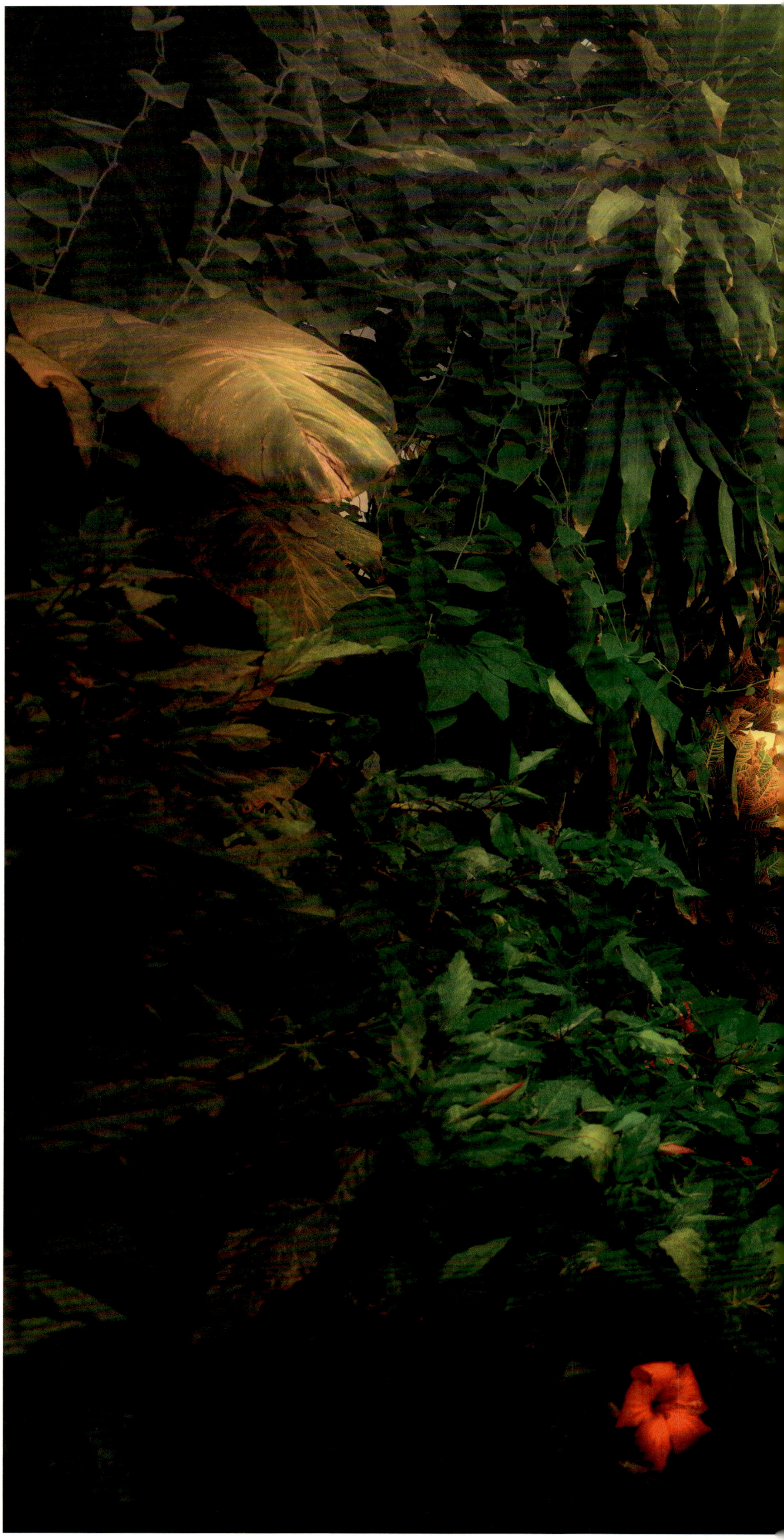

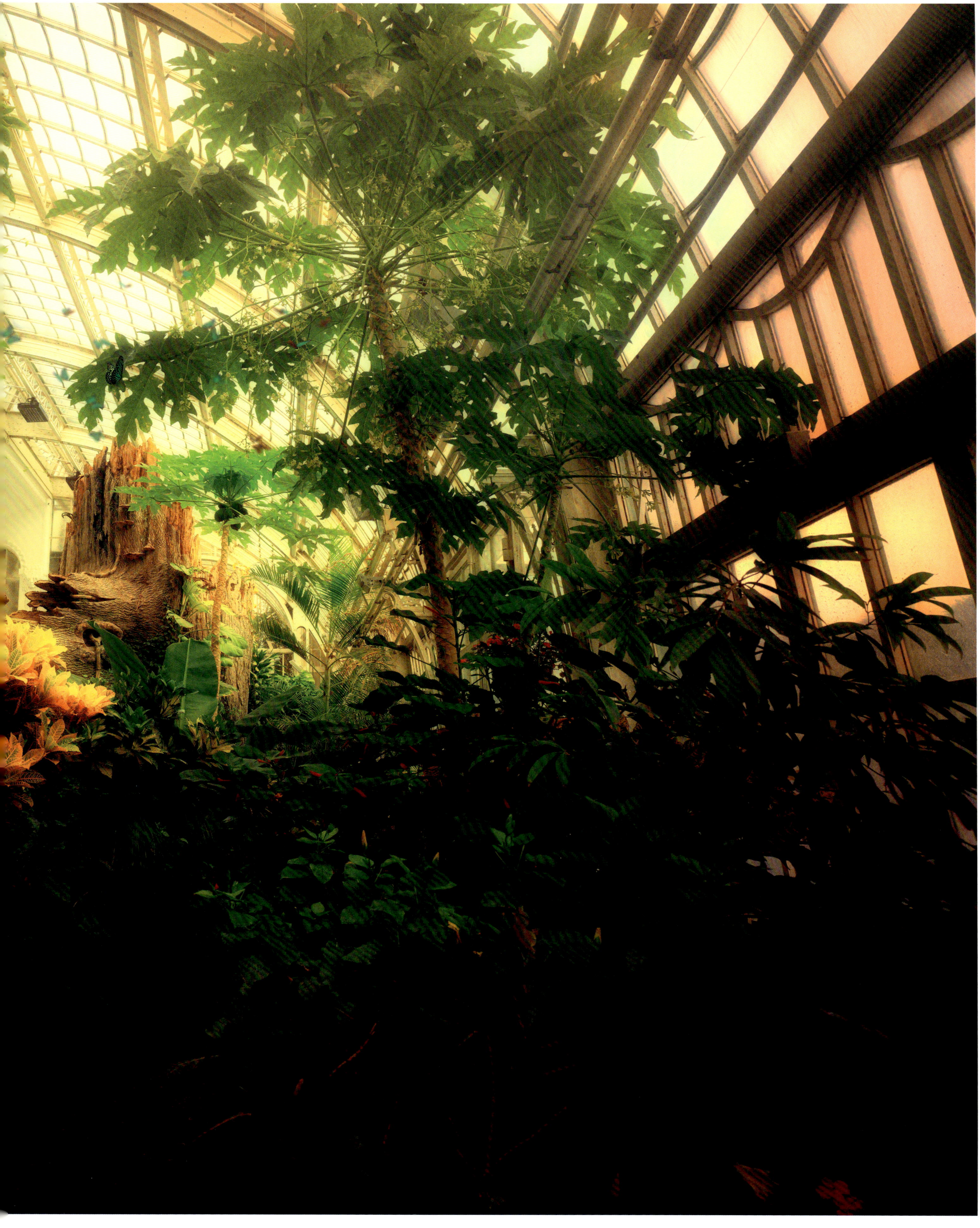

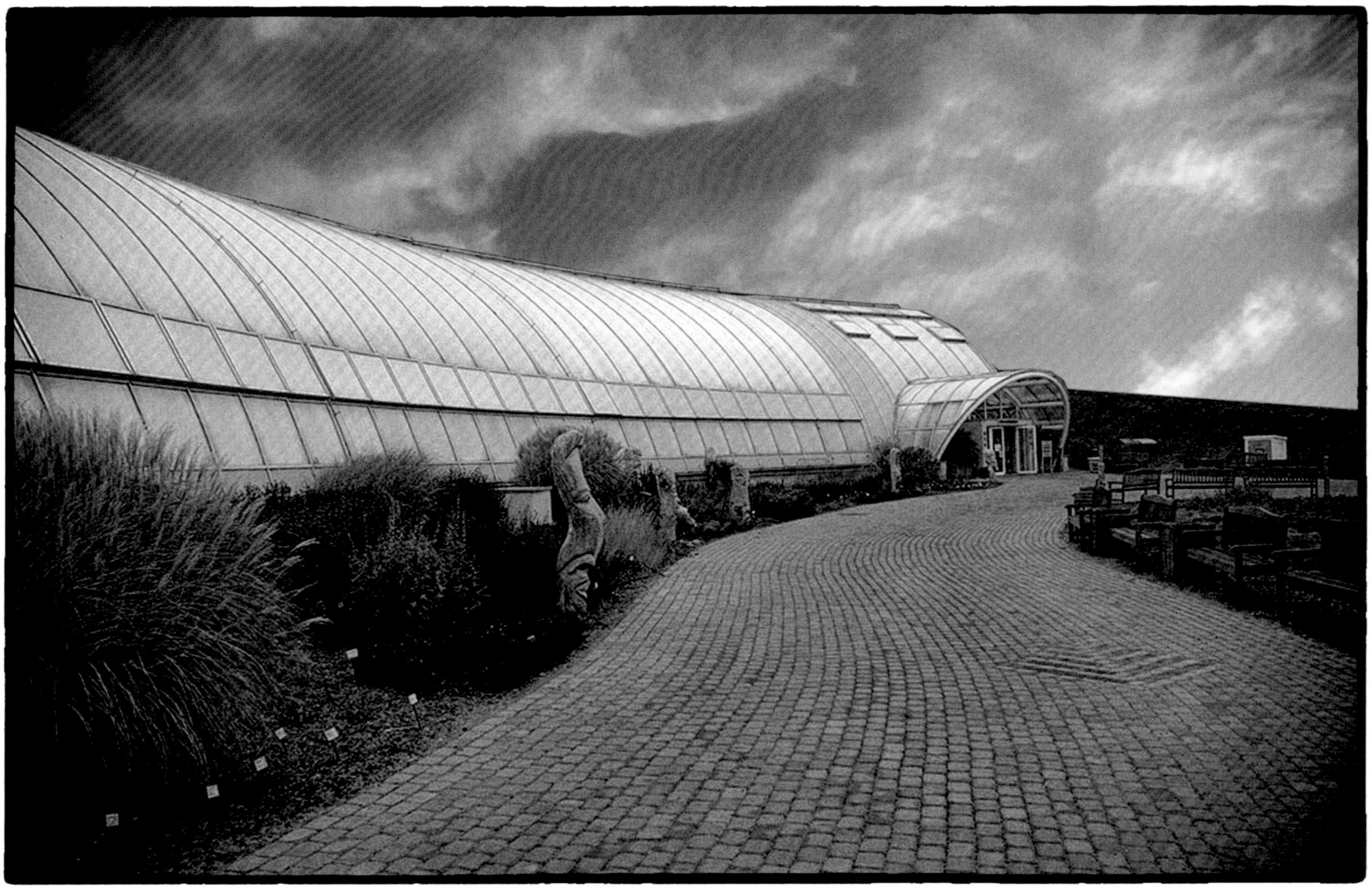

FATA MORGANA

PRAGUE

FATA MORGANA

ORT
Prag, Tschechien

GRÖSSE
130 m lang; 13 m breit

ENTSTEHUNG
1998–2004
Entwurf: Zdeněk Deyl

ARCHITEKTUR
Längliches Gebäude mit Halbtonnengewölbe aus Glas und glatten Außenwänden hinten und vorne. Erst in der Vogelperspektive wird deutlich, dass sich der Grundriss S-förmig an den anschließenden Hang anpasst.

PFLANZEN
Im Inneren werden drei Klimazonen mit der dazugehörigen Pflanzenwelt abgebildet: trockene Tropen und Subtropen, Regenwald der feuchten Tropen und die kühlen Areale der Bergwelt.

BESONDERHEITEN
In Prag gibt es drei Botanische Gärten. Troja, indem sich die Fata Morgana befindet, wurde als letzter 1989 eröffnet. Angelegt auf dem Gelände des historischen Schlossparks Troja gehört auch der Weinberg der Heiligen Klara zum Areal des Botanischen Gartens. Der angebaute Wein kann vor Ort verkostet werden.

LOCATION
Prague, Czech Republic

SIZE
130 m long; 13 m wide

ESTABLISHED
1998–2004
design: Zdeněk Deyl

ARCHITECTURE
Elongated building with a half-barrel vault of glass and smooth exterior walls in the front and rear. It is only from a bird's eye view that it becomes clear that the footprint of the greenhouse is S-shaped to conform to the adjoining slope.

PLANTS
The interior of the greenhouse is divided into three climatic zones featuring the corresponding flora for each: dry tropics and subtropics, humid tropical rain forest, and cool mountain areas.

ADDITIONAL NOTES
Prague is home to three botanical gardens. Troja, where Fata Morgana is situated, was the last to be opened in 1989. Located on the grounds of the historic Troja Castle Park, the Botanical Garden is also home to the St. Clara vineyard. Visitors can enjoy tasting the wine cultivated right there in the vineyard.

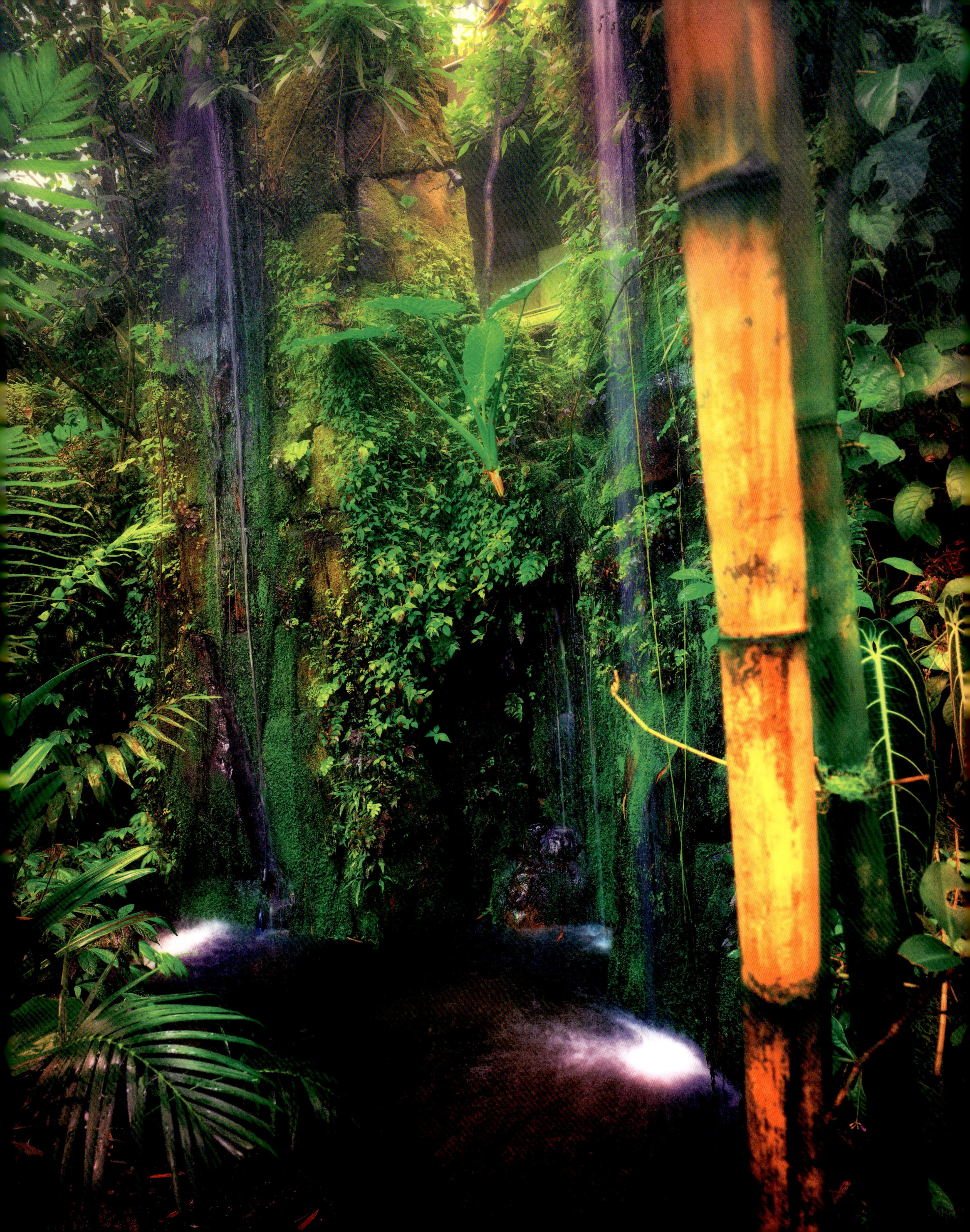

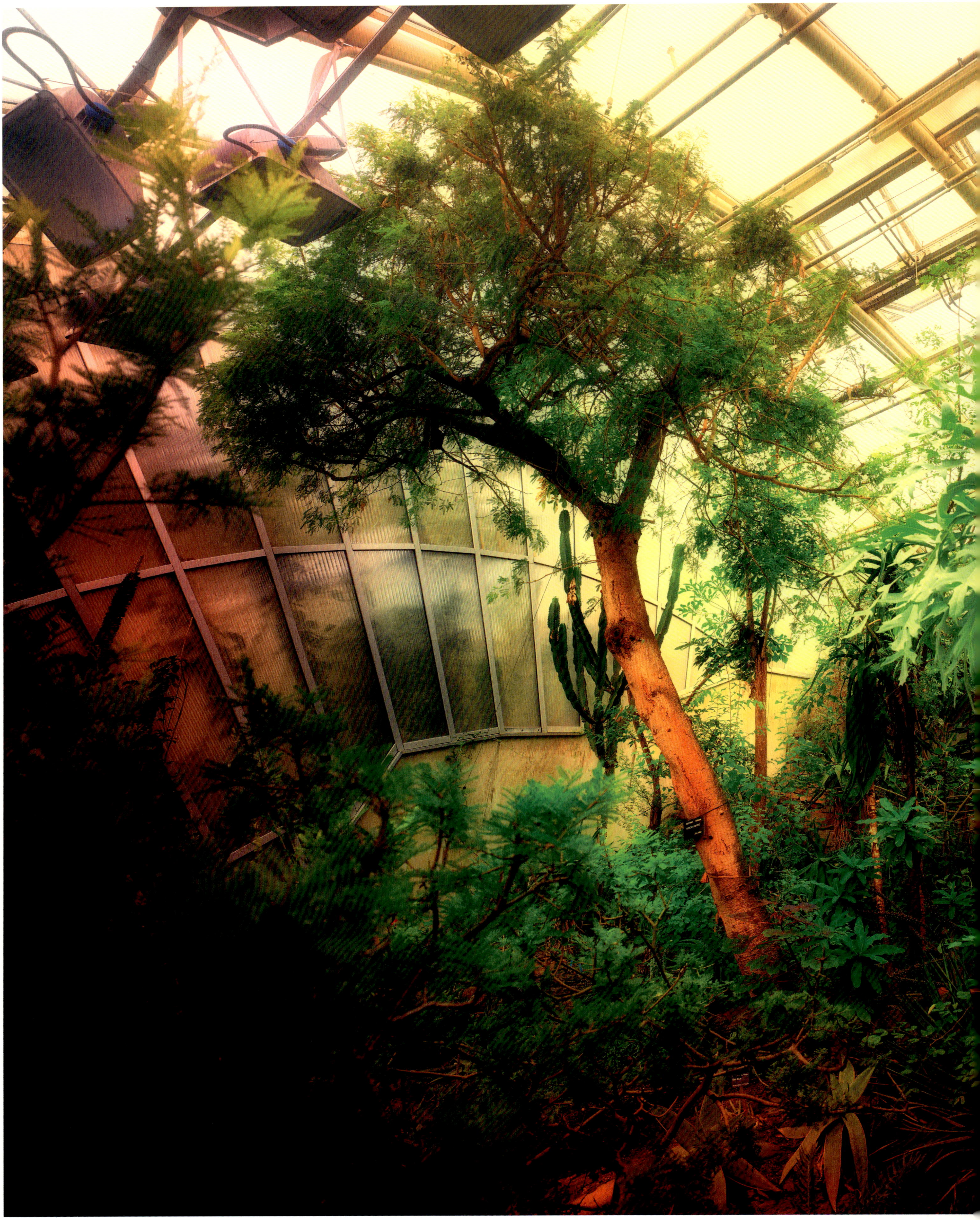

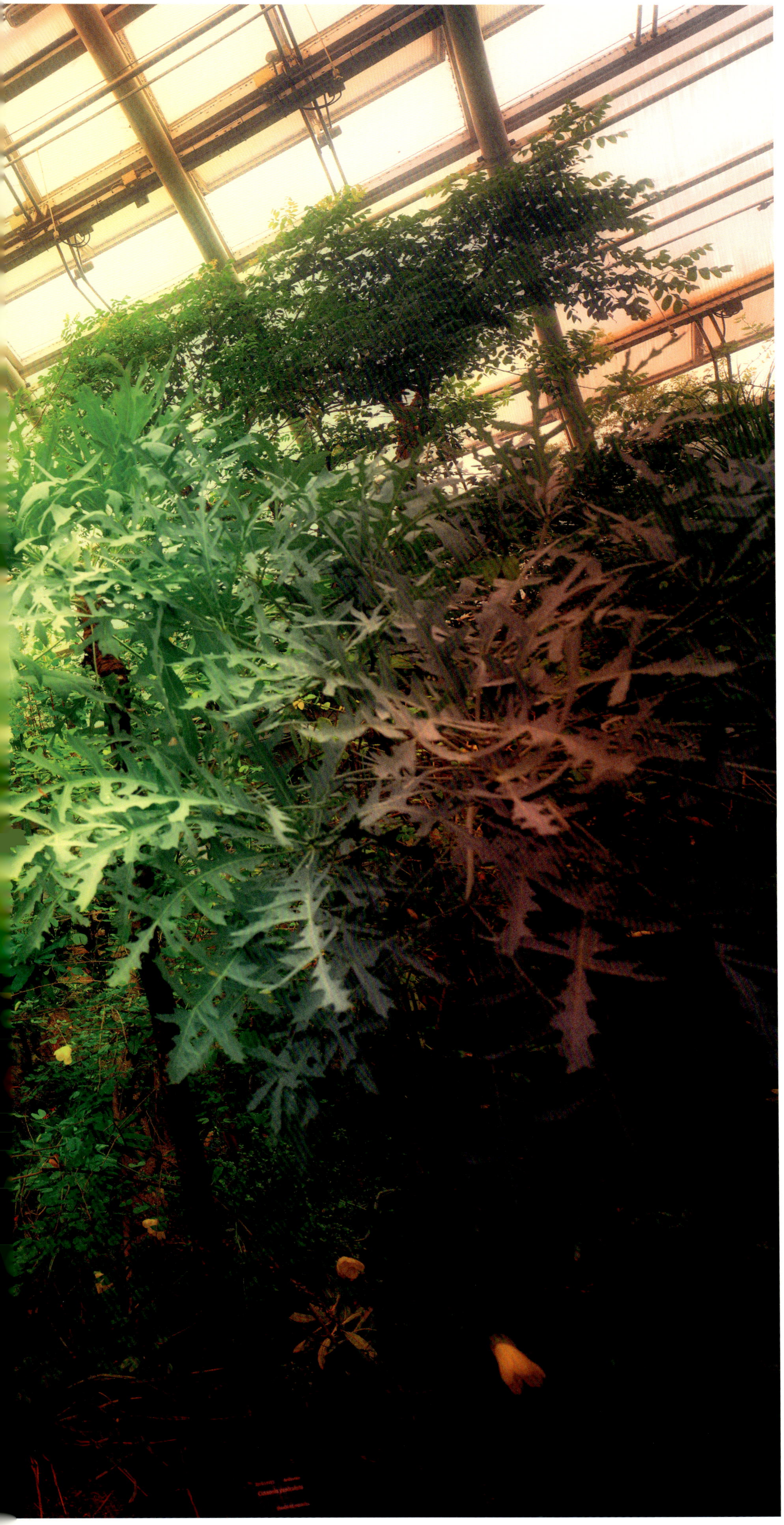

Prag Fata Morgana I
Prag Fata Morgana III ▼

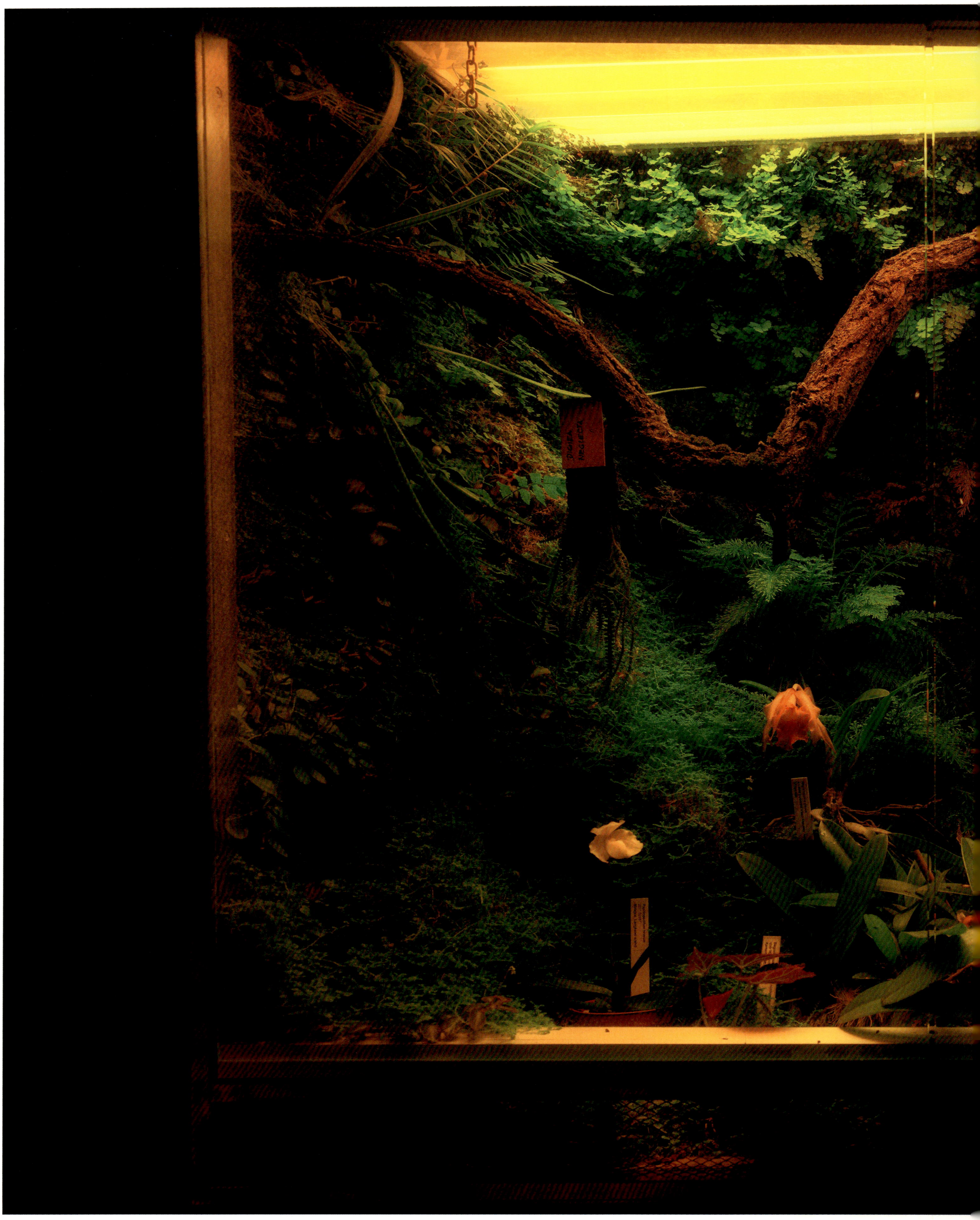

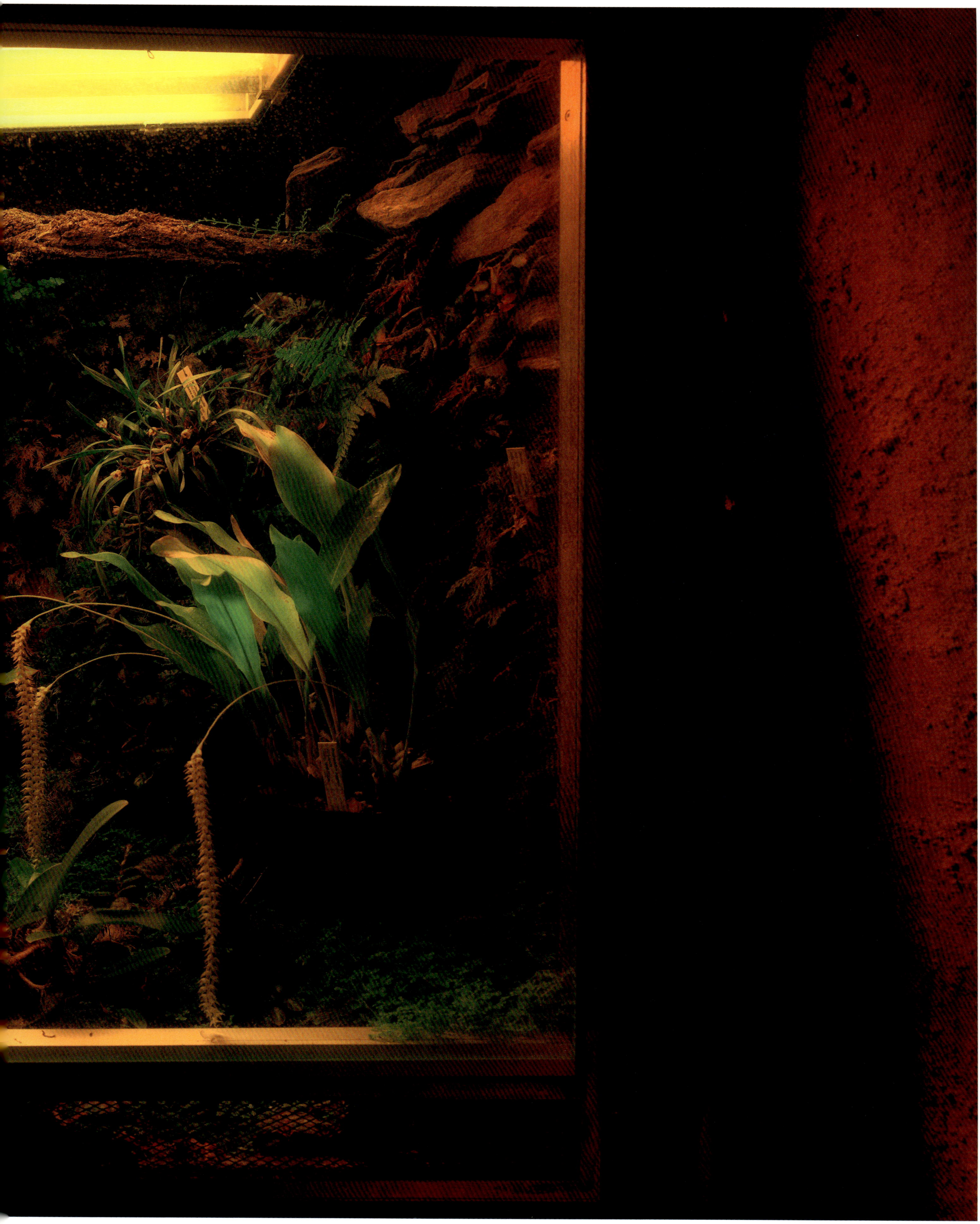

Prag Fata Morgana II
Prag Fata Morgana VII ▼

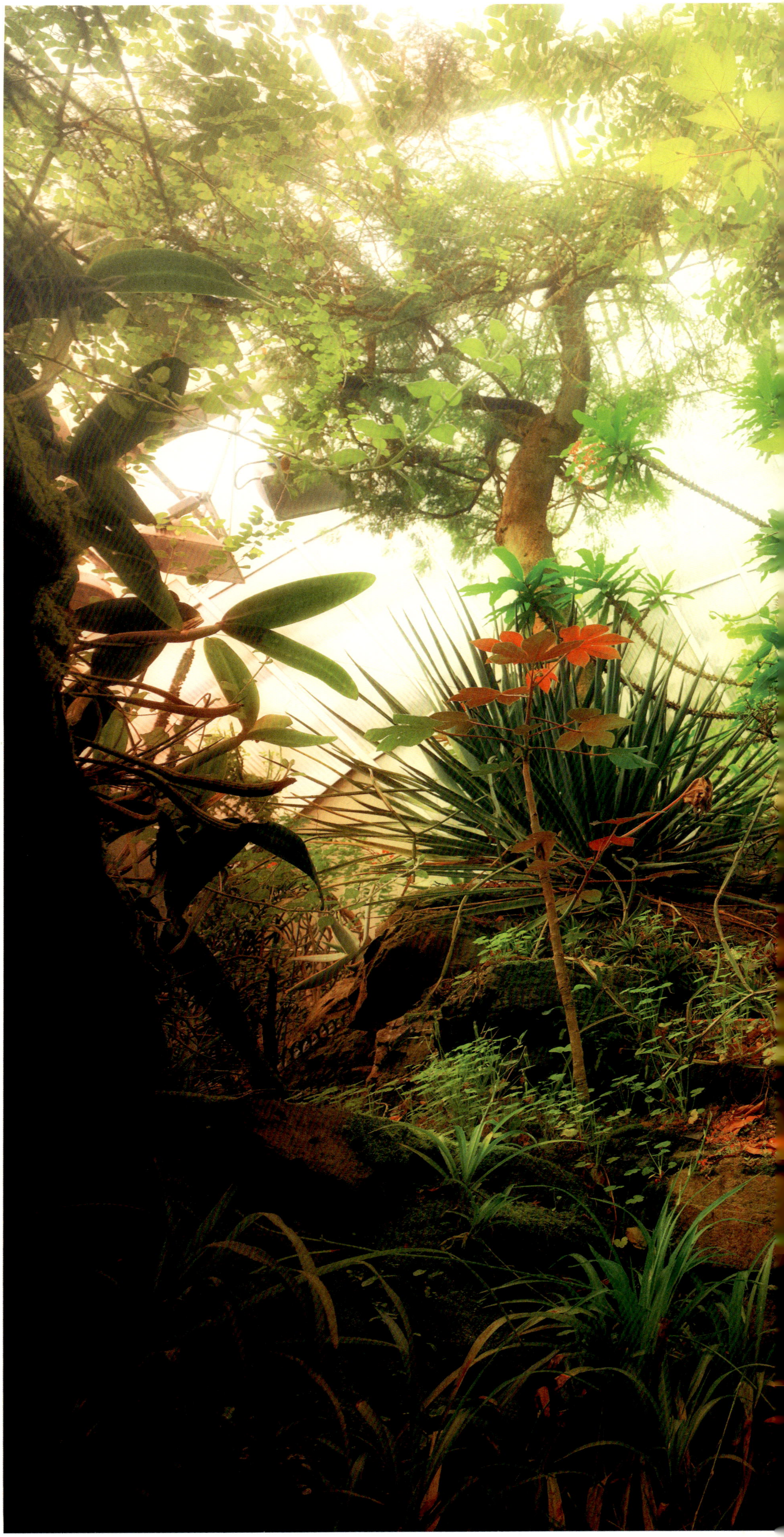

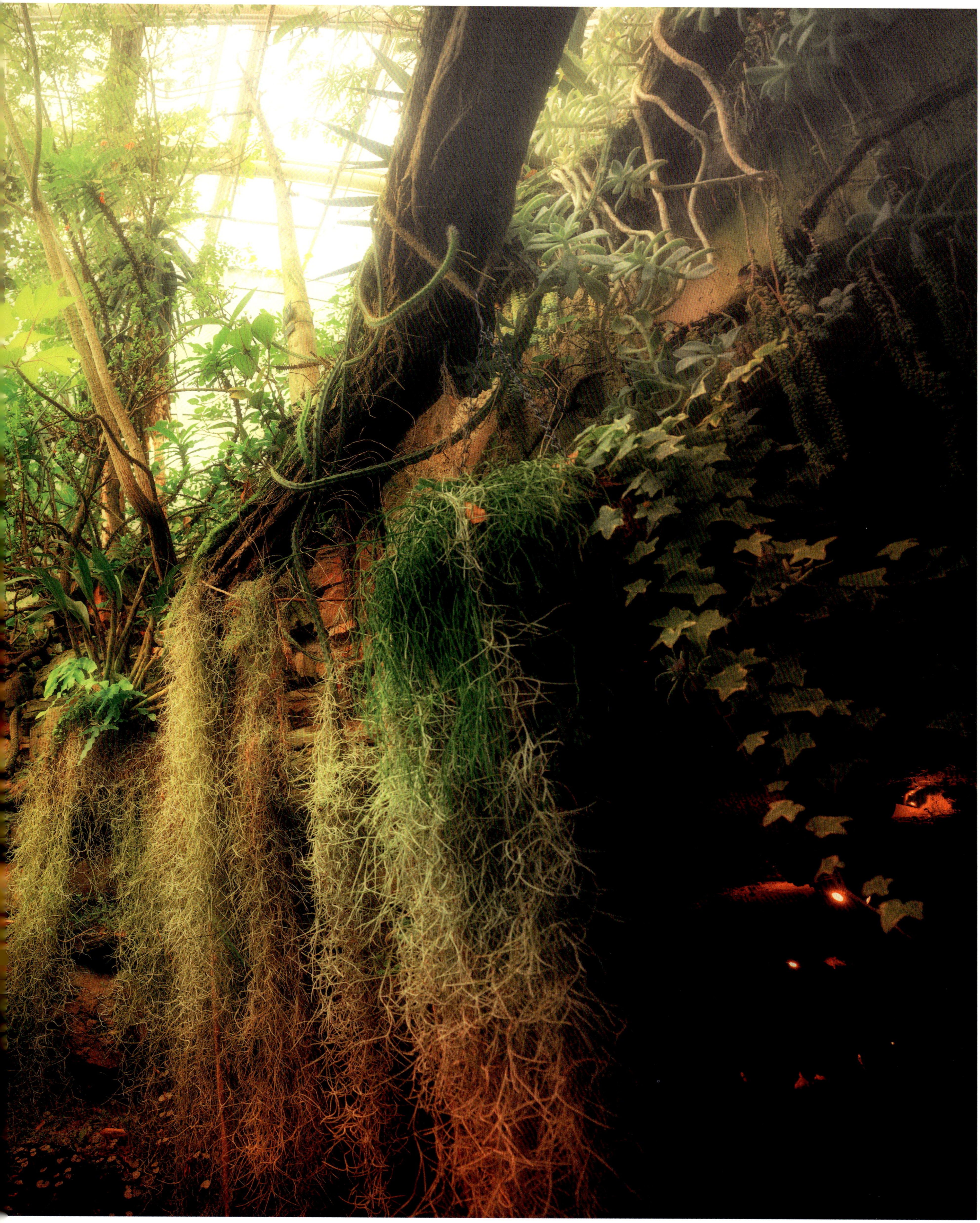

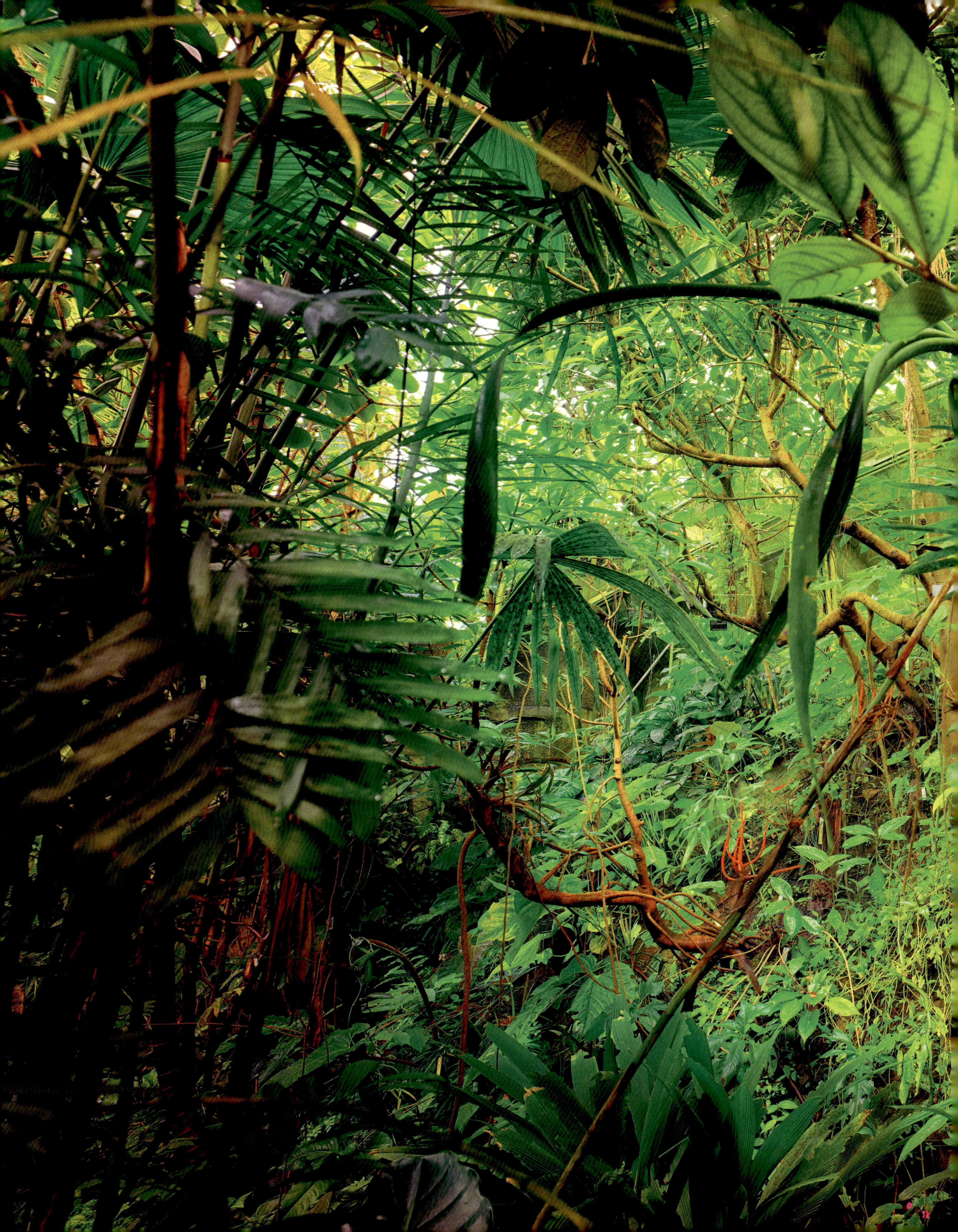

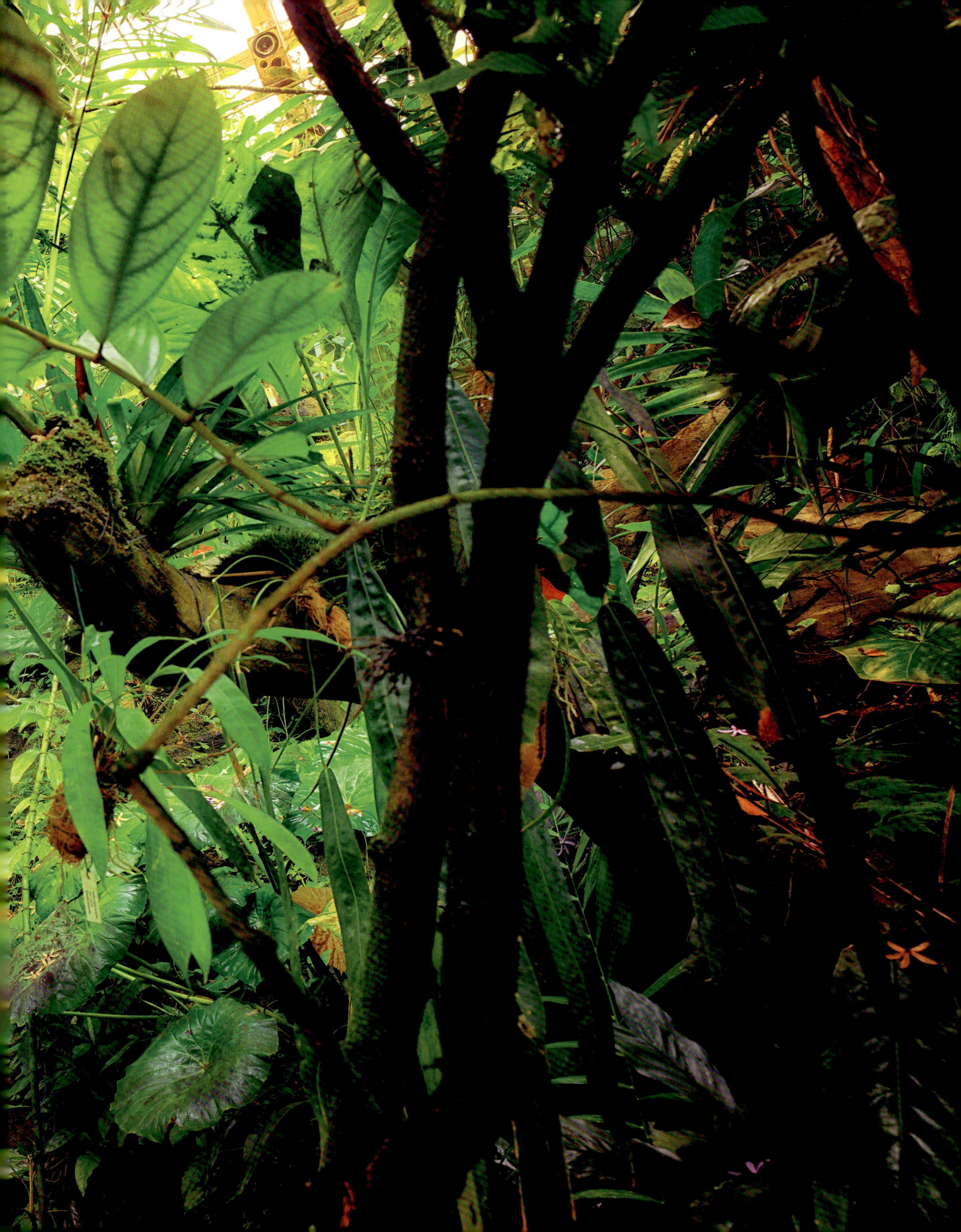

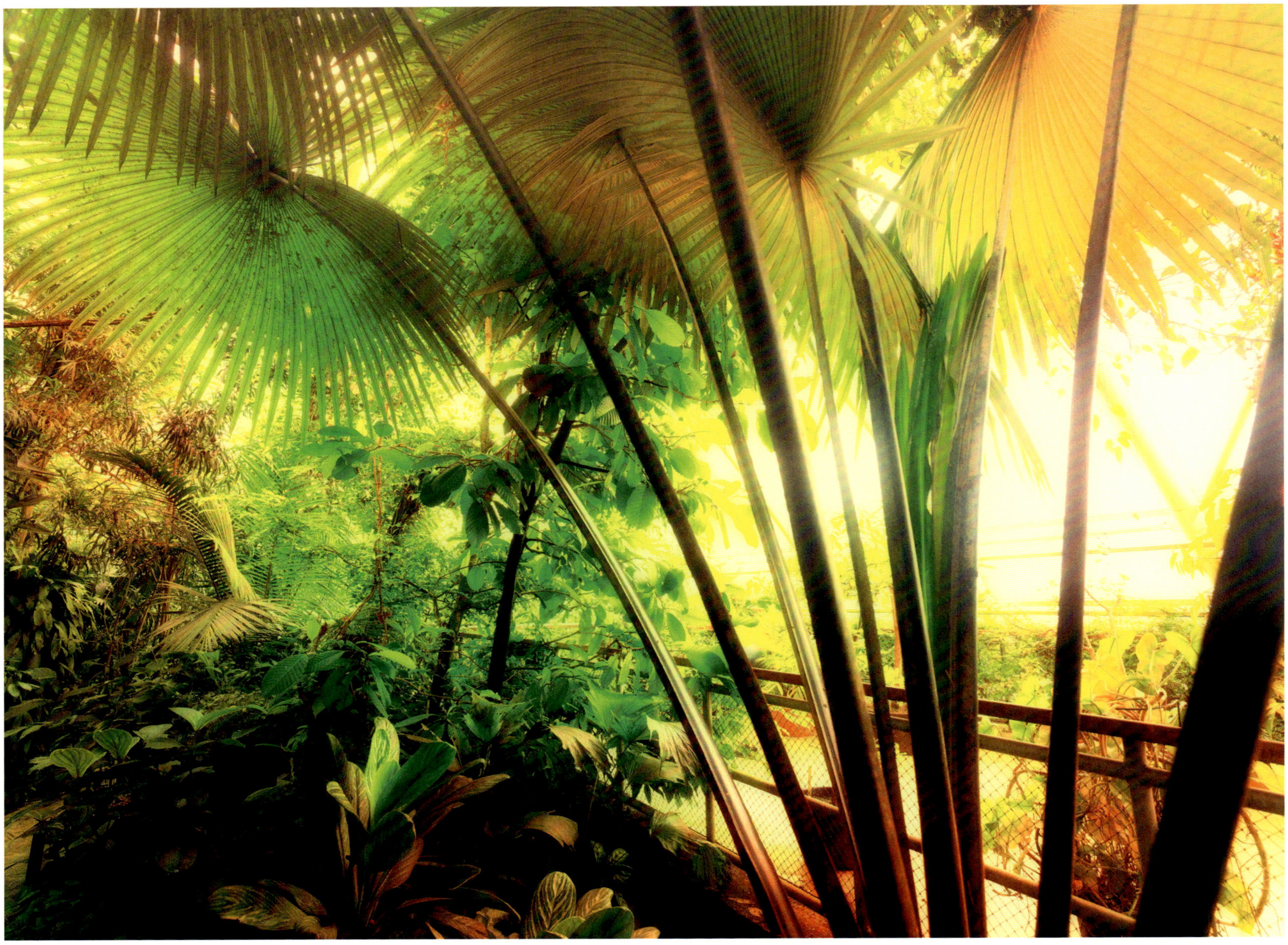

Prag Fata Morgana X · Prag Fata Morgana IX

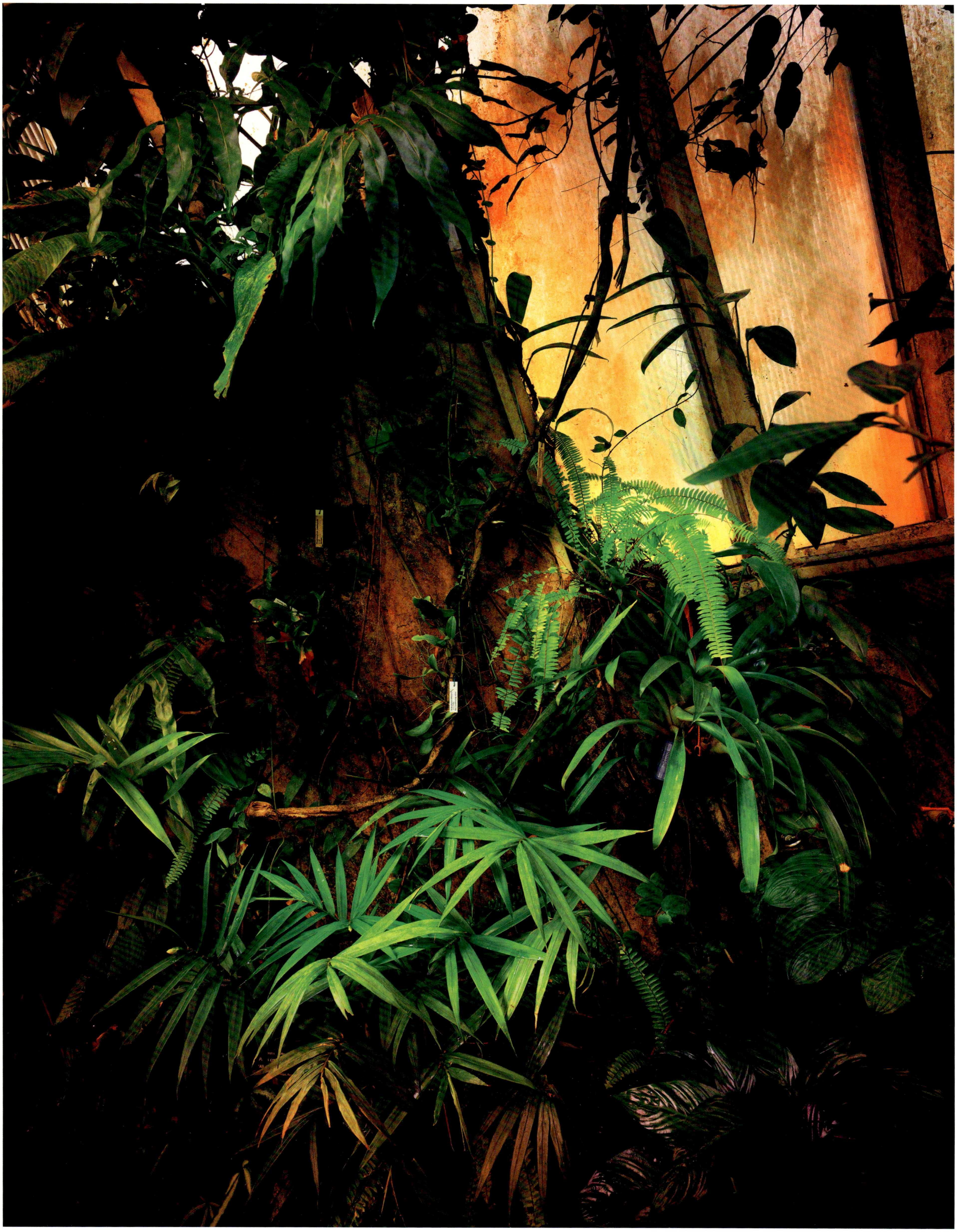

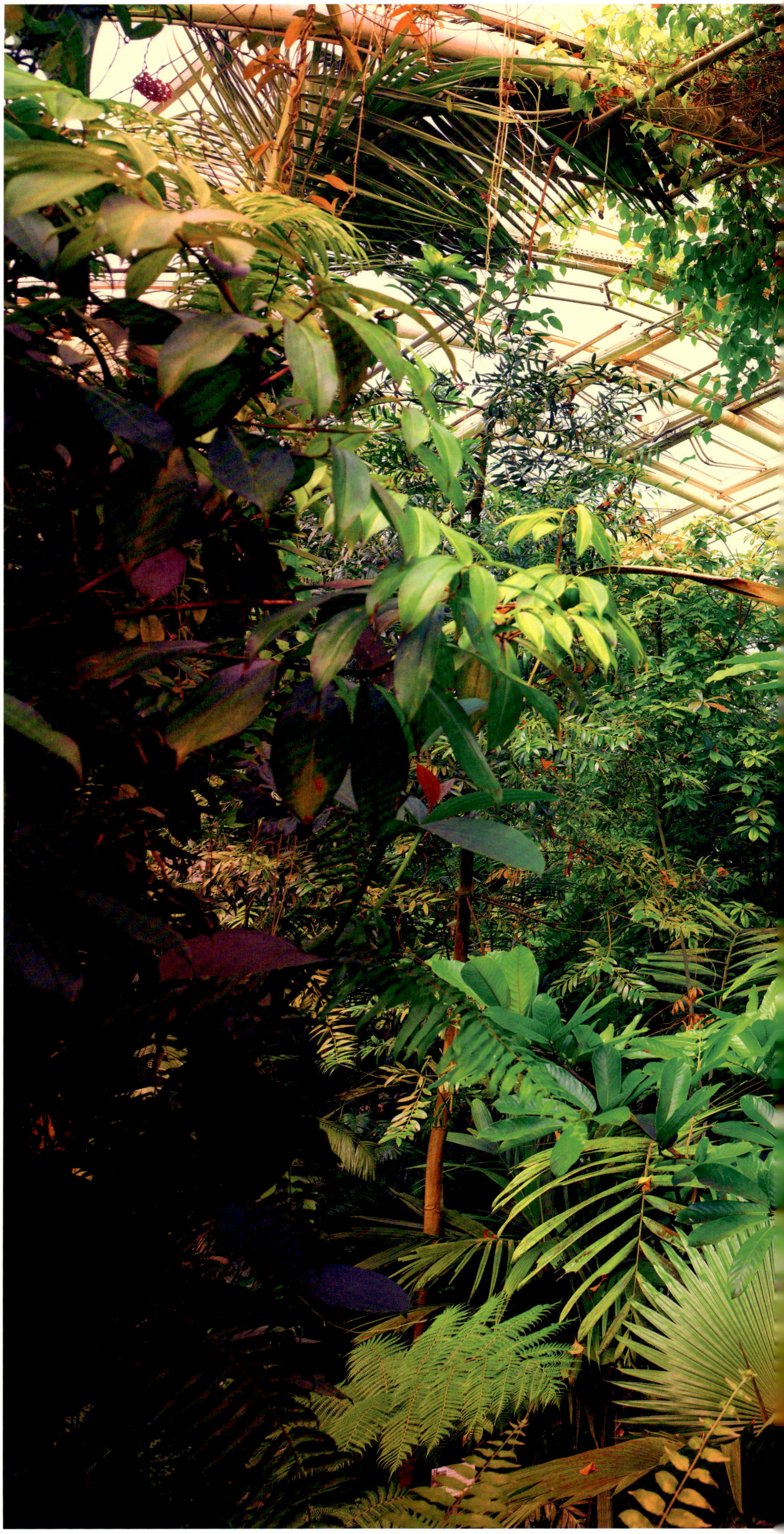

Prag Fata Morgana VI

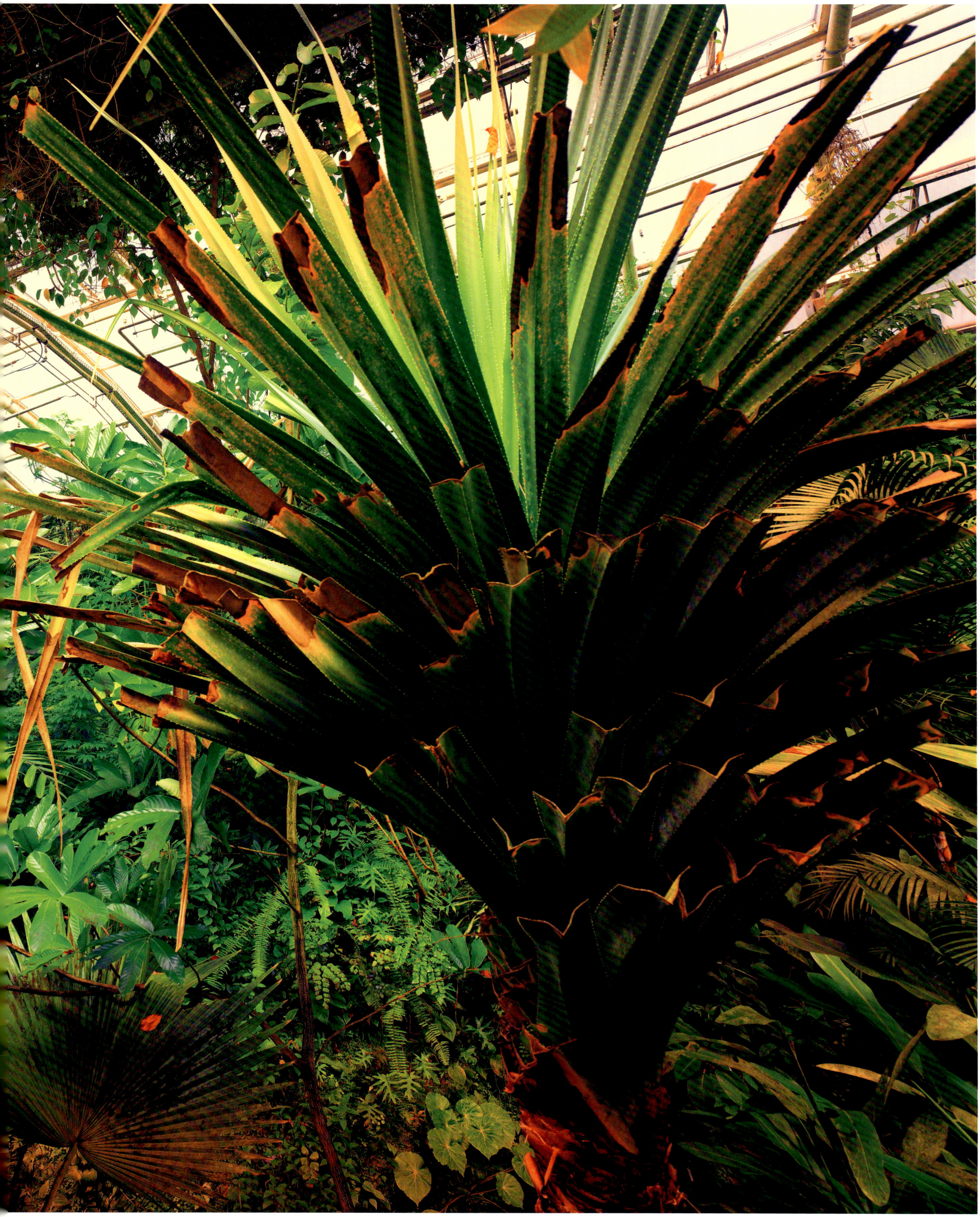

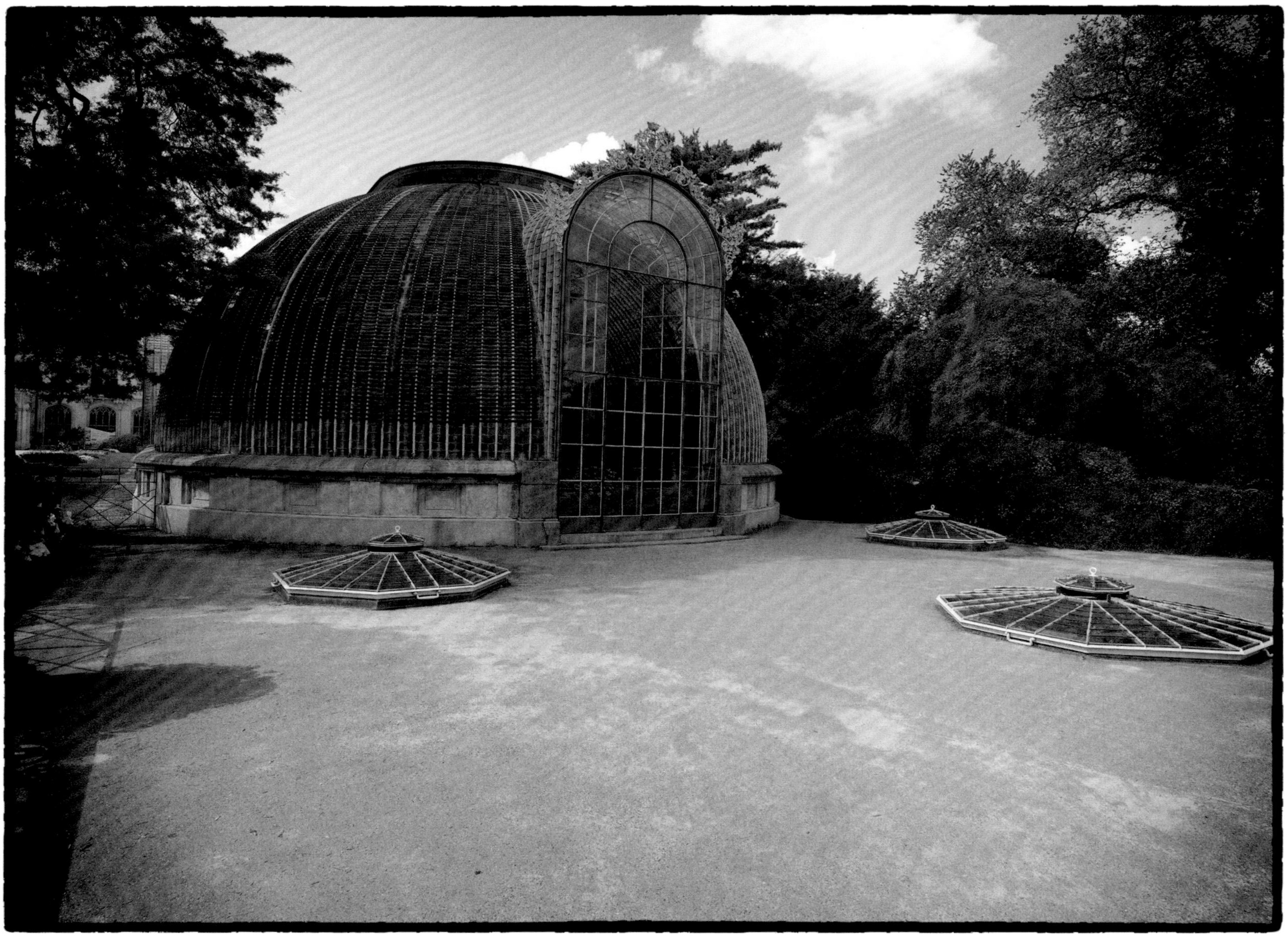

PALM HOUSE BOTANICAL GARDEN

LEDNICE

PALM HOUSE AND BOTANICAL GARDEN

ORT
Lednice, Tschechien

GRÖSSE
92 m lang; 11,5 m breit; 10 m hoch

ENTSTEHUNG
1843–1846
Entwurf: Georg Wingelmüller

ARCHITEKTUR
Angeschlossen an den östlichen Schlossflügel erstreckt sich das Palmenhaus in Ost-West-Ausdehnung auf einem rechteckigen Grundriss mit einem halbrunden Abschluss. Über einer 1,20 m hohen Natursteinmauer erhebt sich durchgehend bis zur Laterne die gewölbte Glasfläche als Halbtonne. Sie wird getragen durch das eiserne Sprossenwerk, in dem die Glasscheiben wie Schuppen übereinandergelegt sind. Die Laterne wird von gusseisernen Säulen, deren Form Bambus imitiert, getragen.

PFLANZEN
Über 200 Pflanzensorten, verschiedene Palmen, Orchideen und andere tropische Pflanzen

BESONDERHEITEN
Einziger kurvenlinearer Glasbau nach den Ideen John Claudius Loudon in Kontinentaleuropa. Lednice gehörte seit dem 13. Jahrhundert bis 1945 dem Fürstenhaus von Liechtenstein und diente als Sommerresidenz. Die durch das Fürstenhaus geschaffene Kulturlandschaft Lednice-Valtice wurde 1996 in die Liste des UNESCO Welterbes eingetragen.

LOCATION
Lednice, Czech Republic

SIZE
92 m long; 11.5 m wide; 10 m high

ESTABLISHED
1843–1846
design: Georg Wingelmüller

ARCHITECTURE
Connected to the eastern wing of the castle, the palm house extends from east to west on a rectangular footprint, terminating in a semicircle. Above a 1.20 m high natural stone wall, the arched glass surface rises continuously up to the lantern, forming a half-barrel design. It is supported by the iron mullions, in which the glass panes are layered like scales. The lantern is supported by cast iron columns shaped to look like bamboo.

PLANTS
Over 200 varieties of plants, various palms, orchids, and other tropical plants

ADDITIONAL NOTES
The only curvilinear glass building based on the ideas of John Claudius Loudon in continental Europe. From the 13th century until 1945, Lednice belonged to the Princely House of Liechtenstein and served as a summer residence. The Lednice-Valtice cultural landscape created by the Princely House was inscribed on the UNESCO World Heritage List in 1996.

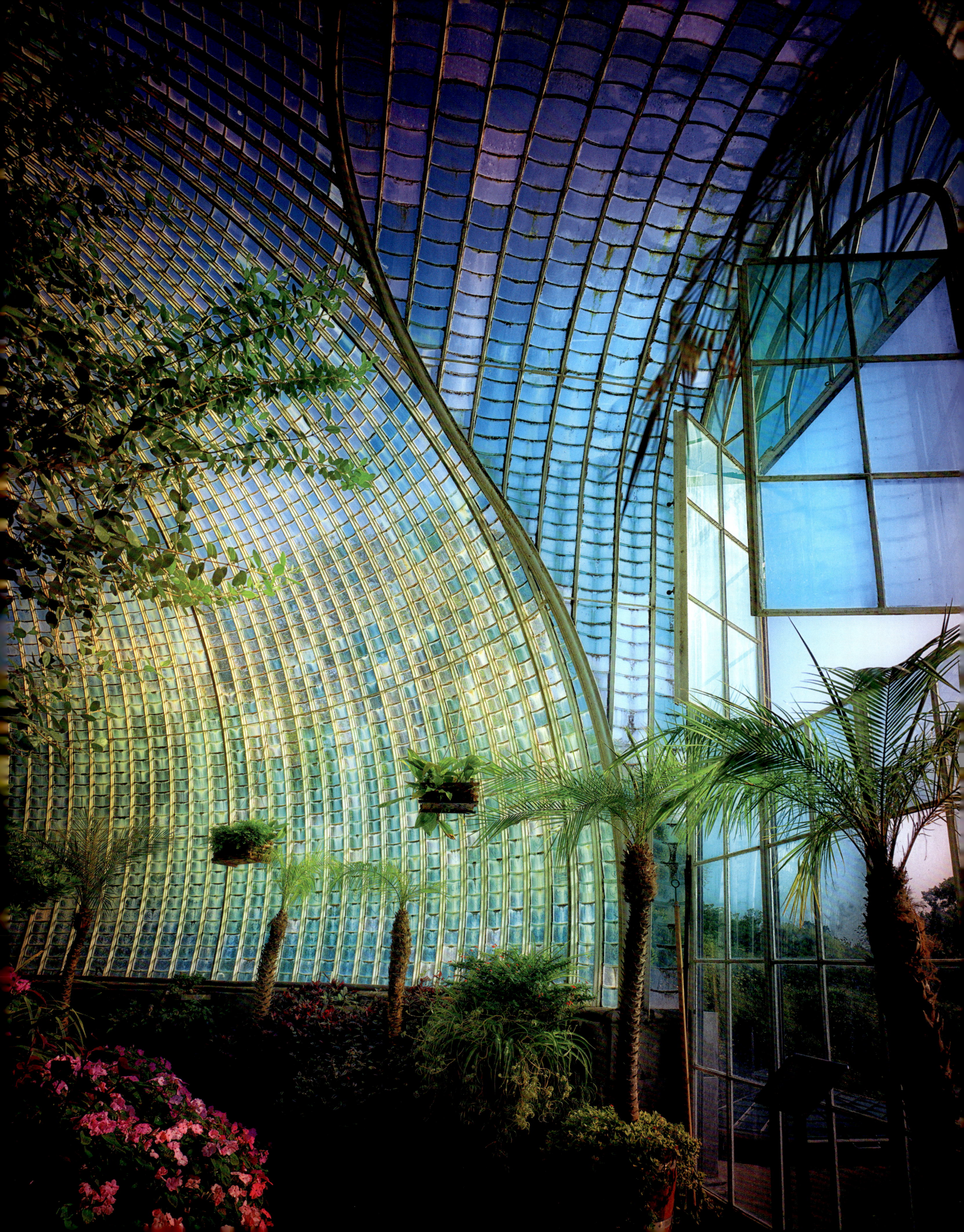

Lednice Palmenhaus XXIII
Lednice Palmenhaus XI ▼

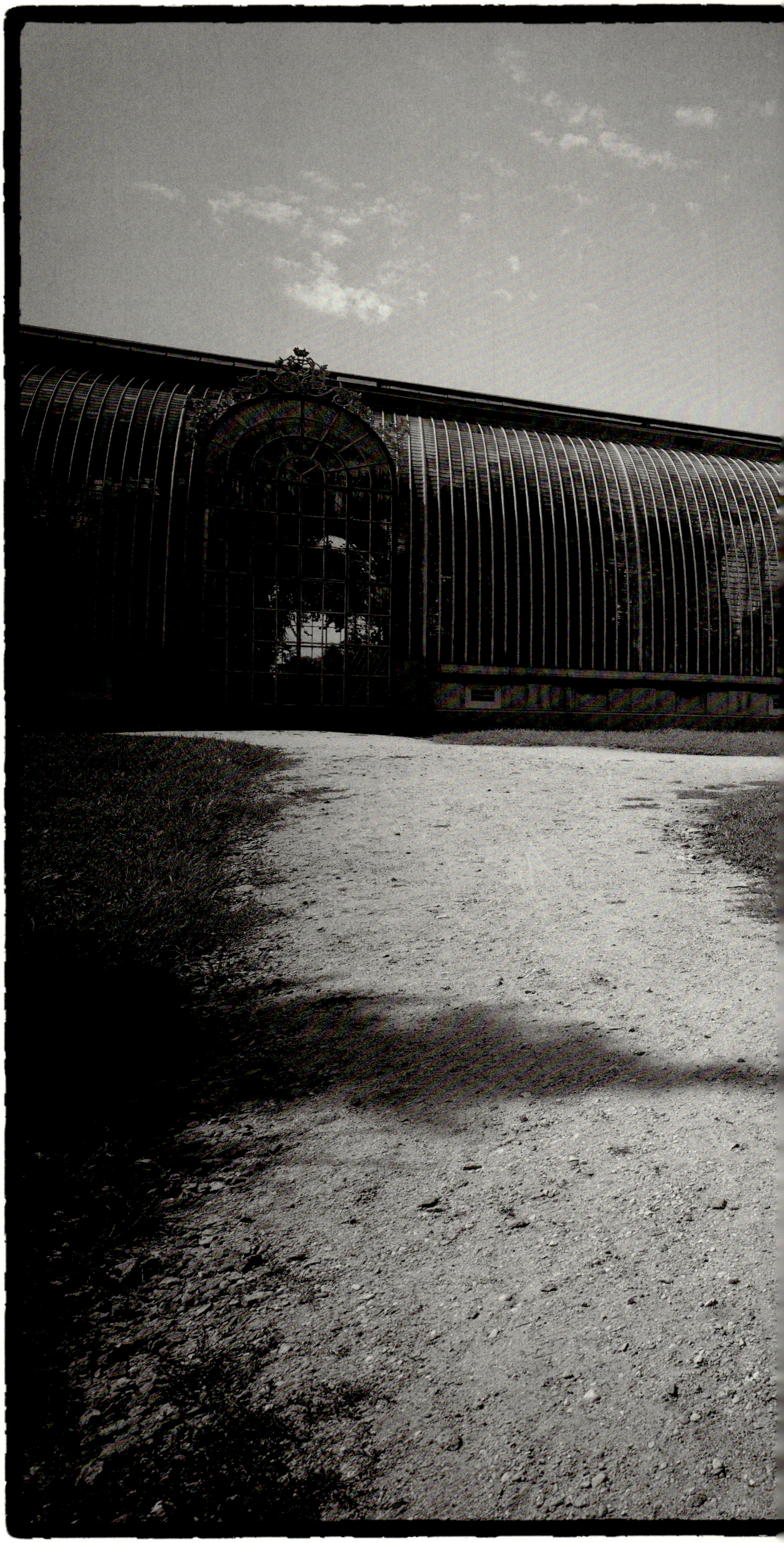

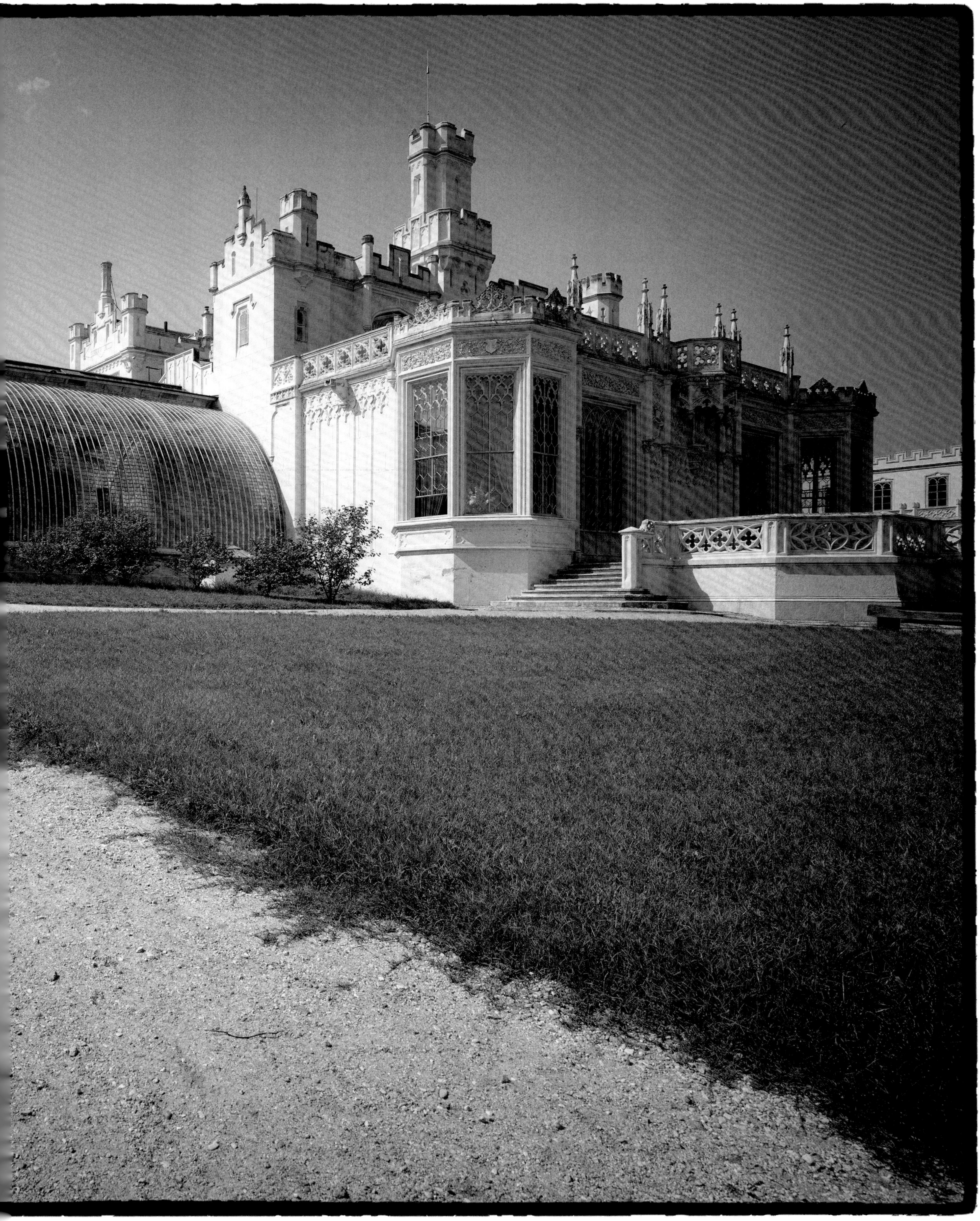

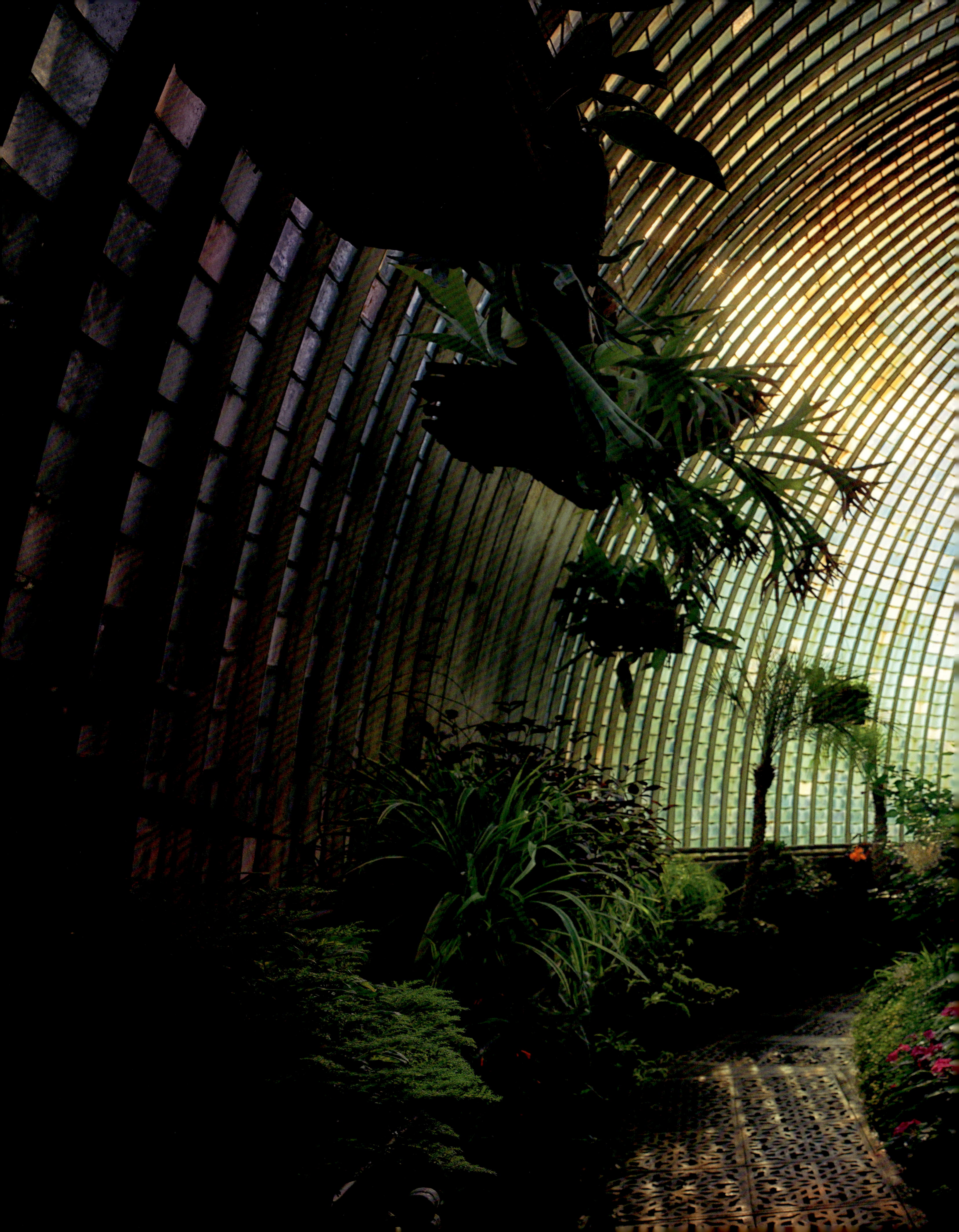

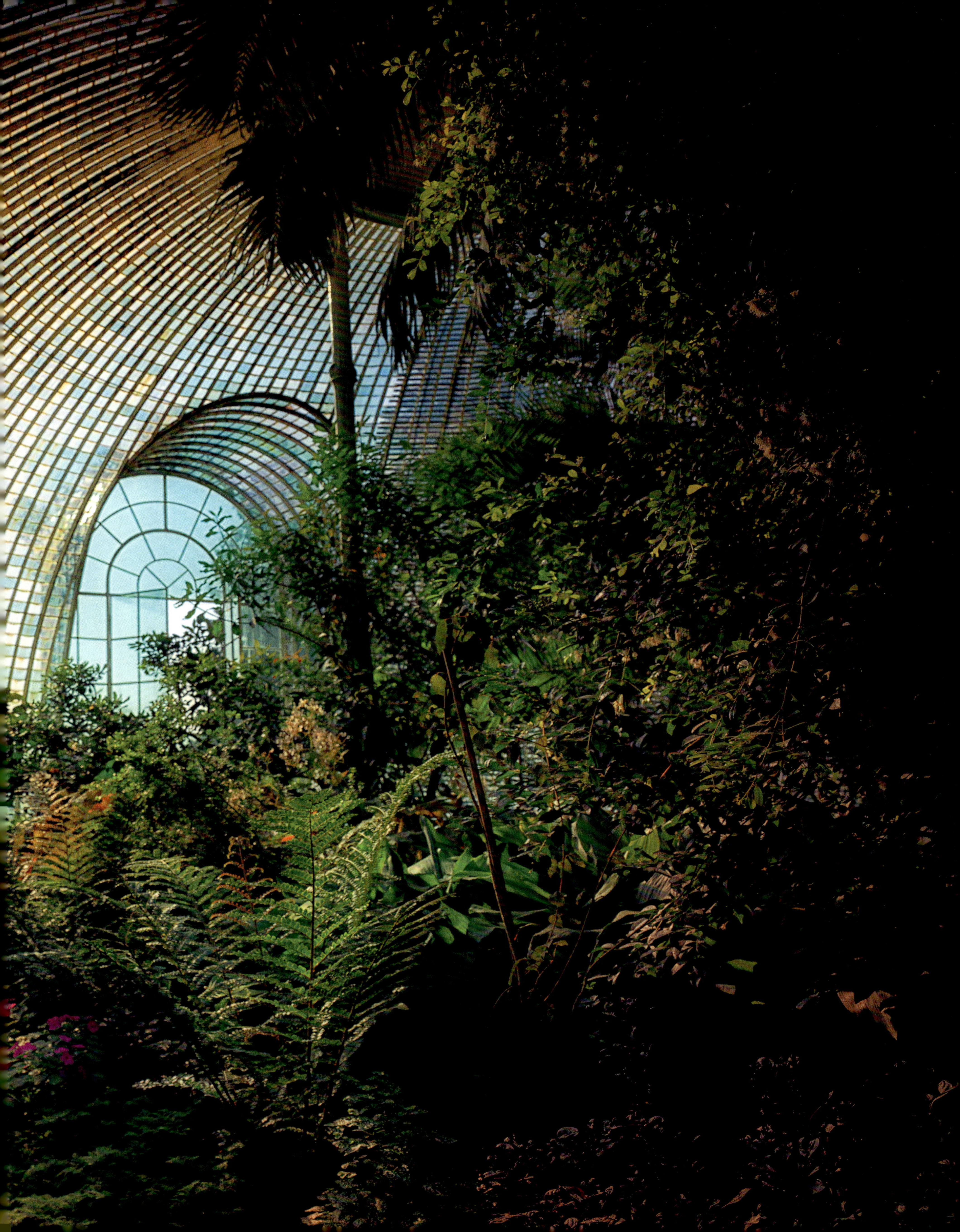

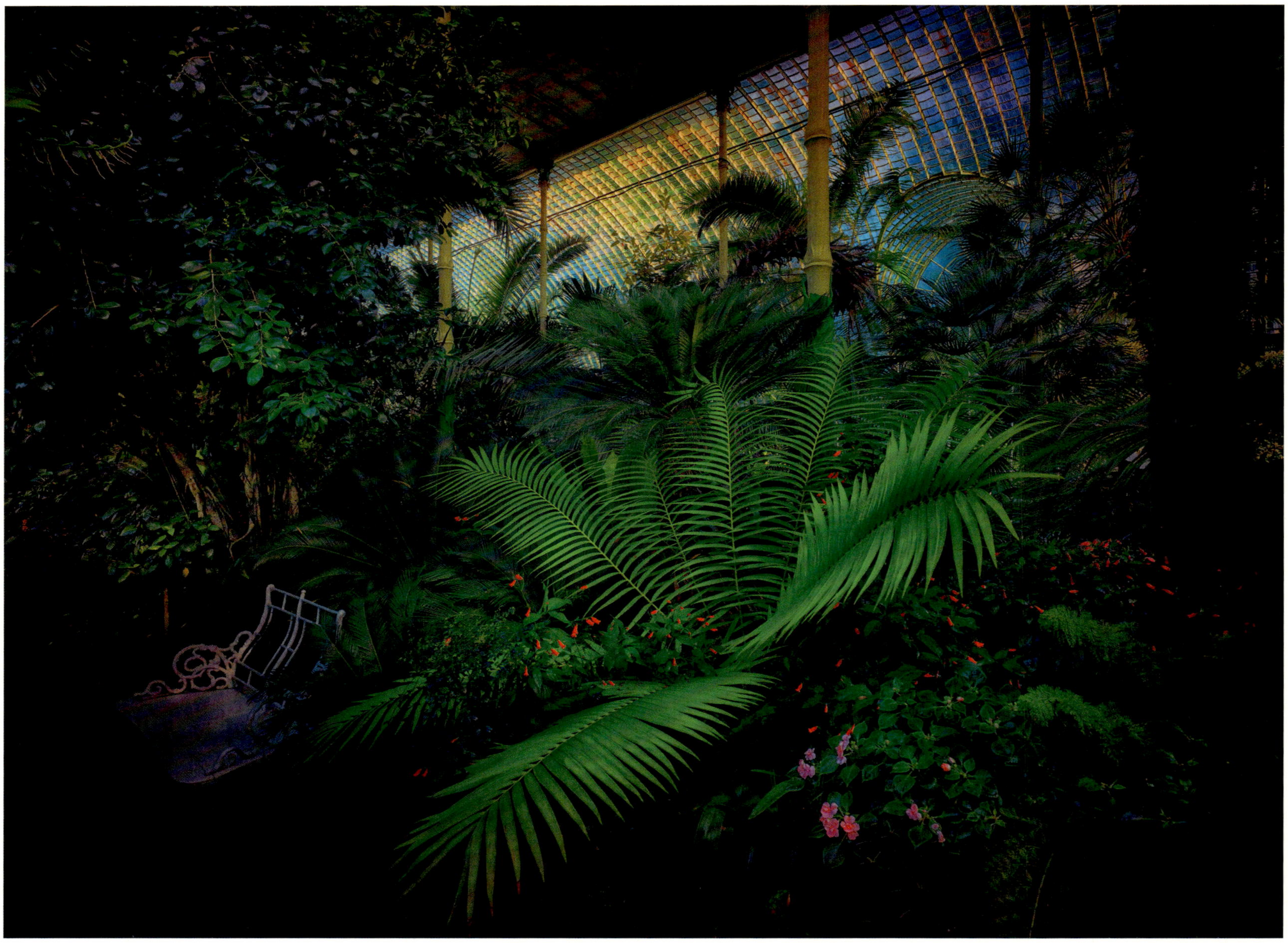

Lednice Palmenhaus XVI • Lednice Palmenhaus XX
Lednice Palmenhaus XVII ▼

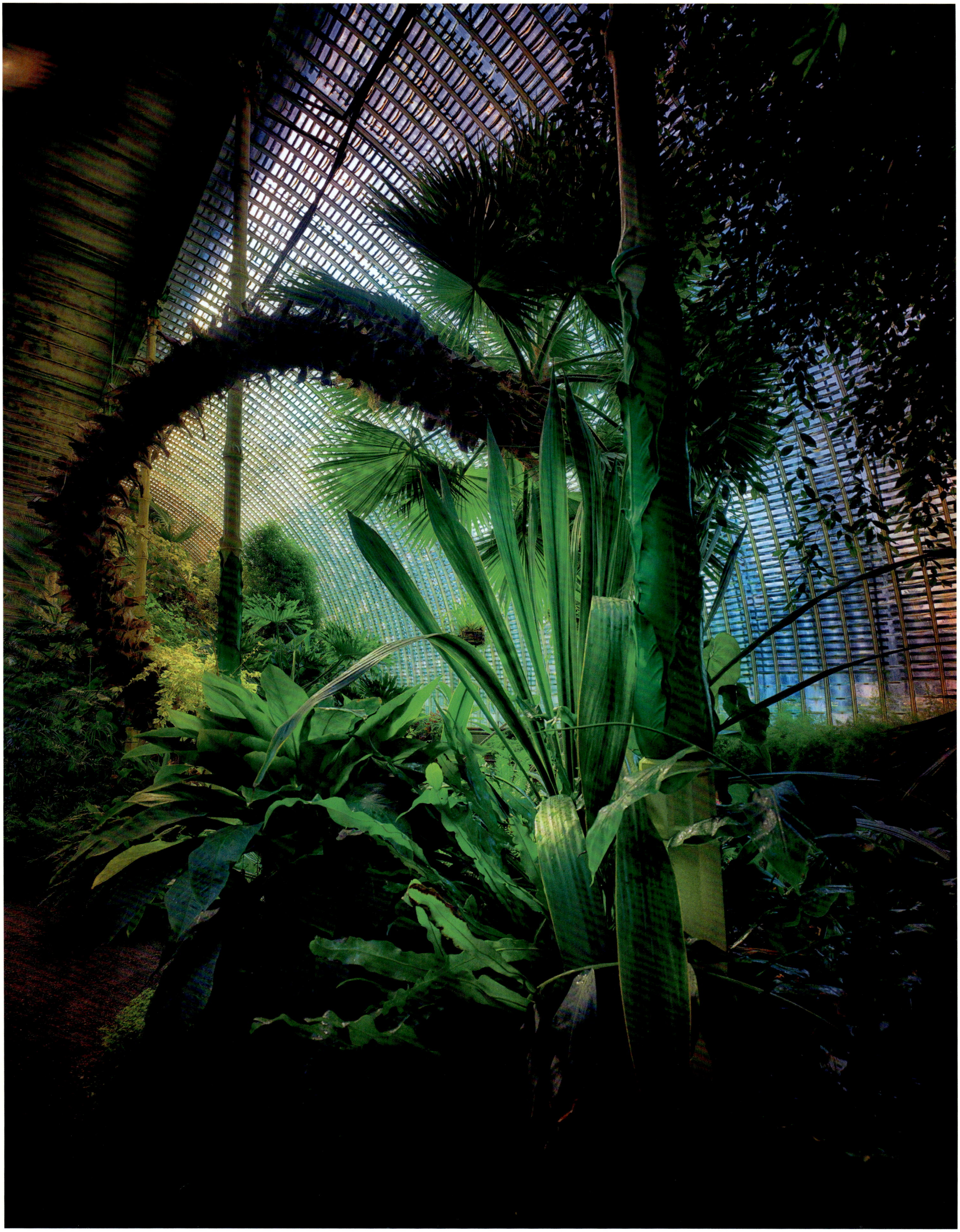

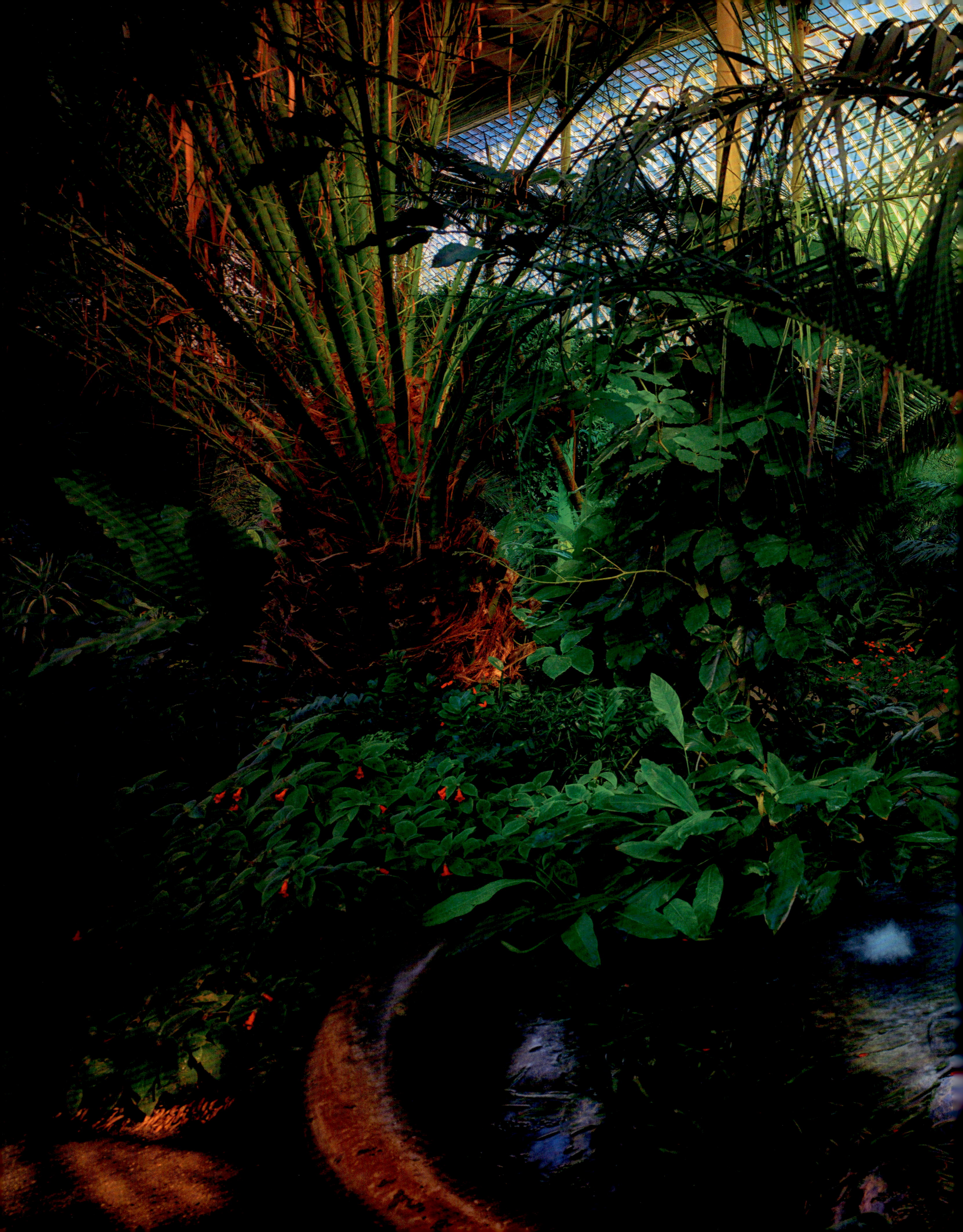

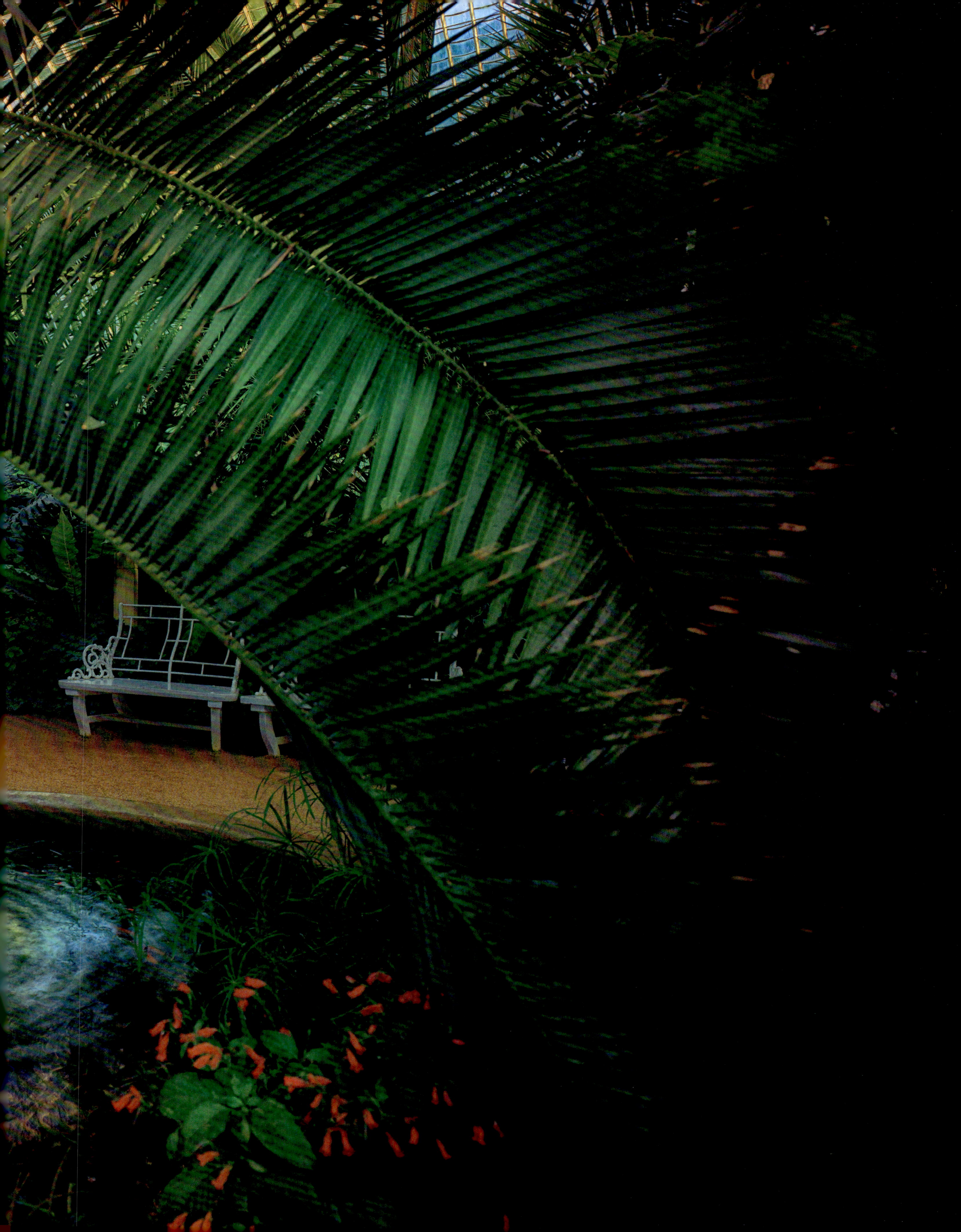

Eine Bildserie wie die *Greenhouses* am Ende in einem Bildband der Öffentlichkeit vorstellen zu können, bewirkt einen zusätzlichen Energieschub im kreativen Prozess, denn nur in einem gedruckten Werk kommt nach meiner Meinung die verbindende Seele einer Bildserie wirklich zum Vorschein.

WERNER PAWLOK

In the end, being able to publicly present a series of images such as *Greenhouses* in the form of a coffee-table book infuses the creative process with an additional boost of energy, because in my opinion only a printed work can truly reveal the unifying soul of a series of images.

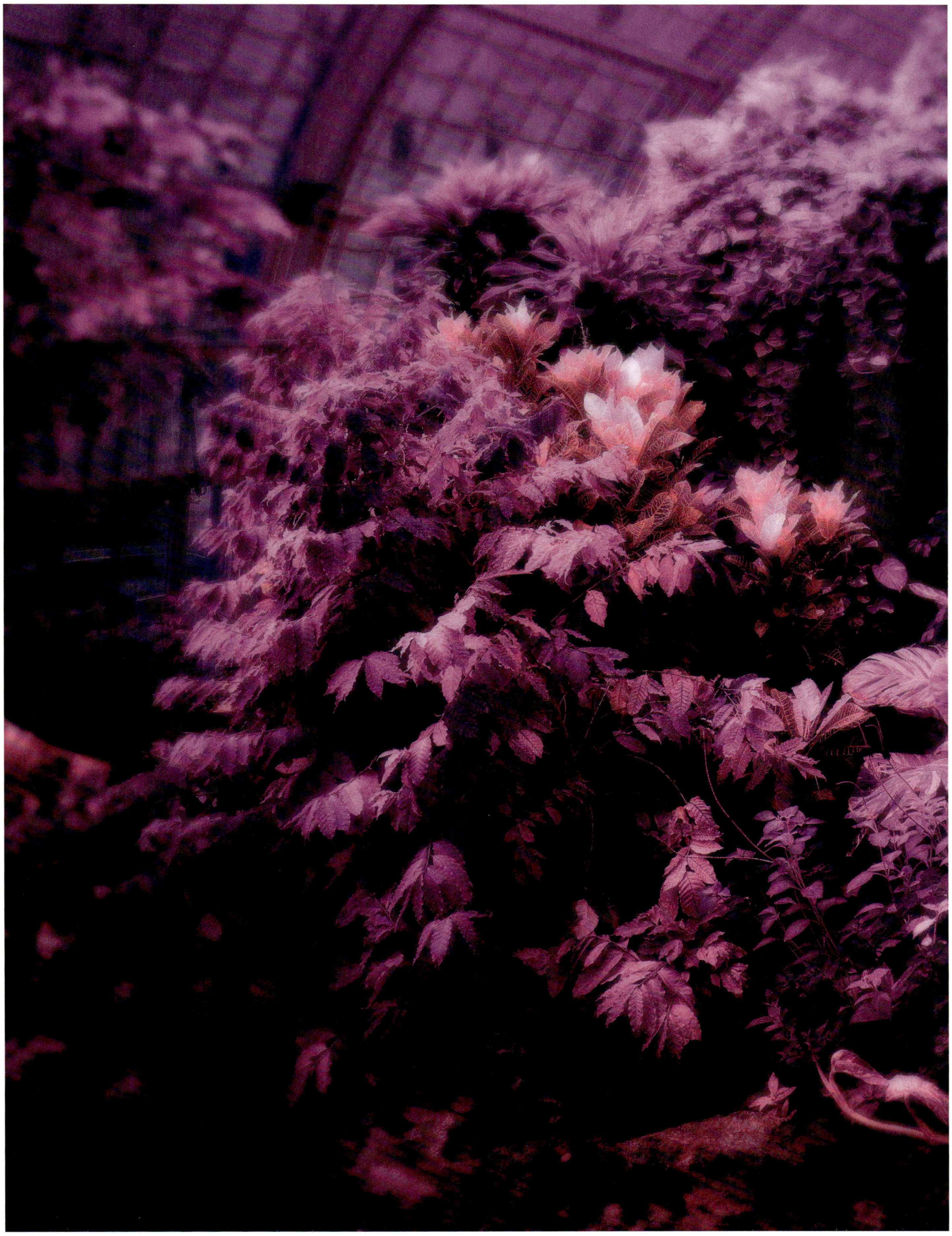

Lednice Park VI

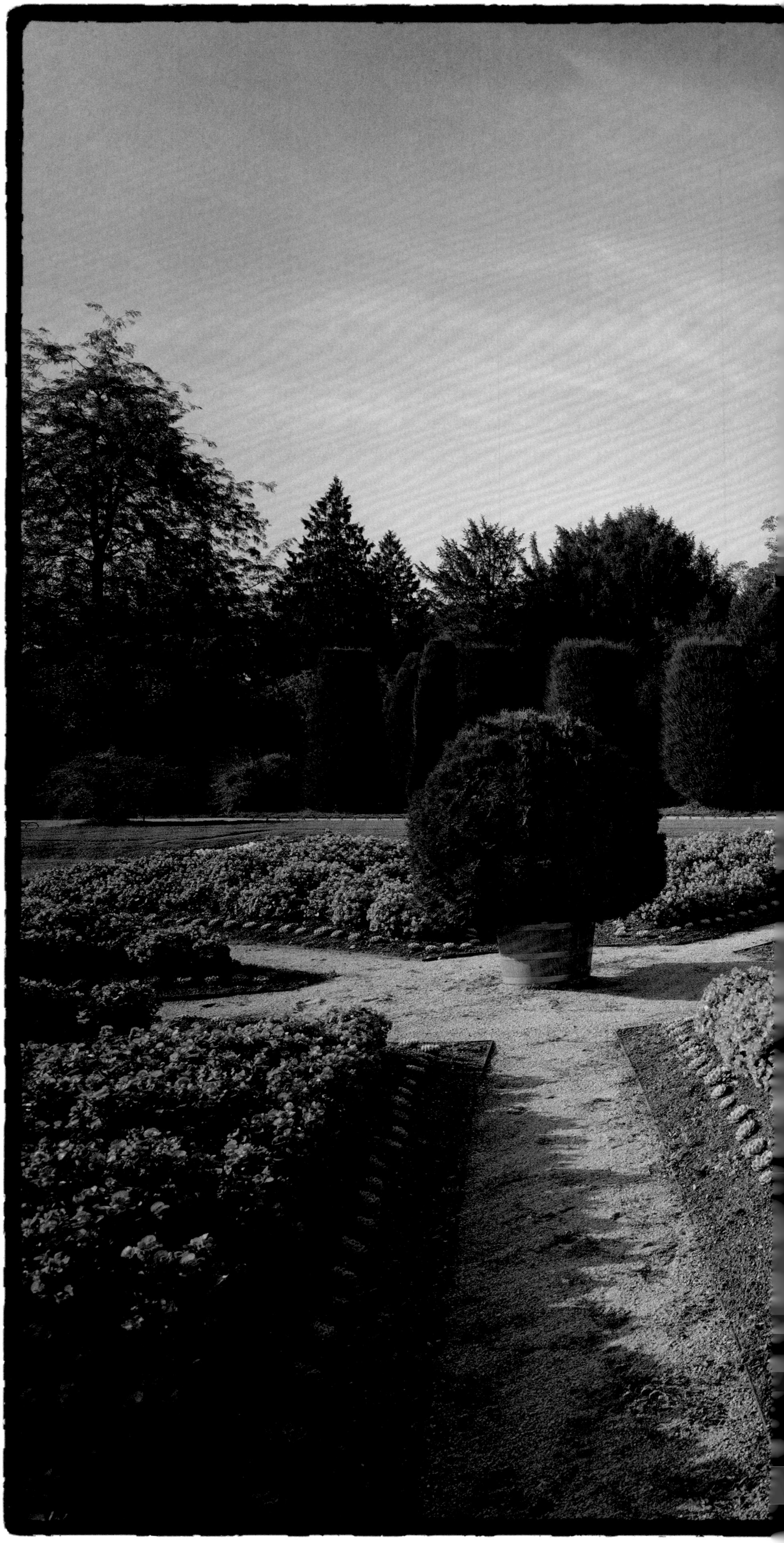

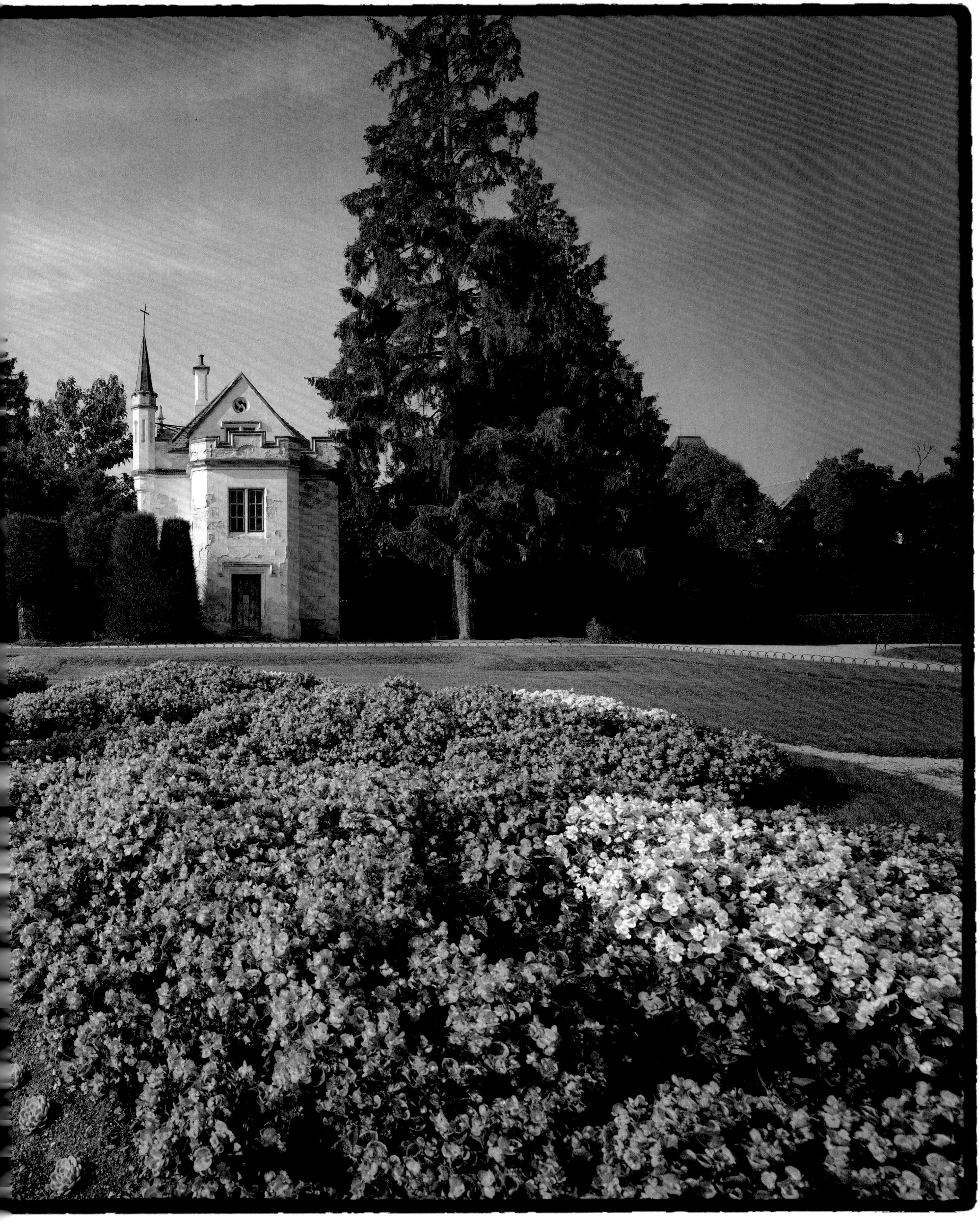

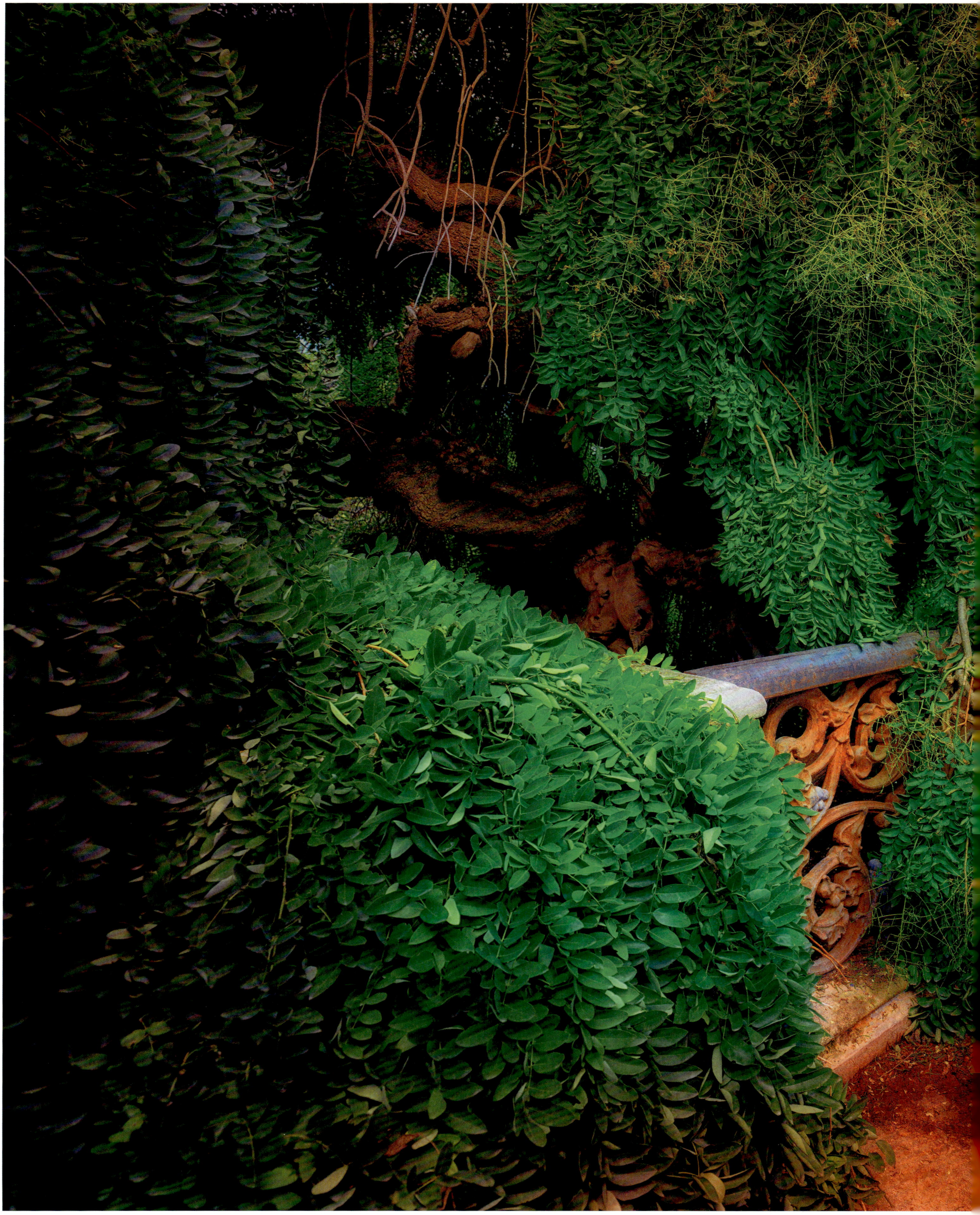

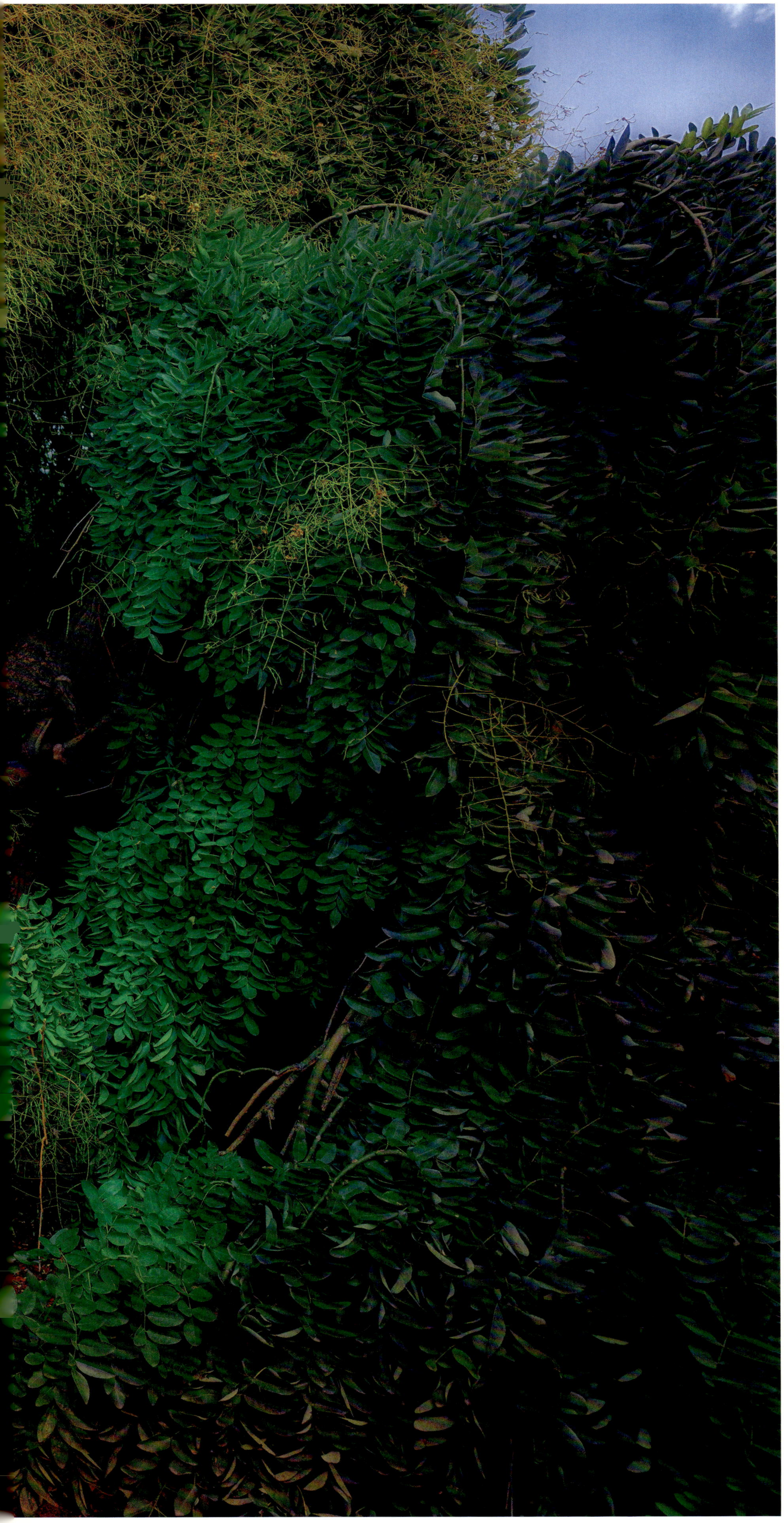

Lednice Park IV
Lednice Palmenhaus XXII ▼

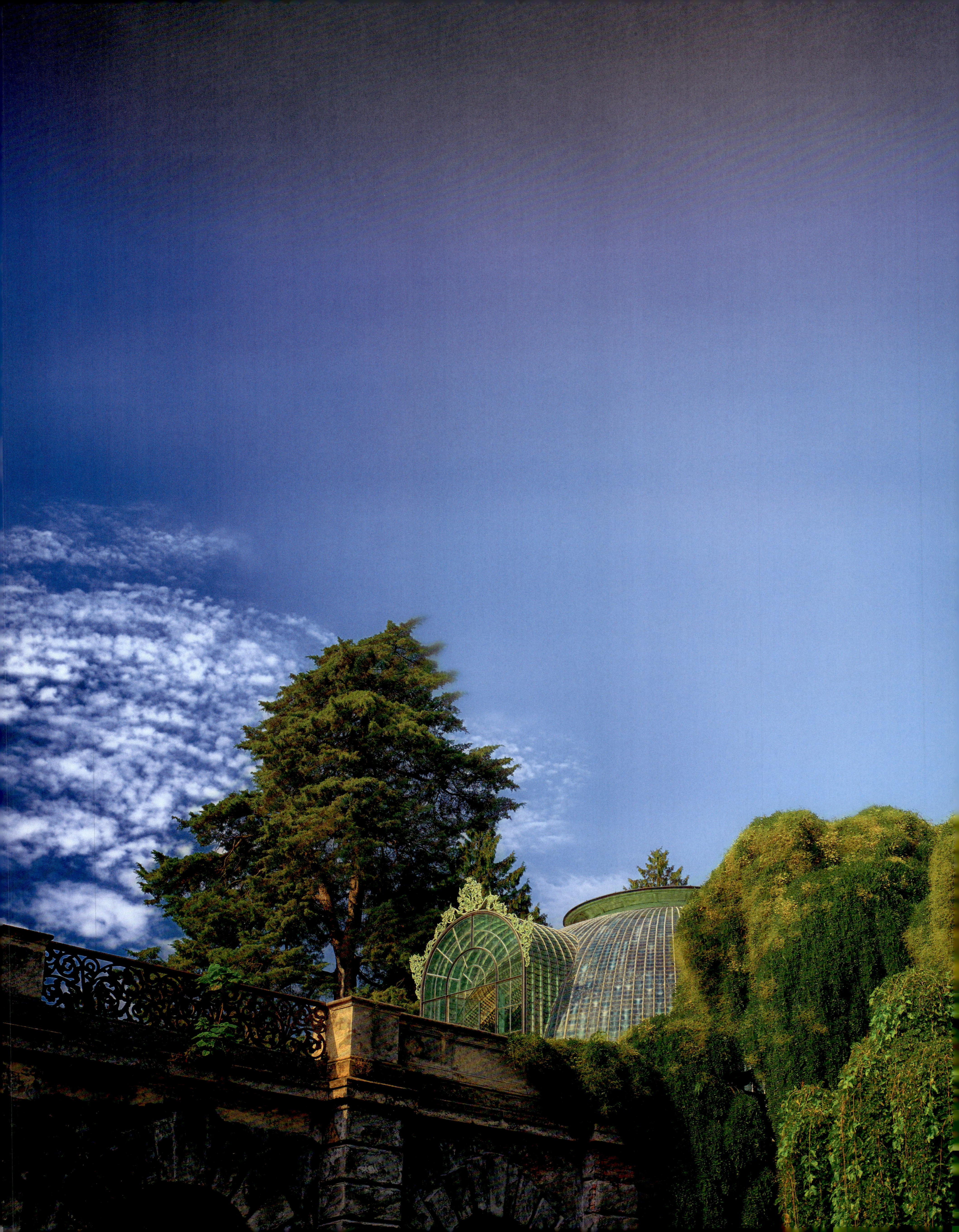

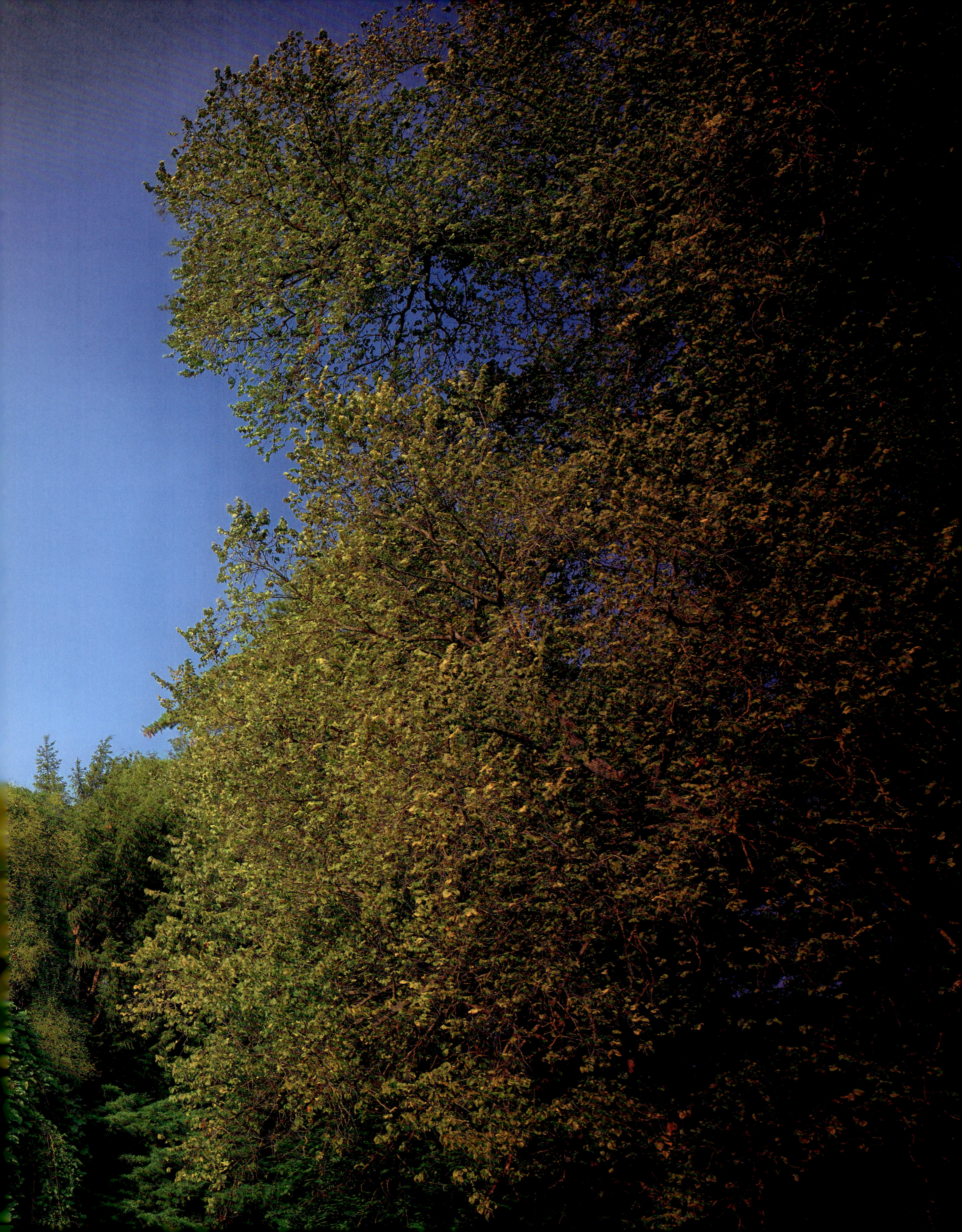

DANK · THANKS

Sehr gerne erinnere ich mich an das erste Telefonat mit Stefanie Penck im Juli 2021, als sie ihr Interesse an meiner Arbeit bekundete. Sehr bald erfolgte ein erstes Kennenlernen bei uns in Stuttgart, das den Weg für unser erstes gemeinsame Projekt frei machen sollte. Sehr wichtig ist es mir, speziell in der heutigen, oft oberflächlichen Zeit, ein Gefühl von Familie zu haben. Gegenseitiges Vertrauen und ein gemeinsames Handeln spielen für mich eine große Rolle. Es freut mich sehr, dass ich mit meinem Werk Teil dieser Familie bin.

Mein Dank gilt allen, die zur Entstehung dieses Buches beigetragen haben. Bedanken möchte ich mich insbesondere bei folgenden Beteiligten:

Allen *Mitarbeitern* der fantastischen Greenhouses, die mich immer herzlich aufgenommen haben, und mir Einblicke in diese wundersame Welt ermöglicht haben.

Die Zusammenarbeit mit dem Team vom *teNeues Verlag* hat viel Freude gemacht. Allen voran danke ich *Stefanie Penck* für die Aufnahme in das Verlagsprogramm sowie *Pit Pauen*, *Nele Jansen* und *Luisa Krause-Rossa* für ihre Unterstützung bei der Zusammenstellung des Buches sowie *Daniel Schäfer* für seine tolle Pressearbeit.

Bei *Bettina Hermann*, die sowohl unsere Reisen perfekt organisierte als auch unterwegs stets wusste, in welche Richtung wir marschieren müssen, und deren Liebe und Partnerschaft ein wesentlicher Bestandteil für die Verwirklichung dieser Serie ist.

Bei den Autoren *Stephan Reisner* für seinen leidenschaftlichen Beitrag sowie bei *Alexandra Schmöger* für Texte zu Struktur und Geschichte der Greenhouses.

Dank an *Gaby Herbrecht*, die mit Greenhouses nun schon mein drittes Buch gestaltete und mit einer unglaublichen Kondition die Layoutphasen des Buches meisterte und nie aufgab an das Gute zu glauben.

Und, nicht zu vergessen, meinen Dank an alle diejenigen, deren Rat und Unterstützung ich in Anspruch nehmen durfte, denn es gibt am Ende mehr Menschen, die sich behilflich zeigen, als man zu Beginn einer solchen Arbeit zu hoffen wagt. Vielen Dank auch an meinen Onkel *Kurt Topitsch* für das coole Portrait und insbesondere an meinen *Vater*, der mir als Kind einen ersten Einblick in diese märchenhafte Welt der Greenhouses gab.

Werner Pawlok

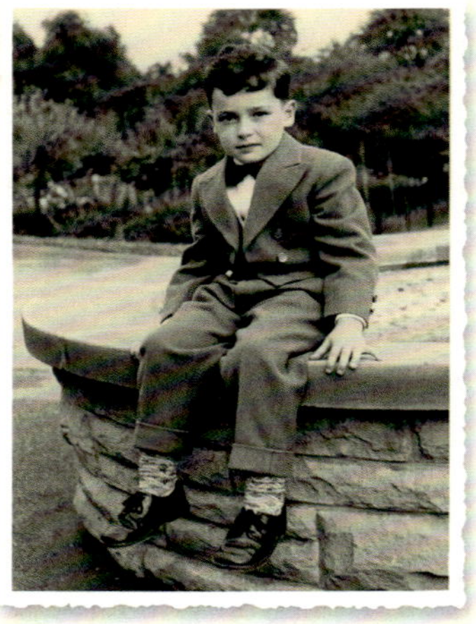

I remember very well the first time I spoke on the phone with Stefanie Penck in July 2021, when she expressed her interest in my work. Soon afterwards, we had our initial in-person meeting in Stuttgart to discuss the prospect of collaborating on a project. A sense of belonging to a family is very important to me, especially these days where so much barely scratches the surface. Working with others in an atmosphere of mutual trust and toward a common goal play an enormous role in my life. I am pleased to be part of this family through my work.

My thanks go to everyone who help bring this book into the world and especially to the following collaborators:

All the *employees* of the fabulous greenhouses, who always welcomed me warmly and gave me glimpses of this wondrous world.

I very much enjoyed working with the *teNeues Verlag* team. Above all, I would like to thank *Stefanie Penck* for adding me to the publisher's catalog as well as *Pit Pauen* and *Nele Jansen*, along with *Luisa Krause-Rossa* for their assistance in putting the book together. Also *Daniel Schäfer* for his outstanding PR work.

I would also like to thank *Bettina Hermann*, who not only organized our trips to perfection by also never hesitated to point us in the right direction while on the road. Her love and partnership were key ingredients in making this series a reality.

Also the author *Stephan Reisner* for his passionate contributions as well as *Alexandra Schmöger* for her pieces on the structure and history of the greenhouses.

My thanks additionally go to *Gaby Herbrecht*, whose work on Greenhouses make this the third time we have collaborated on one of my books. Her incredible stamina took her through the laborious layout phases, and she never lost faith in all that is good.

Not least, I would like to thank everyone whose advice and support I had the privilege to enjoy. In the end, more people are indeed willing to help than one would believe when embarking on such a project. My heartfelt thanks also go to my uncle, *Kurt Topitsch*, for the cool portrait of me and, most especially, to my *father*, who introduced me to this magical world of greenhouses when I was a child.

Werner Pawlok

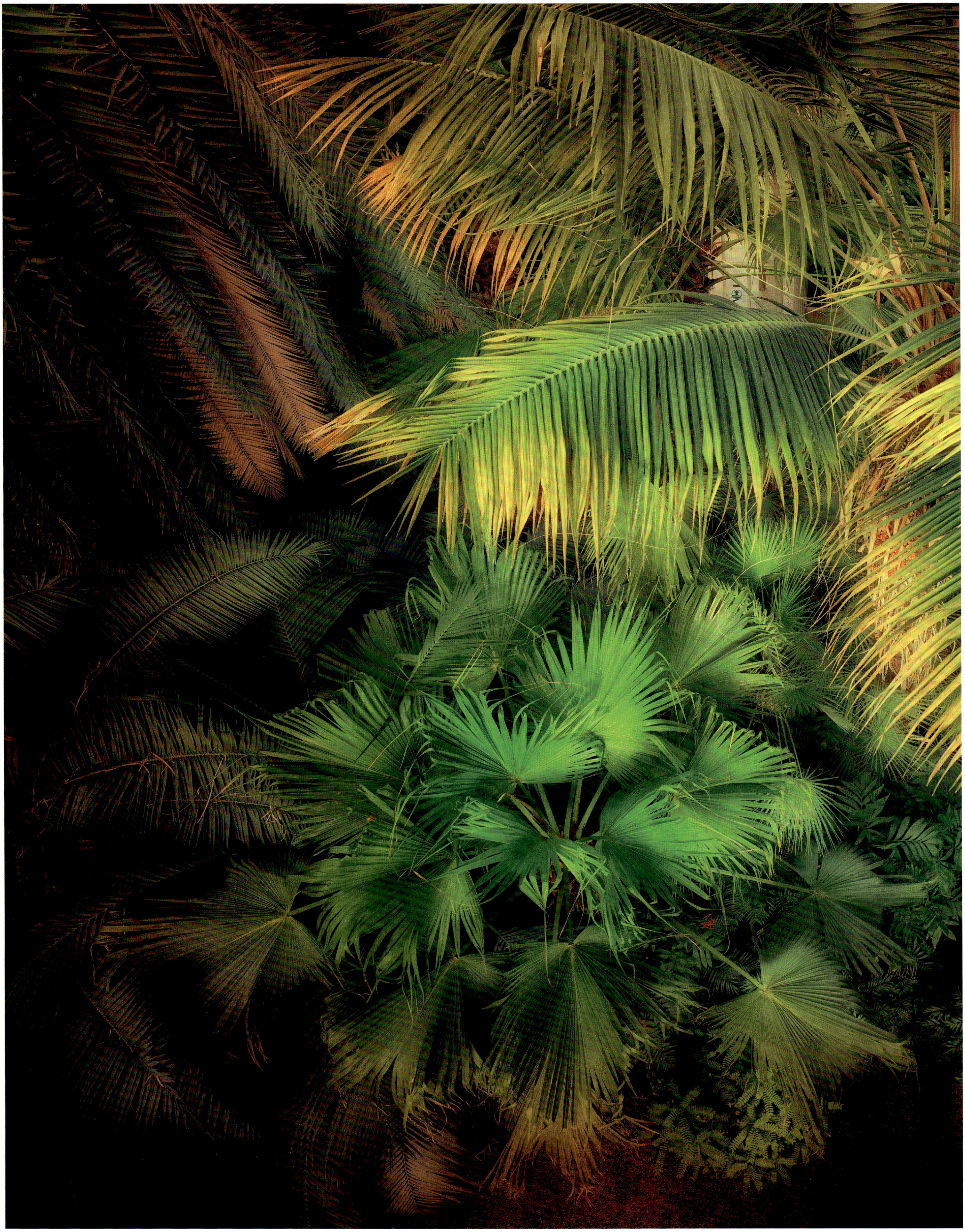

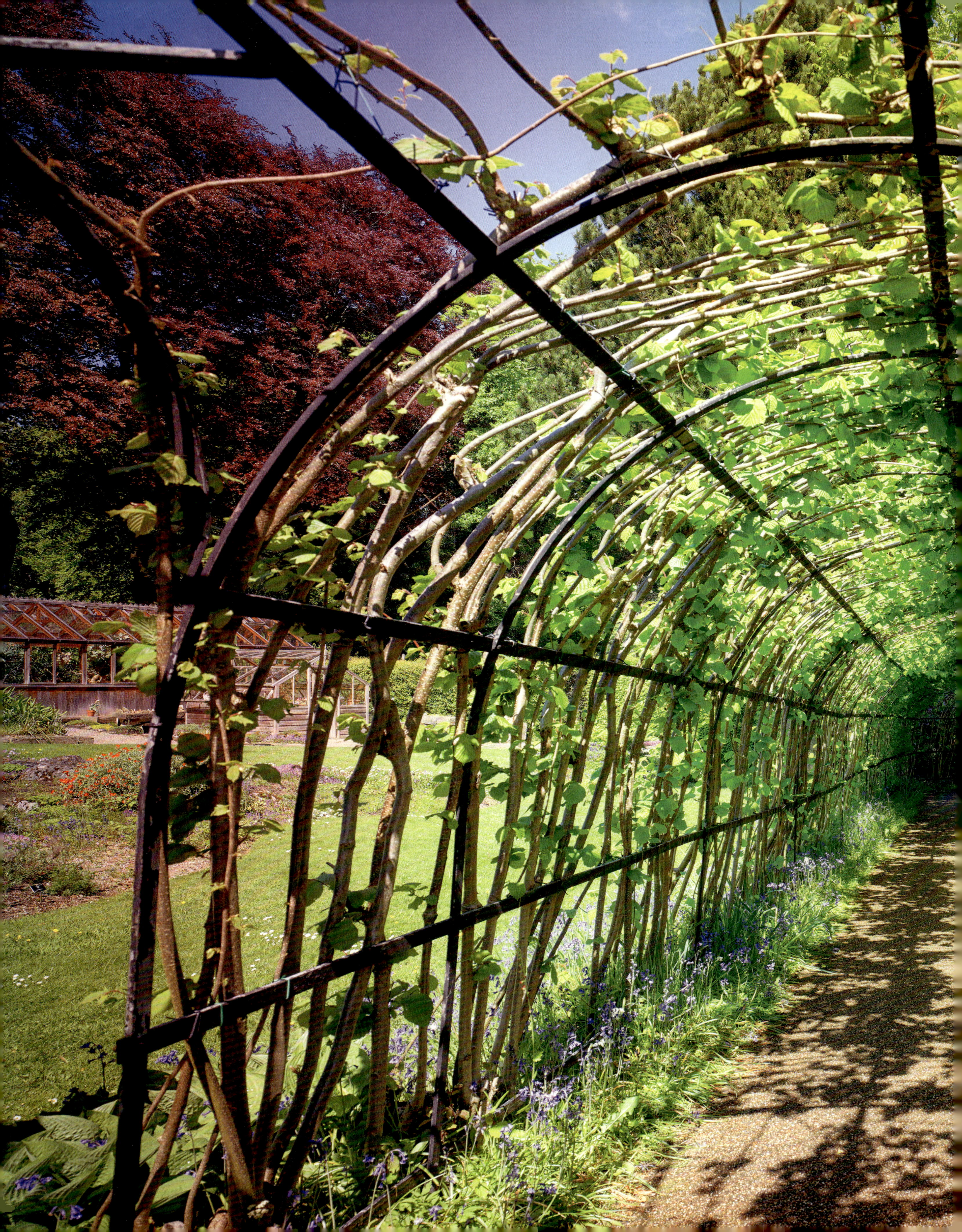

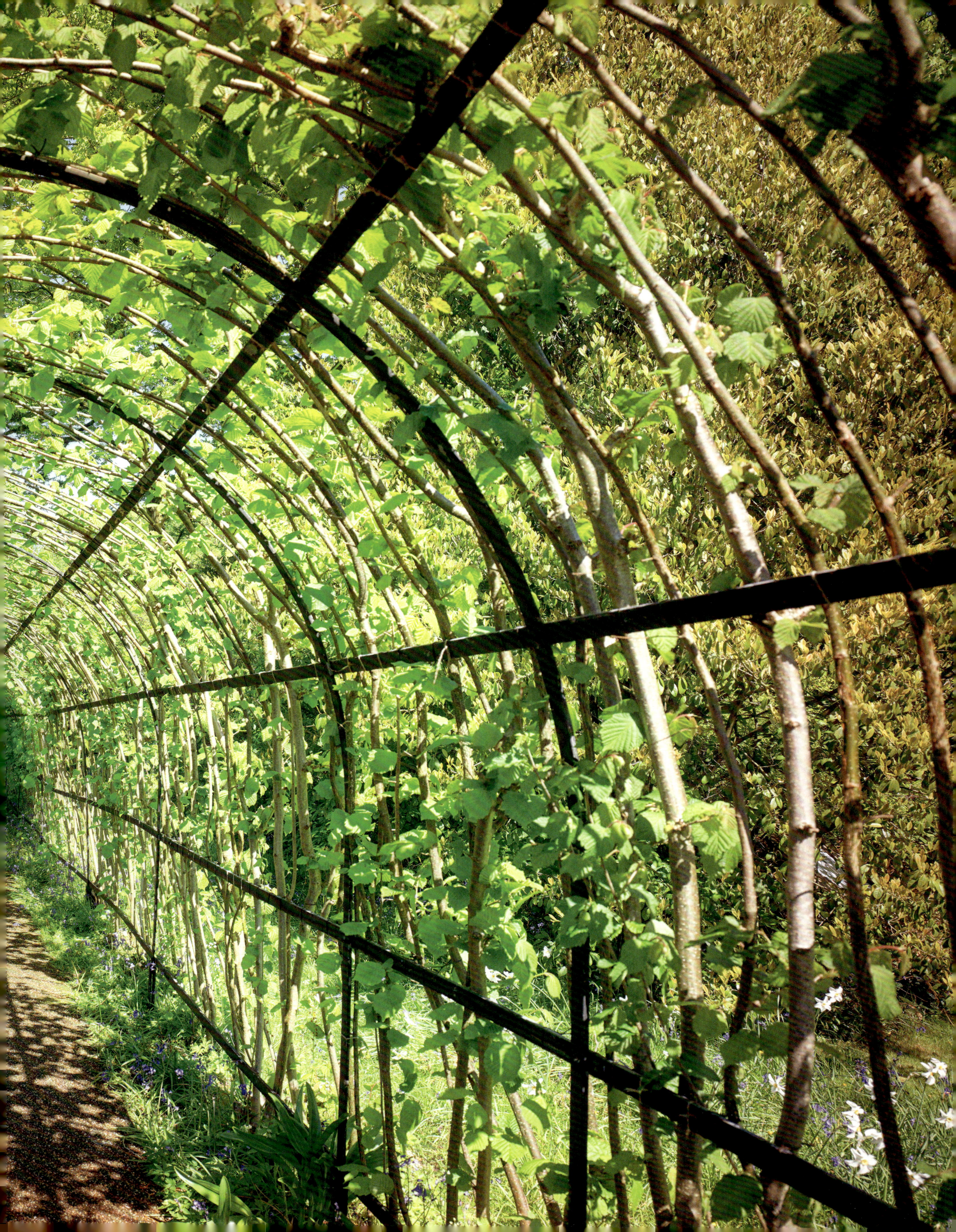

IMPRINT

Project Coordination Photography by Bettina Hermann

Editorial Coordination by Luisa Krause-Rossa, teNeues Verlag
Production by Nele Jansen, teNeues Verlag
Design by VerlagsService Gaby Herbrecht
Color Separation by Robert Kuhlendahl, teNeues Verlag

Texts by Alexandra Schmöger and Stephan Reisner
Translations by WeSwitch GmbH
Proofreading by Luisa Krause-Rossa, teNeues Verlag

ISBN: 978-3-96171-457-5
Library of Congress Number: 2023934493

Printed in Slovakia by Neografia

MIX
Paper | Supporting responsible forestry
FSC® C020353

Bibliographic information published by the Deutsche Nationalbibliothek: The Deutsche Nationalbibliothek lists this publication in the Deutsche Nationalbibliografie; detailed bibliographic data are available on the Internet at dnb.dnb.de.

Published by teNeues Publishing Group

teNeues Verlag GmbH
Ohmstraße 8a
86199 Augsburg, Germany

Düsseldorf Office
Waldenburger Straße 13
41564 Kaarst, Germany
e-mail: books@teneues.com

Augsburg/München Office
Ohmstraße 8a
86199 Augsburg, Germany
e-mail: books@teneues.com

Berlin Office
Lietzenburger Straße 53
10719 Berlin, Germany
e-mail: books@teneues.com

Press Department
presse@teneues.com

teNeues Publishing Company
350 Seventh Avenue, Suite 301
New York, NY 10001, USA
Phone: +1-212-627-9090
Fax: +1-212-627-9511

www.teneues.com

teNeues Publishing Group
Augsburg / München
Berlin
Düsseldorf
London
New York

teNeues

Fußnote S. 38:
Karl Friedrich von Martius, Direktor Botanischer Garten München. Aus: *Genera et species palmarum*, 3-bändig 1824–1836 nach seinem Forschungsaufenthalt in Brasilien erschienen . Zitiert nach: Charles McIntosh: *The Greenhouse, Hothouse and Stove*, London 1838, S. 361.

Footnote p. 38:
Karl Friedrich von Martius, Director of the Munich Botanical Garden. From: *Genera et species palmarum*, 3 volumes, published between 1824 and1836 after his research trip to Brazil . Quoted in Charles McIntosh: *The Greenhouse, Hothouse and Stove*, London, 1838, p. 361.

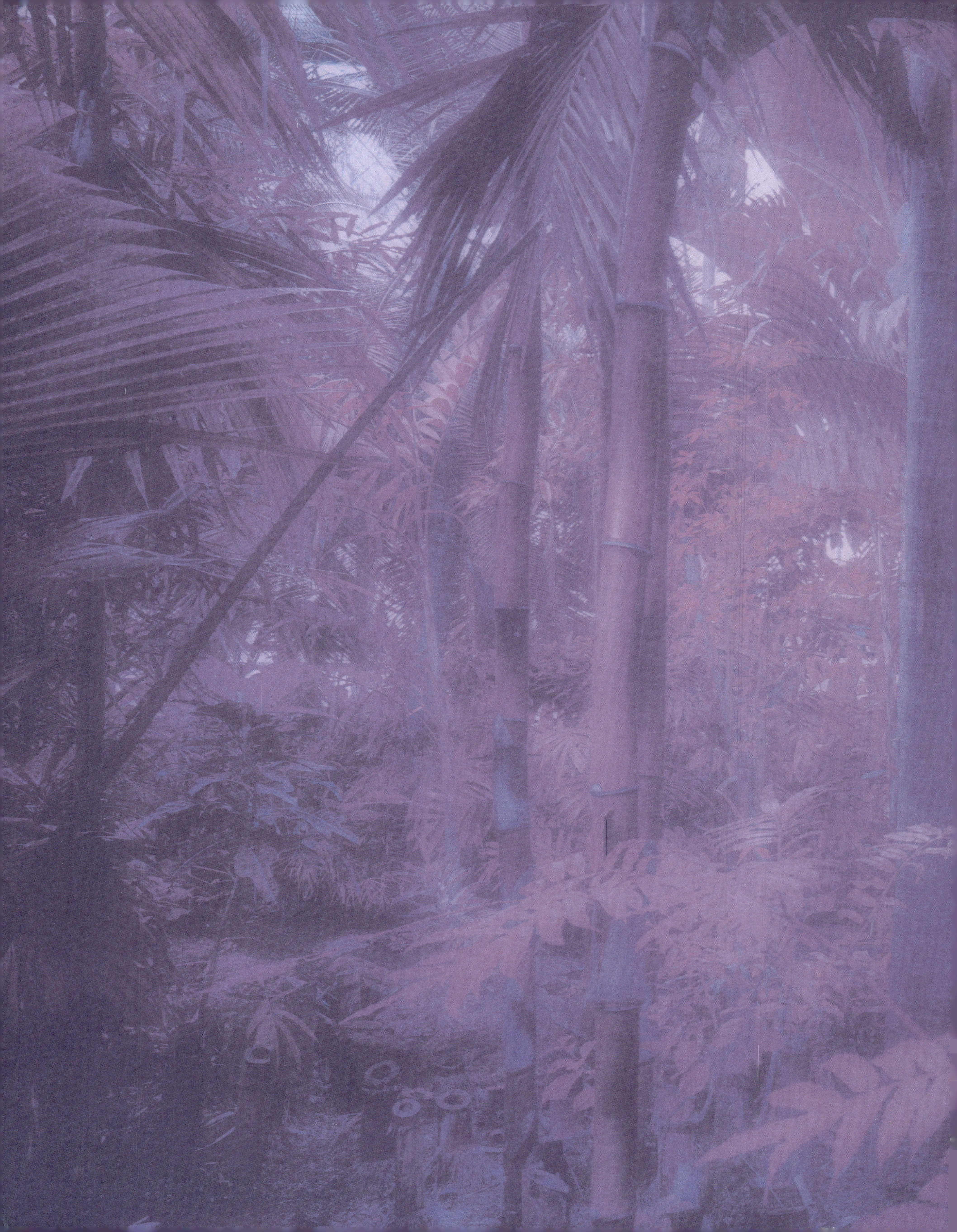